CORPORATE GOVERNANCE AND INSOLVENCY

ELGAR CORPORATE AND INSOLVENCY LAW AND PRACTICE

Series Editors: Andrew Keay, *Professor of Corporate and Commercial Law, University of Leeds, UK* and *Chief Insolvency and Companies Court Judge* Nicholas Briggs

The Elgar Corporate and Insolvency Law and Practice series is a library of works by leading practitioners and scholars covering discrete areas of law in the field. Each title will be analytical in approach, highlighting and unpicking the legal issues that are most critical and relevant to practice. Designed to be detailed, focused reference works, the books in this series aim to offer an authoritative statement on the law and practice in key topics within the fields of company law, corporate governance, corporate insolvency and personal insolvency.

Presented in a format that allows for ease of navigation to a particular point of law, each title in the series is written by specialists in their respective fields, often with insight either from private practice or from an academic perspective.

Titles in the series include:

Creditor Treatment in Corporate Insolvency Law
Kayode Akintola

Insolvency Practitioners
Appointment, Duties, Powers and Liability
Hugh Sims QC, Rachel Lai, Neil Levy, Stefan Ramel, Holly Doyle, James Hannant and Samuel Parsons

Cross-Border Protocols in Insolvencies of Multinational Enterprise Groups
Ilya Kokorin and Bob Wessels

The European Restructuring Directive
Gerard McCormack

Corporate Governance and Insolvency
Accountability and Transparency
Andrew Keay, Peter Walton and Joseph Curl QC

CORPORATE GOVERNANCE AND INSOLVENCY

Accountability and Transparency

ANDREW KEAY

Professor of Corporate and Commercial Law, School of Law, University of Leeds and Barrister, Kings Chambers and 9 Stone Buildings, Lincoln's Inn, UK

PETER WALTON

Professor of Insolvency Law, Wolverhampton Law School, University of Wolverhampton, UK

JOSEPH CURL QC

Barrister, 9 Stone Buildings, Lincoln's Inn and Deputy Insolvency and Companies Court Judge, England and Wales

ELGAR CORPORATE AND INSOLVENCY LAW AND PRACTICE

 Edward Elgar
PUBLISHING

Cheltenham, UK • Northampton, MA, USA

Published by
Edward Elgar Publishing Limited
The Lypiatts
15 Lansdown Road
Cheltenham
Glos GL50 2JA
UK

Edward Elgar Publishing, Inc.
William Pratt House
9 Dewey Court
Northampton
Massachusetts 01060
USA

A catalogue record for this book
is available from the British Library

This book is available electronically in the **Elgar**online
Law subject collection
http://dx.doi.org/10.4337/9781788979344

ISBN 978 1 78897 933 7 (cased)
ISBN 978 1 78897 934 4 (eBook)

Printed and bound by CPI Group (UK) Ltd, Croydon, CR0 4YY

CONTENTS

EXTENDED CONTENTS

9 CREDITORS' AND LIQUIDATION COMMITTEES

ABOUT THE AUTHORS

Andrew Keay is Professor of Corporate and Commercial Law at the University of Leeds and is a barrister practising from Kings Chambers and 9 Stone Buildings, Lincoln's Inn. He has published widely on both corporate governance and insolvency law, including *Board Accountability in Corporate Governance* (Routledge, 2015) and *McPherson and Keay's Law of Company Liquidation* (5th ed, Sweet and Maxwell, 2021). His work has been cited in many superior courts including the UK Supreme Court, the Privy Council, the High Court of Australia and the NZ Supreme Court. He holds several editorial posts including Commonwealth editor of *Gore-Browne on Companies* and an editor for *Bankruptcy and Personal Insolvency Reports.*

Peter Walton is Professor of Insolvency Law at the University of Wolverhampton. He has published widely on all aspects of insolvency law. His work has been cited judicially overseas and domestically including by the UK Supreme Court. His research has been cited in UK Parliamentary debates and been the subject of two House of Commons Early Day Motions. He co-authors a number of student and practitioner texts and is an editor for *Bankruptcy and Personal Insolvency Reports.* He sits on both of the UK's principal insolvency law technical committees. He currently leads INSOL International's Global Insolvency Practice Course.

Joseph Curl QC is a barrister practising at 9 Stone Buildings, Lincoln's Inn. He specialises exclusively in insolvency and restructuring and has appeared in many reported cases. He was appointed a Deputy Insolvency and Companies Court Judge in 2020 and Queen's Counsel in 2021. Between 2018 and 2021 he was an elected member of the Council of R3 and continues to sit on the R3 Technical Committee. He is one of the general editors (with Louis Doyle QC and Professor Andrew Keay) of *Doyle, Keay and Curl: Annotated Insolvency Legislation* published by LexisNexis (10th edn, 2021).

FOREWORD

Sir Alastair Norris

One of the clearest lessons of the pandemic (the background against which this book is published) is that there is no necessary link between insolvency and moral turpitude. Disaster can strike the most prudently directed and rigorously managed businesses. The most carefully taken decisions can, in the event, prove to be wrong.

As disaster looms a whole range of difficult commercial and moral questions must be faced. Should the business close? Or downsize? Or seek additional finance to trade-out the difficulty? Which supplier should be paid? Which customer should be let down? Should more orders be placed when finances are rocky? Should more orders be taken when fulfilment is not assured? And in the great majority of cases the answer to these questions will have a consequential impact upon the lives of the decision takers, as stresses increase, income is lost, guarantees called in and personal friendships disrupted.

When insolvency occurs, these difficulties do not evaporate. The officeholder may be a skilled professional operating within a legal and ethical framework. But that framework cannot provide specific answers to the individual questions which the officeholder faces, whether those questions are matters of apparently minute detail (such as proof of a claim) or of fundamental importance (such as the terms of a pre-pack sale or assessing the interest of shareholders in a restructured business). Nor can that framework shield her or him from the pressure exerted by the expectations of appointors and other stakeholders.

What is needed in this turbulence is a compass to guide management operating in the 'twilight zone' and to aid officeholders seeking to navigate a way to the best outcome. This welcome book provides such. It distils experience into principles which can be applied to those pressing problems. Because its authors are leaders in their field, and meld together the academic and the practical, it does so it does so in a clear, engaging and stimulating way.

This book is a very good idea, well executed. I hope it is the first of many editions.

Sir Alastair Norris
Former Justice of the High Court of England and Wales

PREFACE

There has been a great deal written, and particularly in the last 30 years, about corporate governance in many jurisdictions. The literature has been focused almost totally on solvent companies. In contrast, while much has been said about insolvent companies and aspects of how they are managed, save for some discussions of how companies are governed while subject to Chapter 11 bankruptcies in the United States, the literature has not provided any focus on corporate governance and some of the issues which it throws up. In this book we seek to address this lacuna.

Insolvency is an incredibly important issue in the corporate world. At this very moment there are likely to be millions of companies across the world that are insolvent. That does not mean that their existence will come to an end as many companies move in and out of insolvency on a fairly regular basis. However, many others will need to be restructured to survive while many more will have to be wound up as a precursor to their dissolution on the basis that their insolvency is terminal. While insolvency is an important issue at all times, it is an even more important issue in times of financial crisis or when, as we have had in the past two years, a pandemic in the form of COVID-19, which is causing havoc to the economic well-being of a huge number of businesses, including some of the largest and most profitable around the world. As a consequence of the importance of insolvency, it is critical that the governance of insolvent companies is examined carefully. This is what this book endeavours to do. It considers governance at two points of time. First, when a company is insolvent but remains under the control of its directors and outside any formal insolvency regime. Secondly, when a company is insolvent and subject to a formal insolvency regime. In many of the latter situations an insolvency practitioner will take control of the affairs of the company and the governance focus will shift from the directors to the insolvency practitioner. Thus, the book examines the role and work of directors and insolvency practitioners when the latter hold office, primarily as administrators and liquidators. While focusing on directors and insolvency practitioners the book does consider the position of creditors and contributories as well as the role of official receivers and the Insolvency Service.

As we explain in Chapter 2, there has been a great number of explanations of corporate governance have been provided over the years. We put forward our own for the purposes of this book and for the consideration of corporate governance in the context of insolvent companies. The explanation of corporate governance in insolvency which we offer is: 'the rules, relationships, systems and processes within and by which authority is exercised and controlled in companies for the benefit of pertinent stakeholders'. Again, as we say in Chapter 2, we believe that the two most important features of corporate governance are transparency and accountability, and this is acknowledged in a number of sources. The book, therefore, analyses the law and practice that exists through the lenses of these virtues. Where possible and appropriate we draw attention to where transparency and accountability exist and where they do not (and, perhaps, should).

After saying that, we must emphasise that what the work is designed to be is an analytical doctrinal study of corporate governance in insolvent companies. Except on a few occasions, we do not seek to make normative claims.

We would like to thank Tony Hawitt from Edward Elgar who helped us to begin this project and who has given us great support and gracious indulgence during the writing process. We would also like to thank Sabrina Lynott-May and Sabrina Zaher from Edward Elgar who have assisted us in the production of the final product. We also thank Paula Devine for editing the work.

We have stated the law as it is available to us at 1 May 2021, and, unless otherwise stated, websites cited were live as at this date.

Andrew Keay
Peter Walton
Joseph Curl QC
1 May 2021

TABLE OF CASES

AUSTRALIA

CARIBBEAN

HONG KONG

IRELAND

NEW ZEALAND

UNITED KINGDOM

UNITED STATES

TABLE OF LEGISLATION

UNITED KINGDOM - STATUTORY INSTRUMENTS

1

INTRODUCTION TO *CORPORATE GOVERNANCE AND INSOLVENCY*

A. THE IMPORTANCE OF COMPANIES

While there are other vehicles through which to conduct businesses, such as partnerships, **1.001** arguably there is no other trading entity of a private nature that is more important or more powerful in national and global economies around the world than the company.[1] It is trite to say that companies are a critical part of the commercial environment. Companies carry on large numbers of businesses in the UK and across the world. Companies registered under the UK's various Companies Acts, as David Richards LJ recently acknowledged: 'are the principal medium through which business is carried on in this country'.[2] Such entities have great effects on our daily lives and have an influence over just about all that we do.

The business company has been with us now in the UK in its present form, or close to it, for **1.002** over 150 years and it has dominated commerce for that period. As the Honourable Justice Michael Kirby, (a judge of the High Court of Australia at the time of speaking) once said extra-judicially:

> [T]he idea of an independent corporation, governed by directors and accountable to shareholders, was a brilliant one. It permitted people to rise capital from the public, to invest it without, in most cases,

---

1 This does not include sole proprietorships as they are not entities. Clearly there are many businesses carried on in the UK as sole proprietorships.

2 *BTI 2014 LLC v Sequana S.A.* [2019] EWCA Civ 112, [125].

a danger of personal risk and to engage in entrepreneurial activity which, otherwise, would probably not occur.[3]

1.003 All companies, whether they are large or small, multinational or local, play a fundamental, multi-dimensional and evolving role in promoting economic growth.[4] They have a vital role as the most important institutions for social wealth creation in capitalist economies.[5]

1.004 Companies employ millions of people in the UK alone and make large numbers of contracts with external parties each year. These contracts are often made between companies. Companies provide us with good and services, they employ us and provide benefits to communities. It has led some to claim that the company is one of the greatest inventions of humans and because of its existence society has made unimaginable progress.[6] Mary Stokes sums it up neatly when she states:

> [T]he company has become an organization whose significance almost rivals that of the state. It is the primary institution for organizing and employing much of our capital and labour resources and the primary supplier of goods and services in our community.[7]

1.005 The company is a mechanism that people who want to carry on business collectively can use effectively and productively. The company is popular for a variety of reasons, such as the fact that those who own shares in companies enjoy limited liability, and tax benefits might be available. Some have regarded the company as one of the best systems that man has ever designed.[8] At the end of March 2020 there were 4,350,913 companies registered in the UK.[9] The vast majority of these were private companies, with the remainder being public companies. Some companies are established as not for profit companies, but this book generally is concerned about those companies that are set up for profit.

1.006 What is striking about companies is that they are rather peculiar structures. Whilst obviously not human, they are legal persons. Legal personality is conferred as a result of the process of incorporation and consequently companies are able to do many things which can be done by humans, such as owning property, making contracts, instituting legal proceedings and, most importantly, and unlike humans, enjoying perpetual succession. This last feature of a company

---

3   'The Company Director, Past, Present and Future', address to the Australian Institute of Directors, Hobart, 31 March 1998.
4   Department of the Treasury (Australia), *Submission 134*, 1, and referred to in para 2.34 of the Australian Parliamentary Joint Committee on Corporations and Financial Services, *Corporate Responsibility: Managing Risk and Creating Value*, June 2006.
5   M Blair, 'For Whom Should Corporations Be Run?: An Economic Rationale for Stakeholder Management' (1998) 31 *Long Range Planning* 195, 195.
6   J Micklethwait and A Wooldridge, *The Company: A Short History of a Revolutionary Idea*, (Modern Library, 2003), xv; T. Lin, 'The Corporate Governance of Iconic Executives' (2011) 87 *Notre Dame Law Review* 351, 352.
7   'Company Law and Company Theory' in S Wheeler (ed), *The Law of the Business Enterprise* (Oxford University Press, 1994), 107.
8   R Tricker, *Corporate Governance – Principles, Policies and Practices*, (Oxford University Press, 2009), 8.
9   Companies House statistics: https://www.gov.uk/government/publications/incorporated-companies-in-the-uk-january-to-march-2020/incorporated-companies-in-the-uk-january-to-march-2020 accessed 16 October 2020. 4,064,063 of these companies were on the effective register (this excludes those companies that are in the process of being liquidated or dissolved).

means that they may, conceivably, never cease to exist. Indeed, we have operating in the UK many companies that have existed not only for decades, but centuries.

There are two notions that flow from incorporation of a company and they are important for **1.007** any work that addresses matters relevant to companies and their directors and shareholders. The first is one that we have referred to already. That is the limited liability of investors. Section 74 of the Insolvency Act 1986 ('the Act') provides that on the winding up of a company its shareholders (referred to as 'contributories' in the section) are liable to pay towards the assets of the company what they owe on their shares. Thus, if a shareholder has paid all of what is owed on his or her shares the shareholder can be liable for nothing more. The benefit is clearly that a shareholder knows how much he or she will have to pay if the company fails. The second notion is that of separate legal personality. That is, the company is an entity which is separate from the shareholders and directors. The shareholders and directors are not liable for the debts of the company, as provided for in the classic case of *Salomon v Salomon & Co Ltd*;[10] the company itself is liable.

Companies vary in all sorts of ways. Some are huge and operate across borders. Some are very **1.008** small and really are incorporated partnerships (often referred to as quasi-companies). While there are some different requirements in law that can apply to different companies, for the most part companies, no matter their size and make-up, are treated the same by the UK's prevailing companies' legislation, namely the Companies Act 2006 ('Companies Act'). This is whether the company is a mammoth multinational or a one-person company operating a small business in a small and constrained locality in the UK.

While companies will differ in various ways, the two critical concepts referred to above in 1.07 **1.009** apply to all. There is one other thing that is virtually common to all companies carrying on business and that is they will borrow funds and they incur debts. As a consequence all companies may at some point become insolvent, that is, unable to pay their debts. It is with insolvent companies and, in some parts, those close to insolvency that the book is concerned.

B. THE AIM OF THE BOOK

While a substantial volume of literature has addressed corporate governance in relation **1.010** to solvent companies, relatively little has been written about corporate governance when a company is insolvent, and certainly not in one volume. Publications have dealt with particular aspects of governance but do not deal with governance comprehensively. While some matters will be the same whether a company is solvent or insolvent, clearly there are some different corporate governance issues where insolvent companies are concerned, and this is especially so if the company enters some form of insolvency regime.

This book endeavours to provide a detailed analysis of all relevant corporate governance issues **1.011** as they relate to UK companies that are insolvent. The main focus is on governance when a company has entered an insolvency regime and when a company is insolvent but remains

---

10   [1897] AC 22.

outside of a formal insolvency regime. We have sought to ascertain those areas of corporate insolvency which raise issues and questions of governance and to address them accordingly. This is an ambitious aim as insolvency is a very complicated area of law, given, inter alia, that it involves other fields of law and very different insolvency regimes that have different goals and processes. We seek to examine the issue of governance through the lenses of transparency and accountability. We submit that they are critical virtues in many aspects of life and particularly where power is granted to some person or body. With companies there must be some human or group of humans who are in control of them. With companies that are not subject to an insolvency regime it is the board of directors. Where a company is under an insolvency regime it is an officeholder, who, as discussed later, is a qualified insolvency practitioner.

1.012 This chapter seeks to introduce the topic and then in Chapter 2 we provide a consideration of what corporate governance involves. Chapter 3 then analyses the meaning of insolvency and the law that has developed in relation to it. From Chapter 4 onwards the book deals with those areas that precipitate an examination of specific governance matters.

C. INSOLVENCY AND INSOLVENCY REGIMES

1.013 Insolvency occurs when a company is unable to pay its debts. It is outside the scope of this work to consider why companies become insolvent, but we can say that the most common causes are 'over-trading, making expensive and ill-judged acquisitions, loss of market share, lack of cash flow and the failure of management to respond to changed circumstances'.[11] In the UK the meaning of unable to pay debts is defined in s 123 of the Act. We discuss the way that s 123 has been interpreted and applied by the courts in detail in Chapter 3.

1.014 Suffice it to say, companies can move in and out of insolvency quite frequently and provided that no creditor presses for payment to the point of seeking to have the company placed in some form of insolvency regime, usually administration or liquidation, a company can continue to trade. Of course, creditors might be reluctant to provide more credit to a company in such a position, although often creditors, existing and prospective, or at least some of them, are not aware of the position which a company is actually in.

1.015 A company may continue to operate while insolvent. Unlike with some European countries, the directors of an insolvent company in the UK do not have to place the company in some insolvency regime; it is not a civil wrong or criminal offence to operate while insolvent, although it might lead to the directors being held liable at some point later if the company enters liquidation or administration. Yet, it might become impossible or imprudent to continue to operate as an insolvent company, so the company may itself decide to enter some form of insolvency regime or a creditor might seek an order from a court that the company be forced into an insolvency regime.

1.016 There are a number of insolvency regimes into which a company can enter. As indicated in the last paragraph, this can be voluntary or compulsorily. A company can decide to enter

---

11   Kristen van Zwieten (ed), *Goode on Principles of Corporate Insolvency Law* (5th ed, Sweet & Maxwell, 2019), 457.

administration, and this can be achieved out of court by simply filing documents at court which indicate that the company has appointed an administrator, and naming the person who has consented to act (an intention to appoint must also be filed prior to the notice of appointment where the appointor is the company or directors). In some situations companies may apply for a court order that the company enter administration. On the commencement of administration a person, known as an administrator, will take control of the company's affairs. This person must be a qualified insolvency practitioner ('IP'), and he or she is to be independent from any parties in, or related to, the company itself. There will be discussion of what qualifications are needed for a person to act as an IP, as well as the position, duties and role of an IP, in several chapters, but especially in Chapters 7 and 8. Also, towards the end of this chapter more is said in general terms about IPs.

A company might decide that it is not likely to be able to be rescued from its insolvent position and thus its shareholders or directors vote to place it into liquidation. This is known as creditors' voluntary liquidation.[12] A qualified IP who, as with administration, is independent, is appointed as the liquidator. **1.017**

A company can also decide to try and rescue/restructure itself and to continue trading whilst also entering an insolvency regime and it will do this by proposing a creditors' voluntary arrangement ('CVA') to its creditors. The proposal will put forward a way that the company thinks will allow it to escape its insolvency and also benefit the creditors, or at least give them more benefits than they would get if the company was liquidated. In some cases, and this usually involves large companies, a company might propose what is known as a scheme of arrangement under the Companies Act (pursuant to either Part 26 or Part 26A). Again, this will involve a proposal from the company that is put to meetings of creditors to see if the latter are willing to agree to the proposal. **1.018**

It is important to note that insolvency has become more publicised in the past 30 years compared to earlier times. Also, during this period we have seen more companies enter formal insolvency regimes. This might partly be because more options are available to companies than once was the case. Before the enactment of the Act companies were essentially limited to entering liquidation or entering into a scheme of arrangement. Companies could also enter into an informal arrangement with creditors if they thought that it was appropriate. Certainly in the past 30 years there has been more emphasis on the rescue of insolvent or near insolvent companies than was the case in the past. This can be seen in the inclusion of provisions in the Act which gave birth to administrations and CVAs as insolvency regimes, and it was the rationale for the enactment of the Enterprise Act 2002 when the government, inter alia, made it easier to enter administration by discontinuing the requirement of obtaining an order of the court for a company to enter administration.[13] **1.019**

---

12   The book does not discuss members' voluntary liquidation because to be able to enter this regime the company must be solvent.

13   Inter alia, this endeavoured to make administration more effective and as a vehicle to restructuring.

1.020 Importantly, we have seen recently a response from the Department of Business Energy and Industrial Strategy to proposals it published in 2016[14] to support restructuring. In the Corporate Insolvency and Governance Act 2020 the government introduced a number of reforms, many of which were precipitated by the COVID-19 pandemic that hit the world in 2020. One major part of the legislation did introduce changes that had been foreshadowed in 2016 and involved the introduction of a new form of insolvency regime. This is known as the Moratorium procedure,[15] which can be initiated merely by filing documents in court and will last, initially (it can be extended), for 20 days. It is expected that this would give vulnerable companies respite from creditor attack while they seek to engage in rescuing themselves from their financial malaise.

1.021 Courts,[16] practitioners and academics[17] have all supported rescue at various times. Many have lauded restructuring as optimal and beneficial[18] as it means that the company survives and continues to trade, and this can benefit stakeholders,[19] particularly employees who keep their jobs and suppliers who can retain a customer to whom they can supply their goods. Moreover, rescue is seen as enhancing the wider economy,[20] and it can be attractive to the state as it promotes economic growth.[21] If restructuring can take place outside a formal insolvency process then costs may be saved as well as other possible advantages such as limiting the publicity of the company's distress.

1.022 More frequently a company in difficulty is not rescued but one or more of its businesses are rescued by being sold to buyers who believe that they can trade them profitably.

1.023 A company might not decide to initiate an insolvency regime. There might be attempts out of court to arrive at an informal arrangement with the creditors. These are sometimes known as 'workouts.' If a workout is pursued then directors are subject to the same responsibilities that they had before the workout was commenced. They will also be subject to different and additional responsibilities. We deal with governance issues that affect directors in this kind of case in Chapter 4.

---

14 'Review of the Corporate Governance Framework' May 2016: https://assets.publishing.service.gov.uk/government/uploads/system/uploads/attachment_data/file/525523/A_Review_of_the_Corporate_Insolvency_Framework.pdf accessed, 2 October 2018.

15 Now found in the Act as Part A1.

16 For instance, see *Re Welfab Ltd* [1990] BCC 600, 604.

17 For example, R Maslen-Stannage, 'Directors' duties to creditors: Walker v Wimborne revisited' (2013) 31 *Company and Securities Law Journal* 76, 78; M Epeoglou, 'Comments on Commission's Proposal for a Directive on Preventive Restructuring Frameworks and Second Chance for Entrepreneurs: The Third Step to the European Cross-border Insolvency Saga' (2017) 14 *International Corporate Rescue* 4, 6.

18 S Gilson, J Kose, and H Lang, 'Troubled Debt Restructurings: An Empirical Study of Private Reorganisation of Firms in Default' (1990) 27 *Journal of Financial Economics* 411, 412; L Weiss, 'Bankruptcy Resolution: Direct Costs and Violation of Priority Claims' (1990) *27 Journal of Financial Economics* 285, 288.

19 L Lo Pucki and W Whitfield, 'Corporate Governance in the Bankruptcy Reorganization of Large Publicly Held Companies' (1993) 14 *University of Pennsylvania Law Review* 669, 752. The authors argue that if restructuring does not occur then it could lead to the externalisation of costs to the detriment of non-creditor stakeholders.

20 European Commission, *Recommendation Impact Assessment* (Accompanying the Recommendation on A New Approach to Business Failure and Insolvency) SWD (2014) 61, 26.

21 S Paterson, 'Bargaining in Financial Restructuring: Market Norms, Legal Rights and Regulatory Standards' (2014) 14 *Journal of Corporate Law Studies* 333, 338.

Companies that are insolvent may decide to continue to operate and 'to tough it out'. But some **1.024** of their creditors might well have had enough of not being paid on time or at all, and they might decide, individually or collectively, that action needs to be taken. Creditors with quali-fying charges over company property are able either to commence administration out of court or apply to the court for an administration order. Unsecured creditors are permitted to apply to the court for an administration order but are more likely to petition the court for a winding-up order that will see the commencement of the liquidation of the company. Again, as with the situation where the company initiates administration or liquidation, if a court orders admin-istration a qualified IP is appointed as administrator. Where liquidation commences through a court order the official receiver becomes the liquidator but he or she will usually be replaced by a private IP unless the value in the company's estate is not likely to be sufficient to cover the fees and expenses of an IP.

It should be noted that a creditor who holds a floating charge over company property created **1.025** before 15 September 2003 may appoint an administrative receiver instead of an administrator. Appointments of administrative receivers are now relatively uncommon.

Whether administration is commenced as a result of the company's action or a court order **1.026** the administrator will effectively govern the affairs of the company. The same can be said of the official receiver in liquidations ordered by the court, and in relation to an IP who replaces the official receiver as liquidator at a later point of time. Likewise, a liquidator in a creditors' voluntary liquidation will oversee the affairs of the company.

As foreshadowed earlier in the chapter, the incidence of insolvency regimes has increased over **1.027** the years. In 1960, which is the earliest date from when we have insolvency statistics, there were 1,038 creditors' voluntary liquidations and 525 compulsory liquidations making a total of 1,563 liquidations in England and Wales. No other insolvency regimes existed at that point save for receiverships and schemes of arrangement. From 1960 there was, except for the occasional year, an increase in both kinds of liquidation. For instance, in 1970 there was a total of 3,689 liquidations, in 1980 there were 6,890, and in 1990 there were 15,051 liquidations,[22] with the leap in 1990 probably due to a bad recession that commenced in the UK in the late 1980s and continued until 1992. From 1990 onwards the number of liquidations remained high, never falling below 12,000. In 1992, at the end of the recession there were 24,425. In 2017, there were 15,660,[23] and in 2019, slightly fewer with 15,158 insolvent liquidations.[24] We do not address 2020 figures because in this year the numbers were distorted by the COVID-19 pandemic.

In 1986 administrations and CVAs were introduced. In the early years the number of admin- **1.028** istrations was relatively low, not exceeding 698 per annum. They increased in number in the 2000s when the Enterprise Act 2002 made amendments to the Act to permit the com-

---

22   https://webarchive.nationalarchives.gov.uk/20140716212200/http://www.insolvencydirect.bis.gov.uk/ otherinformation/statistics/historicdata/HDmenu.htm accessed 18 December 2018.
23   https://assets.publishing.service.gov.uk/government/uploads/system/uploads/attachment_data/file/675931/Insolvency _Statistics_-_web.pdf accessed 18 December 2018.
24   See Insolvency Service, Insolvency Statistics – https://www.gov.uk/government/statistics/company-insolvency-statistics -january-to-march-2020 accessed 16 October 2020.

mencement of administration out of court.[25] The highest number reached was in 2008 when there were 4,822 administrations, although this high number was bolstered by the fact that 729 separate managed service companies entered administration.[26] In 2017 there were 1,289 administrations. As with administrations the early years of the life of CVAs saw small numbers. Numbers began to increase substantially in the mid–late 1990s with 1997 posting 629 CVAs. High points were 2003 (726) and 2012 (839).[27] Numbers had fallen to 292 in 2017.[28]

D. CORPORATE GOVERNANCE IN INSOLVENCY

1.029   When a company becomes insolvent, or even is in financial distress that is short of insolvency, the nature of corporate governance will, as indicated earlier, change to some degree at least. If the company remains outside of a formal insolvency regime the directors and the board will continue to govern and control the company and in doing so they will do many of the things that they would have done when the company was solvent. However, the law requires directors to make some changes to the way that they act and the decisions they make. Different considerations must occupy the minds of directors with insolvent companies compared with solvent ones. How they must change and what they should be doing is discussed in detail in Chapter 4. Importantly in an insolvency or near insolvency situation the focus will turn from what are the interests of the shareholders, as the majority of UK case law tends to suggest that the interests of the company are those of the shareholders, to what are the interests of the creditors. If a company is insolvent, then the shareholders' interest in the company is nil as there will not be sufficient to pay the creditors in full and they are entitled to be paid before the shareholders see anything at all.

1.030   If a company enters some formal regime then, as foreshadowed in the previous part of the chapter, an IP who is independent of the directors, shareholders and creditors will take charge of the company and govern it. Having said that, the IP will often be appointed by the directors, the general body of creditors or a secured creditor. Those IPs who become administrators (in an administration) may, in some situations, allow the directors to remain in office and/or consult the directors on some issues concerning the life of the company,[29] but the final decision rests with the administrator, and the directors have no power. In liquidation, liquidators will generally speak with the directors but they are less likely to consult with them, especially given the fact that, unlike with administration where there might be a return to active trading following the end of administration, the end game will be the dissolution of the company. Liquidators are more likely to undertake more detailed investigations of what the directors have done prior to liquidation occurring. Again, any decisions rest with the liquidator. Chapters 7 and 8 will

---

25   https://webarchive.nationalarchives.gov.uk/20140716212200/http://www.insolvencydirect.bis.gov.uk/otherinformation/statistics/historicdata/HDmenu.htm accessed 18 December 2018.

26   Ibid.

27   Ibid.

28   https://www.gov.uk/government/statistics/insolvency-statistics-july-to-september-2018 accessed 18 December 2018.

29   Directors cannot exercise management powers except with the consent of the administrator: Insolvency Act 1986, para 64 of Sch B1. The directors remain subject to the duties imposed on them by Chapter 2 of Part 10 of the Companies Act 2006 (the general duties): *Hunt v Michie* [2020] EWHC 54, [60].

address substantively the appointment of IPs, what IPs must do, what they may do and how they do it.

Administrations and liquidations may have committees who oversee what the administrators **1.031** or liquidators do, and possibly offer advice in relation to the actions that the administrators or liquidators are considering taking. These committees are known as creditors' committees in administration and liquidation committees in liquidation. The role and work of these committees are considered in detail in Chapter 9.

E. THE PLAYERS IN CORPORATE GOVERNANCE IN INSOLVENCY

In this part of the chapter we examine those who are involved in the governance of companies, **1.032** some of whom have already been mentioned. This part seeks to identify clearly who they are and to say something about them. It is only intended to introduce the players and to sketch the role and place these players have. More details will be given about what they do and what they have to do in later chapters. The players discussed below might be referred to as stakeholders. There are others who will or may have a part to play in corporate governance, particularly when the company is solvent, such as the employees. The book does not discuss stakeholders, other than those mentioned below in detail, as their input into corporate governance, where the company is insolvent, is either non-existent or not as potentially substantial as when the company is solvent. Further elucidation of the role and work of the various players will occur in later chapters.

1.   Directors

Before an insolvent company enters an insolvency regime the primary players are the company's **1.033** directors, either individually or as a board. As adverted to earlier, directors may also have a role when the company is in an insolvency regime, but it will be limited.

Directors play a vital role in companies and their importance cannot be overstated in relation to **1.034** corporate governance. The Australian judge, Middleton J, has said that:

> A director is an essential component of corporate governance. Each director is placed at the apex of the structure of direction and management of a company. The higher the office that is held by a person, the greater the responsibility that falls upon him or her. The role of a director is significant as their actions may have a profound effect on the community, and not just shareholders, employees and creditors.[30]

Naturally directors are critical to corporate governance when the company is solvent, but **1.035** where a company is insolvent (or close to it) they still have a significant role to play. While all companies are required by law to have at least one director,[31] the make-up of a board of directors will depend on the constitution of the company and any corporate governance code

---

30   *ASIC v Healey* [2011] FCA 717, [14].
31   Companies Act 2006, s 154(1). Public companies must have at least two directors (s 154(2)). At least one director of a company must be a person (s 155(1)).

that applies, such as the UK Corporate Governance Code[32] for listed public companies or the Wates Corporate Governance Principles for Large Private Companies,[33] but companies are usually given a deal of discretion as to how many directors are appointed. Obviously, the norm is that the larger the company the larger the board, up to a certain size where adding to the board makes it unwieldy.

1.036 The directors of a company sit as a board and act corporately. The board of directors is one of the two organs that make decisions for companies, the other is the general meeting of shareholders.[34] Typically, today, the company's articles of association will vest the board of directors, elected by the shareholders at a general meeting, with very broad general management powers,[35] many of which are then delegated to company managers and officers.[36] Thus decisions are not only taken by the shareholders in general meeting and the board, but also by individuals who manage the company's affairs. In large companies the fact is that shareholders have no interest in managing the company even if they possess significant information about it and its line of business. They leave it to the board whom they appoint to run the company for the shareholders. The wide-ranging powers given to the directors by the articles can only be exercised by the directors, and the only action that the shareholders might be able to take is to pass a special resolution to amend the articles; the shareholders cannot interfere in the exercise of the management power except in very limited circumstances.[37]

1.037 Besides the articles being of critical importance to the role and functions of directors, the common law, specific provisions in the Companies Act, subordinate legislation, and codes of governance are also important as they require directors to fulfil certain duties[38] responsibilities and functions.

(a) Who are they?

1.038 Directors must be at least 16 years of age.[39] There is no upper age limit. Directors do not need any formal qualifications to take up appointments either as executive or non-executive directors; they may have no recognised skills whatsoever. Many directors, particularly of large public companies, will have university degrees but not necessarily relevant to the business in

---

32 Drafted and sanctioned by the Financial Reporting Council, July 2018.

33 Published by the Financial Reporting Council in December 2018.

34 Boards have certainly been a critical element of the company from the time they were first employed: S Watson, 'The Significance of the Source of the Powers of Boards of Directors in UK Company Law' (2011) *Journal of Business Law* 597, 601.

35 For example, see The Companies (Tables A–F) Regulations 1985 SI 1985/805 Table A art 70 and The Companies (Model Articles) Regulations 2008 SI 2008/3229 reg 2 and Sch 1 art 5 (private companies); reg 4 and Sch 3 art 5 (public companies).

36 Susan Watson argues that no significance should be suggested where the powers are provided for in the articles as opposed to a statute: 'The Significance of the Source of the Powers of Boards of Directors in UK Company Law' (2011) *Journal of Business Law* 597, 599. For a legislative delegation, see s 130 of the Companies Act 1993 (NZ).

37 *John Shaw & Sons (Salford) Ltd v Shaw* [1935] 2 KB 113, 134; *NRMA v Parker* (1986) 4 ACLC 609, 613–614; *Auer v Dressel* (1954) 118 NE 2d 590, 594 (NY). See, *Automatic Self-Cleansing Filter Syndicate Co Ltd v Cunninghame* [1906] 2 Ch 34, 44; *Ashburton Oil NL v Alpha Minerals NL* (1971) 123 CLR 614. Also, see art 3 of The Companies (Model Articles) Regulations 2008 (SI 2008/3229).

38 For a discussion of the leading duties affecting directors in UK companies, see Andrew Keay, *Directors' Duties*, (4th ed, LexisNexis, 2020).

39 Companies Act 2006, s 157(1).

which a company is engaged or related to managing businesses. Specialist directors, such as the finance director who is likely to have finance and/or accounting qualifications which enable him or her to do the job for which they have been hired, will possess formal qualifications. An important element for directors, as with other posts in society, is experience. In this regard, a good 'track record' on the part of directors is sought after by companies.

There is no licensing system that is provided for directors. Anyone is able to call himself or **1.039** herself a director. Directors of large companies are often members of professional bodies like the Institute of Directors which runs courses on subjects relevant to directors. But there is no body to which a director is accountable. Any disciplining has to be undertaken within the company.[40] History suggests that it does not occur very often.

Certain people are excluded from acting as directors. These include those who are undischarged **1.040** bankrupts, who are automatically disqualified because of s 11 of the Company Directors' Disqualification Act 1986. Other persons who have been directors are disqualified from acting because they have been disqualified under this legislation, for other reasons.

(b) Types of directors

'Director' is defined in s 250 of the Companies Act and s 251 of the Act as including anyone **1.041** occupying the position of director 'by whatever name called'. This means that a person can be a director if he or she does not have that title. Most directors will be de jure directors, namely, those who have been appointed at law. Their names will appear on the register of directors held by Companies House. Whether a person has been appointed as a director might not always be clear, but that is outside the scope of this book. Going back to the earlier point that a person can be a director even if he or she is not referred to as such and does not attend board meetings, such people might be either de facto or shadow directors.

A de facto director is a person who assumes the functions and status of a director, while never **1.042** being appointed according to law.[41] This might be as a result of some defect in the appointment of a person as a de jure director,[42] but more often than not it covers someone who is not appointed, although he or she is involved in directorial roles. If a person had assumed responsibility to act as a director, then the court would have to determine in what capacity the person was acting.[43] A person will only be held to be a de facto director if it can be established that he or she carried out director-like functions and they are functions that could only be discharged by a director.[44]

---

40   For example, see A Keay, 'Company Directors Behaving Poorly: Disciplinary Options for Shareholders' [2007] *Journal of Business Law* 656.

41   *Re Hydrodan (Corby) Ltd* [1994] BCC 161, [1994] 2 BCLC 180 at 183; *Re Kaytech International Ltd* [1999] 2 BCLC 351; *Re Mea Corp Ltd* [2006] EWHC 1846 (Ch), [2007] BCC 288, [83].

42   This occurred in *Re Canadian Land Reclaiming and Colonizing Co* (1880) 14 Ch D 660. Also, see *Corporate Affairs Commission (NSW) v Drysdale* (1978) 141 CLR 236.

43   *Smithton Ltd (formerly Hobart Capital Markets Ltd) v Naggar* [2014] EWCA Civ 939, [2015] 1 WLR 189, [2014] BCC 482, [36].

44   *Re Hydrodan (Corby) Ltd* [1994] BCC 161; [1994] 2 BCLC 180; *Secretary of State for Trade and Industry v Becker* [2003] 1 BCLC 555.

1.043 In *Re Hydrodan (Corby) Ltd*[45] it was said that a person will not be held to be a de facto director merely if he or she had been involved in managing the affairs of a company and being concerned with tasks that may properly be undertaken by a manager below board level.[46] It was stated in this case that the term de facto director encompasses someone who is held out as a director by the company,[47] although subsequent cases appear to take the view that this is only one element to consider when deciding whether someone is a de facto director or not.[48] The critical matter seems to be that for a person to be classified as a de facto director, he or she has to have been part of the corporate governance structure.[49] To be successful in alleging someone has acted as a de facto director, a claimant must demonstrate that the person assumed the status and functions of a company director and exercised 'real influence' in the corporate governance of the company.[50] It is likely that the nature of the functions or powers which are exercised and the extent of their exercise will be of great importance.[51] The role of a de facto director need not extend over the whole range of a company's activities.[52]

1.044 The cases have made it clear that there is no one decisive test for determining if someone is a de facto director.[53] Courts have to take into account all relevant factors[54] and that has included consideration as to whether the company held out the person as a director,[55] the person used the title of director;[56] the person had possession of appropriate information on which to make decisions, and the person was required to make major decisions.[57] In *Elsworth Ethanol Co Ltd v Hartley*[58] HHJ Hacon (sitting as a High Court judge) said that a court was permitted to consider all relevant factors in arriving at a decision in the person's position. This included whether the person acted as an equal of one or more of the directors.

1.045 It is possible that a person who is involved with a company is regarded as a shadow director. While a de facto director is not mentioned in legislation, the term 'shadow director' is, namely in s 251 of the Act, s 251(2) of the Companies Act and s 22(5) of the Company Directors' Disqualification Act 1986. Section 251(1) of the Act provides that a shadow director is 'a person in accordance with whose directions or instructions the directors of the company are accustomed to act'.

---

45   [1994] BCC 161, [1994] 2 BCLC 180.
46   Ibid., 163, 183.
47   Ibid.
48   *Secretary of State for Trade and Industry v Tjolle* [1998] 1 BCLC 333.
49   Ibid.; *Re Mumtaz Properties Ltd* [2011] EWCA Civ 610, [2012] 2 BCLC 109.
50   *Re Kaytech International plc* [1999] 2 BCLC 351, 423; *Gemma v Davies* [2008] EWHC 546 (Ch), [2008] BCC 812, [40].
51   *Deputy Commissioner of Taxation v Austin* (1998) 16 ACLC 1555, 1559.
52   *Smithton Ltd (formerly Hobart Capital Markets Ltd) v Naggar* [2014] EWCA Civ 939, [2015] 1 WLR 189, [2014] BCC 482, [32].
53   *Revenue and Customs Commissioners v Holland; Re Paycheck Services 3 Ltd* [2010] UKSC 51, [2011] BCC 1; *Re Mumtaz Properties Ltd* [2011] EWCA Civ 610, [2012] 2 BCLC 109; *Smithton Ltd (formerly Hobart Capital Markets Ltd) v Naggar* [2014] EWCA Civ 939, [2015] 1 WLR 189, [2014] BCC 482, [33].
54   *Re Mumtaz Properties Ltd* [2011] EWCA Civ 610, [2012] 2 BCLC 109.
55   Ibid.
56   Ibid.; *Smithton Ltd (formerly Hobart Capital Markets Ltd) v Naggar* [2014] EWCA Civ 939, [2015] 1 WLR 189, [2014] BCC 482.
57   *Secretary of State for Trade and Industry v Tjolle* [1998] 1 BCLC 333.
58   [2014] EWHC 99 (IPEC).

Section 251 of the Act and s 251(2) of the Companies Act state that persons are not deemed to **1.046** be shadow directors just because the directors act on their advice, in situations where the advice is given in a person's professional capacity. Normally this will exclude people such as lawyers, accountants and auditors being regarded as shadow directors. Yet there might be situations where such persons do in fact become shadow directors and so their professional standing is not an absolute exclusion from being a shadow. The rationale behind the notion of shadow directors is to catch those who have real influence over the affairs of companies.[59] However, as with de facto directors, it is not a requirement that the person exercises influence over the whole field of activities of the company before he or she is determined to be a shadow.[60]

Another kind of director that one comes across, sometimes with large companies and more **1.047** particularly joint venture companies, is the nominee director. This is a director who has been nominated to the board by particular parties with the idea that the nominee would represent their interests.[61] Nominee directors are subject to the same duties and responsibilities to which ordinary directors are subject. The right to appoint a nominee might be provided for under the company's constitution or pursuant to contract. In some cases there is no constitutional or contractual right to appoint, but the appointor has so much influence that the persons who have the legal power to appoint will agree to the appointor's desire for representation on the board of directors.

The main issue with nominee directors is: are they to act in the best interests of the company **1.048** as a whole or in the interests of their nominator? We will not engage in discussion of this nice legal issue as it is outside the scope of the book, although highly relevant for solvent companies, but we can say that the English case law makes it clear that nominee directors must not put the interests of their nominators higher than those of the company. Such directors, notwithstanding their position, are required to do that which is in the interests of the company and not what might correspond with the interests of his or her appointors.[62] This is likely to be seen to be embedded in the law now by s 173 of the Companies Act which requires directors to exercise independent judgment in their decisions.[63]

(c) Executive and non-executive directors

While not recognised by the Companies Act, traditionally directors are separated into executive **1.049** and non-executive directors, and the UK Corporate Governance Code and other codes of practice use the terms, as do practitioners and those operating in the commercial world. This is particularly so in relation to larger companies. In small companies the directors are often all executives, and often they are also shareholders.

---

59   *Secretary of State for Trade and Industry v Deverell* [2001] Ch 340, [2000] 2 WLR 907, [2000] 2 BCLC 133 (CA), [35].
60   Ibid.; *Smithton Ltd (formerly Hobart Capital Markets Ltd) v Naggar* [2014] EWCA Civ 939, [2015] 1 WLR 189, [2014] BCC 482, [32].
61   See, E Thomas 'The Role of Nominee Directors and the Liability of their Appointors' in F Patfield (ed) *Perspectives on Company Law* (vol 2, Kluwer, 1997), 235; J De Lacy 'The Concept of a Company Director: Time for a New Expanded and Unified Concept?' [2006] *Journal of Business Law* 276, 284–287.
62   *Selangor United Rubber Estates Ltd v Craddock (No 3)* [1968] 1 WLR 1555, [1968] 2 All ER 1073; *Hawkes v Cuddy; Re Neath Rugby Ltd* [2007] EWHC (Ch) 2999, [2008] BCC 390.
63   See, Andrew Keay, *Directors' Duties,* (4th ed, LexisNexis, 2020), 213–220.

1.050 Executive directors are employed full-time by the company in order to lead the management of the company while non-executives are not employed by the company. The former will often have service contracts and be granted significant management powers. In some companies executive directors might be appointed to specific posts, such as finance director or sales director, and they are given specific tasks related to the day-to-day conduct of the company's business.

1.051 With larger companies non-executives are often appointed to provide expertise and experience for the board and to act on behalf of the shareholders as monitors of the executives. Non-executive directors are often executive directors or former executive directors of other large companies. Companies are entitled to look to non-executives for independence of judgment[64] and supervision of the executives.[65] Whether non-executives (can) achieve all of this is debatable. While executives must give their full endeavours to their company a non-executive's responsibilities are transitory as they are not engaged on a full-time basis and are not commissioned with the task of overseeing the daily operations of the company. They will attend board meetings, and in larger companies act as a member of board committees. While they are required to contribute to developing company strategy their main role might be seen as overseeing the work of the executives and other managers on behalf of the shareholders. A major difficulty for non-executives in medium–large companies is to attain a balance in relation to the primary tasks of non-executives, namely monitoring the executives and contributing to the development of strategy for the company. It can be argued that there is a conflict with these two tasks in that if the non-executives are involved in the latter they may be less active in relation to the former and may be rather reluctant to examine what the executives are doing in carrying out a strategy the devising of which was due to contributions from the non-executives. This can create internal tensions between the two roles.[66]

1.052 While there is no legislative distinction made between executive and non-executive directors, the courts in more recent times have acknowledged the different roles that are played by individual directors and will refer to the two terms in judgments.

(d) Directors in different companies

1.053 While the Companies Act treats all companies the same for most purposes, there is obviously a marked difference between a large multinational company and a one-person company providing goods locally or providing a local service. This is most acute in relation to corporate governance. Most of the academic work that has been done on corporate governance relates to public companies. So let us provide some consideration of them before moving on to small private companies. The types of companies identified are at either end of a broad spectrum. There are, of course, a lot of different kinds of companies in between the two extremes.

---

64 For a study of the issue of independence, see, A Palmiter, 'Reshaping the Corporate Fiduciary Model: A Director's Duty of Independence' (1989) 67 *Texas Law Review* 1351.

65 *Equitable Life Assurance Society v Bowley* [2003] EWHC 2263 (Comm), [2004] 1 BCLC 180, [41].

66 A Licht, 'Corporate Governance' November 2011, 13: http://ssrn.com/abstract=1786382 accessed 20 October 2020. Also, see S Lindenberg, 'Myopic Opportunism and Joint Production: A Relational Approach to Corporate Governance' in A Grandori (ed), *Corporate Governance and Firm Organization*, (OUP, 2004), 212. Although note that J Roberts, T McNulty and P Stiles in 'Beyond Agency Conceptions of the Work of the Non-Executive Director: Creating Accountability in the Boardroom' (2005) 16 *British Journal of Management* S5 tend to play down the conflict that exists with these functions and argue that positive boardroom climate as far as dynamics of the board are concerned is what matters the most.

In much of the literature written in relation to large companies the board is the focus of **1.054**
the company.[67] It is the site of responsibility and authority of the company.[68] The board is
regarded as the heart of the power relations in the company.[69] Jonathan Macey refers to it as
'the epicentre' of corporate governance,[70] and board members can be seen as the 'custodians of
the enterprise objectives of survival and growth'.[71] In more recent times and certainly since the
delivery of the Higgs Report in 2003[72] there have been greater numbers of independent directors on boards, and usually the non-executive directors outnumber the executives. The UK's
Corporate Governance Code requires there to be an appropriate combination of executive and
non-executive directors.[73]

Company law and practice centralises power in the board, and this allows for specialisation **1.055**
and division of labour.[74] It provides for the most cost-effective and efficient way to govern the
affairs of a public company.[75] It is necessary to have centralised authority, particularly for all
but the smallest companies, so that information that is spread all over an organisation might be
provided to one specialised body which can make informed decisions that will enhance a company's business, and can be transmitted to all members of the organisation in an appropriate
way.[76] Of course, the larger the company the more pertinent the foregoing points are.

The general meeting might be endowed with what is usually referred to as reserved powers. **1.056**
For instance, art 4 of the UK's model articles for public companies, which applies to all public
companies (incorporated post-2009) by default where they do not exclude it, provides that the
shareholders may, by special resolution, direct the directors to do something or refrain from
doing something.[77] Obtaining a special resolution is not easy to achieve,[78] but it does potentially
place some curb on board power.[79] In many jurisdictions, of which the UK is one, general
meetings have the power to remove a director,[80] and so some might see the general meeting
having the ultimate power.[81]

---

67   For example, see G Hayden and M Bodie, 'Shareholder Primacy and the Curious Turn Toward Board Primacy' (2010)
     51 *William and Mary Law Review* 2071, 2076.
68   Ibid., 2078.
69   A Licht, 'Culture and Law in Corporate Governance' 6 March 2014, 36: http://papers.ssrn.com/sol3/papers.cfm
     ?abstract_id=2405538 accessed, 19 October 2020.
70   *Corporate Governance,* Princeton, (Princeton University Press, 2008), 51. Macey says that the directors are the governors
     of the company.
71   W Suojanen, 'Accounting Theory and the Large Corporation' (1954) 29 *The Accounting Review* 391, 393.
72   *Review of the role and effectiveness of non-executive directors,* January 2003.
73   Financial Reporting Council, *UK Corporate Governance Code,* July 2018, Principle G: https://www.frc.org.uk/
     getattachment/88bd8c45–50ea-4841–95b0-d2f4f48069a2/2018-UK-Corporate-Governance-Code-FINAL.PDF
     accessed 18 October 2020.
74   R Clark, *Corporate Law,* (Little Brown & Co, 1986), 802.
75   S Bainbridge, 'Director Primacy and Shareholder Disempowerment' (2006) 119 *Harvard Law Review* 1735, 1746.
76   K Arrow, *The Limits of Organization,* (W. W. Norton, 1974), 68–70. Also, see S Bainbridge, 'Investor Activism:
     Reshaping the Playing Field?' May 2008, 8: http://ssrn.com/abstract=1130969 accessed, 19 October 2020; F Gevurtz,
     'The Historical and Political Origins of the Corporate Board of Directors (2004) 33 *Hofstra Law Review* 89, 96.
77   The Companies (Model Articles) Regulations 2008 (SI 2008/3229), Sch 3.
78   It requires the vote by a 75 per cent majority of votes cast at a meeting of the company: Companies Act 2006, s 283.
79   The Companies (Model Articles) Regulations 2008 SI 2008/3229, reg 2 and Sch 1 art 4 (private companies); reg 4 and
     Sch 3 art 4 (public companies).
80   Companies Act 2006, s 168.
81   J Lowry and A Reisberg, *Pettet's Company Law,* (4th ed, Pearson, 2012), 147.

1.057 Notwithstanding the fact that the general meeting might have residual and removal powers, and the shareholders can play an important role in the decision-making of a company,[82] the board is seen as the most important decision-making body,[83] and is regarded as the highest authority in the company. Its members act on behalf of the company, which while it is a legal person needs human beings to act for it. Company law effectively centralises power and authority in the board of directors, and to provide for a centralised structure that controls the company, company law provides the board with exclusive authority and power to manage the affairs of the company.[84] It is traditionally held that this approach is more efficient, especially where there are a large number of shareholders, and typically boards make company decisions.[85]

1.058 Public companies in the UK are traditionally characterised by ownership being separated from control, that is, the shareholders who are regarded as the owners (in a loose sense) do not control the company, the directors do. This means that the board is even more powerful. Centralising power in the board allows for specialisation and division of labour.[86] It provides for the most cost-effective and efficient way to govern the affairs of a public company.[87] This approach is necessary as large organisations cannot achieve their aims by involving their shareholders in regular decision-making.[88] It is also more efficient and less costly than transmitting all of the information on which the decision is based,[89] and avoids the difficulty of getting a large group to make decisions.[90] It also overcomes rational apathy that characterises shareholders in large companies;[91] shareholders will only expend funds and effort to enable them to make informed decisions if the expected benefits of doing so will be greater than the costs,[92] and they can never be sure of that.

1.059 The board is regarded, inter alia, as a mechanism by which the powers exerted by the company's managers (executives and non-board managers) can be controlled, and in achieving this it

---

82 P Davies and S Worthington, *Gower and Davies' Principles of Modern Company Law* (9th ed, Sweet & Maxwell, 2012), 435.

83 Ibid., 383. It is key body according to codes of practice that apply around the world.

84 See F Gevurtz, 'The Historical and Political Origins of the Corporate Board of Directors' (2004) 33 *Hofstra Law Review* 89, 95.

85 M Dooley, 'Two Models of Corporate Governance' (1992) 47 *Business Lawyer* 461, 466–467. Also, see W Bratton and M Wachter, 'The Case Against Shareholder Empowerment' (2010) 158 *University of Pennsylvania Law Review* 653, 660.

86 R Clark, *Corporate Law*, (Little Brown & Co, 1986), 802

87 S Bainbridge, 'Director Primacy and Shareholder Disempowerment' (2006) 119 *Harvard Law Review* 1735, 1746.

88 R Buxbaum, 'The Internal Division of Powers in Corporate Governance' (1985) 73 *California Law Review* 1671, 1671; G Hayden and M Bodie, 'Shareholder Primacy and the Curious Turn Toward Board Primacy' (2010) 51 *William and Mary Law Review* 2071, 2085.

89 K Arrow, *The Limits of Organization*, (W. W. Norton, 1974), 68. Also, see W Bratton and M Wachter, 'The Case Against Shareholder Empowerment' (2010) 158 *University of Pennsylvania Law Review* 653, 660.

90 H Hutchinson, 'Director Primacy and Corporate Governance: Shareholder Voting Rights Captured by the Accountability/Authority Paradigm' (2005) 36 *Loyola University of Chicago Law Journal* 1111, 1201.

91 I Anabtawi, 'Some Skepticism About Increasing Shareholder Power' (2006) 53 *UCLA Law Review* 561, 574, n.61; B Sharfman, 'What's Wrong with Shareholder Empowerment?' (2012) 37 *Journal of Corporation Law* 903, 906; D Ahern, 'Directors' Duties: Broadening the Focus Beyond Content to Examine the Accountability Spectrum' (2011) 33 *Dublin University Law Journal* 116.

92 S Bainbridge, 'The Case for Limited Shareholder Voting Rights' (2006) 63 *UCLA Law Review* 601, 623.

engages in monitoring the work of the managers. The board effectively links the shareholders and the managers of the company.[93]

To permit the board to be granted a broad discretion is not a perfect solution, but undoubtedly **1.060** granting significant discretion to the directors is largely unavoidable. It is simply not possible to formulate a single overarching principle or test to guide directors how to act, as circumstances will be so varied, and the issues that directors encounter are often complex and multifaceted. That is why it is necessary to have flexibility, and to have a model that embraces broad principles rather than specific rules. To perform efficiently directors have to be granted open-ended discretions.[94]

One of the primary concerns in public and large private companies as far as corporate govern- **1.061** ance is concerned, in the eyes of many, is that the way that organs of management are set up and the control that directors have in running the company is that it produces an agency problem. This assumes that the directors are seen as the agents of the 'owners'[95] (the shareholders) of the company. The agency problem is that the directors, because they have control of the company's affairs, may seek to act in their own interests and this will cause loss to the principals, that is the shareholders. This problem is the reason, so the argument goes, for provisions/measures that restrict the directors or call them to account.[96] Directors' duties are prime instances.

The board is regarded as the link between the shareholders and the management of the compa- **1.062** ny,[97] and as an element of this the board is charged with the responsibility of maintaining good corporate governance. Directors operate as members of boards that are granted wide powers to manage a company's affairs. The board is the governing body that is ultimately responsible and accountable for the decisions of the company and its performance.[98]

More specifically the board's role includes:[99] **1.063**

- Selecting and setting the remuneration of the chief executive officer of the company;
- Determining objectives for the company's business, including strategic planning and risk management;
- Formulating strategy and approving business plans;
- Reviewing at intervals the company's progress in achieving its goals;

---

93   P Stiles and B Taylor, *Boards at Work. How Directors View Their Roles and Responsibilities*, (Oxford University Press, 2001), 4.
94   M Whincop, 'A Theoretical and Policy Critique of the Modern Reformulation of Directors' Duties of Care' (1996) 6 *Australian Journal of Corporate Law* 72, 83.
95   Many would disagree with the shareholders being called owners as they only hold shares in the company and do not own it. However, others would point to the fact that this is how the shareholders are perceived in economic theory.
96   Also attempts are often made to align the interests of the directors with those of the shareholders. This is often done by structuring a remuneration package for directors which means their benefits rise or fall with those of the company (and ultimately the shareholders).
97   P Stiles and B Taylor, *Boards at Work: How Directors View Their Roles and Responsibilities*, (OUP, 2001), at 4.
98   R Tricker, *Corporate Governance – Principles, Policies and Practices*, (OUP, 2009) at 7.
99   The following list is derived from A. Keay, *Directors' Duties*, (4th ed, LexisNexis, 2020), 5 which is based on : *AWA Ltd v Daniels* (1992) 10 ACLC 933 at 1013; *Dairy Containers Ltd v NZI Bank Ltd* [1995] 2 NZLR 30 at 79; R P Austin, H A J Ford and I M Ramsay, *Company Directors*, (LexisNexis Butterworths, 2005), 60; A E Onetto, 'Agency Problems and the Board of Directors' (2007) 7 *Journal of International Banking and Financial Law* 414.

- Determining the extent of the company's investment in new ventures;
- Approving revenue and capital expenditure budgets;
- Considering and approving important management decisions;
- Ensuring that the company has accounting and information systems that are adequate to monitor company performance;
- Monitoring the performance of the managers and how the company is performing overall;
- Providing direction to the company;
- Ensuring that proper information is made available to the markets concerning the company's financial position and performance;
- Reporting to the shareholders at appropriate points.

1.064 Of course, as one would expect, much of what is the role of a board depends on the needs and goals of a company at a particular point in time.[100]

1.065 What we have said so far in relation to large companies includes public and large private companies. Some aspects may be relevant to smaller companies and some of the roles mentioned above are applicable to small companies, but the dynamics and practice of smaller private companies is, as far as the board and directors are concerned, quite a bit different. Corporate governance is not quite as formal with smaller companies as it is with larger companies and is different because of other issues such as the size of the membership of the board and the company's general meeting.

1.066 As mentioned earlier, often, with smaller companies, the directors and the shareholders are the same people and these sorts of companies are known as owner/managed companies/firms. Where the shareholders are also the directors, an occurrence that is common particularly with really small companies, ownership and control of the company come together.[101] Small companies have their own unique corporate governance issues and in owner/managed companies, while the agency problem that was discussed above in relation to large companies may not be as prominent, it can exist. However, another agency problem can also exist. That is, the majority shareholder (if one exists) or a coalition of larger shareholders may seek to act to benefit themselves at the expense of the minority shareholders. Such action is likely to involve controlling the board. This type of agency problem is overcome by measures that give minority shareholders power to hold the majority to account and, perhaps, take legal proceedings against the majority. A critical instance is found under s 994 of the Companies Act that provides, inter alia, that:

> a member of a company may apply to the court by petition for an order under this Part on the ground–
>
> (a) that the company's affairs are being or have been conducted in a manner that is unfairly prejudicial to the interests of members generally or of some part of its members (including at least himself), or
> (b) that an actual or proposed act or omission of the company (including an act or omission on its behalf) is or would be so prejudicial.

1.067 Small companies tend to be characterised by less formality as far as most aspects of company law are concerned, including corporate governance. While this might be fine while a company

---

100 Onetto, ibid.
101 These companies are said to have concentrated ownership.

is solvent and the directors control the company, it might not be if the company becomes insolvent and enters some form of insolvency regime. Administrators and liquidators will, as mentioned earlier and discussed in depth later, look very carefully at how the directors have governed the company and may, in their investigations, find actions of directors to be in breach of the Act or the common law and constitute grounds on which to institute legal proceedings in order to recover funds for the creditors.

2.   Shareholders

As mentioned in the previous section of the chapter, the general meeting might be endowed **1.068** with what is usually referred to as reserved powers. For instance, art 4 of the UK's model articles for private companies, and which applies to all companies registered post-2009 by default where not excluded, provides that the shareholders may, by special resolution, direct the directors to do something or refrain from doing something.[102] As noted earlier, obtaining a special resolution is not easy to achieve,[103] but it does potentially place some curb on board power,[104] and it might be easier to pass one in small companies when compared with large ones.

It is only large shareholders in large companies that will usually be able to influence corporate **1.069** governance. For instance, institutional shareholders such as pension funds often have informal discussions with boards of directors and they might make known their concern over particular issues. Boards might change aspects of their corporate governance following such discussions as they do want to lose a large shareholder, which in listed companies can simply sell its shares on the stock exchange if it is not happy with the way that the company is being run by the board. If it does sell it could well lead to a reduction in the share price of the company.

A major restriction on the power of the general meeting of shareholders occurs if a company **1.070** is insolvent or near to it, for in such circumstances the general meeting is not able to ratify any actions of directors that are outside their powers or constitute breaches of their duties, if those actions will prejudice the creditors.[105] This is discussed further in Chapter 4.

Generally speaking, in UK law shareholders do not owe any duties or other responsibilities **1.071** to other shareholders, or to the company itself. An exception to this is the fact that in certain circumstances a majority can be held liable to the minority for indulging in what is known as a fraud on the minority.

If a company enters an insolvency regime the role of the shareholders is generally emasculated. **1.072** In liquidation the shareholders become known as contributories. They may be asked to make a decision on some issues. On what decisions shareholders might be able to have a role in

---

102   The Companies (Model Articles) Regulations 2008 (SI 2008/3229), Sch 1.

103   In the UK it requires the vote by a 75 per cent majority, that is, 75 per cent of the votes cast at the meeting must support the resolution: Companies Act 2006, s 283.

104   The Companies (Model Articles) Regulations 2008 SI 2008/3229, reg 2 and Sch 1 art 4 (private companies); reg 4 and Sch 3 art 4 (public companies).

105   For example, see *Re Horsley & Weight Ltd* [1982] 3 All ER 1045; *Kinsela v Russell Kinsela Pty Ltd* (1986) 4 ACLC 215, (1986) 10 ACLR 395; *Re DKG Contractors Ltd* [1990] BCC 903; *Liquidator of West Mercia Safetywear Ltd v Dodd* (1988) 4 BCC 30; *Official Receiver v Stern* [2001] EWCA Civ 1787, [2002] 1 BCLC 119; *Gold Travel Ltd v Aydin* [2014] EWHC 1587 (Ch); *Bilta (UK) Ltd (in liqtrat) and others v Nazir* [2015] UKSC 23, [2016] AC 1.

governance and what processes are involved in leading to contributories having an input are discussed in Chapter 5. Contributories may become members of a liquidation committee and their position in this committee is considered in Chapter 9.

3. Creditors

1.073 When a company is solvent it is argued, by some commentators, that creditors should have to protect themselves through contract, such as obtaining security over company property or getting personal guarantees from directors, so that if the company fails to pay then the creditor can rely on the security or the guarantee to satisfy the debt owed. Save for any benefits secured through contractual means most creditors have little influence over corporate governance when the company is solvent. Of course, a large creditor, such as a bank might well be able to exert influence. So might repeat creditors, such as suppliers of large amounts of critical goods or services that cannot be accessed elsewhere easily or at all. However, some creditors have little or no power and cannot obtain security. As we see in Chapter 4, the law seeks to deal with that problem.

1.074 Whether a person is a creditor will not be a big issue, for the most part. A creditor is someone owed a debt. According to r 14.1(5) of the Insolvency Rules 2016, which defines 'debt' for the purposes of the liquidation of companies, it is a term which includes any debt or liability that is present or future, whether it is certain or contingent or whether its amount is fixed or liquidated, or is able to be ascertained by fixed rules or as a matter of opinion. Further, it would include liabilities involving the liability to pay money or money's worth, including any liability under an enactment, any liability for breach of trust, any liability in contract, tort or bailment, and any liability arising out of any obligation to make restitution.[106]

1.075 Often companies will have a range of different creditors. Companies usually will have borrowed funds to enable them to operate as money invested by shareholders might not be sufficient. Companies will have usually borrowed as much as they can from leading banks, who will normally require the granting of security. Besides lenders, most companies will have creditors who are landlords, suppliers of goods and/or services, and HM Revenue and Customs (for outstanding corporation tax, and any unremitted VAT and PAYE deductions). Companies might also have more specialist or unusual types of creditor, such as customers who have paid deposits on goods or services yet to be supplied and those having tort claims against the company.

1.076 As is discussed in detail in Chapter 4, the directors of a company are obliged to take into account the interests of creditors when the company is near to or in insolvency (and before the entry into any formal insolvency regime) but despite this the creditors themselves have little power to do anything, unless they are also shareholders. It has been decisively held in the case law that the creditors are not owed a duty by the directors as the directors' duties are to the company itself. This is now codified in s 170(4) of the Companies Act. If a creditor was also a shareholder and he or she had evidence of a breach of duty by the directors in not considering the interests of the creditors when the company is insolvent, then he or she could seek to insti-

---

106 Insolvency Rules 2016, r 14.1(6).

tute a derivative action against the directors.[107] This action is taken on behalf of the company to whom the duties are owed. However, this is all extremely unlikely.

The banks and major lenders to the company, especially if they hold security, are likely to be **1.077** able to wield some influence over what the directors do if the company is in financial distress. Those lenders who hold a floating charge over company assets which can be classed as a qualifying charge, are able to appoint an administrator if there is any breach of the terms of the loan agreement that includes the charge. If the charge on which creditors rely was created prior to 15 September 2003 they can, if the charge permits them to (and it usually will), appoint an administrative receiver.

Suppliers and other trade creditors may press for payment if they are not paid or, alternatively, **1.078** they may decide to withhold the extension of any further credit unless some or all of the money owed to them is paid. This may well have an effect on the governance decisions that directors take.

Generally, any creditor who is owed a debt is permitted to petition the court for a winding-up **1.079** order provided that the company is insolvent, so that the company can be taken into liquidation. This right is often used by creditors as a way of getting companies to pay what they owe or at least consider taking some sort of action to address the financial malaise from which it suffers.

In insolvency regimes creditors will have the power to have an input in relation to some major **1.080** decisions that are proposed to be taken by the IP. The processes involved are considered in Chapter 5 where decision-making is explained. Creditors might act as part of creditors' committees in administration or members of liquidation committees in liquidation. Their role and work is discussed in detail in Chapter 9. In these committees the creditors are able to hold the IP to account and the IP may seek input from the committees in relation to important and critical decisions that might need to be made. Also, provisions in the Act grant creditors the power to apply to the courts to have decisions of IPs reviewed.

4.   Company officers

Directors are the primary officers of the company, but there may be others, and they can play **1.081** a role in corporate governance. There is no detailed definition of 'officer' although both the Act[108] and the Companies Act[109] refer to the expression. Section 1121(1) of the Companies Act provides that 'officer' includes directors, managers and company secretaries. This is only in the context of offences, but later s 1173 states that an 'officer' in relation to a body corporate includes a director, a manager and a secretary, so it makes it plain that these persons are company officers for other purposes. Persons might be regarded as company officers for certain purposes. An auditor is an example. Section 212 of the Act includes, according to *Re Thomas Gerrard and Sons Ltd*,[110] auditors within the expression 'officer' in s 212. Section 1157(1) of the Companies Act envisages that auditors employed by the company may be company officers.

---

107   This would necessitate obtaining the leave of the court to continue an action (s 261 of the Companies Act 2006).
108   For example, s 212 of the Act.
109   For example, s 1173 of the Companies Act.
110   [1968] Ch 455.

1.082   The main officer, besides directors, as far as our study is concerned is the company secretary. The company secretary is responsible for ensuring that an organisation complies with standard financial and legal practice, and maintains high standards of corporate governance. They will advise on governance matters,[111] and they are often perceived as the head of governance. They must possess a complete understanding of the law that affect what they do and the matters that impinge on corporate governance. He or she has a strategic position at the centre of governance operations and liaises between the board of directors and the executive management as well as communicating with shareholders. Company secretaries should act as support to the board to ensure that it has the policies, information and resources to enable the board to function efficiently and properly.[112] Another aspect of their responsibility is, usually, to keep and maintain company registers, such as the register of members.[113] Since April 2008, when most of the provisions of the Companies Act 2006 came into force, private companies are no longer required to have company secretaries, but one would expect to see company secretaries appointed to large private companies and smaller companies still retain the practice.

5.   The community

1.083   While its impact on governance may not be huge, the community in which a company operates (communities for large companies) is clearly a stakeholder in a company and in that role it may influence corporate governance.

1.084   Many communities rely wholly or substantially on the operations of one company. This will usually be a very large company. The decisions the board of that company make will often have an impact on the community. For instance, if a company decides to make a reasonably large number of workers redundant, that will affect the community, particularly when the workers live in the local area. The workers will have less money to spend in shops, some may have to move elsewhere to secure employment and there may be social costs for family and their contacts and involvement in the community. If a company becomes insolvent and enters administration, or even worse collapses totally and enters liquidation, there are likely to be even greater effects on the community.

1.085   The collapse of some companies which operate nationally or internationally can be even greater than that outlined above. Examples are Woolworths and BHS, two High Street retailers that were, until their demise, household names in the UK for years. Not only did the closure of their stores blight the High Street, people all over the UK lost their jobs. Naturally with a multinational company, insolvency can be even more devastating, affecting communities across the world. The collapse of the carmaker MG Rover in 2005 due to its insolvency is a very good instance of a multinational company that has a negative impact on communities locally, nationally and internationally.

1.086   What is often not recognised by the public is that when a company becomes insolvent and stops trading it is not just the people employed by that company and their families that are affected. With large companies there are usually many suppliers, a good proportion of which

---

111   A Alcock (ed), *Gore-Browne on Companies*, (LexisNexis), 41A[4]
112   Financial Reporting Council, *UK Corporate Governance Code*, 2018, Principle I.
113   A Alcock (ed), *Gore-Browne on Companies*, (LexisNexis), 12[2].

rely totally or substantially on a large company to provide it with business. This is known as 'the ripple effect', and can lead to insolvencies at different levels of those people and companies who are involved in supply and production. This happened with MG Rover with a substantial number of job losses and business closures, particularly in the West Midlands. It also led to closures and job losses related to the carmaker's dealerships all over the UK and in several countries in Western Europe. The collapse of the construction company, Carillion, provides a more recent instance of this problem. Those conducting construction businesses rely heavily on sub-contractors such as suppliers of building materials and tradespersons who undertake, for example, electrical, plastering and plumbing work. Again, as with MG Rover, there were a large number of people who lost their jobs, not only in Carillion itself, but also in associated businesses, and businesses either suffered large losses or entered insolvency regimes.

The above illustrates the fact that insolvency is a matter of public interest.[114] **1.087**

6.   Insolvency practitioners/officeholders

UK law has developed to the point where a person may only conduct an insolvency regime, such   **1.088** as a liquidation, where he or she is licensed to act.[115] A person who is so licensed is referred to as an 'insolvency practitioner' (IP),[116] and we use this term when referring in a general way to those who are licensed to act. Where IPs have been appointed to act in insolvency regimes we will refer to them as 'officeholders'.[117] Of course, when referring to specific regimes we will use the term that is appropriate; for instance, liquidator in relation to liquidations.

Once a company enters some form of insolvency regime the primary player is usually going to   **1.089** be the 'officeholder' who is appointed to oversee the company's affairs. This is certainly the case with administration and liquidation, but not, normally, the case in relation to CVAs. While an IP is appointed as the supervisor of the CVA, in most CVAs the IP as officeholder will not have a major role in the governance of the company. The officeholder might have to step in if the terms of the CVA are not complied with, and he or she has the power to petition for a winding up of the company.[118]

To act as an officeholder a person must be appropriately qualified; the issue of qualifications   **1.090** will be addressed in Chapter 8.[119] To act without being qualified is a criminal offence.[120] It should be mentioned at this point that only a human being can be appointed as an officeholder

---

114   A. Keay, 'Insolvency Law: A Matter of Public Interest?' (2000) 51 *Northern Ireland Legal Quarterly* 509.

115   Insolvency Act 1986, s 390.

116   This is a term used in the Act when it is referring to who is able to be appointed to act in relation to formal insolvency regimes and it is now used in the English language version of the recast European Union Regulation on Insolvency Proceedings: Regulation 2015/848.

117   A person may have a licence to act as an IP but does not actually hold an office as a liquidator, etc. Examples are senior employees in firms that take appointments. Appointments are held by partners in the firms and they will be referred to as 'officeholders'.

118   Insolvency Act 1986, s 7(4)(b).

119   Until the Insolvency Act was enacted there were no qualifications specified for IPs. Qualifications was an issue raised and addressed by the *Report of the Review Committee on Insolvency Law and Practice* (1982) Cmnd 8558, London, HMSO (Cork Report).

120   Insolvency Act 1986, s 389(1).

in relation to any insolvency administration.[121] That obviously means that companies and partnerships cannot be appointed.

1.091 The reason that IPs are the primary players in regimes like administration and liquidation is because they will control the company and are accountable to the creditors for what is done. Also, they are, in some regimes, accountable to the court. The practice has been in UK insolvency law to have an independent third person appointed to take control of a company that enters insolvency regime, with the management of the company displaced from power, in comparison with the United States where the management can remain in power, as is the case with Chapter 11 bankruptcies,[122] except where there are serious allegations and proof of management defalcations, whereupon a trustee is appointed by the relevant bankruptcy court.

1.092 On one view, corporate governance in an insolvent company may be regarded as the governance of divergent economic interests and the conflicts that arise from them. Managing and mediating these conflicts in a formal insolvency process, acting with disinterest and fairness, is the role of the officeholder. Maintaining that position while simultaneously achieving commercial objectives, often under considerable time-pressure or in circumstances of imperfect information, is a responsible and challenging task. The officeholder should be above the fray, but the nature of the functions they perform mean that they are peculiarly vulnerable to allegations of conflict of interest themselves.

1.093 At one time IPs were seen only as undertakers, namely only liquidating and overseeing the dissolution of companies. Since the mid-1980s, IPs in the UK have embraced more of a rescue role, trying to save companies. This came about as a result of the *Report of the Review Committee on Insolvency Law and Practice*,[123] known as 'the Cork Report' which was handed down in 1982 and the subsequently enacted Insolvency Act 1986 that provided for new regimes, namely administration and CVAs. It is probably fair to say that the rescue role was given impetus by the changes brought about to the Act by the provisions of the Enterprise Act 2002. Different governance measures are likely to be required when IPs are seeking to rescue a company compared with when they are liquidating it.

1.094 Officeholders are essentially accountable to the creditors in whose interests they will run, rescue or liquidate a company. In regimes that have been commenced by court order the officeholder also is accountable to the court. In some ways officeholders are accountable to the public. For instance, officeholders are subject to a duty to report the unfitness of directors to the Disqualification Unit, situated within the Insolvency Service. The Disqualification Unit then may seek to have a director disqualified through a court order or an undertaking from the director not to act as a director for a specified period of time. Disqualification is largely about protecting the public from people being able to act as directors when they have acted improperly or incompetently.

---

121   Ibid., s 390(1).
122   Under the Bankruptcy Reform Act 1978.
123   (1982) Cmnd 8558, London, HMSO.

The leading organisation which represents IPs and their interests is the Association of Business   **1.095**
Recovery Professionals,[124] and it is generally known as R3. R3 frequently will make submissions to government about insolvency matters and is regularly consulted by the government
and specifically by the Insolvency Service, a part of the Department of Business Energy and
Industrial Strategy. The vast majority of IPs are accountants. It has always been the case that
the accountancy profession has dominated the administration of insolvent estates. This is the
case in most of the Commonwealth and Ireland. In other places in the world lawyers tend to be
appointed.[125] IPs in the UK and Ireland will frequently seek legal advice.

We should note that IPs are often consulted by companies that are insolvent or near to it.   **1.096**
Companies will seek advice as to what they might do and the advantages and disadvantages
of that action. IPs might advise on the various insolvency regimes that are available. In giving
advice the IP is not acting in any statutorily sanctioned role. It is not unusual for the IP to
become the administrator or the liquidator if the company decides to enter administration
or creditors' voluntary liquidation at some later point. In giving advice prior to the entry of
the company into an insolvency regime an IP must ensure that he or she is not able to be
characterised as a shadow director by, for instance, interfering in the running of the company.
For the most part the IP will be saved by s 251(2) of the Companies Act which provides that
persons are not deemed to be shadow directors just because the directors act on their advice, in
situations where the advice is given in a person's professional capacity.

We will not say anything more about IPs as they will feature throughout much of the book and   **1.097**
their work, duties and role will be considered in depth, particularly in Chapters 8 and 9.

7.   The Insolvency Service

The Department of Business, Energy and Industrial Strategy has the oversight of both the   **1.098**
regulation of companies and the administration of insolvencies. The Insolvency Service, which
is an executive agency within the Department of Business, Energy and Industrial Strategy,
fulfils a supervisory role in relation to IPs and the administration of insolvent companies in
general. It will carry out many of the oversight and regulatory responsibilities that redound on
the Secretary of State for Business, Energy and Industrial Strategy. Sections 391D–391T of
the Act set out in some detail what many of these are. Chapter 11 discusses the work of the
Insolvency Service.

The Insolvency Service is subject to the direction and oversight of the Inspector-General and   **1.099**
Chief Executive.

What the Insolvency Service determines by way of implementation of insolvency practice   **1.100**
can affect how IPs carry out their governance role. This is done partly through the issuing
of Statements of Practice (SIPs). SIPs are designed to promote and maintain high standards
of practice by setting what is required practice,[126] and we will mention various SIPs during
the course of the book. A part of the Insolvency Service are official receivers. These officers

---

124   Previously it was known as the Society of Practitioners of Insolvency.
125   For example, the United States and Germany.
126   Insolvency Service, *SIP 1: An Introduction to Statements of Insolvency Practice*, 1 October 2015.

are appointed by the Secretary of State for Business, Energy and Industrial Strategy and are discussed next.

8. Official receivers

1.101 The office of official receiver was established by the Bankruptcy Act 1883.[127] While the role of this officer was originally limited to dealing with personal bankruptcies, it was extended to companies in compulsory liquidation by the Companies (Winding up) Act 1890.[128]

1.102 The official receivers still carry out an important role in relation to personal insolvency, an issue with which we are not concerned in this book. They also undertake an important supervisory role in relation to company insolvencies and particularly in respect of the liquidation of companies. The official receiver is always the first liquidator in compulsory windings up and he or she will continue to act in this capacity until replaced by a private IP.[129] In some liquidations the official receiver will remain as liquidator. This is usually where there is uncertainty as to whether there will be enough funds and assets in the company to pay the remuneration of an IP. An example is Carillion.

1.103 The official receiver might remain as liquidator and not be replaced by a private liquidator (IP) where there are public interest issues at stake, such as with the liquidation of British Steel.[130]

1.104 Besides the role of first liquidator, official receivers act as liquidators where there are vacancies in the post of liquidator from to time.[131] One of their major functions is, in relation to insolvent companies entering liquidation, to investigate, pursuant to s 132 of the Act, the causes of the failure of such companies. Official receivers are at liberty to apply to the court for directions in relation to any matter affecting a liquidation.[132]

1.105 The official receivers are duty bound, like liquidators, pursuant to the Company Directors' Disqualification Act 1986,[133] to report to the Secretary of State for Business, Energy and Industrial Strategy any director, past or present, of an insolvent company who appears to be unfit to be concerned in the management of a company.[134] If there is no liquidation committee for a liquidation then the functions of a committee are vested in the Secretary of State,[135] and in this type of case the functions may be exercised by the official receiver.[136]

---

127 46 & 47 Vict c 52.
128 53 & 54 Vict c 63
129 Insolvency Act 1986, s 136.
130 *Re British Steel Ltd* [2019] EWHC 1304 (Ch). See, A Keay and P Walton, 'British Steel: Is it a wind up?' (2019) 12(4) *Corporate Rescue and Insolvency* 125.
131 Insolvency Act 1986, s 136(3).
132 Insolvency Rules 2016, r 13.3.
133 Company Directors' Disqualification Act 1986, s 7(3).
134 Official receivers are empowered to bring disqualification proceedings: *Re Minotaur Data Systems Ltd* [1999] 2 BCLC 766, 772 (CA).
135 Insolvency Act 1986, 141(5).
136 Insolvency Rules 2016, r 17.28(1)(2).

The official receivers are officers of the court to which they are attached and are answerable to the court for the carrying out of its orders and for the discharge of their statutory functions.[137] **1.106**

The Secretary of State is at liberty to give directions to official receivers as far as the disposal of their business is concerned.[138] The Secretary of State may confer on official receivers further functions.[139] In carrying out the functions of his or her office an official receiver is to act under the directions of the Secretary of State and is an officer of the court when he or she exercises those functions.[140] As a result of the latter capacity, any interference with the work of an official receiver could constitute a contempt of court. As an officer of the court an official receiver is required to act honourably and fairly and must not rely on his or her technical rights under the law.[141] **1.107**

9.   The courts

It might be thought that the courts are not involved in corporate governance, but they are/can in some ways. We will just mention some instances. More detailed discussion is contained in later chapters. First, with some insolvency regimes, namely administrations[142] and compulsory liquidations,[143] the officeholders involved (administrators and liquidators) are officers of the court and, in that capacity, they are representatives of the court and entrusted with the reputation of the court; they are answerable to the court. Being under the control and discipline of the court, the liquidator is required at all times to act in an honest, impartial,[144] and high-minded[145] fashion. **1.108**

Secondly, even when an IP is not acting as an officer of the court, such as the liquidator of a creditors' voluntary liquidation, he or she is able to apply to the court for directions under s 112 of the Act, and accordingly a court can direct a liquidator to take a particular course of action. **1.109**

Thirdly, courts have a supervisory role in relation to all IPs appointed to insolvency regimes. For instance, under s 168(5) of the Act, on an application brought before it, the court is able to reverse or modify (as well as confirm) the decision of a liquidator. Another instance is under **1.110**

---

137 *Re Pantmaenog Timber Co Ltd (in liq; Official Receiver v Wadge Rapps & Hunt* [2003] UKHL 49, [2004] 1 AC 158, [2003] 3 WLR 767, [2003] 4 All ER 18, [2003] 2 BCLC 257, [2004] BPIR 139, [43].

138 Insolvency Act 1986, s 399(6).

139 Ibid., s 400(1).

140 Ibid., s 400(2).

141 This is the Rule in *Ex p James* (1874) 9 Ch App 609. The rule is discussed at length below at [7.113]–[7.120]. The rule applies to official receivers: *Re Opera Ltd* [1891] 2 Ch 154; *Re Wyvern Developments Ltd* [1974] 1 WLR 1097.

142 Insolvency Act 1986, para 5 of Sch B1.

143 *Re Contract Corp; Gooch's Case* (1872) 7 LR Ch App 207, 211; *Re Timberland Ltd; Commissioner for Corporate Affairs v Harvey* (1979) 4 ACLR 259 at 281, 286; *Re Winnis Trading Pty Ltd* (1985) 3 ACLC 39; *Re Australian National Finance Ltd* (1992) 7 ACSR 697; *United Tool & Die Makers Pty Ltd (in liq) JV Marine Motors Pty Ltd* (1991) 9 ACLC 314; *Sydlow Pty Ltd v TG Kotselas Pty Ltd* (1996) 14 ACLC 846.

144 *Re Contract Corp; Gooch's Case* (1871) 7 LR Ch App 207 at 211; *Re National Safety Council of Australia (Victoria Division)* (1989) 15 ACLR 355, (1989) 7 ACLC 602; *Re West Australian Gem Explorers Pty Ltd* (1994) 13 ACSR 104, (1994) 12 ACLC 256.

145 Indeed, Australian authority has stated that a liquidator is expected to dispatch his or her duties in the manner expected of a judge or a court: *Re Timberland Ltd; Commissioner for Corporate Affairs v Harvey* (1979) 4 ACLR 259, 286.

para 74 of Sch BI to the Act where the court might regulate the exercise of the actions of an administrator or require the administrator to do or not to do something.

1.111 Fourthly, courts have power in appointing IPs to certain roles in certain cases or removing them from roles in other cases.

2

THE MEANING AND FEATURES OF CORPORATE GOVERNANCE

A. INTRODUCTION

Obviously, an essential part of the book is corporate governance. A voluminous amount of **2.001** material has been written about the subject and it is a matter that goes to the heart of company law and practice. However, the vast majority of this material has been in the context of solvent companies and it has not touched on insolvent companies at all. It is the contention of this work that corporate governance is a critical aspect of companies that are insolvent. In such a situation different issues come to the fore. This chapter endeavours to discuss the meaning of corporate governance as a concept as well as the features of it, before we plunge into a specific and focused examination of it where companies are insolvent.

One caveat that needs to be sounded is the fact that much of the material that has been **2.002** written by commentators and the reports composed by government, quasi-government and professional bodies address corporate governance in public companies. The fact that public companies and large private companies on the one hand, and most private companies on the other are very different in the way that they are organised and operate are important factors that must not be overlooked.

B. MEANING OF CORPORATE GOVERNANCE

The first thing to note is that there is no universally accepted definition of corporate govern- **2.003** ance, and no one definitive articulation of the concept. It is far from a term of art.[1] It has been

---

1   *Report to the HIH Royal Commission*, 'Directions for the future,' Part III, 2003, para 6.1: http://www.hihroyalcom.gov.au/finalreport/Chapter%206.HTML. In fact his Honour was not comfortable with the phrase because he felt that it had been so widely used that it may have become meaningless.

said to be an ambiguous concept.[2] It evades exact definition.[3] Many definitions have been proferred by government committees, corporate officers, practitioners in various professions and by academics. On the one hand, it has been defined extremely broadly. For instance, the Cadbury Committee in its *Report of the Committee on the Financial Aspects of Corporate Governance* (usually known as 'the Cadbury Report') said that corporate governance was: 'the system by which companies are directed and controlled'.[4] This is a definition which is often relied on. The Chartered Institute of Internal Auditors in the UK has expanded this basic definition and has said that corporate governance is 'the combination of processes and structures implemented by the board in order to inform, direct, manage and monitor the activities of the organisation toward the achievement of its objectives'.[5]

2.004 In Volume I of his Report dealing with the collapse of the once leading large Australian insurance company, HIH, Owen J said that 'corporate governance' describes:

> the framework of rules, relationships, systems and processes within and by which authority is exercised and controlled within corporations. It encompasses the mechanisms by which companies, and those in control, are held to account.[6]

2.005 Later, in Volume III of the Report his Honour said:

> At its broadest, the governance of corporate entities comprehends the framework of rules, relationships, systems and processes within and by which authority is exercised and controlled in corporations. It includes the practices by which that exercise and control of authority is in fact effected.[7]

2.006 In his background report to the Report, Owen J said that:

> Corporate governance refers generally to the legal and organisational framework within which, and the principles and processes by which, corporations are governed. It refers in particular to the powers, accountability and relationships of those who participate in the direction and control of a company. Chief among these participants are the board of directors, and management. There are aspects of the corporate governance regime that have an impact on the relationship between shareholders and the company.[8]

2.007 Professor John Farrar has said that corporate governance is a subject which involves consideration of 'the legitimacy of corporate power, corporate accountability and standards by which the corporation is to be governed and by whom'.[9]

---

2   K Keasey, S Thompson and M Wright, 'Introduction' in K Keasey, S Thompson and M Wright (eds), *Corporate Governance – Economic, Management and Financial Issues*, (Oxford University Press, 1997), 2.

3   J Birds et al, *Boyle and Bird's* Company Law, (7th ed, Jordans, 2009), 357.

4   1992, para, 2.5: http://www.ecgi.org/codes/documents/cadbury.pdf.

5   See http://www.iia.org.uk/en/Knowledge_Centre/Resource_Library/corporate-governance.cfm.

6   *Report to the HIH Royal Commission: The Failure of HIH Insurance* Volume 1: 'A Corporate Collapse and Its Lessons,' Commonwealth of Australia, April 2003, xxxiv: http://www.hihroyalcom.gov.au/finalreport/Front%20Matter ,%20critical%20assessment%20and%20summary.HTML#_Toc37086537.

7   Ibid., para 6.1.

8   Background Paper 11 (HIH Royal Commission) *Directors' Duties and Other Obligations under the Corporations Act* (November 2001) 27, para 76 and quoted in J du Plessis, A Hargovan and M Bagaric, *Principles of Contemporary Corporate Governance*, (2nd ed, CUP, 2011), 4.

9   J Farrar, 'Corporate Governance, Business Judgment and the Professionalism of Directors' (1993) 5 *Corporate and Business Law Journal* 1, 1.

Continuing the broad theme, some commentators have said that it is 'the structures, processes, **2.008**
cultures and systems that engender the successful operation of the organisation'.[10]

The predecessor of the UK's Department for Business Energy and Industrial Strategy, the **2.009**
Department for Business Innovation and Skills, defined corporate governance in a narrower
way and quite extensively as:

> the system by which companies are directed and controlled. It deals largely with the relationship
> between the constituent parts of a company – the directors, the board (and its sub-committees) and
> the shareholders. Transparency and accountability are the most important elements of good corporate
> governance. This includes: the timely provision by companies of good quality information; a clear and
> credible company decision-making process; shareholders giving proper consideration to the informa-
> tion provided and making considered judgments.[11]

The G20 and the Organization for Economic Co-operation and Development have co-operated **2.010**
in providing principles for corporate governance and with these principles they provided
a detailed explanation, saying that:

> Corporate governance involves a set of relationships between a company's management, its board,
> its shareholders and other stakeholders. Corporate governance also provides the structure through
> which the company objectives are set, and the means of attaining those objectives and monitoring
> performance are determined.[12]

Professor Peter Mülbert has defined corporate governance as dealing: **2.011**

> the decision-making at the level of the board of directors and top management (i.e., the management
> board in a two-tier system), and the different internal and external mechanisms that ensure that all
> decisions taken by the directors and top management are in line with the objective(s) of a company
> and its shareholders, respectively.[13]

A company law text has stated that a useful description of corporate governance is that it con- **2.012**
sists of the control mechanisms available for ensuring that managers and directors do not abuse
their corporate powers.[14] Canadian scholar, Janis Sarra, has described corporate governance as
providing:

> [T]he framework for the setting and achievement of the company's overall objectives: engaging strate-
> gic planning and risk management; supervision of corporate officers to prevent shirking or self-dealing
> transactions; and oversight of the relationship between corporate officers and stakeholders with an
> interest in the corporation.[15]

In his private capacity, Sir Adrian Cadbury, who chaired the Cadbury Committee, stated that: **2.013**

---

10   J Cook and S Deakin, 'Stakeholding and Corporate Governance: Theory and Evidence on Economic Performance,'
     ESRC Centre for Business Research, University of Cambridge, 1999.
11   See: http://webarchive.nationalarchives.gov.uk/20090902193559/berr.gov.uk/whatwedo/businesslaw/corp-governance/
     page15267.html.
12   OECD/G20, *Principles of Corporate Governance*, 2015, 91: http://www.oecd.org/corporate/principles-corporate
     -governance.htm.
13   P Mülbert, 'Corporate Governance of Banks after the Financial Crisis – Theory, Evidence, Reform,' April 2010: http://
     papers.ssrn.com/sol3/papers.cfm?abstract_id=1448118 accessed 20 October 2020.
14   J Birds et al, *Boyle and Bird's* Company Law, (7th ed, Jordans 2009), 357.
15   J Sarra, 'Dancing the Derivative Deux Pas, the Financial Crisis and Lessons for Corporate Governance' (2009) 32
     University of New South Wales Law Journal 447, 449.

Corporate governance is concerned with holding the balance between economic and social goals and between individuals and communal goals. The governance framework is there to encourage the efficient use of resources and equally to require accountability for the stewardship of those resources. The aim is to align as nearly as possible the interests of individuals, corporations and society.[16]

2.014 In a discussion paper the Australian Audit Office said that:

Broadly speaking, corporate governance generally refers to the processes by which organisations are directed, controlled and held to account. It encompasses authority, accountability, stewardship, leadership, direction and control exercised in the organisation.[17]

2.015 A different approach taken by Mufleh Al-Sartawi is that corporate governance can be seen as a management tool which enhances the ability of companies to disclose appropriate information for decision-makers such as representatives of shareholders.[18]

2.016 Professor Marc Moore has provided a much narrower explanation and has said that corporate governance can be defined 'as the problem of holding key executive decision-makers in listed companies accountable for their actions'.[19]

2.017 In another book, Moore, writing with Professor Martin Petrin, sees power as critical.[20] They say that corporate governance is concerned first and foremost with the issue of power.

2.018 Professor Amir Licht regards the issue of power as being at the centre of corporate governance and says that 'corporate governance is about institutional regulation of power to protect socially approved entitlements in the corporation'.[21]

2.019 It is perhaps in relation to power that some[22] have referred to the need to introduce appropriate checks and balances in order to have good governance. In order to offset power and authority there has to be evidence of transparency in relation to those who do wield power, most notably the board of directors, as well as ensuring that the board is accountable for what it does. Requiring transparency and accountability provides the checks needed.

2.020 Some commentators have asserted that corporate governance has internal and external aspects to it. That is, the internal relates to how a company is governed within itself and how it deals with issues such as board composition, decision-making by boards and directors, how roles

---

16 'Foreword' in M Iskander and N Chamlou, *Corporate Governance: A Framework for Implementation*, (World Bank, 1999).

17 Corporate Governance in Commonwealth Authorities and Companies, Commonwealth of Australia: http://www.anao .gov.au/uploads/documents/Corporate_Governance_in_Commonwealth_Authorities_and_Companies.pdf accessed 20 October 2020.

18 'Corporate Governance and Intellectual Capital' (2018) 22 *Academy of Accounting and Financial Studies* 1 and referred to in A Rehman and F Hashim in 'Corporate Governance Maturity and Its Related Measurement Framework' Proceedings of the 5th International Conference on Accounting Studies, 16 October 2018, 18.

19 M Moore, 'The End of "Comply or Explain" in UK Corporate Governance?' (2009) 60 *Northern Ireland Legal Quarterly* 85, 85.

20 *Corporate Governance: Law, Regulation and Theory*, (Palgrave, 2017), 4.

21 'Corporate Governance' 16 November 2011, 2: http://ssrn.com/abstract=1786382 accessed 20 October 2020.

22 For example, in the Introduction to the Government's 2016 Green Paper on Corporate Governance the then Prime Minister, Theresa May, stated that 'Good corporate governance is about having the right checks and balances within big business to strengthen decision making and accountability': Department for Business, Energy and Industrial Strategy, *Corporate Governance Reform Green Paper* (November 2016), 2.

are delegated and how managers are overseen. The external relates to regulation of how the company interacts with external parties and how it addresses matters such as markets, dealing with regulatory authorities, reporting and disclosure. Certainly, some commentators have seen both external and internal perspectives in the famous Cadbury Report definition provided earlier.[23]

The discipline of corporate governance has developed from a number of academic disciplines, **2.021** namely law, finance, economics, accounting, organisational behaviour, management and ethics. Clearly there are different interpretations. Yet, the main focus of corporate governance tends to be on directors and the process of management.

The definitions enumerated in this section of the chapter relate to solvent companies, so they **2.022** have the directors/management in focus, but with insolvent companies insolvency practitioners ('IPs') s are also important if companies have entered insolvency regimes.

While it is exceedingly difficult to construct a comprehensive and accurate definition of **2.023** corporate governance we will employ the following for the purposes of this book: 'the rules, relationships, systems and processes within and by which authority is exercised and controlled in companies for the benefit of pertinent stakeholders.'

C. CORPORATE GOVERNANCE DEVELOPMENTS

The term 'corporate governance,' while used in the United States previously,[24] was never really **2.024** used in the UK until the late 1980s or early 1990s. This is not to say that there was not corporate governance until this time. Nothing could be further from the truth. The issue of corporate governance has been of immense concern to the commercial world ever since companies started to trade.[25] There have been measures taken for many years by government, the courts, companies themselves and stakeholders in order to address corporate governance and matters inextricably related to it. For instance, there has been the inclusion in companies' legislation of the power to remove directors from boards, the courts held that directors owed certain kinds of duties to their companies, companies have limited the powers of their directors by including provisions in memorandum and articles of association and shareholders and creditors have required directors to take certain actions in the governing of the company. Nevertheless, the last 25–30 years has seen far more concentration on what corporate governance entails and what must be done in this regard.

---

23   K Lanoo, 'A European Perspective on Corporate Governance' (1999) 37 *Journal of Common Market Studies* 269; C Mallin, 'The Financial Sector and Corporate Governance: the UK Case' (2005) 13 *Corporate Governance: An International Review* 532.

24   It has been suggested that it was term whose use was first recorded in the work of Richard Eells, *The Meaning of Modern Business: An Introduction to the Philosophy of Large Corporate Enterprises*, (Columbia University Press, 1960): D Milman, *Governance of Distressed Firms*, (Edward Elgar, 2013), 27.

25   In economics it is even traced back to the time of Adam Smith (circa 1776): R Adams, B Hermalin and M Weisbach, 'The Role of Boards of Directors in Corporate Governance: A Conceptual Framework and Survey' (2010) 48 *Journal of Economic Literature* 58, 96.

2.025 There are too many developments and trends in corporate governance for all of them to be discussed in a book of this kind. The following are some of the major developments that have occurred in the UK. Of course, others have taken place elsewhere and it might be said that, in light of globalisation, the majority of corporate governance measures that have transpired will affect most countries in the world even if in a limited way. It will be discerned that most of the developments have related to large public companies. As noted in Chapter 1, while there are far more private companies registered in the UK, large public companies wield an immense amount of power and influence and so they often attract the most attention. But, as made clear in Chapter 1, private companies constitute a very important part of the commercial life of the UK and the governance of these companies is critical.

2.026 It has been said, with some good reason, that 'scandals have long been the engines of corporate law reform', and that corporate governance has developed by way of knee-jerk reactions to crises.[26] This has not led to corporate governance developments that are well articulated and balanced.[27]

2.027 Perhaps the earliest major development that we can point to in the modern era of corporate governance was the convening of what became known as the Cadbury Committee, 'The Committee on the Financial Aspects of Corporate Governance', and the delivery of its report in 1992.[28] The Committee was established in May 1991 by the Financial Reporting Council, the Stock Exchange and the accountancy profession in response to continuing concern about standards of financial reporting and accountability, and so the purpose of the Committee was 'to review those aspects of corporate governance specifically related to financial reporting and accountability'.[29] It was convened following some terrible corporate collapses in the UK, such as Polly Peck and Maxwell Communications, the occurrence of other corporate scandals, and criticisms of some of the actions of a number of companies. The work of the Committee led to the drafting of the aforementioned report which constituted a Code of Practice and Principles for Governance.

2.028 Over the 30 years since the Cadbury Report, the growth of interest in corporate governance, worldwide, has been dramatic. It might be said that it contributed to corporate governance development in respect of three major matters, namely the definition of corporate governance, voluntary adoption of codes and the 'comply or explain' approach to governance.[30]

2.029 The definition of corporate governance was discussed earlier in the chapter. The notion of the corporate governance code was really important, as it introduced into the UK's corporate governance a major soft law component. The Corporate Governance Code which the Cadbury Report effectively ushered in and which became more formal by the late 1990s (and named

---

26   R Tomasic, 'Raising Corporate Governance Standards in response to Corporate Rescue and Insolvency' (2009) *Corporate Rescue and Insolvency* (February) 5, 7.

27   Ibid.

28   1 December 1982, Gee Publishing. The Committee was established under the chairmanship of Sir Adrian Cadbury and its Report was known as 'the Cadbury Report'.

29   Ibid., para 1.2. However, the Report's definition of 'corporate governance' did not include an express reference to 'accountability' (para 2.5).

30   N Shah and C Napier, 'The Cadbury Report 1992: Shared Vision and Beyond,' 1: http://wwwdata.unibg.it/dati/corsi/900002/79548-Beyond%20Cadbury%20Report%20Napier%20paper.pdf.

the Combined Code) was not and is not mandatory, but companies have to explain why they have not complied with any particular part of the Code. Adoption of comply or explain means that compliance with a governance code is not mandatory, but what is compulsory is disclosing non-compliance. Comply or explain is designed to permit flexibility in companies.[31] The idea behind it is that it is not possible to raise the standards of corporate governance by simply requiring the assembly of structures and the laying down of rules as companies are all different and should not be subject to rigid rules.[32] Also of importance is the fact that the Code has been highly influential in the drafting of corporate governance codes in many countries around the world. The Cadbury Report has been regarded as 'the cornerstone of the comply-or-explain framework in Europe, long before this system was introduced in European law.'[33]

After the Cadbury Report there were two other major committees convened, the Greenbury and Hampel Committees and following the delivery of the latter Committee's Report a Combined Code was published. This Code was derived from the reports of the Cadbury, Greenbury and Hampel Reports. In 2003, following the collapse of several huge companies in the US a further Committee was convened, the Higgs Committee, which provided a report, 'Review of the Role and Effectiveness of Non-executive Directors,' recommending changes to the Combined Code particularly in respect of the constitution of boards.[34]   **2.030**

The UK Corporate Governance Code, as the Combined Code became known, has been amended regularly by the Financial Reporting Council, and was last amended in July 2018. The 2018 changes reflected concern that directors were not explaining in their reporting how they were discharging their duty under s 172(1) of the Companies Act ('the Act') which required a director to: **2.031**

> act in a way that he considers, in good faith, would be most likely to promote the success of the company for the benefit of its members as a whole, and in doing so have regard (amongst other matters) to –

(a)   The likely consequences of any decision in the long term
(b)   the interests of the company's employees
(c)   the need to foster the company's business relationships with suppliers, customers and others
(d)   the impact of the company's operations on the community and the environment
(e)   the desirability of the company maintaining a reputation for high standards of business conduct, and
(f)   the need to act fairly between the members of the company.

A major development in the UK's corporate governance occurred with the advent Act which addressed a number of substantial issues. Perhaps chief among these was the codification of the duties of directors that had developed through 150 years or more of case law. Especially   **2.032**

---

31   For a broad discussion, see ibid.; M Moore, ''Whispering Sweet Nothings': The Limitations of Informal Conformance in UK Corporate Governance' (2009) 9 *Journal of Corporate Law Studies* 95, 101.

32   S Arcot, V Bruno and A Faure-Grimaud, 'Corporate Governance in the UK: Is the Comply or Explain Approach Working?' (2010) 30 *International Review of Law and Economics* 193.

33   'Study on Monitoring and Enforcement Practices in Corporate Governance in the Member States' conducted by RiskMetrics Group for the EU, 23 September 2009, 22: http://ec.europa.eu/internal_market/company/docs/ecgforum/studies/comply-or-explain-090923_en.pdf.

34   *Review of the role and effectiveness of non-executive directors*, January 2003: http://www.ecgi.org/codes/documents/higgsreport.pdf.

important was the inclusion of s 172(1) and quoted above. This provision, which provides for what is known as enlightened shareholder value, effectively set out the ultimate objective of the company which is to benefit the shareholders while having regard for the interests of stakeholders. Other sections of the legislation prohibited directors from not disclosing conflicts between their interests and those of the company.[35]

2.033   In 2010, in response to criticism of major shareholders, and particularly institutional investors, failing to engage with boards of the companies in which they held shares, the Financial Reporting Council introduced the Stewardship Code. This was designed to encourage shareholders to be more active. As with the UK Corporate Governance Code, the Stewardship Code operates on a comply or explain basis.

2.034   Also in 2010 the Institute of Directors published a Code for unlisted companies, *Corporate Governance Guidance and Principles for Unlisted Companies*.[36] Hitherto there had been a focus only on listed companies and the UK Corporate Governance Code applied and still applies only to listed companies. Obviously, there are many different companies that fall into the classification of unlisted. The range can be from large (but unlisted) public companies to one-person private companies. Therefore, the Guidance has two sets of principles. Phase 1 (Principles 1–9) relates to all unlisted companies and Phase 2 (Principles 10–14) relates to larger more complex unlisted companies. The Institute's Code even included a principle specifically directed at family-controlled companies.[37]

2.035   In late 2016 the government published a Green Paper, *Corporate Governance Reform*,[38] in which it sought responses to action it was proposing to address executive pay, how directors connected with stakeholders (and strengthening the voice of stakeholders) and the governance of large private companies. We deal with the last matter in the next paragraph. The Companies (Miscellaneous Reporting) Regulations 2018 addressed the other two matters that the Green Paper raised. The government also asked the Financial Reporting Council to construct a new draft of the UK Corporate Governance Code, taking into account issues that it had raised in the Green Paper and the response to comments about the Green Paper.[39]

2.036   To address the concerns manifested in the Green Paper of 2016 about the governance of large private companies in 2018 a Code was proposed for large private companies in the wake of the well-publicised demise of BHS and problems in other large private companies in order to strengthen corporate governance in such companies. The Code is known as *The Wates Corporate Governance Principles for Large Private Companies*, and was published by the Financial

---

35   Companies Act 2006, s 175.

36   Available at: https://www.iod.com/news/good-governance-debate/article/corporate-governance-for-unlisted-companies

37   For instance, see Principle 9.

38   Department of Business, Energy and Industrial Strategy, 'Corporate Governance Reform,' November 2016: https://assets .publishing.service.gov.uk/government/uploads/system/uploads/attachment_data/file/584013/corporate-governance -reform-green-paper.pdf.

39   Department of Business Energy and Industrial Strategy, 'Corporate Governance Reform: The Government response to the green paper consultation' August 2017: https://assets.publishing.service.gov.uk/government/uploads/system/ uploads/attachment_data/file/640470/corporate-governance-reform-government-response.pdf.

Reporting Council in December 2018.[40] From January 2019 the Companies (Miscellaneous Reporting) Regulations 2018[41] required private companies of a significant size to disclose their corporate governance arrangements in their directors' report and on their website, including whether they follow a formal code such as the *Wates Corporate Governance Principles*. A company may choose to apply the *Wates Principles*, in order to comply with the Companies (Miscellaneous Reporting) Regulations 2018, where it has more than 2,000 employees or turn-over above 200 million pounds and a balance sheet of more than two billion pounds. Where companies fall within these criteria they must publish a statement of their corporate governance arrangements in the directors' report. If companies do not comply with the *Wates Corporate Governance Principles* they must explain why not. This continues the heavy reliance on comply or explain in UK corporate governance.

As mentioned earlier, most of the developments in corporate governance have related to large companies, whether public or private. Many are irrelevant to small private companies which are owner-managed. In a lot of small companies which are owner-managed the principles of corporate governance are not, or are rarely, considered. Often it is only when a company ends up in an insolvency regime and an IP investigates the company's affairs is corporate governance an issue. It is possible to see this in the many cases that have ended up in court as a result of action taken by a liquidator against directors for what they did or did not do before the company entered liquidation. **2.037**

With small companies that have several shareholders, some of whom may not be directors, corporate governance issues may only come to the fore when a minority shareholder institutes an action under s 994 of the Act claiming that the affairs of the company have been conducted in an unfairly prejudicial manner. In such cases evidence introduced in court often demonstrates poor corporate governance. **2.038**

Family companies can be particularly problematic when it comes to corporate governance. As with many owner-managed companies, there is often a great informality in the way that things are done. This can mean that decisions are made more quickly and there is not the same 'red tape' holding back the company, but this can also mean that there are squabbles about certain issues, such as director remuneration and actions of overbearing patriarchs (and sometimes matriarchs) who control all aspects of the company's life. **2.039**

Often when disagreements between a shareholder and/or directors have got to court, judges have identified from the evidence before them poor corporate governance in the company whose affairs are subject to the proceedings. **2.040**

---

40   See: https://www.frc.org.uk/getattachment/31dfb844–6d4b–4093–9bfe–19cee2c29cda/Wates-Corporate-Governance
     -Principles-for-LPC-Dec-2018.pdf.
41   SI 2018/860.

D. FEATURES OF CORPORATE GOVERNANCE

1.   Generally

2.041   We saw earlier in the chapter that it is difficult to draft a definition and certainly one of which a lot of people will approve of. So, from the definitions of corporate governance provided earlier in the chapter, and the general corporate governance literature itself, it is probably more helpful to draw out a number of features that appear to pervade the definitions and the literature. We do this below. We will address two of the features, transparency and accountability, separately and in detail in the next parts of the chapter.

2.042   While there are different approaches to stating what corporate governance is, there are a lot of overlaps and similarities. The following seem to be critical features of corporate governance:

- Control
- Balance
- Interests – shareholders and stakeholders
- Processes/measures
- Structure/framework
- Power/authority
- Transparency
- Accountability.

2.043   We will mention all of the above features at some point in the book. However, as indicated above, our focus is on the last two, transparency and accountability. It has been said that a wide range of people in various areas of society maintain that these two features are essential to good governance.[42] Laksmi and Kamila have recently identified these concepts as necessary for good corporate governance.[43] We submit that transparency and accountability are critical to corporate governance in general and perhaps even more so when a company is insolvent. There are many contributions to the corporate governance literature as well as government and quasi-government reports and professional association papers that endorse the importance of these features in corporate governance. The UK Corporate Governance Code 2016 stated that transparency and accountability are underlying principles of good corporate governance.[44] In the Introduction to the *Wates Corporate Governance Principles for Large Private Companies* mention is made of the need to improve transparency and accountability in light of large-scale corporate failures. King III, the South African Corporate Governance Code 2009, stated that good corporate governance 'is essentially about effective, responsible leadership. Responsible

---

42   J Fox, 'The Uncertain Relationship Between Tansparency and Accountability' (2007) 17 *Development in Practice* 663, 664; International Council on Mining and Metals, 'Governance and Transparency': https://www.icmm.com/en-gb/society-and-the-economy/governance-and-transparency; L Lumentut et al, 'The Transparency Principle in Realize Good Corporate Governance: Limited Company' (2017) 22 *Journal of Humanities and Social Science* 50, 50.

43   A Laksmi and Z Kamila, 'The Effect of Good Corporate Governance and Earnings Management to Corporate Social Responsibility Disclosure' (2018) 22 *Academy of Accounting and Financial Studies Journal* 1, 2.

44   April 2016, 1.

leadership is characterised by the ethical values of responsibility, accountability, fairness and transparency'.[45] This was, effectively, repeated later in King IV.[46]

We have already indicated earlier in the chapter that the Cadbury Committee was established **2.044** because of concern over a lack of accountability in the corporate world. Interestingly, the Wates Committee was established because of the public need for more accountability and transparency.[47] This suggests that the need for accountability and transparency are prime movers in bringing change in corporate governance.

The concepts of accountability and transparency are central to the definition that we have **2.045** adopted for corporate governance, namely: 'the rules, relationships, systems and processes within and by which authority is exercised and controlled in companies for the benefit of pertinent stakeholders'. As a result of the centrality of transparency and accountability we will focus on these in our examination of corporate governance in insolvency, because while insolvency produces many different issues for consideration, the company continues to exist as a legal entity in insolvency both before and after any insolvency regime is instigated.

Transparency and accountability can facilitate achieving a number of aims. We mention three. **2.046** First, the Company Law Review Steering Group which was directed to undertake a comprehensive examination of UK company law in the late 1990s said that: 'We attach great importance to the potential of company law to achieve a proper measure of corporate responsiveness to wider interests through transparency and accountability.'[48] Secondly, as stated earlier in the chapter, transparency and accountability are able to provide checks on the power and control that is given to, and exercised by, the board of directors and, in an insolvency regime, by IPs. Thirdly, if there is transparency and accountability evident in the governance of companies then it is more likely to engender a greater degree of trust in the actions of directors and IPs.

Moving from pure corporate governance to insolvency governance, it is important to note that **2.047** the UK government in 2001 indicated in a major White Paper proposing significant changes to UK insolvency law, *Productivity and Enterprise: Insolvency – a Second Chance*,[49] that transparency and accountability were important and the fact that the administrative receivership process lacked these characteristics was a reason for terminating its use, save in limited circumstances.[50]

---

45   *King Report on Governance for South Africa 2009*, Institute of Directors in Southern Africa, Principle 1.1: https://cdn .ymaws.com/www.iodsa.co.za/resource/resmgr/king_iii/King_Report_on_Governance_fo.pdf.

46   *King Report on Governance for South Africa 2016*, Institute of Directors in Southern Africa, Principle 1 and at pages 20 and 89: https://cdn.ymaws.com/iodsa.site-ym.com/resource/resmgr/King_IV/King_IV_Report_draft.pdf.

47   Financial Reporting Council, 'The Wates Corporate Governance Principles for Large Private Companies,' December 2018, 3: https://www.frc.org.uk/getattachment/31dfb844–6d4b-4093–9bfe-19cee2c29cda/Wates-Corporate-Governance -Principles-for-LPC-Dec-2018.pdf.

48   Company Law Review, *Modern Company Law for a Competitive Economy*: Strategic Framework, 1999, London, DTI, para 5.1.47.

49   Cm 5234, London, TSO, 2001, 9: https://webarchive.nationalarchives.gov.uk/+/http://www.insolvency.gov.uk/cwp/ cm5234.pdf.

50   Limited to receivership initiated under a charge created before 15 September 2003.

2.048 Transparency and accountability are often referred to as complementary[51] or related concepts.[52] This is a correct perception, but there are differences between them, as the next sections of the chapter demonstrate.

2. Transparency

2.049 Transparency has become a worldwide phenomenon.[53] It is particularly of concern to those in government and public service and it is in these areas where the most studies have occurred. However, as already discussed, it is of critical importance to corporate governance as is evident from the fact that it is regularly referred to in the corporate governance literature and in government reports that have addressed corporate governance issues.

2.050 Transparency is referred to on several occasions in the UK Corporate Governance Code 2018. For instance, appointments to the board of directors are to be based on a transparent process.[54] The same requirement is found in the Wates Report.[55] King IV, the South African Corporate Governance Code, states that: 'Members of the governing body should be transparent in the manner in which they exercise their governance role and responsibilities.'[56] The Association of Chartered Certified Accountants ('ACCA') has said that boards should be transparent,[57] as 'we live in an age of transparency and openness'.[58]

2.051 So transparency is important, but what is transparency? Like accountability, its meaning is not as clear as one would like. It can refer to something being widely available,[59] and in the corporate sphere it can cover reporting and information dissemination.[60] It is linked to openness,[61] and disclosure. It has been said to involve opening up 'working procedures not immediately visible to those not directly involved, in order to demonstrate the good working of an institution'.[62] This could also be applied to the work of an individual. Meijer has said that it is seen as 'an institutional relation or arrangement in which an actor is rendered transparent to another

---

51   For example, see H Hu and D Robinson, 'The New Ambiguity of "Open Government"' (2012) 59 *UCLA Law Review Discourse* 178, 192, 197, 201; T Vishwanath and D Kaufmann, 'Towards Transparency in Finance and Governance, World Bank, 3: https://papers.ssrn.com/sol3/papers.cfm?abstract_id=258978.

52   L Dickinson, 'Privatization and Accountability' (2011) 7 *Annual Review of Law and Social Science* 101, 103.

53   A Meijer, 'Transparency' in M Bovens, R Goodin and T Schillemans (eds), *The Oxford Handbook of Public Accountability*, (OUP, 2014), 508.

54   July 2018, Principle J.

55   Financial Reporting Council, 'The Wates Corporate Governance Principles for Large Private Companies,' December 2018, 14: https://www.frc.org.uk/getattachment/31dfb844–6d4b–4093–9bfe–19cee2c29cda/Wates-Corporate-Governance -Principles-for-LPC-Dec-2018.pdf.

56   *King Report on Governance for South Africa 2016*, Institute of Directors in Southern Africa.

57   ACCA, 'Creating value through governance – towards a new accountability; A consultation' 2014, 26: https://www .accaglobal.com/content/dam/acca/global/PDF-technical/corporate-governance/tech-tp-cvtg.pdf.

58   Ibid., 47.

59   R Bushman and A Smith, 'Transparency, Financial Accounting Information and Corporate Governance' (2003) *FBRNY Economic Policy Review* 65, 66.

60   Ibid., 76.

61   T Vishwanath and D Kaufmann, 'Towards Transparency in Finance and Governance, World Bank, 2: https://papers .ssrn.com/sol3/papers.cfm?abstract_id=258978; L Lumentut et al, 'The Transparency Principle in Realize Good Corporate Governance: Limited Company' (2017) 22 *Journal of Humanities and Social Science* 50 at 50.

62   C Moser, 'How Open is "Open as Possible"? Three Different Approaches to Transparency and Openness in Regulating Access to EU Documents' IHS Political Science Series, No 80, Institute for Advanced Studies, Vienna and referred to by

actor'.[63] This provides us with the notion of the person who is to be transparent being open about what he or she is doing or has done. In the corporate sense it can be said that it 'means openness, a willingness by the company to provide clear information to shareholders and other stakeholders. For example, transparency refers to the openness and willingness to disclose financial performance figures which are truthful and accurate'.[64]

The pervasive idea behind transparency is to not keep things secretive.[65] According to the IMF's Report of the Working Group on Transparency and Accountability, transparency refers to a process by which 'information about existing conditions, decisions and actions is made accessible, visible and understandable'.[66] To others, transparency is perceived as the conducting of business in a manner that ensures that decisions and other information can be seen from the outside.[67] To be transparent means that it is easy to see through.[68] In business it has been said to mean: a situation in which business and financial activities are done in an open way without secrets, so that people can trust that they are fair and honest.[69] According to Transparency International: 'Transparency is about shedding light on rules, plans, processes and actions. It is knowing why, how, what, and how much.'[70]   **2.052**

It is critical that a person to whom an account is made has full and complete information so transparency is a necessary precondition for those giving an account since without access to clear, accurate and up-to-date information, it is impossible to make a determination on how the company is operating and how the one accounting is doing his, her or its job.[71]   **2.053**

An important aspect of transparency is that it entails the flow of timely and reliable information and a lack of transparency is constituted by 'deliberately withholding access to, or misrepresentation of information or failure to ensure that the information provided is of adequate relevance or quality'.[72] Information and disclosure or dissemination is critical.[73] Thus, given   **2.054**

A Meijer, 'Transparency' in M Bovens, R Goodin and T Schillemans (eds), *The Oxford Handbook of Public Accountability* (OUP, 2014), 511.

63   Ibid.

64   Pearse Trust, 'Core Principles of Good Corporate Governance': https://www.pearse-trust.ie/blog/bid/108866/the-core -principles-of-good-corporate-governance.

65   F Steelman Kahn, 'Transparency and Accountability: Rethinking Corporate Fiduciary's Relevance to Corporate Disclosure' (2000) 34 *Georgia Law Review* 505, 505; L. Lumentut et al, 'The Transparency Principle in Realize Good Corporate Governance: Limited Company' (2017) 22 *Journal of Humanities and Social Science* 50, 51.

66   October 1998, v: https://www.imf.org/external/np/g22/taarep.pdf.

67   C Hood, 'Accountability and Transparency: Siamese Twins, Matching Parts, Awkward Couple? (2010) 33 *West European Politics* 989, 989.

68   *Cambridge Dictionary*: https://dictionary.cambridge.org/dictionary/english/transparency.

69   Ibid.

70   'What is Transparency': https://www.transparency.org/what-is-corruption?gclid=EAIaIQobChMIsfuPmvrb3wIV7bftCh2 qxg9bEAAYASAAEgIhXPD_BwE#what-is-transparency.

71   International Institute for Sustainable Development, 'Transparency and Accountability' and available at: http://www.iisd .org/trade/policy/transparency.asp.

72   T Vishwanath and D Kaufmann, 'Towards Transparency in Finance and Governance, World Bank, 3: https://papers .ssrn.com/sol3/papers.cfm?abstract_id=258978 accessed 20 October 2020; A Madhavan, 'Market Microstructure; A Survey' 2000, 21:

73   Madhavan, ibid,, 3:

the above, the following can be seen as characteristics of transparency: accessibility, relevance, quality, reliability and comprehensiveness.[74]

2.055 It can be difficult to measure the level of transparency that exists in any given situation. Information can always be selective. Often those who wish to receive the information are in the position of not knowing whether there has been full disclosure. Those appearing to be transparent may only provide part of the relevant information, which can be misleading.

2.056 Some even assert accountability and transparency to be the same.[75] But with respect, and as discussed shortly, it is submitted that they are not. They overlap in that if there is no transparency, a person or body cannot be truly accountable, and so transparency is an element of accountability.[76] Transparency should lead to accountability, as we see in the next section. It is possible to have transparency without full accountability as the latter presupposes explanation as well as transparency. Transparency involves a disclosure stage which involves the provision of basic information and perhaps the laying bare here what has occurred and this may need to be followed by an explanatory stage if the information needs to be explained to be understood.[77] It is submitted that one can say that, in a sense, accountability and transparency are interdependent.[78]

2.057 Clearly stakeholders in a company want transparency to ensure that they know what is going on and that they are aware of the true state of affairs. Information provided in transparency procedures will help, for instance, shareholders in companies know to whether they should invest further, sell or consider bringing proceedings against the directors. Information in an insolvency procedure should help creditors know that the IP is doing all that he or she can do to investigate the company's affairs thoroughly and what sort of dividend they will ultimately receive. Information is incredibly important to any stakeholder in any venture. Finance theory and law and economics regularly see information asymmetry as a concern for any party. That is, if one party knows more than the other the former has an advantage in any dealings which these parties have with one another, and others, perhaps.

2.058 The benefit of transparency generally is that it can help the dialogue between the ones in control and those who are affected by that control. It may engender greater trust which can reduce costs. The disclosure of what is done by persons or bodies deters corruption and provides a basis for better and more trustworthy performance.[79] As Hildyard J said in the relatively recent case of *Bank St Petersburg PJSC v Arkhangelsky*[80]: 'lack of transparency inevitably gave rise to suspicion'.[81] Therefore, if people and bodies are transparent then they become, potentially,

---

74 T Vishwanath and. Kaufmann, 'Towards Transparency in Finance and Governance, World Bank, 3: https://papers.ssrn .com/sol3/papers.cfm?abstract_id=258978 accessed 20 October 2020.

75 P Kamuf, 'Accountability' (2007) 21 *Textual Practice* 251, 253.

76 R Keohane 'Exploring the Governance Agenda of Corporate Responsibility' (2008) 8 *Corporate Governance* 361, 362.

77 A Keay, *Board Accountability and Corporate Governance*, (Routledge, 2015), 46.

78 IMF, The Report of the Working Group on Transparency and Accountability, October 1998, 5: https://www.bis.org/ publ/othp01b.pdf.

79 O O'Neil, 'Transparency and the Ethics of Communication' in C Hood and D Heald (eds), *Transparency: The Key to Better Governance?* (OUP, 2006), 76.

80 [2018] EWHC 1077 (Ch).

81 Ibid., [1410].

more trustworthy. Also, just like accountability, the existence of transparency on the part of a person or body who have responsibilities will generally enhance the legitimacy of that person (or body), particularly in the eyes of those who deal with the person or who rely on the decisions the person makes in exercising powers and discharging duties and functions.

Transparency is all well and good, but it is potentially of little benefit unless there is an appropriate enforcement procedure or a process allowing a stakeholder to respond, such as to ask for a judicial holding on what has been done or not done. **2.059**

It has been found that increased transparency can benefit a company, but it will also, very often, increase costs,[82] as the person disclosing will have to take time to provide information and possibly give explanations. In some cases, the discloser will need to obtain information from others. Thus, the person in control may argue that the costs involved in being fully transparent are excessive and it is not worth it; the one who is calling for transparency may ultimately lose out. This is perhaps pertinent in an insolvency regime where an officeholder (IP) may argue that to be totally transparent to the satisfaction of the creditors will involve costs that will, in turn, see a reduction in the creditors' dividends. **2.060**

It has been said that transparency is more important in times of uncertainty.[83] One cannot get much greater uncertainty than when a company is near to, or in fact, insolvent and whether operating outside, or within, an insolvency procedure. **2.061**

There are many examples of action being taken to increase transparency. In the corporate governance context we are talking about such things as annual financial statements and answers to questions at annual general meetings. In the insolvency context the matters covered in the Statements of Insolvency Practice (SIP) are prime examples as far as IPs are concerned. SIPs are designed to promote and maintain high standards of practice by setting required practice with which IPs are required to comply.[84] An instance of transparency in the insolvency field was the introduction of SIP 16 on 1 November 2015, designed to bring increased transparency to the pre-pack sale process. SIP 9 specifically refers to the primary importance of transparency for the dealings of IPs. This is discussed in Chapters 7 and 8. **2.062**

One of the many good aspects of transparency is that it is able to illuminate conflicts of interest which have the potential to cause problems, but it could be. This is addressed in the context of directors in insolvent companies in Chapter 4 and IPs in Chapters 7 and 8 where an insolvent company is subject to formal insolvency processes. **2.063**

One final note is that while transparency is a good thing, there care must be taken to ensure that it does not produce an information overload for stakeholders to the point where they are unable to process it. Furthermore, the fact that transparency is regarded as meritorious must not be used by parties as an opportunity to make unreasonable requirements of the one who is **2.064**

---

82   B Hermalin and M Weisbach, 'Transparency and Corporate Governance' 2007, 19: https://ccl.yale.edu/sites/default/files/files/HW_mkts_v5.pdf accessed 20 October 2020.

83   M Lang, K Lins and M Maffett, 'Transparency, Liquidity and Valuation: International Evidence,' 2011, 3: https://papers.ssrn.com/sol3/papers.cfm?abstract_id=1323514 accessed 20 October 2020.

84   Insolvency Service, *SIP 1: An Introduction to Statements of Insolvency Practice*, 1 October 2015.

to disclose to the point where it is oppressive. However, one would think that this would not occur frequently.

3.   Accountability[85]

2.065 'Accountability for conduct is a pervasive feature of human association'[86] but it is a term that tends to get thrown around rather liberally.[87] Nevertheless, it is seen as critical to corporate governance and, together with transparency, has been described as 'the most important elements of good corporate governance'.[88] For instance, in the Introduction to the government's 2016 Green Paper on *Corporate Governance* the then Prime Minister, Theresa May, stated that: 'Good corporate governance is about having the right checks and balances within big business to strengthen decision making and accountability.'[89]The concept of accountability has been at the forefront of corporate governance of large companies, with it being described as '…the cornerstone of governance'.[90] As discussed earlier, one of the major reasons for the establishment of the Cadbury Committee in 1991 was the need for accountability. It is, therefore, not surprising that the Cadbury Report that emanated from the Committee stated that: 'The issue for corporate governance is how to strengthen the accountability of boards of directors to shareholders.'[91] It has been something that has been referred to in various iterations of both the Combined Code on Corporate Governance and the UK Corporate Governance Code. The UK Corporate Governance Code 2016 in fact devoted a whole section to accountability.[92]

2.066 For many years, and particularly since the global financial crisis, the concept of accountability has been used increasingly in government reports, discussion papers and the academic literature on corporate governance.

2.067 Accountability in corporate governance is directed at the board. The board's members, the directors, are accountable for what they do. In solvent companies the position that is usually adopted in the UK is that the board of directors is accountable to the shareholders. In insolvent companies things change. These changes will be discussed in Chapter 4 in detail. When a company is insolvent, and it enters an insolvency regime, the officeholder who is appointed to oversee the company is the main person whose accountability is key. IPs are in control of an insolvency regime and it is imperative that they are seen as being accountable for what they

---

85   For a detailed account of board accountability in corporate governance, see A Keay, *Board Accountability and Corporate Governance* (Routledge, 2015).

86   A Allen, '2003 Daniel J Meador Lecture: Privacy Isn't Everything: Accountability as a Personal and Social Good' (2003) 54 *Alabama Law Review* 1375, 1377.

87   G Brandsma and T Schillemans, 'The Accountability Cube: Measuring Accountability (2012) 23 *Journal of Public Administration and Research and Theory* 953, 971.

88   The definition appears at: http://webarchive.nationalarchives.gov.uk/20090902193559/berr.gov.uk/whatwedo/businesslaw/corp-governance/page15267.html accessed 20 October 2020.

89   Department for Business, Energy and Industrial Strategy, *Corporate Governance Reform Green Paper*, November 2016, 2: https://assets.publishing.service.gov.uk/government/uploads/system/uploads/attachment_data/file/584013/corporate-governance-reform-green-paper.pdf.

90   S Lowe, 'Five Principles of Good Governance – Accountability' (Grant Thornton, 17 July 2018) https://www.grantthornton.co.uk/insights/five-principles-of-good-governance-accountability/.

91   'Report of the Committee on the Financial Aspects of Corporate Governance,' 1 December 1992, para 6.1.

92   April 2016, Section C: https://www.frc.org.uk/getattachment/ca7e94c4-b9a9–49e2-a824-ad76a322873c/UK-Corporate-Governance-Code-April-2016.pdf.

do. This is discussed, particularly in Chapters 7 and 8, in light of specific matters in insolvency practice that are provided for both by the legislature and the courts.

It is worth noting that accountability is a mode of governance used to restrain power to socially acceptable levels, which is a particular answer to a universal problem.[93] In the context of this book, directors and IPs, on whom we focus, are the ones who wield power when a company is insolvent either inside or outside of a formal insolvency procedure. While accountability is a word and concept that is used frequently in our society, its exact meaning is rarely articulated. It has been defined for broad purposes as: 'the fact of being responsible for what you do and able to give a satisfactory reason for it, or the degree to which this happens'.[94] Accountability is essentially an evaluative concept[95] as far as the accountees (the persons receiving an account) and the end result are concerned, namely how have the accountors (the persons giving an account) performed and whether they have adhered to certain standards. It is designed to bridge the gap between action and expectation.[96] **2.068**

The meaning of accountability has been tackled in various fields, and particularly in government, public administration and political science. Several commentators have identified a number of dimensions of accountability. For instance, Koppell identifies the following: transparency, liability, controllability, responsibility and responsiveness.[97] Lloyd, Oatham and Hammer also see four dimensions to making someone more accountable: transparency, participation, evaluation, and complaint and response mechanisms.[98] As we have discussed already, and as the comments of these commentators indicate, transparency is a part of accountability. **2.069**

As far as its meaning in corporate governance is concerned, it has recently been said in one study that accountability is a process and that it encompasses five stages and this produces its comprehensive meaning.[99] These stages are as follows. First, a person or entity (accountor) must be called to account, that is, obliged to recount or report his or her conduct to a third party (the accountee). Secondly, the accountor must provide information to the accountee and this has been referred to as 'accounting for verification',[100] or 'informative accountability'.[101] The disclosing of information in this respect can be seen as contributing to greater transparency.[102] **2.070**

---

93   A Licht, 'Adaptive Accountability: Towards a Culturally Compatible Model of Corporate Governance for East Asia' paper delivered at the BCLBE Conference on Corporate Governance in East Asia UC Berkeley, 4–5 May 2006: http://www.law.berkeley.edu/files/Licht-AdaptiveAccountability.pdf accessed 20 October 2020.

94   *Cambridge Dictionary*: https://dictionary.cambridge.org/dictionary/english/accountability.

95   M Bovens, 'Analysing and Assessing Accountability: A Conceptual Framework' (2007) 13 *European Law Journal* 447, 450.

96   M Scott and S Lyman, 'Accounts' (1968) 33 *American Sociological Review* 46, 46.

97   J Koppell, 'Pathologies of Accountability: ICANN and the Challenge of "Multiple Accountabilities Disorder"' (2005) 65 *Public Administration Review* 94, 96.

98   R Lloyd, J Oatham and M Hammer, *Global Accountability Report*, London, One World Trust, 2007, 11.

99   A Keay, *Board Accountability and Corporate Governance* (Routledge, 2015), Chapter 2.

100 J Uhr, 'Redesigning Accountability: From Muddles to Maps' (1993) 65 *Australian Quarterly* 1, 4.

101 J Kaler, 'Responsibility, Accountability and Governance' (2002) 11 *Business Ethics: A European Review* 327, 328.

102 S Gilman and H Whitton, 'When Transparency Becomes the Enemy of Accountability, Reflections From the Field' 5 December 2013: http://www.clmr.unsw.edu.au/article/ethics/when-transparency-becomes-enemy-accountability-reflections-field accessed 20 October 2020.

But, as mentioned earlier, transparency can occur without accountability.[103] Transparency alone does not alone produce accountability.[104] It is only a part, although a key part,[105] of accountability, but others actions are required for the accountability process. Transparency facilitates the fostering of accountability[106] as it requires, for full accountability, accountors to make their decisions and to give the reasoning underlying those decisions available.[107] Without transparency there can be no effective accountability.[108] The Cadbury Report indicated this when it stated that: 'Boards of directors are accountable to their shareholders...[they]need to do so through the quality of the information which they provide to shareholders...'[109]

2.071   The third stage in the process has been referred to as explanatory accountability.[110] Alongside providing information accountors must explain and justify or excuse their conduct against a set of externally set values or standards. Importantly, 'the step ensures that the accountor has not done something on mere whim or as a matter of a caprice'.[111] This stage is essential to the idea that accountability includes the notion of being answerable, which is seen as a key element of accountability.[112] This aspect of accountability envisages that the justification will involve the accountor endeavouring to persuade the accountee that what has been done or not done is appropriate in the circumstances and is best for the accountee.[113]

2.072   The fourth stage involves an opportunity for the accountee to pose questions concerning the accountor's conduct before passing some kind of judgment.[114] This questioning stage, together with, perhaps, the next part, fulfils what is often meant by the notion of holding someone accountable.[115] This entails undertaking an evaluation of the accountor's actions based on full information supplied and explained by the accountor.

2.073   The final stage can, although it does not have to, involve consequences for the accountor. This is the accountee's response to what the accountor has said in explanation and justification.

---

103   C Hood, 'Accountability and Transparency: Siamese Twins, Matching Parts, Awkward Couple?' (2010) 33 *West European Politics* 989, 991.

104   J Fox, 'The Uncertain Relationship Between Transparency and Accountability' (2007) 17 *Development in Practice* 663, 665.

105   J Koppell, 'Pathologies of Accountability: ICANN and the Challenge of "Multiple Accountabilities Disorder"' (2005) 65 *Public Administration Review* 94, 96.

106   A Meijer, 'Transparency' in M Bovens, R Goodin and T Schillemans (eds), *The Oxford Handbook of Public Accountability*, (OUP, 2014), 512.

107   IMF, 'Report of the Working Group on Transparency and Accountability,' October 1998, v: https://www.bis.org/publ/othp01b.pdf.

108   F Steelman Kahn, 'Transparency and Accountability: Rethinking Corporate Fiduciary's Relevance to Corporate Disclosure' (2000) 34 *Georgia Law Review* 505, 505.

109   'Report of the Committee on the Financial Aspects of Corporate Governance,' 1 December 1992, para 3.4.

110   J Uhr, 'Redesigning Accountability: From Muddles to Maps' (1993) 65 *Australian Quarterly* 1, 4.

111   A Keay, *Board Accountability and Corporate Governance*, (Routledge, 2015), 45.

112   A Quinn and B Schlenker, 'Can Accountability Produce Independence? Goals as Determinants of the Impact of Accountability on Conformity' (2002) 28 *Personality and Social Psychology Bulletin* 472, 472; R. Mulgan, '"Accountability": An Ever Expanding Concept?' (2000) 78 *Public Administration* 555, 569.

113   A Keay, *Board Accountability and Corporate Governance*, (Routledge, 2015), 46.

114   Ibid.

115   R Mulgan, '"Accountability": An Ever Expanding Concept?' (2000) 78 *Public Administration* 555, 569; A Allen, '2003 Daniel J Meador Lecture: Privacy Isn't Everything: Accountability as a Personal and Social Good' (2003) 54 *Alabama Law Review* 1375, 1382.

Consequences, while usually seen as negative, could be positive. The negative consequences that are often envisaged flow from the notion that what has been done is not acceptable. Negative consequences may comprise formal or informal sanctions.[116] Classic examples are liability[117] and removal from office. It has been said that there has to be a threat of some kind of punishment so as to ensure that the accountor explains and justifies truthfully.[118] While negative consequences tend to be emphasised, and they in fact may be implemented, they are not inevitable. All that is needed is that there is a potential for sanctions.[119] It has been said that the possibility of sanctions acts as a reminder of the fact that accountors have a moral obligation for what they do,[120] that is, they show respect for the accountee(s).[121] Some commentators say that the existence of sanctions permits the accountee to control the behaviour of the accountor.[122]

As foreshadowed above, there might not be any consequences; the accountee is merely receiving information and reasons and having the chance to question. The consequences could even be positive.[123] The accountees may affirm what the accountor has done and encourage the accountor to continue to do what he, she or it is doing or approve the strategy that the accountor has adopted or has planned.   **2.074**

Ordinarily accountability in corporate governance, particularly in Anglo-American countries, is focused on the board accounting to the shareholders. The accountability that one envisages in insolvency is somewhat different. While a company remains outside an insolvency regime, albeit insolvent, the directors will continue to be accountable to shareholders to some degree, but for what they are accountable for is different. This is because, as we discuss in Chapter 4, the interests of the creditors intrude when a company is insolvent, and directors are accountable for what they do in relation to the interests of the creditors. As we see in Chapter 4 the creditors cannot hold the directors accountable in terms of liability as creditors have no standing to sue the directors who are acting for the company, but there might be other ways of ensuring there   **2.075**

---

116 J Lerner and P Tetlock, 'Accounting for the Effects of Accountability' (1999) 125 *Psychological Bulletin* 255, 256; L Seidman, 'Ambivalence and Accountability' (1988) 61 *Southern California Law Review* 1571, 1574; R Jones, 'Law, Norms and the Breakdown of the Board: Promoting Accountability in Corporate Governance' (2007) 92 *Iowa Law Review* 105, 118.

117 J Koppell, 'Pathologies of Accountability: ICANN and the Challenge of "Multiple Accountabilities Disorder"' (2005) 65 *Public Administration Review* 94, 96.

118 K Ramana, 'A Framework for Research on Corporate Accountability Reporting,' Harvard Business School Working Paper, 1 October 2012, 7: http://ssrn.com/abstract=1934322 accessed 20 October 2020.

119 S Chesterman, 'Globalisation rules: Accountability, Power and the Prospects for Global Administrative Law' (2008) 14 *Global Governance* 39, 43.

120 M Dubnick, 'Situating Accountability: Seeking Salvation for the Core Concept' 2007, 28: http://pubpages.unh.edu/dubnick/papers/2007/Situacct031307.pdf

121 A Licht, 'Accountability and Corporate Governance' September 2002, 29–30: http://ssrn.com/abstract=328401 accessed 21 October 2020; G Staszewski, 'Reason-Giving and Accountability' (2009) 93 *Minnesota Law Review* 1253, 1286–1287.

122 J Kaler, 'Responsibility, Accountability and Gvernance' (2002) 11 (4) *Business Ethics: A European Review* 327, 329–330. He sees the attribution of blame as a weaker version of coercive accountability and punishment as the stronger version (at 330). Also, see D Beu and M Buckley, 'The Hypothesized Relationship Between Accountability and Ethical Behavior' (2001) 34 *Journal of Business Ethics* 57, 58; M Bovens, 'Two Concepts of Accountability' (2010) 33(5) *West European Politics* 946, 961.

123 See A Keay, 'Stewardship Theory: Is Board Accountability Necessary?' (2017) 59 *International Journal of Law and Management* 1292.

is some accounting. When a company is insolvent but has entered an insolvency regime, the IP is the main accountor.

2.076 We contend that an important aspect of corporate governance is to achieve a balance between authority/power on the one hand and accountability, on the other. People who are in control of companies, directors in a solvent company and an insolvent company before going into an insolvency regime, and IPs in companies subject to insolvency regimes, necessarily must be given authority to get things done. As a check on this authority the ones holding authority needs to be accountable. Also, accountability engenders greater legitimacy of the person or body endowed with powers, and the trust that it can produce, and it is necessary for good corporate governance.[124] Directors and IPs, the subject of much of this book, are endowed with significant power, and to convince people that their role is legitimate they need to provide an accounting of what they have done and why they have done it.

2.077 As mentioned earlier, accountability and transparency are related closely.[125] Transparency might be seen as covering processes that contribute to accountability occurring. It has been said that transparency actually promotes accountability.[126] It is critical that the accountee has full and complete information so transparency is a necessary precondition for accountors to be account-able since without access to clear, accurate and up-to-date information, it is impossible to make a determination on how the company is operating and how the board is doing its job[127] or how the affairs of a company in an insolvency procedure are being managed by an officeholder. So, as mentioned already, in a sense accountability and transparency are interdependent.[128]

2.078 As alluded to in this part and the previous part, there are various mechanisms which exist to ensure that transparency and accountability occur. They are obviously critical. Even more crit-ical is that they are effective. Many of the following chapters will discuss such mechanisms and their benefits and problems. One critical mechanism is the litigation process by which directors and IPs are made accountable for what they have done.

E. CORPORATE GOVERNANCE IN INSOLVENCY

2.079 We made some general and brief comments about corporate governance in insolvency in Chapter 1, where we made the point that when a company becomes insolvent, or is even in financial distress short of insolvency, the nature of corporate governance will change. If the company remains outside a formal insolvency regime, the directors and the board will continue to govern and control the company and in doing so they will do many of the things that they

---

124 A Keay, 'Exploring the Rationale for Board Accountability in Corporate Governance' (2014) 29 *Australian Journal of Corporate Law* 115.

125 J Fox, 'The Uncertain Relationship Between Transparency and Accountability' (2007) 17 *Development in Practice* 663.

126 A Meijer, 'Transparency' in M Bovens, R Goodin and T Schillemans (eds), *The Oxford Handbook of Public Accountability*, (OUP, 2014), and referring to what President Barack Obama said in 2009.

127 International Institute for Sustainable Development, 'Transparency and Accountability': http://www.iisd.org/trade/policy/transparency.asp.

128 IMF, The Report of the Working Group on Transparency and Accountability, October 1998, 5: https://www.bis.org/publ/othp01b.pdf.

would have done when the company was solvent, but other matters will have to be considered. If a company enters an insolvency regime, then, and this applies principally to administration and liquidation, the directors are superseded by the IP as being the one who is in control of the company and the one who is the main player.

While there have been measures taken in the past that involved corporate governance issues in **2.080** insolvency, there has been relatively little discussion about corporate governance in insolvency in the literature, and the government does not appear to have directly considered it until March 2018 when it published proposals to deal specifically with corporate governance and insolvency. In a joint venture between the Department of Business Energy and Industrial Strategy and the Insolvency Service a discussion paper titled, *Corporate Governance and Insolvency*, was published. In many ways the title is misleading as there were a number of matters canvassed in the paper that, arguably, do not deal with corporate governance. While there are other issues of corporate governance in insolvency that could have been considered, it is at least encouraging that it is recognised at the government level that corporate governance is an important issue when insolvency hits.

The issue of governance during a time of insolvency is concerned with the person(s) who are **2.081** directing and influencing processes and who is able/permitted to make the critical decisions that affect the results of these processes. Clearly the main players will be the directors prior to the advent of an insolvency regime and the IP after a regime has commenced, but others will, as we explain in the book, have, in certain situations, an influence over what is done and how it is done.

The fact is that when a company becomes insolvent, and it is controlled by the board, interests **2.082** of stakeholders will conflict and this often makes for difficult governance decisions. The following conflicts occur:

> Shareholders endeavouring to preserve their capital; creditors seeking payment; employees and management looking to retain their jobs; suppliers attempting to keep trade links open…and customers with concerns about pre-paid goods and services not yet delivered or about the company's performance of post-delivery warranties.[129]

Some of these will carry over if the company enters an insolvency regime. It is possible to add **2.083** those in the quote, the interests of IPs where there is an insolvency regime. They will be concerned for their remuneration and expenses as well as their reputation and standing.

Some stakeholders, principally the directors and creditors, may seek to influence forthcoming **2.084** governance decisions in an insolvency regime by endeavouring to appoint someone whom they might perceive to be a tame IP. That is, someone whom they believe they can influence or manipulate into making decisions that favour them in some way. This was one of the many criticisms directed at administrative receivership prior to the enactment of the Enterprise Act 2000. We discuss the independence of IPs later, in Chapter 8.

---

129 M Ross, 'Director's Liability on Corporate Restructuring' in C Rickett (ed), *Essays on Corporate Restructuring and Insolvency*, (Brookers, 1996), 176.

2.085   On several occasions so far we have adverted to the fact there are a great number of small private companies in the UK. They benefit from the twin principles of separate legal entity and limited liability but they are not subject to the same degree of reporting and disclosure as large companies. Many owner-managed companies are treated as the plaything of the 'owner', and the funds of the owner and that of the company are not infrequently mixed. While not good practice, this might not cause any concerns until insolvency occurs and the company enters an insolvency regime. If companies that have been managed in such a way become insolvent then the creditors will want to know what has been happening and how they can ensure that the owner is made responsible for improper conduct.

2.086   Professor David Milman has asked whether there is a link between corporate governance failures and financial distress.[130] It has been asserted that poor corporate governance often ends up leading to companies making huge losses.[131] Adroitly Milman cautions that we must be careful in establishing the link because corporate failure can be due to a number of causes.[132] For instance, as we have already noted, company X can become insolvent as part of the ripple effect, that is, its debtors and possibly its debtors' debtors and so on might collapse and because they cannot repay their debts X cannot continue to fulfil its own liabilities. In such a case company X may have done nothing wrong or imprudent. Other reasons for failure are: failing to understand the business' market; products are no longer wanted; inadequate financing.[133]

2.087   Nevertheless, clearly some companies fail because of poor corporate governance. The demise of large US companies like Enron and WorldCom in the early years of this century are examples. Enron was the fifth largest company in the US at one stage but, inter alia, there were corporate governance shortcomings in the company. For instance, the board of directors failed to monitor sufficiently what the executives and managers were doing.[134] There are UK companies that have fallen into insolvency due to corporate governance failures. Examples in the past are, arguably, Polly Peck and Maxwell Communications and in more recent times, HBOS[135] and Carillion.[136]

2.088   Much of the literature addressing corporate governance in insolvency is American and deals with companies that have entered Chapter 11 bankruptcy. The UK has, at various times, flirted with the idea of embracing a process similar to this type of insolvency regime, but has always declined in the end. Chapter 11 bankruptcy is different from anything that exists in the UK and even differs from the Moratorium procedure, introduced recently through the Corporate Insolvency and Governance Act 2020, which does represent a move closer to the Chapter 11 approach. Chapter 11 allows, save where there is clear evidence of wrongdoing and possibly fraud in the company when a trustee can be appointed, the management of the company to

---

130   D Milman, *Governance of Distressed Firms*, (Edward Elgar, 2013), 37.

131   U Nwagbara, 'En/Countering Corrupt Leadership and Poor Corporate Governance in the Nigerian Banking Sector' (2012) 5 *Indian Journal of Corporate Governance* 133.

132   D Milman, *Governance of Distressed Firms*, (Edward Elgar, 2013), 37.

133   'What Causes Small Businesses to Fail?': http://www.moyak.com/papers/small-business-failure.html.

134   Others, so-called gatekeepers, also failed to do their jobs properly and Enron was given a good bill of health just until it collapsed into bankruptcy. This was largely due to the auditors, but other gatekeepers were also at fault.

135   'An accident waiting to happen: The failure of HBOS' Parliamentary Commission on Banking Standards, Fourth Report of Session 2012–13: https://publications.parliament.uk/pa/jt201213/jtselect/jtpcbs/144/144.pdf.

136   'Carillion,' Second Joint Report of the Business, Energy and Industrial Strategy and work and Pensions Committees Session 2017–19, 9 May 2018: https://publications.parliament.uk/pa/cm201719/cmselect/cmworpen/769/76902.htm.

remain in control of the company, subject to court oversight. This is known as debtor in possession ('DIP'). As the management remains in control in DIP it tends to throw up more and different issues than those which occur in the UK in most insolvency regimes, thus a lot of the American literature and case law is of limited assistance.

3

INTRODUCTION TO INSOLVENCY

A. THE SIGNIFICANCE OF INSOLVENCY

3.001 A company may be notoriously insolvent but the state of insolvency does not have immediate consequences in and of itself. It may be that a company may continue in business for many years being able to pay its debts as they fall due but have significant long-term debt which it may have very little realistic chance of ever paying off.

Where a company is insolvent, it (usually by acting through its directors) may or may not decide   **3.002**
to restructure its debt either formally or informally. It may decide to attempt a formal company
or business rescue. It may decide to call it a day and enter liquidation. Its creditors, or others
with some involvement in the company, may decide to take action to protect their respective
positions. That action may lead to a form of company or business rescue or indeed bring the
company to an end by ensuring the company is wound up.

The company may or may not be able to negotiate effectively with its creditors. The company   **3.003**
may have only a small number of creditors in which case informal bi-lateral agreements may be
sufficient to reach a lasting compromise which permits the company to continue in business.
There may be numerous creditors and those creditors may fall into different classes each with
a different priority for their respective debts. Some formal agreement may be needed in order
to bind a dissenting minority of creditors. The fact that the company is insolvent or likely to
become insolvent may open the door to various statutory regimes which may be used to rescue
the company, its business or precipitate its liquidation.

In this chapter we first consider the meaning of 'insolvency' so that we have an understanding   **3.004**
of how the legislature and the courts have defined the concept. We will then consider ways in
which a company which is either technically insolvent or at least financially distressed (in that
it may not yet be technically insolvent but needs to take action now to avoid insolvency) may
deal with its position.

As we shall see, there are a number of options available to a company. Depending upon the   **3.005**
circumstances, some options will be more realistic and attractive than others. It may be that
the directors will remain in control in running a planned workout outside any formal statutory
framework. The directors may consider a more formal procedure such as a company voluntary
arrangement under the Insolvency Act 1986 or a scheme of arrangement or restructuring
plan under the Companies Act 2006. Such procedures, in allowing the directors to remain in
control of the company, are often referred to as debtor-in-possession procedures and the hope
is that they lead to the rescue of the company. The company may take advantage of a statutory
moratorium on creditor action against the company whilst they put together their company
rescue plan.

On the other hand, it may be that the directors cannot put together a plan to rescue the   **3.006**
company or its business themselves. In such cases, the company may enter administration
where the directors' powers of management are usurped by an administrator who then decides
whether or not a company rescue or a business rescue is possible. Frequently, administration
leads to the company's business being sold onto a buyer but the company itself is wound up
or dissolved. It may be that administration is not the best option. It may be that liquidation is
inevitable. Even in such cases, it may be that the company's business or at least its assets can be
sold on and used by the buyer in a future successful business.

It is often a pre-requisite for entering a formal procedure that a company is insolvent or that   **3.007**
that it is reasonably likely that it will become insolvent.

If directors do nothing (or nothing helpful) and the company eventually enters liquidation (or   **3.008**
some other formal process), the directors may find they have incurred some personal liabilities

for their actions or inactions. Much will depend upon the date when they knew or ought to have known that the company was insolvent or had no reasonable prospect of avoiding insolvency. These potential liabilities are explored in Chapter 4.

3.009 The meaning of insolvency is, therefore, a significant matter and will be considered next.

B. WHAT IS INSOLVENCY?[1]

3.010 A newcomer to the world of insolvency law might reasonably expect there to be a straightforward definition of the term 'insolvency' in the principal statute on the area, the Insolvency Act 1986 ('the Act'). Rather than define 'insolvency' as such, the Act instead adopts and defines the phrase 'inability to pay debts' when referring to a state of insolvency. It is this phrase which permeates the Act in that it is incorporated by reference into multiple other provisions in the Act.

3.011 It has been observed that a clear definition of 'inability to pay debts' is 'fundamental'[2] to any system of insolvency law. A casual perusal of corporate or insolvency law commentaries over the years would initially suggest that the meaning of a company being 'unable to pay its debts' is quite straightforward. Relying upon the ostensibly simple wording of s 123 of the Act,[3] the distinction is made between the 'cash flow' test where a company is unable to pay its debts as they fall due and a 'balance sheet' test where a company's liabilities are greater than its assets.

3.012 Specifically, a company is deemed unable to pay its debts under s 123(1)(e) of the Act: 'if it is proved to the satisfaction of the court that the company is unable to pay its debts as they fall due'. This is the 'cash flow' test.[4]

3.013 Under s 123(2) of the Act a company:

> is also deemed unable to pay its debts if it is proved to the satisfaction of the court that the value of the company's assets is less than the amount of its liabilities, taking into account its contingent and prospective liabilities.

3.014 This is the 'balance sheet' test.

3.015 Matters are not, though, quite that straightforward. Although the Supreme Court[5] has opined on the issue in recent times, there remains some uncertainty in practical terms as to how and to what extent contingent and prospective (or future) liabilities can be considered in applying either test. Although there is no mention of contingent and prospective liabilities under the statutory wording of the 'cash flow' test, the Supreme Court has stated that they may be taken

---

1   The first section of this chapter is partly based upon P Walton '"Inability to pay debts": Beyond the Point of No Return?' (2013) *Journal of Business Law* 212 cited with approval by the Supreme Court in *BNY Corporate Trustee Services Ltd v Eurosail-UK 2007–3BL plc* [2013] UKSC 28; [2013] 1 WLR 1408.

2   Jeremy Hanley MP in the House of Commons debate on the Insolvency Act 1985: HC Deb 28 October 1985 vol 84 c 686.

3   1986 c 45.

4   Cash flow insolvency is usually proven by service of a statutory demand for an unsecured debt exceeding £750 which has not been satisfied within three weeks of service (see s 123(1) of the Act).

5   *BNY Corporate Trustee Services Ltd v Eurosail-UK 2007–3BL plc* [2013] UKSC 28; [2013] 1 WLR 1408.

into account in assessing present ability to pay debts. Problems of how to quantify debts have been encountered by the courts in attempting to take account of future and contingent liabilities when considering the 'balance sheet' test.

The difficulties in interpreting s 123 can be traced back at least as far as the Companies Act 1907,[6] when the definition of 'inability to pay debts' was amended. The amendment permitted the court, for the first time under the Companies Acts, to take account of the company's contingent and prospective liabilities in deciding whether a company was insolvent.   **3.016**

The meaning of 'inability to pay debts' is important in the corporate setting. Most obviously, the definition found in s 123 is important as the main ground upon which a petition for the compulsory winding up of a company is made to the court. The same definition is specifically adopted elsewhere in the Act when considering, for example: petitions for administration orders;[7] applications for a statutory moratorium;[8] adjustment of withdrawals of property from limited liability partnerships;[9] transactions at an undervalue;[10] and preferences.[11] It is also widely adopted in drafting various types of commercial agreement where it is used as a trigger to demonstrate default by a debtor and for permitting a creditor to take enforcement action.[12]   **3.017**

In this first part of the chapter we will consider the historical development of the meaning of 'inability to pay debts' in the corporate context. The development of the law in relation to the ability to *prove* for future and contingent debts goes hand in hand with the ability to *petition* (for liquidation[13]) on the basis of future or contingent debts. Some consideration of the ability to prove will help inform the discussion on the ability to petition. In order to understand the governance obligations of a director of a company which is suffering financial distress, it is crucial to understand the meaning of 'inability to pay debts'.   **3.018**

1.   What are 'future' and 'contingent' debts?

The modern-day problems encountered in interpreting the meaning of 'inability to pay debts', stem, at least in part, from difficulties in understanding the amendments to the statutory regime which introduced references to future and contingent debts. Some understanding of how these types of debts found their way into the Act is helpful in understanding how we ended up with the current version of s 123.   **3.019**

---

6   7 Edw 7 c 50.

7   Insolvency Act 1986, Sch B1, para 11.

8   Ibid., s A6.

9   Ibid., s 214A. It is not used in assessing liability for wrongful trading under s 214.

10   Ibid., ss 238 and 240.

11   Ibid., ss 239 and 240.

12   See e.g., *Re Cheyne Finance plc* [2007] EWHC 2402 (Ch), [2008] 1 BCLC 741 and *BNY Corporate Trustee Services Ltd v Eurosail-UK 2007–3BL plc* [2013] UKSC 28; [2013] 1 WLR 1408, both of which are considered below. Section 123 is also referred to under the provisions of the Companies Act 2006, s 653, when the court is asked to confirm a reduction of capital.

13   The regime governing administration has effectively adopted the rules applicable in liquidation (see e.g., Insolvency Act 1986, Sch B1, para 11 and Insolvency (England and Wales) Rules 2016 (SI 2016/1024) rr 14.14 and 14.44).

3.020   'Future' and 'contingent' debts are generally distinguished from one another on the basis of the certainty of the debt becoming payable. If a debt is for a liquidated sum and is payable at a certain future date, it will usually be classified as a 'future' or 'prospective' debt:

> [A] 'prospective creditor' is a creditor in respect of a debt which will certainly become due in the future, either on some date which has been already determined or on some date determinable by reference to future events.[14]

3.021   In order to be a 'future' or 'prospective' liability, it must arise out of a current transaction or obligation, not a future obligation.[15]

3.022   If the debt is for an unliquidated amount, or if its payment is uncertain or dependent upon some future occurrence, it will usually be seen as a 'contingent' debt. In 1873, Mellish LJ commented: 'a contingent debt refers to a case where there is a doubt if there will be a debt at all'.[16] More recently a contingent creditor has been referred to as 'a person towards whom under an existing obligation, the company may or will become subject to a present liability upon the happening of some future event or some future date'.[17]

3.023   In order to qualify as a 'future' or 'contingent' debt, a liability must be referable to an existing obligation. If the liability is certain it will be classified as a 'future' or 'prospective' debt. If it is uncertain it will be seen as a 'contingent' debt.

3.024   As will be seen below, the corporate insolvency provisions have developed alongside one another so that the law permitting a winding-up order to be made on the basis of a future debt is the same as that for a contingent debt.

2.   Cork recommendations

3.025   The Cork Committee, reporting in 1982, recommended that 'the sole ground upon which the Court may make an Insolvency Order in respect of a debtor, whether individual or corporate, will be that the debtor is unable to pay his or its debts'.[18] Although the 1986 Act does require proof that debtors are unable to pay their debts, the meaning of inability to pay debts varies depending upon the type of petition. Its meaning in the context of a creditor's petition for bankruptcy is different from that where the debtor applies for his or her own bankruptcy. It is different again where the creditor is petitioning for a company's liquidation.[19] This is a long way from the Cork Committee's recommendation that the meaning of 'unable to pay debts' should be the same for individuals and companies.

---

14   *Stonegate Securities v Gregory* [1980] Ch 576, 579 *per* Buckley LJ. See also *Re Sutherland* [1963] AC 235, 263 *per* Lord Guest.

15   *Burford Midland Properties Ltd v Marley* [1994] BCC 604, 609 *per* His Honour Judge Roger Cooke. See also *Re British Equitable Bond and Mortgage Corp* [1910] 1 Ch 574 and *Re European Life Assurance Society* (1869) 9 Eq 122.

16   *Ex parte Ruffle* (1873) 8 Ch D 997, 1001. See also *Holt on the Bankruptcy Laws* (1827, J Butterworth & Sons, London), 162.

17   *Re William Hockley Ltd* [1962] 1 WLR 555, 558 *per* Pennycuick J.

18   *Insolvency Law Review Committee, Insolvency Law and Practice*, Cmnd 858, (HMSO, 1982) ('the Cork Committee'), para 535.

19   See generally the discussion in P Walton '"Inability to pay debts" Beyond the Point of No Return?' (2013) *Journal of Business Law* 212.

The Cork Committee had suggested that a debtor would be deemed unable to pay his or its **3.026** debts in three situations:

(i)   where a judgment debt of at least the prescribed amount has gone unpaid;

(ii)   where a debt of at least the prescribed amount is presently due and payable and the debtor has failed to pay the debt within 21 days of a formal demand; and

(iii)   where the creditor is owed either a contingent or a prospective debt of at least the prescribed amount and that the court is satisfied 'that the ultimate repayment of the debt is in jeopardy because the debtor's liabilities, including contingent and future liabilities, exceed the debtor's assets'.[20]

The Cork Committee gives no real guidance as to how contingent and future liabilities should **3.027** be included within the calculation beyond seeming to suggest that all liabilities are added up. This would only make sense, it is submitted, if a current value is placed upon contingent and prospective liabilities. Once this is done, the liabilities can be set against the value of the company's current assets to see if the company is 'balance sheet' insolvent, that is, the liabilities outweigh the assets.

3.   Proving future and contingent debts

Rules governing company liquidation slowly evolved during the nineteenth century alongside **3.028** the development of the fundamental principles of company law of limited liability and separate corporate personality.[21] Specific provisions dealing with the proof of future and contingent debts appeared in the Companies Act 1862.[22]

Section 158 of the 1862 Act first permitted future and contingent debts to be proved in **3.029** winding up in the following terms:

> all claims against the company, present or future, certain or contingent, ascertained or sounding only in damages, shall be admissible to proof against, a just estimate being made, so far as is possible, of the value of all such debts or claims as may be subject to any contingency or sound only in damages, or for some other reason do not bear a certain value.

Section 158 was drafted in very wide terms to include all possible future and contingent liabil- **3.030** ities.[23] The legislature, by 1862, was therefore clearly of the view that it was possible to assess the current value of any future or contingent debt. The modern equivalent provisions to s 158,

---

20   Cork Committee Report, para 535(c).
21   For a very clear summary of the early legislative history see A Keay *McPherson's Law of Company Liquidation* (2001, Sweet & Maxwell, London), 13–25.
22   25 & 26 Vict c 89.
23   Due to an unrelated perceived injustice flowing from *Kellock's Case* (1868) 3 Ch App 769, (see e.g., the comments in *Re Withernsea Brickworks* (1880) 16 Ch D 340, 341 *per* James LJ and, 343 Lush LJ) s 10 of the Judicature Act 1875 imported into an insolvent winding up, the distributional rules in bankruptcy, which at the time excluded proof for unquantified tort claims. The effect of s 10 was that if the winding up was solvent, a contingent creditor with a tort claim, could prove under s 158 of the 1862 Act, but in an insolvent winding up, the creditor could not prove. The distinction was only remedied following a recommendation by the Cork Committee by the introduction of what are now rr 14.1 and 14.2 of the Insolvency (England and Wales) Rules 2016 which allow tort claimants to prove in bankruptcy and in all types of liquidation.

permitting future and contingent debts to be proved, are found in rr 14.1, 14.2 and 14.14 of the Insolvency (England and Wales) Rules 2016.[24]

4. Rights of future and contingent creditors to petition for a winding-up order

3.031 Until the Companies Act 1907, a future or contingent creditor could not petition for a debtor company's winding up. Under the provisions of s 82 of the Companies Act 1862 a winding-up petition could only be presented by one or more 'creditors' of the company. This was held to mean creditors with a current claim which was presently payable by the company. If the debt relied upon was due under the terms of a current lease,[25] bill of exchange,[26] guarantee,[27] or debenture[28] but the date for payment had not yet arrived, the creditor could not obtain a winding-up order even if the company was notoriously insolvent. This was seen as an undesirable state of affairs by the authors of several contemporary textbooks[29] and of the Loreburn Report.[30]

3.032 The examples given above involve types of 'future' debt which are certain to fall payable at a certain future time as opposed to 'contingent' debts. Contingent debts were, not surprisingly, also subject to the same rule. Jessel MR commented in *Re Pen-y-Van Colliery Co*[31] that: 'I do not think a claim for unliquidated damages... makes a man a creditor entitling him to petition... for a winding-up.'

3.033 As will be seen below, the Companies Act 1907 introduced the ability for a future or contingent creditor to petition for a company's winding up and that provision survives today in the form of s 124 of the Act.

5. Pre-1869 case law on the meaning of 'unable to pay debts'

3.034 Section 5(8) of the Winding-Up Act 1848,[32] and later s 79(5) of the Companies Act 1862, allowed for a winding-up order to be made on the 'just and equitable' ground. This was in addition to specific provision being made for a winding-up order on the basis that the company was 'unable to pay its debts' under s 5(7) of the 1848 Act and s 79(4) of the 1862 Act. On a number of occasions where a winding-up order was requested, the courts considered whether it was permissible to consider the likely prospect of a company becoming insolvent due to contingent liabilities, even if the company was currently able to cover its present debts. Such cases were argued under the 'just and equitable' ground.

---

24   For an example of the court assessing the value of a contingent liability for the purposes of proof see *Re Danka Business Systems plc* [2013] EWCA Civ 92, [2013] Ch 506.

25   *Re United Club Co* (1889) 60 LT 665.

26   *Re W Powell & Sons* [1892] WN 94.

27   *Re Vron Colliery Co* (1882) 20 Ch D 442.

28   *Re Melbourne Brewery and Distillery Ltd* [1901] 1 Ch 453.

29   See e.g., *Palmer on the Companies Act 1907* (1908, Stevens & Sons, London) at 33. Simonson *The Companies Acts 1900 and 1907 with Commentaries* (1908, Effingham Wilson and Sweet & Maxwell, London), 173, *Palmer's Company Precedents* Part II Winding Up (1910, 10th ed, Stevens & Sons, London), 68–9.

30   See the *Report of the Company Law Amendment Committee* (1906) Cd 3052 (the Loreburn Committee), para 43.

31   (1877) 6 Ch D 477, 484.

32   11 & 12 Vict c 45.

In *Ex parte Spackman*,[33] Lord Cottenham LC, in considering the 'just and equitable' ground,   **3.035** explained that the uncertain nature of contingent liabilities meant that they could not be considered in assessing the current solvency of company under the 1848 Winding-Up Act. Lord Cottenham LC decided that the 'just and equitable' ground should be interpreted *ejusdem generis* with the remainder of s 5 which referred, *inter alia*, to a company being unable to pay its debts. The case shows a nascent willingness for the courts to consider a form of 'balance sheet' insolvency.

To similar effect, in *Re National Live Stock Insurance Co*,[34] Turner LJ followed Lord   **3.036** Cottenham's view in *Spackman*, that s 5(8) was to be interpreted *ejusdem generis* with the other subsections of s 5, so that if there was proof of insolvency the company might be wound up. It appears that his Lordship approaches the 'just and equitable' ground as permitting the court to consider whether the company is 'balance sheet' insolvent although his Lordship limits his consideration to whether the assets and likely assets would cover present liabilities. Contingent liabilities were not to be added into this calculation.[35]

The consequence of this line of cases was that the courts appeared open to ordering an   **3.037** insolvency-related 'just and equitable' winding up but only where there was evidence of insolvency on a balance sheet basis. This was limited to considering whether a company's current liabilities outweighed its current assets. Contingent liabilities did not form part of the equation.

6.   *Re European Life Assurance Society* (1869)

The leading case of *Re European Life Assurance Society*[36] extended this line of reasoning. The   **3.038** case involved a life assurance company which had sold a large number of life assurance policies and annuities. The petition was not presented by a creditor but a shareholder. The company's income was considerable but the evidence suggested that its future and contingent liabilities would not be met out of its current assets. The suggestion was that the company had only been able to pay its debts as they fell due in: 'a hand-to-mouth way by applying current income to discharge past liabilities'.[37] James V-C held that in order to show that the company was unable to pay its debts under ss 79(4) and 80 of the 1862 Act, a petitioner could rely only upon debts actually due, for which a creditor could claim immediate payment. As the company was successfully paying its debts as they fell due, it was not 'unable to pay its debts' under ss 79(4) and 80.[38]

The alternative argument, that in the circumstances it would be 'just and equitable' to wind   **3.039** up the company under s 79(5), also failed. His Lordship considered that it might be 'just and equitable' to wind up where the evidence was that it was 'plainly and commercially insolvent[39] –

---

33   (1849) 1 Mac & G 170, 41 ER 1228.
34   (1858) 26 Beav 153, 53 ER 855.
35   (1858) 27 LJ Ch 669 at 674. For cases decided under s 79 Companies Act 1862 to the same effect see e.g., *Re Anglo-Greek Steam Co* (1866) 2 Eq 1 and *Re Suburban Hotel Co* (1867) 2 Ch App 737.
36   (1869) 9 Eq 122.
37   Ibid., 127 *per* James V-C.
38   Ibid., 127.
39   The reference here to 'commercial insolvency' is to 'balance sheet' insolvency even though 'commercial insolvency' is usually viewed in modern times as referring to the inability to pay debts as they fall due, that is, the 'cash flow' test under s 123(1)(e) of the Act.

that is to say, that its assets are such, and its existing liabilities are such, as to make it reasonably certain … that the existing and probable assets would be insufficient to meet the existing liabilities'.[40] His Lordship refused to take into account any possible income from future business.[41]

3.040 On the facts, his Lordship carried out a calculation based upon the company's latest balance sheet. The court added together all current assets, including uncalled share capital (there being no evidence that the company's shareholders would be unable to meet calls) and income due in the future from existing policies. It then deducted from that figure, liabilities under existing policies. For these purposes his Lordship took account of future and contingent liabilities under existing contracts. His conclusion was that the court could not be satisfied: 'that the company will be unable to discharge its liabilities under those contracts when they arise'.[42] No winding-up order was made.

3.041 It is clear from *European Life* that by 1869, a court would consider a winding-up petition based upon the 'just and equitable' ground if a company was 'balance sheet' insolvent. The court would limit itself to giving a current value to assets (including assets which the company would receive in the future under contracts already entered into) and a current value to present, future and contingent liabilities (again under existing contractual arrangements).

7. Insurance companies legislation

3.042 The year following the decision in *European Life*, Parliament acted to regulate generally the workings of life assurance companies by passing the Life Assurance Companies Act 1870.[43] Section 21 of this Act expressly permitted a shareholder or policy holder to petition for the winding up of an assurance company, under the general jurisdiction under the 1862 Act, on the ground that it was 'insolvent'. Section 21 did not use the phrase 'unable to pay its debts'. The reference to the company being 'insolvent' echoes the wording of James V-C in *European Life* and appears to be statutory recognition or codification of his decision.[44] As it does not refer to 'unable to pay debts' specifically but instead to 'insolvent', it seems reasonable to assume it was intended to be confirming James V-C's interpretation of the 'just and equitable' ground.

3.043 Section 21 expressly permitted the court to take account of the company's contingent and prospective liabilities. The court was given a power to suspend proceedings whilst a call was made on shareholders. This appears to be a direct response to James V-C's point in *European Life* that there was no evidence before him that the shareholders were not able to pay a call.

3.044 Section 21 provided a 'balance sheet' test for assessing the solvency of an assurance company. All available and probable assets (including uncalled capital) were to be set against existing and

---

40   (1869) 9 Eq 122, 128.
41   Ibid., 128.
42   Ibid., 131.
43   33 & 34 Vict c 61.
44   Slade J in *Re Capital Annuities Ltd* [1978] 3 All ER 704 commented, 716, that:
      I feel little doubt that this was a deliberate choice of language and that the legislature used the word 'insolvent' in the same sense as that used by James V-C… namely having existing and probable assets insufficient to meet its liabilities, but subject to the rider that, for this purpose, a life assurance company's contingent or prospective liabilities under policies and annuities and other existing contracts should be taken into account, in addition to its existing liabilities.

estimated liabilities. Section 21 is consistent with earlier case law under the Companies Acts in that it does not require a consideration of whether or not a company is likely to trade profitably or not in the future. It required a snapshot of the company's current financial position by comparing the current value of its assets with the current value of its liabilities (including those which were future and contingent).

8.   Companies Act 1907

On the recommendation of the Loreburn Committee[45] in 1906, s 21 of the Life Assurance **3.045** Companies 1870 Act was introduced, *mutatis mutandis*, for companies generally by s 28 Companies Act 1907. The form of words used in s 28 was an abbreviated version of s 21 of the 1870 Act. In determining whether a company was unable to pay its debts, the court could now take into account its contingent and prospective liabilities whatever the type of company.[46]

There is a clear link between James LJ's interpretation of the 'just and equitable' ground in **3.046** *European Life*, the wording of s 21 of the 1870 Act and subsequently s 28 of the 1907 Act through to the statutory provision (s 518 of the Companies Act 1985) in force immediately prior to s 123 of the Insolvency Act 1986. In considering the development of the law in this area Nicholls LJ, in giving the judgment of the Court of Appeal in *Byblos Bank SAL v Al-Khudhairy*[47] commented:

> Subsequently, s 28 of the Companies Act 1907 introduced the requirement to take into account contingent and prospective liabilities in determining whether a company was unable to pay its debts. In my view the exercise described by Sir William James is the exercise required to be done under s 223 [Companies Act 1948] (now s 518 of the Companies Act 1985).[48]

There is a direct link starting from James V-C's judgment in *European Life* through to s 518 **3.047** of the Companies Act 1985 (as originally enacted). The provenance of the distinction between 'cash flow' insolvency and 'balance sheet' insolvency can therefore be traced from 1869 through to 1985. In interpreting the respective statutory provisions case law has, up to this point, kept separate the 'cash flow' test for insolvency from the 'balance sheet' test. Future and contingent debts are only relevant to the 'balance sheet' test and do not form an element of the 'cash flow' test.[49] The 'balance sheet' test involves a simple subtraction of liabilities from assets (as currently valued). Although a company's prospects may be considered by a court in exercising its discretion as to whether or not to order a winding up, they are not to be considered in assessing whether or not it is currently unable to pay its debts under the 'balance sheet' test.[50]

---

45   *Report of the Company Law Amendment Committee* (1906) Cd 3052, para 43.
46   *Re British Equitable Bond and Mortgage Corporation Ltd* [1910] 1 Ch 574.
47   (1986) 2 BCC 99, 549.
48   Ibid., 99, 563.
49   Ibid., 99, 562.
50   Ibid. If it can be shown that the company is unable to pay its debts, the court still possesses a wide discretion not to make an order. This rule goes back at least to the Winding Up Act 1848, see *Ex parte Wise* (1853) 1 Drew 465, 61 ER 530.

9. Insolvency Acts 1985 and 1986

3.048 As explained above the Cork Committee recommended that the definition of 'inability to pay debts' should expressly separate out the 'cash flow' test from the 'balance sheet' test and should apply both tests to both individual and corporate insolvency. The 'balance sheet' test alone was to take account of future and contingent liabilities. It is clear that Parliament did not adopt *all* of these recommendations, for example, no 'balance sheet' test has been applied in the context of individual insolvency. In a corporate context, the initial wording of s 518 of the Companies Act 1985 was altered to what is now s 123. One significant issue is whether the change in the wording was intended to change the meaning of the previous provisions which had been clear since, at the latest, 1907. This matter requires a little analysis.

3.049 As explained above, the wording of s 28 of the 1907 Act was intended to bring into general company law the provisions of s 21 of the 1870 Act. The substantive wording of s 28 found its way into s 518 of the Companies Act 1985 (as originally enacted in March 1985).[51]

3.050 Shortly afterwards, and towards the end of the Parliamentary debates on the Insolvency Act 1985, the wording of s 518 of the Companies Act 1985 was amended. When consolidated, the amended s 518 became s 123 of the 1986 Act. When Parliament considered the amendment to s 518, some disquiet was expressed as to what appeared to be an extension of the definition of insolvency. The government minister answered these concerns by stating:

> We are not seeking to amend the law by this amendment; merely to give effect to that interpretation by the courts, namely, that Section 518 contains both a cash flow and a balance sheet test… The courts do have a discretion whether or not to make an order and it is vital that in exercising that discretion they have regard to contingent and prospective liabilities in the manner I have described, which merely expresses quite clearly the current law and practice in the matter.[52]

3.051 It is tolerably clear from this that the draftsman preferred the wording of the amendment to the wording of the original s 518 and that, although the wording is different, no change in meaning was intended. Section 123, consistently with the Cork Committee recommendation, separates the 'cash flow' test from the 'balance sheet' test which had co-existed in a compendium subsection, since 1907 (or arguably since *European Life*). The express wording of s 123 makes it entirely clear that, as was always the case, the 'cash flow' test takes no account of future or contingent debts. Such liabilities are only relevant in considering the 'balance sheet' test. In this context, they are relevant in that the court will be required to assess the present value of such debts and assign that present value in assessing 'balance sheet' insolvency. The result under s 123(2) is that by placing a current value on future and contingent liabilities, it is possible to say whether the company is currently insolvent. It is not necessary, nor permissible, to assess what will happen in the future. The balance sheet calculation is one made on the present values of assets and liabilities. Even if the company is found to be 'balance sheet' insolvent, the court may

---

51 Companies Act 1985 (1985) which received Royal Assent on 11 March 1985.
52 Lord Lucas of Chilworth, then Under Secretary of State for Trade and Industry in answer to a concern expressed by Lord Milne: HL Deb 23 October 1985 vol 467 cc 1244–9. See also the exchange in the House of Commons to similar effect at HC Deb 28 October 1985 vol 84 c 685. In both exchanges, reference is made to Nourse J's judgment referring to s 518 in 'Re Bond Jewellers' reported as *Re a Company* [1986] BCLC 261.

still exercise its discretion not to make the order if it is convinced that the company's prospects are sufficiently promising.[53]

10. Two post-1986 decisions

In *Re Colt Telecom Group plc*[54] the court was asked to consider a hostile application for an administration order under the pre-Enterprise Act 2002 administration regime. Under s 8 of the Insolvency Act 1986, the court needed to be persuaded that the company was or was likely to become 'unable to pay its debts (within the meaning given to that expression by 123 of this Act).' **3.052**

In considering the 'cash flow' test under 123(1)(e) Jacob J refused to consider future liabilities in assessing the company's supposed inability to pay its debts as they fell due. There was no risk of 'cash flow' insolvency until at least four years into the future and the appellant's evidence was considered: 'shaky, tentative and speculative peering into the middle-distance'.[55] The attempt to introduce future inability to pay debts into the 'cash flow' test was dismissed by his Lordship. In considering the 'balance sheet' test, his Lordship focused on the Financial Reporting Standard relevant to the preparation of the company's balance sheet. His Lordship came down in favour of the company's solvent balance sheet results rather than the appellant's expert evidence. Jacob J's application of s 123(2) involved a literal interpretation of the company's accounting balance sheet. The decision is consistent with previous pre-1986 authority such as the Court of Appeal's decision in *Byblos*. **3.053**

Re Cheyne Finance plc (No 2)[56] involved the court being asked to interpret a security trust deed in the context of security given by a special investment vehicle company. The occurrence of an 'Insolvency Event' would affect the order of priority of payment to certain creditors. The trust deed defined the meaning of 'Insolvency Event' by reference to the wording of s 123(1)(e) but made no reference to s 123(2). At first blush, one might have expected the court to view the test in s 123(1)(e) as a straightforward exercise in considering whether the company was able to pay its debts then due. Only s 123(2) refers to taking account of contingent or prospective debts, so they do not appear to be relevant considerations in considering 'cash flow' insolvency. **3.054**

Briggs J disagreed. His Lordship decided that although the 1986 wording of the 'cash flow' test excluded reference to 'contingent and prospective liabilities' it did now include reference to the payment of debts 'as they fall due.' Relying upon Australian authority,[57] his Lordship decided that this phrase imported an element of futurity into the equation. The conclusion reached was that the 'cash flow' test under 123(1)(e): **3.055**

---

53   Section 122(1) of the Act specifically provides that the court 'may' make an order if, inter alia, the company is unable to pay its debts.

54   [2002] EWHC 2815 (Ch).

55   Ibid., [87].

56   [2007] EWHC 2402 (Ch), [2008] 1 BCLC 741.

57   *Bank of Australasia v Hall* (1907) 4 CLR 1514, *Sandell v Porter* (1966) 115 CLR 666, *Hymix Concrete Pty Ltd v Garrity* (1977) 13 ALR 321, *Taylor v Australia and New Zealand Banking Group Ltd* (1988) 6 ACLC 808, *Cuthbertson v Thomas* (1998) 28 ACSR 310; *Southern Cross Interiors Pty Ltd v Deputy Commissioner for Taxation* (1998) 29 ACSR 130 and *Lewis v Doran* [2005] NSWCA 243.

permits references to debts which will fall due in the future, i.e. in English terminology 'prospective debts', rather than 'prospective or contingent liabilities'. The reason why this question has, unlike in England, been analysed in such detail in Australia is probably that neither the Australian courts nor legislature have developed a balance sheet test of the type found in s 123(2).[58]

3.056 His Lordship relied upon the similarity of the Australian legislation to the new wording of s 123(1)(e) to reach the conclusion that:

> I can see no good reason why the developed understanding in Australia ... should not be recognised when the same phrase is, for the first time, deliberately inserted into the English insolvency test.[59]

3.057 The result of *Cheyne* is therefore that under s 123(1)(e) it is possible, in assessing a company's inability to pay its debts, to consider both its present and future liabilities but not, it seems, its contingent liabilities. *Cheyne* clearly assumes that the change in the wording introduced by s 123 brings with it a change to the previous law.

11. The Supreme Court settles the law

3.058 In light of the above discussion, we now turn to the definitive answer to the issues raised above. Although definitive, the answer does raise some continuing uncertainties. The Supreme Court in *BNY Corporate Trustee Service Ltd v Eurosail-UK 2007–3BL plc*[60] ('*Eurosail*'), for the first time, considered and commented upon the statutory definition of 'inability to pay debts' found in s 123 of the Act. The decision in *Eurosail* is important for a number of reasons. As mentioned above, as well as being a pre-requisite for certain statutory provisions, s 123 is widely adopted in drafting various types of commercial agreement where it is used as a trigger to demonstrate default by a debtor, usually permitting a creditor to take enforcement action. It is in this last context that the *Eurosail* case was fought out. The guidance provided by the Supreme Court is clearly therefore important.

12. Facts of *Eurosail*

3.059 Loan notes were issued by Eurosail-UK 2007–3BL plc ('the company') as part of a securitisation transaction. Note-holders were entitled to interest payments and at a specified date in the future to repayment of capital. The proceeds of the notes issue (£660m) were used by the company to purchase a portfolio of sub-prime mortgage loans secured on residential property in England and Scotland (valued at the time of acquisition at approximately £650m).

3.060 The terms of the loan notes provided for the trustee representing the note-holders to serve on the company, an enforcement notice upon the occurrence of any event of default. The effect of the service of an enforcement notice was to make all liability (interest and capital) on the notes due and payable immediately. Without an enforcement notice, the company would only have to repay the capital owed on the notes in question in 2045. One of the events of default listed was the company becoming unable to pay its debts within the meaning of s 123(1) or (2). Although the company continued to pay interest due under the notes its balance sheet

---

58   [2007] EWHC 2402 (Ch), [2008] 1 BCLC 741, [41].
59   Ibid., [54].
60   [2013] UKSC 28, [2013] 1 WLR 1408 (SC).

suggested that it would struggle to pay all its long-term prospective liabilities (the repayment of the note-holders' capital).

The case was fought between different classes of note-holder principally upon the meaning **3.061** of s 123 and how it applied to these circumstances. If the company was currently unable to pay its debts under s 123, the relative priority of note-holders would be altered. In both the High Court[61] and the Court of Appeal[62] the claimant note-holders failed to establish that the company was unable to pay its debts under s 123. They then appealed unsuccessfully to the Supreme Court.

13.   Court of Appeal decision

The main issue addressed by the Court of Appeal was how to take account of future and **3.062** contingent liabilities when assessing the 'balance sheet' test under s 123(2). Section 123(1)(e) was irrelevant on the facts as there were no current liquidity problems. The Court of Appeal regarded the wording of s 123 as materially different to its predecessors. It was therefore capable of being interpreted anew without the court being bound by authority decided under predecessor provisions. In giving the leading judgment of the court, Lord Neuberger MR rejected a mechanistic approach to s 123(2). His Lordship refused to hold that the 'balance sheet' test for insolvency was always satisfied whenever a company's liabilities outweighed its assets. On the facts, the company appeared to have a balance sheet deficit of between £75m and £130m. His Lordship held that a company was only 'balance sheet' insolvent when it had reached 'the point of no return because of an incurable deficiency in its assets'. In the circumstances of the case, due to the many variables and the length of time which needed to elapse before the capital sums became payable, the Court of Appeal upheld the High Court's decision that the company was not currently unable to pay its debts under s 123(2). The company could not be said to have reached the 'point of no return'.

Toulson LJ agreed with Lord Neuberger MR that s 123(2) was not satisfied on the facts but **3.063** chose different language from the Master of the Rolls to describe the 'balance sheet' test. Instead Toulson LJ referred to a fairly strict 'balance sheet' approach but one which required 'proper allowance' for future and contingent liabilities. The question was whether the company could reasonably be expected to be able to meet those liabilities. Toulson LJ pointed out that the more distant the liabilities, the harder this will be to establish.

14.   Supreme Court disagrees with Court of Appeal

The Supreme Court's main judgment was given by Lord Walker. Lord Walker's reasoning **3.064** differed significantly from that of Lord Neuberger MR in the Court of Appeal. The Supreme Court expressly rejected the 'point of no return' test for 'balance sheet' insolvency and instead favoured an approach similar to Toulson LJ.

---

61   [2010] EWHC 2005 (Ch), [2011] 1 WLR 1200.
62   [2011] EWCA Civ 227, [2011] 1 WLR 2524.

3.065   Lord Walker went through in some detail the legislative history of s 123, deriving 'great assistance' from academic commentary.[63] His Lordship identified that the Court of Appeal's decision to treat s 123 as a new section unencumbered by the courts' interpretation of its predecessor provisions was contrary to Parliamentary intention. The change in wording brought about in 1985 was expressly stated in Parliamentary debates as intended to clarify the courts' previous interpretation not to change it.

3.066   Lord Walker provided an historical analysis detailing many of the points explained above, beginning with the Companies Act 1862 which contained the predecessor of today's 'cash flow' test but no 'balance sheet' test. Under the terms of the 1862 Act, in order to prove a company's inability to pay its debts, a creditor had to show that debts 'absolutely due' had not been paid. In *European Life* James V-C had accepted that the 'just and equitable' ground for a winding-up order could include 'balance sheet' insolvency if a company's existing and probable assets would be insufficient to meet its existing liabilities. No account could be taken of future or contingent liabilities even though, on the facts of the case, the life assurance company in question had very significant future and contingent liabilities.

3.067   His Lordship explained how Parliament had intervened in relation to life offices by passing the Life Assurance Companies Act 1870 which permitted a life assurance company to be wound up on the basis of 'balance sheet' insolvency taking into account 'contingent and prospective' as well as current liabilities. A version of the 1870 provision was introduced for all companies by the Companies Act 1907. It was clear to his Lordship from contemporary Parliamentary debates and the view of the Loreburn Committee of 1906 that the 1907 provision was intended to bring the principle of the 1870 Act into company law generally. The 1907 provision's wording remained unchanged through successive Companies Acts until 1985, when, as mentioned above, Parliament changed the wording, without intending to alter its meaning.

3.068   Lord Walker examined the small number of cases since 1907 where the courts considered how to take account of prospective and contingent debts. It is clear from those decisions that the courts, in applying the 'balance sheet' test will not merely add up the face value of such liabilities (without some discount to take account of deferment and contingencies) and then require a company to be able to show it has sufficient assets to cover that amount. The difficulty for a petitioning creditor is to know how to discount the value of such future and contingent debts to enable the 'balance sheet' calculation to be made accurately.

3.069   Lord Walker referred to the chaos which accompanied the passing of the Insolvency Acts 1985 and 1986 but accepted that the change in wording made in 1985 to what is now s 123 made 'little significant change in the law'. This is a rather strange comment as the Parliamentary debates show that no change at all was intended. Despite this, it is clearly Lord Walker's view that some change was made. This change appears in his Lordship's explanation of the 'cash-flow' test under s 123(1)(e). His Lordship fully endorses Briggs J's judgment in *Cheyne Finance* where it was held that the wording of s 123(1)(e), which includes a reference to debts 'as they fall due' looks to the future. As explained above, previous authority had always limited the 'cash flow' test to debts presently owed only. Future or contingent debts could not be taken into account. The 'cash flow' test, according to Briggs J and endorsed by Lord Walker, would

---

63   In particular, P Walton "'Inability to pay debts": Beyond the Point of No Return?' [2013] *Journal of Business Law* 212.

include not only debts immediately payable but also those payable in the reasonably near future. According to Lord Walker, the moment the reasonably near future becomes the future, and so beyond the reach of s 123(1)(e), depends upon the facts of each case.

Lord Walker went on to explain how the 'cash flow' test and the 'balance sheet' interact. Once the court moves beyond the reasonably near future, the 'cash flow' test can no longer be sensibly used and so a comparison of present assets with present and future liabilities (discounted for contingencies and deferment) (the 'balance sheet' test) becomes the only sensible test. It is, as Lord Walker admits, very far from an exact test but the burden of proof must be on the party which asserts 'balance sheet' insolvency. The problem which Lord Walker did not answer is how a creditor should go about quantifying contingent and prospective liabilities to the satisfaction of the court. **3.070**

15. The law is settled

We now have some certainty as to the meaning of 'inability to pay debts'. When establishing **3.071** that a company is unable to pay its debts under s 123(1)(e) and s 123(2), it is possible to look first, at whether the company in question has paid its debts which are due or will be able to pay its debts falling due in the reasonably near future (this is the new formulation of the 'cash flow' test with an added futurity element). The second possibility is to look beyond the reasonably near future to see if the company's present assets are outweighed by its liabilities (present, future and contingent) (the 'balance sheet' test).

Lord Walker's judgment does provide some much needed clarification. It explicitly overrules **3.072** the 'point of no return' test favoured in the Court of Appeal by Lord Neuberger MR and it explains how the 'cash flow' test and 'balance sheet' test are to operate in future. It does, however, leave a number of questions or issues unresolved.

It appears that Lord Walker does not fully accept Parliament's intention not to change the **3.073** law in 1985 when it changed the wording to what became s 123. His Lordship's view is that a change was made to the 'cash flow' test. Prior to *Cheyne Finance*, it had been assumed, ever since *European Life*, that only presently due debts could be considered in assessing a company's 'cash flow' solvency. There was never any future element. The introduction by Briggs J of a futurity element appears to have been made without the court being aware of Parliamentary statements that no change in the law had been intended.

Under s 123(1)(e), a company must be unable to pay its debts which are either immediately **3.074** payable or are payable in the reasonably near future (contingent debts may or may not be included).

Lord Walker's explanation of the 'balance sheet' test under s 123(2) shows a sensible return to **3.075** the orthodoxy of needing to show that a company has insufficient assets to be able to meet its liabilities (including prospective and contingent liabilities) but refuses to enter into any attempt to calculate with any certainty the value of future or contingent liabilities.

3.076 The difficulty in trying to prove 'balance sheet' insolvency, in the terms explained by Lord Walker, wherever there are significant future or contingent liabilities, will be close to insuperable.

3.077 Although there are therefore practical issues around how parties may take advantage of the modern interpretation of 'inability to pay debts', the courts have, of course, adopted it and have attempted to apply it. In *Re Casa Estates (UK) Ltd*[64] the Court of Appeal explained that the two tests for 'cash flow' and 'balance sheet' insolvency were part of a single exercise to determine whether a company was unable to pay its debts. On the facts of *Casa*, it was not enough when applying the 'cash flow' test to ask only whether the company was for the time being paying its debts as they fell due. It was appropriate on the facts for the court to ask how the company was managing to pay its debts for the time being. It was counterintuitive that a company that managed to stave off cash flow insolvency by going deeper and deeper into long-term debt was not insolvent. If, as the court had found, the company was only able to continue to pay its debts as they fell due by taking on new long-term debts which is used to pay off old debts, in any commercial sense it was insolvent, whether on a 'cash flow' or a 'balance sheet' basis.[65]

3.078 This reasoning may be of significance in cases of so-called 'zombie companies' where the company is kept alive but is not profitable. If it is only kept alive by paying its current debts due to taking on long-term debt, it may be said to be 'balance sheet' insolvent, and according to *Casa*, also 'cash flow' insolvent.

3.079 It is regrettable that the statutory definition of 'inability to pay debts' is not always easy to apply to a given company. Directors of companies need to understand when a company is insolvent or likely so to become. The lack of certainty in this area makes it more difficult for directors to understand fully their obligations towards the company and more importantly to the company's creditors. These obligations are fully considered in Chapter 4 below.

C. WORKOUTS

3.080 Although we have seen many large companies fail due to insolvency in recent years, few have gone under without some attempt being made to turn around their fortunes. It is often seen that the larger the debt owed by a company, the less likely its financial backers are to pull the rug from under it unless all else fails. The failure of a large concern will often have a significant impact upon its financiers. There are frequently multiple banks or other financiers who to varying degrees have supported the company. The financial failure of such large companies will have a social cost as well as affecting those who have supported it financially.

3.081 Large companies who are financially distressed or indeed technically insolvent have a number of options they may pursue. As we shall see in the next section, they may enter some formal debtor-in-possession statutory procedure such as a company voluntary arrangement, a scheme

---

64 [2014] EWCA Civ 383, [2014] BCC 269.

65 For further examples of how the courts have used the *Eurosail* test see *Synergy Agri Holdings Ltd v Agform Ltd* [2020] EWHC 343 (Ch), *Burnden Holdings (UK) Ltd (In Liquidation) v Fielding* [2019] EWHC 1566 (Ch), [2020] BPIR 1; and *Evans v Jones* [2016] EWCA Civ 660, [2016] 3 WLR 1480.

of arrangement or a restructuring plan. Their best option, in terms of trying to save the business and the jobs of its workers, may be to enter administration or even liquidation.

In the case of smaller companies, there is often one major or senior creditor who may be in a strong position either to support a rescue plan or to pull the plug. It may not make much difference what other creditors wish to do, if the major creditor has prior security over the company's assets and decides to take steps to enforce that security. It is rather different where there are multiple financiers in the picture. Although it is still possible for the lender with the best security to act to look after its own position at a potentially significant cost to junior lenders, it is also likely to be the case that in the next large corporate failure the respective positions of the creditors may be reversed. A more collegiate approach to working out the problems of the distressed company may be in everyone's interests. Each of the financiers may agree to act for the common good in a transparent and accountable manner.   **3.082**

In the early 1970s we saw the creation of what is usually called the 'London Approach'.[66] The Bank of England took a lead role in orchestrating the restructuring of a number of large failed companies. The idea was that the Bank of England could act as a trusted intermediary in helping to put together financial rescue packages which considered the future of the distressed companies but also engendered a level of trust and co-operation between the major lenders. In 1990 the Bank of England, along with a number of major London-based banks, created and adopted certain principles of best practice called the 'London Rules' which developed into what is now referred to as the 'London Approach'.   **3.083**

The 'London Approach' has two distinct phases. In the first phase a company gives notice to its banks that it is in financial trouble and is looking to initiate what is called a 'workout', whereby the company, with its financiers' support, will attempt to trade out of its difficulties. The lenders are then asked to agree collectively a form of standstill or moratorium on actions against the company. The banks agree not to take enforcement action against the company and also agree to continue to support the company financially. The banks will agree between themselves that any fresh finance provided will have priority status over pre-existing debt. Whilst the workout is in operation, the company's financial position is fully investigated and the results of this investigation are used by the banks to decide what happens next. This activity occurs behind closed doors and is not made public so as to avoid a loss of confidence in the company. It may be that some form of restructuring is subsequently agreed. If the investigation leads to the conclusion that the company cannot be saved, the costs of the process up to this point will be shared equally between the participating banks.   **3.084**

Where a rescue package is pursued, one of the lenders will take a lead in the negotiations and be the intermediary between the various interested parties. If negotiations are successful the final result may take the form of a debt waiver or debt equity swap. The financial benefit in avoiding a formal insolvency will be shared amongst the different lenders.   **3.085**

The co-operative approach typified by the 'London Approach' does require the lenders to act in concert. A more recent development and, to some extent, a consequence of globalisation is   **3.086**

---

66   For a full explanation of the creation and operation of London Approach see J Armour and S Deakin 'Norms in Private Insolvency: The 'London Approach' to the Resolution of Financial Distress' (2001) 1 *Journal of Corporate Law Studies* 21.

the market in distressed debt which appeared at the beginning of the new millennium.[67] Mainly US-based investors brought to the UK the US practice of purchasing debt from lenders. The idea of this market, in simple terms, is for the investor (or 'vulture fund' as they have been labelled) to take an assignment of the debt owed by a company to various lenders. This distressed debt will be sold for a value below its par value as it is distressed debt and unlikely to be paid in full (at least at the time of the purchase of the debt).

3.087   The power acquired by the purchasing investors is then used to negotiate some form of deal with the company, for example, a restructuring of the company's debt and equity. Assuming the restructure is a success, the value of the purchased debt will thereby increase in value and may be realised or traded on at a profit. The restructuring of the company may involve a debt-equity swap where the investor swaps its debt for an equity shareholding in the debtor company. The investor may then use its position as a significant shareholder to influence the restructure. Again, if the plan is a success, the shareholding may be sold on at a profit. The decision as to whether or not to purchase distressed debt will depend upon a sophisticated valuation of the value of the company and the aim is to purchase debt for a value below the likely value of the business.

3.088   The distressed debt market is clearly efficient in that its participators benefit financially and the businesses over which they take control are often turned around. There is clearly a lack of accountability to anyone, outside general legal restrictions, on the activity of distressed debt investors.

3.089   Despite the introduction of a market in distressed debt, co-operation between creditors is still reasonably common. There have been international attempts to encourage global norms for such negotiations, which bear similarity with the 'London Approach'. INSOL International has produced a *Statement of Principles for a Global Approach to Multi-Creditor Workouts II*[68] which has the support of a number of global lenders as well as the Bank of England. It has eight principles which are:

(1)   Where a debtor is found to be in financial difficulties, all relevant creditors should be prepared to co-operate with each other to give sufficient time, referred to as a 'standstill period' to the debtor for proposals to be formulated and assessed.

(2)   During the standstill period, all relevant creditors should agree to a moratorium on actions to enforce their claims against the debtor or (otherwise than by disposal of their debt to a third party) to reduce their exposure to the debtor. Their position relative to other creditors and each other should not be prejudiced during this period.

(3)   During the standstill period, the debtor should not take any action which might adversely affect returns to relevant creditors.

---

67   For an analysis of the development of the distressed debt market where there is little or no place for the collegiate approach of the 'London Approach' see S Paterson 'Bargaining in Financial Restructuring: Market Norms, Legal Rights and Regulatory Standards' (2014) 14 *Journal of Corporate Legal Studies* 333.

68   The second edition dates from 2017 and updates the original version from 2000. It is available on the INSOL International website.

(4)   The interests of relevant creditors are best served by co-ordinating their response to a debtor in financial difficulty. Such co-ordination is facilitated by selecting representatives and by the appointment of professional advisers to advise and assist them.

(5)   During the standstill period, the debtor provides reasonable and timely access to information relating to its assets, liabilities, business and prospects, in order to enable evaluation of its proposals.

(6)   Proposals should reflect applicable law and the relative legal positions of relevant creditors.

(7)   Information obtained for these purposes is kept confidential.

(8)   Any additional funding provided during the standstill period is given priority status as compared to other indebtedness of relevant creditors.

As with any negotiation, each case will progress (or not) according to its own individual cir-   **3.090** cumstances. A collective approach may lead to a successful planned workout or some (or all) creditors may instead opt to trade on their debt. It is clearly important that between themselves, the creditors are transparent in their dealings even though they remain undisclosed publicly. If any of the creditors breaches the agreement, the whole plan is likely to fail. Each creditor has to be accountable to one another for keeping to the agreed plan.

Directors of companies which are subject to such processes will need to ensure they keep a close   **3.091** eye on the companies' solvency and ability to remain a going concern. Taking expert and legal advice will be crucial in making justifiable decisions and to avoid the types of liability discussed in the next chapter.

D. STATUTORY PROCEDURES

As explained in Part A of this chapter, there are a number of different formal procedures which   **3.092** a company in financial distress may enter. These procedures are statutory and are governed either by the Insolvency Act 1986 or the Companies Act 2006. The reason for this divergence of statutory authority is largely historical. Although the Insolvency Act 1986 was designed to include all the procedures available to an insolvent debtor, the Scheme of Arrangement, dating from the nineteenth century, had always been available to enable the restructuring of both solvent and insolvent companies and, after 1986, consequently remained in the Companies Act. When the Restructuring Plan was introduced in 2020, as it was so closely modelled on the Scheme of Arrangement, it was passed as an addition to the Companies Act 2006 rather than the Insolvency Act 1986. It applies in a grey area between solvency and insolvency as the company in question must have encountered, or be likely to encounter, financial difficulties that are affecting, or will or may affect, its ability to carry on business as a going concern.

Prior to looking at the available statutory procedures, it may be helpful to make some general   **3.093** points. The insolvency regime in general recognises that different creditors have different priority rights. A secured creditor usually holds a strong position in any insolvency and has various powers and rights to be paid out ahead of other creditors. Traditionally a secured creditor will have the benefit of a debenture document which contains a mixture of fixed and floating charges.[69]

3.094 A fixed charge (or mortgage) typically fixes on or attaches to a particular asset or class of assets. Any asset subject to a fixed charge cannot be dealt with by the debtor without the consent of the secured creditor (the holder of the fixed charge). A floating charge is said to float or hover above a class of assets until such time that it becomes fixed in nature when it is said to crystallise. Until a floating charge crystallises, the assets subject to it may be dealt with by the company in the normal course of business without the consent for each dealing from the holder of the floating charge.[70]

3.095 A floating charge is usually expressed to be over the company's undertaking which has been interpreted as including all the company's property both present and future, including the right to carry on the business of the company. When a company becomes insolvent, a fixed charge is paid out ahead of a floating charge so is seen as a better security. Although not the strongest of security rights in terms of priority, a floating charge usually gives the secured creditor the power to appoint an administrator who will take control of the charged assets and will attempt, amongst other things, to realise them to pay off secured (and other) creditors. The power to appoint an administrator is available to the holder of a qualifying floating charge which is a charge over the whole or substantially the whole of a company's property, both present and future.[71]

3.096 The insolvency regime gives primacy to secured creditors but unsecured creditors have a number of significant rights in the legislation. By way of example, they will often get to vote on: whether to approve an administrator's proposals; whether to approve a proposal for a company voluntary arrangement, scheme of arrangement or restructuring plan; who is appointed as liquidator; and how an insolvency officeholder is to be remunerated. In the past, creditors have made these decisions by passing resolutions at creditors' meetings. In procedures contained within the Insolvency Act 1986, such meetings are now rare in practice as creditors' decisions are made either by the deemed consent procedure or by a procedure which does not require a physical meeting. Physical meetings are still possible but have to be specifically requested by a requisite majority of creditors.

---

69   For the history of secured borrowing see generally R Gregory and P Walton 'Fixed and Floating Charges – A Revelation' (2001) LMCLQ 123.

70   See in particular the leading cases of *Agnew v Commissioner of Inland Revenue (Re Brumark Investments Ltd)* [2001] 2 AC 710 and *Re Spectrum Plus Ltd (National Westminster Bank plc v Spectrum Plus Ltd)* [2005] 2 AC 680.

71   The power to appoint an administrator replaced the previous power available to the holder of a floating charge over the whole or substantially the whole of a company's undertaking to appoint an administrative receiver under s 29(2) of the Insolvency Act 1986. The Enterprise Act 2002 introduced s 72A of the 1986 Act which states (subject to some very rare exceptions) that the remedy of appointing an administrative receiver is no longer be available to holders of floating charges executed on or after 15 September 2003. The passage of time means that as there are so few floating charges executed prior to 15 September 2003 still in force the possibility of appointing an administrative receiver is rarely encountered in practice. Even where such a floating charge does exist the debenture holder has the option to appoint an administrator instead of an administrative receiver and will frequently choose that option anyway. Administration has therefore effectively replaced administrative receivership. Administrative receivership will not be considered further in this chapter.

All decisions of creditors in corporate Insolvency Act 1986 procedures are now made by **3.097** decision procedures which may or may not include an actual meeting being held. The default position is that no creditors' meeting will be held.

Section 246ZE(1) of the Insolvency Act 1986 provides that a decision of the creditors may be **3.098** considered using any qualifying decision procedure that the officeholder thinks fit, except that it may not be made by a creditors' meeting unless such a meeting is requisitioned by the requisite majority of creditors. A creditors' meeting may only be held if it is requested by a minimum number of creditors. That minimum number is 10 per cent in value of the creditors, 10 per cent in number of the creditors or ten creditors.

The decision of the creditors will be made using either the deemed consent procedure or a qual- **3.099** ifying decision procedure. The deemed consent procedure permits a decision to be made by notifying creditors of the intended decision (e.g., the approval of an administrator's proposal) and if that decision is not effectively objected to, it is deemed to have been made. The deemed consent procedure applies to any decision unless 10 per cent by value of the creditors object before the date stated for the deemed consent procedure to take effect. In the absence of the 10 per cent objection, the deemed consent is effective.

Deemed consent can generally be used for all decisions (except for fixing the basis of the **3.100** officeholder's remuneration). Where deemed consent cannot be used, or where it is effectively objected to or where the officeholder decides not to use it, a decision is instead made by one of five qualifying decision procedures listed in the Rules, namely: (a) correspondence; (b) electronic voting; (c) virtual meeting; (d) physical meeting; or (e) any other decision-making procedure which enables all creditors who are entitled to participate in the making of the decision to participate equally. For most decisions, a majority in value of unsecured creditors in favour of any decision is sufficient for it to be passed.

Decisions of classes of creditors under the Companies Act 2006 procedures are still made by **3.101** calling physical meetings.

As explained in Part A, the various statutory procedures available to a financially distressed **3.102** company may allow the management team to remain in control of the company's operations (debtor-in-possession) or may require the appointment of an independent insolvency practitioner who takes over. The following discussion therefore distinguishes between these two categories.

It has long been a desire of insolvency policy-makers to attempt to create a system which **3.103** encourages corporate rescue. This concept in itself may be divided between attempts to rescue the company itself (company rescue) and attempts to rescue the business even if the company does not survive following the transfer of the business to a buyer (business rescue). It is frequently the result of administration, and perhaps surprisingly, liquidation, that a business is rescued. Company rescue is encountered less frequently but is the main aim of debtor-in-possession procedures.

The following consideration of the various statutory procedures is designed to provide only an **3.104** outline guide and to emphasise any potential strengths or weaknesses on matters of accountability and transparency. It is important for directors of companies in financial distress to understand the options available to such companies and to understand the procedures which must be followed in order for such procedures to be entered and operated within the legal framework. There are many potential pitfalls for company directors when considering procedural and substantive rules which must be followed in each respective procedure.[72] For more detailed consideration of the procedures, readers are directed to more specialist publications.[73]

E. FORMAL DEBTOR-IN-POSSESSION PROCEDURES

1.   Moratorium

3.105   Although the government had been considering the introduction of a form of pre-insolvency moratorium for a number of years,[74] its hand was forced by the COVID-19 pandemic. As part of its reaction to the economic crisis, in a bid to give more emphasis and support to attempts at company rescue, the Corporate Insolvency and Governance Act 2020 ('the 2020 Act') introduced a short-term (initially 20 business days) stay or moratorium on creditor actions. The moratorium is designed to allow a company's management team a breathing space free from creditor harassment to put together a plan to rescue the company. That plan may involve a proposal for a company voluntary arrangement under the Insolvency Act 1986 or a scheme of arrangement or restructuring plan under the Companies Act 2006.

3.106   The 2020 Act introduced the new moratorium by way of a new Part A1 to the Insolvency Act 1986. The moratorium is a standalone procedure and is not linked to any other procedure although it is intended it will often be used as the precursor for another procedure. The moratorium is a debtor-in-possession procedure whereby the directors remain in control of the company, subject to the supervision of a monitor. The intention behind entering the moratorium is to rescue the company as a going concern not merely to lead to a business rescue.

---

72   It is perhaps useful to have a broad understanding of how commonly each of these proceedings are encountered in practice. As statistics have been affected by the COVID-19 pandemic, the following statistics, taken from the Insolvency Service website look only to Insolvency Act 1986 procedures during the pre-pandemic period and provide yearly numbers for 2019: compulsory liquidations: 2,970; creditors' voluntary liquidations: 12,060; administrations: 1,814; company voluntary arrangements: 351. As the statutory moratorium under the Insolvency Act 1986 only came into force in 2020, it is too early to see how frequently it will be used but early experience suggests there may be as few as only a handful annually. Anecdotally, it seems that there are between ten and 20 schemes of arrangement under the Companies Act 2006 each year. The new restructuring plan introduced in 2020 under the Companies Act 2006 may impact on the number of schemes of arrangement. It is anticipated that there may be a similar number of restructuring plans per annum as there are schemes (between ten and 20).

73   See e.g., A Keay, L Doyle and J Curl QC *Insolvency Legislation: Annotations and Commentary 2021* (9th ed., LexisNexis), D Milman and P Bailey *Sealy and Milman Annotated Guide to the Insolvency Legislation 2020* (23rd ed., Sweet & Maxwell) and A Keay and P Walton *Insolvency Law Corporate and Personal* (2020, 5th ed., LexisNexis).

74   *A Review of the Corporate Insolvency Framework: A Consultation on Options for Reform* (May 2016) was followed by a similar consultation in 2018. In its response to its consultations on insolvency law reform (Insolvency and Corporate Governance – Government Response 26th August 2018) the government stated an intention to introduce a short-term moratorium available to virtually all companies which were not yet technically insolvent. The moratorium would permit a breathing space for companies to consider a rescue package or a more beneficial winding up of its assets. The requirement that the procedure be a pre-insolvency procedure to this effect was not retained in the final Moratorium where the company must be unable to pay its debts or likely so to become.

Directors can apply for a moratorium by filing relevant documents in court.[75] The directors are **3.107** required to state that they wish to apply for a moratorium and that the company is, or is likely to become, unable to pay its debts (as defined under s 123 of the Insolvency Act 1986). No court hearing is required. The moratorium is subject to the agreement to act and continued supervision of a monitor. The monitor must be a licensed insolvency practitioner who will be an officer of the court.[76] The monitor has to state that the company is an eligible company and that, in his or her view, it is likely that a moratorium would result in the rescue of the company as a going concern. Guidance on the duties of monitors has been produced by the Insolvency Service.[77]

Interestingly, the idea of the new procedure being a pre-insolvency procedure, that is, only **3.108** available to companies who are not yet insolvent, did not find its way into the legislation. The idea that the company must be able to pay its debts as they fall due during the moratorium has remained. It is possible to view the moratorium as having a limited appeal to companies who are financially distressed. If they can pay their debts for the foreseeable future anyway, there may not be any great demand for the use of the moratorium.

Early experience of the moratorium suggests it may not prove popular. This is partly due to **3.109** the point made above but also due to concerns over the quite detailed provisions which apply to its operation. Insolvency practitioners are generally risk averse and the potential benefits of the moratorium may be outweighed by concerns about the risks run by the moratorium monitor and directors. This was often the reason put forward for the lack of use of the moratorium's immediate predecessor[78] (which was repealed by the 2020 Act) which was a form of moratorium specifically linked to the proposed creation of a company voluntary arrangement for small companies only.[79] It may be that the new moratorium proves to be a victim of its own robust requirements to ensure the monitor is accountable for any wrongs committed whilst the company is being monitored.

If there is an outstanding winding-up petition[80] (or the company is an overseas company[81]) the **3.110** directors will have to apply to court for a moratorium and the court will only make an order, where there is an outstanding winding-up petition, where it is satisfied that the moratorium would achieve a better result for the company's creditors, as a whole, than would be likely if the company were wound up (without first being in a moratorium).[82]

Assuming no court hearing is required, the process of filing relevant documents at court leads **3.111** automatically to a moratorium for an initial period of 20 business days and the nominated insolvency practitioner becomes monitor at that point.[83] As soon as reasonably practicable after

---

75   Insolvency Act 1986, ss A3 and A6.
76   Ibid., s A34.
77   See *Insolvency Act 1986 Part A1: Moratorium A Guide for Monitors* Published 26 June 2020 available at: https://www.gov
      .uk/government/publications/insolvency-act-1986-part-a1-moratorium-guidance-for-monitors.
78   Insolvency Act 1986, Sch A1 (repealed).
79   P Walton, C Umfreville and L Jacobs *Company Voluntary Arrangements: Evaluating Success and Failure* May 2018 R3
      Research Report.
80   Insolvency Act 1986, s A4.
81   Ibid., s A5.
82   Ibid., s A4(5).
83   Ibid., s A7(2).

a moratorium comes into force, the directors must notify the monitor of that fact. Failure to do so without reasonable excuse will result in the directors in default committing an offence.[84]

3.112   The monitor must then notify various parties that the moratorium has come into effect:

(a)   the registrar of companies,

(b)   every creditor of the company of whose claim the monitor is aware,

(c)   in a case where the company is or has been an employer in respect of an occupational pension scheme that is not a money purchase scheme, the Pensions Regulator, and

(d)   in a case where the company is an employer in respect of such a pension scheme that is an eligible scheme within the meaning given by s 126 of the Pensions Act 2004, the Board of the Pension Protection Fund.

3.113   A monitor who fails, without reasonable excuse, to give these notices commits an offence.[85]

3.114   During the moratorium, the company must display prominently the fact that the company is subject to a moratorium and the identity of the monitor in any business premises, on any websites and on every business document. Any failure to do so results in an offence being committed by the company and any officer of the company who without reasonable excuse authorised or permitted the contravention.[86]

3.115   The initial 20-business day period can be extended by the directors for a further period of 20 business days by the filing of further relevant papers in court[87] (or with creditor consent by way of a creditors' qualifying decision by pre-moratorium creditors for a maximum period of up to one year in total[88]). In either case there is no court hearing but in both cases the directors must make a statement that all debts which have fallen due during the moratorium have been paid, and that, in their view, the company is, or is likely to become, unable to pay its pre-moratorium debts. The directors' statement must be accompanied by a statement from the monitor that, in the monitor's view, it is likely that the extension to the moratorium will result in the rescue of the company as a going concern. An extension beyond one year is possible but that does require an application to the court.[89]

3.116   The moratorium is also extended where consideration of a CVA is pending in which case the moratorium lasts until the CVA proposal has been considered (whether it is approved or rejected).[90] In addition, the court may extend a moratorium if a scheme of arrangement or restructuring plan is being considered.[91]

---

84   Ibid., s A8(1) and (4). Under s A17, they must also notify the monitor of any extension or if the moratorium comes to an end.

85   Ibid., s A8(2), (3) and (5).

86   Ibid., s A19.

87   Ibid., s A10. The documents must be filed after the first 15 business days but before the initial period expires.

88   Ibid., s A11.

89   Ibid., s A13.

90   Ibid., s A14

91   Ibid., s A15.

Companies will not be eligible[92] to apply for a moratorium if: **3.117**

- they are already subject to an insolvency procedure;
- a winding-up petition is outstanding (unless the court orders otherwise);
- if, at any time in the period of 12 months ending with the filing date, a moratorium of the company was in force; and
- if, at any time in the period of 12 months ending with the filing date, the company was subject to a CVA or was in administration.

Certain specific types of company are also ineligible for a moratorium[93] (e.g., insurance com-   **3.118**
panies; banks; electronic money institutions; recognised investment exchanges and clearing
houses; securitisation companies; parties to capital market arrangements; public-private partnership project companies; and overseas companies with corresponding functions).

The procedure effectively requires the company to be able to pay debts as they fall due during   **3.119**
the moratorium. The moratorium provides a stay on actions in relation to debts incurred
prior to the moratorium only.[94] The moratorium does not prevent enforcement of creditor
actions in relation to debts incurred during the moratorium but does impose restrictions on the
enforcement or payment of the debts which are pre-moratorium debts for which a company has
a payment holiday during the moratorium.[95]

The stay on enforcement of pre-moratorium debts (that is, debts falling due before the mora-   **3.120**
torium and which fall due during the moratorium by reason of a pre-moratorium obligation)
applies except in so far as they consist of amounts payable in respect of:

(a)   the monitor's remuneration or expenses;
(b)   goods or services supplied during the moratorium;
(c)   rent in respect of a period during the moratorium;
(d)   wages or salary arising under a contract of employment;
(e)   redundancy payments; or
(f)   debts or other liabilities arising under a contract or other instrument involving financial
       services.[96]

The role of the monitor is to monitor the company's affairs for the purpose of forming a view   **3.121**
as to whether it remains likely that the moratorium will result in the rescue of the company as
a going concern.[97] If such a rescue is no longer likely the monitor must bring the moratorium
to an end. Similarly, the monitor must terminate the moratorium if he or she thinks that the
company is unable to pay any of its moratorium debts (or pre-moratorium debts for which
the moratorium does not provide the company a payment holiday).[98] The remuneration of
the monitor, including for any pre-appointment work, is a contractual matter between the
company and the monitor.

---

92   Ibid., Sch ZA1, para 2.
93   Ibid., s A2 and Sch ZA1, paras 3–18.
94   Ibid., s A18.
95   Ibid., ss A28 and A53.
96   Ibid., s A18(3).
97   Ibid., s A35.
98   Ibid., s A38.

3.122   The actions and remuneration of monitors (and the actions of directors) may be challenged by, amongst others, the company's creditors in the court. The court has wide powers to confirm, reverse or modify any act or decision of the monitor and so could itself order the moratorium to come to an end or indeed reverse the monitor's decision to bring the moratorium to an end. It has similarly wide powers in relation to a challenge to directors' actions which permit the court to regulate the management of the company, to require directors to refrain from certain actions or even once again to bring the moratorium to an end.[99]

3.123   A number of offences may be committed by an officer of the company either before or during the moratorium if they have made false representations to obtain the moratorium or have acted outside the limitations of their powers during it.[100]

3.124   During the moratorium, the company cannot generally enter liquidation or administration;[101] no landlord can exercise a right of forfeiture; generally security rights cannot be enforced; and, again, generally no legal process may be instituted or continued against the company.[102] Floating charges will not crystallise during the moratorium[103] and the directors may continue to run the company in the ordinary course of business with any major decisions being subject to the consent of the monitor or the court.[104]

3.125   A moratorium comes to an end if the company enters into a scheme of arrangement or restructuring plan under Parts 26 or 26A of the Companies Act 2006 or enters into a relevant insolvency procedure (e.g., a company voluntary arrangement, administration or liquidation).[105]

3.126   There is little doubt that the moratorium is a transparent procedure. It must be widely publicised so that those dealing with the company are aware of its existence. It contains a number of checks and balances within its processes which require the directors and monitor to take very seriously not only publicity aspects of the process but also the potentially serious consequences of the monitor failing to identify a company which is failing to meet its moratorium liabilities or who fails to recognise circumstances occurring where that the company can no longer be rescued.

2.   Company voluntary arrangement

3.127   The Cork Committee identified in 1982 a need for a simple procedure to be introduced, where the will of the majority of creditors in agreeing to a debt arrangement could be made binding on an unwilling minority.[106] This gave rise to the company voluntary arrangement (CVA). Sections 1–7B of the Insolvency Act 1986 contain the primary legislation governing CVAs. Part 2 of the Insolvency Rules 2016[107] contains most of the relevant secondary legislation.

---

99   Ibid., ss A42–A45.
100   Ibid., ss A46–A48.
101   Ibid., s A20.
102   Ibid., s A21.
103   Ibid., s A52.
104   Ibid, s A22 – A33.
105   Ibid., s A16.
106   Cork Committee Report, Chapter 7.
107   Insolvency (England and Wales) Rules 2016 (SI 2016/1024) ('Insolvency Rules 2016').

The CVA is designed to rescue the company.[108] A CVA must take the form of a scheme of **3.128** arrangement (whereby a company promises full payment to creditors whose debts are currently due but instead of paying immediately the payments are delayed and usually spread over a period of time) or a composition of debts (where only a percentage of the debts owed are promised to be paid) or a combination of the two.[109] It is common for unsecured creditors to accept the promise of payment of, for example, 50 per cent of the debt owed over a three-year period, under the terms of a CVA, as they are likely to receive less than that percentage (if anything) if the company is instead immediately placed into liquidation. Although there is no formal requirement for a company to be insolvent to enter into a CVA, it is unlikely that creditors would accede to a CVA if the company were not insolvent (or likely to become insolvent in the near future).

It is most commonly the directors of a company who propose a CVA but it is possible for an **3.129** administrator[110] to put forward a CVA proposal.

Where the directors propose a CVA they must approach an insolvency practitioner to act as **3.130** 'nominee'. The nominee's role is to opine on the proposal (and will frequently assist with its drafting in the role of adviser as distinct from nominee[111]). If the nominee's opinion is that the proposal has 'a reasonable prospect of being approved and implemented'[112] that opinion will be filed at court and the proposal will be put to the members and creditors of the company. The report to the court is largely a matter of record only. The court does not become judicially involved in the CVA unless a problem arises. Assuming the report is positive, the nominee will summon a meeting of the company's members and seek a decision from the company's creditors as to whether they approve the proposal. The decision of the creditors cannot be by deemed consent procedure. It must be made by a qualifying decision procedure.[113]

As it is usual for the nominee to have had a hand in the drafting of the proposal, it is almost **3.131** certain that the report to the court will be positive. It is important for the nominee to remain objective and maintain a fair balance between the company and its creditors and other stakeholders. The nominee is not the agent of the debtor company. If a nominee fails to live up to the professional standards of a nominee he or she may have to pay all or part of any costs incurred in proceedings relating to the nominee's lack of professionalism.[114]

If the proposal is being put forward by an administrator, the administrator will act as nominee **3.132** and there is no need to file any report at court. The administrator may instead without further formality put the proposal to the members and creditors.[115]

---

108   Although in practice it is often used as a mechanism to provide for an orderly realisation of a company's assets and so can sometimes be seen as a planned form of winding up.
109   Insolvency Act 1986, s 1.
110   It is also possible for a liquidator to propose a CVA but this rarely ever happens.
111   For a full consideration of the varying roles of an insolvency practitioner in the context of a CVA, including planning, obtaining approval and supervising the CVA, see *Paymex Ltd v HMRC* [2012] BPIR 178.
112   Insolvency Rules 2016, r 2.9(2).
113   Insolvency Act 1986, s 3(3).
114   See, e.g., the IVA cases *Re a Debtor (no 222 of 1990) ex parte Bank of Ireland (No 2)* [1993] BCLC 233 and *AB Agri Ltd v Curtis* [2016] BPIR 1297.
115   Insolvency Act 1986, s 3(2).

3.133 One of the major concerns which creditors have about CVAs is their distrust of the assessment of the nominee. Many creditors see the nominee as having a conflict of interest in that if the nominee has helped to negotiate and draft the CVA, and if the nominee is to act as supervisor in the event the CVA is approved, the nominee's assessment of the CVA may not be as independent as the creditors might wish. Whether or not this concern is founded on fact or mere subjective suspicion it is important for the nominee to be able to explain fully why he or she is supportive of the proposal. Some creditors, such as commercial landlords, have in the past asked their trade body to provide its view on CVAs (especially in large retail CVAs).[116] There is a view amongst creditors that some further independent assessment, in addition to the nominee's opinion, is often helpful.

3.134 The remuneration of the nominee and supervisor including for any pre-appointment work is a contractual matter between the company, the creditors and the insolvency practitioner, details of which will be included in the CVA proposal.

3.135 The members' meeting is conducted according to the voting rights in the company's articles. An ordinary resolution is required to approve the CVA.[117]

3.136 As far as the creditors' vote on the proposal is concerned, it is only the unsecured creditors who get to vote on the CVA proposal. If the unsecured creditors agree to it by a majority of at least 75 per cent in value of those creditors voting, the CVA becomes binding upon the company and all the unsecured creditors (even those who voted against the proposal or were unaware of the CVA proposal because, e.g., they did not receive notice of the creditor decision procedure as they were future or contingent creditors at the time).[118] A resolution will normally be invalid if those voting against it include more than half in value of the creditors who are not persons connected with the company.[119]

3.137 Secured creditors are only bound if they agree to be bound[120] and a CVA may not be approved which fails to recognise the priority of preferential creditors.[121] It is common for secured creditors not to take an active interest in a CVA proposal but to reserve its position. If it is not treated with appropriate priority it can, of course, take steps to enforce its security if it has not agreed to its terms. The protection given to preferential creditors is of note. As unsecured creditors, they still get to vote on the CVA and retain the additional protection that if their priority position is not recognised by the terms of the CVA they may complain to the court. As HMRC is now once again the major preferential creditor,[122] it may decide to wield its power as an unsecured creditor for its own benefit without considering the interests of other stakeholders. If HMRC

---

116 See the discussion in P Walton, C Umfreville and L Jacobs *Company Voluntary Arrangements: Evaluating Success and Failure* May 2018 R3 Research Report.
117 Insolvency Rules 2016, r 2.35 and 2.36.
118 Insolvency Act 1986, s 4A states that the proposal is approved if either: (1) both the creditors and members vote in favour of it; or (2) if the proposal is approved only by the creditors (in which case, any member may, within 28 days, apply to the court to object if, e.g., the terms of the proposal are unfairly prejudicial to the interests of the member). Section 4A effectively ensures the creditors' vote takes primacy over any differing view at the members' meeting.
119 Insolvency Rules 2016, r 15.34. For the meaning of 'connected' see Insolvency Act 1986, s 249.
120 Insolvency Act 1986, s 4(3).
121 Ibid., s 4(4).
122 Finance Act 2020, s 98.

wants to be paid its debt reasonably quickly, it may decide to vote down a CVA and rely upon its preferential status in an ensuing liquidation. This is a real concern with the reintroduction of the Crown preference and a concern which existed previously before the Crown's preferential status was abolished by the Enterprise Act 2002.[123]

Creditors (or members) may apply to the court if the CVA's terms are unfairly prejudicial (e.g., **3.138** if unsecured creditors, other than preferential creditors, are treated differentially under the terms of the CVA) or if there was some material irregularity in the procedure leading up to its approval (e.g., if valid votes of creditors are not counted for some reason).[124] It is important that the nominee does not support a CVA which he or she knows is unfairly prejudicial as there may be costs and professional conduct implications.[125]

As an officer of the court, the actions of the nominee or supervisor are subject to the control of **3.139** the court but no private law action such as a negligence action, may be brought by a creditors against the nominee or supervisor.[126] The court is able to exercise control over the insolvency practitioner under the powers provided within the Insolvency Act 1986. No private law actions are possible, as they are against Insolvency Act officeholders such as administrators and liquidators.[127]

Once approved, the CVA is given effect to under the supervision usually of the nominee who **3.140** becomes the 'supervisor' upon the CVA being approved. Its terms are then carried out in much the same way as any other commercial contract. It is common for a CVA to permit the business of the company to continue with the directors remaining in day-to-day management control with a proportion of the company's debts being paid off by monthly instalments (often over a period ranging from three to five years). If all creditors are paid what the CVA has promised, the CVA will complete. If the company does not satisfy the terms of the CVA, for example, if it is unable to keep up with monthly payments, the CVA's terms will often have provisions for how to deal with its termination. A CVA which terminates will often lead to the company entering a subsequent insolvency procedure, most often a liquidation.

The CVA procedure in itself contains no moratorium on actions against the company whilst **3.141** the CVA proposal is prepared and considered. Creditors may therefore frustrate a possible CVA by enforcing their rights prior to the decision-making procedures convened to approve the proposal. In cases where a moratorium would be helpful in allowing time to permit the CVA to be put to the creditors, the company may consider the above statutory moratorium

---

123 See the analysis in A Keay and P Walton, 'The Preferential Debts' Regime in Liquidation Law: In the Public Interest?' (1999) 3 *Company, Financial and Insolvency Law Review* 84.

124 Insolvency Act 1986, s 6. See e.g., *Re Primlaks (UK) Ltd (No 2)* [1990] BCLC 234, *IRC v Wimbledon Football Club Ltd* [2004] 1 BCC 638, *Sea Voyager Maritime Inc v Bielecki* [1999] 1 BCLC 133, *Somji v Cadbury Schweppes plc* [2001] 1 BCLC 498, *Prudential Assurance Co Ltd v PRG Powerhouse Ltd* [2007] EWHC 1002 (Ch), [2007] BCC 500, *Gertner v CFL Finance* [2018] EWCA Civ 1781and *Discovery (Northampton) Ltd v Debenhams Retail Ltd* [2019] EWHC 2441 (Ch), [2020] BCC 9.

125 In *Mourant v Sixty UK Ltd* [2010] BCC 882 the court took a dim view of the terms of the proposal and reported the insolvency practitioners involved in its creation to their professional bodies (see *R (on the application of Hollis) v Association of Chartered Certified Accountants* [2014] BPIR 1317).

126 *King v Anthony* [1998] 2 BCLC 517.

127 See *Irvine v Duff & Phelps Ltd* [2019] EWHC 2780 (Ch) where the position of an IVA supervisor was contrasted with that of a trustee in bankruptcy.

procedure, where the directors will remain in control, or alternatively decide to place the company into administration, where an external insolvency practitioner will be appointed administrator but where again, there is the benefit of a statutory moratorium. The moratorium on creditor enforcement action may permit the administrator, who will have taken over the directors' management role, some respite from creditor harassment whilst he or she attempts to achieve the primary purpose of administration, that is, to rescue the company. From the directors' viewpoint, putting the company into administration so as to ensure a stay on creditor action, has the marked weakness that the administrator controls the company and the process, not the directors. It may also prove to be expensive due to the administrator's fees.[128]

3.142   In order to ensure creditor confidence a CVA must be transparent and convincing. The Insolvency Rules require a long list of matters to be included within the proposal but in addition, and overriding everything, the proposal will need to give a transparently accurate picture of the company's existing state of affairs and its business plan going forward. For example:

-   Are the assets valued independently?
-   Are any third party funds being put into the CVA and, if so, are they reliable?
-   Are suppliers and customers still in place?
-   How are creditors under executory contracts such as leases to be treated both under the CVA and in terms of calculating their voting rights as creditors?

3.143   Importantly, the proposal must be realistic. Too often, directors are overly optimistic about the future and how much the company can pay back. During its term, the assets and income subject to it will need to be held securely. The financial results for creditors must be better than they would receive under alternative insolvency procedures. Certain creditors, for example, HMRC, have standard demands regarding the content of a CVA and how long they will wait for payment. Depending upon the company's own tax compliance record, HMRC may or may not be supportive of a CVA proposal. From the company's point of view, it will want a full discharge from its liabilities.

3.144   CVAs are not as popular as perhaps they ought to be. One of the likely reasons for this is that they are traditionally quite expensive to draft. Each CVA is essentially a bespoke product and therefore potentially out of the reach of many small companies in financial distress. As the CVA itself is not required to be registered at Companies House, there is little opportunity for practitioners to learn from the drafting approaches of others. The insolvency profession's trade body, R3, has recently produced a precedent primarily aimed at small and medium-sized companies whose businesses have been affected by the pandemic.[129] It is hoped that the availability of such a precedent will bring some uniformity and transparency to CVAs and lead to an increased popularity.

---

128   It is interesting to note that the Cork Committee's view was that a CVA proposed by directors would only be likely where for some reason it was not appropriate to appoint an administrator and where the CVA was a simple one and would prove of value to small companies (Cork Committee para.430).

129   https://www.r3.org.uk/technical-library/england-wales/technical-guidance/r3-standard-form-covid-19-cva-proposal/.

3. Scheme of arrangement

An alternative to a CVA, and another possible debtor-in-possession option, is for a company   **3.145**
to enter into a scheme of arrangement under Part 26 of the Companies Act 2006. Although
designed and intended for the re-organisation of solvent companies, such schemes, which have
been around since the nineteenth century, are often used for the re-structuring of insolvent
companies but can be used by a company which is not insolvent. The procedure involves a great
deal of court involvement as well as creditor consent and so is usually only seen in cases where
a company has significant assets. Creditors are split into different classes and each class of
creditor must consent to the scheme.

A scheme can bind all of a company's creditors (or just the classes of creditors who are   **3.146**
included within it). Although potentially an alternative to a CVA, such a scheme is usually
more complex, expensive and time-consuming to draft and agree than a CVA. It can be made
binding upon members of a class of creditors (e.g., secured creditors) even where not all the
class consents to it. This is different to a CVA which cannot be made binding upon any secured
creditor without its consent. A scheme tends to be used only in respect of reasonably large
companies and can involve full-scale company reconstructions. There is no specific provision
for a moratorium[130] on creditor actions during the planning period for a scheme and so it may
be necessary to combine a scheme with first putting the company into administration.[131] This
prevents creditors from acting to frustrate the purposes of the scheme. As a preparatory step for
a scheme, the company is sometimes placed into liquidation or provisional liquidation where
the court is asked to stay all proceedings against the company while the liquidator acts to obtain
the approval of the company, its creditors and the court.[132]

The procedure to enter into a Part 26 scheme is court led and therefore subject to a deal of   **3.147**
judicial scrutiny. It is commenced with an application to the court, usually referred to as the
convening hearing. The company, a creditor, a member, an administrator or a liquidator may
apply to the court. The scheme may affect the respective rights of the company and its creditors
(or a class of creditors) and/or the company and its members (or a class of them). The court
may order that meetings of creditors (or classes of creditors) and/or members (or classes of
members) affected by the proposed scheme be convened. Care is required when 'determining
the correct classes of creditor, for which purpose the relevant criteria are the existing rights of
creditors and their rights as affected by the scheme'.[133] If the rights of creditors are such as to
make it impossible for them to consult together with a view to their common interest, then
the scheme has to be regarded as a number of linked arrangements and separate meetings are
required. However, just because a scheme treats creditors differently does not necessarily mean
that the rights are so dissimilar that persons have to be put in different classes.[134] The court will

---

130   See *Booth v Walkden Spinning and Manufacturing Co Ltd* [1909] 2 KB 368.
131   See *Polly Peck International plc (No 3)* [1996] BCC 486, *Re T & N Ltd (No 2)* [2006] 2 BCLC 374 and *Re Lehman
      Brothers International (Europe)* [2018] EWHC 1980 (Ch), [2019] BCC 115.
132   In such cases, where a petition for winding up has been presented to the court and a scheme is proposed, the court will
      usually order the winding-up proceedings to stand over and stay proceedings against the company pending the consider-
      ation of the scheme (*Bowkett v Fuller's United Electric Works Ltd* [1923] 1 KB 160).
133   Per David Richards J in *Re T & N Ltd* [2005] 2 BCLC 488 at [79]. See also *Practice Statement (Companies: Schemes of
      Arrangement under Part 26 and Part 26A of the Companies Act 2006)* [2020] BCC 691.
134   *Re Hawk Insurance Co Ltd* [2001] EWCA Civ 241, [2002] BCC 300.

look closely at the class compositions suggested by those proposing the scheme and may alter the suggested class composition.[135]

3.148 Each meeting (or class meeting) must approve the scheme by a majority in number and a majority of three-quarters in value of the creditors or members present and voting.[136] After the meetings have approved the scheme there is a second hearing. If the court sanctions the scheme at this hearing, it becomes binding on all the company's creditors or members (as the case may be) who are subject to the scheme. The court will look to ensure that the procedure has been carried out correctly and also that the scheme is fair to all creditors bound by it, including those who voted against it. The meaning of 'fairness' in this context has a very similar meaning to 'fairness' when considering claims that a CVA is 'unfairly prejudicial'. The court will not just 'rubber stamp' the decision of the creditors but will need to be satisfied that an intelligent and honest person could reasonably have approved the scheme.[137]

3.149 In *Re Sunbird Business Services Ltd*[138] the court refused to sanction the scheme due to the inadequacies of the statement explaining the scheme's effect, as required by s 897 of the Companies Act 2006. The statement had failed to state the material interests of the company directors. In addition, the directors had asserted that if the company was wound up, the unsecured creditors would receive a negligible or very low return. However, no specific information was given to the creditors to enable them to evaluate whether that assertion was objectively justified. The directors' views had not been independently verified and so the scheme was not sanctioned by the court. It is important that the scheme and its accompanying documentation are transparent. If they are not, the court will not sanction the scheme.

3.150 In most corporate insolvency situations, a scheme does have some potential advantages over a CVA. A 'company' which can enter into a scheme in this context is any company which is capable of being wound up under the Act.[139] Importantly, this includes any foreign company which, though not registered under the Companies Act 2006, has a 'sufficient connection' with England or Wales.[140] The hurdle of 'sufficient connection' appears to be reasonably easy to get over. For example, in *Re Syncreon Group BV*[141] a Dutch company had made changes to the governing law of its financing arrangements so that they were no longer subject to New York law but instead were subject to the law in England and Wales. This change provided sufficient connection to the jurisdiction of England and Wales to allow the court to consider a scheme.

3.151 Until very recently, although Insolvency Act 1986 procedures such as a CVA were subject to the EU Regulation on Insolvency Proceedings, the scheme was not. It could therefore be

---

135 See *Re Codere Finance 2 (UK) Ltd* [2020] EWHC 2441 (Ch) for an example where the court decided that a single class of creditors was appropriate where the differences between the creditors was not so material as to fracture the class.
136 Companies Act 2006, s 899.
137 See, e.g., *Re NN2 Newco Ltd* [2019] EWHC 1917 (Ch) at [10] and *Re Noble Group Ltd* [2018] EWHC 3092, [2019] BCC 349 (Ch) at [17].
138 [2020] EWHC 2493 (Ch).
139 Companies Act 2006, s 117.
140 *Re Rodenstock GmbH* [2011] EWHC 1104 (Ch), [2012] BCC 459.
141 [2019] EWHC 2412 (Ch).

used by companies which did not have their centres of main interests in the UK.[142] A great many overseas companies have used the Part 26 scheme to restructure in preference to using the restructuring mechanisms available under their respective domestic legal regimes.[143] It is unclear whether this trend will continue following the UK's departure from the European Union. Much will depend upon how straightforward it will be to obtain recognition of the UK court order sanctioning the scheme in foreign jurisdictions but it seems that the principal overseas legal jurisdictions will continue to recognise a scheme. As part of its decision to sanction a scheme, the court will require evidence that the scheme will have a substantial effect in relevant overseas jurisdictions.

A scheme usually enables the directors to remain in managerial control of the company.[144] **3.152** Schemes are sometimes used in situations where a fully consensual, unanimous agreement of creditors has not been possible. In practice, there may be a small number of 'hold out' creditors who try to negotiate particularly favourable terms for themselves. The alternative, the scheme, may therefore be seen as a kind of backup plan to be used if the minority will not agree to the consensual agreement. Unlike a CVA, it may be made binding on minority secured creditors against their will, if a majority in number and 75 per cent in value of the secured creditor class approve it. Also, unlike a CVA, as the terms must be considered fair before a scheme will be sanctioned by the court, its terms are automatically considered judicially. A CVA's terms are only considered by the court if a creditor (or other person with standing) brings an action claiming unfair prejudice or material irregularity.

4.   Restructuring plan

The restructuring plan was introduced by the 2020 Act by the creation of a new Part 26A of the **3.153** Companies Act 2006. It looks very similar to the Part 26 scheme but also displays a discernible influence from the US's Chapter 11 with its distinctive ability to 'cram down' a class of creditors who have voted against the plan (and so allow the plan to be sanctioned by the court despite that class's dissent). Such a cram down is not possible with a scheme.

Similar to schemes, a plan requires an initial convening hearing application to the court which **3.154** is asked to order class meetings of creditors (and members). Assuming the class meetings are ordered and approve the plan, the court is then asked to sanction the plan and it is then given effect by court order.

---

142   It was not listed (in Annex A) as one of the insolvency proceedings covered by the EC Regulation on Insolvency Proceedings 2000 (1346/2000) as recast by the EU Regulation (2015/848) of the European Parliament and of the Council of 20 May 2015 on insolvency proceedings.

143   See, e.g., *Re Syncreon Group BV* [2019] EWHC 2412 (Ch), *Re NN2 Newco Ltd* [2019] EWHC 1917 (Ch), *Re Noble Group Ltd* [2018] EWHC 3092, [2019] BCC 349 (Ch), *Re Far East Capital Ltd SA* [2017] EWHC 2878 (Ch), *Re Global Garden Products Italy SpA* [2016] EWHC 1884 (Ch), *Re Metinvest BV* [2016] EWHC 1868 (Ch), *Re Van Gansewinkel Groep BV* [2015] EWHC 2151 (Ch), [2015] Bus LR 1046, *Re Apcoa Parking Holdings GmbH* [2014] EWHC 3849 (Ch), [2015] 2 BCLC 659, *Re Zodiac Pool Solutions SAS* [2014] BCC 569, *Re Magyar Telecom BV* [2013] EWHC 3800 (Ch), [2015] 1 BCLC 418, *Re Primacom Holding GmbH (No 1)* [2011] EWHC 3746 (Ch) and *(No 2)* [2012] EWHC 164 (Ch) and *Re Rodenstock GmbH* [2011] EWHC 1104 (Ch), [2012] BCC 459.

144   D Milman 'Schemes of Arrangement and Other Restructuring Regimes Under UK Company Law in Context' (2011) 301 *Company Law Newsletter* 1.

3.155   The plan is a debtor-in-possession procedure. It allows a company in financial difficulties to enter into an arrangement or reconstruction. Similarly to Part 26 schemes, Part 26A applies to all companies, including overseas companies which are liable to be wound up in England and Wales.

3.156   A compromise or arrangement under Part 26A is only available where:[145]

(1)   the relevant company has encountered, or is likely to encounter, financial difficulties that are affecting, or will or may affect, its ability to carry on business as a going concern (this appears to be a widely defined provision which would seem to include a great many trading companies); and

(2)(a)

    (i)   that a compromise or arrangement is proposed between the company and its creditors, or any class of them, or

    (ii)   its members, or any class of them, and

(b)   the purpose of the compromise or arrangement is to eliminate, reduce or prevent, or mitigate the effect of, any of the said financial difficulties.

3.157   On the application[146] of the company, any creditor or member of the company, a liquidator or administrator, the court may order that a meeting of the creditors or class of creditors, or the members, or a class of members, be summoned in such manner as the court directs. The rules for deciding upon the class composition are the same as for schemes. The overriding principle is that a class should consist of those whose rights are not so dissimilar as to make it impossible for them to consult together with a view to their common interest. The question whether or not consultation is possible depends on whether there is more that unites the relevant creditors than divides them.[147]

3.158   Section 901C of the Companies Act 2006 makes express provision for who must be permitted to participate in a class meeting. Included is every creditor or member of the company whose rights are affected by the compromise or arrangement. Not included is any person who the court is satisfied does not have a genuine economic interest in the company.

3.159   The court may sanction the compromise or arrangement if a number representing 75 per cent or more in value of the creditors or class of creditors, or members or class of members (as the case may be) agree to terms of the plan. This differs from a scheme which requires a majority in number as well as 75 per cent or more in value of each class to approve the scheme.

3.160   The other main characteristic which distinguishes the plan from a scheme is the ability of the court to cram down a dissenting class who does not approve the plan. Unlike a scheme which must be approved by each class meeting in order to be capable of being sanctioned by the court, s 901G includes a provision for a plan to cram down a dissenting class. In circumstances where

---

145   Companies Act 2006, s 901A.
146   Ibid., s 901C.
147   *Re Virgin Atlantic Airways Ltd* [2020] EWHC 2191 (Ch) and [2020] EWHC 2376 (Ch), [2020] BCC 997 per Trower J at [40–48]. See also the same approach in *Re PizzaExpress Financing 2 plc* [2020] EWHC 2873 (Ch).

one or more classes dissent, if Conditions A and B below are met, the fact that the dissenting class has not agreed to the plan will not prevent the court from granting sanction.[148]

3.161 Condition A is the court is satisfied that, if sanctioned, none of the dissenting class would be any worse off than they would be in the event of the 'relevant alternative' (which will usually be a liquidation or administration).

3.162 Condition B is that the compromise or arrangement has been agreed by 75 per cent in value of at least one class of creditors or members, as the case may be, who would receive a payment, or have a genuine economic interest in the company, in the event of the 'relevant alternative'.

3.163 As long as Conditions A and B are satisfied, one class of creditor can impose, via a court order, the plan on all classes of creditor, even dissenting creditor classes.

3.164 If the proposal is put forward as a plan, the court will be able to sanction the plan as the class that voted against it would be no worse off than they would be in the next most likely outcome (which is usually likely to be liquidation). The court therefore has an absolute discretion to sanction the plan but may still refuse to sanction if it is just and equitable to do so.

3.165 Plans and schemes have much in common. They must both be registered at Companies House to be effective.[149] They are subject to many similar rules and share a Practice Statement.[150] The big differences are that plans: are only available if a company is in, or is likely to encounter, financial difficulties; do not require a majority in number to be approved; do not require that every class of creditor or member approve them; and have the capacity to cram down a dissenting class. Both are subject to significant scrutiny by the court.

F. FORMAL PROCEDURES UNDER THE CONTROL OF AN INSOLVENCY PRACTITIONER

1. Administration

3.166 The historical development of administration is a story of a bit player in the world of corporate rescue who has taken centre stage. When administration was first introduced following the recommendations of the Cork Committee it was seen as filling a potential gap. It had been recognised by Cork that a company's business was often saved by the appointment of a receiver who would often be able to sell on the business as a going concern and thereby realising the company's assets in an efficient way which also saved jobs and economic activity.

---

148   For the first judicial consideration of the power to cram down a class of creditors see Trower J's judgment in *Re Deepocean 1 UK Ltd* [2021] EWHC 138 (Ch).

149   Companies Act 2006, ss 899 and 901F.

150   *Practice Statement (Companies: Schemes of Arrangement under Part 26 and Part 26A of the Companies Act 2006)* [2020] BCC 691.

3.167   Although the appointment of an administrative receiver[151] was for many years the remedy of choice for secured creditors with a floating charge over a company's undertaking, this remedy was effectively abolished by the Enterprise Act 2002 for holders of floating charges created on or after 15 September 2003.[152] For holders of floating charges created on or after that date, their power to enforce[153] their floating charge is now limited to the out-of-court appointment of an administrator (rather than an administrative receiver). An administrator owes duties to all creditors. An administrative receiver owes a primary duty to the appointing floating charge holder. This was one of the main reasons behind the policy to replace administrative receivership with administration. Prior to the Enterprise Act 2002, a court order was always required in order to put a company into administration. This power remains and it is also possible for the directors or members of a company to place it into administration.[154]

3.168   One of the great strengths of administration is that an external insolvency practitioner is appointed to take over the company's operations from its directors.[155] The experienced views and actions of such a person are seen as bringing a fresh hope for either the survival of the company or at least the survival of its business. As part of this, the administrator may decide to dismiss or appoint a director.[156]

(a) Overview of the process[157]

3.169   Administration is a temporary procedure designed to give the company some time free from creditor harassment during which the administrator may be able to rescue the company or business or at least improve matters for creditors relative to their likely position in an immediate winding up. In reality, a great many administrations do not involve any period of trading under the administrator, rather a sale of the business is conducted often on day one of the administration (a practice referred to as pre-packaged administration, where the deal for the sale is agreed before the administrator is appointed and on appointment the administrator executes the agreement).

3.170   In outline, an administration involves the following stages:

(1)   An administration commences when an administrator is appointed. The appointment may be made out-of-court by the holder of a qualifying floating charge or by the company or by the directors. In addition, the appointment may be made by the court making an administration order.

---

151   As defined in Insolvency Act 1986, s 29.

152   Insolvency Service statistics show that administrative receivership has virtually disappeared with only one such appointment made in 2018 and a further one only in 2019.

153   The power to appoint an administrator is seen as an exercise of the floating charge holder's power of enforcement (*Arlington Infrastructure Ltd (in administration) v Woolrych* [2020] EWHC 3123 (Ch)).

154   For a consideration of this development see, e.g., A. Keay and P. Walton *Insolvency Law Corporate and Personal* (2020, 5th ed., LexisNexis) Chapters 6 and 7.

155   Insolvency Act 1986, Sch B1, para 64 – a company (or any of its officers) in administration may not exercise any management power without the consent of the administrator.

156   Ibid., Sch B1, para 61.

157   The procedural rules applying to administration may be found principally in Sch B1 of the Insolvency Act 1986 and Part 3 of the Insolvency Rules 2016.

(2) As soon as the administrator is appointed, a wide-ranging moratorium comes into effect which prevents creditors taking any form of enforcement action against the company whether by court action, repossession of goods or enforcement of security.

(3) The appointment of the licensed insolvency practitioner administrator is publicised and the fact of the administration must appear on all company correspondence and websites. The administrator takes over the management of the company from the directors.

(4) The administrator will require the directors (or others) to provide a statement of affairs of the company.

(5) The administrator must prepare a proposal designed to achieve one or more of the statutory purposes of administration.

(6) Depending upon the circumstances, the creditors may be asked to vote on the proposal. If approved, the administrator will put it into effect. If not agreed, the administrator may attempt to put forward further proposals or may take steps to terminate the administration.

(7) If the proposal successfully leads to the rescue of the company, the administrator will vacate office allowing the directors back in (this is very rare in practice).

(8) If the business is successfully sold on to a buyer (which is commonly the case) the administrator may distribute the proceeds to creditors according to the statutory order then take steps to end the administration (usually by conversion to a liquidation or by going straight to dissolution).

(9) Unless extended the administration will end automatically after 12 months.

An administrator cannot be appointed if the company is already in administration or liquidation. **3.171**

Some of these points are further explained below in this chapter largely for background purposes. The main corporate governance issues, such as those dealing with appointment, powers and duties, remuneration and liabilities of administrators are looked at in detail in Chapters 7 and 8. **3.172**

(b) Administration order

The following may apply to the court for an administration order:[158] **3.173**

(a) The company;
(b) The directors of the company;
(c) One or more creditors whether they are owed debts which are current, future or contingent;
(d) Court officials where the company has failed to pay a fine;
(e) A combination of the above;
(f) Any liquidator of the company; or
(g) The supervisor of a CVA.

The court has a discretion whether or not to make the order but may only do so if satisfied that: **3.174**

(a) the company is or likely to become unable to pay its debts within the meaning of s 123 of the Insolvency Act 1986 on either the cash flow or balance sheet basis (there is no

---

158 Insolvency Act 1986, Sch B1, paras 12 and 13.

need for the court to be satisfied of this if the application is made by a qualifying floating charge holder with the power to appoint out-of-court); and

(b)   the administration order is reasonably likely to achieve one of the three statutory purposes of administration.

3.175   The appointment takes effect either when the order is made or at a time specified in the order.

(c) Out-of-court by the holder of a qualifying floating charge

3.176   The holder of a qualifying floating charge must file at court a notice of the appointment which includes a statutory declaration confirming that the floating charge has become enforceable. The notice of appointment must identify the administrator who must consent to act and confirm his or her belief that one or more of the statutory objectives is reasonably likely to be achieved. The appointment is effective once all the requisite documentation has been filed at court.[159] An appointment cannot be made by the holder of a qualifying floating charge unless it has given two business days' notice to the holder of any prior floating charge.

3.177   No out-of-court appointment may be made by the holder of a qualifying floating charge where:

(a)   a provisional liquidator is in office; or

(b)   an administrative receiver has been appointed.

(d) Out-of-court appointment by the company or its directors

3.178   The company may resolve in general meeting to appoint an administrator or the board may pass a board resolution to similar effect.[160] Prior to the appointment taking effect, the company or directors must serve a notice of intention to appoint on any holder of a qualifying floating charge at least five business days prior to the appointment. This provides the floating charge holder with the opportunity either to agree with the proposed appointment or to appoint its own administrator. In practice, holders of qualifying floating charges are often content for the directors to appoint the administrators subject to their agreement as to who is to be the administrator. A copy of the notice of intention to appoint must be filed at court along with, amongst other things, a statement that the company is or is likely to become unable to pay its debts and is not in liquidation. Whether or not there is a holder of a qualifying floating charge, the person making the appointment must file a notice of appointment with the court which is accompanied by a statement from the administrator that he or she agrees to act as such and that in his or her opinion the administration is reasonably likely to achieve one or more of the statutory objectives. The appointment takes effect when all the requisite documents are filed at court.[161]

---

159   Ibid., Sch B1, para 14.

160   Ibid., Sch B1, para 22 et seq.

161   The procedure which must be followed by the directors has been the subject of a good deal of case law which contemplates whether or not a defect in following these procedural rules may be seen as merely a procedural defect which does not affect the validity of the appointment or is fundamental to the validity of the appointment. For an understanding of these issues, reference may usefully be made to the following cases: *Re Skeggs Beef Ltd* [2019] EWHC 2607 (Ch); *Re SJ Henderson & Co Ltd and Triumph Furniture Ltd* [2019] EWHC 2742 (Ch); *Re Symm & Co Ltd* [2020] EWHC 317 (Ch); *Strategic Advantage SPC v Rutter* [2020] EWHC 3171 (Ch) and *Re NMUL Realisations Ltd* [2021] EWHC 94 (Ch).

No out-of-court appointment may be made by the company or its directors in certain **3.179** circumstances:

(1)   where the company has been in administration in the previous 12 months where the appointment was made by the company or its directors;
(2)   a petition for the winding up of the company has been presented to the court;
(3)   an application for an administration order has been made to the court; or
(4)   an administrative receiver is in office.

Where any of these restrictions prevents an out-of-court appointment, the person wishing to **3.180** make the appointment may have to apply to the court for an administration order.

One interesting aspect of an appointment by the directors (or company) is that an interim mor- **3.181** atorium[162] is effective from the time when a copy of the notice of intention to appoint is filed with the court.[163] The interim moratorium continues until the appointment is made or ten business days have passed without an appointment being made. If there is no holder of a qualifying floating charge to whom notice of intention to appoint must be given, the company or directors may proceed to an immediate appointment and so render the interim moratorium irrelevant. The power to file a notice of intention to appoint cannot be used tactically to produce a temporary ten-day moratorium (or a succession of such moratoria) if no settled intention to appoint an administrator exists. To use the power in this way would be seen as an abuse of power.[164]

(e)   Purpose of administration

An administrator must act with one or more of three statutory objectives in mind. The objec- **3.182** tives are listed in para 3 of Sch B1 of the Insolvency Act 1986 and are listed in order of primacy. The first objective is to consider rescuing the company as a going concern. If the administrator thinks that objective is not reasonably practicable (or thinks that a better result for the company's creditors as whole would be achieved by pursuing the second objective) he or she may move to the second objective, that of achieving a better result for the company's creditors as a whole than would be likely if the company were wound up (without first being placed into administration). If the administrator thinks that the second objective is not reasonably practicable he or she may pursue the third objective, that of realising property in order to make a distribution to one or more secured or preferential creditors (as long as he or she does not unnecessarily harm the interests of the creditors of the company as a whole).

---

162   To similar effect an interim moratorium under Insolvency Act 1986, Sch B1, para 44 comes into effect in the case of an application to the court for an administration order as soon as the application is made and continues until the order is made or until the application is dismissed. If the administration is commenced by an appointment by a floating charge holder under Insolvency Act 1986, Sch B1, para 14, the interim moratorium is effective from the date a copy of the notice of intention to appoint is filed at the court. It continues until either the appointment is made or the period of five business days since the filing expires without an appointment being made. This is frequently a superfluous provision as the appointment by a floating charge holder under para 14 is effective when a notice of appointment is filed at court. The substantive moratorium comes into effect at this point. There is usually no need under a para 14 appointment to file a notice of intention to appoint with the court. A notice of intention to appoint will only be required to be served where there is a holder of a prior ranking floating charge.
163   Insolvency Act 1986, Sch B1, para 27.
164   *JCAM Commercial Real Estate Property XV Ltd v Davis Haulage Ltd* [2017] EWCA Civ 267.

3.183 In practice, the second objective is the one most commonly pursued by administrators. It focuses on achieving a better return to unsecured creditors as well as repaying secured creditors. The final result of the second objective, usually a sale as a going concern, looks very much like the optimum conclusion of an old school administrative receivership.

3.184 The first objective involves rescuing the company as a going concern with the retention of all or a material part of the business of the company together with a restoration to solvency with all the creditors being paid in full. Unlike an administrative receiver who owes a primary duty to the appointing secured creditor, an administrator must have regard to the interests of all of the company's creditors and can only limit his or her ambition to seeking to realise assets to repay a secured creditor (the third objective) if he or she thinks that it is not reasonably practicable to achieve anything else (and must not, even in that case, unnecessarily harm the interests of the creditors as a whole).

3.185 Much is left subjectively to what the administrator 'thinks' is the best way forward. Only if an administrator's decision to pursue one objective as opposed to another is in bad faith or perverse, will it be open to attack by creditors.[165] It is entirely possible and reasonable for an administrator to change his or her mind about which objective to pursue during the administration due to changing circumstances or a changed understanding of the company's circumstances.[166]

(f) Effect of opening administration proceedings

3.186 Due to the nature of administration being a collective procedure whereby the administrator will usually take control of all the company's assets and act in the interests of all the company's creditors, it is usually incompatible for an administration to co-exist with other insolvency procedures. If the court makes an administration order, any outstanding winding-up petition is dismissed.[167] If a company goes into administration as a result of an appointment by a qualifying floating charge holder, any outstanding winding-up petition is suspended.

3.187 When an administration order takes effect, any administrative receiver must vacate office, and any receiver of part of the company's property must vacate office if required to by the administrator. An administrator must be careful not to decide to remove a fixed charge receiver unless there is a good reason to do so. If the value of the charged assets in the receivership is likely to leave a shortfall owing to the appointing charge holder and the property is not needed for the administration, the removal is unlikely to be justified.[168] Although an administrator must carry out the administration taking into account and balancing the rights of all creditors, both secured and unsecured, an administration should not be conducted for the benefit of the unsecured creditors at the expense of a secured creditor. The receiver's rights to remuneration and any entitlement to an indemnity are protected even if removed by the administrator.

---

165 *Davey v Money* [2018] EWHC 766 (Ch).
166 *Moulds Fencing (Torksey) Ltd v Butler* [2020] EWHC 2933 (Ch).
167 Insolvency Act 1986, Sch B1, para 40.
168 Ibid., Sch B1, para 41. In *Promontoria (Chestnut) Ltd v Craig* [2017] EWHC 2405 (Ch), [2018] BCC 551, the court ordered the re-appointment of receivers where it described the administrators' decision to remove the receivers as irrational.

The administrator is an agent[169] of the company and must on appointment take custody or **3.188** control over all the property to which he or she thinks the company is entitled.[170] This will usually include assets subject to a security such as assets subject to fixed and floating charges but will not include book debts which have been effectively assigned to a receivables financier as such book debts will not belong to the company. An administrator may dispose of items subject to a floating charge with the security transferring to the acquired proceeds or replacement items.[171] Goods subject to a fixed charge or hire purchase or retention of title contracts may be disposed of with the consent of the chargee or owner or by an application to the court under paras 71 or 72 of Sch B1 of the Insolvency Act 1986. This power is useful where the administrator is trying to realise the assets in question as part of a sale of the business as a going concern.[172] The court will only make an order if it thinks that the disposal is likely to promote the purpose of the administration. As a condition of making such an order the net proceeds of the sale of the secured asset and any extra amount required, so as to produce a total amount equal to the asset's market value as determined by the court, must be paid to the owner or secured creditor.

(g) Moratorium

While a company is in administration a moratorium[173] prevents certain actions against the **3.189** company:

(a)   no resolution may be passed for the winding up of the company;

(b)   no winding-up order may be made against the company (other than on public interest grounds);

(c)   no step may be taken to enforce security[174] over the company's property except with the consent of the administrator or the permission of the court;

(d)   no step may be taken to repossess goods in the company's possession under a hire-purchase agreement (which term includes retention of title contracts) except with the consent of the administrator or the permission of the court;

(e)   a landlord may not exercise a right of forfeiture by peaceable re-entry in relation to premises let to the company except with the consent of the administrator or the permission of the court;

(f)   no legal process (including any legal proceedings or execution of any judgment) may be instituted or continued against the company or property of the company except with the consent of the administrator or the permission of the court; and

(g)   no administrative receiver may be appointed.

According to Nicholls LJ in the leading case *Re Atlantic Computer Systems plc*[175] the purpose of **3.190** the moratorium is to 'give the administrator time to formulate proposals and lay them before

---

169   Ibid., Sch B1, para 69.

170   Ibid., Sch B1, para 67.

171   Ibid., Sch B1, para 70.

172   For examples of these applications see: *O'Connell v Rollings* [2014] EWCA Civ 639 and *Re Sky Building Ltd* [2020] EWHC 3139 (Ch).

173   Insolvency Act 1986, Sch B1, paras 42 and 43.

174   The term 'security' is defined in s 248 of the Insolvency Act 1986 as meaning 'any mortgage, charge, lien or other security' (for which see generally *Bristol Airport plc v Powdrill* [1990] Ch 744).

175   [1992] Ch 505.

the creditors, and then implement any proposals approved by the creditors'.[176] The moratorium is procedural in nature in that, although the power to enforce rights is suspended, those rights are not extinguished.

3.191   Whenever a creditor wishes to enforce any of its rights against a company in administration, it may do so with the consent of the administrator or permission of the court. If an administrator has no use for an asset he or she may, for example, permit a retention of title supplier to repossess it. If the administrator is unwilling to allow a creditor to enforce its rights during the administration, the creditor must ask for permission of the court. When considering such an application the court will attempt to carry out a balancing exercise in deciding whether or not to permit such action. Nicholls LJ in the *Atlantic Computers* case set out a number of principles relating to applications by creditors for permission to enforce their rights. The principles or guidelines have been followed in numerous cases subsequently. The principles are as follows:

(1)   it is in every case for the person who seeks permission to make out a case to be given leave;

(2)   the moratorium is intended to assist the company, under the management of the administrator, to achieve the purpose of the administration. If granting permission to a lessor of land or the hirer of goods (a lessor) to exercise proprietary rights and repossess land or goods is unlikely to impede the achievement of that purpose, permission should normally be given;

(3)   in other cases when a lessor seeks possession the court has to carry out a balancing exercise, balancing the legitimate interests of the lessor and the legitimate interests of the other creditors of the company;

(4)   in carrying out the balancing exercise great importance is normally to be given to the proprietary interests of the lessor. The underlying principle is that an administration for the benefit of unsecured creditors should not be conducted at the expense of those who have proprietary rights which they are seeking to exercise;

(5)   it will normally be a sufficient ground for the grant of permission if significant loss would be caused to the lessor by a refusal. If substantially greater loss would be caused to others by the grant of permission, or loss which is out of all proportion to the benefit which permission would confer on the lessor, that may outweigh the loss to the lessor caused by a refusal;

(6)   in assessing these respective losses the court will have regard to matters such as: the financial position of the company, its ability to pay any rental arrears and continuing rentals, the administrator's proposals, the period for which the administration has already been in force and is expected to remain in force, the effect on the administration if permission were given, the effect on the applicant if leave were refused, the end result sought to be achieved by the administration, the prospects of that result being achieved, the history of the administration so far and the conduct of the parties;

(7)   in considering these matters it will often be necessary to assess how probable the suggested consequences are;

(8)   this list is not exhaustive;

(9)   the above considerations may be relevant not only to the decision whether permission should be given but also to a decision to impose terms if permission is granted;

---

176   Ibid., 542.

(10) the above considerations will also apply to a decision on whether to impose terms as a condition for refusing permission.

Despite the restrictions on creditors enforcing their rights against a company in administration, there are therefore a number of checks and balances in place to protect their interests. Although, for example, owners of hire purchase goods can be prevented from repossessing them during the administration, they may be allowed to repossess if it is fair so to do. Similarly, any application to the court to sell such items will only be successful if the creditor's interests are fully protected. **3.192**

(h) Effect on employees

The appointment of an administrator does not automatically terminate any contracts of employment. Employees retain their contractual and statutory rights against the company. **3.193**

Of course, any contractual rights against the company may prove to be of limited or no value in the event that the company is unable to pay any of its unsecured creditors (which includes its employees). There are three main ways in which an employee of a company in administration is protected. **3.194**

Although an administrator may decide to dismiss employees (as is frequently the case), if an employee is kept on for 14 days after the administrator's appointment, the employee's contract is deemed to be adopted by the administrator. Under para 99 of Sch B1 of the Insolvency Act 1986, any 'wages or salary' due to the employee by the company after the contract of employment is adopted has what is usually called 'super priority' in that the wages or salary owed must be paid out ahead even of the administrator's own fees and expenses. The liability is charged on any property held by the administrator. For these purposes, 'wages or salary' includes holiday pay, sickness pay and contributions to occupational pension schemes. **3.195**

In addition, an employee who is owed money relating to services rendered prior to the appointment of the administrator is a preferential creditor and so will be paid some of the money ahead of any floating charge holder and any unsecured creditors. These rights are limited to the four months prior to the appointment and importantly are also limited to a maximum payment of £800 in total.[177] **3.196**

The third main protection is under general employment legislation such as the Employment Rights Act 1996 whereby an employee has a right not to be unfairly dismissed, a right to be paid compensation if made redundant and a right to be paid arrears of wages. These rights are subject to a number of limitations but where the company is unable to pay these amounts the Government operated Redundancy Payments Service ensures the employees are paid what is owed. **3.197**

If, as is commonly the case, the company's business is transferred to a buyer, the effect of the Transfer of Undertakings (Protection of Employment) Regulations 2006[178] is broadly to **3.198**

---

177 Insolvency Act 1986, Sch 6 and Sch B1, para 65.
178 SI 2006/246.

transfer the employees' contracts of employment on existing terms to the buyer. Any rights the employee had against the former employer are therefore enforceable against the new employer.

(i) Formulation and submission of proposals

3.199 The administrator is under a general duty to make a statement setting out proposals for achieving the purpose of administration.[179] The statement must include amongst other things:

(a) details of the administrator's appointment;

(b) if a statement of affairs has been submitted, a copy or summary of it, (and an explanation of why there was no statement of affairs if one was not provided);

(c) a full list of the company's creditors;

(d) a statement of how it is proposed that the purpose of the administration will be achieved, and how it is proposed that the administration will end, including, where it is proposed that the administration will end by the company moving to a creditors' voluntary winding up details of the proposed liquidator (who will usually be the administrator);

(e) a statement of the method by which the administrator has decided to seek a decision from creditors as to whether they approve the proposals;

(f) the manner in which the affairs and business of the company have, since the administrator's appointment, been managed and financed, and will, if the administrator's proposals are approved, continue to be managed and financed.[180]

3.200 Where applicable, the proposals must explain why the administrator thinks that the objectives of rescue or a better result than an immediate liquidation cannot be achieved. The proposal may include a proposal for a company voluntary arrangement (CVA) under the Act or a proposal for a scheme or plan under the Companies Act 2006.

3.201 The proposal must include a statement of the basis on which it is proposed that the administrator's remuneration should be fixed by a decision of the creditors (or creditors' committee if there is one).

3.202 The administrator must send a copy of the proposals to the Registrar of Companies, every creditor of the company of whose claim and address he or she is aware and every member of the company of whose address he or she is aware. He or she must send out the statement of proposals as soon as reasonably practicable, and in any event within eight weeks of the date the company entered administration.

(j) Approval of the proposals

3.203 The administrator must generally seek a decision from the creditors as to whether or not they approve the administrator's proposals. The initial decision date for that decision must be within ten weeks of the date the company entered administration, subject to extension as for sending out proposals.[181]

---

179 Insolvency Act 1986, Sch B1, para 49.
180 For full details of the proposal see Insolvency Rules 2016, r 3.35.
181 Insolvency Act 1986, Sch B1, para 51.

(k) Publicity

During the administration of a company, all its business documents which will include its   **3.204**
orders and invoices (whether hard copy or electronic) and any websites must state the name of
the administrator and that he or she is managing the company's affairs.[182]

(l) Pre-packs

A 'pre-packaged' sale (or 'pre-pack' administration) process has been judicially described in the   **3.205**
following terms:

> Pre-packs are increasingly common and highly controversial. The term refers to a sale of all or part of
> the business and assets of a company … negotiated 'in principle' while it is not subject to any insol-
> vency procedure, but on the footing that the sale will be concluded immediately after the company has
> entered into such a procedure, and on the authority of the insolvency practitioner appointed.[183]

A pre-pack therefore commonly involves a financially distressed company entering into an   **3.206**
agreement along with a prospective administrator to sell the business of a company immediately after the administrator is appointed. The sale is usually on day one of the administration
and will not therefore allow for the administrator to prepare proposals or have those proposals
considered and voted upon by the company's creditors. The deal is negotiated in secret and the
first the creditors hear of it is after the company has entered administration and the business
has already been sold.

The advantages of pre-packs are that they provide certainty for suppliers, customers and   **3.207**
employees: they preserve goodwill and alleviate the need to fund continuing trading during an
administration. However, there are also concerns about pre-packs. Where a pre-pack is agreed,
the administrator will not have been able to expose fully the business to the market in the course
of the sale process. A pre-pack also limits consultation with creditors and raises concerns about
transparency, particularly if the business is being sold to persons previously involved in the
ownership or management of the company.

In light of these concerns, the Joint Insolvency Committee in consultation with the Insolvency   **3.208**
Service and professional and trade bodies, issued Statement of Insolvency Practice 16 (SIP
16)[184] which sought to increase transparency in the pre-pack process by setting out various
matters to be borne in mind by insolvency practitioners. In particular, SIP 16:

(a)   emphasises that administrators should be mindful of the interests of unsecured cred-
       itors and clear about the nature and extent of their relationship with directors in the
       pre-appointment period;
(b)   emphasises that, when considering the manner of disposal of the business or assets,
       administrators should bear in mind the requirements of para 3 of Sch B1 of the
       Insolvency Act 1986 which provides, amongst other things, that the administrator must
       perform his or her functions in the interests of the company's creditors as a whole and,
       where the purpose of administration is to make a distribution to one or more secured or

---

182   Ibid, Sch B1, para 45.
183   *Re Kayley Vending Ltd* [2009] EWHC 904 (Ch), [2009] BCC 578 at [2] per HHJ Cooke.
184   Available at: https://insolvency-practitioners.org.uk/uploads/documents/f30389ce35ed923c06b2879fecdb616a.pdf.

preferential creditors, the administrator is under a duty to avoid unnecessarily harming the interests of creditors as a whole;

(c)   highlights the importance of giving unsecured creditors a detailed explanation and justification of why a pre-packaged sale was undertaken, so that they can be satisfied that the administrator has acted with due regard for their interests;

(d)   provides a detailed list of information which should be disclosed to creditors in all cases where there is a pre-packaged sale. If there are exceptional circumstances which justify not providing such information, the administrator should provide the reasons why it has not been provided.

3.209   SIP 16 is designed to enable unsecured creditors to understand the pre-packaged sale process and to evaluate (and potentially challenge) its use by the administrator.

3.210   In response to pressure from creditor groups and the media, the Insolvency Service commissioned an independent report into pre-packs which reported in 2014. The Graham Review[185] made a number of recommendations which were brought into force voluntarily by the insolvency practitioner profession. A re-drafted SIP 16 contains an appendix detailing marketing essentials which need to be considered in connected party pre-packs in order to ensure that a proper price is paid for the business when sold to, for example, the existing management team, informed by an independent valuation. Principles of marketing are now included. In addition, the 'Pre-Pack Pool' was set up.[186] Purchasers of a business via a pre-pack were able to ask an independent expert to assess their business plan prior to going ahead with the purchase. It was thought that if this voluntary process became widespread, there would be greater confidence in the way pre-packs operate generally.

3.211   Despite these measures, pre-packs remain a controversial practice and the government has consulted[187] on whether to exercise its statutory power to create regulations with provisions relating to sales to connected persons by an administrator. The resulting Administration (Restrictions on Disposal etc. to Connected Persons) Regulations 2021[188] now make it compulsory for any connected party sale within the first eight weeks of the administration either to be agreed to by the company's creditors or to have been the subject of an independent assessment by an evaluator.

3.212   The continued notoriety of connected party pre-packs is fuelled by suspicions that both the administrators and directors are acting in each other's best interests and not the creditors in general. Examples of connected party pre-packs where the court has identified conflicts of interest support these suspicions. The administrators in these cases are not always seen as entirely independent of the directors, especially when appointed by those directors to complete a sale to those directors. Although SIP 16 has gone some way to increase the transparency of pre-packs, there remains concerns that administrators and management teams are not always

---

185   Available at: https://www.gov.uk/government/publications/graham-review-into-pre-pack-administration.

186   This idea appears to have been adopted from a suggestion put forward by M Wellard and P Walton 'A Comparative Analysis of Anglo-Australian Pre-packs: Can the Means Be Made to Justify the Ends?' (2012) 21 *International Insolvency Review* 143.

187   Available   at: https://www.gov.uk/government/publications/pre-pack-sales-in-administration/pre-pack-sales-in-administration-report.

188   SI 2021/427.

transparent in their dealings or indeed accountable for their actions.[189] Governance issues around pre-packs are considered further in Chapter 8.

(m) Closure of administration[190]

It is possible that the successful completion of an administrator's proposals may lead to the   **3.213** administration coming to an end and the management of the company is then returned to the directors. This level of success is rare in practice. The most commonly encountered successful result of an administration is where the business is sold on to a buyer and, once the proceeds of sale are distributed amongst the creditors, the company itself is left as an empty shell which may need to be wound up or dissolved.

If an administrator appointed by an order of the court thinks that the purpose of the admin-   **3.214** istration has been sufficiently achieved he or she shall make an application to the court for an order to the effect that the appointment is to come to an end from a specified time. If the administrator has been appointed out-of-court, and he or she thinks the purpose of the administration has been sufficiently achieved, he or she files a notice with the court and with the Registrar of Companies which brings the administration to an end.

The administration may be converted into a creditors' voluntary liquidation where the admin-   **3.215** istrator forms the view that there will be a distribution to unsecured creditors. If the administrator forms the view that there is no property for distribution to the unsecured creditors the administrator must take steps to dissolve the company.

2. Liquidation

(a) Overview of liquidation

Liquidation is a terminal procedure that leads to the company being dissolved and ceasing to   **3.216** exist. It may be used by solvent companies where the participators wish to bring the business to an orderly end and to receive payment of the surplus funds once all the assets are realised and all the creditors have been paid. More commonly, a company that enters liquidation will be insolvent and therefore unable to pay all its creditors. In such circumstances, the purpose of liquidation is to ensure that all the company assets are got in; any questionable circumstances leading up to its liquidation are investigated and appropriate action taken to swell the assets of the company and, if necessary, to punish any wrongdoers; and the assets are realised and distributed to the creditors in the most efficient manner subject to the statutory order of distribution. A liquidator will not usually look to trade the company's business and has a power only to continue the business to the extent that it is needed for a beneficial winding up.

The main corporate governance issues facing liquidators, such as those dealing with appoint-   **3.217** ment, powers and duties, remuneration and liabilities are looked at in detail in Chapters 7 and 8.

---

189   See, e.g., *Re Ve Interactive Ltd* [2018] EWHC 186 (Ch) and *Re Zinc Hotels (Holdings) Ltd* [2018] EWHC 1936 (Ch); [2018] BCC 968 at [73–85].
190   See Chapter 7 below and generally Insolvency Act 1986, Sch B1, paras 83–86.

(b) Opening of liquidation proceedings

3.218 Liquidation may be commenced voluntarily by the company's members (termed voluntary liquidation and there is no involvement of the court unless its assistance is called upon) or it may be commenced by a petition to the court which may order the company to be wound up (termed compulsory liquidation or winding up by the court).

(c) Voluntary liquidation

3.219 A voluntary liquidation is an out-of-court procedure which commences on the passing by the company of:

(a)   a special resolution that the company be wound up voluntarily; or
(b)   when the period (if any) fixed for the duration of the company by its constitution has expired, or some other event occurs on the happening of which the articles provide that the company shall be dissolved, an ordinary resolution that the company be wound up voluntarily (this is rare in practice).

3.220 There are two types of voluntary liquidation – members' voluntary liquidation where the company is solvent and creditors' voluntary liquidation where the company is insolvent. Both are commenced by a members' special resolution (75 per cent of members voting) although in a members' voluntary liquidation, the members decide who is to be the liquidator. The creditors will be paid in full in a members' voluntary liquidation and therefore have little involvement in the liquidation. In a creditors' voluntary liquidation, although the members may choose a liquidator, the creditors may nominate an alternative and it is their choice who is appointed. As the members will not receive anything from an insolvent liquidation, it is the creditors who effectively have various powers as part of the process.

3.221 Under s 84 of the Act, a members' voluntary liquidation takes place when a declaration of solvency has been sworn by a majority of the directors before the passing of the winding-up resolution that those directors have conducted a full enquiry into the company's affairs and formed the opinion that it will be able to pay its debts, together with interest at the official rate, in full within a stated period not exceeding 12 months from the date of the commencement of the winding up (the date of the members' resolution). The members decide who is appointed as liquidator (as with all officeholders, the liquidator must be a licensed insolvency practitioner). Under s 89 of the Act, any director who makes a declaration of solvency without having reason-able grounds for believing that the company will be able to pay its debts in full within the period stated in the declaration of solvency, is liable to a fine or imprisonment or both. If the debts are not paid or provided for in full within the period stated in the declaration, it will be presumed that the director did not have reasonable grounds for his opinion unless he proves the contrary. In such circumstances, the members' voluntary liquidation comes to an end and is converted into a creditors' voluntary liquidation. There is always a potential risk that a company's debts together with the expenses of a winding up may be in excess of what the directors thought likely. What they thought would be a members' voluntary liquidation may be converted into a creditors' voluntary liquidation with the potential for criminal liability of the directors who misjudged the situation.

3.222 A creditors' voluntary liquidation is a voluntary liquidation which is not preceded by a decla-ration of solvency.

The purpose of a creditors' voluntary liquidation is to realise the company's assets and, after the payment of costs, to distribute the proceeds among the creditors according to their respective rights and interests. **3.223**

In a creditors' voluntary winding up, at the same time that the members pass the resolution to wind up the company, they will usually also nominate a person to be liquidator. Under s 100 of the Act, the company's creditors may nominate their own choice of liquidator and the company's directors are under a duty to seek such a nomination from the creditors. The liquidator will be the person nominated by the creditors, or where no person is so nominated, the person (if any) nominated by the company. Under the Insolvency Rules 2016, the creditors' nomination must be sought either by way of the deemed consent procedure or a virtual meeting. **3.224**

Under s 99 of the Insolvency Act 1986, the directors must make out a statement of the company's affairs and send it to the company's creditors within seven days of the day on which the company passes a resolution for voluntary winding up. **3.225**

Under r 6.19 of the Insolvency Rules 2016, when the decision is sought from the company's creditors as to nominations for the position of liquidator, the convener of the decision must at the same time invite the creditors to decide whether a liquidation committee should be established. The creditors may appoint a liquidation committee of up to five persons. It is often more convenient for the liquidator if a committee is appointed, since the liquidator then has a small group of people to whom he or she may turn for advice if necessary; and the liquidator will otherwise have to convene creditors' decision-making procedures to fix the liquidator's remuneration. As in administration, the committee has the power to fix the liquidator's remuneration and the process for so doing is effectively the same as for administrators. **3.226**

(d) Winding up by the court

A compulsory liquidation is a winding up of a company by order of the court. 'Compulsory liquidation' or 'compulsory winding up' are the terms generally used, but the relevant legislation refers to winding up 'by the court'. While compulsory liquidations are, generally speaking, intended to achieve the same purposes as voluntary liquidations there are some very important differences in the procedures, resulting in part from the fact that in fulfilling his or her functions the liquidator is acting as an officer of the court as well as an officer of the company. **3.227**

A petition may be presented to the court by a number of different parties (listed in s 124 of the Act) on a number of different grounds (listed in s 122 of the Act). The most frequent petitioner in practice is a creditor whose petition will be based upon the most frequent ground, that the company is unable to pay its debts (as defined in s 123 of the Insolvency Act 1986). A very small number of petitions are made by shareholders or directors on the 'just and equitable' ground, usually where the company participators in a quasi-partnership company have fallen out and cannot continue to work together. The vast majority of compulsory liquidations involve companies which cannot pay their debts. **3.228**

When the court makes a winding-up order, the Official Receiver (a government employee) is usually appointed as the first liquidator. If the Official Receiver (or a majority of creditors) so decides, the Official Receiver may be replaced as liquidator by a private sector, licensed insolvency practitioner. Historically, the Official Receiver would look to hand over the liquidation **3.229** of a company to a private sector liquidator whenever the company had sufficient assets to cover the fees of the private sector liquidator. If that was not the case, the Official Receiver would complete the liquidation and the costs of so doing would fall on the public purse. It is now the policy of the Official Receiver to hand over cases which require the specialist skills of a private sector liquidator, otherwise the Official Receiver will usually remain as liquidator unless the creditors resolve to replace him.

3.230   At the hearing of a winding-up petition, the court has a wide discretion and may:

(a)   make a winding-up order;
(b)   dismiss the petition;
(c)   adjourn the hearing conditionally or unconditionally;
(d)   make an interim order; or
(e)   make any other order it thinks fit.

3.231   If the debt due to the petitioning creditor is genuinely disputed, the court will normally dismiss the petition on the basis that a winding-up hearing is not a convenient forum to determine disputes over debts. Where the company has a genuine cross-claim, which the company has not been able to litigate, which equals or exceeds the petition debt, the court will usually dismiss the petition.

3.232   If an administration order is considered to be preferable to a compulsory winding up of the company, those concerned should apply for an administration order as soon as possible, which will prevent a winding-up order being made until the alternative application has been determined.

3.233   Under s 129 of the Act, where a winding-up order is made, the liquidation is deemed to have commenced at the date of the petition not the date of the winding-up order.

(e) Effect of opening liquidation proceedings

3.234   Under s 130 of the Act, as soon as a company enters compulsory liquidation, creditors are prevented from taking or continuing any legal action against the company without permission of the court. Under s 128 of the Act, any attachment or execution put in force against the company after the commencement of the liquidation, is void. Under s 130 of the Act, any disposition of the company's property, transfer of shares or alteration in the status of members after the commencement of the winding up is also void, except to the extent the court orders otherwise. Although these provisions do not explicitly apply in a voluntary winding up, a voluntary liquidator may apply to the court under s 112 of the Act to ask the court to apply any provision applicable to a compulsory winding up, in the voluntary winding up.

3.235   In all types of liquidation, the function of the liquidator is essentially the same. He or she will take over control of the company and get in its assets. He or she has a large number of powers scattered throughout the Insolvency Act 1986 to require a statement of affairs, investigate the affairs of the company (including powers to examine former officers of the company in court), to compel delivery of assets or records belonging to the company and to take action against anyone who may be liable to the company. The liquidator has a number of specific actions available which are considered below in Chapter 4.

The liquidator is subject to similar reporting obligations as an administrator and effectively the **3.236** same regime concerning the liquidator's remuneration.

(f)   Order of asset distribution in liquidation

A liquidator may only realise assets which belong to the company. If debts have been effectively **3.237** assigned to a receivables financier or assets are subject to hire purchase or retention of title contracts, the liquidator will have no right to those assets. Depending upon the circumstances, the holder of a qualifying floating charge may choose to enforce its charge by appointing an administrator which will usually prevent a liquidator being appointed until the administration is completed. It is possible for such a charge holder to consent to the appointment of a liquidator rather than an administrator, in which case the liquidator may realise the charged assets as part of the liquidation and pay out the floating charge holder according to the charge holder's priority.

The liquidator has a statutory duty to distribute the proceeds of the realisation of the company's **3.238** assets in the following order:

1. Expenses of winding up, including the liquidator's remuneration (s 115 and rr 6.42 and 7.108 of the Insolvency Rules 2016);
2. Preferential creditors, as defined in ss 386, 387 and Sch 6;
3. Floating charge holder and the 'prescribed part';[191]
4. Unsecured creditors;
5. Shareholders.

(g)   Closure of liquidation

Once the liquidator has realised the estate and distributed it according to the statutory **3.239** order, the liquidator will make a final report to the creditors and deliver a final notice to the Registrar of Companies who will usually dissolve (strike off) the company from the Register of Companies three months later.

(h)   Phoenix trading

The concept of 'phoenix' trading comes from the image of a phoenix rising from the ashes. **3.240** It is used to describe the practice where a company has been wound up as insolvent and the old business is bought by the previous management group of the company and trades under a new name (which is often similar to the old company's name), often from the same premises using the same assets. The practice is frowned upon as it is used often to take advantage of the reputation of the old company so as to encourage people to do business with what appears to be a longstanding company. Such companies have been known to rise from the ashes on successive occasions always leaving a string of unpaid unsecured debts.

---

191   Before any payment can be made to any floating charge holder, the liquidator must first consider the application of s 176A of the Act. Section 176A applies to a company with a floating charge created on or after 15 September 2003 and the company has gone into liquidation. Where the company's net property does not exceed £10,000, the prescribed part is 50 per cent of that property. However, in such circumstances, where the property is less than the 'prescribed minimum' of £10,000 and the liquidator (or administrator) thinks that making a distribution to unsecured creditors would be disproportionate to the benefits, then the duty to make the distribution of the prescribed part does not apply. Where the company's net property exceeds £10,000, the prescribed part is the sum of 50 per cent of the first £10,000 in value, plus 20 per cent of the excess in value above the £10,000, subject to a maximum amount of the prescribed part of £800,000.

3.241   Although phoenix trading bears some similarity to pre-packaged administrations, they are rather different in that there are a number of provisions in place to ensure that pre-packs are used to safeguard value for creditors of the old company and to ensure, as far as possible, that the business of the new company has a reasonable chance of success. The potential liability on directors of the old company who purchase its business and trade using a similar name look ostensibly quite severe. A breach of the restriction on a company's directors engaging in phoenix activity in breach of ss 216 and 217 of the Insolvency Act 1986 imposes criminal liability and personal liability on the directors for the new company's debts. Perhaps somewhat surprisingly, the apparent rigour of this restriction may be completely avoided by the directors in a number of ways, most usually by the publication of a notice to the old company's creditors and in the Gazette prior to the sale of the business to the connected party controlled new company.[192]

3.242   Although largely under the radar when compared with the very public debate on pre-pack administration, such phoenix activity is common in practice with hundreds of such sales each year. The restrictions under ss 216 and 217 are not particularly logical and may be sidestepped relatively easily.

---

192   See the exceptions listed in Part 22 of the Insolvency Rules 2016 in particular r 22.4.

4

GOVERNANCE WHERE THE COMPANY IS INSOLVENT BUT NOT IN AN INSOLVENCY REGIME

A. INTRODUCTION

A company can become insolvent at any time in its life, and if it does then under UK law there **4.001** is nothing that prevents it from continuing to trade. While there is no proscription in UK law that prohibits a company from operating, there are some matters which the law requires directors to take into account in making decisions and ultimately deciding what actions the company should take when the company is insolvent. Directors must realise that it cannot be totally 'business as usual' for the company when it is insolvent, and they may well need to seek the advice of accountants, legal practitioners, perhaps other professionals, and even, in some situations, IPs (Insolvency Practitioners).

4.002   This chapter considers what issues directors have to consider that impinge on corporate governance when a company is insolvent but is not subject to an insolvency process such as liquidation. It also examines those matters that the law requires directors to take into account, what they are actually to do in response to these legal requirements when the directors' company is insolvent and what limits are placed on directors in the decisions that they make about trading.

4.003   The chapter examines the position that the directors find themselves in before a company enters a formal insolvency regime, and it explores the actions that might be initiated in the courts against directors. This is done because what actions can be taken should affect the way that directors manage their companies. The provisions discussed in the chapter as well as the institution of legal proceedings can foster transparency in that directors may be required to disclose information and they can make directors accountable for what they have done or not done. While the chapter addresses the relevant law, it does not purport to provide an exhaustive account of the law that applies to these actions but focuses on the governance elements that relate to such actions and which must be fulfilled to ensure that these legal actions will not be able to be instigated by a subsequently appointed officeholder if the company ends up in an insolvency regime. To do this some discussion of the law underpinning the actions must be provided. In addition to considering the position of the company and directors when the company is insolvent, in a few places the chapter discusses, albeit briefly, aspects of the position of directors when their company is near to, or risks, becoming insolvent.

4.004   The chapter does not seek to provide either a detailed exposition of the duties of directors or the legislative provisions that are examined. The discussion goes as far as is necessary to explain how they affect the corporate governance of companies when they are insolvent. We are particularly interested in how directors should behave in order to ensure that they adhere to rules relevant to corporate governance and to wider aspects of the law. The issue of legal liability is an important element of corporate governance and we endeavour to provide sufficient discussion to enable readers to ascertain the nature of liability and what has to be established for liability to be imposed.

4.005   At the outset we need to emphasise that we are envisaging the situation where the company is still operating (perhaps at a different level than previously) but is insolvent. When this situation occurs the interests of the shareholders, directors and creditors are likely to diverge so it can make governance extremely difficult. It is relevant for us to reiterate our loose definition of corporate governance, namely: 'the rules, relationships, systems and processes within and by which authority is exercised and controlled in companies for the benefit of pertinent stakeholders' as this will guide our discussions to a large extent. This definition is considered in this book in the context of accountability and transparency. Much of that which is discussed below involves aspects of accountability, that is the provisions that are considered require directors to do certain things and have, within them, the notion of directors accounting for what they have done or not done.

In this chapter 'the authority' mentioned in our definition of corporate governance relates to   **4.006**
the directors and we are focusing in the chapter on the rules and processes which control the
directors in the period when their company is insolvent.

B. THE COMPANY SECRETARY

In public companies, which must have appointed a company secretary,[1] one of the primary roles   **4.007**
of the company secretary, as mentioned in Chapter 1, is to advise on governance matters. It,
therefore, means that the person holding this post should be advising directors of their duties
and responsibilities when the company is insolvent, and how they may impact on corporate
governance. This advice is likely to change, when compared with where the company is solvent.

C. PROFESSIONAL ADVICE

Besides seeking advice from the company secretary (if there is one) it will be advisable, in   **4.008**
many situations involving their management of a company's affairs, for the directors of public
companies to seek the advice of certain professional advisers. This might be advisable not only
to assist directors in addressing the financial position of the company but also to demonstrate,
if administration or liquidation follows at some point, that they were being prudent in getting
advice. It might go some way to helping directors defend any action brought by an administrator or liquidator at a later date.

Of course, the directors of private companies might well also be advised to seek the counsel   **4.009**
of professional advisers. In fact, obtaining professional advice, such as from accountants and
lawyers, is perhaps even more important for the directors of smaller private companies who
do not have the same support as the directors of public companies which often have corporate
counsel, internal accountants and auditors and fellow directors with finance qualifications and
experience, as well as a company secretary. The concern that the directors of small private companies may well have will be the costs involved in seeking advice. Professional services are often
costly, particularly where the company's position is unclear and/or its records are not in a good
state. It is also probably more imperative that directors who have no, or little, understanding of
aspects of finance and law seek advice.

The employment of expert insolvency advice and the process involved in securing it is explained   **4.010**
in the Australian decision of *Ten Network Holdings Ltd (Administrators Appointed) (Receivers
and Managers Appointed)*[2] by the Federal Court of Australia. Certainly, if there is any notion
of directors contemplating potential insolvency, they should be encouraged to engage with
appropriately qualified professionals early to develop restructuring plans which will maximise
the chance of rescuing a viable business or returning as much value as possible to the relevant
stakeholders should the later appointment of an administrator or liquidator prove necessary.[3]

---

1   It is prudent for large private companies also to have company secretaries, and many do.
2   [2017] FCA 914.
3   Ibid., [35].

D. DIRECTOR CONSIDERATIONS IN THE TWILIGHT ZONE

1. Introduction

4.011   If a company is near to insolvency or insolvent there are many issues with which directors will be concerned. The focus of their attention is likely to be on how to ride out the storm. This period is sometimes referred to as the 'twilight zone'.[4] We will use this expression in this chapter to denote the period of insolvency (or near insolvency) of a company prior to the advent of an insolvency regime.

4.012   An insolvent or doubtfully solvent company becomes a rich breeding ground for conflicts of interest. Such conflicts may arise between shareholders and creditors, between senior and junior secured creditors, between secured and unsecured creditors, or even between creditors who have the same rights. Shareholders may be more inclined to favour trying to trade out of financial distress, having nothing left to lose from doing so, and running the risk of depleting whatever value is left in the company. A secured creditor may prefer to curtail its losses rather than risk increasing them. Once doubts emerge about a company's ability to pay its debts, unsecured creditors will find (or at least perceive) themselves to be in competition with each other for payment. Those who exercise the most pressure are likely to get paid first. Unsecured creditors may even try to procure security.[5] Once these distress-related conflicts emerge, the kind of corporate governance that exists during times of solvency may become difficult without the commencement of a formal insolvency process.

4.013   When operating in the twilight zone directors will have to make many of the same decisions that they have to when their company is solvent. Having said that, clearly there will be some decisions that are different and it is likely that the same kind of decisions have to be approached in a different manner and with a different mindset.

4.014   It would be advisable for directors to review areas of expenditure and to contemplate how cash flow might be improved, such as agreeing a change of terms of trade with trading partners, selling assets and, perhaps, in parlous circumstances, reducing the size of the workforce. Directors might well consider taking personal austerity measures, such as reducing salaries or operating on more of a hand-to-mouth basis except where this is not viable. This is particularly the case in smaller companies. Directors must realise that if their company ends up in insolvent liquidation the liquidator might be minded to bring proceedings against them and courts have

---

4   INSOL International, 'Directors in the Twilight Zone IV' 2013. See, D Milman, 'Strategies for Regulating Managerial Performance in the "Twilight Zone" – Familiar Dilemmas: New Considerations' (2004) *JBL* 493; R Purslowe, 'Decisions in the Twilight Zone of Insolvency' (2011) *13 University of Notre Dame in Australia Law Review* 113. Also, see the articles contained in volume 1 of the journal, *Journal of Business and Technology Law* in 2007 that included papers presented at a conference on the issue of the twilight zone.

5   See, e.g., *Robert Petroleum Ltd v Bernard Kenny Ltd* [1983] 2 AC 192. Lord Brightman (Lord Diplock, Lord Edmund-Davies, Lord Keith and Lord Roskill concurring) held (at 206) that such conduct was not sharp practice on the part of the creditor and a creditor of a company that runs into financial difficulties has every right to seek to obtain security for himself. Moreover, a creditor of a distressed company may well be in a position to demand security and is justified in doing so: *Re MC Bacon Ltd* [1990] BCC 78, 83.

not been impressed with directors who have continued to take unreasonable or unsustainable salaries and failing to engage in actions that are likely to minimise losses.[6]

Directors might decide to establish a separate committee charged with overseeing the correction of the company's fortunes and this would involve recommending measures to be taken to overcome the company's malaise.   **4.015**

It is probably wise for directors to engage with the company's stakeholders, and particularly its creditors so that the latter might gain an understanding of why the company might fail to meet any payments due. Directors should also inform the shareholders and perhaps inquire whether they might be in a position to invest new funds in the company. Of course, many shareholders might take the view that this would be 'throwing good money after bad' but in some situations they might see the future as positive if the company can persevere and get through the insolvency period.   **4.016**

While operating in the twilight zone the directors might consider restructuring the company and in doing so enter into an informal arrangement with creditors. Restructuring involves 'a process by which the liabilities of a company in financial difficulties are restructured so as to enable the company, and, therefore, value, to be preserved and for its business to be carried on as a going concern'.[7] Jason Harris describes it as the situation 'where a company has become over-leveraged with debt and needs to alter the nature of some or all of the debt obligations so as to facilitate the company to return to profitability at some point in the future'.[8]   **4.017**

Restructuring may consist of several stages which may well include the assessment of problems of the company and selection of a particular rescue option. Naturally, the kind of restructuring that may be sought will depend on a number of elements such as the size of the company, market conditions, the financial state of the company, and the attitude of creditors. In large companies, restructuring can be extremely complicated.   **4.018**

Any arrangement that eventuates from discussions concerning restructuring outside of formal insolvency procedures is often known as 'a workout'. A 'workout' is the designation of an out-of-court, privately arranged restructuring on a going-concern basis of all, or substantially all, of a company's liabilities, laid down in an agreement when insolvency looms.[9] A workout might involve one or more of a number of strategies, but they usually include one or more of the following: debt for equity swaps, debt re-scheduling, asset sales, write-offs, cost reductions, of equipment and plant, injection of new capital,[10] payment holidays and compromises. The   **4.019**

---

6   See, e.g., *Secretary of State v van Hengel* [1996] 1 BCLC 545; *Re Ward Sherrard Ltd* [1996] BCC 418; *Roberts v Frohlich* [2011] EWHC (Ch) 257, [2012] BCC 407.

7   B Hedger and C Howard, *Restructuring Law and Practice*, (2nd revised ed, LexisNexis, 2014), para 1.2.

8   J Harris, 'Reforming Insolvent Trading to Encourage Restructuring; Safe Harbour or Sleepy Hollows?' (2016) 27 *Journal of Banking and Finance Law and Practice* 294, 298.

9   B Wessels and S Madaus, 'Rescue of Business in Insolvency Law,' (European Law Institute, 2017), 75: https://www.europeanlawinstitute.eu/fileadmin/user_upload/p_eli/Publications/Instrument_INSOLVENCY.pdf accessed 23 October 2020.

10   J Harris, 'Reforming Insolvent Trading to Encourage Restructuring; Safe Harbour or Sleepy Hollows?' (2016) 27 *Journal of Banking and Finance Law and Practice* 294, 298; World Bank Group and the United Nations Commission on International Trade Law, *Creditor Rights and Insolvency Standard* (the World Bank Group, 2005) (the latter referred to in

essential aspect is that the company is restructured on the basis of contractual relations rather than being subjected to a formal insolvency procedure, although a formal procedure may, in due course, be employed to implement the arrangement arrived at by the parties. Endeavouring to implement a workout can be fraught with problems, many of which are not within the scope of this book. What is of importance is to recognise that while seeking to get agreement for, and the implementation of, a restructuring agreement the directors will be subject to a number of responsibilities such as adhering to the general duties that are imposed on directors under the Companies Act 2006 ('the Companies Act') and the directors will have to be careful that they do not engage in wrongful trading, as is proscribed by s 214 of the Act.

4.020 The directors should always keep in mind the need, perhaps, to take the company into some formal insolvency regime. It is often difficult for directors to know whether or not it is premature to do so, a matter discussed later in the context of wrongful trading. Directors can find themselves in a dilemma. They may feel that they are in a 'no win' situation. If they do take the company into a formal insolvency regime they may be criticised for taking this action prematurely because the company could have been rescued. On the other hand, if they do not take this action they might be subject to legal action at a later date if the company does in fact become the subject of an insolvency process. In making their decisions it is imperative that directors are aware of their duties and other legal responsibilities. They then must make appropriate decisions based on complying with their duties and the fulfilment of their responsibilities. At some point though it might appear to be necessary to embrace a formal regime.

4.021 When lending to small companies it is customary for creditors which have substantial leverage to require the directors to give personal guarantees under which they agree to pay up the loan if the company fails to do so. This means that the directors have a vested interest in seeing the creditor whose debt they have guaranteed paid if the fortunes of the company look decidedly bleak. This can cause a complication for directors. They can find themselves in a type of conflict situation; that is, to pay the creditor who holds their guarantee will be in the interests of the directors, but to pay other creditors might be best for the company's business and continued trading. What they need to ensure is that they make decisions which are in the best interests of the company and not what suits them. In the type of scenario just posited it is possible that the directors' interests and those of the company will conflict. If that is the case then the director has to be aware of this and ensure that he or she does act in the best interests of the company or risk possible legal action at some point in the future.

4.022 When a company is solvent directors will usually be concerned with pleasing the shareholders. The reason for this is that the shareholders have the power to refrain from re-electing them or even removing them. Besides this, when the company is solvent the shareholders must be the focus of the directors' attention, as envisaged by s 172(1) of the Companies Act, and they will also need to consider the interests of stakeholders, again as required by s 172(1). In insolvency, directors might come under pressure from both shareholders and creditors. Shareholders might want directors to take excessive risks because, as those entitled to the residue of the company, they have lost their investment unless the company is able to return to profit, and only extreme risk might produce profits.

R Purslowe, 'Decisions in the Twilight Zone of Insolvency – Should Directors be Afforded a Safe Harbour?' (2011) 13 *University of Notre Dame Australia Law Review* 113, 133).

When a company becomes insolvent the interests of stakeholders, as we noted in Chapter 2, **4.023** will conflict. As Mike Ross states:

> Shareholders endeavouring to preserve their capital; creditors seeking payment; employees and management looking to retain their jobs; suppliers attempting to keep trade links open...and customers with concerns about pre-paid goods and services not yet delivered or about the company's performance of post-delivery warranties.[11]

Directors have a number of incentives to avoid a formal insolvency regime. Primarily, they **4.024** are: the loss of reputation (directors will be known for overseeing a company's insolvency), particularly for directors whose livelihood depends on their positions as directors; scrutiny of their stewardship of the company's affairs with possible concomitant legal proceedings; possible disqualification. Disqualification is a particular concern for those directors of SMEs as the case law tells us that it is the directors of these sorts of companies who are, predominantly, the directors against whom proceedings are brought. It is a matter discussed towards the end of the chapter.

The directors of a company have the power to declare dividends in favour of shareholders. In **4.025** smaller companies which are effectively manager-owned there is a practice of directors being paid for their services, at least partly, by way of dividends.[12] The practice is that directors receive payments throughout the financial year and initially they are regarded as dividends but where the company does not have adequate distributable reserves they are re-labelled as salary. Dividends are only able to be paid out of profits available for that purpose and determined by accounts which have been prepared properly in accordance with the Companies Act.[13] This is an issue which is discussed in more detail later in the chapter.

While courts are wary of employing hindsight in considering the actions of directors against **4.026** whom proceedings have been brought, usually many years after the actions for which are they said to be liable, directors must consider the likely effects of their decisions and all of the extant circumstances. In doing this it would be sensible to retain notes and all documents and advice that relate to their decisions so that they can justify what they did at a later date, if necessary.

The final thing to say in this section of the chapter and by way of introduction to some of the **4.027** issues discussed below is that the directors are not, unlike in many European countries, necessarily going to be liable if they continue to trade while their company is insolvent. As Chadwick J (as he then was) said in *Re C S Holidays Ltd*:

> The companies legislation does not impose on directors a statutory duty to ensure that their company does not trade while insolvent; nor does that legislation impose an obligation to ensure that the company does not trade at a loss... Directors may properly take the view that it is in the interests of the company and of its creditors that, although insolvent, the company should continue to trade out of its difficulties. They may properly take the view that it is in the interests of the company and its creditors

---

11   'Director's Liability on Corporate Restructuring' in C Rickett (ed), *Essays on Corporate Restructuring and Insolvency* (Brookers, 1996), 176.

12   For an instance, see *Global Corporate Ltd v Hale* [2018] EWCA Civ 2618.

13   See *Progress Property Co Ltd v Moorgarth Group Ltd* [2010] UKSC 55, [2011] BCC 196.

that some loss-making trade should be accepted in anticipation of future profitability. They are not to be criticised if they give effect to such a view.[14]

2.   Creditor pressure

4.028   Absent compliance with restrictive covenants in a loan contract, directors will not usually focus overly on creditors of the company when the company is clearly solvent. Obligations to creditors should take care of themselves in profitable companies. The only issues directors might be concerned about is whether creditors have discharged their part of the contract with the company, such as delivering goods of merchantable quality according to what was agreed. Directors may have to liaise with the company's largest lenders from time to time particularly in relation to financing of the day-to-day affairs of the company, and perhaps in refinancing at certain points in the life of the company.

4.029   Many creditors, particularly in large companies, may know little about the financial state of the company. It is likely to be only when their debt is not paid within a reasonable period of the due date that they are likely to start to get worried and to inquire about non-payment. Of course, in some industries, word will get around that company X is experiencing financial difficulties and this might alert creditors to take some sort of self-help action/remedy against X. While general creditors can be activist, the most likely to be active are those who purchase debts of the company from creditors under arrangements that involve or are similar to factoring. Today there are more professional distress investors taking positions in companies with the idea of buying distressed debts at a discount to resell immediately or benefitting from a higher dividend as a result of an insolvency plan with the sole purpose of making a profit.[15]

4.030   Most companies will have borrowed against assets and the lender will often be the company's banker. The bank will usually have taken fixed and floating charges against the assets and so it will be imperative for directors to liaise with the bank if the company is insolvent in order to delay the advent of a possible receivership or administration. Companies often use funds owed to HMRC, in respect of employees' PAYE deductions and VAT received on sale of its goods and/or services that is to be refunded to HMRC,[16] as operating capital and directors must realise that HMRC might be more intense in its claims for recovery than other creditors. Certainly, HMRC has the resources and knowledge to engage in debt recovery and has a history of taking liquidation proceedings against companies.

4.031   Once a company fails to discharge its debts on time or within a reasonable period after the due date for payment, pressure will come from creditors. The type of pressure can vary. It might come in the form of a polite inquiry (at first) as to when payment is to be expected. Other creditors might be a little more robust and demand payment within a short period past the due date for payment. If these types of action bring no result then often solicitors will be instructed

---

14   [1997] 1 WLR 407, 414.

15   J S Athanas, M L Warren and E P Khatchatourian, 'Bankruptcy Needs to get its Priorities Straight: A Proposal for Limiting the Leverage of Unsecured Creditors' Committees when Unsecured Creditors are "Out-of-the-Money"' [2018] *ABI Law Review* 93, 101.

16   The Crown will now have a priority to repayment for such sums in a liquidation. It had such a priority until 2003 when the priority was removed. The priority was restored from 1 December 2020.

and they will send a demand letter threatening legal action if payment is not made within a specified period.

Directors have to try and deal with all of these forms of creditor pressure as well as 'keeping the **4.032** show on the road'. Many will say that the best thing is for directors to speak to creditors and try to assuage the latter's concerns. This might entail explaining what the company's financial position is (in general terms) and what the company is proposing to do about non-payment. Ignoring creditor pressure is usually counselled against as it likely to infuriate creditors and end up merely delaying the inevitable demand and/or winding-up petition.

What directors have to take into account is that most creditors will engage in self-dealing as **4.033** they have no obligation or duty (usually) to other creditors of the debtor company, and they are 'axiomatically self-interested'.[17] This self-dealing might take a number of forms. For instance, it might entail engaging in hold-out tactics where a restructuring outside of a formal insolvency regime is being proposed. Outside of such a regime it is necessary to obtain the support of all creditors to a restructuring or else it only takes one creditor to refuse to agree to a workout and to petition for a winding-up order in order to scupper any restructuring.[18]

E. DIRECTORS' DUTIES

As mentioned at various points in the book already we have emphasised the fact that directors **4.034** are subject to duties and responsibilities. This chapter majors on one particular duty and several responsibilities that are pertinent to companies in financial distress. But besides these, directors must keep in mind the general duties that are set out in Chapter 2 of Part 10 of the Companies Act, namely ss 171–177. These will apply to directors who are managing companies which are insolvent to the same extent as solvent companies, with the possible exception of s 172(1).[19] We understand from s 178 that all of the duties, except for s 174, are fiduciary duties; s 174 addresses the duty of care. The duties codified, for the most part, what existed at common law and in equity and that had been developed over 150 years or so in the case law. Section 170(3) provides that the duties are owed to the company. Section 170(4) explains that the duties in this Part of the Act are to be interpreted and applied in the same way as common law rules or equitable principles and regard is to be had to the corresponding common law rules and equitable principles in interpreting and applying the duties.

The codified duties are not necessarily exhaustive and there is no bar to other duties being **4.035** imposed by the courts on directors. This appears to be recognised by s 178(2) for it refers to 'any other fiduciary duty owed to a company by its directors,' besides those in Chapter 2 of Part 10.

---

17   J Lipson, 'Governance in the Breach: Controlling Creditor Opportunism' (2011) 84 *Southern California Law Review* 1035, 1049.

18   This is unless the court decided in its discretion to refrain from making such an order. This would only be likely where there is support for restructuring from a majority of independent creditors. See Andrew Keay, *McPherson and Keay's The Law of Company Liquidation* (5th ed, Sweet & Maxwell, 2021), 186–190.

19   See Companies Act, s 172(3).

4.036   Of particular interest in relation to a company that is experiencing insolvency, leaving aside s 172(3) to which we will come shortly, might be ss 171(b) and 175. The former provides that directors are only to exercise powers for the purposes for which the powers were conferred upon them. The latter provision requires directors to avoid conflicts of interest, that is, where their interests may conflict with those of the company.

4.037   While the general duties of directors are still owed in insolvency when the directors' company continues to operate under their control, there has been uncertainty as to whether they do when the company is placed in some form of insolvency regime. It has been clear for some time that if an administrative receiver is appointed the directors still owe duties, certainly as far as duties of loyalty and obligations in relation to conflict of duties are concerned.[20] It might be thought that where an administrator is appointed and directors virtually lose their management powers, for those powers are vested in the administrator,[21] that directors are no longer subject to duties. However, in *Hunt v Michie*[22] ICC Judge Barber in fact held that directors remain subject to the duties when their company enters administration. In the situation where a liquidator is appointed to a company by court order the Court of Appeal in *Measures Brothers Ltd v Measures*[23] held that the appointment of the directors is terminated automatically.[24] This would suggest, therefore, that the general duties of the directors end (with some other duties imposed by legislation applying for the period of the liquidation only).[25] Where the directors' company enters voluntary liquidation it is submitted that the office of director does not come to an end because the Act permits directors to exercise certain powers in some circumstances after the commencement of winding up, and this conclusion is supported by the decision in *Midland Counties District Bank Ltd v Attwood*.[26] In *Hunt v Michie*[27] Judge Barber specifically held that the duties of directors survive the company's entry into voluntary liquidation, as with administration.[28]

4.038   While any subsequent administrator or liquidator of a company usually brings proceedings against directors for breaches occurring outside the twilight zone, save where there is a breach of s 172(3), as indicated above directors must comply with these duties while managing companies in the twilight zone. Apart from s 172(3), we will not undertake any analysis of the general duties of directors as they are outside the scope of the book and are dealt with in detail elsewhere.[29] However, from time to time we might mention one or more of them.

---

20   Ultraframe (UK) Ltd v Fielding [2005] EWHC 1638 (Ch), [2006] FSR 17, [1329].
21   Insolvency Act 1986, Sch B1, paras 59–64.
22   [2020] EWHC 54 (Ch), [60].
23   [1910] 2 Ch 248.
24   Ibid., 254, 256 and 259.
25   Section 170(2) of the Companies Act provides that a person who ceases to be a director continues to be subject to the duty in s 175 (duty to avoid conflicts of interest) as far as the exploitation of any company property, information or opportunity of which he or she became aware when he or she was still a director is concerned. Also, directors remains subject to the duty in s 176 (duty not to accept benefits from third parties) in respect of things done or omitted by them before the cessation of office.
26   [1905] 1 Ch 357.
27   [2020] EWHC 54 (Ch).
28   Ibid., [60].
29   For a detailed discussion of them, see Andrew Keay, *Directors' Duties* (4th ed, LexisNexis, 2020); Simon Mortimore (ed), *Company Directors: Duties, Liabilities, and Remedies* (3rd ed, OUP, 2016).

F. THE PROTECTION OF CREDITORS

When a company enters the twilight zone is there a need to be concerned about the creditors?   **4.039**
Many have argued, primarily in the United States, that creditors do not need any special protection,[30] because, for instance, creditors have a number of avenues that they can take when
agreeing to extend credit. These comments have not been limited to academics. In the Court
of Appeal decision, *BTI 2014 LLC v Sequana S.A.*[31] David Richards LJ said, in giving the
judgment with which the other judges concurred, that: 'Creditors can be assumed to look after
their own interests when deciding to deal with a company and there are a range of protective
measures, such as the taking of security, for which they can bargain.'[32] The sorts of things that
creditors can do is, as David Richards LJ suggested, to take security over the property of the
debtor, and they might even require personal guarantees from directors of corporate debtors
and the inclusion of restrictive covenants in lending contracts.

Nevertheless, the law in the UK has tended to endeavour to protect creditors. It has done this   **4.040**
in four ways. First, it has provided in the Act that certain transactions entered into prior to
a company entering administration or liquidation can be impugned. This is designed to ensure
that in an administration or liquidation there will be a distribution according to the terms
of the Act, and this will involve a pari passu distribution to the creditors if funds permit and
once creditors with some sort of priority, such as employees, have been paid. Secondly, various
Companies Acts have included prohibitive provisions. For instance, placing restrictions on
the payment of dividends to shareholders. Thirdly, in more recent years, the law has protected
creditors from loss when their corporate debtor is in financial strife. This has been achieved
through provisions such as s 214 of the Act, providing for liability for wrongful trading,
and requiring directors to consider the interests of creditors. Fourthly, the common law has
provided, for more than 40 years, that in insolvency the directors must take into account the
interests of the company's creditors. We will not engage in consideration of the normative
question of whether creditors should be protected outside contractual provisions and self-help
procedures. Rather, we will focus on what provision has been made to protect creditors where
the provision impacts potentially, on directors managing a company in the twilight zone as this
affects governance of the company. We will seek to examine the provisions and, in the course
of doing so, identify any weaknesses that might exist or appear to exist and how they affect the
process of corporate governance. We do not purport to deal with the provisions in the Act that
allow for the adjustment of transactions in a liquidation or administration.[33]

In the next parts of the chapter we consider responsibilities that directors have when their   **4.041**
company is insolvent and what limits are placed on their actions. What directors do might
precipitate the initiation of legal proceedings against them by a liquidator or administrator if
the company subsequently enters either liquidation or administration. What we are mainly

---

30   F Tung, 'The New Death of Contract: Creeping Corporate Fiduciary Duties for Creditors' (2008) 57 *Emory Law Journal*
     809; H Hu and J Westbrook, 'Abolition of the Corporate Duty to Creditors (2007) 107 *Columbia Law Review* 1321.
31   [2019] EWCA Civ 112, [2019] 2 All ER 784, [2019] BCC 631, [2019] 1 BCLC 347, [2019] BPIR 562.
32   Ibid., [127].
33   For in-depth consideration of these provisions, see, e.g., J Armour and H Bennett, *Vulnerable Transactions in Corporate
     Insolvency* (Hart Publishing, 2003); R Parry et al, *Transactional Avoidance in Insolvencies* (3rd ed, OUP, 2018); Andrew
     Keay, *McPherson and Keay's The Law of Company Liquidation* (5th ed, Sweet & Maxwell, 2021), Chapter 11.

concerned with in these Parts is what directors need to do (or avoid doing) in managing the company. That is, how the obligations under which directors are subject affects the nature of corporate governance. Whether proceedings will subsequently be taken against directors if the company moves into a formal legal procedure is a matter for the relevant officeholder. In this chapter we do not consider directly the issues that confront an officeholder in deciding whether or not to institute proceedings. That is covered in Chapter 7.

4.042 What follows does not purport to be an exhaustive analysis of the obligations applying to directors. We are going to focus, as far as possible, on the corporate governance elements that present themselves in the course of a discussion of the obligations and the law that has developed in relation to them. Consequently, greatest attention is paid to the duty directors owe to take account of the interests of creditors, how directors are to avoid wrongful trading and fraudulent trading, what would involve directors engaging in entering into transactions designed to defraud creditors and how directors are to ensure that they do not approve the payment of unlawful distributions to shareholders. Furthermore, in light of these responsibilities we consider how directors are to act and what they need to consider. It is in relation to these issues where the most focus is on what directors have to do as part of their corporate governance responsibilities.

G. DUTY TO TAKE ACCOUNT OF CREDITORS' INTERESTS

4.043 We now begin consideration of the first of several obligations which directors have when their company is insolvent. The first is found in s 172(3) of the Companies Act. Of the obligations considered in this chapter, it is this provision, and the accompanying law developed in relation to it that, arguably, effectively incorporates and leads to one of the greatest, if not the greatest, consideration of corporate governance issues. Section 172(3) provides that: 'the duty imposed by this section [s 172(1)] has effect subject to any enactment or rule of law requiring directors, in certain circumstances, to consider or act in the interests of creditors of the company'. One of the 'certain circumstances' is, as we discuss shortly, the insolvency of the company.

4.044 It is good to put the subsection in context. It is obviously part of the same section as s 172(1), a provision that been subject to a substantial amount of debate, commentary and discussion.[34] Section 172(1) provides as follows:

> A director of a company must act in a way that he considers, in good faith, would be most likely to promote the success of the company for the benefit of its members as a whole, and in doing so have regard (amongst other matters) to –
>
> (a)   the likely consequences of any decision in the long term

34 See, e.g., Andrew Keay, *The Enlightened Shareholder Value Principle and Corporate Governance* (Routledge, 2013), Chapter 4; S Kiarie, 'At Crossroads: Shareholder Value, Stakeholder Value and Enlightened Shareholder Value: Which Road Should the United Kingdom Take?' (2006) 17 *ICCLR* 329; A Keay, 'Enlightened Shareholder Value, the Reform of the Duties of Company Directors and the Corporate Objective' [2006] *LMCLQ* 335; D Fisher 'The Enlightened Shareholder – Leaving Stakeholders in the Dark: Will Section 172(1) of the Companies Act 2006 Make Directors Consider the Impact of Their Decisions on Third Parties?' (2009) 20 *ICCLR* 10; A Alcock, 'An Accidental Change to Directors' Duties?' (2009) 30 *Company Lawyer* 362; A Keay, 'Tackling the Issue of the Corporate Objective : An Analysis of the United Kingdom's "Enlightened Shareholder Value Approach"' (2007) 29 *Sydney Law Review* 577; N Grier, 'Enlightened Shareholder Value: Did Directors Deliver?' (2014) *Juridical Review* 95.

(b)   the interests of the company's employees
(c)   the need to foster the company's business relationships with suppliers, customers and others
(d)   the impact of the company's operations on the community and the environment
(e)   the desirability of the company maintaining a reputation for high standards of business conduct, and
(f)   the need to act fairly between the members of the company.

This provision is critical and highly relevant to corporate governance, when a company is **4.045** solvent. When a company is insolvent then, as we see below, the provision is trumped by s 172(3).

1.   Background to the duty

The obligation that is found in s 172(3) may be traced back to 1976. In that year the Australian **4.046** High Court (the court at the apex of the Australian judicial system) decided a case called *Walker v Wimborne*.[35] The facts and much of the decision are not very notable for our purposes. What was notable is that in a dictum Mason J said that the directors of an insolvent company in discharging their duty to the company must take account of the interests of its shareholders *and* its creditors.[36]

Thus, over a number of years it became a rule of law in many parts of the Commonwealth **4.047** (including the UK) and Ireland that directors must consider the interests of creditors when their company is insolvent. After significant debate in the Company Law Review Steering Group ('the CLRSG') in the late 1990s, which had been established by the UK government to undertake a comprehensive examination of UK company law and what action needed to be taken in respect of companies legislation, a majority of the CLRSG in its Final Report advocated the inclusion of reference to this rule of law in any new legislation that was to be enacted.[37] It stated that:

> In providing a high level statement of directors' duties, it is important to draw to directors' attention that different factors may need to be taken into consideration where the company is insolvent or threatened by insolvency. To fail to do so would risk misleading directors by omitting an important part of the overall picture.[38]

There is now, as Rose J noted at first instance in the decision in *Bti 2014 Llc v Sequana SA*,[39] **4.048** a long line of cases which have been based on a claim under the rule of law referred to in s 172(3),[40] either alone or in conjunction with other causes of action.

Any action that is brought against directors under s 172(3) is commenced on behalf of the **4.049** company. Nearly all cases have been instigated by liquidators, so the following refers to liquidators when reference is being made to the claimants in an action under the duty. Proceedings are

---

35   (1976) 137 CLR 1.
36   Ibid., 7.
37   For a discussion of the various comments of the CLRSG over several years concerning the inclusion of the obligation in prospective legislation, see, Andrew Keay, *The Enlightened Shareholder Value Principle and Corporate Governance* (Routledge, 2013), 65–76.
38   *Modern Company Law for a Competitive Economy: Final Report* Vol 1, (DTI, 2001), para 3.12.
39   [2016] EWHC 1686; [2017] 1 BCLC 453.
40   Ibid., [465].

generally commenced pursuant to s 212 of the Act where a liquidator is acting[41]. Applications made under this provision are referred to as misfeasance applications. There are a number of practical advantages to liquidators in bringing proceedings in the name of the liquidator under s 212 rather than causing the company to pursue the same causes of action in its own name.

2.   The rationale for the duty

4.050   Notwithstanding the fact that the rule of law referred to in s 172(3) has become an important weapon in the hands of liquidators and administrators, because they are likely to be the only ones who will bring proceedings against directors under the provision, and this is borne out by the case law, there has been little said about the reason for the existence of the rule. What principle or policy underpins the rule?

4.051   A large portion of the literature, and mainly it is American, has stated that the reason for this protection is that the shareholders are no longer the owners of the residual value of the firm, having been, in effect, transplanted by the creditors, whose rights are transformed into equity-like rights.[42] Thus, at this point, the creditors are the residual claimants of the company's assets[43] and the ones who have the most valid interest in the company's assets.[44] It is asserted that when their companies are in difficulty, directors could be expected, to embrace actions which involve more risk;[45] this was the position stated by the CLRSG.[46]

4.052   The theory suggests that directors might engage in excessive risk-taking,[47] and, in effect, gamble with what are the creditors' funds in the hope of securing a rescue for the company,[48] and gaining benefits for the shareholders, in due course. Directors might well incur more debt, and this will reduce what the existing creditors will ultimately receive. Shareholders could well be in favour of such an approach taken by the directors because the directors' strategy might pay off, even if the chances are slim, and if it does then it would produce sufficient to pay the

---

41   Proceedings are actually initated under Part 12 of the Insolvency Rules 2016.

42   S Schwarcz, 'Rethinking a Corporation's Obligations to Creditors' (1996) 17 *Cardozo Law Review* 647, 668; R de R Barondes, 'Fiduciary Duties of Officers and Directors of Distressed Corporations' (1998) 7 *George Mason Law Review* 45, 46.

43   F Easterbrook and D Fischel, *The Economic Structure of Corporate Law* (Harvard University Press, 1991), 60.

44   J William Callison, 'Why a Fiduciary Duty Shift to Creditors of Insolvent Business Entities is Incorrect' (2007) 1 *Journal of Business and Technology Law* 431, 432.

45   See, C C Nicolls, 'Liability of Corporate Officers and Directors to Third Parties' (2001) 35 *Canadian Business Law Journal* 1, 35; R F Hartman, 'Situation Specific Fiduciary Duties for Corporate Directors: Enforceable Obligations or Toothless Ideals' (1993) 50 *Washington and Lee Law Review* 1761, 1771; R de R Barondes, 'Fiduciary Duties of Officers and Directors of Distressed Corporations' (1998) 7 *George Mason Law Review* 45, 46; J Armour, 'The Law and Economics of Corporate Insolvency : A Review' (2001) ESRC Centre for Business Research, University of Cambridge, Working Paper No 197, p 1.

46   *Modern Company Law for a Competitive Economy: Final Report* Vol 1 (DTI, 2001), para 3.15.

47   See, F Easterbrook and D Fischel, *The Economic Structure of Corporate Law* (Harvard University Press, 1991), 60; V Jelisavcic, 'A Safe Harbour Proposal to Define the Limits of Directors' Fiduciary Duty to Creditors in the "Vicinity of Insolvency"' [1992] *Journal of Corporation Law* 145, 148; R de R Barondes, 'Fiduciary Duties of Officers and Directors of Distressed Corporations' (1998) 7 *George Mason Law Review* 45, 50; R D Valsan and M A Yahya, 'Shareholders, Creditors, and Directors' Fiduciary Duties: A Law and Finance Approach' (2007) 2 *Virginia Law and Business Review* 1, 10.

48   B Morgan and H Underwood, 'Directors' Liability to Creditors on a Corporation's Insolvency in Light of the Dylex and Peoples Department Stores Litigation' (2004) 39 *Canadian Business Law Journal* 336, 338.

creditors and provide some benefits for shareholders. This is because, as rehearsed above, the shareholders have nothing to lose,[49] as they cannot expect dividends or return of capital if nothing is done. Where there are owner-managed companies then, of course, the directors are likely to think of their position as shareholders and in an insolvency situation they, in their capacity as shareholders, have nothing to lose as there is little or no equity left in the company.[50]

Because of the concepts of separate legal entity and limited liability the directors are insulated **4.053** from liability, ordinarily, if their actions fall flat. Of course, as far as owner-managed companies are concerned the owner-director(s) might well have given personal guarantees to lenders and so the above type of behaviour is not likely to occur, save where the director does not realise his or her position and the likelihood of personal liability eventuating. Of course, a director subject to a guarantee might choose to pay off lenders holding such guarantees.

The fact is that when one considers the UK case law the duty has not been invoked in the **4.054** circumstances identified in the material set out above. The case law demonstrates that there are two broad situations in which the UK courts have held that the rule of law applies. First, where directors have sought to engaging in self-dealing, perhaps involving a transfer of company assets or funds to themselves or associates.[51] Secondly, where they have either turned a blind eye to their company's financial predicament or clearly just ignored it.[52]

The absence of case law on the rationale discussed above might chime with two matters. First, **4.055** professional directors might well refrain from engaging in risky activity lest the company does enter insolvent liquidation and this could well affect their reputations, thus meaning that they will find it hard to obtain another post. Allied to this is the fact that they might be subject to disqualification proceedings which if successful would mean that professional directors would lose their livelihood. Secondly, as mentioned earlier, with directors of owner-managed companies, they may well refrain from engaging in excessively risky action if they have granted guarantees to lenders. Perhaps the only instance where they may engage in excessive risk-taking is where the amount of debt owed is high and surpasses significantly what is owed to the lenders holding guarantees for in such a case the directors' personal liability will get no worse if they fail in their gamble with the company's affairs.

In *Walker v Wimborne* Mason J did not articulate any reason for his dictum. However, sub- **4.056** sequent case law arguably has done so. It appears to suggest that the rationale for the duty is simply to provide a form of protection for creditors. This was probably first articulated in the

---

49   L Lin, 'Shift of Fiduciary Duty upon Corporate Insolvency: Proper Scope of Directors' Duty to Creditors' (1993) 46 *Vanderbilt Law Review* 1485, 1489; P Davies, 'Directors' Creditor-Regarding Duties in Respect of Trading Decisions Taken in the Vicinity of Insolvency' (2006) 7 *EBOR* 301, 306.

50   See, C D Kandestin, 'The Duty to Creditors in Near-Insolvent Firms: Eliminating the '"The Near Insolvency" Distinction' (2007) 60 *Vanderbilt Law Review* 1235. Where professional directors are involved, they might well wish to refrain from engaging in risky activity lest the company does enter liquidation as this could well affect their reputations.

51   See, e.g., *Liquidator of West Mercia Safetywear Ltd v Dodd* [1988] 4 BCC 30; *GHLM Trading Ltd v Maroo* [2012] EWHC 61 (Ch); *Re HLC Environmental Projects Ltd (in liq)* [2013] EWHC 2876 (Ch), [2014] BCC 337; *Ball v Hughes* [2017] EWHC 3228 (Ch); *Joint Liquidators of CS Properties (Sales) Ltd* [2018] CSOH 24.

52   See, e.g., *Re Idessa (UK) Ltd* [2011] EWHC 804 (Ch), [2012] BCC 315. Also, see *Roberts v Frohlich* [2011] EWHC (Ch) 257, [2012] BCC 407 which may partly fit within this classification.

Australian case of *Kinsela v Russell Kinsela Pty Ltd*,[53] a case that has been regularly cited with approval in the UK for the past 30 years or so. In *Kinsela* Street CJ of the New South Wales Court of Appeal said that:

> In a solvent company the proprietary interests of the shareholders entitle them as a general body to be regarded as the company when questions of the duty of directors arise. If, as a general body, they authorise or ratify a particular action of the directors, there can be no challenge to the validity of what the directors have done. But where a company is insolvent the interests of the creditors intrude. They become prospectively entitled, through the mechanism of liquidation, to displace the power of the shareholders and directors to deal with the company's assets. It is in a practical sense their assets and not the shareholders' assets that, through the medium of the company, are under the management of the directors pending either liquidation, return to solvency, or the imposition of some alternative administration.[54]

4.057   The first UK appellate case to deal with the duty, *Liquidator of West Mercia Safetywear Ltd v Dodd*,[55] expressly approved of what Street CJ said. In the UK Supreme Court in *Bilta (UK) Ltd (in liquidation) v Nazir and others (No 2)*,[56] Lords Toulson and Hodge gave the above comments in *Kinsela* their support. They said in obiter that: 'The principle [obligation to consider creditor interests] and the reasons for it were set out with great clarity by Street CJ in *Kinsela v Russell Kinsela Pty Ltd*.'[57]

4.058   Lords Toulson and Hodge in *Bilta (UK) Ltd* said that the purpose of s 172(3) is to ensure that: 'the directors should not be off the hook if they act in disregard of the creditors' interests'.[58]

4.059   More recently, when considering the duty in some depth, David Richards LJ (in giving the leading judgment and approved of by Longmore and Henderson LJJ) in *BTI 2014 LLC v Sequana S.A.*[59] said that: 'the prospective interest of creditors in the assets of an insolvent company put forward by Street CJ in *Kinsela* and expressly adopted by this court in *West Mercia* is not simply the only rationale authoritatively established in this jurisdiction but continues to attract support'.[60] It should be noted that the decision of the Court of Appeal was appealed to the Supreme Court. At the time of going to press the appeal had been heard but no decision delivered.

4.060   All of the foregoing suggests that, as far as the courts are concerned, the rationale, or at least the predominant rationale, for the provision is simply to provide protection for the creditors. Certainly, this notion is in accord with what the CLRSG said in 1999 when it stated that duties of directors was subject to an overriding obligation to ensure that creditors are not wrongfully exposed to insolvency.[61]

---

53   (1986) 4 ACLC 215.
54   Ibid., 221.
55   [1988] 4 BCC 30.
56   [2015] UKSC 23, [2016] AC 1.
57   Ibid., [123].
58   Ibid., [130].
59   [2019] EWCA Civ 112, [2019] 2 All ER 784, [2019] BCC 631, [2019] 1 BCLC 347, [2019] BPIR 562.
60   Ibid., [217].
61   Company Law Review, *Modern Company Law for a Competitive Economy: The Strategic Framework*, (DTI, 1999), para 5.1.6.

3.   Who is subject to the duty?

Clearly de jure directors, namely those who have been appointed at law, are subject to the duty. **4.061**
Also, de facto directors, that is persons who assume the functions and status of a director,[62]
while never being appointed according to law,[63] are subject to the duty.[64] This might be a particular matter of concern for de facto directors as they may well not have the same opportunities
or constitutional power to make decisions about the company at a time when special considerations are called for.

Unlike de facto directors, who are not mentioned in either the Companies Act or the Act, **4.062**
shadow directors are. They are specifically defined in s 251 of the former legislation and s 251
of the latter (and in similar terms). Moreover s 170 of the Companies Act, which introduces
the part of the Act that deals with the general duties of directors, refers to them, and states in
s 170(5) that: 'the general duties apply to shadow directors where, and to the extent that, the
corresponding common law rules or equitable principles so apply'. It is clear from the cases
that the duty of care dealt with in s 174, will apply. But it is not clear that shadow directors are
subject to fiduciary duties. This is a matter that needs to be considered as s 172(3) constitutes
a fiduciary duty.

As far as the issue of whether shadow directors can be liable for breach of fiduciary duties **4.063**
there is conflicting case law. In a nutshell there are more cases in favour of liability. In *Yukong
Line Ltd of Korea v Rendsburg Investments Corp of Liberia (No 2)*[65] Toulson J (as he then was)
was strongly of the view that fiduciary duties did apply to shadow directors. Subsequently,
in *Ultraframe (UK) Ltd v Fielding*,[66] Lewison J (as he then was) was not so persuaded. In
more recent times two cases tend to support the former view. In *Secretary of State for Business
Innovation and Skills; Re UKLI Ltd*[67] Hildyard J seemed to suggest that a shadow director might
owe such duties. This approach was also taken by Newey J (as he then was) in *Vivendi SA v
Richards*.[68] His Lordship concluded that there were a number of reasons for adopting the view
that shadow directors do commonly owe fiduciary duties to at least some degree.[69] However, in
another recent decision, Morgan J in *Instant Access Properties Ltd (in liquidation) v Rosser*[70] said
that he, like Lewison J, did not think that an attempt to define the duties of a typical shadow
director was helpful. His Lordship said that: 'it may be preferable to ask instead whether in all
the circumstances of the case the individual [the shadow director] owed fiduciary duties, and if
so what duties, to a company'.[71]

---

62   It was common ground in *Instant* (see n 70 below) that de facto directors owe the same duties as de jure directors.
63   *Re Hydrodan (Corby) Ltd* [1994] 2 BCLC 180, 183; *Re Kaytech International Ltd* [1999] 2 BCLC 351; *Re Mea Corp Ltd*
     [2006] EWHC 1846 (Ch), [2007] BCC 288, [83].
64   See, for instance, see *Ultraframe UK Ltd v Fielding* [2005] EWHC 1638 (Ch), [2006] FSR 17, [1257]; *Primlake Ltd v
     Matthews Associates* [2006] EWHC 1227 (Ch), [2007] 1 BCLC 686, [284].
65   [1998] BCC 870.
66   [2005] EWHC 1638 (Ch), [1284].
67   [2013] EWHC 680 (Ch), [48].
68   [2013] EWHC 3006 (Ch).
69   Ibid., [142].
70   [2018] EWHC 756 (Ch), [2018] BCC 751, [259].
71   Ibid.

4.064   In the most recent case to consider this issue, *Standish v Royal Bank of* Scotland[72] Trower J acknowledged that shadow directors could be liable for breach of their fiduciary duties but, as with Newey J in *Viviendi* and Morgan J in *Instant Access,* he placed an important limitation on the scope of liability, namely that shadow directors can only be said to owe fiduciary duties in relation to that part of the company affairs in which they gave instructions or directions.[73] Thus, there still remains uncertainty over this issue and we await clear direction from the Court of Appeal.

4.   When does the obligation arise?

4.065   Section 172(3) requires different things of directors than does s 172(1). Therefore, it is important for directors to know when they have become subject to the application of s 172(3) or else they might well be confronted with making a decision at a time when they are unsure whether they should aim to fulfil the requirements of s 172(1) or the requirements of s 172(3). If there is doubt, then it might well pay directors to act conservatively and make a decision that takes account of creditors' interests. Why do we say this when, conceivably, such action of the directors could, if it is later found that the duty under s 172(3) had not in fact arisen, precipitate the shareholders instituting a derivative action on the basis that the directors were in breach of s 172(1)? There are, in our submission, three reasons why this is highly unlikely.

4.066   First,[74] shareholders need to obtain the permission of the court to prosecute such an action, and this process will involve cost to a shareholder and this fact together with the fact that permission has not been granted on a great many occasions might cause a shareholder to decide not to proceed.[75] Secondly, shareholders may well not have any knowledge of what directors have done by way of breach for some period, and by the time that they become aware and take advice the company might well have entered either administration or liquidation, or the company will have recovered, possibly justifying the action of the directors. Thirdly, directors might not in fact be in breach of the duty in s 172(1). The subsection requires directors to have regard to several factors set out in s 172(1)(a)–(f), but it also states that the factors in paras (a)–(f) are not to be seen as exhaustive of the directors' consideration. It appears very arguable that directors may have regard to creditors' interests (provided that in doing so it involves promoting the success of the company for the ultimate benefit of the members) and it might be thought to be prudent and proper that directors especially take creditors' interests into consideration when there are some doubts over the financial position and future of the company.

4.067   The problem is that there is no precise point at which time the duty arises, and this is, arguably, the most contentious and vague issue that is related to the duty. It can be contended that this has caused directors some difficulty in knowing when they are subject to the duty, and likewise

---

72   [2019] EWHC 3116 (Ch).

73   Ibid, [54] – [55]

74   The following section draws on parts of A Keay, 'Directors' Duties and Creditors' Interests' (2014) 130 *Law Quarterly Review* 443.

75   See A Keay and J Loughrey, 'An Assessment of the Present State of Statutory Derivative Proceedings' in J Loughrey (ed), *Directors' Duties and Shareholder Litigation in the Wake of the Financial Crisis* (Edward Elgar, 2013), Chapter 7; A Keay, 'Assessing and Rethinking the Statutory Scheme for Derivative Actions Under the Companies Act 2006' (2016) 16 *Journal of Corporate Law Studies* 39.

it has been difficult for liquidators to know when to institute proceedings against directors. This was acknowledged in the Court of Appeal in *BTI 2014 LLC v Sequana S.A* ('*Sequana*').[76] by David Richards LJ when he said that: 'the present structure of section 172, and the wording of section 172(3), implicitly recognise that a precise statement of the trigger is difficult'.[77]

Importantly for the purposes of this book, there is absolute certainty in the case law that when   **4.068** a company is insolvent the duty arises.[78] To be comprehensive we will consider other triggers, albeit briefly. Before doing so, it needs to be said that even the insolvency trigger point can be problematic, for while insolvency is the most precise point offered as the point when the duty arises, its precision is only relative.[79] Determining whether a company is insolvent is often not an easy task as was made evident in Chapter 3.[80] It is especially difficult when the company has contingent or even prospective liabilities. Added to the difficulty of establishing what insolvency actually involves is the fact that many companies can often move in and out of the state of insolvency. An important issue to note in this regard is that in small companies company accounts are often poorly maintained or not kept at all, thus it makes it even more difficult to determine whether a company is in fact insolvent. A major concern is that a company could be insolvent, and the directors do not realise it, and they continue to act as if the company was solvent. David Richards LJ in *Sequana* said the directors may often not know, nor be expected to know, that the company is actually insolvent until sometime after it has occurred.[81] Admittedly, there should be plain signs that a company is in serious difficulty if not insolvent, but directors might not be willing to face up to reality. A further factor is that while increasingly courts are indicating that it is necessary for directors to understand company accounts,[82] many do not and manifest the ostrich approach of putting their heads in the sand, not wanting to broach the issue of insolvency head-on. The failure to appreciate the state of a company accounts and what they mean can even occur in large companies.[83]

Clearly courts have held on many occasions that directors can be subject to the duty when the   **4.069** company is short of being insolvent but in financial difficulty. Over the years there have been several descriptive phrases invoked by courts to explain the point when the duty arises. In only

---

76   [2019] EWCA Civ 112, [2019] 2 All ER 784, [2019] 1 BCLC 347, [2019] BPIR 562.
77   Ibid., [202]. The decision of the Court of Appeal was appealed to the Supreme Court. At the time of going to press the appeal had been heard but no decision delivered.
78   This was made clear in ibid., but was fairly clear anyway before the decision as evidenced by the following cases: *Colin Gwyer v London Wharf (Limehouse) Ltd* [2002] EWHC 2748 (Ch), [2003] 2 BCLC 153; *Re Capitol Films Ltd (in admin)* [2010] EWHC 2240 (Ch), [2011] 2 BCLC 359; *Re Oxford Pharmaceuticals Ltd* [2009] EWHC 1753 (Ch), [2010] BCC 838; *Roberts v Frohlich* [2011] EWHC 257 (Ch), [2012] BCC 407, [2011] 2 BCLC 625; *Re HLC Environmental Projects Ltd* [2013] EWHC 2876 (Ch).
79   It is not precise for a number of reasons, such as the need for consideration to be had for liabilities that are due in the reasonably near future. See Re Cheyne Finance plc [2007] EWHC 2402 (Ch), [2008] 1 BCLC 741, [2008] BCC 182. For a detailed and useful discussion of the issue of insolvency, particularly in relation to a breach of duty to consider creditors' interests, see *Bell Group Ltd (in liq) v Westpac Banking Corporation (No 9)* [2008] WASC 239, especially [1061]–[1151].
80   See the comments of Briggs J (as he then was) in Re Cheyne Finance plc [2007] EWHC 2402 (Ch), [2008] 1 BCLC 741 and those of the Supreme Court in *BNY Corporate Trustee Services Ltd v Eurosail – UK 2007–3BL plc* [2013] UKSC 28, [2013] 1 WLR 1408.
81   [2019] EWCA Civ 112, [2019] 2 All ER 784, [2019] 1 BCLC 347, [2019] BPIR 562, [218].
82   D Milman, 'Strategies for Regulating Managerial Performance in the "Twilight Zone" – Familiar Dilemmas: New Considerations' (2004)] *JBL* 493, 497.
83   For instance, see the Australian case of *ASIC v Healy* [2011] FCA 717.

the second Court of Appeal decision to discuss the duty and the first for over 30 years, *Sequana*, David Richards LJ, with whose judgment Longmore and Henderson LJJ agreed, accepted that the duty can apply before a company becomes insolvent.[84] The judge said that on the subject of identifying a trigger short of insolvency: 'However, for good reason, not least because it has rarely been necessary, judges have shied away from a single form of words, preferring instead a variety of expressions such as those that I have mentioned.'[85]

4.070   Various different formulations were mentioned in courts as being the basis for the triggering of the duty.[86] An example is the company verging on insolvency.[87] Clearly there are overlaps between the formulations and many were extremely close in meaning. In *Re HLC Environmental Projects Ltd*[88] John Randall QC (sitting as a deputy High Court judge) said, after referring to many of the formulations, that they added up to the same thing.[89] In *Sequana*[90] David Richards LJ identified a problem with the different formulations as they suggest a temporal test. His Lordship said that:

> If the test is that insolvency is 'imminent', or if similar words are used, it suggests that actual insolvency will be established within a very short time. That may well describe many situations in which the duty is triggered, but it does not or may not cover the situation where, although the company may be able to pay its debts as they fall due for some time, perhaps a considerable time, to come, insolvency is nonetheless likely to occur and decisions taken now may prejudice creditors when the likely insolvency occurs.[91]

4.071   Importantly David Richards LJ rejected the argument that the duty was triggered where there was a real as opposed to a remote risk of insolvency.[92] He felt that this, if allowed, would provide for a much lower threshold for the application of the duty.[93] His Lordship adopted, with the concurrence of the other members of the court, the following as the test for when the duty arises, namely when the directors know or should know that the company is or is likely to

---

84   Ibid., [213].
85   Ibid., [216].
86   See, *Nicholson v Permakraft (NZ) Ltd* (1985) 3 ACLC 453, 459; *Re New World Alliance* (1994) 51 FCR 425, 444–445, (1994) 122 ALR 531; *The Liquidator of Wendy Fair (Heritage) Ltd v Hobday* [2006] EWHC 5803, [66]; *Geneva Finance Ltd v Resource and Industry Ltd* (2002) 20 ACLC 1427; *Eastford Ltd v Gillespie, Airdrie North Ltd* [2010] CSOH 132, [22]; *Colin Gwyer v London Wharf (Limehouse) Ltd* [2002] EWHC 2748 (Ch), [2003] BCC 885; *Kinsela v Russell Kinsela Pty Ltd* (1986) 4 ACLC 215, 223, (1986) 10 ACLR 395, 404; *Winkworth v Edward Baron Development Ltd* [1986] 1 WLR 1512; *Facia Footwear Ltd (in admin) v Hinchliffe* [1998] 1 BCLC 218; *Williams v Farrow* [2008] EWHC 3663 (Ch); *Linton v Telnet Pty Ltd* [1999] NSWCA 33, (1999) 30 ACSR 465; *Re MDA Investment Management Ltd* [2003] EWHC 227 (Ch), [2004] EWHC (Ch) 42, [2005] BCC 783; *Re Idessa (UK) Ltd* (sub nom *Burke v Morrison*) [2011] EWHC 804 (Ch), [2012] BCC 315, [55].
87   See, e.g., *Colin Gwyer v London Wharf (Limehouse) Ltd* [2002] EWHC 2748 (Ch), [2003] BCC 885, [74].
88   [2013] EWHC 2876 (Ch), [2014] BCC 337.
89   And approved on other occasions by, e.g., by Rose J at first instance in *BTI 2014 LLC v Sequana SA* [2016] EWHC 1686 (Ch).
90   [2019] EWCA Civ 112, [2019] 2 All ER 784, [2019] 1 BCLC 347, [2019] BPIR 562.
91   Ibid., [219].
92   Ibid., [214], [215]. This was one of the grounds for the appeal to the Supreme Court against the Court of Appeal's judgment.
93   Ibid., [214].

become insolvent.[94] According to the judge, in this context 'likely' means probable, not some lower test.[95]

While the courts have laid down some tests short of insolvency, there remains uncertainty and in 'the absence of a defined trigger can leave directors facing very difficult judgment calls'.[96] As nearly all judges hearing matters in relation to this duty have said, each case must be considered on its own facts.   **4.072**

We are focused on the position where a company is insolvent and while the fact of insolvency is not a matter of certainty, as we noted in earlier, it does provide more certainty than where the company is in bad shape but not legally insolvent.   **4.073**

5.   The content of the duty

(a) Introduction

Once a company is insolvent (or close to it) and the duty has been triggered, it is necessary for directors to think carefully what changes, in relation to their governance of the company, are needed. This is where the real corporate governance issue arises.   **4.074**

For some time, there has been uncertainty as to how creditors' interests are to be taken into account. Are they to be considered along with shareholders or are they to be considered as more important than shareholders? There have been suggestions in some UK and Commonwealth cases that the creditors' interests are to be taken into account with those of the shareholders. If that approach is implemented, then how do the directors make decisions while concerned for the interests of the two different stakeholders?   **4.075**

(b) Creditors' interests: are they paramount?

It would seem that all but one of the cases decided in the UK have taken the view that when a company is insolvent the rule of law to which s 172(3) refers requires directors to regard the creditors' interests as paramount. This can be seen plainly in a number of first instance English decisions, such as *Re Pantone 485 Ltd*,[97] *Colin Gwyer v London Wharf (Limehouse) Ltd*,[98] *Re Capitol Films Ltd (in administration)*,[99] *Re Oxford Pharmaceuticals Ltd*,[100] *Roberts v Frohlich*[101] and *Re HLC Environmental Projects Ltd*.[102] Although this approach was mentioned by the English Court of Appeal in *Sequana*,[103] it did not receive its unreserved imprimatur and the court did not have to consider what the duty required directors to do. Nevertheless, what was   **4.076**

---

94   Ibid., [220].
95   Ibid.
96   Clifford Chance, 'The Role of Directors in a Restructuring: is it Getting Tougher?' (2015) *Corporate Rescue and Insolvency* 208, 208.
97   [2002] 1 BCLC 266, [69].
98   [2002] EWHC 2748 (Ch), [2003] 2 BCLC 153, [74].
99   [2010] EWHC 2240 (Ch), [2011] 2 BCLC 359, [49].
100   [2009] EWHC 1753 (Ch), [2010] BCC 838, [92].
101   [2011] EWHC 257 (Ch), [2012] BCC 407, [2011] 2 BCLC 625, [85].
102   [2013] EWHC 2876 (Ch), [92].
103   [2019] EWCA Civ 112, [2019] 2 All ER 784, [2019] BCC 631, [2019] 1 BCLC 347, [2019] BPIR 562.

said pointed strongly in the direction of the Court accepting paramountcy where a company is insolvent. In giving the leading judgment in *Sequana,* David Richards LJ said that:

> As I have earlier mentioned, an important issue is whether, once the creditors' interests duty [that referred to in s 172(3)] is engaged, their interests are paramount or are to be considered without being decisive. This is not straightforward, and there has been a good deal of discussion about it in some of the cases and in the academic literature. It is not an issue that arises on the facts of this case and, in my view, it should be addressed on the facts of cases where it must be decided. I therefore express no view on it, save to say that where the directors know or ought to know that the company is presently and actually insolvent, it is hard to see that creditors' interests could be anything but paramount.[104]

4.077   This comment, together with the comments in earlier first instance decisions, makes it very hard to assert that when a company is insolvent the directors are not to regard the interests of the creditors as paramount. We might add that there is a divergence of opinion in first instance decisions as to whether paramountcy applies where a company is not insolvent but in a dire financial position or near insolvency.

4.078   Notably, it was agreed by the parties in *BTI 2014 LLC v Sequana SA*[105] at first instance that the content of the duty of directors does not vary according to the degree of risk of insolvency. There is no suggestion in the judgment at first instance or on appeal in *Sequana* that this was not correct.

4.079   It has been suggested that perhaps the pre-eminence of creditors' interests can be regarded as being consistent with s 172(3) in that this provision trumps s 172(1) when the relevant circumstances exist as s 172(1) is subject to any rule of law requiring directors to consider or act in the interests of creditors.[106] There are certainly some attractions to the courts applying a paramountcy approach where the company is insolvent. First, when the company is insolvent the creditors are clearly the primary stakeholders as all of the company property would be distributed to the creditors on a winding up. Secondly, this kind of approach is easier for the directors to apply as their focus is largely on what will benefit the creditors, not that ascertaining what is in the interests of creditors is itself an easy task, a matter we will take up shortly. If paramountcy did not exist then the directors might be forced, at least, to balance the interests of the creditors and shareholders, which would be, potentially, difficult. It can be hard enough to balance the interests of different types of creditors let alone trying to balance across broad stakeholder groups. Thirdly, it assists possible claimants such as liquidators in determining whether directors have complied with the obligation that is imposed on them.

4.080   Whilst it might be quite clear that the creditors' interests are paramount, what that actually means in practice might not be so clear. The word 'paramount' means something that is more important than anything else,[107] so we can conclude that the creditors' interests are to be seen as pre-eminent. Thus, this would suggest that directors must put the interests of creditors before any other concern or interest, including those of the shareholders, but it does not mean that it would necessarily be to the total exclusion of others' interests. However, in obiter in the Court

---

104   Ibid., [222].
105   [2016] EWHC 1686 (Ch) and noted by the Court of Appeal in an appeal in that case: [2019] EWCA Civ 112, [2019] 2 All ER 784, [2019] 1 BCLC 347, [2019] BPIR 562, [119].
106   A Keay, 'Directors' Duties and Creditors' Interests' (2014) 130 *LQR* 443, 443.
107   J Pearsall, *New Oxford Dictionary of English* (OUP, 2001), 1346.

of Appeal in *Brady v Brady*[108] Nourse LJ did say that where the company is insolvent the interests of the company are in reality the interests of existing creditors *alone*. While not mentioning the paramountcy of creditors' interests when a company is insolvent, Lesley Anderson QC (sitting as a deputy judge of the High Court) in *Re Idessa (UK) Ltd*[109] said that the interests of the creditors overrode those of the shareholders, and there probably is little difference between this and saying the interests of the creditors are paramount. The Irish Supreme Court in *Re Frederick Inns Ltd*[110] also seemed to require paramountcy.

The problem is that if the directors are not to see the creditors' interests as paramount how do **4.081** they possibly manage the company? The alternative is that they are to run the company taking into account the interests of the shareholders and creditors. As noted already, we submit that that would be exceedingly difficult.

In so many ways the interests of the shareholders and the creditors are likely to require directors **4.082** to act in totally different ways. The shareholders might well welcome directors engaging in excessive risk if there is some chance of redeeming the company's fortunes, while the creditors would not wish to see such an approach. In cases where the courts which have said that directors owe a duty to consider the interests of the shareholders and creditors have not considered how directors can do that. Obviously, what will be done will often depend on a company's affairs, the state of the business and the prospects for the business, but when it comes down to it the interests of the two stakeholder groups will not be at one or close to it. Arguably, the courts are imposing upon the directors a very difficult, perhaps unreasonable, task if they expect them to take into account both groups.

(c) What should directors do?

From a corporate governance perspective, it is of critical importance to determine how directors **4.083** are to conduct themselves when they are the subject of s 172(3). In considering this we need to accept that a company's position will change from time to time with the result that the circumstances that dictate what directors are to do will vary.[111] The courts[112] have made it clear when dealing with a solvent company that a director will only be held liable for a breach of s 172(1) if he or she fails to act in good faith and the courts have said that it might be harder for the directors to maintain that they acted in good faith when the company has incurred a substantial detriment. The same is likely to apply when a company is insolvent or in financial difficulties and the creditors have sustained a significant loss.[113] It is even more likely to be the case where the directors have benefitted personally from what they have done.[114]

The first thought that the directors should have when considering a course of action is: how will **4.084** this affect the creditors? Perhaps we can say that nothing should be done that prejudices the

---

108   (1987) 3 BCC 535, 552.
109   [2011] EWHC 804 (Ch), [2012] BCC 315, [54].
110   [1993] IESC 1, [47].
111   *Bell Group Ltd (in liq) v Westpac Banking Corporation (No 9)* [2008] WASC 239, [4440].
112   *Regentcrest plc v Cohen* [2002] 2 BCLC 80, 105; *Extrasure Travel Insurances Ltd v Scattergood* [2003] 1 BCLC 598.
113   *Roberts v Frohlich* [2011] EWHC 257 (Ch), [2012] BCC 407, [2011] 2 BCLC 625. Also see, *Dryburgh v Scotts Media Tax Ltd* [2011] CSOH 147, [94].
114   See *Re HLC Environmental Projects Ltd* [2013] EWHC 2876 (Ch).

interests of creditors. In the appeal in the Australian decision of *Westpac Banking Corporation v Bell Group Ltd (in liquidation) (No 3)*,[115] Drummond AJA said that:

> if the circumstances of the particular case are such that there is a real risk that the creditors of a company in an insolvency context would suffer significant prejudice if the directors undertook a certain course of action, that is sufficient to show that the contemplated course of action is not in the interests of the company.[116]

4.085   Other cases have suggested that the directors are not to be prejudiced by the action of the creditors, a reasonably recent instance being the decision in *Joint Liquidators of CS Properties (Sales) Ltd*.[117]

4.086   Indeed, we could say that everything that the directors do must provide an advantage for creditors or at least not be disadvantageous. The consequence is that the company's affairs are to be administered in such a way as to ensure that actions will enhance the wealth of creditors, or certainly not to derogate from their wealth. According to Leslie Kosmin QC (sitting as a deputy judge of the High Court),[118] directors, in the process of taking into account the interests of creditors, have to consider the impact of any decision on the ability of the creditors to recover the sums due to them from the company.[119] Paramountcy cannot simply entail directors refraining from disposing of assets improperly or diverting property to insiders in the company, which are obviously actions detrimental to the creditors (and arguably to the shareholders and a breach of other duties, save where all of the insiders constitute the entire shareholding body), but it extends to all of the duties that are owed, and functions undertaken, by directors. There will be very obvious breaches of duty, such as where directors decide to enter into a transaction that could not possibly benefit the creditors, as occurred in *Colin Gwyer v London Wharf (Limehouse) Ltd*,[120] but many other actions or inactions of directors are not going to be as clear-cut as they were in that case.[121]

4.087   It is clear from the cases that for a director to be in breach, there is no need to establish that he or she deliberately ignored the interests of the creditors; if it does not occur to the director to take account of a creditor's interest then that would suffice for a potential breach.[122]

4.088   The required reaction of directors to the existence of a state of affairs that would attract the operation of s 172(3) could be varied. In some cases it could be reducing expenditure and 'tightening the corporate belt', something that Lesley Anderson QC said should have happened in *Re Idessa (UK) Ltd*.[123] In others it might involve not commencing a project unless it was

---

115   [2012] WASCA 157.
116   Ibid., [2047].
117   [2018] CSOH 24. Also, see *Nicholson v Permakraft (NZ) Ltd* (1985) 3 ACLC 453.
118   *Colin Gwyer v London Wharf (Limehouse) Ltd* [2002] EWHC 2748, [2003] 2 BCLC 153.
119   Ibid., [81]. This view was also voiced by Lesley Anderson QC (sitting as a deputy High Court judge) in *Re Idessa (UK) Ltd* [2011] EWHC 804 (Ch), [2012] BCC 315, [120].
120   [2002] EWHC 2748, [2003] 2 BCLC 153, [80].
121   See, *Facia Footwear Ltd (in admin) v Hinchliffe* [1998] 1 BCLC 218, 228.
122   *Colin Gwyer v London Wharf (Limehouse) Ltd* [2002] EWHC 2748 (Ch), [2003] 2 BCLC 153, [78]; *Re HLC Environmental Projects Ltd* [2013] EWHC 2876 (Ch), [89].
123   [2011] EWHC 804 (Ch), [2012] BCC 315, [92], [112].

adequately funded,[124] or seeking refinancing that could support either a continuation of profitable trading of the company or the successful reorganisation of the company's affairs, as the termination of trading followed by the disposal of the assets of the companies on a forced sale basis could lead to heavy losses for the creditors.[125] It might be that the creditors' only chance of being paid in full (or even a reasonable portion of the debt) lies in a continuation of trading, but obviously it will be necessary for directors to weigh up the likely success of a restructuring given the state of the company's financial affairs and the information and advice available to them. In doing this the benefit for the creditors must be in the minds of the directors and not the continuing viability of the business,[126] or the interests of others, such as the employees.[127] Yet in other cases a company may be so insolvent that the directors cannot reasonably expect the company to survive and that it is appropriate to put the company into administration or liquidation as the directors in *Colin Gwyer*[128] perhaps should have done in the circumstances which confronted them.

Whether or not directors should cease trading depends substantially on the facts. Adopting such   **4.089**
an approach has some attractions for directors as it is likely to safeguard them, but the argument against it is that it might lead to the premature end for companies that have the potential to recover. Whether it is in fact appropriate or not to end trading or place the company in administration or liquidation is likely to depend heavily on the depth of the insolvency and, in light of market conditions and financing, the prospects of the company.

Can we say that taking into account the interests of creditors is akin to the directors in s 172(1)   **4.090**
being required to have regard for the factors set out in paras (a)–(f) of that provision or does it mean something different? It is submitted that it is different because in s 172(1) the factors are not the end concern of directors. The end concern is the interests of the members. Whereas under s 172(3) the interests of the creditors are not to be taken into account in achieving some other objective; the end concern of the directors would appear to be the creditors' interests. As indicated above, the case law suggests in many places that the directors are to consider the impact actions might have on creditors and they are not to prejudice the creditors. This suggests something more than merely having regard to creditor interests. Drummond AJA, who provided the most forthright of the judgments in the appellate court in *Westpac Banking Corp v Bell Group Ltd (in liquidation)(No 3)*,[129] said that directors have a duty to ensure that creditor interests are properly protected and these interests are not to be considered only as one of a number of stakeholder groups.[130] This latter comment probably accords with the law under s 172(3). Thus, to comply with s 172(3) it would appear that the interests of the employees and other stakeholders would not be taken into account in any directorial decision if that action were to prejudice creditors. It is not within the scope of the book to consider whether this is normative or not.

---

124   See, e.g., *Roberts v Frohlich* [2011] EWHC 257 (Ch), [2012] BCC 407, [2011] 2 BCLC 625.
125   *Facia Footwear Ltd (in admin) v Hinchliffe* [1998] 1 BCLC 218, 228.
126   *Sydlow Pty Ltd v Melwren Pty Ltd* (1993) 13 ACSR 144.
127   However, in *Re Welfab Engineers Ltd* [1990] BCC 600 Hoffmann J took account of employee interests.
128   [2002] EWHC 2748, [2003] 2 BCLC 153, [80].
129   [2012] WASCA 157.
130   Ibid., [2029].

4.091   As the responsibilities of directors are multifarious and the decisions that they make highly dependent on circumstances and the nature of their company, it is not possible to discuss specific actions that are to be taken by directors. However, we might note that the sorts of actions that directors might have to consider and then decide whether they accord with benefitting the creditors or not are as follows. First, the directors of an insolvent company might consider restructuring their company in an attempt to alleviate the insolvency problem.[131] Restructuring in this context involves a restructuring of debt and it is generally encouraged in order to try to save jobs and prevent further insolvencies, namely those of businesses that rely on the insolvent company in some way. Directors will be obliged to consider how any restructuring will affect the creditors primarily and not the other stakeholders. The frequent call from governments that leads to encouragement for restructuring as a way of preserving jobs and ensuring that communities are not affected (or, on occasions, devastated) is not really a matter with which directors should concern themselves where s 172(3) applies. This might be unpalatable to some who would like to see restructuring in order to prevent the prejudicing of stakeholders in general, while others would justify it on the basis that it is the creditors' money that is at stake and so no restructuring should occur that might be detrimental for creditors.

4.092   Secondly, the directors might be confronted with having to consider whether to pay certain creditors while the company is insolvent. The case law provides, of which *GHLM Trading Ltd v Maroo*[132] is an example, that directors must have regard for the interests of the creditors as a class. It has been argued that in paying creditors of the company care must be had for the overall interests of creditors.[133] It is obviously in the interests of the creditor who is paid, but it will not be in the interests of the remaining unsecured general creditors who will, if the company enters liquidation, have to be content with receiving less than 100p in the pound. Thus, it is submitted, that the payment of a creditor in full must only occur after considering the benefits to the creditors as a whole. Certain payments will be beneficial. For example, the paying of a creditor who refuses to supply any further goods to the company where those goods are critical to the continuation of the company's business are beneficial save where it is clear that the carrying on of the business is not viable. If the business shows signs of being able to recover, then it can be argued that the payment of the creditor mentioned above is necessary and in the interests of the creditors.

4.093   The decisions of directors must be taken in the context of the material available to them and the situation that existed at the relevant time.

(d) The interests of which creditors?[134]

4.094   Even if creditors' interests are to be seen as paramount, one particular problem that directors might have in some companies is the existence of many different creditor groups or classes, all with different kinds of interests, for the interests of creditors are not identical.

---

131   For more detailed discussion of restructuring in this context, see A Keay, 'Financially Distressed Companies, Restructuring and Creditors' Interests: What is a Director to do?' (2019) *LMCLQ* 297.

132   [2012] EWHC 61, [2012] 2 BCLC 369.

133   See, A Keay, 'Financially Distressed Companies, Preferential Payments and the Director's Duty to Take Account of Creditors' Interests' (2020) 136 *LQR* 52.

134   This section draws on A Keay, 'Directors' Duties and Creditors' Interests' (2014) 130 *LQR* 443.

It is not enough to identify that a party has an economic interest in an insolvency; the nature of **4.095**
that interest is relevant. For example, there are likely to be significant differences between the
interests of a bank with a charge over company assets compared with unsecured trade creditors.
This was mentioned by Snowden J when he stated:

> ...the inherent potential conflict between the interests of a secured creditor in achieving a sale at a level
> which sees it paid out, and the interests of the unsecured creditors in holding out or doing more to
> achieve a sale at a higher level.[135]

There might well even be a difference within actual classes of creditors. For instance, the inter- **4.096**
ests of an unsecured creditor who has lent money to the company might well have a different
perspective on an arrangement than a trade creditor, such as one who has built its business
around supplying the company. Different creditors might well have different agenda and they
are dealt with in different ways by the law, particularly on winding up.[136] Thus, what is in the
best interests of the creditors is, potentially, an even more complex issue where there are creditors with different aims and interests. Nevertheless, directors cannot be taken to know of the
preferences of creditors unless they have been expressed to them or they are obvious. Absent
this, directors would probably be expected to turn their mind to the legal rights that creditors
have and might have if there were a liquidation of the company. Therefore, it might be argued
that directors are in breach if they indiscriminately, or discriminately, pay some unsecured
creditors and not others of the same class.[137]

On occasions it can be difficult for directors to know what action to take where the interests of **4.097**
different creditors might conflict. Much will depend on the position of the creditors, how much
they are owed and what action is being contemplated.

In determining how to deal with the various kinds of creditors, with different interests, some **4.098**
assistance might be obtained from cases dealing with schemes of arrangement[138] where there
may be multiple groups of creditors with different interests and expectations and these may
well conflict. It is contended that the comments of Mann J in *Re Bluebrook Ltd*,[139] a scheme of
arrangement case, are important for our purposes. In this case a scheme of arrangement was
proposed, which restructured a group of companies in the interests of the senior lenders and
left the mezzanine lenders in one company in the group without any benefit. The mezzanine
lenders opposed the application to court for approval of the scheme. One of the grounds was
that the directors had breached their duty in failing to promote the interests of the mezzanine

---

135   *Davey v Money* [2018] EWHC 766, [2018] Bus LR 1903, [442]. In the earlier case *Re Capitol Films Ltd (in admin)*
[2010] EWHC 2240, [2011] 2 BCLC 359, the same judge (when sitting as a deputy High Court judge) had identified
the tension in administration between the interests of a fixed chargeholder, who may prefer to defer the sale of a secured
property, and the interests of the floating chargeholder and unsecured creditors, who are likely to benefit from the immediate sale of a business as a going concern, including the property that is the subject of the fixed charge: at [36]. Conflicts
may also arise between the holders of different tranches of secured debt: see *Re Bluebrook* [2009] EWHC 2114, [2010]
1 BCLC 338.

136   This issue is dealt with in greater depth in Andrew Keay, *Company Directors' Responsibilities to Creditors* (Routledge,
2007), 235–241.

137   See, A Keay, 'Financially Distressed Companies, Preferential Payments and the Director's Duty To Take Account of
Creditors' Interests' (2020) 136 *LQR* 52.

138   Addressed by Part 26 of the Companies Act 2006.

139   [2009] EWHC 2114 (Ch), [2010] 1 BCLC 338.

lenders. Counsel for the mezzanine lenders argued that directors of an insolvent company do not owe duties to particular sections of the creditors only.[140] The judge accepted that argument, but rejected the claim on the basis that the mezzanine lenders were 'out of the money' in that they had no economic interest in the company.[141] An example of what directors must do or not do falls from what Mann J said, namely that if a company is insolvent then a consideration of whether or not to preserve the business as a going concern must be guided by the interests of the creditors and not by consideration of the interests of some third party who has no claim.[142] The judge said that the directors:

> entered into arrangements with the section of *secured* creditors with priority over *subordinated* creditors who, on the facts as known to them, would not have any interest in the assets because of their subordination. That is entirely different from the situation where directors advance the cause of one creditor at the expense of other creditors who thereby lose a benefit they would otherwise have.[143]

4.099   It is submitted that the upshot of what his Lordship said in relation to schemes can be applied to directors considering creditors in an insolvency type situation. Applying what his Lordship said in this context, directors are to take into account the commercial realities of the company and they do not have to consider the interests of those creditors who are 'out of the money', namely a creditor who has no possibility of recovering money owed, even in a liquidation. Of course, it might not be possible in many cases for directors to know which creditors' money is effectively at stake and, therefore, who is actually out of the money, so that is always something of which they must be wary.

4.100   Sometimes the value of a creditor's interest might be difficult to ascertain. In *Wessely v White*[144] the judge said that in dealing with s 172(3) a subjective test applies as to what directors did and as to whether there has been a breach of duty in the situation where 'no material interest has been overlooked'.[145] If creditors are out of the money then they do not have 'a material interest' and, it follows, it can be overlooked.

4.101   Therefore, where a company is insolvent and it has, besides general unsecured creditors, creditors of another class, such as one or more secured creditors, it might be argued that if the company's funds/assets do not cover the debts owed to the secured creditors the directors should not take into account the unsecured creditors' interests as their money has gone, just like the shareholders' funds. That is, they are out of the money, and any trading would involve using the funds of the secured creditors and it would be at their risk. In such a position it might be thought appropriate that, in order to protect the interests of the secured creditors, the directors should take the company into administration or liquidation. To trade on and risk further funds might suit junior and unsecured creditors who have the hope that the company might be turned around, but it would not usually be favoured by secured creditors. Of course, determining who is out of the money is an exercise that might be difficult as directors would have to value the

---

140   Ibid., [67].
141   Ibid., [25], [80] and referring to *Re Tea Corp Ltd* [1904] 1 Ch 12.
142   Ibid., [67].
143   Ibid.
144   [2018] EWHC 1499 (Ch).
145   Ibid., [40].

company's assets and business to ascertain if certain creditors are out of the money. The matter of value can be a vexed exercise.

While it would seem that directors might ignore the interests of creditors where they are not **4.102** in the money and by some way, *Re Bluebrook Ltd*[146] indicates directors must ensure that they do not discriminate between creditors within a particular class. This is a sentiment that has been stated in the cases involving the director's obligation to creditors. In *Re Pantone* Richard Field QC (sitting as a deputy High Court judge) said that a director is not in breach if he or she acts consistently with the interests of the general creditors but inconsistently with the interests of a creditor or a section of creditors with special rights in a liquidation,[147] hence it follows that if a director favours one creditor or a section of creditors to the prejudice of the general creditors as a whole, then he or she is in breach. This approach was followed by Newey J in *GHLM Trading Ltd v Maroo*,[148] when he said that where a company is insolvent then the director's duty involves having regard for the interests of the creditors as a class. His Lordship said that: 'If a director acts to advance the interests of a particular creditor, without believing the action to be in the interests of creditors as a class, it seems to me that he will commit a breach of duty.'[149]

Conversely then, and as mentioned earlier, we might conclude that a director can advance the **4.103** interests of a specific creditor provided that he or she believes that it will be in the interests of creditors as a class. If, for instance, one or more creditors benefit from a restructuring at the expense of others, then it suggests that there is a breach, except where the latter were out of the money.

What about the interests of future, contingent and prospective creditors? Are they relevant? At **4.104** present there is no definitive answer to this. The clearest view that we have in relation to future creditors is that of Lord Templeman in *Winkworth v Edward Baron Development Co Ltd*.[150] His Lordship plainly said: '[A] company owes a duty to its creditors, present and future.'[151]

In *Fulham Football Club Ltd v Cabra Estates plc*,[152] the Court of Appeal stated that: 'The duties **4.105** owed by the directors are to the company and the company is more than just the sum total of its members. Creditors, both present and *potential*, are interested' (our emphasis). The use of the word 'potential' suggests that an obligation was owed to future creditors of the company, although it must be noted that in this case the court was not considering the usual case where a company is insolvent or close to it and the comment was very much made in passing. Yet in a case which considered the duty, the majority of a bench of the Australian High Court in *Spies v The Queen*[153] said that comments in the authorities suggest that the directors owed a duty to the company to consider the interests of creditors and potential creditors of the company.

---

146   [2009] EWHC 2114 (Ch), [2010] 1 BCLC 338.
147   Ibid., [73].
148   [2012] EWHC 61, [2012] 2 BCLC 369.
149   Ibid., [168]. Also, see *Capital For Enterprise Fund A LP and another v Bibby Financial Services Ltd* [2015] EWHC 2593 (Ch), [89].
150   [1986] 1 WLR 1512, [1987] 1 All ER 114.
151   Ibid., 1516, 118.
152   [1994] BCLC 363, 379.
153   [2000] HCA 43, (2000) 201 CLR 603, (2000) 173 ALR 529, [93].

4.106 Nevertheless, there are indications from the decision of Cooke J In *Nicholson v Permakraft (NZ) Ltd*,[154] that the duty was owed to current and continuing trade creditors, and it would be much more difficult to make out a duty to future new creditors, on the basis that future creditors have to take a company as they find it when they decide to do business with it.[155] However, the judge's view has not attracted a lot of support in later cases.

4.107 In the New South Wales Court of Appeal, Young CJ in Eq, in *Edwards A-G*.[156] seemed to imply that, at the moment he was giving his judgment, future creditors were not covered by the duty, but his Honour said that a court might extend the principles devised in relation to the duty and hold that a company in a precarious financial position might not only owe duties to the shareholders and creditors but also to likely future creditors.

4.108 Most recently, in the UK Supreme Court decision of *Bilta (UK) Ltd (in liquidation) and others v Nazir*,[157] Lords Toulson and Hodge JJSC stated,[158] in the context of considering duties owed by directors when their company is insolvent, that the directors do have a duty to take account of the interests of prospective creditors of their company. The comment was obiter, and the other judges did not consider the matter. Also, in *Angel Group Ltd v Davey*[159] Fancourt J said that when a company is insolvent or bordering on insolvency the directors must have proper regard for the interests of prospective creditors. In the Western Australian Court of Appeal in *Bell Group*[160] the majority view of the court suggested that every creditor's interest needs to be taken into account.

6. Exculpation from liability

4.109 As with all breaches of duty a director may ask a court to invoke the terms of s 1157 of the Companies Act. This permits a court to excuse an officer from liability arising out of his or her negligence, breach of duty or breach of trust on the basis that he or she had acted honestly and reasonably, and, as a consequence of his or her actions, ought fairly to be excused from liability. Naturally each case has to be taken on its merits as to whether s 1157 can be applied.[161]

7. Comment

4.110 While many would argue that the directors of a solvent company should be accountable to the company entity,[162] the preponderance of UK case law provides, in effect, that directors are accountable to the shareholders, as it states in s 170(3) of the Companies Act that the duties of directors are owed to the company as a whole and that has been taken to mean the

---

154 (1985) 3 ACLC 453.
155 Ibid., 459.
156 [2004] NSWCA 272, [153].
157 [2015] UKSC 23, [2016] AC 1.
158 Ibid., [123].
159 [2018] EWHC 1781 (Ch), [89].
160 [2012] WASCA 157.
161 For a discussion of the provision, see Andrew Keay, *Directors' Duties*, (4th ed, LexisNexis, 2020), Chapter 17.
162 See, e.g., Andrew Keay, *Board Accountability in Corporate Governance* (Routledge, 2015), Chap 4.

shareholders.[163] From a governance perspective it is interesting to note that when a company is insolvent the directors owe a duty to consider the interests of the creditors and they are paramount; the directors are not accountable to the creditors. They actually remain accountable to the shareholders, just as they were when the company was solvent. However, the nature of what the directors are accountable for changes. That is, when the company is insolvent the directors are no longer accountable to promote the success of the company for the benefit of the shareholders, but they are to account for what they have done as far as considering the interests of the creditors. Nevertheless, this is rather academic because it is unlikely that there will be a general meeting of the shareholders during insolvency and even if there is a meeting it is even more unlikely that the directors will disclose what they have been doing to further the interests of the creditors.

The discussion of the duty just considered might seem to place, potentially, significant burdens **4.111** on directors who might be under substantial stress, and directors might have the feeling that they are under great pressure from the duty, but that perception might well be incorrect for several reasons, three of which we mention here. First, the case law has indicated that provided that the directors, acting in good faith, consider the interests of the creditors they are not going to be liable. Secondly, even if they did not consider the interests of creditors, or a court disbelieves the directors when they saw that they did take into account creditor interests, they will not be liable provided that a court takes the view that an honest and intelligent director would have believed that the decision was for the benefit of the creditors.[164]

Thirdly, in the leading judgment in the Court of Appeal decision in *Sequana*[165] David Richards **4.112** LJ expressed some concern for the plight of directors and that they should not be hindered in engaging in entrepreneurism,[166] thus courts might be willing to show some leniency to directors provided that they have not acted in a totally irresponsible manner.

H. WRONGFUL TRADING

1. Introduction

Thus far we have been considering the responsibility of directors where the company is insol- **4.113** vent. We continue to do so in this part of the chapter, but we must note that the obligation that we discuss here might, like the duty to take account of creditors' interests, arise before a company is actually insolvent. This part of the chapter deals with an obligation imposed on directors by the Act to refrain from engaging in wrongful trading.

---

163 See, e.g., *Re Smith & Fawcett Ltd* [1942] Ch 304; *Greenhalgh v Arderne Cinemas* [1951] Ch 286, 291; *Peters American Delicacy v Heath* (1939) 61 CLR 457; *Parke v Daily News Ltd* [1962] Ch 927, 963; *Gaiman v National Association for Mental Health* [1971] Ch 317, 330.
164 *Colin Gwyer & Associates Ltd v London Wharf (Limehouse) Ltd* [2002] EWHC 2748 (Ch), [2003] BCC 885, [87], applying to an insolvent or near insolvent company what was said in Charterbridge Corp Ltd v Lloyds Bank Ltd [1970] Ch 62 in relation to a solvent company.
165 [2019] EWCA Civ 112, [2019] 2 All ER 784, [2019] 1 BCLC 347, [2019] BPIR 562.
166 For instance, see ibid., [200].

4.114 The term 'wrongful trading' is not mentioned in the Act and the use of it is, in our view, inappropriate because the Act does not require directors to act wrongfully in the sense of culpably for them to be liable. The trading that offends against what is the wrongful trading section in the Act, s 214 is, perhaps, better referred to as 'irresponsible' or 'illicit'.[167] Nevertheless, the term 'wrongful trading' is used widely in case law[168] and the literature in the area and thus we employ it in the chapter.

4.115 The rule that implements a prohibition against wrongful trading affects the management and control that directors have within companies and the issue of wrongful trading, like the duty to account for creditors' interests, is worthy of some extended consideration.

4.116 Wrongful trading is proscribed by s 214 of the Act. It provides that the liquidator of a company that is in insolvent liquidation (effectively the situation where a company's assets are not sufficient to pay its debts at the time of liquidation[169]) may commence proceedings against the company's directors, and seek an order that the directors make such contribution to the company's assets as the court thinks proper.[170] Directors will only be liable if at some time before the commencement of the winding up of the company, they knew or ought to have concluded that there was no reasonable prospect that the company would avoid going into insolvent liquidation.[171] If a liquidator can establish this, a defence exists in that directors are not liable if the court is satisfied that after the directors first knew or ought to have concluded that there was no reasonable prospect that the company would avoid going into insolvent liquidation, they took every step with a view to minimising the potential loss to the company's creditors as they ought to have taken.[172] It is on this defence that we will spend some time as it could well affect what the directors do in terms of governance.

4.117 Wrongful trading only became a matter of concern for directors when s 214 of the Act came into force in 1986. The provision was introduced in order to encourage directors to minimise the losses of creditors when their company is in financial difficulty. Administrators now also have the right to bring proceedings for wrongful trading. This right came about through the enactment of s 117 of the Small Business, Enterprise and Employment Act 2015 which provided for a new section in the Act, s 246ZB. For ease of exposition, we will only refer, for the most part, to s 214. The law developed in relation to this provision will apply equally to s 246ZB. We will refer to liquidators taking action but obviously what we say could well apply to administrators.

4.118 Section 214 can be perceived as a form of regulation that is designed to have directors undertake certain actions in order to prescribe how the directors are to behave to produce a particular

---

167 The latter term was employed by A Keay and M Murray, 'Making Company Directors Liable: A Comparative Analysis of Wrongful Trading in the United Kingdom and Insolvent Trading in Australia' (2005) 14 *International Insolvency Review* 27.

168 For instance, see the recent case of *Nicholson v Fielding* (unreported, 15 September 2017, Deputy Registrar Prentis, Ch D), 2017 WL 04225693, [24].

169 Section 214(6) of the Act. This is a balance sheet test.

170 Section 214(1).

171 Section 214(2).

172 Section 214(3).

outcome.[173] In this regard, the wrongful trading provision was introduced in order to necessitate directors taking action in order to address the situation where directors ascertain their company is in difficulty and they do nothing to protect creditors' interests; directors are to be required to engage in better and more diligent monitoring of the health of their companies. Thus, the section was introduced not to penalise directors for the fact that their company had become insolvent, but to require directors to do something where they saw that their company was in difficulty, and perhaps insolvent.

Effectively, s 214 provides a stick approach to make directors more accountable and to induce **4.119** the raising of directorial standards. The provision is not intended to be a provision that compensates creditors by proscribing wrongful trading, but it is an attempt to ensure that wrongful trading does not actually occur so that such compensation is unnecessary. The provision can be seen as an attempt to 'align the interests of managers of firms [although it is not limited to the managers alone] on the verge of insolvency with the interests of the firm's creditors'.[174] The section is 'premised on conduct by directors which does not meet the standard of competence objectively to be expected of directors'.[175] Of course, if directors fail to act appropriately then compensation may be ordered and this will ultimately benefit the creditors.

As with the duty to take account of the interests of the creditors, directors are forced, when, **4.120** they know or ought to conclude that there is no reasonable prospect that the company would avoid going into insolvent liquidation (or insolvent administration), to have consideration for the interests of creditors, for if a company is heading for insolvent liquidation the creditors of the company, as we have seen already, are effectively the ones who have a residual claim over the company's assets,[176] that is, a claim by those whose wealth directly rises or falls with changes in the value of the company.[177]

How s 214 affects corporate governance is seen in the defence that is available to directors **4.121** under s 214(4) and mentioned above. Before considering that and what effects the wrongful trading provision has on corporate governance, we need to establish what the provision means and how it is applied. We do so briefly.

The provision was an implementation of the recommendations of the Cork Committee in **4.122** its 1982 Report.[178] There had been grave concerns at that time concerning the practical use of fraudulent trading, now contained in s 213 of the Act but then part of the Companies Act 1948, as this only covered actions where there was an intent to defraud. There were perceived inadequacies with fraudulent trading in dealing with irresponsible trading[179] and courts were reluctant to find directors and others liable for fraudulent trading given that they were saying

---

173   K Yeung, 'Private Enforcement of Competition Law' in C McCrudden (ed), *Regulation and Deregulation* (Clarendon Press, 1999), 40.

174   R Mokal, 'On Fairness and Efficiency' (2003) 66 MLR 452, 461.

175   *Brooks v Armstrong* [2017] EWHC 2893 (Ch), [2017] BCC 99, [139].

176   S Schwarcz, 'Rethinking a Corporation's Obligations to Creditors' (1996) 17 *Cardozo Law Review* 647, 668.

177   D Baird, 'The Initiation Problem in Bankruptcy' (1991) 11 *International Review of Law and Economics* 223, 228–229; S Gilson and M Vetsuypens, 'Creditor Control in Financially Distressed Companies' (1994) 72 *Wash ULQ* 1005, 1006. Until there is financial strife a company's residual claimants are its shareholders.

178   Insolvency Law Review Committee, *Insolvency Law and Practice*, Cmnd 858, (HMSO, 1982).

179   Ibid., [1776]–[1780].

that the respondents were dishonest. The Cork Committee was concerned that unsecured creditors were not protected adequately and it took the view that compensation ought to be available to those persons who experience loss due to unreasonable behaviour as well as fraudulent action.[180] It was concerned that the existing fraudulent trading provision had failed in curbing directors running up losses when their companies were in deep financial difficulty.[181]

4.123   It is appropriate to mention at this point that the Corporate Insolvency and Governance Act 2020, which partly was enacted in reaction to the COVID-19 pandemic which commenced in 2020, suspended liability for wrongful trading for the period from 1 March 2020 until 30 September 2020. The Corporate Insolvency and Governance Act provided that a court is to assume that a director is not responsible for the worsening of a company's financial position or that of the company's creditors during this period.[182] The objective behind what the government did was to remove the deterrent of personal liability in order that directors did not have to take it into account when deciding whether or not a company whose business has been impacted by the effects of the pandemic should continue trading, and this was to try and prevent companies from entering insolvency regimes unnecessarily. In November 2020 the government introduced a further suspension of liability for the period from 26 November until 30 April 2021.[183] On 21 March 2021 the government in reg 2 of the Corporate Insolvency and Governance Act 2020 (Coronavirus) (Extension of the Relevant Period) Regulations 2021[184] further extended the suspension of liability for wrongful trading to 30 June 2021. This suspension will provide some comfort for directors, although there might be some concern that there is a period of about two months (30 September to 26 November 2020) where the suspension does not apply. It should be noted that while wrongful trading is suspended a director must still during the periods of wrongful trading suspension take into account the interests of creditors as discussed earlier.

2.   What is wrongful trading?

4.124   It will be recalled that directors are liable for wrongful trading and, therefore, liable to make contributions to the assets of the company if at some time before the commencement of the winding up of the company, they knew or ought to have concluded that there was no reasonable prospect that the company would avoid going into insolvent liquidation.[185] What is conveyed here is the idea that if the circumstances in the last sentence exist then the directors must possibly look at changing what is being done on the basis that how the company is being run is not working. Thus, the following might constitute engaging in wrongful trading: the paying of overly generous dividends, selling company assets at an undervalue and the payment of excessive remuneration to directors, as well as the incurring of liabilities when the directors knew or ought to have known that the company was likely not going to be able to satisfy those liabilities and existing liabilities.[186] In relation to remuneration it should be noted that in *Re*

---

180   Ibid., [1777].
181   Ibid., [1776]–[1778].
182   See s 12 of the Corporate Insolvency and Governance Act 2020.
183   This was provided for by reg 2 of the Corporate Insolvency and Governance Act 2020 (Coronavirus) (Suspension of Liability for Wrongful Trading and Extension of the Relevant Period) Regulations 2020 (SI 2020/148).
184   SI 2021/375.
185   Section 214(2) of the Act.
186   S Griffin, *Personal Liability and Disqualification of Company Directors*, (Hart Publishing, 1999).

Purpoint Ltd[187] the court was critical of one of the directors for the excessive remuneration that he received. However, directors do not, it would seem from what Snowden J said in *Re Ralls Builders Ltd*,[188] have to give up receiving reasonable salaries for their work.[189]

Due to the fact that the word 'trading' is not actually referred to in s 214, it might be argued **4.125** that activity that falls short of what might usually be seen as actual trading, such as selling assets with a view to winding up the company or failing to collect debts owed, can form the basis of an action.

3.   The components for a claim

For a claim to be made the company must have entered insolvent liquidation.[190] According **4.126** to s 214(6) insolvent liquidation means that the company, at the time of winding up, was in a position where its debts and liabilities, together with the expenses of winding up, exceeded its assets. So, a balance sheet test, as provided for under s 122(2) is included.[191] While the majority of liquidations do involve insolvent companies, we must note that if a company was not insolvent within the meaning of s 214(6) no proceedings could be brought.

We have already noted that the respondent must be a director (or former director). 'Director' **4.127** should include a de facto, one would think, given the definition of 'director' in the Act, and this is confirmed by *Re Hydrodan (Corby) Ltd*.[192] Section 214(7) specifically provides that a shadow director can be guilty of wrongful trading.

Trading when insolvent does not automatically determine that directors are liable for wrongful **4.128** trading,[193] although it should mean that the directors will be taking different steps to ensure that they do not fall foul of s 214. Rather, as we have mentioned, it must be established, given s 214(2), that at some time prior to the commencement of winding up the respondent knew or ought to have concluded that there was no reasonable prospect of the company avoiding going into insolvent liquidation. Subjective knowledge, that is actual knowledge of there being no reasonable prospect of avoidance of insolvent liquidation, is not the only test. A director can also be liable if a court reasons that the directors should have concluded that liquidation could not be avoided. This may well prevent a director who is either shirking or incompetent from being able to elude liability. It also means that if the director has taken professional advice in relation to the company's malaise it is possible that a court might be more ready to decide that the directors ought to have concluded that there was no reasonable prospect of the company avoiding insolvent liquidation.[194]

---

187   [1991] BCC 121, 125;, [1991[BCLC 491, 495.
188   [2016] EWHC 243 (Ch), [2016] BCC 293.
189   [2016] EWHC 243 (Ch), [2016] BCC 293 at [248].
190   Section 214(2)(a) of the Act.
191   For a discussion of this test, see Chapter 3; Kristen van Zwieten (ed), *Goode on Principles of Corporate Insolvency Law*, (5th ed, Sweet & Maxwell, 2019), [4.06]; Andrew Keay, *McPherson and Keay's Law of Company Liquidation*, (5th ed, Sweet & Maxwell, 2021) [3.05] – [3.37].
192   [1994] BCC 161, 162.
193   *Re Sherborne Associates Ltd* [1995] BCC 40; *Secretary of State for Trade and Industry v Gash* [1997] 2 BCLC 341.
194   See, *Re Ralls Builders Ltd* [2016] EWHC 243 (Ch), [2016] BCC 293.

4.129   Section 214(4) expands on s 214(2) (and s 214(3)) and it sets out the approach that a court must take in assessing a claim, and provides that the facts that a director ought to know or ascertain, and the conclusions which ought to be reached are those that a reasonably diligent person would take or have taken and who has the general knowledge, skill and experience that may reasonably be expected of a person who carries out the same functions as are carried out by the respondent director, and, in addition, that person has the general knowledge, skill and experience that the respondent director possesses. All of this provides for a combination of both subjective and objective elements. The objective element of the provision is marked by the reference to the reasonably diligent person and the general knowledge, skill and experience that may reasonably be expected of a person who carries out the same functions as the respondent. Thus, if a director carries out a specialist role, such as finance director, his or her actions will be considered in light of the reasonably diligent director who would have the skill and experience of a person who is qualified to act in that specialised role.

4.130   The subjective element introduces the general knowledge, skill and experience of the director, himself or herself, namely something that is specific to the respondent director. The inclusion of the subjective element does mean that there is a reduction in the standard of knowing or ascertaining. In fact, it raises it if the director is experienced. So, if a director is not very experienced or does not have qualities that match that of the reasonable person, he or she is not able to take advantage of that fact and be protected from liability; ignorance or lack of experience is not an excuse.[195]

4.131   All of the above means that directors are not going to be held liable merely because they agreed to their company continuing to trade. The issue is far more nuanced.

4.132   It is critical that a particular time is established from which the director should have realised that insolvent liquidation was inevitable.[196] So, the key issue is clearly: at what time did the director know or should have concluded that there was no reasonable prospect of the company avoiding insolvent liquidation? Clearly a director is not going to be able to rely solely on a feeling that things would get better. He or she would have to be able to point to something that indicated to the reasonable person in his or her position that the company's position would either improve or, at least, not deteriorate. The director could not rely on the fact that he or she had a good faith belief that the company's position would be ameliorated.

4.133   The director must be proved to have known that the company had no reasonable prospect of avoiding insolvent liquidation. The phrase 'reasonable prospect' is elusive.[197] It is difficult for directors in many situations, leaving aside those cases where their company is clearly hopelessly insolvent and could not possibly recover, or the slide into insolvency appears to be unable to be stopped, to determine whether insolvent liquidation is the company's fate. One would think that directors have to consider the overall position of the company and its accounts accompanied by some professional finance advice to be able to come to a view. Importantly, one would think, directors would have to consider what plans the company has, what are the company's

---

195   *Re Brian D. Pierson (Contractors) Ltd* [1999] BCC 26, 55, [2001] BCLC 275, 309.

196   For a discussion about the point when the liquidator will argue that insolvent trading commenced, see A Keay, 'Wrongful Trading and the Point of Liability' (2006) 19 *Insolvency Intelligence* 132.

197   F Oditah, 'Wrongful Trading' (1990) LMCLQ 205, 208.

prospects as far as its business goes, what is the general market situation for its products and the state of the market overall as far as it affects the company and its business, and whether funds are likely to be received in the short term. Certainly, temporary cash-flow problems should not be seen as meaning, necessarily, that the company is heading for insolvent liquidation,[198] but, obviously continual problems in this regard must be seen as warning signs. Just returning to the issue of accounts, directors must keep on top of the financial position of their companies, and, in accordance with what the law now requires of directors, they must be able to understand company accounts.[199] If they are not able to do so, then they must employ someone who can advise them appropriately.[200]

The case law suggests that it is not likely that directors who have made an effort to understand the position of their company and where they have actually considered whether there should be a continuation of business, will be held liable.[201] Indeed, in *Re Continental Assurance of London plc*[202] Park J said that the typical case in which directors have been held to be liable is where the directors have: '[C]losed their eyes to the reality of the company's position, and carried on trading long after it should have been obvious to them that the company was insolvent and that there was no way out for it.'[203] Unreasonable expectations of directors are not usually held by courts. Hoffmann J said in *Re CU Fittings Ltd*[204] that: 'directors immersed in the day to day task of trying to keep their business afloat cannot be expected to have wholly dispassionate minds'. However, he later said that: 'there comes a point at which an honest businessman recognises that he is only gambling at the expense of his creditors on the possibility that something may turn up'.[205] **4.134**

It is probably advisable that directors record all their decisions and what information they have sought and considered, as well as why decisions were taken. It would also be advisable that directors obtain all available information about the company, and that should include not only what is available to them, but what ought to be available,[206] and that which they could have reasonably obtained,[207] such as documents or information concerning the financial state of the company. **4.135**

In determining what directors did, why they did it and whether their actions infringed s 214, courts will possess hindsight and the courts have acknowledged that they must acknowledge that and be wary of making assumptions about the circumstances and that the directors should have been able to foresee the consequences of their decisions.[208] Courts must consider the **4.136**

---

198   Ibid.
199   See, *Re DKG Contractors Ltd* [1990] BCC 903; *ASIC v Healy* [2011] FCA 717.
200   *Re Hitco 2000 Ltd* [1995] 2 BCLC 63.
201   For instance, see *Re Sherborne Associates Ltd* [1995] BCC 40; *Re Continental Assurance of London plc* [2001] BPIR 733.
202   [2001] BPIR 733.
203   Ibid., 769.
204   [1989] BCLC 556, 559.
205   Ibid.
206   P Fidler, 'Wrongful Trading after Continental Assurance' (2001) 17 I L & P 212, 215.
207   *Re Produce Marketing Consortium Ltd* (1989) 5 BCC 569, 595.
208   *Re Sherborne Associates Ltd* [1995] BCC 40, 54; *Re Brian Pierson Ltd* [1999] BCC 26, 50, [2001] BCLC 275, 303; *Re Idessa (UK) Ltd* [2011] EWHC 804 (Ch), [2012] BCC 315; *Re Ralls Builders Ltd* [2016] EWHC 243 (Ch), [2016] BCC 293, [173].

decisions of the director in the context of the material and information available to him or her and the kind of circumstances that existed at the relevant time. The case law tends to suggest that the courts have not used hindsight to the detriment of respondents, with directors being, in some cases, given the benefit of any doubts that might exist. While hindsight should be eschewed, the court should adopt rational expectations of what the future might hold.[209] All of this does not mean that a court is prohibited from considering what actually happened.[210]

4.137 While courts will expect certain minimum standards are to be attained in whatever the company, for example, to cause accounting records to be maintained,[211] courts will have regard for the kind of company managed by the director, as well as the type of business in which it was involved[212] and the kind and role of directors concerned. Courts will expect less general knowledge, skill and experience of a director of a small company than a person who is a director in a large company that has extensive resources.[213] Allowances are likely to be made in the case of non-executive and part-time directors.[214] Probably, as indicated earlier, more might be expected of some directors, with particular knowledge and/or experience in specialist fields.

4.138 It must be emphasised that the obligation imposed on directors in s 214 does not provide directors with a duty to ensure that their company does not trade while insolvent. Chadwick J in *Re C S Holidays Ltd*[215] said that:

> The directors may properly take the view that it is in the interests of the company and of its creditors that, although insolvent, the company should continue to trade out of its difficulties. They may properly take the view that it is in the interests of the company and its creditors that some loss-making trade should be accepted in anticipation of future profitability. They are not to be criticised if they give effect to such a view.[216]

4.139 The fact that a company was insolvent at some point and then continued to trade does not, according to *Re Ralls Builders Ltd*,[217] necessarily lead to the conclusion that a director with knowledge of that fact is liable if the company subsequently failed to survive. It is not out of the ordinary for a company to have a balance-sheet deficit from time to time but despite this have a real chance of trading out of the difficulty or otherwise recovering from the deficiency and, as a consequence, avoiding insolvent liquidation. In a similar manner, companies often experience cash-flow difficulties and fail to pay their creditors on time but are able to overcome those problems in some way.[218]

---

209 *Re Hawkes Hill Publishing Co Ltd* [2007] BCC 937, [41].
210 *Jackson v Casey* [2019] EWHC 1657 (Ch), [184].
211 *Re Produce Marketing Consortium Ltd* (1989) 5 BCC 569, 595.
212 Ibid., 594; *Re Sherborne Associates Ltd* [1995] BCC 40, 54; *Re Brian Pierson Ltd* [1999] BCC 26, 50, [2001] BCLC 275, 303.
213 *Re Produce Marketing Consortium Ltd* (1989) 5 BCC 569, 594–595.
214 L Sealy and D Milman, *Annotated Guide to the Insolvency Legislation*, (second revised 7th ed., Sweet & Maxwell, 2004), 227.
215 [1997] 1 WLR 407.
216 Ibid., 414.
217 [2016] EWHC 243 (Ch); [2016] BCC 293.
218 Ibid., [168].

4.   The defence

If directors act in such a way that they can invoke what the defence covers then it is likely **4.140**
that they will not be the subject of legal proceedings and, more importantly, they are acting in
a manner in which they are required. That is, the appropriate corporate governance practice is
being adhered to.

The only defence that is available to a claim under s 214 is found in s 214(3) and provides **4.141**
that the court must be satisfied that after becoming aware that the insolvent liquidation of
the company could not be avoided, the director took 'every step with a view to minimising
the potential loss to the company's creditors as [on the assumption that he had knowledge
that there was no reasonable prospect that the company would avoid going into insolvent
liquidation]…he ought to have taken'. The principal concern with this is that it is vague – what
constitutes every step? Of importance is the fact that it is virtually impossible to know, until
a court hears a case and gives its judgment, whether a director has in fact fulfilled the requirement. Nevertheless, it is not prudent to throw one's hands up in despair; some attempt must be
made to try and discern what would qualify as 'every step'. Of course, it is usually going to be
fact-specific so it is difficult to generalise.

In determining whether the defence is made out or not the court is required by s 214(4) to **4.142**
consider if the director took the steps which a reasonably diligent person who has the general
knowledge, skill and experience that may reasonably be expected of a person who carries out
the same functions as are carried out by the respondent director, and, the general knowledge,
skill and experience that the respondent director possesses. This is the same kind of factor that
applies in deciding whether a director falls within the condition for liability.

Thus, what must directors do to ensure that they act properly and do not fall foul of s 214? **4.143**
This is likely to depend on a number of matters, such as the financial position of the company,
the nature of its business(es) and the state of the market, particularly that which governs the
services or goods which the director's company provides. The defence effectively means that
directors, when they know or ought to have concluded that there is no reasonable prospect
of their company avoiding entering insolvent liquidation, will have to change how they are
managing their companies. They must take steps to redress their company's position. If their
actions fail to do so but a court regards the directors as having taken appropriate measures, then
they will not be held liable. What we can say with some certainty, as mentioned earlier, is that
a director must not bury his or her head in the sand and do nothing. Doing nothing is simply
not an option.

If the directors do trade on they need to be able to demonstrate that doing so was intended to **4.144**
reduce the net deficiency of the company and also it was done in a manner that would minimise
the risk of loss to individual creditors.[219] This means that directors need to take action which
protects new creditors.[220] If they do not then they can be held liable.[221] It has been suggested

---

219   *Re Ralls Builders Ltd* [2016] EWHC 243 (Ch), [2016] BCC 293, [245].
220   Ibid., [279].
221   Ibid.

that one thing that could be done is to establish a trust account for deposits on new purchase orders in a retail situation.[222]

4.145   'Every step' was 'intended to apply to cases where, for example, the directors take specific steps with a view to preserving or realising assets or claims for the benefit of creditors, even if they fail to achieve that result'.[223] This is all well and good, but it does not really assist directors. And, it is not possible to look at the cases and identify guidelines. On the surface the demand of s 214(4) may be seen as too great in that it is possible that even the most diligent director might not take 'every step'. Consequently, as Professor Sir Roy Goode has said, 'every step', may mean no more than, given the reference in s 214 to the reasonably diligent person, requiring the taking of 'every reasonable step'.[224]

4.146   The first thing we might say is that it would be prudent for any director to take appropriate professional advice. This could be from accountants, lawyers or others. There are instances where courts have clearly smiled on directors who have done so,[225] and been critical of directors when they have not taken advice or not heeded it. The director in *Re Brian Pierson Ltd*,[226] who was found liable, had ignored indications, although not warnings, from professional advisers concerning the financial malaise of the company and .in *Re Purpoint Ltd*,[227] the director found liable had simply not heeded professional advice.

4.147   It must be noted that even if a director takes professional advice, follows that advice as best as he or she could and, notwithstanding that advice and its implementation, the company enters insolvency liquidation the director may still be held liable as the advice is not guaranteed to absolve a director. However, it should go an appreciable way to doing so.[228] It is imperative that the directors obtain advice from an appropriate person. For instance, obtaining advice from a general legal practitioner who does not work regularly or at all in the insolvency field may well be considered as not appropriate and that more specialised practitioners should be giving advice. Furthermore, seeking advice solely from a legal practitioner might not be appropriate as the advice of an accountant or even a qualified IP might well be critical.

4.148   Directors might contemplate a restructuring of their companies' affairs. This could entail one or more of a number of actions as discussed earlier in the chapter.[229]

4.149   Directors must be careful in being passive, for even if there are no professional warnings about the state of the company's finances from in-house accountants or auditors that does not absolve a director from liability, particularly if there are other factors that suggest the state of the finances may constitute a problem for the company.[230]

---

222   R Tett and H Fielding, 'A Masterclass in Construction: Ralls Builders and Wrongful Trading' (2016) *CRI* 95 at 97.
223   *Re Brian Pierson Ltd* [1999] BCC 26, 54; [2001] BCLC 275, 308.
224   *Principles of Corporate Insolvency Law*, (2nd ed., Sweet & Maxwell, 1997), 471.
225   For example, *Re Bath Glass Ltd* [1988] BCLC 329; *Re Douglas Construction Services Ltd* [1988] BCLC 397; *Re Continental Assurance Co of London plc* [2001] BPIR 733.
226   [1999] BCC 26, 54, [2001] BCLC 275, 308.
227   [1991] BCC 121, [1991] BCLC 491.
228   See F Oditah, 'Wrongful Trading' [1990] *LMCLQ* 205, 208.
229   See [4.17]–[4.19].
230   *Re Brian D Pierson* [1999] BCC 26, 54, [2001] BCLC 275, 308.

Directors might consider resignation, although it is often seen as the last resort, for if a director **4.150** does resign he or she loses the opportunity to be a voice at board meetings, to obtain confidential information, and the director can no longer influence the direction of the company's affairs. Also, if a company has commenced wrongful trading when he or she resigns, the director's liability could be greater because of what is done subsequent to his or her resignation. Moreover, it might be said that resigning is 'designed to protect the interests and integrity of the individual director, rather than seeking to confer any benefit on the company in respect of minimising the potential loss of its creditors'.[231]

Nevertheless, resignation might be a valid consideration where his or her advice or recommen- **4.151** dations have not been heeded. In *Secretary of State for Trade and Industry v Taylor*[232] Chadwick J said, while hearing a director disqualification case, that in such a situation it was prudent for a director to resign.[233] However, the judge did add that simply because a director does not resign does not necessarily mean that he or she will be held liable.

Obviously, a court will have to weigh up what was the reason behind the resignation and what **4.152** other options might have been available to the director. If a director is of the view that the company is heading for insolvent liquidation, but he or she is alone in this view, then the director faces an uphill battle. So, resignation might be the most appropriate action for the director to take. This action should follow only after the director has expressed his or her concern at a board meeting or in some other formal way, and he or she has ensured that what he or she has to say is minuted or recorded in some fashion.

It might be thought that liquidation is *the step* that should be taken. While liquidation might **4.153** minimise further company losses, it might not be the most beneficial action as far as the creditors are concerned. For instance, in liquidation if assets are sold off piecemeal pursuant to a 'fire sale', the liquidator will recover less than if the assets were sold off strategically, or as part of a sale of the business.

Administration might be seen as another safe course of action. Directors might, quite properly, **4.154** now regard administration more favourably than liquidation as an escape route from possible wrongful trading. With administration there is the possibility of the company being rescued whereas in liquidation the focus will be on closing the business and selling off the company's property. The administration route was taken in *Re Chancery plc*,[234] one of the few instances we have in case law of the directors of a public company going close to engaging in wrongful trading. Harman J, in making an administration order,[235] adverted to the serious risk that the directors would have been taking of running foul of s 214 by continuing to trade.[236] A liquidator (or administrator) will only seek a contribution from directors to the time when the company entered administration (or liquidation), so at least that step might restrict the liability of a director where he or she is held liable.

---

231 S Griffin, *Personal Liability and Disqualification of Company Directors,* (Hart Publishing, 1999), 77.
232 [1997] 1 WLR 407.
233 Ibid., 412.
234 [1991] BCC 171.
235 This was before the Act was amended to permit directors taking their company into administration without the need for a court order.
236 [1991] BCC 171, 172.

4.155   It has been said often, and referred to earlier, that the drawback with placing the company in some form of formal insolvency regime can be premature as the company might still have the potential of being rescued. And the mere fact that the directors continue to trade does not necessarily mean that they have not taken every step.[237]

4.156   In placing the company in formal insolvency proceedings, the directors' concern over personal liability might outweigh consideration of the future of the company. If directors did place their company in an insolvency regime, then in some situations, and it is suggested that they would have to be fairly extreme, directors might be subject to liability for wrongful trading as the action might not be regarded as minimising creditor losses. Another possibility is that in taking the company into a formal insolvency process the directors are breaching their duty to promote the success of the company for the benefit of the members (s 172(1)) or, if the directors are subject to the duty under s 172(3) and their focus must have been on the creditors' interests, they are breaching that duty as the action is not in the interests of creditors. We mentioned this issue earlier in the chapter.[238] It is likely that liability would rarely be imposed and only in cases where the directors panicked or totally misread the situation and the company clearly could have returned to profitable trading if appropriate action had been taken. The fact that administration is a regime which allows for rescue in the appropriate case means that directors may be less likely to be held liable. Although a query whether they might be liable for some of the costs associated with administration in a case where they should have seen that entering administration was premature. But all of this means that if directors have any concerns that their decision to place a company in a formal insolvency process might be premature, they should probably choose administration over liquidation.

4.157   It is contended that it is likely to be more appropriate for directors to place the company in administration rather than to embark on some form of rescue process save where they believe that it has a good chance of success. The process of seeking to put in place some arrangement with creditors, such as a company voluntary arrangement or an informal scheme can be dangerous as this could take a while to finalise and during this period the losses to creditors could be growing, and, of course, any one of the creditors could petition for a winding-up order which would scupper the restructuring.

4.158   While the termination of the company's business might seem appropriate it can in fact be the worst thing, especially in the short term, as it may be detrimental for all concerned, particularly the creditors.[239] This is especially the case where the company can make gains in the short term and this might rescue the company from its parlous state. It also might not be the best action to take where a company is to be placed in administration or liquidation. If placed in administration it would mean that one option of resuscitating the business has gone as it is usually difficult and not beneficial to open up a business that has closed as clientele might well have been lost and the business is likely to have lost reputation and credibility. Even if liquidation is envisaged closure of the business might not be the wisest move as the liquidator might find it

---

237   V Finch, 'Directors' Duties: Insolvency and the Unsecured Creditor' in Clarke, A (ed), *Current Issues in Insolvency Law*, (Stevens, 1991), 96.

238   See [4.20].

239   See, *Re Hefferon Kearns Ltd (No 2)* (1993) 3 IR 191.

more difficult to realise company assets. However, in some limited cases termination may well be the best option.

It would seem that many of the things that one would expect of a director when subject to the duty under s 172(3) of the Companies Act would apply to a director who is obliged to take every step to with a view to minimising the potential loss to the company's creditors as he or she ought to have taken.   **4.159**

It is plain that what a director might do very much depends on a company's specific position and it is impossible to generalise, but the following actions might be appropriate (and, in some cases, in addition to other measure mentioned earlier): adopting a frugal approach to business, as well as in relation to the taking of directors' own salary entitlements;[240] calling a creditors' meeting in order to advise them of the state of the company;[241] convening regular board meetings to review the position of the company and ensure that discussions and processes are clearly documented, including an indication that creditor interests are taken into account in the decisions made; assessing the reasons for the company's financial woes and addressing them in some positive way(s); regularly assessing and monitoring the financial position of the company; ensuring that the company's accounts are properly kept up to date; operating more cautiously and, in some cases, for the company to reduce the volume of its trading activities.[242]   **4.160**

Finally, on the issue of the defence, are directors able to rely on s 1157 of the Companies Act that permits a court to excuse officers from liability arising out of their negligence, breach of duty or breach of trust on the basis that they had acted honestly and reasonably, and, as a consequence of their actions, ought fairly to be excused from liability. Whether directors are able to do so is rather uncertain.   **4.161**

There are cases that say that s 1157 (or its precursor, s 727 of the Companies Act 1985) does not apply as it is incompatible with the objective nature of the test found in s 214, namely that the action of the director could not be said to be reasonable.[243] Notwithstanding this, in *Re D'Jan of London Ltd*[244] where Hoffmann LJ held that the test in s 214(4) was to be used in determining whether a director had breached his or her duty of care and skill, his Lordship said that a director found liable could be relieved under s 1157. Also, while s 214 undoubtedly includes an objective approach, it also has a subjective element and s 1157 has subjective components[245] in that it requires consideration of the respondent's state of mind in examining the issue of honesty.   **4.162**

Even if relief were possible under s 1157, it is likely that it would be employed in few situations, for, directors have tended to be found liable only when they are irresponsible, and in such cases the courts are likely to refrain from excusing them from liability on the basis that the directors   **4.163**

---

240   D Milman, 'Strategies for Regulating Managerial Performance in the Twilight Zone – Familiar Dilemmas: New Consideration' (2004) *JBL* 493, 505.

241   The following are taken from A Keay, *Company Directors' Responsibilities to Creditors* (Routledge, 2007), 119.

242   See, *Re Continental Assurance of London plc* [2001] BPIR 733, 769.

243   *Re Produce Marketing Consortium Ltd* (1989) 5 BCC 569; *Re Brian D. Pierson (Contractors) Ltd* [1999] BCC 26, [2001] BCLC 275, and see the comments of Nelson J in *Bairstow v Queens Moat Houses plc* [2000] BCC 1025.

244   [1993] BCC 646.

245   R Bradgate and G Howells, 'No Excuse for Wrongful Trading' (1990) *JBL* 249, 251 n 11.

ought not to be excused. If s 1157 can be used it would allow judges to find directors liable under s 214 in cases short of irresponsibility, yet they could excuse them under s 1157. This approach maintains the integrity of s 214 but permits courts to excuse those directors whose conduct is viewed as being not completely irresponsible. Nevertheless, a judge does not need to fall back on s 1157 where of the opinion that a director should be excused from liability. The judge can achieve the same result as excusing liability under s 1157, if he or she were to reduce or make no order for contribution against a director under s 214, for the judge has a discretion, provided by s 214(1), as to whether he or she thinks a contribution should be made.[246] The subsection clearly permits a judge to refrain from ordering a director to make a contribution.

5. Loss

4.164   The issue of establishing loss and for what directors might be held liable, while matters of substantial importance are not of critical importance for the purposes of this book, hence, we only touch on it. After saying that, the issue, of course, is critical for directors and what they might be ordered to pay, if anything.

4.165   In *Re Continental Assurance Co of London plc*[247] Park J said that it was necessary for a liquidator to establish some connection between the wrongfulness of the directors' conduct with the company's losses which the liquidator seeks to recover. Park J said that more had to be established than mere nexus between an incorrect decision to carry on trading and a particular loss sustained by the company.[248] The judge pointed out that the required nexus will often be obvious, such as where a director turns a blind eye to inherent loss-making.[249] Not all losses suffered by a company after the directors wrongly decide to continue trading can necessarily be claimed by a liquidator.[250] The law will limit liability to those consequences which can be linked to the wrongful action(s).[251] Liquidators are required to show that there was a net deficiency in company assets when comparing the company's position as at the time when wrongful trading is alleged to have commenced and the position when trading actually ceased.[252]

4.166   In *The Liquidator of Marini Ltd v Dickensen*[253] the court said that in determining loss the appropriate test was not whether new debt was incurred after the date on which it was decided that the respondent knew or ought to have concluded that the company could not avoid insolvent liquidation, but whether the company was in a worse position at the date of liquidation than it would have been if trading had ceased when, on the liquidator's claim, it should have done.

4.167   In *Re Ralls Builders Ltd*[254] Snowden J indicated that it does not necessarily follow that directors should be liable to make a contribution to the company's assets if they ought to have concluded that there was no reasonable prospect of the company avoiding insolvent liquidation and there

---

246   An example is *Re Ralls Builders Ltd* [2016] EWHC 243 (Ch), [2016] BCC 293.
247   *Re Continental Assurance of London plc* [2001] BPIR 733, 844.
248   Ibid.
249   Ibid.
250   Ibid.; *The Liquidator of Marini Ltd v Dickensen* [2004] BCC 172, [2003] EWHC 334 (Ch), [68].
251   *Re Continental Assurance of London plc* [2001] BPIR 733, 845.
252   Ibid., 821, 844; *The Liquidator of Marini Ltd v Dickensen* [2004] BCC 172, [2003] EWHC 334 (Ch), [68].
253   Ibid.
254   [2016] EWHC 243 (Ch), [2016] BCC 293.

was a loss.[255] The judge made it plain that any liability of a director to make a contribution was to be calculated on the basis of the loss to the company overall and the amount by which the position of the creditors as a whole had worsened. His Lordship said that merely because the end result of the directors' trading was that the position of new creditors was worse than that of existing creditors was not pertinent to determining whether a contribution should be ordered to be paid by directors.[256]

The final thing to say is that Snowden J in *Re Ralls Builders Ltd* said that there must be some **4.168** causal connection between the amount of any contribution ordered to be paid and the continuation of trading. Thus, the judge went on to say that: 'Losses that would have been incurred in any event as a consequence of a company going into a formal insolvency process should not be laid at the door of directors…'[257]

6. Conclusion

The general feeling tends to be that wrongful trading has not contributed a lot to director **4.169** accountability. The cause of action is complicated and determining loss can be highly problematic for an officeholder. The vast majority of cases have been brought against the directors of very small private companies and it leads one to think that it is unlikely that proceedings will be brought against public company directors and even less likely against a listed company director. The directors of public companies are likely to be able to obtain more and better advice when a company is in difficulty. However, even with small private companies there are many obstacles for liquidators and administrators to have deal with and consequently it can deter some officeholders from taking action. Clearly, directors must ensure that they address their company's financial problems and not ignore them, and assess whether continuing trading, whether in the same manner or in a modified fashion, is going to enable them to avoid wrongful trading. It might well be that other action, such as placing the company in administration is the more prudent action to take.

I. FRAUDULENT TRADING

1. Introduction

A longstanding obligation that redounds on directors is not to engage in fraudulent trading. **4.170** Directors (and others) may be liable for fraudulent trading either under the criminal law or the civil law. For many years, and as recently as the Companies Act 1948 which applied until 1985, there was one section that imposed both criminal and civil liability and in both civil and criminal proceedings the elements of the section had to be established beyond reasonable doubt.[258]

---

255 Ibid., [219].
256 Ibid., [279]. The judge accepted the fact that this was an apparent shortcoming in s 214, but it was a matter for Parliament to remedy.
257 Ibid., [242].
258 *Re Maidstone Buildings Ltd* [1971] 1 WLR 1085, 1094.

Now there are two provisions, one dealing with civil sanctions and the other criminal sanctions, but they are essentially the same provision.[259]

4.171 Section 993 of the Companies Act provides that if a business is carried on with intent to defraud creditors of the company or creditors of any other person, or for any fraudulent purpose, every person who is knowingly a party to this is committing an offence. Section 213 of the Act provides something similar, but it only provides for civil liability requiring guilty parties to contribute to the company's assets. An application under s 213 can only be brought by a liquidator,[260] so we are talking about a company that has entered liquidation. This will usually mean insolvent liquidation, but it does not have to. The liquidator or a company that entered members' voluntary liquidation would have power to institute proceedings, probably against former directors of the company, although it is highly unlikely. Also, administrators are permitted by a relatively new provision, s 246ZA, to instigate proceedings. Section 246ZA is in the same terms as s 213. We will refer to s 213 in this part of the chapter, but what is said should generally be seen as applicable to s 246ZA.

4.172 We will generally focus on the civil provision. Unlike the wrongful trading provision which limits liability to directors, past and present, any persons who are knowingly parties to the fraudulent trading can be the subject of proceedings under s 213. While it is probable, certainly based on history, the most likely respondents to an action will be the directors and other officers of the company.[261] As a result, and given the thrust of the book, we will refer to respondents as directors even though other persons could also be named as respondents in a fraudulent trading action brought by a liquidator or administrator.

4.173 The primary aim of s 213 is to compensate those who have lost out due to the actions of persons, who are identified in the section, engaging in fraudulent trading.[262] As with the duty referred to in s 172(3) of the Companies Act, s 213 is directed at protecting creditors.

4.174 There is no need for a company to have been insolvent when directors (or others) engaged in fraudulent trading for a liquidator to succeed, so it can relate to an action that was undertaken outside insolvency, just as we saw with the duty to take account of creditor interests. But, as the company has to be in liquidation for proceedings to be instigated, and this is usually due to insolvency, proceedings are mounted because the creditors have been prejudiced in some way.

2. The provisions

4.175 Fraudulent trading is provided for in two subsections in s 213. The first states the conduct that makes up fraudulent trading, and this is that there was either intent to defraud creditors or a fraudulent purpose in the carrying on of the business of the company. The subject of the fraud are the creditors of either the company or any other person. Section 213(2) then states who

---

259 *Bernasconi v Nicholas Bennett & Co* [2000] BCC 921, 924.

260 This does not include a provisional liquidator: *Re Overnight Ltd; Goldfarb v Higgins* [2009] EWHC 601 (Ch).

261 There is every indication that the persons who can be said to be the 'directing mind' of the company are liable, more often than not, to be the subject of proceedings. See *R v Miles* [1992] Crim L R 657. Also, see *Re Supply of Ready Mixed Concrete (No 2)* [1995] 1 AC 456; *Meridian Global Funds Management Asia Ltd v Securities Commission* [1995] BCC 942.

262 *Bank of India v Morris* [2005] EWCA Civ 693, [2005] 2 BCLC 328, [2005] BPIR 1067, [111].

may be liable in civil actions and for what they can be liable. First, the persons who are able to be sued are those who are knowingly parties to the carrying on of a business of a company with intent to defraud creditors. Secondly, such persons are liable to make such contributions to the company as the court thinks proper.

Section 993 of the Companies Act provides for the same first subsection as s 213. Section 993(2) then states that the provision applies whether or not the company is in liquidation. The third subsection includes the criminal penalties that may be imposed on a person found liable. If a person is charged under indictment the penalty can be severe.   **4.176**

Sections 213 and 993 appear to be quite broad, in that it provides that they both cover 'any business of the company [that] has been carried out'. This is broader than merely stating 'the business of the company'.[263]   **4.177**

Unlike with wrongful trading there is no specific defence provided for in the fraudulent trading sections. Thus, there is no prescribed behaviour that directors need to embrace. Having said that, clearly ss 213 and 993 direct directors not to engage in any kind of action in running the company's business that would involve intending to defraud creditors. This means that directors have to know what fraudulent trading entails.   **4.178**

3.   Liability

There will not be any liability if a company merely continues to engage in trading while it is insolvent, except where the company obtains credit when the directors know that there was no good reason to think that funds would be available to pay the debt when it became payable.[264] This can be applied to the failure to pay trade creditors and not remitting moneys, deducted from employees' salary, to the revenue authorities, or the failure to pay VAT when receiving money for goods sold,[265] and continuing to incur liabilities when the company is clearly insolvent and with no prospect of being able to discharge them as the company is obviously heading for administration or liquidation.[266] Of course, in such a case there might be liability for wrongful trading.   **4.179**

A claim for fraudulent trading under s 993 can succeed even if it is not possible to establish that anyone has suffered a loss.[267] Whereas with the civil liability provision, in order for a contribution to be ordered to be paid by a court, a liquidator or administrator has to establish a loss to creditors and that there is a nexus between the loss because of the fraudulent trading and the contribution that is being sought from the person allegedly involved in the fraudulent trading.[268] If the requisite nexus can be established, then the sum that is to be ordered to be   **4.180**

---

263   *Hardie v Hanson* [1960] HCA 8, (1960) 105 CLR 451.
264   *R v Grantham* [1984] 2 QB 675, 682–683; *R v Waite* (2003) WL 21162167, [5] (CCA).
265   *Re L Todd (Swanscombe) Ltd* [1990] BCLC 454.
266   *Re William C. Leitch Bros Ltd* [1932] 2 Ch 71, 77.
267   *R v Grantham* [1984] QB 675, 683–684.
268   Morphitis v Bernasconi [2003] EWCA Civ 289, [2003] BCC 540, [53].

paid is limited to the amount of the debts of the creditors proved to have been defrauded by the fraudulent trading.[269]

4.181   There are three elements that need to be established by a liquidator for liability under s 213. These are:

- the business of the company in liquidation has been carried on with intent to defraud creditors or for any other fraudulent purpose;
- the respondent participated in the carrying of business;
- the respondent participated knowingly.[270]

(a)   An intent to defraud[271]

4.182   While courts have given 'intent to defraud' and 'fraudulent purpose' a wide meaning,[272] they are the most problematic elements of the fraudulent trading provision. The intention to defraud or acting for any fraudulent purpose must accompany the carrying on of the business. The reason that it is problematic is the difficulty in knowing what intent to defraud and fraudulent purpose mean, and what must be established by a liquidator in order to succeed in the claim is that the director has engaged in one or the other. This problem has existed as long as the provision has been enacted.

4.183   One commentator has submitted that the greatest obstacle to the use of fraudulent trading proceedings is the requirement of fraud or dishonesty.[273] The onus of proving an intent to defraud, which involves dishonesty,[274] can be extremely hard to discharge.[275] It was a primary reason for the introduction of the wrongful trading provision. All of this means that many directors will not have to worry that they are acting in breach of the provision.

4.184   Fraud is difficult to define for it has different meanings in different contexts.[276] Initially it is necessary to appreciate that for anyone to be liable for fraud he or she must be proved to have been engaging in dishonesty,[277] a concept that is associated with fraud. Fraud is said to connote dishonesty involving, according to current notions of fair trading among commercial men, real moral blame.[278]

---

269   *Re a Company No 001418 of 1988* [1991] BCLC 197, 203.
270   *Re BCCI International SA; Morris v Bank of India (No 14)* [2003] EWHC 1868 (Ch), [2004] 2 BCLC 236, [11].
271   For a detailed discussion of the expression, see A Keay, 'Fraudulent Trading: The Intent to Defraud Element' (2006) 35 *Common Law World Review* 121.
272   *Re William C. Leitch Bros Ltd* [1932] 2 Ch 71; *R v Kemp* [1988] QB 645, 654–655.
273   F Oditah, 'Wrongful Trading' [1990] LMCLQ 205, 206.
274   *R v Grantham* [1984] QB 675, [1984] 2 WLR 815, [1984] BCLC 270.
275   *Bank of India v Morris* [2005] EWCA (Civ) 693, [2005] 2 BCLC 328, [2005] BPIR 1067, [101].
276   J Farrar, 'Fraudulent Trading' (1980) *JBL* 336, 339.
277   *Re Cox and Hodges* (1982) 75 Cr App R 291 (CCA); *R v Grantham* [1984] QB 675, [1984] 2 WLR 815, [1984] BCLC 270; *Bank of India v Morris* [2005] EWCA (Civ) 693, [2005] 2 BCLC 328, [2005] BPIR 1067, [8].
278   *Re Patrick & Lyon Ltd* [1933] Ch 786, 790; *R v Grantham* [1984] QB 675, [1984] 2 WLR 815, [1984] BCLC 270; *Re a Company No 001418 of 1988* [1991] BCLC 197.

The test for intent to defraud is a subjective test,[279] so the state of a person's mind is at issue. **4.185** Consequently, if it can be proven that a director had knowledge of fraud then it follows that he or she was acting dishonestly.[280] It has to be established that the respondent had an intent or a reckless indifference as to whether creditors were defrauded.[281]

Notwithstanding the fact that a subjective test applies, there is case law that indicates that **4.186** objective factors are not without importance. What has been at issue is both when objective factors can be considered and to what extent. In several older decisions the courts were, effectively, inferring intent to defraud, based on something close to recklessness.[282] In *Bernasconi v Nicholas Bennett & Co*[283] Laddie J seemed to accept this view as he said that to be liable the respondent had to evince an intent or, as an alternative, a reckless indifference as to whether creditors were defrauded.[284] The circumstances pertaining to what is being alleged as fraudulent trading must be taken into account and, if a respondent's subjective view is found not to be reasonable, he or she might be found liable. But it has been said that courts must be careful in invoking the concept of the hypothetical decent honest man and what he would have done in the circumstances, as there might be a temptation to treat shortcomings by the respondent as a failure to comply with the necessary objective standard of conduct.[285] Lord Hoffmann said in *Aktieselskabet Dansk Skibsfinansiering v Brothers*[286] that dishonesty depended on an assessment of all the facts and stated that it was much safer to focus on the respondent before the court and to ask whether that person had been dishonest. The Court of Appeal decision in *R v Grantham*[287] seems to suggest that courts can take into account objective considerations when respondents incur debts at a time when they know that their company will clearly not be able to make repayment, or where there is considerable risk that the company will not be able to repay.

The majority of UK authority holds that a court may infer that the respondent had an intent **4.187** to defraud either where the respondent, when incurring a debt, was aware that there was no good reason for thinking that the debt could be satisfied, or where the respondent knew that there was a risk that the creditor may not get paid. Lord Hoffmann, primarily in *Aktieselskabet Dansk Skibsfinansiering,* a decision of the Hong Kong Court of Final Appeal, seemed to require the respondent to be in receipt of a personal gain from a transaction before he would acquiesce to the making of any inference. If the former approach is correct, then directors must be very careful in incurring debts.

As far as the standard of honesty is concerned in civil law, the courts have tended to apply what **4.188** can be referred to as 'the combined approach', something that has been employed in considering liability under the limb of dishonest assistance when a party is involved in assisting a breach

279 *Bernasconi v Nicholas Bennett & Co* [2000] BCC 921; *Re BCCI International SA; Morris v Bank of India (No 14)* [2003] EWHC 1868 (Ch), [2004] 2 BCLC 236.
280 *Re BCCI; Morris v State Bank of India* [2004] EWHC 528 (Ch), [2004] 2 BCLC 279, [2004] BCC 404.
281 *Bernasconi v Nicholas Bennett & Co* [2000] BCC 921.
282 See, e.g., *Re Gerald Cooper Chemicals Ltd* [1978] Ch 262.
283 *Bernasconi v Nicholas Bennett & Co* [2000] BCC 921.
284 Ibid., 924.
285 *Aktieselskabet Dansk Skibsfinansiering v Brothers* [2001] 2 BCLC 324, 334 (HKCFA).
286 Ibid.
287 [1984] QB 675.

of fiduciary duty.[288] In *Aktieselskabet Dansk Skibsfinansiering v Brothers* Lord Hoffmann appeared to accept that while respondents are not liable unless they knew that they were acting dishonestly, the standard of honesty is not the respondent's; it is the ordinary standards of reasonable and honest people.[289] So, while a court will consider the subjectivity of the respondent's mind, the ordinary standards of reasonable and honest people are not excluded because a person is not able to set the standards of what is honest. A person is unable to escape a finding of dishonesty simply because he or she sees nothing wrong in a particular kind of behaviour.[290] In the latest appellate case to consider the matter, *Ivey v Genting Casino*,[291] Lord Hughes (with whose judgment all the judges agreed) said that:

> When dishonesty is in question the fact-finding tribunal must first ascertain (subjectively) the actual state of the individual's knowledge or belief as to the facts. The reasonableness or otherwise of his belief is a matter of evidence (often in practice determinative) going to whether he held the belief, but it is not an additional requirement that his belief must be reasonable; the question is whether it is genuinely held. When once his actual state of mind as to knowledge or belief as to facts is established, the question whether his conduct was honest or dishonest is to be determined by the fact-finder by applying the (objective) standards of ordinary decent people. There is no requirement that the defendant must appreciate that what he has done is, by those standards, dishonest.[292]

(b) Fraudulent purpose

4.189 It has been held that the expression is extremely wide.[293] A person is not liable merely because he or she nominated a person as a director who committed fraudulent trading, or because he or she had the opportunity of influencing the conduct of the affairs of the company. Directors are not, necessarily, liable for fraudulent trading while engaging in trading when the company is insolvent. It may well depend on whether the directors have been reckless in incurring debts. If there is no recklessness, and there is no intent to defraud involved, a liquidator might well prefer to proceed against directors under the wrongful trading provision.

(c) Party to the carrying on of a business

4.190 According to *Re Maidstone Buildings Ltd*[294] being a party to the carrying on of business involves nothing more than participating, taking part or concurring in the business of the company. It might well exclude those who might know about the fraudulent conduct, but who do not get involved.[295] Clearly for the most part any directors subject to action will usually be a part of carrying on the business. However, a director might seek to argue that he or she was not involved in the part of the business that is subject to scrutiny. Would it depend in why the director was not involved? Was it due to inertia, laziness or because he or she was being kept out of the loop? Courts today are more ready to hold directors liable for inertia than in the past, but would a court hold a director liable for fraudulent trading where there is a need for an element of wrongdoing rather than laziness or incompetence? It is not likely.

---

288 See *Twinsectra Ltd v Yardley* [2002] UKHL 12, [2002] 2 AC 164.
289 *Aktieselskabet Dansk Skibsfinansiering v Brothers* [2001] 2 BCLC 324, 333.
290 *Royal Brunei Airlines Snd Bhd v Tan* [1995] 2 AC 378, 389.
291 [2017] UKSC 67, [2018] AC 391, [2018] 3 WLR 1212.
292 Ibid., [74].
293 *R v Kemp* [1988] QB 645, 654–655.
294 [1971] 1 WLR 1085.
295 Ibid., 1094.

It might be said that while directors would not be able to escape liability for wrongful trading, **4.191** they could escape liability for fraudulent trading. The same might be said where a director has not been informed about the part of the business that has involved actions that constitute fraudulent trading. Again, a director might be held liable for wrongful trading in such a case unless it could be said that any reasonable inquiries he or she made would not have been fruitful. In the situation where the fraudulent activity relates to the mainstream business of the company, it is likely that it would be very difficult for a director, save where he or she registered unequivocal dissent to the action that the company has taken, to argue that he or she was not a party to the carrying on of business.

For fraudulent trading to have been committed, it is not necessary for the liquidator to prove **4.192** that there has been a course of conduct, as a single transaction or act is able to constitute the basis for action under s 213.[296] While fraudulent trading will usually involve an intent to defraud the company's creditors in general, it can occur when business is being carried on to defraud just one creditor, but one cannot say that whenever a fraud on a creditor is perpetrated while carrying on business it is inevitable that a breach of s 213 occurs, as the business must have been carried on with intent to defraud.[297] It has been made clear by the Court of Appeal[298] that Parliament had not sought to hold liable a person for fraudulent trading when any creditor had been defrauded in the course of carrying on business. The very business itself must have been conducted with the aim of defrauding creditors.

(d) 'Knowingly'

The courts may only impose liability on a person if he or she was 'knowingly' a party to the **4.193** carrying on of business. It has been held by the Court of Appeal that the liquidator is required to demonstrate dishonesty on the part of the respondent,[299] and if a person is found to have knowingly participated, then he or she is acting dishonestly.[300] To be knowingly parties to the fraud, people do not have to know every detail of the fraud or how it is to be perpetrated,[301] so a director who is not kept fully in the loop but is aware of what is going on to some extent, may be liable. To be liable a director must have had the relevant knowledge contemporaneously with assisting in the fraud.[302] If the alleged fraudulent trading involved a series of transactions, it has been held that it would be appropriate to look at a director's conduct as a whole in determining state of mind,[303] but it would appear that a court must evaluate a person's state of mind in relation to each transaction.[304] Thus, it would seem that the way that a transaction is structured can go some way to indicating whether or not there was knowledge of fraud.

It is possible in a company that directors might 'wash their hands' of a matter and try to ignore **4.194** what is going on. In such cases they might well still be liable. This is because the courts have

---

296 Re Gerald Cooper Chemicals [1978] Ch 262, *R v Lockwood* (1986) 2 BCC 99,333, 99,341, *Morphitis v Bernasconi* [2003] EWCA Civ 289, [2003] BCC 540.
297 Morphitis, ibid., [46]–[47].
298 Ibid., [46].
299 *Bank of India v Morris* [2005] EWCA Civ 693, [2005] 2 BCLC 328, [2005] BPIR 1067, [8].
300 *Re BCCI International SA; Morris v Bank of India (No 14)* [2003] EWHC 1868 (Ch), [2004] 2 BCLC 236, [12].
301 Re BCCI; Morris v Bank of India (No 15) [2004] 2 BCLC 279, 297; [2004] BCC 404, 419.
302 Ibid., 297; 419.
303 The Court of Appeal in *Bank of India v Morris* [2005] EWCA Civ 693, [2005] 2 BCLC 328, [2005] BPIR 1067, [71].
304 Ibid.

not been lenient on passive directors in more recent years and directors could be said to be knowingly a party to fraud, if it can be established that they had 'blind-eye' knowledge, namely deliberately shutting their eyes to the obvious, in that it was obvious to them that fraud was involved.[305] Blind-eye knowledge involves a suspicion that a fraud exists and a deliberate decision to avoid confirming that it exists, and that the suspicion is well-grounded.[306] In *Manifest Shipping Company Ltd v Uni-Polaris Co Ltd*[307] Lord Scott said that: 'In summary, blind-eye knowledge requires, in my opinion, a suspicion that the relevant facts do exist and a deliberate decision to avoid confirming that they exist.'[308] In *Royal Brunei Airlines Snd Bhd v Tan*,[309] it was said that it was dishonesty for a person 'deliberately to close his eyes and ears, or deliberately not to ask questions, lest he learn something he would rather not know, and then proceed regardless'.[310] But it is necessary to distinguish between a person who has a conscious appreciation of the true nature of the business that is occurring, and someone who fails, even negligently, to appreciate the fraud.[311] It is only in the former that a person is liable.

4.   What constitutes fraudulent trading?

4.195   If directors agree to their company paying uncommercial sums to a party with the intention of ensuring that property were put out of the reach of creditors, then this could be regarded as fraudulent trading, and possibly a breach of s 423 of the Act, an issue that we will come to shortly.

4.196   Failure to take action cannot constitute fraud, as some positive action must be taken for there to be liability.[312] Thus, if the company secretary neglects to inform the directors that the company is insolvent, and what the consequences are in continuing to trade, that person is not liable, as there is no positive conduct. A director would not be liable for fraudulent trading merely by declining to pay a company debt.

4.197   A single transaction or act may serve as the basis for a successful action,[313] and, therefore, if a director were to order goods from a trade supplier with the intention of deceiving the supplier in that the director had no intention of paying for them, this would constitute an intent to defraud.[314]

---

305   See, ibid.
306   Ibid.
307   [2003] 1 AC 469.
308   Ibid., [116].
309   [1995] 2 AC 378.
310   Ibid., 389 per Lord Nichols.
311   *Re BCCI International SA; Morris v Bank of India (No 14)* [2003] EWHC 1868 (Ch), [2004] 2 BCLC 236.
312   *Re Maidstone Buildings Ltd* [1971] 1 WLR 1085.
313   Re Gerald Cooper Chemicals [1978] Ch 262.
314   Ibid.

5.   Court order

A court is only permitted to make a compensatory order and is not able to include a punitive **4.198**
element.[315] The Court of Appeal in *Morphitis v Bernasconi*[316] said that the contribution to the
assets was to be shared amongst the creditors and should reflect the loss which had been caused
to the creditors by the carrying on of the business in the way that gave rise to the exercise of
the power.[317]

J. TRANSACTIONS DEFRAUDING CREDITORS

1.   Introduction

While often considered in the context of the avoidance/adjustment provisions in the Act, that is   **4.199**
provisions that allow liquidators and administrators to challenge transactions entered into prior
to liquidation or administration,[318] s 423 of the Act is discussed here, albeit to a very limited
degree,[319] as its provisions may warrant some consideration by directors of insolvent companies.
Section 423 provides, in effect, as far as our purposes are concerned, that directors are not to
enter into transactions that defraud creditors. Thus, like the matters discussed previously in the
chapter it places limits on what directors are allowed to do when their company is insolvent, or
at least provides possible repercussions if the directors do what is proscribed by the Act.

It needs to be said at the outset that the heading that is given to the section in the legislation,   **4.200**
'Transactions defrauding creditors', and which we employ here as it is the normally acceptable
way to describe the transactions involved, is in fact incorrect as it suggests, wrongly, that there
must be some dishonesty perpetrated by the respondent for a claim to succeed. This is not the
case.[320] Simply the conditions laid down by the section have to be established and this does not
include, necessarily, any dishonesty. Certainly, a claimant under s 423 does not have to prove
dishonesty, although he or she may seek to allege it. If so, a pleading of dishonesty must be
made.

Directors will only be liable under the provision where they have benefitted from the trans-   **4.201**
actions covered by s 423. If directors have not benefitted, they may be subject to liability for
breach of the duty to take into account the interests of the creditors, discussed earlier in the
chapter.

---

315   Morphitis v Bernasconi [2003] EWCA Civ 289, [2003] BCC 540, [55].
316   Ibid.
317   Ibid.
318   Such as preferences or transactions at an undervalue.
319   For more discussion, see R Parry et al, *Transaction Avoidance in Insolvencies* (2nd edn, OUP, 2011); J Armour,
     'Transactions Defrauding Creditors' in J Armour and H Bennett (eds), *Vulnerable Transactions in Corporate Insolvency*
     (Hart Publishing, 2003); Andrew Keay, *McPherson and Keay's Law of Company Liquidation* (5th ed, Sweet & Maxwell,
     2021), [11-112]–[11-130].
320   *Watchorn v Jupiter Industries Ltd* [2014] EWHC 3003 (Ch), [3].

2.   The provision

4.202   Although contained within the Act, s 423 deals with a claim that may be made against persons who benefit from transactions entered into by directors of companies and individual debtors prior to insolvency occurring. To bring proceedings under s 423 one does not necessarily have to be a liquidator or any other kind of officeholder. Nevertheless, we will consider the section from a corporate perspective and assuming that a company is insolvent.

4.203   There are two main aspects of the provision for the purposes of this chapter. The section essentially provides that certain transactions can be avoided if they were entered into for the purpose of putting assets beyond the reach of creditors.

3.   Transaction at an undervalue

4.204   The first main aspect of the provision for the purposes of the chapter is that directors might be attacked pursuant to s 423 for entering into transactions that are at an undervalue. A debtor company enters into a transaction at an undervalue if: a gift is made or the transaction does not provide the company with any consideration; or the transaction is entered into for a consideration the value of which, in money or money's worth, is significantly less than the value, in money or money's worth, of the consideration provided by the company.

4.   Purpose

4.205   The second main aspect of s 423, and one that has caused a substantial amount of uncertainty and debate over many years, is that in entering into the transaction at undervalue the debtor company has the purpose of putting its assets beyond the reach of creditors.[321]

4.206   It was said at first instance in *BTI 2014 LLC v Sequana SA*[322] by Rose J that the: 'purpose of a person in entering into a transaction is a matter of the subjective intention of that person: what did he aim to achieve?' This was subsequently affirmed by the Court of Appeal.[323] Rose J said that for a company to have the required purpose there must be a majority of the directors who acted with that purpose.[324]

4.207   As far as the nature of the purpose goes, Arden LJ, in the Court of Appeal case of *IRC v Hashmi*,[325] said that what a claimant must establish is that the debtor had the purpose required in s 423, that is, he or she intended positively that the assets would be put out of the reach of creditors.[326] She opined that for something to constitute a purpose, under s 423, it must be a real substantial purpose and not something that was a consequence of what the debtor

---

321   Section 423(3). For a discussion of the law in detail, see A Keay, 'Transactions Defrauding Creditors: The Problem of Purpose Under Section 423 of the Insolvency Act' (2003) *The Conveyancer and Property Lawyer* 272.

322   [2016] EWHC 1686 (Ch), [502].

323   [2019] EWCA Civ 112, [2019] 2 All ER 784, [2019] 1 BCLC 347, [2019] BPIR 562, [66].

324   *BTI 2014 LLC v Sequana SA* [2016] EWHC 1686 (Ch), [494].

325   [2002] EWCA Civ 981, [2002] BPIR 974, [2002] 2 BCLC 489.

326   Ibid., 504.

(company) did.[327] So, if the evidence indicated that a debtor entered into a transaction for a purpose other than to prejudice his or her creditors, but the consequence of the entering into the transaction was to prejudice creditors, the claimant would not succeed. This approach has generally been applied.

In another Court of Appeal decision, *JSC BTA Bank v Ablyazov*,[328] Leggat LJ (with whom **4.208**
Coulson and Gloster LJJ agreed) said that:

> The description of the requisite purpose as a 'substantial' purpose was not necessary to the decision of the Court of Appeal in the Hashmi case and to my mind it risks causing confusion. The word 'substantial' is not used in section 423 and I can see no necessity or warrant for reading this (or any other) adjective into the wording of the section. At best it introduces unnecessary complications and at worst introduces an additional requirement which makes the test stricter than Parliament intended.[329]

His Lordship went on to say that: **4.209**

> It is sufficient simply to ask whether the transaction was entered into by the debtor for the prohibited purpose. If it was, then the transaction falls within section 423(3), even if it was also entered into for one or more other purposes. The test is no more complicated than that.[330]

Where the debtor is a company it will be the purposes of the directors in entering into the **4.210**
transaction that is likely to be critical. Thus, it would seem that there is no need to establish that the debtor company's 'substantial purpose' in entering into the impugned transaction was to place assets beyond the reach of creditors, but simply to establish that the purpose in entering into the transactions was to place assets beyond creditors' reach. And it does not matter, for the claimant's case, that the company may have possessed other purposes.

5.   Conclusion

As far as corporate governance is concerned, s 423 limits what the directors may do. They must **4.211**
be careful that they do not enter into a transaction at an undervalue with the purpose of putting the assets of their company out of the reach of creditors, and this is likely to be of greater importance when their company is insolvent.

K. UNLAWFUL DISTRIBUTIONS

An important issue of corporate life, especially for the shareholders, is that the shareholders will **4.212**
be paid some return on their investment in companies. Thus, from time to time, and in large companies often bi-annually, the directors will put before the shareholders a resolution that a dividend be paid to shareholders. In doing this the directors must be careful that they do not breach the requirement in the Companies Act concerning the payment of dividends, to which we will come shortly. The fact is that only realised profits can be taken into account when

---

327   Ibid., 505. This approach has been subsequently applied. See, e.g., *Gil v Baygreen Properties Ltd* [2004] EWHC 1732 (Ch), [2005] BPIR 95; *Random House Ltd v Allason* [2008] EWHC 2854 (Ch).
328   [2018] EWCA Civ 1176, [2019] BCC 96, [2018] BPIR 898.
329   Ibid., [14]
330   Ibid.

determining whether dividends may be paid, and this obviously excludes estimated profits. All of this means that directors should not pay out dividends when their company is insolvent.[331]

4.213   It needs to be said that while perhaps the most frequent distribution made by companies, dividends are not the only kinds of distributions that are subject to specific rules in the Act.[332] As mentioned earlier in the chapter, in smaller companies which are effectively manager-owned there is a practice of directors being paid for their services, at least partly, by way of dividend.[333] The practice is that directors receive payments throughout the financial year and initially they are regarded as dividends but where the company does not have adequate distributable reserves they are re-labelled as salary. These payments are distributions, and the Companies Act prohibits certain types of distributions.

4.214   The legislation defines 'distribution' as meaning every description of distribution of a company's assets to its members, whether in cash or otherwise.[334] For instance, in *Re Implement Consulting Ltd*[335] it was held that payments made to directors of the company pursuant to Employment Benefit Trust Schemes were unlawful distributions. The legislation does go on to exclude from its reach certain kinds of distribution,[336] such as the issue of fully or partly paid-up bonus shares. One of the primary reasons for the law prohibiting distributions is to prevent a return of capital to shareholders at a time when they are behind the creditors in terms of who gets paid and in what order from the company's assets, and so to protect creditors.

4.215   Whilst it is fine for distributions to be made out of profits when a company is solvent, it is another thing when the distributions are made from capital and/or the company is insolvent. The capital of the company is regarded as a pool from which creditors should be able to get paid if the company is struggling. Also, if the company is insolvent the company's assets and funds are spoken for – they are the creditors who will not get paid in full (unless, on occasions, they have some sort of security or priority status under the Act).

4.216   The general rule, as noted above, is that a company may only make a distribution out of profits.[337] According to s 830(2):

> A company's profits available for distribution are its accumulated, realised profits, so far as not previously utilised by distribution or capitalisation, less its accumulated, realised losses, so far as not previously written off in a reduction or reorganisation of capital duly made.[338]

4.217   This requirement is, according to s 830(3), subject to specific provisions the examination of which is outside the scope of the book. Whether there are profits available must be determined by reference to the company's last annual accounts and to particular items in such accounts.[339]

---

331   See *Re Halt Garage (1964) Ltd* [1982] 3 All ER 1016.
332   See *Progress Property Co Ltd v Moorgarth Group Ltd* [201UKSC 55, [2011] 1 WLR 1, [2011] 2 BCLC 332.
333   For an instance, see *Global Corporate Ltd v Hale* [2018] EWCA Civ 2618.
334   Companies Act 2006, s 829(1).
335   [2019] EWHC 2855 (Ch).
336   Companies Act 2006, s 829(2).
337   Ibid., s 830(1).
338   Ibid., s 830(2).
339   Ibid., s 836(1).

In determining whether a distribution contravenes the Companies Act or not, s 830 indicates **4.218** that reference is to be had to the following items as stated in the relevant accounts:

(a)   profits, losses, assets and liabilities;
(b)   provisions of the following kinds –
    (i)   where the relevant accounts are Companies Act accounts, provisions of a kind specified for the purposes of this subsection by regulations under section 396;
    (ii)   where the relevant accounts are IAS accounts, provisions of any kind;
(c)   share capital and reserves (including undistributable reserves).

For the most part 'the relevant accounts' will be the company's last accounts (separate from any **4.219** group accounts),[340] properly prepared in conformity with the Companies Act, and circulated to the members as required by s 423. Of note is the fact that the requirements and rules contained in the Companies Act are supplemented by the common law principle that distributions cannot be paid out of capital. Section 851(1) provides that: 'Except as provided in this section, the provisions of this Part are without prejudice to any rule of law restricting the sums out of which, or the cases in which, a distribution may be made.'

Directors of public companies must satisfy two additional elements before making a distribu- **4.220** tion, namely that they may only distribute: (1) if the amount of the company's net assets is not less than the aggregate of its called up share capital and undistributable reserves; (2) if, and to the extent that, the distribution does not reduce the amount of the company's assets to less than the aggregate.[341] The undistributable reserves are: the company's share premium account; the company's capital redemption reserve; the amount by which the company's accumulated, unrealised profits exceed the company's accumulated, unrealised losses; any other reserve that the company is stopped from disturbing by any legislation or under its articles.[342]

The consequence of a distribution being in breach of the Companies Act is that if at the time of **4.221** the distribution the member knows or has reasonable grounds for believing that it is in breach, he or she is liable to repay it to the company, or in the case of a distribution made otherwise than in cash, to pay the company a sum equal to the value of the distribution at that time.[343] Members might also be liable for knowing receipt if it can be established that the directors breached their duties in making the distribution and the members know that what was received was traceable to a breach of fiduciary duty.[344] Furthermore, members could be held liable under s 423 of the Act on the basis that the payment of a dividend is a transaction defrauding creditors if the company can be said to have had as its purpose in paying the dividend an intention to put assets beyond the reach of creditors.[345]

---

340   Ibid., s 836(2).
341   Ibid., s 831(1).
342   Ibid., s 831(4).
343   Ibid., s 847(2). For a case that dealt with this, see *It's a Wrap (UK) Ltd v Gula* [2006] EWCA Civ 544, [2006] 2 BCLC 634.
344   *El Ajou v Dollar Land Holdings plc* [1994] 2 All ER 685, 700. For an example, see *Precision Dippings Ltd v Precision Dippings Marketing Ltd* [1985] BCLC 385. For a discussion of 'knowing receipt' in the context of directors' breach of duty, see Andrew Keay, *Directors' Duties* (4th ed, LexisNexis, 2020), Ch 15.
345   This was argued in *Johnson v Arden* [2018] EWHC 1624 (Ch).

4.222   The recipient of the benefit may not be the only one affected if the benefit is a breach. While the Companies Act does not provide that the directors are liable for unlawful distributions the common law does, and most actions are taken against the directors, who might also be, especially in small–medium sized companies, the members in receipt.[346] The directors could be liable for that part of the distribution that is unlawful.[347] The basis for this is that the directors are regarded as the trustees of the company's property and the payment would constitute an unlawful distribution of the company's assets.[348] If a director is held liable then the order will be that the director must repay the funds paid out by way of dividends or other distributions.[349] It is usually pleaded that directors who grant unlawful distributions are in breach of duty or breach of trust and action is instituted pursuant to s 212 of the Act (the so-called 'misfeasance provision').[350]

4.223   Where there are unlawful distributions an action could also be brought, when the company is insolvent, on the basis of a breach of the duty to take account of the interests of the creditors,[351] something discussed earlier.

4.224   Whether a distribution is unlawful or not is a matter of substance and not form.[352]

4.225   The prospect of liability should focus the minds of directors and should, also, help them to resist pressure from shareholders for the distribution of dividends if the company has insufficient profits to satisfy a dividend.

4.226   It is not intended to go into great detail as far as the law is concerned. What is critical from a governance perspective is that the directors must be mindful of when they can make distributions to members out of company funds. They need to satisfy themselves that their company has distributable profits from which distributions can be made. This involves, inter alia, taking into account those matters referred to above and enumerated in s 830. Naturally, if a company is insolvent it will not have distributable profits, so no dividends or other distributions should be paid out.

4.227   Directors who are concerned about acting properly might be fearful of the unlawful distribution provisions, but they should take some comfort from the fact that Zacaroli J in *Burnden Holdings (UK) Ltd v Fielding*[353] held that directors would only be liable if they had known or ought reasonably to have known that the distribution entailed a misapplication of company finds.[354] Thus, there is not a rule of strict liability, that is, directors are not necessarily liable merely because an unlawful distribution has been made. Also, of some solace for directors is the fact that his Lordship said that directors were entitled to rely on the opinion of others and,

---

346   See, e.g., *Global Corporate Ltd v Hale* [2018] EWCA Civ 2618, [2019] BCC 431.
347   *Liquidator of Marini Ltd v Dickenson* [2003] EWHC 334 (Ch), [2004] BCC 172.
348   *Belmont Finance Corp Ltd v Williams Furniture Ltd* [1980] 1 All ER 393, 405; *Bairstow v Queen's Moat Houses plc* [2001] 2 BCLC 531, [44], [50], [51].
349   *Re Paycheck Services 3 Ltd* [2010] UKSC 51, [2010] 1 WLR 2793, [2011] 1 BCLC 141, [48]–[49].
350   Proceedings are actually instituted under Part 12 of the Insolvency Rules 2016.
351   *Angel Group Ltd v Davey* [2018] EWHC 1781 (Ch), [75].
352   *Progress Property Co Ltd v Moorgarth Group Ltd* [2010] UKSC 55, [2011] 1 WLR 1, [2011] 2 BCLC 332, [27].
353   [2019] EWHC 1566 (Ch).
354   Ibid., [139].

in particular, the auditors concerning the accuracy of statements that appear in the company's accounts.[355]

L. DIRECTORS' DISQUALIFICATION

1. Introduction

As we have seen earlier in this chapter, directors who continue to allow their companies to trade whilst insolvent, or where insolvency is likely, run a number of specific risks. They may find that they are ordered by the court to contribute to the assets of the company should it eventually enter into a formal insolvency process. **4.228**

The risk of disqualification under the Company Directors Disqualification Act 1986 (CDDA) may be added to the considerations already discussed in this chapter. The process of directors' disqualification itself often takes into account the interests of various stakeholders but is primarily motivated by what is in the public interest.[356] **4.229**

Court-ordered directors' disqualification was introduced in 1928[357] initially as a bolt-on to what was at the time the new law on fraudulent trading. It has undergone numerous additions and amendments over the years. Its link to a court's power to order compensation for fraudulent trading fell away and its main area of operation today is the disqualification of directors of insolvent companies whose behaviour is deemed 'unfit'. Since 2015, a finding of unfitness in such cases also allows the court to order compensation to individual creditors or for the benefit of creditors generally. The link between compensating creditors and disqualification has therefore been renewed albeit in a new form. **4.230**

Disqualification prevents a person from acting as a director or being involved in the management of any company. Disqualification is not limited to certain types of business activity nor restricted to any particular sector. It is economy-wide, restricting involvement in the management of any company regardless of the sector in which it operates or the business it conducts.[358] Disqualification might be seen as an ultimate agent of accountability requiring a director to explain why he or she should not be disqualified for what they have done. **4.231**

It should be recognised that the law on directors' disqualification is in effect a discrete system of law. A breach of fiduciary, common law or statutory duty may contribute to a court's decision **4.232**

---

355 Ibid.
356 CDDA, s 22 extends the application of the Act to effectively all conceivable varieties of director of all conceivable types of corporate body.
357 Sections 75 and 76 of the Companies Act 1928 gave effect to recommendations made by the Greene Committee Cmd 2657 (1925–6). This ground for disqualification survives in a different form today under s 4(1)(a), CDDA.
358 The effect of disqualification is to prohibit a person from acting as a director, as receiver, or being concerned or taking part in the promotion, formation or management of a company (without the permission of the court) or to act as an insolvency practitioner (which is an absolute restriction so that there is no power in the court to permit it) – ss 1(1)(b) and 1A(1)(b) CDDA. A director who has been found unfit under s 6 CDDA, and disqualified (or disqualified under any of the other provisions of the CDDA), may apply to the court under s 17 CDDA to seek the court's leave to continue to act notwithstanding the disqualification order.

to disqualify a director but it is not an ordained requisite. A director of an insolvent company may be found to be unfit to be director, even without any finding by the court that he or she has breached any specific duties.

4.233   A majority of litigation brought against directors generally is intended either to punish directors (if a criminal offence has been committed) or to compensate those who have suffered loss due to the directors' breach of duty. Although there is a public interest to support all such insolvency-related litigation, the aim of disqualification proceedings is primarily to protect the public. Disqualification achieves this by acting as a deterrent to others and by taking unfit directors 'off the road'.[359] Morritt LJ has stated that:

> the whole purpose of the 1986 Act is to protect the public from the future activities of those who for the prescribed reasons have shown themselves to be unfit to act as directors of a company.[360]

4.234   Disqualification generally prevents a director from continuing to act as a director and therefore takes away from that director the privilege of using a limited liability business medium. Although this may be seen as a punishment of the director (especially when a disqualification order is made as part of the sentencing function of a criminal court), its primary function is to protect the public from future actions of the director in question.

4.235   Since 2015, an unfit director of an insolvent company may, in addition to being disqualified, also be order to pay compensation to creditors. In such cases, although compensation is ordered, again, the main purpose of the disqualification is the protection of the public. The compensation is additional to the proceedings' main purpose.[361]

4.236   Disqualification may be seen as an important mechanism to raise standards and encourage responsible decision making. Henry LJ in *Re Grayan Building Services Ltd*[362] expressed this point in these words:

> The concept of limited liability and the sophistication of our corporate law offers great privileges and great opportunities for those who wish to trade under that regime. But the corporate environment carries with it the discipline that those who avail themselves of those privileges ... must accept the standards laid down and abide by the regulatory rules and disciplines in place to protect creditors and shareholders. And, while some significant corporate failures will occur despite the directors exercising best managerial practice, in many, too many, cases there have been serious breaches of those rules and disciplines, in situations where the observance of them would or at least might have prevented or reduced the scale of the failure and consequent loss to creditors and investors.[363]

---

359   For a consideration of the court's view that the aim of disqualification is to protect the public see e.g., *Re Migration Services International Ltd* [2000] BCC 1095 and *Re Pantmaetong Timber Co Ltd* [2003] UKHL 49, [2004] 1 AC 158. The period of disqualification reflects the level of risk to the public that a person poses.

360   *Secretary of State for Trade and Industry v Bannister* [1996] 1 All ER 993, 998. See also *Re Lo-Line Electric Motors Ltd* [1988] Ch 477 and *Re Sevenoaks (Retail) Ltd* [1991] Ch 164. In *Re Westmid Packing Services Ltd (No 3)* [1998] BCC 836 the Court of Appeal said that while the primary purpose of disqualification was to protect the public, there might be cases where there was a delay in bringing proceedings and this meant that the public was no longer at risk, but disqualification ought to be ordered so as to reflect the gravity of the conduct in question and to act as a deterrent.

361   For an encyclopaedic consideration of directors' disqualification in general see the online or looseleaf service, *Mithani on Disqualification* (LexisNexis).

362   [1995] Ch 241.

363   See also *Re Swift 736 Ltd* [1993] BCLC 896, 900 per Sir Donald Nicholls V-C.

To similar effect, emphasising a director's individual responsibility for mismanagement, **4.237** Timothy Lloyd J in *Re Atlantic Computers plc*[364] stated:

> The point of a disqualification order is, by depriving the respondent of the liberty to take part in the management of a business carried on with the privilege of limited liability, to protect the public both from misconduct of a business by that director and also by deterrent effect in relation to other company directors … A consistent theme in the cases under the Act is that, while the court must consider the extent of a respondent's responsibility … a director cannot avoid his responsibility by leaving the management to another or others ….

2.   Grounds for disqualification under the CDDA

The law on directors' disqualification has been the subject of nearly a century of fairly regular **4.238** piecemeal amendment.[365] A significant re-writing of the law came about with the CDDA in 1986 (along with all other aspects of insolvency law) due to the Cork Committee's recommendations.[366] Further significant additions, in the context of insolvency, were made by the Insolvency Act 2000[367] and the Small Business, Enterprise and Employment Act 2015.[368]

One of the consequences of the piecemeal development of the law on disqualification is that **4.239** there are a number of grounds for an order which cover similar ground. In outline, the grounds for disqualification under CDDA fall into six general categories (only the first three are directly relevant in the context of insolvency):

(1)   undischarged bankrupts (or those subject to a bankruptcy restrictions order or a debt relief restrictions order) are disqualified automatically. This also applies to those who are in default in relation to payment under a county court administration order (where the court revokes the order);[369]

(2)   where directors of insolvent companies are found by a court to be unfit to be concerned in the management of a company, the court must disqualify under s 6. Section 6 has turned out to be the most important provision in terms of numbers of disqualifications and in terms of relevance to directors of insolvent companies. It is discussed further below. Directors may also be disqualified, under s 8, based upon a finding of unfitness in cases where the companies in question are not insolvent. Such cases may be brought following an

---

364   Unreported, 15 June 1998 but quoted by Norris J in *Secretary of State for Business, Enterprise and Regulatory Reform v Sullman* [2008] EWHC 3179 (Ch); [2010] BCC 500, [2].

365   See the Companies Act 1928 following the Greene Committee, Cmd 2657 (1925–6); the Companies Act 1948 following the Cohen Committee, Cmd 6659 (1945); the Insolvency Act 1976 and Companies Act 1976 (and the subsequent Companies Act 1981) following the Jenkins Committee, Cmnd 1749 (1962). The maximum period of disqualification was extended from five years to 15 years by the Companies Act 1981.

366   Cmnd 8558 (1982), paras 1813–1837.

367   Primarily introducing the possibility of a defendant director offering an undertaking with the enforceability of a court order without the time and expense of a court hearing.

368   The 2015 Act introduced the possibility of compensation orders linked to disqualification in insolvency cases (ss 15A–15C CDDA), disqualification based upon offences committed overseas (s 5A CDDA) and effectively allowing for a person to be held jointly liable for the unfit behaviour of a person acting on that person's instructions (ss 8ZA–8ZE). For the background to the 2015 amendments to the CDDA see the government consultation paper *Transparency and trust: enhancing the transparency of UK company ownership and increasing trust in UK business – discussion paper* (July 2013 BIS/13/959) and also the *Government response to the consultation Transparency and trust: enhancing the transparency of UK company ownership and increasing trust in UK business – Government Response* (April 2014 BIS/14/672).

369   CDDA, s 11.

investigation into the companies in question but are not limited to such circumstances.[370] A person may also be disqualified if a person who was disqualified under either s 6 or s 8 for unfitness was acting in accordance with instructions or directions from that person;[371]

(3)   directors may be disqualified where they have been found liable for wrongful trading or fraudulent trading;[372]

(4)   directors may be disqualified who have been convicted for indictable offences (including fraudulent trading) connected with the promotion, formation, management or liquidation of a company;[373]

(5)   to similar effect, persistent non-compliance with provisions requiring the filing of documents may lead to disqualification;[374] and

(6)   directors may be disqualified for breach of competition law.[375]

3.   Section 6 CDDA – unfitness

4.240   Most disqualifications are made in civil proceedings based upon the unfitness of directors of insolvent companies under s 6.[376] If the court finds unfitness, it must disqualify. It does not have a discretion not to, as it does have, for example, under s 8. Section 6 provides that three conditions must be satisfied in order for a person to be disqualified:

(i)   the company has at any time become insolvent within the meaning of s 6 (this includes entering any form of liquidation where the company's assets are insufficient to cover all debts and expenses of the winding up, administration or administrative receivership);

(ii)   the defendant was a director of the company;

(iii)   the defendant's conduct as a director was such as to make him or her unfit to be concerned in the management of a company.

4.241   Each case requires a three-stage process to be carried out: (1) does the conduct in question amount to misconduct; (2) if so, does it justify a finding of unfitness;[377] and (3) if so, what period of disqualification, being not less than two years, should be ordered?[378]

---

370   Until the amendments made by the Small Business, Enterprise and Employment Act 2015, s 8 could only be used against directors where it appeared from 'investigative material' that their conduct in relation to a company made them unfit. It is now possible for disqualification under s 8 based upon any information properly put before the court which demonstrates unfitness.

371   CDDA, ss 8ZA–8ZE.

372   CDDA, s 10. The court's analysis in *Re Bath Glass Ltd* [1988] BCLC 329, 333, emphasises that when considering unfitness under s 6, the court may look at a director's decision to allow a company to continue to trade whilst insolvent, but this did not require a finding of wrongful trading along with all of its detailed requisites.

373   CDDA, ss 2 and 4 and in relation to overseas offences, s 5A.

374   CDDA, ss 3 and 5.

375   CDDA, s 9A.

376   Insolvency Service statistics suggest that there are over 1,000 disqualifications under s 6 annually whilst the combined total disqualifications under all the other sections rarely goes above 100.

377   Ordinary commercial misjudgment in itself will not demonstrate unfitness (*Re Lo-Line Electric Motors Ltd* [1988] Ch 477, 486).

378   This formulation is taken from Blackburne J in *Re Structural Concrete Ltd* [2001] BCC 578.

The first stage requires an investigation into the conduct of the director. The court will only **4.242** look at the conduct put before the court.[379] Once the court has assessed the conduct it must then decide whether or not it satisfies the label 'misconduct'.[380] In making that judgment the court has regard to the matters listed in paras 1–4 (in all cases) and in addition, paras 5–7 (where the defendant was a director) of Sch 1 of CDDA:[381]

Para 1   The extent to which the person was responsible for the causes of any material contravention by a company or overseas company of any applicable legislative or other requirement.

Para 2   Where applicable, the extent to which the person was responsible for the causes of a company or overseas company becoming insolvent.

Para 3   The frequency of conduct of the person which falls within paragraph 1 or 2.

Para 4   The nature and extent of any loss or harm caused, or any potential loss or harm which could have been caused, by the person's conduct in relation to a company or overseas company.

Para 5   Any misfeasance or breach of any fiduciary duty by the director in relation to a company or overseas company.

Para 6   Any material breach of any legislative or other obligation of the director which applies as a result of being a director of a company or overseas company.

Para 7   The frequency of conduct of the director which falls within paragraph 5 or 6.

The matters listed in the Schedule are not an exhaustive list. In addition to, or as examples of, **4.243** those listed in the Schedule, it is common to rely upon other matters, each of which, if made out, may be seen as badges of unfitness. The following are broad categories of the types of conduct the court will look for:

(i)   trading while insolvent at the risk of the company's creditors;[382] undercapitalisation of the company;[383] trading with 'phoenix' companies;[384]

(ii)   non-payment of Crown debts to the detriment of the Crown;[385]

---

379   *Re Deaduck Ltd, Baker v Secretary of State for Trade and Industry* [2000]; 1 BCLC 148. *Re Finelist Ltd* [2004] BCC 877, [17]–[19] *Re Sutton Glassworks Ltd* [1996] BCC 174, 176. Besides considering the actions of the director in relation to the company that had become insolvent a court may have regard to the director's conduct in relation to other companies (including overseas companies). The court will only be concerned with evidence of the conduct of the person as a director, including conduct as a shadow or de facto director, therefore ruling out any evidence concerning conduct that related to other positions held by the director, or other situations in which he or she found himself or herself.

380   In *Re Pinemoor Ltd* [1997] BCC 708, 710 Chadwick J explained that care was required in distinguishing between facts that can be established by direct evidence, inferences which the court may draw from those facts and matters which amount to unfitness.

381   Section 12C requires the court to consider the matters listed in Sch 1 in assessing whether conduct is unfit. (which is to be used in s 6 proceedings but also when considering whether to disqualify under ss 2–4, 5A, 8 or 10) and, if so, in determining the period of disqualification.

382   *Re Sevenoaks Stationers (Retail) Ltd* [1991] Ch 164; *Re Synthetic Technology Ltd* [1993] BCC 549; *Re Richborough Furniture Ltd* [1996] 1 BCLC 507; *Re Living Images Ltd* [1996] 1 BCLC 348; *Re City Pram and Toy Co Ltd* [1998] BCC 537.

383   *Re Chartmore Ltd* [1990] BCLC 673; *Re Austinsuite Furniture Ltd* [1992] BCLC 1047; *Re Pamstock Ltd* [1994] 1 BCLC 716.

384   *Re Douglas Construction Services Ltd* [1988] BCLC 397; *Re Keypak Homecare Ltd (No.2)* [1990] BCC 117; *Re Travel Mondial (UK) Ltd* [1991] BCLC 120.

385   *Re Dawson Print Group Ltd* [1987] BCLC 601; *Re Sevenoaks Stationers (Retail) Ltd* [1991] Ch 164; *Secretary of State for Trade and Industry v McTighe (No. 2)* [1996] 2 BCLC 477; *Secretary of State for Business, Energy and Industrial Strategy v Steven* [2018] EWHC 1331 (Ch).

(iii)   excessive directors' remuneration at a time of insolvency;[386] preferences and other breaches of fiduciary and/or statutory duty;[387]

(iv)   failure to maintain adequate accounting records and failure to file statutory returns;[388] misuse of the company's bank account;[389] and

(v)   failure to co-operate with the insolvency officeholder.[390]

4.244   If the facts show misconduct, the second stage requires the court to consider whether it warrants a finding of unfitness. If the director has taken legal or other expert advice and followed that advice, a finding of unfitness is not likely.

4.245   In *Re Bath Glass Ltd*[391] Peter Gibson J said:

> To reach a finding of unfitness the court must be satisfied that the director has been guilty of a serious failure or serious failures, whether deliberately or through incompetence, to perform those duties of directors which are attendant on the privilege of trading through companies with limited liability. Any misconduct qua director may be relevant, even if it does not fall within a specific section of the Companies Act or the Insolvency Act.

4.246   In *Re UKLI Ltd*[392] Hildyard J held:

> [A] finding of unfitness does not depend upon a finding of lack of moral probity: the touchstone is lack of regard for and compliance with proper standards, and breaches of the rules and disciplines by which those who avail themselves of the great privileges and opportunities of limited liability must abide … Although the touchstone of unfitness should reflect the public interest in promoting and raising standards amongst those who manage companies with the benefit of limited liability, the test is always whether the conduct complained of makes the defendant unfit, and not whether it is more generally in the public interest that a person be disqualified: thus, for example, the question is whether the present evidence of the director's past misconduct makes him unfit, not whether the defendant is likely to behave wrongly again in the future.

4.247   Where a court comes to the conclusion that a director is unfit, it must impose a term of disqualification. The range that can be considered is from two years to not more than 15 years. The courts have a discretion as to the period which they will impose, but the discretion is to be exercised in accordance with relevant principles. The following will be taken into account by a court: the seriousness of the conduct; the extent of the conduct; and the role the person played in the company.

---

386   *Re Stanford Services Ltd* [1987] BCLC 607; *Re McNulty's Interchange Ltd* [1989] BCLC 709; *Official Receiver v Stern* [2002] 1 BCLC 119.

387   *Re Austinsuite Furniture Ltd* [1992] BCLC 1047; *Re CSTC Ltd* [1995] BCC 173; *Re Grayan Building Services Ltd* [1995] Ch 241.

388   *Re Bath Glass Ltd* [1988] BCLC 329; *Re Pamstock Ltd* [1994] 1 BCLC 716; *Secretary of State for Trade and Industry v Goldberg* [2004] 1 BCLC 597; *Secretary of State for Business, Energy and Industrial Strategy v Al-Safee* [2018] EWHC 509 (Ch).

389   *Re Pamstock Ltd* [1994] 1 BCLC 716; *Re Firedart Ltd* [1994] 2 BCLC 340; *Re Hitco 2000 Ltd* [1995] 2 BCLC 63; *Re Finelist Group Ltd (No 2)* [2005] BCC 596.

390   *Re Tansoft Ltd* [1991] BCLC 339; *Secretary of State for Trade and Industry v McTighe (No 2)* [1996] 2 BCLC 477.

391   [1988] BCLC 329, 333.

392   [2015] BCC 755, 790.

In *Re Sevenoaks Stationers (Retail) Ltd* [393] the Court of Appeal laid down guidelines for the   **4.248**
setting of disqualification periods. The court said that there are three categories. First, there
were particularly serious cases to which a period in excess of ten years should be attached.
Second, where there were cases which involved serious matters, but which did not warrant the
top penalties, a disqualification period of between six and ten years was appropriate. Third,
the range of two to five years was to be applied to cases where the misconduct established was
not of a particularly serious kind. It is permissible for a court, in coming to a decision in s 6
proceedings, to take account of the fact that the defendant gave false evidence to the court.[394]

4.   Procedure under section 6 CDDA

The Secretary of State for Business, Energy and Industrial Strategy (or the official receiver on   **4.249**
the Secretary of State's instructions where the company has entered compulsory liquidation)[395]
initiates proceedings and will seek a finding from a court under section 6 that a person is unfit
for office.

The evidence which is usually used in disqualification proceedings, certainly where a company is   **4.250**
insolvent, comes from the duty imposed upon all liquidators, administrators and administrative
receivers to submit a report on directors' conduct to the Secretary of State.[396] The report must
be submitted online within three months of the company's insolvency. The officeholder must
report on each person who had been a director of the company within the previous three years.
The report must detail any conduct which may assist the Secretary of State in deciding whether
to bring disqualification proceedings. If the Secretary of State decides to bring proceedings
under section 6, he or she must do so within three years of the company entering insolvency.[397]

5.   Disqualification undertakings

When s 6 proceedings were first instituted in the late 1980s and 1990s, they were very expen-   **4.251**
sive. They required a High Court hearing and, whether disqualified or not, the cost and time
spent on such cases left some directors without the means to continue in business. There were
relatively informal attempts at this time to try to reduce the costs and the time involved in
obtaining a disqualification. It became a common practice, in the 1990s, for targeted directors
to give undertakings to the Secretary of State that they would not act as a director for a specified
period of time. Such informal undertakings did not have the force of law behind them and there
were concerns that the public interest might not have been best served by excluding the court
from such deliberations.

The Insolvency Act 2000 gave statutory recognition to a system of disqualification undertak-   **4.252**
ings. Section 1A(1) of the CDDA now provides that the Secretary of State may accept an
undertaking, which may include an agreement by a person not to act as: a director; a receiver
of a company's property; an insolvency practitioner; or in any way take part in the management

---

393   [1991] Ch 164.
394   *R v Moorgate Metals Ltd* [1995] BCLC 503.
395   CDDA, s 7.
396   CDDA, s 7A.
397   CDDA, s 7(2).

of a company unless leave of the court is secured. A disqualification undertaking is enforceable as if it were a disqualification order made by the court. Breach of either a disqualification order or undertaking is a criminal offence[398] and the person in breach will be personally liable for the debts of any new company in which he or she is involved.[399]

4.253 The Secretary of State must, before he or she may accept an undertaking, judge that the conduct of the director makes him or her unfit to be involved in the management of a company and that accepting an undertaking is in the public interest. It is possible for a court order to vary an undertaking that has been given.[400]

6. Compensation orders

4.254 In what may be seen as part of the public interest nature of CDDA proceedings, ss 15A–15C permit the court, whilst disqualifying a director of an insolvent company on any ground, which of course includes s 6 (or in a subsequent application brought within two years of any such disqualification), also to order that person to compensate creditors for the loss his or her conduct caused.

4.255 The compensation order may be made in favour of specific creditors who have suffered loss or more generally in favour of creditors generally. The overall effect of the court exercising this discretion is both to protect the public from unfit directors but additionally to compensate those creditors who have suffered loss due to the unfit conduct of those directors. It is a potentially an extremely useful tool to be used against errant directors for the benefit of creditors.

4.256 The compensation order regime provides two separate remedies for a director's culpable conduct. For example, as well as disqualifying a director under s 6, and so protecting the public from further unfit conduct by that person, it also provides compensation to the victims of the director's unfit conduct. This is likely also to have a deterrent effect. Directors may be tempted to risk disqualification. If it leads to a disqualification undertaking, the director may not be affected financially to any significant degree. If the risk of a compensation order is real, those directors may feel less inclined to risk disqualification.

4.257 Thus far, the Secretary of State seems inexplicably reluctant to use the power to apply for compensation orders in disqualification proceedings. It is, of course, quite reasonable that the Secretary of State would not wish to tread on the toes of insolvency officeholders if they are already litigating a matter. Compensation orders are therefore extremely unlikely to be requested where the finding of unfitness, upon which the disqualification order is made, is based upon the same facts as existing or prospective litigation being brought by an officeholder. This avoids the risk of a director being held liable twice for the same conduct.

4.258 At the time of writing, there has only been one reported case, which is believed to be the only case where the Secretary of State has applied for a disqualification compensation order. In

---

398 CDDA, s 12.
399 CDDA, s 15.
400 CDDA, s 8A.

Re Noble Vintners Ltd[401] a sole director was found to have misappropriated company funds of £559,484. He had moved to Northern Cyprus and was disqualified for 15 years in his absence. A compensation order in the sum of £559,484 was made. The Secretary of State had identified 28 unpaid creditors whose total losses were quantified as £460,067. This amount was ordered to be paid to the Secretary of State on behalf of those named creditors. In addition, £99,417 was ordered to be paid to the liquidator of the company as a contribution to the assets of the company (and which would cover the liquidator's fees and expenses as well as allowing for a dividend to creditors).

The compensation order regime is an entirely new, free-standing regime which provides for **4.259** a single basis for liability. It is intended to give monetary redress directly to creditors affected by a director's unfit conduct. Liability is based not upon loss to the company but on loss to its individual creditors, such loss being measurable in monetary terms. There has to be a causal link between the loss and unfit conduct, but the misconduct does not have to be the predominant cause. Using hindsight and common sense but without considering forseeability, the court has to be satisfied that the misconduct caused the loss. Loss is assessed as at the date of the final hearing of the compensation order claim.

The court pointed out that the new compensation order regime permits a court to order **4.260** a payment even where the unfit conduct does not cause loss to the company itself. It also enables recoveries to be made in cases where one creditor (or class of creditors) is paid ahead of another creditor (or class of creditor). The court recognised that this is potentially significant in the context of disqualification, where a regular ground is that a director caused the company to pay other creditors ahead of the Crown, and thereby to trade to the Crown's detriment. As this allegation is commonly found in disqualification proceedings, there appears no reason why the court could not begin to make compensation orders in favour of the Crown on a regular basis.

This interpretation goes some way to distinguishing the compensation regime from the reme- **4.261** dies available to an officeholder under the Insolvency Act 1986. It includes breaches of duty or specific statutory provisions but covers the entirety of the unfit conduct and so its reach goes beyond those breaches of duty. Importantly, the court will only look at unfit conduct which has caused loss. The court may consider the respective liability of other directors and any amount of financial contribution already made in recompense for the misconduct. There would be no double liability imposed based upon the same conduct.

Checks and balances exist within the statutory machinery so that any officeholder will be served **4.262** with notice of any application for a compensation order and may appear to contest the claim if it is likely to be detrimental to any action being brought or considered by the officeholder based upon the same misconduct.

The court has to consider whether a payment to individual creditors is appropriate, or whether **4.263** a contribution to the insolvency estate is more appropriate (or, as in *Noble Vintners*, a combination of both).

---

401   [2019] EWHC 2806 (Ch), [2020] BCC 198.

7. Conclusion

4.264 Although directors' disqualification does occur in the context of solvent companies, the large majority of disqualifications relate to companies which have entered a formal insolvency proceeding. Directors need to understand the risks they run when a company's solvency is in question. Even if a company appears solvent whilst a going concern, it may be that once in liquidation, the various costs and expenses of the winding up, when added to the company's general debts, pushes the company out of what looked likely to be a solvent winding up into insolvent liquidation. The risk of s 6 proceedings in particular then becomes very real.

4.265 Of all the disqualification provisions, s 6 is the most significant in terms of numbers of disqualifications and application in the context of insolvency. The big risk to a director of a company which is likely to enter an insolvency process is disqualification under s 6. Procedurally, such disqualification has been simplified since the beginning of the millennium and made less time-consuming and expensive with the introduction of the undertakings regime. A great many disqualifications are now agreed under the undertaking process where there is no court hearing.

4.266 Breach of a disqualification order of undertaking is a serious matter for a director. The director will have committed a criminal offence and be personally liable for the debts of any company whose management he or she has been involved in.

4.267 The Secretary of State is sometimes seen as only taking steps to disqualify those who are pejoratively referred to as 'low hanging fruit'.[402] There is a common belief amongst different insolvency stakeholders that directors responsible for large-scale or complex patterns of misconduct are not often pursued under the CDDA. There is some evidence to suggest that the Secretary of State may be trying to change this perception with the announcement that proceedings are being taken against directors of Carillion plc.[403]

4.268 In recent times, the potential consequence of disqualification proceedings is no longer limited to just disqualification, serious though such restrictions are to anyone who wishes to trade with the benefit of limited liability. The original idea from the Companies Act 1928 to link disqualification to personal liability for fraudulent trading survives to this day in the form of s 4 CDDA but is rarely used in practice. However, this century-old concept has developed to the point where there is now the potentially very serious financial risk of a disqualified director being ordered to compensate creditors directly (or indirectly) who have suffered loss due to the director's misconduct.

4.269 Although there is currently no suggestion that applying for a compensation order will become the norm in disqualification cases, if it were to, it would very much increase the risk run by directors of companies of doubtful solvency.

---

402 P Walton *Insolvency Litigation and the Jackson Reforms – an update* (May 2016) a research report commissioned by R3 (with the support of ACCA, ICAEW, ICAS, ILA, IPA, IRS, JLT Specialty Ltd, Willis Taylor Watson), 29.

403 https://www.gov.uk/government/news/carillion-directors-disqualification-proceedings.

5

DECISION-MAKING IN INSOLVENT REGIMES

A. INTRODUCTION

5.001 Once a company enters a formal insolvency process (whether under the Insolvency Act 1986 ('the Act') or the Companies Act 2006), it is clearly critical that appropriate checks and balances are in place to ensure that decisions made are arrived at in a transparent manner and that where those decisions are questionable, there exist powers in interested stakeholders to hold those decision-makers to account. It is a significant strength of the insolvency regime that decisions are generally made in a transparent way which enables others to consider fully the reasons for such decisions.[1] Where appropriate, the regime provides for court oversight, either as an inherent part of the process or in the form of an application to court by concerned stakeholders in order to have such decisions independently assessed.

5.002 The role of insolvency practitioners as officeholders in making decisions is fully considered below in Chapters 7 and 8. This chapter outlines the situations where insolvency practitioners have powers to make decisions. In some procedures (administration and liquidation) the insolvency practitioner will be in control of the company and will therefore be in a position to make all managerial decisions. This chapter will also consider the powers of other stakeholders to make important decisions such as the company's directors, shareholders and creditors. Such powers are usually limited to the appointment and supervision of insolvency practitioners in administration and liquidation but are more extensive in the debtor-in-possession procedures. This discussion will build upon the outlines of each of the statutory insolvency procedures in Chapter 3, Parts D, E and F and will concentrate on an explanation of decision making in each of those insolvency procedures. It will consider the permissible limits within which such deci-

---

1   As part of the checks and balances the general requirements throughout the Insolvency Act 1986 for insolvency office-holders to provide information at the commencement of proceedings and regular updated reports to creditors (and others) are significant in allowing creditors (or others) to make a reasonably informed decision as to whether or not to take remedial action.

sions are made and also consider how decisions may be called into question or countermanded by other stakeholders whether by court action or otherwise.

5.003 Board and shareholder decisions are generally made in accordance with a company's articles of association. The mechanics of creditor decision making are explained above in Part D of Chapter 3.

B. FORMAL DEBTOR-IN-POSSESSION PROCEDURES

1. Moratorium

5.004 The moratorium procedure is a debtor-in-possession procedure which means the directors remain in managerial control of the company. Although in control they are subject to certain controls where either the court's permission or the monitor's consent is needed.

5.005 The initial decision to obtain a moratorium will be made by the company's directors. The court will not usually be actively involved.[2] The directors file the requisite documents in court and that filing brings into force the moratorium (for an initial period of 20 business days).[3] The documents filed must include a notice that the directors wish to obtain a moratorium. The directors must also make a statement that, in their view, the company is, or is likely to become, unable to pay its debts (within the definition found in s 123 of the Act).[4]

5.006 The monitor, a licensed insolvency practitioner, must make a statement that he or she consents to act as monitor and that the company is an eligible company.[5]

5.007 The proposed monitor must also make a statement that, in his or her view, it is likely that the moratorium will result in the rescue of the company as a going concern.[6] The likely result of rescue as a going concern[7] is in very similar terms to the primary objective of administration and will be interpreted in the same manner. It will require the monitor to be of the view there is a real prospect[8] that rescue will occur.

---

2   Under Insolvency Act 1986, ss A4 and A5 respectively where the company is subject to a winding-up petition or is an overseas company the directors will need to apply to court.

3   Insolvency Act 1986, s A7(1)(a). The moratorium comes into effect automatically when the relevant documents are filed with the court. Directors are under a duty to notify the monitor when the moratorium comes into force. A failure to do so without a reasonable excuse is an offence under s A8.

4   Ibid., s A6.

5   Not all companies are eligible for a Moratorium. A list of companies which are not eligible is found in Sch ZA1. The monitor will need to ensure that he or she has confirmed eligibility before making this statement.

6   Insolvency Act 1986, s A6. Companies who are regulated under the Financial Services and Markets Act 2000 will also need to provide a reference to the written consent of the appropriate regulator under s A49.

7   Although both *Davey v Money* [2018] EWHC 766 (Ch), [2018] Bus L R 1903 and *Re Zinc Hotels (Holdings) Ltd* [2018] EWHC 1936 (Ch) suggest that the primary objective of administration under para 3(1)(a) of Sch B1 of the Act requires restoration of the company as a going concern, *Lehman Brothers International (Europe) (in admin)* [2020] EWHC 1932 (Ch) suggests a return to solvency without being a going concern will be sufficient.

8   *Re Harris Simons Construction Ltd* [1989] 1 WLR 368.

It is important for any proposed monitor to become informed as to the company's situation otherwise the monitor will not be able to make these statements. As with other roles taken on by insolvency practitioners, the monitor needs to exercise professional judgment in relation to the reliability of information provided and how to react to it. **5.008**

After the moratorium becomes effective, the monitor must monitor the company. The monitor's role is to act in a supervisory capacity to ensure that it remains likely that the company can be rescued as a going concern. The monitor may demand relevant information from the company's directors for this purpose.[9] If such information is not forthcoming or is deficient or delayed, the monitor may decide to bring the moratorium to an end by filing a notice at court.[10] **5.009**

The monitor may also decide to file a notice at court terminating the moratorium if the monitor no longer thinks rescue remains a likely result or conversely if rescuing the company as a going concern has been achieved.[11] **5.010**

The remuneration of a monitor is a contractual matter between the company and the monitor. The monitor's remuneration is not decided upon by a separate decision of the creditors but is agreed between the monitor and the company's directors. **5.011**

During the moratorium the payment of pre-moratorium debts (subject to certain exceptions[12]) is restricted unless the monitor consents. Debts falling due during the moratorium must be paid (along with pre-moratorium debts for which the company does not have a payment holiday under s A18 of the Act). If the monitor thinks that the company is unable to pay such moratorium debts, the monitor must again bring the moratorium to an end by filing a notice at court. For the purposes of making this decision the monitor must disregard any debts that the monitor has reasonable grounds for thinking are likely to be paid within five days of the decision, and any debts in respect of which the creditor has agreed to defer payment until a time that is later than the decision.[13] **5.012**

The company may dispose of property that is not subject to a security, in the ordinary way of its business, if the monitor consents, or if the disposal is in pursuance of a court order. The monitor may give consent to the disposal only if he or she thinks that it will support the rescue of the company as a going concern.[14] **5.013**

---

9   Insolvency Act 1986, s A36.
10   Ibid., s A38.
11   Ibid., s A38. A moratorium comes to an end under s A16 if the company enters into a scheme of arrangement or restructuring plan under Parts 26 or 26A of the Companies Act 2006 or enters into a relevant insolvency procedure (e.g., a company voluntary arrangement, administration or liquidation).
12   Ibid., s A18. Total payments of non-excluded pre-moratorium debts may be made under s A28 of not more than the greater of £5,000 or 1 per cent of the value of the unsecured debts owed by the company at the start of the moratorium. The monitor may give consent to the company to make payments of pre-moratorium debts above these limits but only if the monitor thinks that it will support the rescue of the company as a going concern.
13   Ibid., s A38(1)(d).
14   Ibid., s A29. Under s A26 the monitor may consent to the company granting security.

5.014   In the case of property that is subject to a security interest, the company may only dispose of the property with the permission of the court or in accordance with the terms of the security.[15]

5.015   Any decision by the directors to borrow money or obtain credit during the moratorium needs to be transparent. It is an offence for the company to obtain credit of £500 or more unless the person providing the credit has been informed that a moratorium is in force in relation to the company.[16]

5.016   The directors may decide that they need to extend the term of the moratorium for a further 20 business days under s A10.[17] They may obtain creditor consent via a creditors' qualifying decision procedure (only pre-moratorium creditors may vote) for an extension (or series of extensions) beyond 40 business days up to one year in total from commencement under s A11. In order to vote, creditors must provide the directors with proof of their debt. A majority in value of secured creditors must approve the extension as well as a majority in value of unsecured creditors.[18] It is an unusual quirk of the moratorium process that the directors and not the monitor deal with the creditor voting process.

5.017   On the application of the directors, the court may extend a moratorium for any period under s A13.[19]

5.018   Creditors cannot generally take legal action against the company subject to a moratorium in relation to pre-moratorium debts although the court may give creditors permission so to do. The court will rely upon the case law under the administration moratorium in considering whether or not to allow creditor action to occur.[20]

5.019   Creditors are provided with little information about the moratorium beyond the fact that it is happening and the identity of the monitor. However, a creditor (director or member) is provided with a power to apply to the court to challenge an act, omission or decision by the monitor.[21] This power is similar to the power to challenge the decisions of a supervisor in the context of a company voluntary arrangement.[22]

---

15   Ibid., s A31. This power mirrors the power available under administration found in para 71 of Sch B1. Under s A30, the disposal of hire purchase goods is subject to a power very similar to that found in administration under para 72 of Sch B1 whereby the court may order disposal subject to certain safeguards for the owner.

16   Ibid., s A25.

17   The directors must state that all moratorium debts that have fallen due have been paid or otherwise discharged and that the company is still, or is likely to become, unable to pay its debts. The monitor must state that he or she is of the view that an extension to the moratorium is likely to result in the rescue of the company as a going concern.

18   Insolvency Act 1986, s A12 and Insolvency Rules 2016, r 5.31. A decision to consent to an extension is not made if, of those voting either a majority of the pre-moratorium creditors who are unconnected secured creditors vote against or a majority of the pre-moratorium creditors who are unconnected unsecured creditors vote against.

19   Under s A14 a moratorium is extended whilst a company voluntary arrangement is being considered by creditors and under s A15 the court which is considering, for example a scheme of arrangement or restructuring plan under the Companies Act 2006, may extend the moratorium allowing the court to consider sanctioning such a rescue.

20   See *Re Atlantic Computer Systems plc* [1992] Ch 505.

21   Insolvency Act 1986, s A42.

22   Ibid., s 7.

A creditor (or member) may apply to the court on the grounds that the company's affairs, **5.020** business and property are being or have been managed in a way that has unfairly harmed the applicant's interests.[23] The court may make any order it thinks fit. The court's order may, amongst other things, regulate the management of the directors, require the directors to stop taking the action complained of, or require a decision of the company's creditors. This power is similar in its terms to that available against an administrator.[24]

2.   Company voluntary arrangement

The terms of a company voluntary arrangement ('CVA') must be transparent and clear. In **5.021** order to garner the support of a company's creditors, the terms of a CVA must be fair and the statutory process to obtain its approval must be carried out carefully and openly. The position of the insolvency practitioner as the person in between the company and its creditors is crucial. He or she must be meticulous and open in dealings with all parties.

A CVA may be proposed by an administrator (or a liquidator) but the vast majority of proposals **5.022** are made by the company's directors. The decision to put forward a CVA is therefore made by whoever is in managerial control of the company.

Where the directors propose a CVA they must approach an insolvency practitioner to act as **5.023** 'nominee'. The nominee must give his or her opinion on the proposal. If the nominee's opinion is that the proposal has 'a reasonable prospect of being approved and implemented' that opinion is filed at court and the proposal is then put to the members and creditors of the company.[25] The directors will therefore usually remain in managerial control of a company in CVA subject to the supervisor's role vis-à-vis the CVA itself. The supervisor will not usually take any active role in the company's management itself.

If the proposal is being put forward by an administrator, the administrator will act as nominee **5.024** and no report is filed at court. The administrator puts the proposal to the members and creditors.

A meeting of the company's members is summoned and a qualifying creditors' decision is **5.025** sought to approve the proposal. The decision of the creditors cannot be by deemed consent procedure. An ordinary resolution of the members must be passed and a creditors' majority of 75 per cent or more in value of the unsecured creditors voting is needed. A resolution in favour of the CVA will usually be invalid if those voting against it include more than half in value of the creditors who are not persons connected with the company.[26]

Section 4A of the Act states that the proposal is approved if either: (1) both the creditors and **5.026** members vote in favour of it; or (2) if the proposal is approved only by the creditors. Section

---

23   Ibid., s A44.
24   Ibid., Sch B1, para 74.
25   The need for the nominee to display complete impartiality in the assessment of the proposal has been emphasised by the wording of Statement of Insolvency Practice 3.2 which was revised in 2021.
26   Insolvency Rules 2016, r 15.34. For the meaning of 'connected' see Insolvency Act 1986, s 249.

4A effectively ensures the creditors' vote takes primacy over any differing view at the members' meeting.

5.027 The members' meeting is conducted according to the voting rights in the company's articles. An ordinary resolution is required to approve the CVA.

5.028 A creditor's voting rights depend upon the amount of the creditor's unsecured debt as at the decision date (or the date of the company going into liquidation or administration as the case may be). If a creditor is fully secured, he or she may still vote on the decision but the value of the vote is nil. If a creditor's debt is partly secured, he or she may vote in respect of the unsecured part. Preferential creditors, such as HMRC, being unsecured, are permitted to vote on the proposal.

5.029 The Insolvency (England and Wales) Rules 2016 ('the Rules') make a distinction between debts which are for an unliquidated or unascertained amount and debts which are disputed on the other.

5.030 A creditor who is owed a debt for an unliquidated amount or a debt whose value is not ascertained may still vote. For the purposes of voting, the unliquidated or unascertained debt shall be valued at £1 unless the person convening the decision (the convener) agrees to put a higher value on the debt.[27] Future debts can usually be readily valued by applying a reasonable discount (if the rules in liquidation are followed such a discount might be 5 per cent per annum). Contingent debts are trickier.[28] Where the contingency makes it impossible to put a current value on the contingent debt the convener will have no choice but to put a value of £1 on it. The convener is obliged to consider the evidence and if it permits him or her safely to attribute to a claim a minimum value higher than £1 then he or she should do so.

5.031 The convener may admit or reject a claim and, where there is a dispute over the debt and the convener is in doubt, he or she must allow the vote, but mark it as objected to. If the objected vote is subsequently found to be invalid, the court may order a new decision-making process be held.[29]

5.032 After the members' meeting has been held and the creditors have decided whether or not to approve the proposal, the chair of the meeting and the convener of the creditors' decision report the respective results to the court under s 4(6) and (6A). An application against any decision of the chair or convener, for example, in disallowing a creditor's vote, must be made to the court within 28 days of the reports being made to the court.

5.033 The remuneration of the nominee and supervisor is a contractual matter between the company, the creditors and the insolvency practitioner, details of which will be included in the CVA proposal. The remuneration is therefore subject to the creditors' approval but the statutory

---

27 Ibid., r 15.31(3).
28 The position of creditors under executory contracts such as continuing leases have proven particularly controversial, see e.g., *Discovery (Northampton) Ltd v Debenhams Retail Ltd* [2019] EWHC 2441 (Ch), [2020] BCC 9.
29 Insolvency Rules 2016, r 15.33(3).

machinery for approving an officeholder's remuneration under the Rules does not apply to CVAs.

Once approved, it is usually the nominee who, under the terms of the CVA, becomes the **5.034** supervisor, although it is possible for the creditors to approve a different insolvency practitioner to be supervisor. The supervisor will have a broad range of powers to agree creditor claims, to receive money from the company and to distribute that money to the creditors according to the terms of the CVA. The supervisor will usually be given powers of enforcement against the company with the ultimate weapon of being enabled to petition for the company's winding up if it breaches the terms of the CVA.

Under s 6, a person entitled to vote either at the members' meeting or on the creditors' quali- **5.035** fying decision procedure (whether or not that person had notice) may apply to the court on the grounds that:

(1)   the CVA unfairly prejudices the interests of a creditor, member or contributory of the company; or
(2)   that there has been some material irregularity at or in relation to the members' meeting or creditors' qualifying decision procedure.

On a finding of unfair prejudice or material irregularity, the court may revoke or suspend the **5.036** approval of the CVA and/or order that a further meeting of the company be called or a further creditors' decision-making procedure be carried out to consider the original or a revised proposal.

Unfair prejudice must relate to the terms of the CVA itself. Adopting the useful heuristics **5.037** found in *Prudential Assurance Co Ltd v PRG Powerhouse Ltd*[30] a creditor's position under the terms of a CVA may be compared to others from both a 'vertical' and a 'horizontal' angle. The vertical angle requires the court to compare the creditor's position under the CVA to the position the creditor would have been in under a winding up. The *Powerhouse* case itself involved an attempt to strip away guarantees which had been provided to creditors by parties connected to the company in question. The effect under the CVA was that the guaranteed creditors would have been in a worse position than if the company had been wound up. Horizontal comparison is with other creditors or classes of creditors under the terms of the CVA. Generally, unless there are convincing reasons to support differential treatment, creditors of the same class will normally be treated equally.[31] Where a nominee has indicated support for a CVA proposal which displays such clear unfair prejudice, as well as the CVA being open to attack, the nominee may be found to have breached his or her professional duties and be reported by the court to his or her professional body.[32]

---

30   [2007] EWHC 1002 (Ch), [2007] BCC 500 at [75].
31   Although differential treatment of the landlords under leases where the profitability of the tenanted premises varied significantly was permitted in *Discovery (Northampton) Ltd v Debenhams Retail Ltd* [2019] EWHC 2441 (Ch), [2020] BCC 9. The court emphasised that it was not possible for a CVA to interfere with proprietary rights such as the right to forfeit the lease.
32   As happened in *Mourant v Sixty UK Ltd* [2010] BCC 882.

5.038 A 'material irregularity' at or in relation to either the company meeting or in relation to the relevant qualifying decision-making procedure requires an irregularity that would or could have made a material difference to the way the CVA was assessed by those voting upon it.[33] Minor breaches of the statutory requirements do not normally amount to material irregularities especially where they would make no difference to the result of the vote. For example, if a creditor is not given notice of the qualifying decision procedure this would normally be an irregularity in relation to the decision procedure. If the creditor in question was only owed a small amount and therefore his or her vote would have made no difference to the result, the irregularity would be unlikely to be seen as material.[34]

5.039 Challenges under s 6 must usually be made within 28 days from the date of the report to court of the decisions made by the members and creditors.[35]

5.040 Various statutory duties are owed by the insolvency practitioner who will frequently act in more than one capacity, that is, as nominee, chairman or convener, and supervisor. The insolvency practitioner will therefore have to carry out an initial appraisal of the proposal, call and hold a members' meeting, convene a creditors' qualifying decision procedure and then supervise the voluntary arrangement in accordance with the Act and the terms of the arrangement. Any breach of the statutory duties owed by a person acting in any of these capacities gives creditors the right to apply to court. The court has wide powers, for example, to remove and replace a nominee or supervisor, to overturn a decision of the supervisor and to regulate the supervision of the arrangement generally.[36]

5.041 The statutory power to apply to the court under s 6 is an exhaustive remedy which precludes other forms of challenge. The duties owed by the insolvency practitioner in all the different statutory roles are created by statute and the statute contains appropriate protections and remedies for aggrieved parties. In addition, as an officer of the court, the court itself has wide powers to control the proper performance of the statutory powers. There can be no private law action for breach of these statutory duties.[37]

3.   Scheme of arrangement

5.042 Schemes of arrangement may be extremely complex documents involving large multinational corporate groups but can also be seen in relatively simple straightforward SME restructurings. The decisions which need to be made are in theory quite straightforward but, as with many things, in certain situations, they may become less clear.

5.043 Schemes of arrangement are found in Part 26 of Companies Act 2006. They require a decision to approve a proposed restructuring or compromise between a company and its creditors (or

---

33   See the leading IVA case of *Somji v Cadbury Schweppes plc* [2001] 1 BCLC 498 and *Gertner v CFL Finance* [2018] EWCA Civ 1781.

34   See the IVA case *Re A Debtor (no 259 of 1990)* [1992] 1 All ER 641.

35   Insolvency Act 1986, s 6(3).

36   See generally, ibid., ss 6 and 7.

37   See also *Irvine v Duff & Phelps Ltd* [2019] EWHC 2780 (Ch) where the position of an IVA supervisor was contrasted with that of a trustee in bankruptcy.

any class of them) or its members (or any class of them). The scheme must also be sanctioned by the court.

When considering a scheme, it is important to make a distinction between members' schemes, **5.044** which are usually solvent restructurings, and creditors' schemes, where some form of compromise of a company's debts is agreed where the company is financially distressed.

The decision to propose a scheme will nearly always be made by a company's directors. **5.045** An application will consequently be made to the court by the company (acting through its directors) under s 896 of Companies Act 2006. It is possible but very rare for a company in administration or liquidation to apply to the court with a proposed scheme. It is also possible, but equally unlikely, for a member or creditor to make an application to the court. In realistic terms, the application will be made by the company acting through its directors having received advice from their legal and accountancy advisors.

At the first, convening, hearing, the court may order a meeting of the creditors or class of **5.046** creditors (or of the members of the company or class of members as the case may be) to be summoned in such manner as the court directs.

Where such a meeting is summoned, the notice calling the meeting must include an explan- **5.047** atory memorandum explaining the effect of the proposed scheme. It must detail any interest of the company's directors in the scheme. Importantly, it must state the effect of the scheme on those with like interests where the effect differs. Under s 897 of Companies Act 2006, any default in these obligations results in an offence being committed by the company and every officer in default.

In many cases a crucial consideration is how to determine 'the correct classes of creditor, for **5.048** which purpose the relevant criteria are the existing rights of creditors and their rights as affected by the scheme'.[38] In deciding upon the different classes of creditor it must be possible for them to consult together with a view to their common interest.[39] The scheme is then seen as a number of linked arrangements and separate class meetings are called.[40] A scheme may treat creditors within the same class differently and this does not necessarily mean that the rights are so dissimilar that persons have to be put in different classes.[41] The court will look closely at the class compositions suggested by those proposing the scheme and may alter the suggested class

---

38   Per David Richards J in *Re T & N Ltd* [2005] 2 BCLC 488 at [79]. See also *Practice Statement (Companies: Schemes of Arrangement under Part 26 and Part 26A of the Companies Act 2006)* [2020] BCC 691.

39   A class of creditors 'must be confined to those persons whose rights are not so dissimilar as to make it impossible for them to consult together with a view to their common interest' (*Sovereign Life Assurance v Dodd* [1892] 2 QB 573, 583). See also *Re UDL Holdings Ltd* [2002] 1 HKC 172, 184–85 and *Re Telewest Communications plc (No 1)* [2004] BCC 342 at [19]–[22] and [37].

40   In *Re Indah Kiat International Finance Co BV* [2016] EWHC 246 (Ch), [2016] BCC 418 at [28]–[30], Snowden J explained:

   The primary purpose of following the Practice Statement is to enable scheme creditors to have an effective opportunity to appear at the convening hearing at which the constitution of the classes is determined … These purposes can self-evidently only be served if the notice of the convening hearing to creditors is adequate.

41   *Re Hawk Insurance Co Ltd* [2001] EWCA Civ 241, [2002] BCC 300.

composition.[42] The court will not at the convening hearing consider the merits or fairness of the scheme which is left to the sanction hearing.[43]

5.049   One particular issue which has been the subject of judicial debate in recent times is the practice for a scheme company to offer so-called 'lock-up' or 'consent' fees to scheme creditors if they agree at an early stage of negotiation to vote in favour of the scheme. The concern is that such payments to some members only of a class may cause the class to 'fracture' as all its members may no longer have an identity of interest.

5.050   In *Re ColourOz Investment 2 LLC*[44] Snowden J observed:

> in principle a consent fee of this nature will not fracture a class provided that it is made available to all scheme creditors, and provided also that it does not induce creditors to commit to vote in favour of a scheme which they might otherwise reject.[45]

5.051   A majority in number representing 75 per cent in value of the creditors or class of creditors (or members or class of members as the case may be), present and voting at the meeting summoned must agree to the compromise or arrangement. If such approval is given, an application is then made to the court under s 899 of Companies Act 2006 to sanction the scheme. The application will usually be made by the company acting through its directors.

5.052   In *Re Noble Group Ltd*[46] Snowden J followed the established approach in respect of how the court approaches a sanction hearing for a Part 26 scheme of arrangement by providing a four-stage test as follows:

(i)   At the first stage, the Court must consider whether the provisions of the statute have been complied with. This will include questions of class composition, whether the statutory majorities were obtained, and whether an adequate explanatory statement was distributed to creditors.

(ii)   At the second stage, the Court must consider whether the class was fairly represented by the meeting, and whether the majority were coercing the minority in order to promote interests adverse to the class whom they purported to represent.

(iii)   At the third stage, the Court must consider whether the scheme is a fair scheme which a creditor could reasonably approve. Importantly it must be appreciated that the Court is not concerned to decide whether the scheme is the only fair scheme or even the 'best' scheme.

(iv)   At the fourth stage the Court must consider whether there is any 'blot' or defect in the scheme that would, for example, make it unlawful or in any other way inoperable.

5.053   A creditor may appear at the sanction hearing if the creditor believes there is any unfairness or if there is some other 'blot' on the scheme.[47] The meaning of unfairness in this context has

---

42   See *Re Codere Finance 2 (UK) Ltd* [2020] EWHC 2441 (Ch) where the court decided that a single class of creditors was appropriate where the differences between the creditors was not so material as to fracture the class.

43   *Re ColourOz 2 Investment LLC* [2020] EWHC 1864 (Ch), [2020] BCC 926. Para 6d of the Practice Statement requires the company to draw to the attention of the court at the convening hearing any issues not going to merits or fairness, but which might lead the court to refuse to sanction the scheme, sometimes referred to as a 'blot' on the scheme.

44   [2020] EWHC 1864 (Ch), [2020] BCC 926 at [98].

45   See also *Re Primacom Holding GmbH* [2013] BCC 201, *Re DX Holdings Ltd* [2010] EWHC 1513 (Ch), *Re JSC Commercial Co Privatbank* [2015] EWHC 3299 (Ch) and *KCA Deutag UK Finance plc* [2020] EWHC 2779 (Ch).

46   [2018] EWHC 3092 (Ch) at [17].

47   A 'blot' in this context refers a technical or legal defect which demonstrates either an inherent contradiction in the scheme's own terms or that it is unlawful (*Re Co-operative Bank plc* [2017] EWHC 2269 (Ch) at [22]).

effectively the same meaning as unfair prejudice does in the context of CVAs considered in the previous section.[48]

If sanctioned by the court, the scheme is binding upon all creditors or class of creditors (or members or class of members as the case may be) and the company.[49] **5.054**

4.   Restructuring plan

The procedure and decision-making processes contained within Part 26A Companies Act 2006 which lead to the court sanctioning a restructuring plan are intended to be broadly the same as for schemes under Part 26.[50] The same Practice Statement[51] applies to both. In both there will be a convening hearing where the court considers, amongst other things, the composition of creditor classes. As with Part 26 schemes, the convening hearing will not consider the merits of fairness of the plan. That will occur at the sanction hearing. **5.055**

As explained in Chapter 3, there are some differences. Under Part 26A, a company must satisfy the two statutory conditions set out in s 901A of the 2006 Act (Conditions A and B). **5.056**

(2)   Condition A is that the company has encountered, or is likely to encounter, financial difficulties
       … affecting its ability to carry on business as a going concern.
(3)   Condition B is that—
       (a) a compromise or arrangement is proposed between the company and
            (i)   its creditors, or any class of them, or
            (ii) its members, or any class of them, and
       (b) the purpose of the compromise or arrangement is to eliminate, reduce or prevent, or mitigate
           the effect of, any of the financial difficulties.

Under Part 26A there is no requirement for a restructuring plan to be approved by a majority in number of the relevant class of plan creditors. The required majority is simply 75 per cent by value of plan creditors present and voting. **5.057**

In addition, Part 26A includes provision for what is usually called 'cross-class cram down'. Under s 901G where the court may still sanction a restructuring plan even if one of the classes does not agree to the plan by the required 75 per cent in value, if two conditions are met (rather confusingly drafted as Condition A and Condition B but completely different to those found under s 901A explained above). **5.058**

---

48   See *Re T & N Ltd* [2005] BCLC 488 where David Richards J observed at [82]:
      While I am wary of laying down in advance of a hearing on the merits of any scheme or CVA any particular rule, there
      is one element which can be mentioned at this stage. I find it very difficult to envisage a case where the court would
      sanction a scheme of arrangement, or not interfere with a CVA, which was an alternative to a winding up but which
      was likely to result in creditors, or some of them, receiving less than they would in a winding up of the company.
49   Companies Act 2006, s 900 gives the court a number of powers to facilitate a scheme which involves the transfer of the
      company's undertaking or property to another company.
50   *Re Virgin Atlantic Airways Ltd* [2020] EWHC 2191 (Ch).
51   *Practice Statement (Companies: Schemes of Arrangement under Part 26 and Part 26A of the Companies Act 2006)* [2020] BCC
      691.

5.059   Condition A under s 901G is that the court is satisfied that, if the restructuring plan were to be sanctioned, none of the members of the dissenting class would be any worse off[52] than they would be in the event of what is called the 'relevant alternative' which is usually but not necessarily a liquidation. Condition B is that the plan has been agreed by 75 per cent in value of at least one other class of creditors who would receive a payment or have a genuine economic interest in the company in the event of the relevant alternative.

5.060   The case of *Re DeepOcean 1 UK Ltd*[53] was the first to consider the court's power to cram down a class and the guidance provided at both the convening and sanction hearing is valuable to see how the court assesses the procedure and decisions made in such circumstances.

5.061   The following were listed by the court in the convening hearing in *Re DeepOcean 1 UK Ltd*[54] as matters which would be considered at a convening hearing under Part 26A:

(1)   Jurisdictional requirements (that the company is liable to be wound up under the Act);
(2)   Conditions A and B under s 901A;
(3)   Class composition;
(4)   Any other issues not going to merits or fairness which might cause the court to refuse to sanction the restructuring plans; and
(5)   Practical issues regarding the adequacy of notice, documentation and proposals for the meetings of creditors.

5.062   In the sanction hearing judgment in *Re Deepocean 1 UK Ltd*[55] Trower J provided a helpful checklist of what the court will consider when asked to sanction a restructuring plan (and how this process differs slightly from that used for a scheme):

(1)   The court will look to see whether the terms of the statute have been complied with.[56]
(2)   The court will look to see that conditions A and B in s 901A(1) are met in relation to the company.
(3)   The court would take a similar approach to questions of class composition as it would in a scheme of arrangement.[57]
(4)   The court will ensure that any terms of the convening order have been complied with, for example, that the creditor class meetings have been summoned in accordance with the

---

52   The phrase 'any worse off' was described as: 'a broad concept and appears to contemplate the need to take into account the impact of the restructuring plan on all incidents of the liability to the creditor concerned, including matters such as timing and the security of any covenant to pay' in *Re Deepocean 1 UK Ltd* [2021] EWHC 138 (Ch) at [35].
53   [2020] EWHC 3549 (Ch) (convening hearing) and [2021] EWHC 138 (Ch) (sanction hearing).
54   [2020] EWHC 3549 (Ch) at [29].
55   [2021] EWHC 138 (Ch) at [57]–[67].
56   The starting point is whether the company is within the meaning of Part 26A (that is, a company which is liable to be wound up under the Insolvency Act 1986) see the convening judgment in *Re Deepocean 1 UK Ltd* [2020] EWHC 3549 (Ch) at [36]–[38].
57   The convening hearing judgment in *Re Deepocean UK 1 Ltd* [2020] EWHC 3549 (Ch) at [50]–[57] discussed and approved four separate classes of creditors, namely separate classes for secured creditors, landlords, vessel owners and unsecured creditors respectively. At the sanction hearing the court recognised that there may be some cross-class cram down cases in which there is artificiality in the creation of classes to ensure that the requirements of the s 901G are satisfied. In cases where this only becomes apparent when the s 901G power is sought to be exercised at the sanction stage, the court will be prepared to revisit the conclusion that it reached on classes at the convening hearing ([2021] EWHC 138 (Ch) at [41]).

order and that the accompanying explanatory statement was sufficiently full and comprehensive so as to provide creditors with all the information they might reasonably require.

(5)   Where the statutory majorities are not met at each meeting the cross-class cram down provisions of section 901G must be considered. This differs from the procedure for a Part 26 scheme where no cross-class cram down is possible.

(6)   The court retains a discretion whether to sanction the restructuring plan or not. It may consider that a low turnout at a meeting which has agreed a plan is capable of undermining the conclusion that the vote was representative, particularly where creditors were unable to engage rather than chose not do so or where votes were cast in favour due to some collateral interest rather than in good faith with a view to the interests of the class as a whole.

(7)   The court will look to ensure the Plan is fair and equitable and this is especially the case where the court is asked to cram down a class.[58]

(8)   The court will also ensure there is no blot on the plan.

(9)   Finally, the court must be satisfied that the plan is likely to be substantially effective in relevant jurisdictions outside England and Wales.

If sanctioned by the court, and assuming no cram down is required, the plan is binding upon all creditors or class of creditors (or members or class of members as the case may be) and the company.[59]   **5.063**

If the plan is not agreed by a number representing at least 75 per cent in value of a class of creditors (or members as the case may be), if the cram down Conditions A and B under s 901G are satisfied, the court may still sanction the plan which will thereby become binding upon all creditors or class of creditors (or members or class of members as the case may be) including the dissenting class and the company.[60]   **5.064**

C. FORMAL PROCEDURES UNDER THE CONTROL OF AN INSOLVENCY PRACTITIONER

Where a company is under the control of an officeholder (administration and liquidation) the day-to-day management of the company will be in hands of the officeholder. An administrator (under Sch 1 and various provisions in Sch B1) and a liquidator (primarily under Sch 4) have wide powers to manage and realise a company's assets.[61] These powers and the decisions to exercise them by the officeholder are discussed in detail in Chapter 7.   **5.065**

The officeholder may decide to use available powers to ask for the court's assistance in ensuring a company's property and records are delivered up and that the duty of directors to co-operate   **5.066**

---

58   The court is likely to apply the 'vertical' comparison adopted from company voluntary arrangement case law for the purposes of establishing unfair prejudice under s 6 of the Insolvency Act 1986 (see *Discovery (Northampton) Limited v Debenhams Retail Ltd* [2020] BCC 9 at [12]).

59   Companies Act 2006, s 901F.

60   Ibid., s 901G(2).

61   An officeholder will commonly decide to sell a company's business to a connected party. Such sales are subject to detailed controls when made by an administrator as discussed in the section below. Where such sales are made by a liquidator there are fewer controls (see the discussion at 3.255 et seq above).

is enforced which may involve a private or public examination in court.[62] Depending upon the results of the officeholder's enquiries, he or she may decide to take enforcement action against connected or third parties where there is evidence of wrongdoing (some of the actions available to officeholders are considered in Chapter 4 above).

5.067   The officeholder, especially an administrator, may decide to trade the company's business for a period of time and so may decide to enter into or continue supply contracts[63] and adopt existing employment contracts.[64]

5.068   The commercial judgment of the officeholder will inform what decisions are made in this respect. This is also the case where an officeholder decides, rather than to take action as officeholder but to assign an officeholder action[65] or company action to a third-party funder. The officeholder may decide to delegate some functions but remains responsible if he or she does not exercise reasonable care. These powers and duties (along with others) are fully explored in Chapter 8.

5.069   In administration the creditors may decide to form a creditors' committee and in liquidation such a body is called a liquidation committee. Such committees are not common in practice and where they exist have relatively limited decision-making roles beyond agreeing an officeholder's remuneration. The rules on how the creditors decide to remunerate officeholders are explained in Chapter 7.

5.070   The mechanisms for deciding whether or not to put a company into administration or liquidation are considered in detail in Chapter 7. Some of these decisions are also mentioned in this section.

5.071   The rules on how creditors (or others) who decide to take steps to remove an officeholder operate are considered in Chapter 8. It is noteworthy that in administration the creditors must apply to court to remove an administrator[66] but in both creditors' voluntary liquidation and compulsory liquidation, creditors have rights to remove a liquidator both via a court order but also by passing a creditors' qualifying decision to that effect.[67]

5.072   The remainder of this chapter considers some of the other decisions which are made in respectively administration and liquidation. It is noteworthy that creditors have a greater say in how specific decisions in administrations are made than they do in liquidation. This is largely due to the differing nature of administration and liquidation. Administration is designed to allow a company's business to be continued along with continuing and new liabilities being incurred and considered. Liquidation is nearly always the end of the road for a company and so is designed to realise assets and distribute their proceeds. Creditor involvement in specific decision-making is not so necessary or desirable.

---

62   Ibid., ss 234–236 and s 113.
63   Ibid., ss 233–233B.
64   In administration, Insolvency Act 1986, Sch B1, para 99 provides employees with super priority, that is a right to be paid wages and salary under adopted contracts of employment ahead even of the administrator's own fees and expenses.
65   Insolvency Act 1986, s 246ZD.
66   Ibid., Sch B1, para 88.
67   Ibid., ss 171–172.

1. Administration

Decisions in an administration may be made by creditors, either secured or unsecured, by the members, by the directors or of course, by the administrator. The following discussion concentrates on how the regime seeks to ensure that such decisions are subject to reasonable oversight by those with a legitimate interest to protect. **5.073**

As explained in outline in Chapter 3 and in more detail in Chapter 7, an administrator may be appointed by the court on the application of various interested parties.[68] The most common applicants would be the company's directors and more rarely a secured creditor. **5.074**

The holder of a 'qualifying floating charge' may appoint an administrator out of court under para 14 of Sch B1. A floating charge will be 'qualifying' for these purposes if either on its own or together with other securities it relates to the whole or substantially the whole of the company's undertaking. The charge may be enforced by the appointment of an administrator[69] as soon as the charge has become enforceable under its own terms.[70] **5.075**

Under para 22 of Sch B1 either the company itself (by a members' ordinary resolution in general meeting or equivalent, such as a written resolution for private companies under s 288 of Companies Act 2006) or the directors may appoint an administrator. An appointment by the directors includes an appointment made by a majority of the directors.[71] In practice, a secured creditor who has the power to appoint an administrator out of court will frequently invite, or consent to, the directors of the company appointing an administrator of whom the creditor approves. Although the directors will formally make the appointment the decision will be controlled by the secured creditor. **5.076**

In the process leading up to, and immediately after, the entry of a company into administration the proposed administrator has an important decision to make. He or she must, before appointment, state that it is his or her opinion that 'the purpose of the administration is reasonably likely to be achieved'.[72] Following the appointment, the administrator must then consider and decide which of the three statutory objectives listed in para 3 of Sch B1 will be pursued. It is perfectly possible for changing events during the administration to cause an administrator to change his or her mind as to which of the statutory objective can be achieved.[73] **5.077**

Within eight weeks of appointment the administrator must send a statement of proposals to the creditors (and members), which will explain how the purpose of the administration is to be achieved.[74] The proposal must also explain how it is proposed that the administration will end, including where it is proposed that the administration will end by being converted into **5.078**

---

68   Ibid., Sch B1, paras 12 and 13.
69   The appointment of an administrator by a qualifying floating charge holder is a form of enforcement (*Re ARL 009 Ltd (Co No.11113979)* [2020] EWHC 3123 (Ch)).
70   Insolvency Act 1986, Sch B1, para 16.
71   Ibid., Sch B1, para 105.
72   Insolvency Rules 2016, r 3.2.
73   *Re Taylor Pearson (Construction) Ltd (in admin)* [2020] EWHC 2933 (Ch) at [15].
74   Insolvency Act 1986, Sch B1, para 49. The statement must explain why, if this is the conclusion the administrator has reached, the administrator thinks that neither of the purposes mentioned in para 3(1)(a) or (b) (company rescue or

a creditors' voluntary liquidation, the details of the proposed liquidator, who will invariably be the administrator. The administrator very commonly is named as the proposed successive liquidator. The creditors' decision on the proposals must be made within ten weeks of the appointment.[75]

5.079   The decision whether or not to approve the proposals by the creditors will be made using either the deemed consent procedure or a qualifying decision procedure where a simple majority in value of those unsecured creditors who vote is needed for approval.[76] A resolution is invalid if those voting against it include more than half in value of the creditors to whom notice of the decision procedure was delivered who are not connected to the company.[77]

5.080   Under para 52(1) of Sch B1, there is no requirement to seek a decision of the creditors on the administrator's proposals[78] if the administrator thinks that:

(1)   the company has sufficient property to pay all the creditors in full; or

(2)   the company has insufficient property to make any payment to unsecured creditors (other than under s 176A – the prescribed percentage deduction in favour of unsecured creditors of monies available to a floating charge holder); or

(3)   the administration cannot achieve either rescue of the company or a better result for creditors generally than under an immediate winding up (the purposes listed in para 3(1) (a) and (b) respectively).

5.081   The decision not to require a decision from the creditors on the proposals is subject to the right under para 52(2) that creditors holding at least 10 per cent of the company's total debts may require the administrator to seek a decision of the creditors as to whether or not they approve the statement of proposals. Under r 15.18(2) such creditors have only eight days to decide to requisition a decision and the creditors must pay the expenses of the requisitioned decision.[79] It is not uncommonly the case, where the administrator believes there will be no return to the unsecured creditors (apart from under s 176A), for the administrator to inform the creditors that he or she is not going to seek a decision of the creditors on the proposal due to para 52(1). Unless 10 per cent of the creditors wish a decision to be made, the administrator can then assume that the proposal is approved.

5.082   Failure by the creditors to approve the proposal will usually lead to the court discharging the administrator and the court may, for example, order the company be wound up.[80]

---

a better deal for the creditors generally than an immediate winding up would achieve) can be achieved. The detailed requirements of the statement of proposals are listed in Insolvency Rules 2016, r 3.35.

75   Ibid., Sch B1, para 51.

76   Ibid., Sch B1, para 51. Secured creditors cannot vote on the administrator's proposals if they are fully secured. There is no restriction on preferential creditors voting. Owners of goods under hire purchase, chattel leasing or conditional sale agreements, can generally vote only the amount of debt outstanding under the respective agreements at the date of the administration (Insolvency Rules 2016, r 15.32).

77   Insolvency Rules 2016, r 15.34(2).

78   Under ibid., r 3.38(4) the proposals are deemed to have been approved in such circumstances.

79   Ibid., rr 15.18 and 15.19.

80   Insolvency Act 1986, Sch B1, para 55.

Where an administrator believes that a swift sale of the company's undertaking or assets is **5.083** needed before any proposals can be considered by the creditors, the courts have decided such a decision is permissible and is one for the commercial judgment of the administrator. It is not a decision which the court will make on behalf of the administrator who cannot therefore treat the court as a form of bomb shelter to hide in away from creditor complaints.[81]

This reasoning has led to the practice of pre-packaged administration where a company's **5.084** business is sold usually on day one of the administration on the terms of a pre-arranged and pre-negotiated deal. One consequence of a pre-pack is that the creditors never get to have a meaningful vote on the deal as it happens before they are given notice of it. This practice has long been controversial especially where the buyer is a person connected to the company. The provisions of Statement of Insolvency Practice 16 have led to more transparency in the process and a requirement that businesses are properly valued and marketed prior to a sale.

The decision to pre-pack is ultimately one for the administrator and the duties owed in such **5.085** circumstances are considered in Chapter 8.

The Administration (Restrictions on Disposal etc. to Connected Persons) Regulations 2021[82] **5.086** contain a specific requirement, where the decision is to conduct a 'substantial sale' to a connected person, either to obtain the approval of the creditors (as part of the statement of the administrator's proposals) or the approval of an independent evaluator[83] in order that such sales may go ahead within the first eight weeks of the administration. The evaluator's qualifying report must contain certain prescribed provisions, most importantly, a statement that the evaluator is (or is not, as the case may be) satisfied that the consideration to be provided for the relevant property and the grounds for the substantial disposal are reasonable in the circumstances. A copy of the qualifying report must be given to the proposed administrator who must be satisfied that the evaluator had sufficient relevant knowledge and experience to make the qualifying report.[84] The meaning of 'connected person' for the purposes of the Regulations adopts the definition found in s 435 of the Act.

The practical effect of the 2021 Regulations is likely to be that the decision of the administrator **5.087** to pre-pack a sale to a connected party will become subject to the approval of an independent third party (the evaluator). It is unlikely that creditor approval will be sought often as the whole point of a pre-pack sale is that it needs to be conducted speedily without notice in order to maintain the business as a going concern.

During administration the statutory moratorium prevents virtually all creditor enforcement **5.088** action against the company but there are two exceptions to this rule.

---

81   *Re T & D Industries Plc* [2000] 1 WLR 646 and *Re Transbus International Ltd* [2004] 1 WLR 2654.
82   SI 2021/427.
83   Reg 3. An evaluator must have the benefit of professional indemnity insurance and must themselves be satisfied that their relevant knowledge and experience is sufficient for the purposes of making a qualifying report (Part 3 of the Regulations).
84   Reg 6. Under Reg 8, where a previous report has been made, the evaluator is required to consider it in their report. This provision and various related provisions are intended to make it difficult for a connected party to 'shop around' for a positive report without disclosing other reports.

5.089 First, the administrator may decide to agree to the action being taken. This may be the case where, for example, some of the company's machinery is held under a hire purchase contract, the administrator has no use for the machinery and the owner wants to repossess.

5.090 Secondly, if the administrator decides not to agree to the lifting of the moratorium, the creditor or other third party must apply to the court for permission to take action. The leading case on how the court is to approach the exercise of its discretionary power to grant permission is *Re Atlantic Computer Systems plc*[85] where the Court of Appeal explained how the court would go about deciding whether or not to lift the moratorium:

(1) The party seeking permission must always make out a case.

(2) Where the party is seeking permission to exercise its proprietary rights over its own property, such as by repossessing its own goods, then if this repossession is unlikely to impede the purpose of the administration, the court would normally grant permission.

(3) In other cases, the court must undertake a balancing exercise. The interests of the party claiming to repossess must be balanced with the interests of the other creditors.

(4) As part of this balancing exercise due weight needs to be given to the owner's proprietary rights. The owners of such property should not have to finance indirectly the administration for the benefit of unsecured creditors.

(5) It will usually be the case that permission will be granted if significant loss would be caused to the owner by refusal. However, as part of the balancing exercise, if substantially greater loss would be caused to others by the grant of permission, that may outweigh the projected loss caused to the owner. The court will consider: the company's financial position; its ability to make payments under the agreements (arrears and current liabilities); the administrator's proposals; the effect on those proposals of granting permission; the effect on the owner of refusal; the duration of the administration and the conduct of the parties.

2. Liquidation

5.091 Section 165 (in the case of voluntary liquidation) and s 167 (in the case of compulsory liquidation) provide that a liquidator may exercise any of the powers specified in Sch 4 to the Act. These powers may all be exercised by the liquidator without any approval of the creditors.[86]

5.092 Once a company has entered insolvent liquidation, the assets of the company are said to be held on trust for the creditors.[87] It might therefore be reasonable to expect creditors to have many and varied decision making powers within such a process. Apart from the decision as to who is the liquidator, creditors do not in reality have much in the way of specific decision-making powers within an insolvent liquidation (whether it is a creditors' voluntary liquidation or compulsory liquidation). That is not to say, however, that their views are ignored in a liquidation.

---

85   [1992] Ch 505.

86   Small Business, Enterprise and Employment Act 2015, s 120 abolished the need to acquire the sanction or approval of the creditors (or others) which was previously needed for the exercise of some of these powers. In a compulsory liquidation where there is a liquidation committee the liquidator (if not the Official Receiver) must inform the committee of any disposal of assets to a connected person and if he or she decides to instruct a solicitor must inform liquidation committee (see s 167 and Chapter 8 below).

87   See the discussion below in Chapter 7.

Section 168 of the Act provides that a liquidator in a compulsory liquidation may seek a decision from the creditors on any matter. This may assist a liquidator in that if he or she is to engage in, for example, a potentially expensive legal action, being able to demonstrate the prior support of creditors if the decision is subsequently questioned will be of some comfort to the liquidator. A voluntary liquidator will also be wise to seek the views of creditors prior to taking a potentially contentious action. **5.093**

Although there are few instances in a liquidation where creditors have specific powers to make decisions, there are provisions which allow their views to be considered. Section 168 requires a compulsory liquidator to seek a decision on any matter when requested to do so by at least one-tenth in value of the creditors even though the courts may override this duty.[88] Section 195 allows the court to have regard to the wishes of the creditors (or contributories) as to all matters relating to a winding up. The court may direct that a creditors' qualifying decision procedure be instigated for the purpose of ascertaining those wishes. **5.094**

As explained in Chapter 7, although a creditors' voluntary liquidation is usually commenced by a members' resolution to wind up,[89] it is the creditors who get to decide who is to be the liquidator. They may or may not agree with the members' nomination (or not agree that a former administrator should be appointed in a subsequent liquidation) and their decision as to who is to be liquidator will take precedence. **5.095**

The first liquidator in a compulsory liquidation will nearly always be the Official Receiver.[90] The Official Receiver is under a duty to consider whether to seek nominations from the creditors for the purpose of replacing the Official Receiver as liquidator. The Official Receiver must exercise this power if requested so to do by one-quarter in value of the creditors.[91] **5.096**

Section 176ZA and the Rules passed under it[92] provide for floating charge holders (and preferential creditors) effectively to decide whether or not litigation will be brought by a liquidator. It does this by varying the general rule under s 176ZA(1) that the expenses of the winding up have priority over a floating charge and preferential creditors. Litigation expenses incurred by the liquidator may not be paid out of floating charge assets without the approval of the floating charge holder and preferential creditors. Without such approval a liquidator will be reluctant to engage in litigation which needs to be funded by the insolvent estate. **5.097**

D. CONCLUSION

It is clear that decisions made in the different procedures are dominated by different stakeholders. Not surprisingly, secured creditors usually either do not need decision-making powers as **5.098**

---

88   *Re Barings plc* [2001] 2 BCLC 159.
89   It may begin as a members' voluntary liquidation which is later shown not to be solvent and is therefore converted into a creditors' voluntary liquidation under s 96 Insolvency Act 1986 or be converted from administration to creditors' voluntary liquidation under para 83 Sch B1 Insolvency Act 1986.
90   Insolvency Act 1986, s 140 provides for a different outcome at the discretion of the court where the winding-up order is made in relation to a company that is in administration or subject to a CVA.
91   Ibid., s 136.
92   Insolvency Rules 2016, rr 6.44–6.48 and 7.112–116.

their position is already protected or they are given the whip hand in making decisions. The Companies Act procedures are dominated by the court's supervision. The court is under a duty to make sure that all schemes and plans are fair. The court only gets to consider the fairness of a CVA if (usually) a creditor decides to take action. Some decisions are left to the professional judgment of insolvency practitioners but in areas such as pre-pack administration, a recent policy shift now requires decisions to enter into connected party sales by an administrator, to be approved by the creditors or be subject to the independent assessment of an evaluator. Where a form of company or business rescue is intended, creditors usually control the big decisions whether that is an extension of a moratorium, the approval of a CVA or an administrator's proposals or an officeholder's remuneration.

6

DIRECTORS IN FORMAL INSOLVENCY

A. INTRODUCTION

Once a company enters into a formal insolvency procedure the directors' position necessarily **6.001** changes. How it changes depends upon which procedure is entered. If a company enters a debtor-in-possession procedure such as a moratorium, company voluntary arrangement, scheme of arrangement or restructuring plan, directors may have duties to provide information and to be under the general supervision of others but they will usually remain in managerial control of the company. In insolvency procedures where the directors' managerial powers are usurped by an officeholder, such as administration or liquidation, the directors do not usually automatically cease to be directors. They will remain subject to various duties to provide information and to co-operate even though their managerial powers and duties will usually cease or be curtailed.

Some duties owed by directors occur in essentially the same way in more than one insolvency **6.002** procedure.[1] For example, directors will be required to provide a statement of the company's affairs where the company enters a company voluntary arrangement, administration or liquidation.[2] Breach of this obligation leads to criminal liability in administration and liquidation.

In this chapter we will consider the obligations and position generally of directors once their **6.003** companies enter any of the formal insolvency procedures under the Insolvency Act 1986 ('the Act') or the Companies Act 2006. Directors remain accountable for their conduct after their

---

1   Finance Act 2020, Sch 13 introduced a new potentially significant liability for directors of present companies if they were previously also directors of companies which entered an insolvency process. The 2020 Act provides, in certain circumstances, for the directors to be personally liable for outstanding tax liabilities of both the old and the new companies.

2   See Insolvency Act 1986, s 2(3)(b) (company voluntary arrangement), Sch B1, para 47 (administration), s 99 (creditors' voluntary liquidation) and s 131 (compulsory liquidation).

company has entered an insolvency process. Transparency in their dealings with others is as important as ever during these processes as the consequences of culpable behaviour may have criminal as well as civil consequences.

B CODIFIED COMMON LAW AND FIDUCIARY DUTIES REMAIN APPLICABLE

6.004   It is clear that whether a company enters a debtor-in-possession procedure or a procedure under the control of an officeholder, directors remain subject to their codified duty of care and fiduciary duties owed to their companies.[3]

6.005   This position is perhaps self-evidently the case where directors remain in control of the company with powers to make significant decisions. It is less obvious that such duties should continue to apply in companies whose management has been taken over by an officeholder such as in administration or liquidation.[4]

6.006   In *Re System Building Services Group Ltd*[5] a company had been in administration which was subsequently converted into a creditors' voluntary liquidation. It was dissolved but later restored to the register. The administrator, who had also acted as liquidator, had been adjudged bankrupt. The new liquidator of the restored company brought an action against the company's directors for breach of duty (there being no commercial justification for taking action against the bankrupt administrator/liquidator).

6.007   The court held that the codified directors' duties owed by directors to their companies and creditors found in ss 170–177 of the Companies Act 2006 survive the company's entry into administration and voluntary liquidation. The codified duties are separate from the duties owed by an administrator or liquidator.[6] Directors therefore remain subject to such duties whether or not they continue to have any active involvement in the management of the company during the administration or voluntary liquidation.

6.008   There has been no authority on whether directors of a company in compulsory liquidation remain subject to the duties mentioned here. It would make sense that they are for the sake of consistency, but it is acknowledged that they do not have as many opportunities of taking unilateral action that the directors in voluntary liquidation do, prior to the appointment of a liquidator.

---

3   See generally the in-depth treatment of these duties in A Keay *Directors' Duties* (LexisNexis, 4th ed, 2020) and Chapter 4 above.
4   The Companies Act 2006, s 193 states that the provisions of s 190 requiring shareholder consent for substantial property transactions do not apply to directors whose companies are in administration or liquidation. This exception to s 190 recognises that once in administration or liquidation, dispositive decisions are made on behalf of the company by the officeholder.
5   [2020] EWHC 54 (Ch).
6   See the discussion and explanation for this conclusion [2020] EWHC 54 (Ch) at [46]–[60].

C. FORMAL DEBTOR-IN-POSSESSION PROCEDURES

1.   Moratorium

As explained in Chapter 5, the moratorium procedure will usually be instigated by the directors **6.009** of the company filing the requisite documents at court.[7] As part of this documentation, the directors must make a statement that, in their view, the company is, or is likely to become, unable to pay its debts (within the definition found in s 123 of the Act).[8]

A director commits an offence if, for the purpose of obtaining a moratorium (or an extension **6.010** of a moratorium) he or she makes any false representation or fraudulently does, or omits to do, anything.[9]

Directors will remain in post and retain their managerial powers subject to the following **6.011** exceptions:

(i)   The monitor may demand relevant information from the company's directors for this purpose;[10]
(ii)   During the moratorium the payment of pre-moratorium debts (subject to certain exceptions[11]) is restricted unless the monitor consents;
(iii) Property that is not subject to a security may only be disposed of, in the ordinary way of its business, or if the monitor consents, or if the disposal is in pursuance of a court order. The monitor may give consent to the disposal only if he or she thinks that it will support the rescue of the company as a going concern.[12]
(iv)   In the case of property that is subject to a security interest, the company may only dispose of the property with the permission of the court or in accordance with the terms of the security;[13]

---

7   Insolvency Act 1986, s A6. The directors may also decide to extend the moratorium with or without creditor consent. Whether creditor consent is sought (it will be if the extension is to be for more than a further 20 business days) under ss A10, A11 and A12 the directors must effectively replicate the documents filed when the moratorium was first made. In addition, the directors must state that all moratorium debts that have fallen due during the moratorium so far have been paid or otherwise discharged and that the company is still, or is likely to become, unable to pay its debts. The monitor must state that he or she is of the view that an extension to the moratorium is likely to result in the rescue of the company as a going concern. In any application for an extension to the court, the directors will, in addition to producing effectively the same documentation, need to explain whether or not the creditors have been consulted.
8   Ibid., s A6.
9   Ibid., s A47.
10   Ibid., s A36. Under s A38 a failure to provide such information to the monitor may lead to the monitor deciding to terminate the moratorium.
11   Ibid., s A18. Total payments of non-excluded pre-moratorium debts may be made under s A28 of not more than the greater of £5,000 or 1 per cent of the value of the unsecured debts owed by the company at the start of the moratorium. The monitor may give consent to the company to make payments of pre-moratorium debts above these limits but only if the monitor thinks that it will support the rescue of the company as a going concern.
12   Ibid., s A29. Under s A26 the monitor may consent to the company granting security.
13   Ibid., ss A29 and A31. This power mirrors the power available under administration found in para 71 of Sch B1. Under ss A30 and A32, the disposal of hire purchase goods is subject to a power very similar to that found in administration under para 72 of Sch B1 whereby the court may order disposal subject to certain safeguards for the owner.

(v) It is an offence for the company to obtain credit of £500 or more unless the person providing the credit has been informed that a moratorium is in force in relation to the company.[14]

6.012 A creditor (or member) may apply to the court on the grounds that the company's affairs, business and property are being or have been managed in a way that has unfairly harmed the applicant's interests.[15] The court may make any order it thinks fit. The court's order may, amongst other things, regulate the management of the directors, require the directors to stop taking the action complained of, or require a decision of the company's creditors. This power is similar in its terms to that available against an administrator.[16]

6.013 Directors need to be aware of possible offences they may commit during or in anticipation of a moratorium. An officer of the company (including a shadow director[17]) commits an offence if he or she does any of the following (or is privy to another who does any of the things listed in cases of (iii), (iv) and (v)):[18]

(i) conceals company property whose value is at least £500, or conceals any debt due to or from the company;
(ii) fraudulently removes company property whose value is at least £500;
(iii) conceals, destroys, mutilates or falsifies any document affecting or relating to the company's property or affairs;
(iv) makes any false entry in any document affecting or relating to the company's property or affairs;
(v) fraudulently parts with, alters or makes any omission in any document affecting or relating to the company's property or affairs; or
(vi) pawns, pledges or disposes of any company property which had been obtained on credit and has not been paid for (unless the transaction is in the ordinary way of the company's business).

6.014 It is a defence if the officer can prove he or she had no intent to defraud or in the case of (iii) and (iv) to prove he or she had no intent to conceal the situation or to defeat the law.[19]

6.015 These provisions are based on the provisions applicable in liquidation under s 206 of the Act and, as with that provision, unusually require the director accused of misconduct to prove the defence rather than require the prosecution to prove the charge.[20]

---

14 Ibid., s A25. The company and any officer in default who without reasonable excuse permitted the obtaining of credit is guilty. Under s A26, there is a similar restriction with similar consequences on the company granting security without the consent of the monitor.
15 Ibid., s A44.
16 Ibid., Sch B1, para 74.
17 Ibid., s A46(5).
18 Ibid., s A46(2).
19 Ibid., s A46(3).
20 The burden of proof on the director may be discharged on a balance of probabilities rather than beyond reasonable doubt (*R v Carr-Briant* [1943] KB 607).

2.   Company voluntary arrangement

Although it is possible for a company voluntary arrangement ('CVA') to be proposed by an administrator or liquidator, in practice, it is nearly always proposed by the company's directors.   **6.016**

As considered in Chapter 5, the roles of the nominee and supervisor (usually the same person) are significant in terms of assisting with the drafting of a proposal, often liaising with creditors, reporting, calling meetings and convening creditor decisions as well as supervising the terms of the CVA if approved.   **6.017**

The directors remain in managerial control of the company. Although the CVA is subject to the oversight of the supervisor, the supervisor will not usually have any power to interfere in the day-to-day management of the company's operations.   **6.018**

It is quite common for CVAs to place restrictions upon what directors may do during the term of a CVA. For example, creditors may insist that directors receive no pay increase and the members no dividend during the CVA.   **6.019**

Similar consequences ensue for fraudulent directors in the context of promulgation of a CVA as they do for a moratorium. Under s 6A of the Act an officer of the company, such as a director, commits an offence if, for the purpose of obtaining approval of the CVA, he or she: **6.020**

(i)   makes any false representation; or
(ii)   fraudulently does, or omits to do, anything.[21]

3.   Scheme of arrangement and restructuring plan

As has been noted judicially, schemes of arrangement and restructuring plans (under Parts 26 and 26A respectively of the Companies Act 2006) have much in common.[22] The position of directors is essentially the same in each. In each procedure the directors remain in managerial control of the company and, subject to the terms of any sanctioned scheme or plan, will continue to carry out their role as before.   **6.021**

The Companies Act 2006 does place identical, specific extra obligations on directors in the context of schemes and plans. When the explanatory statement is prepared for dissemination amongst the creditors (and members) along with the notice of the respective meetings, it must state, amongst other things: **6.022**

(i) any material interests of the directors of the company (whether as directors or as members or as creditors of the company or otherwise), and (ii) the effect on those interests of the compromise or arrangement, in so far as it is different from the effect on the like interests of other persons.[23]

---

21   Insolvency Act 1986, s 7A imposes a duty on the CVA supervisor to report to the Secretary of State any past or present officer of the company who has committed an offence in connection with the CVA.

22   See, e.g., *Re Virgin Atlantic Airways Ltd* [2020] EWHC 2191 (Ch), *Re Gategroup Guarantee Ltd* [2021] EWHC 304 (Ch) and *Re Deepocean 1 UK Ltd* [2020] EWHC 3549 (Ch) and [2021] EWHC 138 (Ch).

23   Companies Act 2006, ss 897(2)(b) and 901D(2)(b) respectively for schemes and plans.

6.023   If the company defaults upon this obligation, it and any officer in default commits an offence.[24]

6.024   If the company (or officer of the company) defaults in this obligation, it may be due to the refusal of a director to supply the necessary particulars of his or her interest in which case the company has a valid defence.[25] In such circumstances, the director in default commits an offence having breached the specific duty to give notice to the company of such matters.[26]

6.025   Although these duties may be breached, the court has a discretion to allow the default to be corrected. The default does not, in itself, necessarily lead to the scheme or plan not being sanctioned by the court. The requirement is to be read purposively so that the need for the notice of the meetings to 'be accompanied by' an explanatory statement containing this information could include the possibility of the statement being supplemented by a further document in an appropriate case.[27]

D. FORMAL PROCEDURES UNDER THE CONTROL OF AN INSOLVENCY PRACTITIONER

6.026   When a company enters administration or voluntary liquidation the directors are not automatically removed from office.[28]

6.027   When a company enters compulsory liquidation the appointments of directors are automatically terminated and so their powers also cease at this point.[29]

6.028   Once in administration directors may no longer exercise any management powers without the consent of the administrator or liquidator.[30]

6.029   When a company enters creditors' voluntary liquidation, all the powers of the directors cease.[31]

---

24   Ibid., ss 897(5) and 901D(5) respectively for schemes and plans.
25   Ibid., ss 897(7) and 901D(7) respectively for schemes and plans.
26   Ibid., ss 898 and 901E respectively for schemes and plans.
27   *Re Sunbird Business Services Ltd* [2020] EWHC 2493 (Ch) at [67]–[70]. In cases where a supplemental circular is needed to make good a material omission, it must still comply with the notice period specified at the convening order for the meeting. In *Sunbird*, the court did not exercise its discretion in favour of sanction as the problems went beyond this omission. The general paucity of information provided to creditors fell short of what the court considered a fair process and so the scheme was not sanctioned by the court.
28   Under Insolvency Act 1986, Sch B1, para 61 an administrator may remove a director and may appoint a director (whether or not to fill a vacancy). Under Insolvency Act 1986, Sch 4, a liquidator has the power to carry on the business of the company so far as is necessary for its beneficial winding up and may appoint agents to do any business the liquidator is unable to do. Directors remain in theory under a duty to make requisite updates to a company's statutory books and to file various updating forms at Companies House (see Companies Act 2006, ss 1135 and 1136).
29   *Measures Brothers Ltd v Measures* [1910] 2 Ch 248.
30   Insolvency Act 1986, Sch B1, para 64. The administrator's consent for a director to exercise a management power may be general or specific (see *Re ASA Resource Group plc* [2020] EWHC 1370 (Ch) at [30]–[31]). Directors do not have a power to bring misfeasance proceedings against an administrator under Insolvency Act 1986, Sch B1, para 75.
31   Ibid., s 103. This is subject to an exception to the extent that the liquidation committee (or absent that, the creditors) sanction their continuance.

There are a number of provisions which provide for directors (or other officers of the company) **6.030** to be made liable criminally for fraudulent conduct where a company is in liquidation. These provisions are considered below. They are intended to act as a deterrent to directors whose behaviour is culpable and are in addition to the mainly civil liability provisions considered in Chapter 4.

1.   Administration

It is perhaps surprising that the administration regime does not replicate the fraud-related **6.031** offences which directors (as officers of the company) may be liable for in a liquidation and which are considered below.

The reason for this apparent lacuna appears to be that there is no real need for such duplication. **6.032** If a director behaves fraudulently prior to or during an administration, the administrator has a number of powers either to retrieve property from directors, take action against directors or put the company into liquidation.

Section 211 of the Act, considered below, is worded in such a way that if a company enters **6.033** winding up, subsequent to an administration, any false representation or other fraud committed for the purpose of obtaining the consent of company's creditors to any agreement with reference to the company's affairs, including any such agreement relating to the administration of the company, will be an offence.

2.   Liquidation

Sections 206–211 of the Act provide for criminal liability in relation to malpractice by directors **6.034** (or other officers of the company) in the context of liquidation.

Section 206 concerns fraudulent conduct committed by a director (or other past or present **6.035** officer[32]) of the company in the 12 months prior to the commencement of the liquidation or after the liquidation commences. The conduct listed in s 206 is where the director has done any of the following (or is privy to another who does any of the things listed in cases of (iii), (iv) and (v)):

(i)   concealed company property worth at least £500, or concealed any debt due to or from the company; or
(ii)   fraudulently removed any company property whose value is at least £500; or
(iii)   concealed, destroyed, mutilated or falsified any book or paper affecting or relating to the company's property or affairs; or
(iv)   made any false entry in any book or paper affecting or relating to the company's property or affairs; or
(v)   fraudulently parted with, altered or made any omission in any document affecting or relating to the company's property or affairs; or

---

32   This term includes a shadow director under s 206(3).

(vi) pawned, pledged or disposed of any property of the company which has been obtained on credit and has not been paid for (unless the pawning, pledging or disposal was in the ordinary way of the company's business).

6.036 It is a defence for the officer to prove that he or she had no intent to defraud or in relation to points (iii) and (iv) to prove that he had no intent to conceal the state of affairs of the company or to defeat the law.[33]

6.037 Section 207 provides for an offence where an officer of a company has done either of the following within the five years prior to the commencement of the winding up:

(i) made or caused to be made any gift or transfer of, or charge on, or has caused or connived at the levying of any execution against, the company's property; or

(ii) concealed or removed any company property since, or within two months before, the date of any unsatisfied judgment or order for the payment of money obtained against the company.

6.038 Once again it is a defence if the director (or other officer) proves that he or she had no intent to defraud the company's creditors.

6.039 Section 208 moves on to offences which may be committed by any past or present officer of the company in the course of the winding up itself. An offence is committed if he or she:

(i) does not to the best of his or her knowledge and belief fully and truly discover to the liquidator all the company's property, and how and to whom and for what consideration and when the company disposed of any part of that property (apart from in the ordinary course of business); or

(ii) does not deliver up to the liquidator all company property in his or her possession; or

(iii) does not deliver up to the liquidator all company books and papers in his or her possession; or

(iv) knowing or believing that a false debt has been proved by any person in the winding up, fails to inform the liquidator as soon as practicable; or

(v) after the commencement of the winding up, prevents the production of any book or paper affecting or relating to the company's property or affairs; or

(vi) after the commencement of the winding up he or she attempts to account for any part of the company's property by fictitious losses or expenses.[34]

6.040 It is a defence for the officer in question to prove that he or she had no intent to defraud or to conceal the state of affairs or to defeat the law.

6.041 Under s 209 an officer of the company being wound up commits an offence if he or she destroys, mutilates, alters or falsifies any books, papers or securities, or makes or is privy to the making of any false or fraudulent entry in any register, book of account or document belonging to the company with intent to defraud or deceive any person.

---

33 See the comments above at 6.15 where the offences in a moratorium have replicated those in liquidation under s 206.

34 The officer of the company is deemed to have committed that offence if he or she has so attempted in connection with any qualifying decision procedure or deemed consent procedure of the company's creditors within the 12 months immediately preceding the commencement of the winding up (s 208(2)).

Under s 210, any past or present officer[35] commits an offence if he or she makes any material **6.042** omission in any statement of the company's affairs (whether made before or after the commencement of the winding up). There is a defence if the officer can prove there was no intent to defraud.

Under s 211, any past or present officer[36] commits an offence if he or she makes any false **6.043** representation or commits any other fraud for the purpose of obtaining the consent of the company's creditors or any of them to an agreement with reference to the company's affairs or to the winding up. He or she is deemed to have committed the offence if, prior to the winding up, he or she has made any false representation, or committed any other fraud, for that purpose.

E. CONCLUSION

As explained in detail in Chapter 4, directors' behaviour prior to a company entering an insol- **6.044** vency process may lead to action being taken against them.

Directors must be wary of potential liabilities due to their conduct both 'liveside' and after their **6.045** company enters a formal insolvency procedure. Common law and fiduciary duties continue to apply even in cases where directors lose managerial control over the company in a formal insolvency.

A number of other potential liabilities, many of them criminal in nature, will apply if directors **6.046** do not deal transparently and fairly with insolvency officeholders and creditors, during formal insolvency procedures. Attempts to hide assets, misrepresent facts and destroy documentary evidence lead to serious consequences for those directors.

---

35   This includes a shadow director under s 210(3).
36   Again this phrase includes a shadow director (s 211(2)).

7

THE ROLE AND WORK OF INSOLVENCY PRACTITIONERS IN INSOLVENT REGIMES

A. INTRODUCTION

When a company enters some kind of formal insolvency regime an insolvency practitioner   **7.001**
('IP') will be appointed to undertake certain duties. He or she is described in this chapter as an
officeholder.

Some officeholders will be appointed in relation to a regime which is effectively   **7.002**
a debtor-in-possession regime whereby the directors remain in control of the affairs of the
company, subject to some oversight from an officeholder. Examples of officeholders acting in
this type of situation are supervisors in company voluntary agreements (CVAs) and monitors
in companies operating under Part A1 moratoria. There are some duties that are imposed on
officeholders in these sorts of arrangements but they do not raise any substantial corporate governance issues mainly because the officeholders do not have control of the company. In contrast
there are two formal regimes, liquidation and administration that do raise substantial corporate
governance issues. Officeholders appointed as liquidators or administrators take control of
a company and as a result they have multifarious duties and powers that are critical in corporate
governance terms. While directors have broad discretion if their company is not subject to
liquidation or administration, when either of these regimes are entered into the discretion is
transferred to the officeholder. Clearly liquidators and administrators have wide discretion in
how they conduct the affairs of a company.

This chapter focuses on the role and work of liquidators and administrators. We are particularly   **7.003**
concerned with the appointment of these officeholders, their duties and powers, and how they
are remunerated. In the process of considering these matters we will seek to address corporate
governance issues that relate to our definition of that term. Chapter 8 will then address other
pertinent matters relative to corporate governance, such as removal. This chapter does not
purport to deal with the powers and duties of liquidators and administrators in great detail; we
endeavour to identify them and provide some brief outlining of them. Specialised works can be
consulted for greater detailed discussion of powers and duties.[1]

In Chapter 3 we dealt with the kinds of insolvency regimes that exist in the UK system and we   **7.004**
explained what they entail and how they commence. We shall not repeat that in this chapter.
Our focus will be on officeholders and how they are appointed and how they are to conduct
themselves.

B. APPOINTMENT OF OFFICEHOLDERS

1.   Appointment of voluntary liquidators

It will be recalled that a voluntary liquidation may either be a members' voluntary liquidation   **7.005**
(MVL) or a creditors' voluntary liquidation (CVL). As a company must be solvent to be able

---

1   See, e.g., A Keay, *McPherson and Keay's The Law of Company Liquidation* (5th ed, Sweet & Maxwell, 2021), Chapters
     8 and 9; T Robinson and P Walton Kerr and Muir Hunter on Receivership and Administration (21st ed, Sweet &
     Maxwell, 2020).

to enter the former, we will not discuss the regime or the appointment of a liquidator to that regime and indeed we will not consider it in relation to other matters broached in this chapter.[2]

7.006 Despite its name, CVL may not be commenced by creditors. A creditor may only initiate insolvent winding up by means of a winding-up petition. The reference to 'creditors' in the term CVL refers to the fact that the economic interest in the liquidation is with the creditors, not the members, by reason of the company's insolvency. Where the company is insolvent, there will be a deficiency of assets for the creditors and nothing to distribute to the members. As such, only the creditors have an interest in the assets and the governance of the company in CVL reflects this, subject to the wider powers of the liquidator and ultimately any direction given by the court.

7.007 There are a number of routes by which a company may enter CVL. First, a voluntary liquidation will proceed as a CVL where a resolution for voluntary winding up is passed by the members and no declaration of solvency is made by the directors. Secondly, where a voluntary liquidation has commenced and a declaration of solvency has been made, that MVL may be converted into a CVL where it subsequently transpires that the company is in fact insolvent. Thirdly, a company may exit from administration into CVL where the administrator thinks that the total amount which each secured creditor of the company is likely to receive has been paid or set aside for that creditor; and that a distribution (other than by way of the prescribed part in s 176A(2)(a)) will be made to unsecured creditors.[3]

7.008 Once CVL has commenced, the appointment of a liquidator is under the control of the creditors.

7.009 Where no declaration of solvency is made, within a week of the resolution to wind up, the directors must prepare a statement of affairs in the prescribed form and send it to the company's creditors.[4] The members may nominate a person to be liquidator at the meeting at which the resolution for voluntary winding up is passed, but are not required to do so.[5] This reflects the members' lack of economic interest by reason of the company's insolvency where the company is in CVL. The real power to appoint is vested in the creditors of the company, who are each also entitled to nominate their own choice to be liquidator[6] and the directors of the company are required to seek such a nomination from the creditors,[7] using either the deemed consent procedure or by holding a virtual meeting.[8]

7.010 Where an initial nomination is made by the members under s 100(1), that nominee takes office as liquidator,[9] but his or her powers are heavily circumscribed. Section 166 of the Insolvency

---

2   For a detailed discussion of members' voluntary liquidations, see A Keay, *McPherson and Keay's The Law of Company Liquidation* (5th ed, Sweet & Maxwell, 2021), 43–48.
3   Insolvency Act 1986, Sch B1, para 83.
4   Ibid., s 99. Further formalities for a statement of affairs made by the directors are found at Insolvent Rules 2016, rr.6.3, 6.4.
5   Ibid., s 100(1).
6   Ibid., s 100(1A).
7   Ibid., s 100(1A), (2A).
8   Insolvency Rules 2016, r 6.14.
9   Ibid., r 6.20(2).

Act 1986 provides that the powers conferred by s 165 (which include the ability to exercise all the key powers of a liquidator set out in Parts 1–3 of Sch 4 to the Insolvency Act 1986 shall not be exercised, save with sanction, until the creditors have had their opportunity to nominate a person to be liquidator. Moreover, where the members do not make a nomination, s 114 provides that the powers of the directors are nonetheless significantly curtailed by the resolution for winding up.

Both ss 114 and 166 were introduced to eradicate the practice of 'centrebinding', which was **7.011** named after the case *Centrebind Ltd v Inland Revenue Commissioners.*[10] In that case, which was decided under the pre-1986 regime, the Inland Revenue Commissioners raised as a preliminary objection the point that there had been no valid appointment of a voluntary liquidator where the members had appointed a liquidator but no subsequent meeting of creditors had been held. Plowman J dismissed the objection and held that where such an appointment had been made, 'until something is done about it at the instance of the creditors', the person appointed by the members was the liquidator of the company.[11] This left an undue level of governance control in an insolvent company with the members. To bridge the gap, s 166 restricted the actions of a liquidator appointed under such a members-only procedure and s 114 prevents the directors from doing very much after a liquidation has commenced where no liquidator has been appointed or nominated by the members. Both provisions are designed to compel those in control of the company to make haste in complying with their obligation to ensure that the creditors are heard at an early stage, reflecting that the economic interest in an insolvent company is with the creditors.

A decision on the identity of the CVL liquidator must be made quickly: the decision date **7.012** must be not earlier than three days after the delivery of the notice seeking a decision, but not later than 14 days after the resolution to wind up the company;[12] and the statement of affairs need only be delivered to the creditors on the business day prior to the decision date.[13] The decision-making machinery is dealt with elsewhere in Chapter 5. For present purposes, in the case of a CVL appointment, where the deemed consent procedure[14] is used and 10 per cent or more of the creditors object, the directors must seek a decision from the creditors on the nomination of a liquidator by holding a physical meeting.[15]

In *Cash Generator Ltd v Fortune,*[16] ICC Judge Jones considered a case where a party claiming **7.013** to be a creditor applied to challenge the status of liquidators appointed using the machinery in s 100 of the Insolvency Act 1986 without the applicant having been given notice of the deemed consent procedure. On the liquidators' case, notice had not been given because the directors had not appreciated that the applicant was a creditor. The applicant contended that such non-compliance with s 100 meant that the liquidators had been appointed only by the company and the creditors' nomination was a nullity. If that were so, then the liquidators were

10   [1967] 1 WLR 377.
11   [1967] 1 WLR 377, 379D–E.
12   Insolvency Rules 2016, r 6.14(3).
13   Ibid., r 6.14(7).
14   See Insolvency Act 1986, s 246ZF.
15   Insolvency Rules 2016, r 6.14(4). Further formalities concerning the provision of information to creditors and the appointment of a CVL liquidator are set out in r 6.14.
16   [2018] EWHC 674 (Ch), [2019] 1 BCLC 475.

subject to s 166. Judge Jones held that although the requirement in s 100(1B) that the directors seek a nomination for a person to act as liquidator from the company's creditors is expressed in mandatory language, a failure on the part of the directors to comply with that requirement did not render the creditors' nomination a nullity.[17] The decision was based on the obvious practical difficulty that would flow from any other outcome. This is because there is always a prospect that one or more persons claiming to be creditors will not be given notice, most obviously where (as in *Cash Generator* itself) those in control of the company are not aware of the claim. A contrary finding would have meant that the validity of many CVL appointments would be open to question.[18]

7.014 Section 100(2) provides that the liquidator shall be the person nominated by the creditors or, where no person has been so nominated, the person (if any) nominated by the company. There may be multiple nominations from the creditors. It is possible that the members' nominee will enjoy support from some of the creditors, but not all, and a contested vote will be required. Alternatively, entirely new competing nominations may emerge from different factions of creditors. In those situations, the matter is decided by taking votes of the creditors until a majority is reached.[19] If there are more than two nominees, this may require multiple votes and the elimination of the nominee with the least support until a majority is achieved,[20] although in practice this is unusual. Where a decision is being made at a meeting, the chair may at any time put to the meeting a resolution for the joint nomination of any two or more nominees.[21] It is not uncommon for such joint appointments to be made, with nominees of differing factions holding office as joint liquidators. While any IP appointed as a liquidator should show the same disinterest and even-handedness between all stakeholders irrespective of the source of their nomination, it is common for conflicted interests to be wary of each other's nominees for liquidator and, depending on the circumstances, joint appointments may sometimes be an appropriate way to manage such antagonisms.[22] A CVL liquidator's appointment takes effect from the date of the passing of the resolution to wind up or, where the creditors make an alternative appointment, from the relevant decision date.[23]

7.015 Where a voluntary liquidation has commenced as an MVL but has to be converted to a CVL, the MVL liquidator must also seek a nomination from the creditors for a person to be liquidator by a decision procedure or by the deemed consent procedure.[24]

7.016 The procedural requirements are similar to those for seeking the creditors' nomination where the winding up proceeds from the outset as a CVL.[25] In the case of conversion from MVL to CVL, the essence of the procedure from a governance point of view is the same as with a winding up that has proceeded throughout as a CVL: the members get to choose first and the

---

17   Ibid., [9].
18   Ibid., [14].
19   Insolvency Rules 2016, r 6.18.
20   Ibid., r 6.18(1)(c).
21   Ibid., r 6.18(2).
22   Although joint appointments are not necessarily a solution to alleged conflicts, a point addressed further in Chapter 8.
23   Insolvency Rules 2016, r 6.20(2).
24   Insolvency Act 1986, s 95(4B), (4C). The formal requirements for seeking the creditors' nomination on conversion from MVL to CVL are found at Insolvency Rules 2016, rr 6.11–6.13.
25   Insolvency Rules 2016, rr 6.11–6.13.

creditors then decide whether to accept the members' nominee or substitute their own. Subject to the intervention of the court, the creditors' right to choose trumps that of the members. This reflects that it is now the creditors', not the members', liquidation.

The MVL becomes a CVL when either the creditors nominate a person to be liquidator, or the **7.017** procedure by which the nomination was to have been made by the creditors concludes with no nomination having been made.[26] Where the creditors make a nomination, that person becomes the liquidator; where no nomination is made, the existing MVL liquidator continues as CVL liquidator.[27]

Whether a company enters CVL by means of conversion from MVL, or has been in CVL **7.018** from the outset, the right of the creditors to choose the liquidator is not absolute. In the case of conversion from MVL, s 96(4) provides that where the creditors nominate a person other than the existing liquidator (i.e., other than the choice of the members), any director, member or creditor of the company may apply within seven days of the nomination for an order that the existing liquidator is to be liquidator instead of, or jointly with, the person nominated by the creditors, or appointing some other person to be liquidator. Where the winding up has been by way of CVL from the outset, s 100(3) provides that where 'different persons' are nominated (in context, this appears to mean different persons nominated, respectively, by the creditors and the company, as opposed to different persons nominated by competing factions of creditors), the same class of applicants may seek similar relief.

In both types of voluntary winding up, there is a presumption in favour of granting such an **7.019** application where it is made by a qualifying floating chargeholder (QFCH) within the meaning of para 14 of Sch B1 to the Act. Both s 96(4A) (which applies in the case of conversion from MVL to CVL) and s 100(4) (where the winding up commenced as a CVL) provide that where such an application is made by a QFCH the court shall grant it unless the court thinks it right to refuse the application because of the particular circumstances of the case. This underlines the elevated position in the hierarchy of governance rights in insolvency enjoyed by such a chargeholder, which is discussed in more detail in the discussion of the appointment of an administrator below.

2.   Appointment of voluntary liquidator and compulsory winding up

There is nothing to prevent a resolution for voluntary winding up from being passed while **7.020** a winding-up petition remains outstanding. But the commencement of voluntary winding up in such circumstances will not, of itself, prevent the court from making an order for that company's compulsory winding up. That is so whether the petition is presented before or after the resolution for voluntary winding up is passed. The right of any creditor or contributory to seek winding up by the court in these circumstances is specifically preserved by s 116 of the Act.

The principal reason that a petition for a compulsory winding-up order may be pursued **7.021** despite a resolution for voluntary winding up having been passed, or such a petition presented despite a company already being in voluntary liquidation, is because one of the remaining

---

26   Insolvency Act 1986, s 96(1).
27   Ibid., s 96(3).

differences[28] between voluntary and compulsory winding up is the automatic obligation on the official receiver (OR) (who becomes liquidator as soon as an order for compulsory winding up is made[29]) to investigate the causes of the failure and the general affairs of a company in compulsory liquidation.[30] No equivalent provision for mandatory investigation exists in voluntary liquidation. A creditor that suspects wrongdoing by the directors, thinks there are matters worth investigating, or who considers that the CVL liquidator may be insufficiently sceptical or inquisitive (perhaps because the creditor fears the voluntary liquidator is too close to the directors who commenced the CVL), may be inclined to take this course. This is more likely to happen where the dissentient creditor is in the voting minority and is otherwise unable to influence the identity of the liquidator.

7.022   An order for compulsory winding up may be sought when the company is already in voluntary liquidation. Whether an order will be made for compulsory winding up is, as with every winding-up petition, a matter of judicial discretion.[31]

3.   Appointment of liquidator in compulsory winding up

7.023   On a winding-up order being made by the court, in most cases[32] the OR becomes the liquidator and continues in office until another person becomes liquidator.[33] Similarly, the OR automatically becomes liquidator to fill any vacancy.[34]

7.024   Section 139 of the Insolvency Act 1986 provides that both the creditors and the contributories may nominate a person to be liquidator, thereby replacing the OR, but the choice of the contributories shall prevail where no person has been nominated by the creditors.[35] This provision self-evidently reflects that the economic interest in the liquidation estate is with the creditors, with the members' interest extinguished by reason of the insolvency.

7.025   As with voluntary liquidation, it is not uncommon in practice for the choice of the members to be supported by one section of the creditors against the choice of another. This will tend to arise in cases where there is an overlap in identity between members and creditors, and disputes may arise over their motives for their choice and its implications for the class interest.

7.026   A residual ability to apply to court exists in s 139(4), similar to those found in s 96(4) (where a winding up is converted from MVL to CVL) and s 100(3) (where a winding up has been in CVL throughout), for the choice of the contributories to be appointed either instead of, or jointly with, the person nominated by the creditors, or for some alternative appointment to be

---

28   For many purposes, the differences between compulsory and voluntary winding up are considerably reduced by the effect of s 112 of the Insolvency Act 1986, see para 8.040.
29   Insolvency Act 1986, s 136.
30   Ibid., s 132.
31   For a discussion of the issues that may be taken into account, see A Keay, *McPherson and Keay's The Law of Company Liquidation* (5th ed, Sweet and Maxwell, 2021), 183–194.
32   Insolvency Act 1986, s 140 provides for a different outcome where the winding-up order is made in relation to a company that is in administration or subject to a CVA.
33   Ibid., s 136(2).
34   Ibid., s 136(3).
35   Ibid., s 139(3).

made.[36] Unlike the provisions that apply in CVL, however, only creditors and members may apply and standing is not conferred on directors. The obvious reason for excluding directors is that a winding-up order terminates the directors' office,[37] whereas voluntary liquidation merely leads to the cesser of their powers.[38] Moreover, there is no mention of any rights for QFCHs nor any presumption in their favour, as are found in both MVL[39] and CVL.[40]

Two governance functions of s 139(4) (which apply equally to s 96(4) and s 100(3) in CVL) may be identified. First, s 139(4) is clearly intended to deal with circumstances where there is a compelling reason why an officeholder other than the choice of the majority of creditors should be appointed as liquidator. Secondly, authority indicates that the section may also be used where something has gone wrong with the machinery of the appointment of the liquidator and the creditors' meeting has for some reason failed accurately to discern the wishes of the majority of creditors.[41] **7.027**

The nomination process discussed above may be circumvented by the OR at any time while the OR is liquidator by making an application to the Secretary of State for the appointment of a liquidator.[42] It is open to the Secretary of State either to make an appointment or decline to make one.[43] There is no express requirement on the OR to take the views of the creditors before asking the Secretary of State to make an appointment, but in practice such views will be highly material. Where nominations have been sought from the creditors and the contributories using the machinery referred to in the previous paragraph and no person has been chosen to be liquidator as a result, then the OR is under a duty to decide whether to refer the need for an appointment to the Secretary of State. **7.028**

Where a winding-up up order is made in relation to a company that is either in administration or subject to a CVA, s 140 provides that the court may appoint the administrator or the CVA supervisor as liquidator.[44] The section confers a discretion to bypass the normal procedure in ss 136 and 139, but does not confer on the court any general power to appoint as liquidator or additional liquidator a person who has not occupied the position of administrator or supervisor.[45] There are obvious reasons of economy and efficiency for this. In many cases, the administrator or the supervisor will be the obvious person to act as liquidator, as they will have extensive knowledge of the company and duplication of work as between the liquidation and the preceding process will be minimised. The gateway is, however, discretionary rather than automatic. Circumstances may readily arise where one or more creditors oppose the appointment of the outgoing administrator or supervisor and instead prefer the appointment of a fresh **7.029**

---

36   Ibid., s 139(4).
37   *Measures Brothers Ltd v Measures* [1910] 2 Ch 248.
38   See Insolvency Act 1986, s 91(2) (in the case of MVL) and s 103 (in the case of CVL).
39   Ibid., s 96(4A).
40   Ibid., s 100(4).
41   *Mardas v The Official Receiver, The Times*, 10 November 1989.
42   Insolvency Act 1986, s 137(1). Insolvency Rules 2016, r 7.57.
43   Ibid., s 137(3).
44   Ibid., s 140.
45   In *Re Exchange Travel (Holdings) Ltd* [1993] BCLC 887, 892b–c. The case referred directly only to the position of an administrator, as this was the context of the case, but the same principle would plainly also be applied to a CVA supervisor.

pair of eyes. For instance, the administrator or supervisor may have been the nominee of the directors, whose conduct the creditors wish to have investigated. Alternatively, the administrator may have been the nominee of a QFCH and some of the unsecured creditors may desire an investigation into the circumstances of the appointment or some feature of the administration itself, such as the degree of scrutiny given to the secured creditor's claim.

4.   Appointment of administrators

(a) Introduction

7.030   An administrator is a person appointed under Sch B1 of the 1986 Act to manage a company's affairs, business and property.[46] Such a person must be a licensed IP.[47] A company 'enters administration' when an administrator of the company is appointed[48] and is 'in administration' while an administrator is appointed.[49] An administrator is an officer of the court however appointed,[50] which means the administration is under the court's inherent jurisdiction over its own officers, as well as subject to the rule in *Ex parte James*.[51] The administrator invariably acts as agent of the company[52] and has wide discretionary powers to manage the company while it is in administration.[53]

7.031   The administration regime is heavily codified by Sch B1 of the Insolvency Act 1986 and it provides three principal ways in which an administrator may be appointed: first, by the court under para 10; secondly, out of court by the holder of a qualifying floating charge under para 14; and, thirdly, out of court by the company or its directors under para 22.[54]

7.032   As a starting point, an administrator cannot be appointed if the company is already in liquidation.[55] There are two exceptions to that. Firstly, where a company is in liquidation (whether voluntary or compulsory), the liquidator of that company may make an application to the court for an administration order.[56] Secondly, where a company is in compulsory winding up (but not where it is in voluntary winding up[57]) the holder of a qualifying floating charge may make an application to court for an administration order.[58]

---

46   Insolvency Act 1986, Sch B1, para 1(1).
47   Ibid., Sch B1, para 6; ss 388(1)(a), 390.
48   Ibid., Sch B1, para 1(2)(b).
49   Ibid., Sch B1, para 1(2)(a).
50   Ibid., Sch B1, para 5.
51   *Ex parte James; In re Condon* (1874) LR 9 Ch App 609, CA.
52   Insolvency Act 1986, Sch B1, para 69. See *Davey v Money* [2018] EWHC 766, [2018] Bus LR 1903, [385].
53   Ibid., Sch B1, para 59; Sch 1.
54   Ibid., Sch B1, para 2.
55   Ibid., Sch B1, para 8. Sch B1, para 39 provides that the court must also dismiss an administration application where the company is already in administrative receivership, whether the receiver was appointed before or after the administration application was made (Sch B1, para 39(2)), unless the person who appointed the receiver consents (Sch B1, para 39(1)(a)) or the court thinks that the security under which the appointment was made would be liable to be released or discharged under the antecedent transaction machinery in the Insolvency Act 1986 (Sch B1, para 39(1)(b)–(d)).
56   Ibid., Sch B1, para 38.
57   This limitation is clear from Insolvency Act 1986, Sch B1, paras 8(2) and 37(1).
58   Insolvency Act 1986, Sch B1, para 37.

The scheme in Sch B1 provides for the relative rights of the secured creditors, unsecured cred-   **7.033**
itors and the company to determine who is appointed as administrator.[59] Most notably, Sch
B1 imposes a clear hierarchy of rights on those with an interest in a company when it comes to
causing that company to enter administration and in choosing the identity of any administrator. When a company is in financial distress, these rights are key corporate governance rights.
An important factor in determining where those rights reside is whether or not there exists any
qualifying floating charge (QFC) over the company. The rights of the holder of such a charge
are firmly at the top of the governance hierarchy in a number of ways that will be addressed
below. As Henry Carr J explained in *Re Zinc Hotels (Holdings) Ltd*:[60] 'The general approach in
Schedule B1 is that where there is a qualifying floating charge, the floating charge-holder has
the right to decide who the administrator should be.'[61]

A QFCH's right to appoint an administrator out-of-court replaced such chargeholders' ability   **7.034**
to appoint an administrative receiver, which was removed in relation to charges created on or
after 15 September 2003 on the coming into force of the modernised administration regime in
Sch B1 of the Insolvency Act 1986, which was introduced by the Enterprise Act 2002. Lewison
J described the reforms to the appointment process as follows:

> Schedule B1 is part of a package of measures intended to encourage enterprise. That package includes
> the facilitation of the raising of credit. Part of the *quid pro quo* was to make it easier for creditors to
> appoint administrators, hence the current power to appoint administrators without having to apply to
> the court.[62]

The QFCH's dominance in an administration is constrained by Sch B1 in an important way   **7.035**
that it was not under an old-style administrative receivership. The purpose of any administration is to achieve one of the hierarchy of objectives in para 3(1) of Sch B1.[63] Paragraph 3(1)
gives priority to the rescue of the company as a going concern[64] and requires an administrator's
functions to be performed in the interests of the company's creditors as a whole.[65] This stands
in contrast to an old-style administrative receiver's limited function in ensuring that the secured
debt was repaid, which served only the interests of the secured creditor. The tension in Sch B1
between the QFCH's primacy in the hierarchy of rights in administration and the simultaneous
restraint on its dominance is a crucial feature in the governance of companies where administration is contemplated.

A particular advantage that a QFCH enjoys when making an out-of-court appointment under   **7.036**
para 14 of Sch B1 over other forms of appointment is that there is no need to demonstrate
insolvency.[66] On the other hand, a QFCH cannot simply appoint an administrator to realise
its security without regard for wider interests: an administrator appointed out of court by the
QFCH must, like any other administrator, pursue the objectives in para 3(1)(a) (rescue as

---

59   Ibid., [54].
60   *Re Zinc Hotels (Holdings) Ltd.* ibid.
61   Ibid., [54].
62   *BCPMS (Europe) Ltd v GMAC Commercial Finance plc* [2006] EWHC 3744, [6].
63   Insolvency Act 1986, Sch B1, para 111(1).
64   Ibid., Sch B1, para 3(1).
65   Ibid., Sch B1, para 3(2).
66   When seeking a court appointment, the QFCH is also (unlike any other appointing party) spared the burden of demon-
     strating insolvency under ibid., Sch B1, para 11(a) by Sch B1, para 35.

a going concern) and 3(1)(b) (a better result for the creditors as a whole than would be likely if the company were wound up without first being in administration) if it is 'reasonably practicable' to do so.

7.037 Given the centrality of the QFC to the governance and control of companies in administration, whether commenced in or out of court, a discussion of such charges is necessary, before turning to the specific forms of appointment that may be made.

(b) The qualifying floating charge

7.038 The floating charge is a device of great importance in the financing of trading companies in the United Kingdom. It charges a company's undertaking, including its present and future assets, which represent a circulating fund. The charge metaphorically 'floats' over this fund until it is crystallised into a fixed charge by, most commonly, an event of default. It developed in line with the rapid growth in corporate activity during the mid-Victorian period.[67] In *Illingworth v Houldsworth*[68] Lord Macnaghten described the floating charge as:

> ambulatory and shifting in its nature, hovering over and so to speak floating with the property which it is intended to affect until some event occurs or some act is done which causes it to settle and fasten on the subject of the charge within its reach and grasp.[69]

7.039 Lord Millett examined the history of the floating charge in detail in the Privy Council decision *Agnew v Commissioner of Inland Revenue*[70] and explained its operation and role as follows:

> The thinking behind the development of the floating charge was that compliance with the terms of a fixed charge on the company's circulating capital would paralyse its business...A fixed charge gives the holder of the charge an immediate proprietary interest in the assets subject to the charge which binds all those into whose hands the assets may come with notice of the charge. Unless it obtained the consent of the holder of the charge, therefore, the company would be unable to deal with its assets without committing a breach of the terms of the charge...In short, a fixed charge would deprive the company of its access to its cash flow, which is the life blood of a business...
>
> The floating charge is capable of affording the creditor, by a single instrument, an effective and comprehensive security upon the entire undertaking of the debtor company and its assets from time to time, while at the same time leaving the company free to deal with its assets and pay its trade creditors in the ordinary course of business without reference to the holder of the charge. Such a form of security is particularly attractive to banks, and it rapidly acquired an importance in English commercial life...[71]

7.040 By the turn of the twentieth century, the floating charge was sufficiently developed for Romer LJ to give the following classic explanation of its characteristics in *Re Yorkshire Woolcombers Association Ltd*:[72]

> I certainly think that if a charge has the three characteristics that I am about to mention it is a floating charge. (1) If it is a charge on a class of assets of a company present and future; (2) if that class is one which, in the ordinary course of the business of the company, would be changing from time to time;

---

67 For a full consideration of the historical development of the floating charge see R Gregory and P Walton 'Fixed and Floating Charges - A Revelation' [2001] *Lloyds Maritime and Commercial Law Quarterly* 123.
68 [1904] AC 355, 358.
69 Ibid., 358.
70 [2001] 2 AC 710.
71 Ibid., [7]–[9].
72 [1903] 2 Ch 284.

and (3) if you find that by the charge it is contemplated that, until some step is taken by or on behalf of those interested in the charge, the company may carry on its business in the ordinary way as far as concerns the particular class of assets I am dealing with.[73]

High authority in recent years, including the House of Lords in *Re Spectrum Plus Ltd*[74] and the Court of Appeal in *SAW (SW) 2010 Ltd v Wilson*,[75] has emphasised that it is the third of the characteristics identified by Romer LJ that plays the predominant part in distinguishing a floating charge from a fixed charge. **7.041**

As mentioned above, central to the regime in Sch B1 is the concept of the QFC.[76] This is defined as a 'floating charge' that 'qualifies' by meeting one of the criteria in para 14(2) of Sch B1. Despite its centrality to the regime, 'floating charge' is not defined as a concept in the Insolvency Act 1986 beyond the circular reference in s 251 that states only: '"floating charge" means a charge which, as created, was a floating charge…'. **7.042**

Whether or not a charge was, as created, a 'floating charge' within this definition will be determined by reference to case law, which indicates that the passage from *Re Yorkshire Woolcombers* set out above will be treated as the appropriate working definition, as explained in *Re Spectrum Plus Ltd*.[77] **7.043**

In order to be a floating charge that 'qualifies', the charge must be created by an instrument that satisfies at least one of the criteria in para 14(2). These include an instrument that expressly provides that para 14 applies,[78] empowers the holder to appoint an administrator,[79] or includes an instrument which purports to empower the holder to appoint an administrative receiver.[80] The power to appoint an administrator under the last-mentioned provision was intended to supersede the holder's power to appoint a receiver, which applied prior to the introduction of the new regime in the Enterprise Act 2002.[81] **7.044**

The validity and enforceability of such a charge by the QFCH are considered further below. **7.045**

(c) Appointment of administrators by the court

Applications for a court appointment under para 10 of Sch B1 may be made by a company itself,[82] its directors[83] or the QFCH[84] (these being the same parties as may make an appoint- **7.046**

---

73   Ibid., 295; cited with approval in *Re Spectrum Plus Ltd* [2005] 2 AC 680, [99].
74   [2005] 2 AC 680 [106]–[107], [111].
75   [2018] Ch 213 [22].
76   Insolvency Act 1986, Sch B1, para 14.
77   [2005] 2 AC 680 [106]–[107], [111].
78   Insolvency Act 1986, Sch B1, para 14(1)(a).
79   Ibid., Sch B1, para 14(1)(b).
80   Ibid., Sch B1, para 14(1)(c).
81   *Re Secure Mortgage Corp Ltd v Harold* [2020] EWHC 1364, [20].
82   Insolvency Act 1986, Sch B1, para 12(1)(a).
83   Ibid., Sch B1, para 12(1)(b).
84   Applying under the general gateway for creditors Insolvency Act 1986, Sch B1, para 12(1)(c).

ment out of court[85]), by unsecured creditors of the company,[86] the supervisor of a company voluntary arrangement over the company,[87] or by a previously appointed liquidator.[88]

7.047　Depending on the circumstances, parties that are entitled to appoint out of court may sometimes choose to seek a court appointment, rather than proceed under the apparently more straightforward out-of-court route discussed below. Where the circumstances are particularly contentious or have attracted adverse publicity, for example, a court appointment may be perceived as a safer route to avoid challenges or criticism later that may have serious consequences. It may be the appointor itself that seeks this additional level of certainty, or perhaps the IP who has been lined up to become administrator may require the comfort of a court appointment as a condition of agreeing to take the appointment. For example, in *Hellenic Capital Investments Ltd v Trainfix Ltd*,[89] the company had filed forms with the registrar of companies claiming that the sum secured by the QFC had been repaid. Although the QFCH disputed this and could have appointed out of court under para 14, it recognised that any proposed administrator would be reluctant to accept an out-of-court appointment in those circumstances and would require the comfort of a court order.[90]

7.048　A party making an application to court for an administration order must, as soon as reasonably practicable, notify a number of parties.[91] The most significant of these parties is any person who is or may be entitled to appoint out of court under para 14, i.e., any person who is or may be a QFCH.[92] On receiving that notice, as a consequence of its position at the top of the hierarchy of governance rights in administration, the QFCH is entitled to take control of the situation if it chooses to do so. First, the QFCH may simply make an out-of-court appointment under para 14, with its own nominee taking office as administrator, and thereby outflank the existing administration application.[93] Secondly, the QFCH may apply under para 36 for a person other than the person specified in the existing application to be appointed as administrator,[94] with a statutory presumption in favour of the QFCH's choice.[95] In this way, most of the governance power remains firmly with the QFCH where an application is made for a court appointment, even where the QFCH is not the applicant.

85　Under Insolvency Act 1986, Sch B1, paras 14 and 22 respectively.
86　Ibid., Sch B1, para 12(1)(c).
87　Ibid., Sch B1, para 12(5); s 7(4)(b); Insolvency Rules 2016, r.3.5.
88　Ibid., Sch B1, para 38.
89　[2015] EWHC 3713, [2016] BCC 493.
90　Ibid., [7].
91　Insolvency Act 1986, Sch B1, para 12(2).
92　Ibid., Sch B1, para 12(2)(c). Notification must also be given to any person who has appointed, or is or may be entitled to appoint, an administrative receiver: Sch B1, paras 12(2)(a)–(b). An existing administrative receivership brings into play Sch B1, para 39, which provides that an administration application must be dismissed where a company is in administrative receivership, save where the appointing creditor consents or the court thinks that the security is liable to be avoided under Insolvency Act 1986, ss 238–240, 242–243 or 245. Administrative receivership is now so rare in practice that this aspect is not considered in detail in this book.
93　It should be noted that a QFCH also enjoys similar rights to take control where an application for an out-of-court appointment is made under Insolvency Act 1986, Sch B1, para 22 by the company or its directors. In that case, Sch B1, para 26 provides that five business days' notice of intention to appoint under Sch B1, para 22 must be given to any QFCH and Sch B1, para 33 provides that the QFCH may outflank such an appointment by making an appointment under Sch B1, para 14 right up until the para 22 appointment takes effect.
94　Insolvency Act 1986, Sch B1, para 36(1).
95　Ibid., Sch B1, para 36(2).

An administration order under para 10 of Sch B1 may only be made where the court is satisfied **7.049** of two conditions: first, that the company is or is likely to become unable to pay its debts (i.e., an insolvency requirement);[96] and, secondly, that the administration order is reasonably likely to achieve the purpose of administration.[97] The burden is on the applicant in both cases, but case law indicates that the standard by which the court must be 'satisfied' is different for the two limbs: the insolvency requirement must be demonstrated on the balance of probabilities, whereas the applicant need show only a 'real prospect' that an administration order would achieve the purpose of administration.[98]

In a further pointer towards the governance control enjoyed by the QFCH, the insolvency **7.050** requirement in para 11(a) is disapplied by para 35(2)(a) of Sch B1 where the application for an administration order is made by the QFCH.[99] Accordingly, a QFCH may seek a court appointment without any need to show that the company is unable to pay its debts. This mirrors the absence of any need to show insolvency where a QFCH makes an appointment out of court under para 14. Paragraph 35 will be useful where the QFCH or the proposed administrators desire the comfort of a court appointment where there exists the possibility of the enforceability of the security being attacked. Mr Robert Ham QC (sitting as a deputy judge of the High Court) explained in *Re St John Spencer Estates & Development Ltd*[100] that:

> The purpose of the para 35 procedure is in my view to provide secured lenders with a simple and assured route to realise their security where the company is in default, and to enable any doubts as to the enforceability of the security to be determined in advance without the administrators being exposed to any risk that an appointment out-of-court was invalid.[101]

The deputy judge also made the observation that where the floating charge is enforceable, the **7.051** QFCH has a *prima facie* right to an order for the appointment of administrators, unless there are countervailing considerations.[102] That said, the cases show that on an application for an administration order under para 10 by the QFCH, although the formal requirement for insolvency is disapplied by para 35, the issue of insolvency remains relevant to the exercise of the court's discretion under para 13 in relation to what order to make.[103] This point is considered further below. In all other cases where the court appointment of administrators is sought, the insolvency requirement in para 11(a) must be satisfied on the balance of probabilities.

As noted above, in addition to the insolvency requirement in para 11(a) of Sch B1, the court **7.052** must also be satisfied under para 11(b) that the administration order is reasonably likely to achieve the purpose of the administration. To satisfy this further requirement, the applicant need show only that there is a 'real prospect' that the purpose will be achieved. In *Baltic House*

---

96   Ibid., Sch B1, para 11(a).
97   Ibid., Sch B1, para 11(b). The purpose of administration being the achievement of one of the three objectives in Sch B1, para 3(1).
98   *Hellenic Capital Investments Ltd v Trainfix Ltd* [2015] EWHC 3713, [2016] BCC 493, [11]. See also *Re Harris Simons Construction Ltd* [1989] 1 WLR 368 and *Re SCL Building Services Ltd* (1989) 5 BCC 746.
99   Insolvency Act 1986, Sch B1, para 35. In order to take advantage of this disapplication, the QFCH's application must include a statement that the application is made in reliance on Sch B1, para 35.
100 [2012] EWHC 2317, [2013] 1 BCLC 718.
101 Ibid., [39].
102 Ibid.
103 *Hellenic Capital Investments Ltd v Trainfix Ltd* [2015] EWHC 3713, [2016] BCC 493 [11], [21].

Developments Ltd v Cheung,[104] His Honour Judge Eyre QC (sitting as a High Court judge) described this as a 'comparatively low hurdle' and summarised the test under para 11(b) as follows:

> The burden is on the applicant to show such a real prospect. I remind myself that the real prospect does not have to be established on the balance of probabilities. The applicant does not have to show it is more likely than not that such a result will be achieved, but there must be something more than speculation. There must be something of substance and reality.[105]

7.053   There is no need, at this point, for the administrator to identify the particular objective in para 3 by which the purpose is to be achieved, which may be uncertain at this stage.[106] It should also be noted that, where a QFCH applies for an administration order under para 10, only the insolvency requirement in para 11(a) is disapplied; the need to show under para 11(b) a real prospect that the statutory purpose will be achieved continues to apply with its usual equal force. In *Strategic Advantage SPC v High Street Rooftop Holdings Ltd*,[107] the court rejected a QFCH's argument that para 11(b), as well as para 11(a), was disapplied in an application by a QFCH for an administration order.

7.054   If the court is satisfied of the two limbs of para 11 of Sch B1, then the jurisdiction to make an administration order is engaged. This remains, however, a matter of judicial discretion. On the hearing of an administration application, para 13 enables the court either to make an administration order[108] or any other order that the court thinks appropriate.[109] Specific provision is included for the court to make an interim order,[110] which may include restrictions on the powers of the company or its directors,[111] or to treat the application as a winding-up petition and make any order that it could make under s 125 of the Insolvency Act 1986.[112]

7.055   Sir Geoffrey Vos C emphasised the wide nature of the discretion in *Rowntree Ventures Ltd v Oak Property Partners Ltd*:[113]

> It is necessary first in my judgment to understand that the discretion provided to the court in paragraph 13 of Sch B1 is of a wide and general nature, not constrained in any way…The circumstances are likely to be infinitely variable. The interests of secured creditors, preferential creditors, unsecured creditors and the company itself will change from case to case.[114]

7.056   Inevitably, similar factors will be relevant to the exercise of the judicial discretion in para 13 to those that go to the requirement in para 11(b) that it is reasonably likely that the purpose

---

104   [2018] EWHC 1525, [2018] Bus LR 1531. See also *Auto Management Services Ltd v Oracle Fleet UK Ltd* [2008] BCC 761, [3].
105   Ibid., [36].
106   *Key2Law (Surrey) LLP v De'Antiquis* [2011] EWCA Civ 1567, [2012] BCC 375, [98].
107   [2020] EWHC 2572 (Ch), [13].
108   Insolvency Act 1986, Sch B1, para 13(1)(a).
109   Ibid., Sch B1, para 13(1)(f).
110   Ibid., Sch B1, para 13(1)(d).
111   Ibid., Sch B1, para 13(1)(3).
112   Ibid., Sch B1, para 13(1)(e).
113   [2017] EWCA Civ 1944, [2018] BCC 135.
114   Ibid., [24].

of administration will be achieved.[115] Judge Eyre QC held in *Baltic House Developments Ltd v Cheung* that the degree of risk of a worse outcome in administration compared with liquidation was relevant to the exercise of the discretion.[116] In that case, the judge found that there was no jurisdiction to make an administration order where the condition in para 11(b) was not satisfied, but would not have exercised his discretion in favour of an order even if it had been, by reason of creditor opposition and the marginal nature of any arguable benefit.[117] Similar reasoning was evident in *Doltable Ltd v Lexi Holdings plc*,[118] where Mann J held that even if it had been arguable that the case could be brought within the statutory purpose and the condition in para 11(b) satisfied, the discretion would have been exercised against making an administration order in circumstances where the substance of the matter was a dispute between the applicant company and its secured creditor.[119]

Where a court appointment is sought and there is a dispute between stakeholders over who the **7.057** administrator should be, the appropriate starting point in resolving it depends upon the identity of the parties to the dispute. In *Oracle (Northwest) Ltd v Pinnacle (UK) Ltd*,[120] the contest was between the company's directors and its unsecured creditors, with the secured creditors remaining neutral. Patten J held that in such a case, the court should resolve the matter in favour of the wishes of creditors, 'for whose benefit in the end the administration is'.[121] This is a reflection both of the general principle that in an insolvent company the real economic interest in the company is with the creditors, combined with the express statutory priority given by Sch B1 to the interests of creditors in administration.[122]

The starting point is different where the contest is between competing factions of creditors. In **7.058** *Med-Gourmet Restaurants Ltd v Ostuni Investments Ltd*,[123] the applicants for the order were two directors of the company, whose proposed administrators enjoyed the support of a majority of creditors. That nomination was opposed by a number of creditors, who pointed to the fact that the creditors supporting the directors' candidates included former directors, members of their families and others who had personal relationships with them.[124] Lewison J referred to *Oracle (Northwest) Ltd v Pinnacle (UK) Ltd*[125] and remarked that where the only contest is between the directors' nominee and the creditors' nominee, plainly the creditors will prevail. But where there is a conflict between creditor and creditor, the majority of creditors do not have the absolute right to choose the identity of the administrators.[126] Lewison J departed from the views

---

115   See *Auto Management Services Ltd v Oracle Fleet UK Ltd* [2008] BCC 761, [3]; [2018] EWHC 1525, [2018] Bus LR 1531, [28].
116   [2018] EWHC 1525, [2018] Bus LR 1531, [28]–[30].
117   Ibid., [43].
118   [2005] EWHC 1804, [2006] BCC 918.
119   Ibid., [42].
120   [2008] EWHC 1920 (Ch), [2009] BCC 159.
121   Ibid., [21].
122   Insolvency Act 1986, Sch B1, para 3.
123   [2010] EWHC 2834 (Ch), [2013] BCC 47.
124   Ibid., [5].
125   [2008] EWHC 1920 (Ch), [2009] BCC 159.
126   [2010] EWHC 2834 (Ch), [2013] BCC 47, [9].

of the majority creditors on the basis that there appeared to be circumstances that required independent investigation.[127] Lewison J observed that:

> There is a public interest in office-holders charged with the administration of an insolvent estate not only acting but being seen to be acting in the best interest of the creditors generally; and ensuring that all legitimate claims that the company may have are thoroughly investigated.[128]

7.059   The principles at work in these cases is identical to those discussed above in relation to contested winding-up petitions where a company is already in CVL. The court's approach to resolving other disputes over the identity of the officeholder is discussed further in Chapter 8.

(d) Appointment out-of-court by the QFCH

7.060   The ability to appoint an administrator out of court, without a number of the fetters that apply to such appointments by the company or its directors, gives the QFCH a high level of governance control over the administration process. The role of the QFCH in administration is a nuanced one. In many ways, the QFCH holds the whip-hand and is unquestionably at the top of the hierarchy of governance rights in administration, but this is tempered by the additional protections for unsecured creditors and the wider interests represented by the company imposed by Sch B1.

7.061   In order to make an appointment under para 14, at the time of the appointment the appointor must be the person in whom the rights to the QFC are vested;[129] the charge in question must be valid as a QFC;[130] and enforceable.[131] The 'validity' of a QFC for these purposes does not depend on the company having had any available uncharged assets at the time of the creation of the QFC; what matters is the terms of the charge itself.[132] Further, the enforceability of the charge is concerned with whether the QFCH has a *right* to enforce, rather than with the question whether there are any *assets* against which the QFCH can enforce at the time of appointment.[133] This underlines the court's reluctance to fetter the QFCH's ability to make a quick appointment or to cause such appointments to become embroiled in fact-based disputes prior to an appointment being made.

7.062   The existence of a good faith dispute on substantial grounds over whether or not the charge is enforceable does not preclude the appointment of an administrator: in *BCPMS (Europe) Ltd v GMAC Commercial Finance plc*,[134] Lewison J rejected an argument that, by analogy with the presentation of a bankruptcy or winding-up petition, the existence of a bona fide dispute rendered any attempt by a QFCH to appoint out of court an administrator in the face of that

---

127   The evidence showed that the company had granted debentures shortly before the presentation of the administration application and one of the applicant directors had given misleading information to the court about the true state of the finances of the company.

128   [2010] EWHC 2834 (Ch), [2013] BCC 47, [14].

129   *Re Secure Mortgage Corp Ltd v Harold* [2020] EWHC 1364, [20].

130   Insolvency Act 1986, Sch B1, para 14.

131   Ibid., Sch B1, para 16.

132   *SAW (SW) 2010 Ltd v Wilson* [2018] Ch 213, [24]–[26].

133   Ibid., [33]. See also *Adjei v Law for All* [2011] EWHC 2672, [2011] BCC 963, where the consequences of a company's directors' failure to give notice under Insolvency Act 1986, Sch B1, para 26 to a QFCH, despite that QFCH's debt having been paid off, were discussed.

134   [2006] EWHC 3744 (Ch).

dispute an abuse of process.[135] In a firm nod towards the primacy of the rights of the QFCH in administration, Lewison J rejected the analogy with bankruptcy and winding up[136] and held:

> The appointment of an administrator by a secured creditor is often a hostile act [opposed] by the company's management. In my judgment it would be a serious impediment to the realisation of assets for the payment of secure creditors if they could be precluded from appointing an administrator merely because the debt was disputed, even if the dispute was in good faith…A debenture and the powers of a debenture holder derive from a contract between the lender and the borrower. The borrower consents to the grant to a lender of powers of enforcement, including the appointment of administrators…[137]

A similar approach was taken in *Barclays Bank plc v Choicezone Ltd*.[138] Newey J referred to the mortgage case *National Westminster Bank plc v Skelton*[139] as authority for the proposition that the existence of a cross-claim on the part of a mortgagee, even where it exceeds the amount of the mortgage debt, will not by itself defeat a right to possession enjoyed by the holder of a legal charge. That principle meant that cross-claims on the part of a company could not render a floating charge unenforceable.[140] These cases serve to demonstrate the importance of the governance rights enjoyed by a QFCH in administration. **7.063**

Directors of a company who wish to resist an appointment on the grounds of cross-claim or invalidity of the charge are not, however, shut out altogether. While para 64 of Sch B1 precludes an officer or director, once a company has entered administration, from exercising any management power without the consent of the administrator, this does not prevent such a person challenging a purported administration appointment.[141] Should it later turn out that the dispute was well-founded and the floating charge was not in fact enforceable, then the appointment will have been invalid.[142] Where an invalid appointment has been made, the person purporting to have made the appointment is required to indemnify the person who purported to act as administrator.[143] That may have serious consequences for the appointor, who may find themselves personally liable to indemnify the IP whose purported appointment they caused, which may include the costs and expenses of the administration.[144] **7.064**

It is no impediment to an appointment by a QFCH under para 14 that the entirety of the company's assets is already subject to a prior floating charge that has crystallised; Sch B1 specifically anticipates this.[145] Where a QFCH wishes to appoint, they must first give two days' written notice to the holder of any prior QFCH,[146] or obtain the prior holder's consent to the **7.065**

---

135   *BCPMS (Europe) Ltd v GMAC Commercial Finance plc* [2006] EWHC 3744, [48], [66]–[68].
136   Ibid., [67].
137   *BCPMS (Europe) Ltd v GMAC Commercial Finance plc* [2006] EWHC 3744, [66], [68].
138   [2011] EWHC 1303, [2012] BCC 767.
139   [1993] 1 WLR 72.
140   *Barclays Bank plc v Choicezone Ltd* [2011] EWHC 1303, [2012] BCC 767, [10]–[11].
141   *Closegate Hotel Development (Durham) Ltd v Mclean* [2013] EWHC 3237 (Ch), [2014] Bus LR 405. *Re Secure Mortgage Corp Ltd v Harold* [2020] EWHC 1364, [24].
142   *BCPMS (Europe) Ltd v GMAC Commercial Finance plc* [2006] EWHC 3744, [62].
143   Insolvency Act 1986, Sch B1, para 21.
144   Ibid., Sch B1, para 21.
145   *SAW (SW) 2010 Ltd v Wilson* [2018] Ch 213, [30], [32].
146   Insolvency Act 1986, Sch B1, para 15(1)(a). 'Prior' means either created first or treated as having priority by agreement between the respective QFCHs: Insolvency Act 1986, Sch B1, para 15(2).

appointment.[147] This illustrates that where there are multiple QFCHs, ordinary rules of priority apply between them. A subsequently created QFC will yield to an earlier QFC in the hierarchy of governance rights in administration.

7.066   There is no need for the QFCH to give advance notice to the company or its directors before appointing an administrator out of court under para 14. This may be contrasted with the position in both an application for a court appointment under para 10 or an out-of-court appointment by the company or its directors under para 22, where five business days' notice of intention to make such an appointment must be given to any QFCH. That notice provision enables any QFCH, if it wishes, to overtake the proposed appointment by making its own under para 14.[148] The QFCH's ability to make an out-of-court appointment without giving notice, and the requirement that it should in turn receive notice of other proposed appointments, are further strong pointers towards the QFCH's position at the top of the hierarchy of governance rights in administration.

7.067   A QFCH is also not precluded from making an appointment under para 14 of Sch B1 where there is an outstanding winding-up petition or administration application.[149] Moreover, a QFCH (only) may make an application to court for an administration order (but not appoint out of court) where a company is in compulsory (but not voluntary) winding up under para 37. This is a further key difference between the rights enjoyed by a QFCH to appoint under para 14 and those of the company or its directors under para 22. Moreover, such an out-of-court appointment by a QFCH would suspend an undisposed of winding-up petition under para 40(1)(b), as well as preventing the appointment being made on the administration application.

7.068   An appointment under para 14 of Sch B1 commences when the requirements of para 18 are completed.[150] These comprise the filing of a notice of appointment and specified accompanying documents.[151] First, the person making the appointment must make a statutory declaration to the effect that they hold a QFC,[152] that each QFC relied on in making the appointment is or was enforceable on the day of the appointment,[153] and that the appointment was in accordance with Sch B1.[154] The making of a false statement in this declaration carries criminal penalties.[155] Secondly, the administrator must make a statement consenting to act and stating that in his or her opinion the purpose of administration is reasonably likely to be achieved,[156] although in so doing the administrator is entitled to rely on information supplied by the directors, unless he or she has reason to doubt its accuracy.[157]

---

147   Ibid., Sch B1, para 15(1)(b).
148   Ibid., Sch B1, para 12(1)(c) (for an application for a court appointment) and Sch B1, para 26(1)(b) (for an out-of-court appointment under Sch B1, para 22).
149   Ibid., Sch B1, para 17 cf Sch B1, para 25.
150   Ibid., Sch B1, para 19.
151   Ibid., Sch B1, para 18.
152   Ibid., Sch B1, para 18(2)(a).
153   Ibid., Sch B1, para 18(2)(b).
154   Ibid., Sch B1, para 18(2)(c).
155   Ibid., Sch B1, para 18(7).
156   Ibid., Sch B1, para 18(3).
157   Ibid., Sch B1, para 18(4).

(e) Appointment out-of-court by the company or its directors

An administrator may be appointed out of court under para 22 of Sch B1 by a company[158] or **7.069** its directors.[159] There are a number of ways in which such an appointment is restricted in ways that an appointment under para 14 by a QFCH is not. These demonstrate the subordinate position of the directors both to the creditors' interest generally and the QFCH specifically in the hierarchy of governance rights in administration.

Paragraph 25 of Sch B1 provides that no appointment may be made under para 22 where either **7.070** a winding-up petition has been presented[160] or an application for an administration order under para 10 has been made[161] and not yet disposed of, or an administrative receiver is in office.[162] This is considerably more restrictive than the equivalent provision in relation to out-of-court appointments by a QFCH, which precludes appointment by a QFCH only where a provisional liquidator has been appointed or an administrative receiver is in office.[163]

A key difference between QFCH appointments under para 14 and company or director **7.071** appointments under para 22 lies in the need to file a notice of intention to appoint under para 26 of Sch B1. This requires a person who proposes to make an appointment under para 22 to give five business days' notice of intention to make the appointment to any person who is or may be entitled to appoint an administrator under para 14,[164] which is a reference to any QFCH that may exist. Notice must be given not only of the intention to appoint, but also of the identity of the proposed administrator.[165] As noted above, there is no requirement to give equivalent notice where a QFCH proposes to make an appointment under para 14. This provision further underlines the dominant position of the QFCH under Sch B1, in that it gives the QFCH an opportunity to take control of the situation, if it wishes, by appointing its own choice of administrator under para 14. It should be noted that para 33 spells out that a para 14 appointment may be made right up until a para 22 appointment takes effect, giving a QFCH the maximum possible amount of time and latitude within which to decide what to do.

A practice developed of the repeat filing of notices of intention to appoint under para 26 in **7.072** order to obtain the protection of the statutory moratorium on the institution of legal proceedings against the company under paras 43 and 44 of Sch B1. In *JCAM Commercial Real Estate Property XV Ltd v Davis*,[166] the Court of Appeal regarded this as technically speaking an abuse

---

158   Ibid., Sch B1, para 22(1).
159   Ibid., Sch B1, para 22(2).
160   Ibid., Sch B1, para 25(a); although Sch B1, para 25A qualifies this by providing that Sch B1, para 25(a) does not prevent an appointment if the petition was presented after the person proposing to make the appointment filed the notice of intention to appoint under Sch B1, para 27.
161   Ibid., Sch B1, para 25(b).
162   Ibid., Sch B1, para 25(c).
163   Ibid., Sch B1, para 17.
164   Ibid., Sch B1, para 26(1)(b). Similar notice must also be given to any person who is or may be entitled to appoint an administrative receiver of the company. Administrative receivership is now so rare in practice that this aspect is not considered further.
165   Ibid., Sch B1, para 26(3)(a).
166   [2017] EWCA Civ 267, [2018] 1 WLR 24.

of process and held that in order to give notice under para 26, the person giving the notice had to propose or intend unconditionally to appoint an administrator.[167]

7.073   It is necessary to comply with para 26 and serve a QFCH even where there is reason to think the QFC is invalid or unenforceable.[168] Compliance with para 26 is mandatory and failure to comply may have severe consequences.[169]

7.074   An appointment under para 22 of Sch B1 may only be made where the company is or is likely to become unable to pay its debts. Paragraph 27 provides that a person who gives notice of intention to appoint under para 26 must file a copy of the notice at court as soon as reasonably practicable and must accompany it with a statutory declaration dealing with the company's insolvency.[170] There is no equivalent insolvency requirement where a QFCH causes the appointment of an administrator, either out of court or by an administration application.[171] Where there is no one entitled to notice of the intention to appoint under para 26, and accordingly nothing to file at court under para 27, confirmation of the company's insolvency must instead be included in a statutory declaration accompanying the notice of appointment filed under para 29.[172]

7.075   Paragraph 28 imposes a narrow time window during which the appointment may be made: the five business days' notice in the para 26 notice of intention to appoint must have expired[173] or each of the persons to whom notice was given must have consented;[174] but the appointment may not be made after the period of ten business days beginning with the date on which the notice of intention was filed at court under para 27(1).[175]

7.076   The appointment of the administrator under para 22 of Sch B1 commences[176] upon the filing at court of a notice of appointment under para 29. This is in almost identical form to the equivalent provision at para 18 where a QFCH makes an appointment under para 14. The person making the appointment must make a statutory declaration under para 29(2) and, where no notice of intention to appoint was required to be given under para 26, the appointor's statutory declaration must include that the company is or is likely to become unable to pay its debts.[177] An appointor making such a statement must have a conscientious belief in its truth with the risk that he might commit perjury if he does not, although it is not a necessary pre-requisite to the validity of the appointment that what the appointor declares to be the case is in fact correct.[178]

---

167   Ibid., [64].
168   *Jackson v Thakrar* [2007] EWHC 2173 (TCC), [93]–[101].
169   *Minmar (929) Ltd v Khalastchi* [2011] EWHC 1159, [2011] BCC 485, *Adjei v Law for All* [2011] EWHC 2672, [2011] BCC 963; but cf *Re Tokenhouse VB Ltd* [2020] EWHC 3171 (Ch), [2021] BCC 107; *Re Zoom UK Distribution Ltd (in administration)* [2021] EWHC 800 (Ch).
170   Insolvency Act 1986, Sch B1, para 27(2).
171   Ibid., Sch B1, para 35.
172   Ibid., Sch B1, para 30.
173   Ibid., Sch B1, para 28(1)(a).
174   Ibid., Sch B1, para 28(1)(b).
175   Ibid., Sch B1, para 28(2).
176   Ibid., Sch B1, para 31.
177   Ibid., Sch B1, para 30.
178   *Re Hat & Mitre plc (in admin)* [2020] EWHC 2649 (Ch), [101].

The notice by the appointor must also be accompanied by a statement by the administrator **7.077** confirming that he consents to act and that the purpose of the administration is reasonably likely to be achieved.[179] As is the case under the equivalent provision under para 18(4) for QFCH appointments, para 29(4) provides that the administrator may rely on information supplied by the directors of the company, unless the administrator has reason to doubt its accuracy. Authority indicates that the courts will regard such an appointment as the directors' responsibility and their appointed administrators will not be held responsible where they have taken what the directors have told them at face value.[180] Where an invalid appointment is made under para 22, the appointor may be required under para 34 to indemnify the IP purportedly appointed, reflecting in substantially identical terms the equivalent in para 21 for invalid appointments purportedly made under para 14.

(f)   Validity of appointment

The out-of-court process has generated a considerable number of cases where some error of **7.078** procedure has given rise to uncertainty over whether or not there has been a valid appointment of administrators. A number of conflicting first instance decisions, many argued on one side only or reached without citation of relevant prior authorities, exist on a number of aspects of the regime. This body of case law could easily give rise to a lengthy chapter on its own without shedding much light on the current position. The authorities up to mid-2020 were carefully analysed in detail in the judgment of His Honour Judge Davies-White QC (sitting as a High Court judge) in *Re A.R.G. (Mansfield) Ltd.*[181]

Following the decision of Norris J in *Re Euromaster Ltd*,[182] a reasonably settled approach has **7.079** developed over the last few years at least at the level of general principle. The question is whether the defect is one of procedure or one of a more fundamental nature going to the power to appoint. Cases in the former category may be capable of cure, whereas purported appointments in the latter category will be invalid. Where a purported appointment is invalid, the court may be prepared to rectify the situation by making an order for the retrospective appointment of administrators. There remains, however, a lack of clarity as to where exactly the line should be drawn. At the time of writing, recent decisions appear to indicate a greater judicial willingness to find defects capable of cure on facts that may once have fallen on the other invalidity side of the line.[183] It is submitted that, short of a decision of the Court of Appeal on the point, this approach is to be welcomed. It is further submitted that, from a practical point of view, the approach taken by Mann J in *Petit v Bradford Bulls (Northern) Ltd (in administration)*[184] of assuming an invalid appointment and making a retrospective order to regularise the position whatever the technically correct position, has much to commend it.

---

179   Insolvency Act 1986, Sch B1, para 29(3).
180   *Re BW Estates Ltd* [2015] EWHC 517 (Ch), [2016] 1 BCLC 708, [27]–[29].
181   [2020] EWHC 1133 (Ch), [2020] BCC 641.
182   [2012] EWHC 2356 (Ch), [2012] BCC 754.
183   *Re Tokenhouse VB Ltd* [2020] EWHC 3171 (Ch), [2021] BCC 107; *Re NMUL Realisations Ltd* [2021] EWHC 94 (Ch); *Re Zoom UK Distribution Ltd (in admin)* [2021] EWHC 800 (Ch).
184   [2016] EWHC 3557 (Ch), [2017] BCC 50.

C. REMUNERATON OF OFFICEHOLDERS

1.   General matters

7.080   An administrator or liquidator is entitled to receive remuneration for services rendered in relation to the winding up of the company.[185] Statement of Insolvency Practice ('SIP') 9, titled 'Payments to insolvency office-holders and their associates from an estate', makes it clear that the nature of an insolvency officeholder's position renders transparency and fairness of primary importance in all their dealings[186] and hence the Insolvency Rules 2016[187] covering remuneration seek to meet this objective. SIP 9 provides that: 'Information provided by an officeholder should be presented in a manner which is transparent, consistent throughout the life of the appointment and useful to creditors and other interested parties, whilst being proportionate to the circumstances of the appointment.'[188] The primary principle that governs remuneration might be seen as ensuring that payments to an administrator or liquidator, and expenses incurred by an administrator or liquidator are fair and reasonable reflections of the work necessarily and properly undertaken.[189]

7.081   The following explanation and analysis of officeholder remuneration will concentrate on the rules applicable to liquidators rather than referring continually to both administrators and liquidators for ease of exposition. The vast majority of rules and principles which apply to liquidators apply equally to administrators. Where there is any significant difference, the position in administration will be noted.

7.082   The liquidator is not entitled to be paid until the liquidation is completed,[190] but, especially if the winding up is protracted, a liquidator may seek to take interim fees from realised assets.

7.083   The remuneration of a voluntary liquidator who acts before the appointment of a liquidator under a court order in relation to the same company may be allowed by the courts to rank ahead of the expenses of the winding up for a compulsory liquidation and referred to in r 7.108(4)(a) of the Insolvency Rules 2016.[191] Where the voluntary liquidator was appointed after the

---

185   Insolvency Rules 2016, r 18.16(1).

186   Para 1. SIP 9 was effective from 1 April 2021.

187   All references to rules are to the Insolvency Rules 2016 unless it is otherwise stated.

188   Ibid., para 13.

189   Ibid., para 6.

190   *Re New Zealand Times Co* [1941] NZLR 677, holding that the period of limitation of action begins to run only after winding up is complete and not as each transaction is carried out. And an administrator is entitled to draw agreed remuneration during the course of the administration (*Spring Valley Properties Ltd v Harris* [2001] BCC 796; [2001] BPIR 709 decided under the pre-Enterprise Act 2002 administration regime but the reasoning of which would apply in interpreting para 99 of Sch B1).

191   Rule 7.109. Where an administration is a pre-pack administration, information about the administrator's pre-appointment costs must be provided in the administrator's statement of proposals under r 3.35(10)(a) and approved under r 3.52. The initial decision to approve or not the pre-appointments costs is one for any creditors' committee. If there is no such committee (or if it does not make a decision or makes a decision upon quantum that the administrator considers inadequate) the determination falls to the company's creditors. The creditors will decide by a decision procedure or in a case where the administrator has made a statement under para 52(1)(b) of Sch B1, by the consent of each secured creditor or (if a distribution to preferential creditors is intended) by the consent of each secured creditor and a decision procedure of the preferential creditors.

presentation of the winding-up petition, the remuneration of the voluntary liquidator cannot be withheld unless the payment of remuneration is successfully challenged.[192]

The remuneration of the liquidator is payable from the company's assets as part of the expenses of winding up. Where there are insufficient assets to pay the expenses of winding up, the expenses are paid out in accordance with the order of priority enumerated in r 6.42(4) for creditors' voluntary liquidations and r 7.108(4) for compulsory liquidations. Under para 99 of Sch B1, an administrator's remuneration and expenses are charged upon and payable out of property the administrator had custody or control of immediately prior to the termination of the administrator's appointment. The remuneration and expenses have priority over any floating charge but are subject to any liabilities incurred under contracts entered into by the administrator or under adopted contracts of employment. The remuneration of the liquidator is mentioned in rr 6.42(4)(h) and 7.108(4)(o). It is not a high priority. An administrator's remuneration also appears at a comparably low point on the list of priority of expenses in administration under r 3.51(2)(i).   **7.084**

The liquidator is only entitled, under these Rules, to any amount not exceeding that which is payable under Sch 11 to the Rules but these limitations imposed by Sch 11 do not apply to administrators. If a liquidator has a claim that exceeds that governed by Sch 11, it will rank almost last.[193] The rationale for this approach is that the liquidator is best placed to know what the eventual position is likely to be, and can, where necessary, ensure that he or she will be paid by refusing to proceed with the winding up unless the creditors or shareholders are prepared to guarantee remuneration.[194]   **7.085**

The court has in compulsory liquidation a discretion as to the order in which the expenses of winding up are to be paid,[195] but it will not be exercised so as to enable liquidators to take or retain their remuneration in priority to other expenses which would normally rank ahead of remuneration except in exceptional circumstances.[196] In *Re Salters Hall School Ltd (in liq)*,[197] it was stated that where there is an insufficiency of assets to cover the expenses of winding up the liquidator is not entitled to retain remuneration out of the assets. Remuneration has been given greater priority where the liquidator's services were rendered by way of salvage, or where the liquidator was paid at a time when there was no reason to suppose that the assets would be insufficient to pay all the costs of winding up.[198]   **7.086**

---

192 *Re A.V. Sorge & Co Ltd* (1986) 2 BCC 99, 306.
193 See, rr 6.42(4)(j) and 7.108(4)(q).
194 *Re Beni-Felkai Mining Co* [1934] Ch 406, 422.
195 Section 156. The same right would exist in voluntary liquidations due to s 112; also see rr 6.43 (creditors' voluntary liquidations) and 7.109 (compulsory liquidations). The equivalent to s 156 in administration is found in r 3.51(3).
196 *Re Linda Marie Ltd (in liq)* (1988) 4 BCC 463, 472.
197 *Re Salters Hall School Ltd (in liq)* [1998] 1 BCLC 401, [1998] BCC 503.
198 *Re Beni-Felkai Mining Co* [1934] Ch 406, 422. A liquidator would appear to have a lien on company property for unpaid remuneration and expenses: see *Nationwide News Pty Ltd v Samalot Enterprises Pty Ltd* (1986) 5 NSWLR 227, (1986) 4 ACLC 386. Compare *Re Stockbridge* [1923] NZLR 221.

7.087   In the past,[199] where a liquidator has not been appointed it has been held that he or she is not entitled to remuneration.[200] Claims for remuneration on a *quantum meruit* basis have been rejected, although liquidators have been allowed to claim on an inferred contract to the extent that their work was shown to have been beneficial to the company or to have been utilised by subsequent liquidators with full knowledge of the circumstances. This is unjust and the correctness of the position has since been doubted.[201] In Australia the decisions in *Nationwide News Pty Ltd v Samalot Enterprises Pty Ltd*[202] and *Re Deisara Pty Ltd (in liquidation),*[203] suggest that a liquidator would be entitled to payment of reasonable remuneration. The cases involved provisional liquidators, but there is nothing to suggest that the reasoning and final decision in each case cannot be applied to liquidators. In *Monks v Poynice,*[204] a case dealing with the defective appointment of a receiver, Young J of the New South Wales Supreme Court said that the receiver should be entitled, on an equitable basis, to reasonable remuneration as his service had conferred benefit. The same reasoning could be applied equally to liquidators.

7.088   Certainly, if a liquidator were appointed in breach of the Rules,[205] by improper solicitation of the post, then no remuneration is to be paid out of the assets of the company.

7.089   A liquidator is not able to claim remuneration for work not properly incurred.[206] Naturally no remuneration will be payable in relation to work which either falls outside the ambit of a liquidator's duties, such as assisting directors in the preparation of a statement of affairs,[207] or that was not necessary.[208] A liquidator will not be able to claim for work done or costs incurred as a result of ignorance of the law or gross want of care;[209] liquidators will be denied remuneration or their costs where they have not exercised a reasonable amount of skill,[210] or where they have not conducted a winding up cost-effectively.[211]

7.090   Liquidators should bear in mind that, according to SIP 9, any requests for additional information about payments to a liquidator should be treated by the liquidator in a fair and reasonable way.[212] Any provision of additional information should be proportionate to the circumstances of the case.[213] This obviously contributes to fulfilling the need for transparency and also lays the groundwork for accountability.

---

199   *Re Allison, Johnson & Foster Ltd* [1904] 2 KB 327.
200   Ibid., 330.
201   See *Craven-Ellis v Canons* [1936] 2 KB 403, particularly per Greer LJ, 415; *Re Wood & Martin (Bricklaying Contractors) Ltd* [1971] 1 WLR 293, 297; compare also *Re Introductions Ltd (No 2)* [1969] 1 WLR 1359.
202   *Nationwide News Pty Ltd v Samalot Enterprises Pty Ltd* (1986) 5 NSWLR 227, (1986) 4 ACLC 386.
203   *Re Deisara Pty Ltd (in liq)* (1992) 7 ACSR 737.
204   *Monks v Poynice* (1987) 8 NSWLR 662.
205   Insolvency Rules 2016, r 5.16, 6.35 or 7.75
206   *Reiter Bros Exploratory Drilling Pty Ltd* (1994) 12 ACLC 430, 434.
207   Ibid., 433.
208   Ibid., 436; *Burns Philp Investment Pty Ltd v Dickens (No 2)* (1993) 10 ACSR 626, 629.
209   *Re Silver Valley Mines* (1882) 21 Ch D 389, 391 per Brett LJ.
210   Ibid., 392 per Cotton LJ.
211   *Conlan v Adams* [2008] WASCA 61.
212   SIP 9 applies equally to administrators as it does to liquidators.
213   SIP 9, para 38.

2.   How is it fixed?

The fixing of remuneration of liquidators in all kinds of liquidations (and administrations) is   **7.091**
covered in Part 18 of the Rules. In compulsory winding up and creditors' voluntary winding
up the amount of the liquidator's remuneration is, in the first instance, to be arrived at by the
liquidation committee, if there is one.[214] If there is no committee, or it makes no determination,
remuneration is fixed by a decision of the creditors by a decision procedure.[215] The liquidator,
the partners and employees of the liquidator and officers and employees of the company of
which the liquidator is a director, officer or employee are not entitled to vote on the decision
procedure.[216] A similar regime applies in administration under r 18.18. The only significant
difference is in cases where the unsecured creditors will not receive any dividend apart from
under the s 176A prescribed part. In such cases the unsecured creditors do not get to decide
upon the administrator's remuneration. Instead, the administrator will make a statement under
para 52(1)(b) of Sch B1 and where there is no effective creditors' committee decision, the
decision will be made by each secured creditor or if a distribution is intended to be made to
preferential creditors, by each secured creditor and a decision of the preferential creditors in
a decision procedure.

If the liquidator in a compulsory liquidation has requested the creditors to fix the basis of remu-   **7.092**
neration and they have failed to do so or if the remuneration is not fixed as above within 18
months after the date of the liquidator's appointment, the remuneration is to be in accordance
with r 18.22(2). This paragraph provides that the liquidator is entitled to such sum as is arrived
at by applying the realisation scale set out in Sch 11 to the Rules to the moneys received by the
liquidator from the realisation of the assets of the company (including any VAT on the realisation but after deducting any sums paid to secured creditors in respect of their securities and
any sums spent out of money received in carrying on the business of the company), and adding
to the sum arrived at such sum as is arrived at by applying the distribution scale set out in Sch
11 to the value of assets distributed to creditors of the company (including payments made in
respect of preferential debts) and to contributories.

If the creditors fail to fix the basis for the liquidator's remuneration in a creditors' voluntary   **7.093**
liquidation, the liquidator may apply to the court for it to be fixed.[217] An application may not
be made more than 18 months after the date of the liquidator's appointment.[218] According to
Practice Direction: Insolvency Proceedings 2020,[219] the objective in any remuneration application
is to ensure that the amount and/or basis of any remuneration fixed by the court is fair, reasonable and commensurate with the nature and extent of the work properly undertaken or to be
undertaken by the officeholder in any given case and is fixed and approved by a process which is
consistent and predictable. The principles that are to be employed in achieving this are listed in
the *Practice Direction*.[220] On an application, the liquidator is to provide the information and evi-

---

214   Insolvency Rules 2016, r 18.20(1)–(2).
215   Ibid., r 18.20(3If a company was in administration prior to entering liquidation then r 18.20(4) and (5) apply.
216   Ibid., r 15.16(1)–(2). This restriction also applies in administration.
217   Ibid., r 18.23(1). This provision also applies in administration.
218   Ibid., r 18.23(3).
219   [2020] BCC 698, [2020] BPIR 1211, para 21.1.
220   Ibid., para 21.2.

dence referred to in paras 21.4.1–21.4.12 of the *Practice Direction*. This will form the basis for the liquidator's explanation and justification of his or her remuneration claim and ensures the liquidator is accountable. The evidence that must be placed before the court in an application should also include the documents listed in para 21.7 of the *Practice Direction*. Except where the court orders otherwise, the costs of an application, including those of any assessor, are to be paid out of the assets under the control of the liquidator.[221]

7.094 Where the liquidator is a private insolvency practitioner, rather than the OR, remuneration may be calculated using one of three methods. These are set out in r 18.16(2).[222] First, it may be set as a percentage of the value of the assets with which the liquidator has dealt or the assets which are realised, distributed or both realised and distributed by the liquidator.[223] Secondly, on the basis of the time properly spent by the practitioner and his or her staff in dealing with matters relating to the winding up.[224] Thirdly, as a set amount.[225] The basis of remuneration may be one or a combination of those methods just set out and different methods or percentages may be fixed in respect of different things done by the liquidator.[226]

7.095 Rule 18.16(4) provides that it if the liquidator in a compulsory or creditors' voluntary liquidation proposes to take all or any part of the remuneration on a time basis, the liquidator must, prior to the determination of which of the bases set out in r 18.16(2) are to be fixed, deliver to the creditors a fees estimate and details of the expenses the liquidator considers will be, or are likely to be, incurred.[227] Fees estimates should be based on all of the information available to the liquidator at the time that the estimate is provided and may not be presented on the basis of alternative scenarios and/or provide a range of estimated charges.[228] SIP 9 states that any estimate should: 'clearly describe what activities are anticipated to be conducted in respect of the estimated fee. When subsequently reporting to creditors, the actual hours and average rate (or rates) of the costs charged for each part should be provided for comparison purposes'.[229] Again, transparency is in mind in providing for this.

7.096 A liquidator in a compulsory or creditors' voluntary liquidation must deliver to the creditors certain information before the determination of which of the bases for remuneration is or are to be fixed, unless the information has already been delivered.[230] The information that the liquidator is required to give is the work that he or she proposes to undertake and of the expenses that are considered will be, or are likely to be, incurred.[231] All of these requirements are clearly designed to enhance transparency. The matters to be determined in fixing the basis of remuneration are: which of the bases is or are to be fixed and (where appropriate) in what

---

221 Ibid., para 21.9.
222 These rules also apply in administration.
223 Insolvency Rules 2016, r 18.16(2)(a).
224 Ibid., r 18.16(2)(b).
225 Ibid., r 18.16(2)(c).
226 Ibid., r 18.16(3).
227 Ibid., r 18.16(4). Under r 18.30, the fees estimate may only be exceeded with the permission of those who first fixed the basis for remuneration.
228 Statement of Insolvency Practice 9, 'Payments to insolvency office-holders and their associates from an estate,' para 25.
229 Ibid., para 24.
230 Insolvency Rules 2016, r 18.16(6). This requirement also applies to administrators.
231 Ibid., r 18.16(7).

combination; the percentage or percentages (if any) to be fixed; and the nature of the specified amount if that basis is chosen.[232] Rule 18.16(9) states that 'in arriving at that determination' (of the remuneration), regard must be had to several factors, included in the rule. It is not clear whether 'that determination' refers to the basis of fixing remuneration or is it to the percentage to be applied? It is submitted that the better view is the former, that is, it refers to the factors which are to be applied when considering the remuneration, namely whether it is based on time or percentage.[233] The matters that are set out in r 18.16(9) are: the complexity of the winding up; any responsibility of an exceptional kind which fell on the liquidator; the effectiveness with which the liquidator appears to be carrying out or appears to have carried out his or her duties; and the value and nature of the assets with which the liquidator has had to deal.

Where the liquidator sells assets on behalf of a secured creditor then, unless the liquidator has agreed otherwise with the secured creditor, the liquidator is entitled to take from the proceeds of sale a sum by way of remuneration and the remuneration is to be determined according to Sch 11 to the Rules.[234]   **7.097**

If there is more than one liquidator then how any remuneration is to be shared is a matter for the liquidators.[235] If agreement cannot be reached, then the issue may be referred to the court, to the liquidation committee or to the creditors (who will make a decision by decision procedure).[236] In hearing a dispute a court may well decide to apportion the fees equally.[237] The sharing of remuneration is usually not a problem as in most cases where there are joint liquidators they are members of the same firm of accountants and the destination of the remuneration will depend on the firm's own internal processes and agreements.   **7.098**

Where the remuneration has been determined by a liquidation committee the liquidator may request the creditors to increase the rate or amount or change the basis in accordance with rr 18.25–18.27 or apply to the court for an order increasing the rate or amount or changing the basis for calculating remuneration in accordance with r 18.28.[238] If the liquidation committee has fixed remuneration and the liquidator makes a request to the creditors for approval of the remuneration the creditors are to decide this pursuant to a decision procedure.[239] On the motion put to creditors, the following are unable to vote: the liquidator, the partners and employees of the liquidator and officers and employees of the company of which the liquidator is a director, officer or employee.[240]   **7.099**

A liquidator may make an application to the court for it to increase the rate or amount or change the basis of the remuneration where the basis of his or her remuneration has been fixed by: the liquidation committee (and the liquidator has requested that the rate or amount be increased or the basis changed by decision of the creditors (via a decision procedure), but the   **7.100**

---

232   Ibid., r 18.16(8).
233   See Nicholls, 'Holding on to Your Money—Remuneration and How to Keep it' (1999) 15(1) *I L & P* 12, 13.
234   Insolvency Rules 2016, r 18.38(1)–(2). This rule has no application to administrators.
235   Ibid., r 18.17. This also applies to joint administrators.
236   Ibid., r 18.17.
237   *Re Langham Hotel Co* (1869) 20 LT 163.
238   Insolvency Rules 2016, r 18.24. These rules also apply, with minor modifications, to administration.
239   Ibid., r 18.25(2).
240   Ibid., r 15.16(1)–(2). This also applies in administration.

creditors have not changed it); a decision of the creditors (by a decision procedure), under r 18.20(4) and (5) or r 18.22; or by the company in general meeting, where there is a members' voluntary winding up.[241] We are not concerned with the members' voluntary situation.

7.101 In a creditors' voluntary liquidation if the liquidator applies to the court, he or she must give at least 14 days' notice of the court application to members of the liquidation committee.[242] If there is no committee the liquidator shall give at least 14 days' notice of the application to such one or more of the company's creditors as the court may direct.[243] The committee, the creditors or the contributories (as the case may be) may nominate one or more of their number to appear or be represented and heard at the hearing of the liquidator's application.[244] The court may, if it appears to be a proper case, order the costs of the liquidator's application, including the costs of any member of the liquidation committee appearing or being represented on it, or of any creditor or contributory so appearing or being represented on it, to be paid as an expense of the estate.[245]

7.102 The liquidator is required to explain in the application to the court why the remuneration allowed was insufficient, and then the liquidator must demonstrate that the case was one in which an increase was deserved.[246] This indicates an element of accountability. More recently, and in relation to the situation where a fixed fee was set for the liquidation work, Registrar Jones (as he then was) said in *Re Central A1 Ltd*[247] that provided that there is no argument that a fixed fee was or is an inappropriate basis upon which to determine the remuneration, the assessment should be made on the basis of:

> the reasonableness for necessary work of a pre-agreed fee which will not change with the time the work in fact takes or the amount the service is used. For that purpose, account should be taken of the fact that a fixed fee will or is likely to involve an element of risk on both sides. In due course the work may prove to be harder or easier than envisaged, the hours spent longer or shorter and the fee may prove miserly or generous in the light of subsequent performance. Nevertheless, the fee remains fixed and any assessment must be on that basis taking account objectively of the information available at the time.[248]

7.103 The registrar proceeded to lay out general guidance for such assessments. He said that they will normally involve a need to identify precisely what work was agreed to be undertaken by the liquidators; to determine whether that work was necessary (taking into account the circumstances); and to determine in relation to the necessary work what was a reasonable fixed fee bearing in mind the actual hours in which the liquidators were engaged in work, what it was reasonable to agree at the time knowing (to the extent this was known or reasonably capable of being ascertained) the company's situation in relation to the work to be carried out and all other factors which should be taken into account when agreeing a fixed fee.[249] This would entail the

---

241 Ibid., r 18.28(3). Administrators may make an equivalent application under r 18.28(2).
242 Ibid., r 18.28.(6)(a)(i).
243 Ibid., r 18.28(6)(a)(ii).
244 Ibid., r 18.28(7).
245 Ibid., r 18.28(8).
246 *Re Tony Rowse NMC Ltd* [1996] 2 BCLC 225, [1996] BCC 196.
247 *Re Central A1 Ltd* [2017] EWHC 220 (Ch), [2017] BCC 69.
248 Ibid., [49].
249 Ibid., [50].

liquidator being accountable for what had been done. The registrar also said that a court is to apply the following principles: 'justification; benefit of doubt; professional integrity; value of service; fairness and reasonableness; proportionality of information and remuneration; and the relevance of professional guidance'.[250] These principles are now contained in para 21.2 of the *Practice Direction*.

If a secured creditor or an unsecured creditor (with either the agreement of 10 per cent in value   **7.104** of the creditors (including themselves) or the permission of the court) believes that remuneration fixed for a liquidator is excessive, the basis fixed for the liquidator's remuneration under rr 18.16 and 18.20 is inappropriate, or the expenses incurred by the liquidator are in all the circumstances excessive,[251] they may apply to the court for an order reducing the liquidator's remuneration.[252] The application by a creditor must be made no later than eight weeks after receipt of the progress report under r 18.3, or final report or account under r 18.14 whichever first reports the charging of the remuneration or the incurring of the expenses in question.[253] With an application that is outside the eight weeks, the court has power to extend time in appropriate cases.[254] Where the court gives permission to a creditor to apply, it must fix a venue for the application to be heard,[255] and the applicant must, at least 14 days before the hearing, deliver to the liquidator a notice stating the venue and it is to be accompanied by a copy of the application and of any evidence on which the applicant intends to rely.[256] If the court thinks that there is no sufficient cause shown for a reduction, it may dismiss the application without giving notice to any party other than the applicant.[257] If the court finds that the application has merit, it must make one or more of the following orders:

- an order reducing the amount of remuneration which the liquidator was entitled to charge;
- an order reducing any fixed rate or amount;
- an order changing the basis of remuneration;
- an order that some or all of the remuneration or expenses in question be treated as not being expenses of the liquidation;
- an order that the liquidator or the liquidator's personal representative pay to the company the amount of the excess of remuneration or expenses or such part of the excess as the court may specify;[258] and/or
- any other order that it sees fit.[259]

Unless the court otherwise orders, the costs of the application shall be paid by the applicant and   **7.105** not be an expense of the liquidation.[260]

---

250   Ibid., [51].
251   The grounds for an application are detailed in r 18.34.
252   Insolvency Rules 2016, r 18.34(2)(a)(b). Equivalent applications may be made in administration based upon the same grounds (r 18.18 fixes the basis for remuneration in administration).
253   Ibid., r 18.34(3). Rule 18.6 provides for the timing of progress reports in administration.
254   *Re Birdi (in bankruptcy)* [2019] EWHC 291 (Ch), [2019] BPIR 498, [69]–[70].
255   Insolvency Rules 2016, r 18.36(2).
256   Ibid., r 18.36(3).
257   Ibid., r 18.37(1).
258   Ibid., r 18.37(4)(a)–(e).
259   Ibid., r 18.37(4)(f).
260   Ibid., r 18.37(6).

7.106   In compulsory and creditors' voluntary liquidations, members of the company do not participate in fixing the remuneration of the liquidator. Also, they have no right to have recourse to
the court if they are dissatisfied with the remuneration fixed by the liquidation committee or
the creditors. Effectively the liquidator is accountable to the creditors for his or her remuneration claim.[261]

7.107   With applications to court in relation to remuneration that are based on time, the applications
should include the time spent on work done and indicate the description of work performed so
that the court has sufficient detail on which to form an opinion as to whether the remuneration
claimed was reasonable.[262] Again this all adds to greater transparency and accountability.

7.108   If a compulsory liquidation order is made at a time when a voluntary liquidation is being conducted, then the court is able to review the remuneration of the voluntary liquidator.[263] Where
a compulsory winding up succeeds a voluntary liquidation and the remuneration and expenses
of a voluntary liquidator (who was appointed earlier) are allowed by the court, they are to rank
with the expenses set out in r 7.108(4)(a).

7.109   The courts have a very wide jurisdiction to fill in gaps left by the Rules where the circumstances
that have arisen were not envisaged, and so if there is a situation where there is a regime for
setting of remuneration outside court involvement but no one is able or willing to determine
remuneration, the courts can do so.[264]

3.   What scale is used?

7.110   Rule 8.16(2) and (3) state, as mentioned earlier, that remuneration can be fixed on a percentage, time or set amount basis or it can be determined on a combination of these methods.
While the Rules provide these alternative methods for determining remuneration, historically
the practice has been to fix remuneration on a percentage basis calculated upon the value of
assets realised or distributed. It has been said that the courts favour this method because this
means that remuneration is calculated according to results achieved.[265] Thus, a small estate pays
a small sum and a large estate a large sum,[266] depending on the amount of divisible assets,[267]
whereas the time spent by the liquidator and his or her staff has been regarded as affording
a most unreliable test[268] which is to be used only where the assets realised are so small that
assessment on a percentage basis would not operate to give a fair remuneration for the work
involved.[269] The cases that support these points are all rather old and the fact is that liquidators

---

261   The same restriction applies in administration.
262   *Re Kal Assay Southern Cross Pty Ltd* (1993) 9 ACSR 245.
263   *Re A.V. Sorge & Co Ltd* (1986) 2 BCC 99, 306, 99, 309. This case was dealing with r 195 of the Companies (Winding-up)
Rules 1949 but r 7.109 of the present Rules is to similar effect.
264   *Re Future Route Ltd* [2017] EWHC 3677 (Ch), [24].
265   *Re Carton Ltd* (1923) 39 TLR 194, 197.
266   *Re Mysore Reefs Gold Mining Co* (1886) 34 Ch D 14, 17.
267   Which means assets realised and free to be divided, not assets actually divided among creditors and shareholders: ibid.,
21.
268   *Re Carton Ltd* (1923) 39 TLR 194, 197.
269   Ibid. See *Practice Direction: Insolvency Proceedings* [2020] BCC 698, [2020] BPIR 1211, para 21.1.

have tended to prefer a time basis; it appears that in England the time basis is now, and has been for some time, more common and is more accepted by courts.[270]

D. OFFICEHOLDERS' POWERS AND DUTIES

1.   Introduction

This section will essentially examine the statutory powers and duties of officeholders, before considering their general duties, although it also deals with what is known as the rule in *Ex parte James* which does not fit comfortably under most subjects but is an important principle applying to how officeholders discharge their functions.   **7.111**

Where differences exist between the duties and powers of different officeholders, these are often explicable by the distinct nature and objectives of the various processes. For instance, liquidation is a terminal process usually expected to lead to dissolution; administration is designed as a rescue process with the principal objective of restoring the company as a going concern. The offices have been described as 'poles apart'.[271]   **7.112**

2.   The rule in *Ex parte James*

We start with what has become known as the rule in *Ex parte James*. This is conveniently dealt with here as it concerns the standards by which (some) officeholders are required to act, although it is not strictly speaking a duty. The rule developed from the case, *Ex parte James; In re Condon*,[272] which concerned a trustee in bankruptcy, and has subsequently been applied to other types of insolvency officeholder where they are also officers of the court. It requires such officeholders to act as the court would act and to observe a higher standard of conduct than other parties.[273]   **7.113**

Compulsory liquidators are officers of the court, both as a matter of common law[274] and legislation.[275] Schedule B1 expressly provides that administrators, however they are appointed, are also officers of the court.[276] Voluntary liquidators, however, are not officers of the court.[277] A court-appointed receiver is an officer of the court, but a receiver appointed out of court is not. Authority confirms that CVA[278] supervisors (as well as IVA supervisors[279]) are officers of the court.   **7.114**

---

270 See Nicholls, 'Holding on to Your Money—Remuneration and How to Keep It' (1999) 15(1) *I L & P* 12, 13.

271 *Lindholm, Re Opes Prime Stockbroking Ltd* [2008] FCA 1425, [61].

272 (1874) LR 9 Ch App 609, CA.

273 *Lehman Bros Australia v MacNamara* [2020] EWCA Civ 321, [2021] Ch 1, [101].

274 *Re Contract Corporation, Gooch's Case* (1871–72) LR 7 Ch App 207, 211.

275 Insolvency Rules 2016, r 7.76(1).

276 Insolvency Act 1986, Sch B1, para 5. See also *Re Atlantic Computer Systems plc* [1992] Ch 505, 529.

277 *Re Hill's Waterfall Estate and Gold Mining Company* (1896) 1 Ch 947, 953–4; *Re Knitwear (Wholesale) Ltd* [1988] Ch 275, 289E.

278 *Appleyard Ltd v Ritecrown Ltd* [2007] EWHC 3515 (Ch), [2009] BPIR 235, [38], [48].

279 *King v Anthony* [1999] BPIR 73, 78.

7.115   The cases indicate that the rule in *Ex parte James* is based on the principle that the court may exercise control over the conduct of its own officers and may give directions to that end.[280] It will not permit officers of the court to act in a way that, although lawful and in accordance with enforceable rights, does not accord with the standards that 'right-thinking people' would think should govern the conduct of the court itself or its officers.[281] The rule does not give effect to rights but operates in favour of a party that the court considers would otherwise suffer injustice. It is capable of derogating from the rights of other parties interested in the assets available for distribution.[282]

7.116   In practical terms, the rule in *Ex parte James* has, for instance, required officeholders to repay money that it would be unjust for the estate to retain,[283] or to keep a promise that was not legally enforceable,[284] or not to enforce a binding contractual agreement,[285] or to admit a proof for a higher sum than was due under a settlement deed that contained a clerical error in the estate's favour.[286]

7.117   Recent high authority has confirmed that the rule in *Ex parte James* may be engaged on something much less than actual wrongdoing by an officeholder. In a comprehensive review of the rule in *Lehman Bros Australia v MacNamara*,[287] David Richards LJ pointed out that it must extend to more than simply assisting those with an enforceable right to recover money, or preventing officers of the court from acting dishonestly, for if that were all it did, there would be no need for any rule as other remedies would be available.[288] It is now settled that the test for the rule to engage is 'unfairness',[289] which is an objective standard calling for judgment or evaluation in its application to particular facts.[290] In *Lehman Bros Australia v MacNamara*, the Court of Appeal specifically rejected a higher test of 'unconscionability', which connoted oppression and wrongful exploitation of one party by another,[291] and is not required for the rule in *Ex parte James* to apply.

7.118   Determining exactly where an officeholder should draw the 'unfairness' line may not always be easy to resolve in practice. When dealing with an insufficiency of assets, questions of 'unfairness' may well be in the eye of the beholder and deciding where a loss should fall by reference to any measure other than the formal legal position is an unenviable task for any officeholder. There are, it is submitted, real issues of transparency over a rule based on unfairness to individual parties (as distinct from unfairness to interest classes as a whole) that may not otherwise

---

280   *Re Mirror Group (Holdings) Ltd* [1992] BCC 972, 976G–H.
281   *Lehman Bros Australia v MacNamara* [2020] EWCA Civ 321, [2021] Ch 1, [35].
282   *Re Knitwear (Wholesale) Ltd* [1988] Ch 275, 289B–C.
283   This was the factual situation in *Ex parte James* itself: (1874) LR 9 Ch App 609, 610, 614.
284   *Re Wyvern Developments Ltd* [1974] 1 WLR 1097, 1106F.
285   *Re Young* [2017] BPIR 1116, [46].
286   *Lehman Bros Australia v MacNamara* [2020] EWCA Civ 321, [2021] Ch 1, [104].
287   [2020] EWCA Civ 321, [2021] Ch 1.
288   Ibid., [40].
289   *Re Nortel GmbH (in administration)* [2013] UKSC 52, [2014] AC 209, [122]; *Lehman Bros Australia v MacNamara* [2020] EWCA Civ 321, [2021] Ch 1, [64].
290   *Lehman Bros Australia v MacNamara* [2020] EWCA Civ 321, [2021] Ch 1, [66].
291   Ibid., [65].

have an enforceable economic interest in the estate. This is particularly so where the ambit of the concept is at large until there has been a court determination.

Where a dispute is, as a matter of substance, one arising between an insolvent company's **7.119** creditors and a party seeking to invoke the rule in *Ex parte James*, it is not obvious why the estate should be worse off, or stakeholder outcomes detrimentally altered, by reason of the commencement of a formal insolvency process and the interpolation of an officeholder held to a higher standard than those who would otherwise be in control of the company. It is sub-mitted that in almost any case where an officeholder considers that the rule in *Ex parte James* may require them to decide not to enforce a legal right capable of bestowing a benefit on an insolvent company's stakeholders, the prudent course will be to seek directions from the court to approve such a course of action.[292] Without such protection, a decision by an officeholder not to enforce such a right to the detriment of an insolvent company's stakeholders would usually disclose a case at least of negligence, so it is likely to be essential.

A further serious objection to the rule in *Ex parte James* as it has evolved in the case law is the **7.120** extent to which a compulsory liquidator or administrator may be expected to behave differently on identical facts compared with a voluntary liquidator by reason of the former, but not the latter, being an officer of the court. In *Re Agrimarche Ltd (in creditors' voluntary liquidation)*,[293] Lewison J drew attention to the oddity of the same IP being subject to a radically different standard of conduct when acting as an administrator (where the rule would apply) from that which would be expected on the company moving from administration into CVL (where the rule would not apply).[294] In *Re South West Car Sales Ltd (in liquidation)*,[295] having noted that the voluntary liquidators before the court were not officers of the court, His Honour Judge Weeks QC (sitting as a High Court judge) nonetheless decided that 'it would be right' to give the same directions as would have been given to compulsory liquidators.[296] On the facts, Judge Weeks decided not to require the liquidators to return the money in issue, but nonetheless considered that the court had 'undoubted jurisdiction' under the rule in *Ex parte James* to do so.[297] Although the decision is difficult to reconcile with the Court of Appeal's conclusion in *Re T H Knitwear (Wholesale) Ltd*[298] that the rule in *Ex parte James* does not apply to voluntary liquidators (which does not appear to have been cited in *Re South West Car Sales Ltd*), it is respectfully submitted that the outcome is clearly the desirable one. It would be wrong for the principled governance of an insolvent company or the outcomes for its stakeholders to be affected by whether the company happens to be in voluntary or compulsory liquidation.

292   For a consideration of directions' applications, see [7.243]–[7.264]
293   [2010] EWHC 1655 (Ch), [2010] BCC 775.
294   Ibid., [25].
295   [1998] BCC 163.
296   Ibid., 170H.
297   Ibid., 171.
298   [1988] Ch 275, 289E.

3. To whom are an officeholder's duties owed?

7.121 In the case of liquidators and administrators, the essential starting point is that these office-holders act as agents[299] when a company is in liquidation or administration and their duties are owed to that company. Save in exceptional cases, neither a liquidator nor an administrator owes a direct duty to individual creditors in these collective insolvency processes.[300] In this respect, the position of an officeholder is analogous to that of a company director.[301] Directors, like liquidators and administrators, owe duties to the company in relation to which they are appointed and there is no direct duty to the members or the creditors.[302] In each case, however, the specific content of the duty is affected by the company's (in)solvency position.[303] As a general rule, for practical purposes, the interests of a company are to be equated with the interests of those with the ultimate economic interest in whatever value remains in the company. In a solvent company where all the creditors will be paid, it is the members that have the relevant interest.[304] Where the company is insolvent or likely to become so, the relevant interest lies with the creditors.[305] To discharge duties owed to an insolvent company, an insolvency officeholder must, like the director of an insolvent company before it enters into a formal insolvency process, act in the interests of the company's creditors.[306] Nonetheless, the duty itself is owed to the company and, save in exceptional circumstances, the officeholder does not owed direct duties to, and is not a trustee for, individual creditors or shareholders.

7.122 This principle is of longstanding in the liquidation context. In *Knowles v Scott*,[307] a new company was incorporated to receive a transfer of the assets of an existing company and the old company entered solvent voluntary winding up. Shareholders in the old company were entitled to receive cash and shares from the new company in exchange for the assets transferred to it. A shareholder in the old company, who had suffered a delay in receiving his shares in the new company, brought an action against the liquidator of the old company on the footing that the liquidator was a trustee for the shareholder in relation to the shares and dividends in question.[308] The claim was dismissed. Despite observing that 'in a sense and for certain pur-

---

299 For the status of liquidators as agents, see *Knowles v Scott* [1891] 1 Ch 717, 723 and *Mahomed v Morris (No 2)* [2001] BCC 233, para 29; for administrators see para 69 of Sch B1 to the 1986 Act and *Davey v Money* [2018] EWHC 766 (Ch), [2018] Bus LR 1903, [385].

300 This requires a special relationship ([141]) or special circumstances ([146]): *Oldham v Kyrris* [2004] BCC 111, [141]–[146].

301 *Oldham v Kyrris* [2004] BCC 111, [143]; *Charalambous v B&C Associates* [2009] EWHC 2601 (Ch), [2013] BCC 491, [14]. It is emphasised that directors and officeholders do not, of course, owe the same duties for all purposes: *Re Lehman Bros Europe Ltd (No 9)* [2017] EWHC 2031 (Ch), [65].

302 The court applies the same approach to determining the existence of direct duties on the part of insolvency officeholders towards individual creditors as it applies in the context of company directors towards shareholders: *Oldham v Kyrris* [2004] BCC 111, [143], [146]. For examples of that approach in the company director context, see *Peskin v Anderson* [2001] BCC 874 and *Sharp v Blank* [2015] EWHC 3220, [2017] BCC 187.

303 In the case of administration, Sch B1, para 3 provides further and additional content to the duty to the company, which is addressed below.

304 Companies Act 2006, s 172(1); *BTI 2014 LLC v Sequana SA* [2019] EWCA Civ 112, [2019] 1 BCLC 347, [2019] BPIR 562, [126]–[127].

305 *BTI 2014 LLC v Sequana SA* [2019] EWCA Civ 112, [2019] 1 BCLC 347, [2019] BPIR 562, [220].

306 See Chapter 4 for a discussion of the obligations of directors in times of insolvency.

307 [1891] 1 Ch 717.

308 As early as 1891, the plaintiff shareholder's leading counsel (Richard Haldane QC, later Lord Chancellor) felt compelled to describe his client's claim against the liquidator as 'no doubt a novel one': [1891] 1 Ch 717, 719.

poses' a liquidator was a trustee, Romer J's view was that a liquidator was not a trustee 'in the strict sense in which the Plaintiff must use the term to enable him to succeed in this action',[309] i.e., not a trustee for the individual creditors or members entitled to share in the distribution of the assets of the company.[310] Lord Diplock later held in *Ayerst (Inspector of Taxes) v C & K Construction) Ltd*[311] that where the assets of a company in liquidation are described as 'trust property', or a liquidator is referred to as a 'trustee', this means no more than that a company in liquidation ceases to have any beneficial interest in its assets.[312] Such assets, held Lord Diplock, resembled trust property in that they could not be used or disposed of by their legal owner (i.e., the company) for its own benefit and instead must be used or disposed of for the benefit of other persons.[313] Those assets were, therefore, subject to a statutory trust. But the liquidator does not owe the duties of a trustee towards those ultimately beneficially interested in the trust assets,[314] nor does the statutory trust confer any direct beneficial interest in those assets on the individual creditors.[315]

7.123 This hybrid treatment appears always to have been grounded in the pragmatic governance concern that officeholders must be allowed to manage and administer insolvent companies without having to deal with unproductive interventions from those without a sufficient interest. As Romer J had observed in *Knowles v Scott*:

> If a liquidator were held to be a trustee for each creditor or contributory of the company, his liability would indeed be onerous, and would render the position of a liquidator one which few persons would care to occupy.[316]

7.124 The principle in *Ayerst* has been applied many times and continues to represent the position.[317] Accordingly, the relevant duties of the liquidator are owed to the company, notwithstanding the fact that those duties require the liquidator to distribute the assets to those with the ultimate economic interest in them.

7.125 Turning from liquidators to administrators, while Lord Diplock held in *Ayerst* that a liquidator is not a trustee 'in the strict sense',[318] the authorities indicate that an administrator does not attract the label of 'trustee' at all.[319] Paragraph 69 of Sch B1 specifically spells out that an administrator is an agent for the company in administration, with no further provision indicating that an administrator is also to be regarded as a trustee in any sense. Snowden J held in *Davey v Money* that in making specific provision for an administrator's status in para 69, the legislature must be taken to have been well aware of the difference between agents and trustees

---

309   [1891] 1 Ch 717, 722.
310   *Leon v York-O-Matic Ltd* [1966] 1 WLR 1450, 1453C; *Ayerst (Inspector of Taxes) v C & K (Construction) Ltd* [1976] AC 167, 178E.
311   [1976] AC 167.
312   Ibid., 181A.
313   Ibid., 180E–F.
314   Ibid., 180E.
315   *Re Buckingham International plc (in liq) (No 1); Mitchell v Carter* [1997] BCC 907, 912.
316   [1891] 1 Ch 717, 722.
317   *Re Oasis Merchandising Services Ltd* [1998] Ch 170, 181A-B; *Re Longmeade Ltd (in liq)* [2016] EWHC 356, [2016] Bus LR 506 [53]; *Re MF Global UK Ltd (in special admin)* [2012] EWHC 3068 (Ch), [2013] 1 WLR 903, [32].
318   *Ayerst (Inspector of Taxes) v C & K (Construction) Ltd* [1976] AC 167, 180D–F.
319   *Re Lehman Bros Europe Ltd (No 9)* [2017] EWHC 2031 (Ch), [84].

and to have understood the consequences of specifying that an administrator was to be the former rather than the latter.[320]

7.126 Moreover, there are sound reasons of principle to support the view that there is no statutory trust for creditors in administration. The statutory trust in liquidation has been described as a 'legal construct';[321] it is a recognition of the fact that winding up is a terminal process and a company in liquidation is on a path to dissolution unless something happens to take it off that path.[322] Once a company is in liquidation, it has no further use for its assets on its own behalf and these are to be applied solely in accordance with the statutory scheme of distribution for creditors, or creditors and shareholders, as the case may be.[323]

7.127 The position is significantly different in administration[324] and gives rise to one of the key principled distinctions for governance purposes between liquidation and administration. While a company may exit administration into either liquidation[325] or dissolution,[326] neither of those outcomes forms any part of the purpose of administration nor the functions of an administrator. There are a number of other ways that an administration may end[327] and the aspiration of the administration regime is to directly opposite effect: the highest statutory objective of administration is to rescue the company as a going concern.[328] If that primary objective is to have any chance of realisation, and if it ultimately happens, the company will self-evidently need its assets for its own purposes. For these reasons, it appears certain that there is no statutory trust in administration.[329] On this view, it might appear that an administrator is, if anything, even more remote than a liquidator from any suggestion of a direct duty to individual creditors.

7.128 The substance and content of an administrator's duty is codified by Sch B1 in a way that a liquidator's duty is not. Paragraph 3 of Sch B1 has been described as the 'the substantive cornerstone of the administration regime'[330] and is the primary source of the administrator's statutory duties. It sets out the priorities that drive the governance of a company in administration. Paragraph 3(1) identifies three 'objectives' and imposes a duty on the administrator to pursue one of them. The 'purpose' of administration is defined by para 111(1) of Sch B1 to mean one of these objectives.[331] Paragraph 3(1) provides as follows:

---

320   Insolvency Act 1986, Sch B1, para 69. See *Davey v Money*, [385]. There is no equivalent statutory specification for the position of liquidators, which is derived from the case law summarised above.

321   *Bloom v Harms Offshore AHT "Taurus" GmbH & Co KG* [2010] Ch 187, [24].

322   See Chapter IX of the Insolvency Act 1986: s 201 for voluntary winding up; ss 202–205 for compulsory winding up.

323   *Ayerst (Inspector of Taxes) v C & K (Construction) Ltd* [1976] AC 167, 177D; *Re Atlantic Computer Systems plc* [1992] Ch 505, 527.

324   *Re Atlantic Computer Systems Plc* [1992] Ch 505, 527–528.

325   Via Insolvency Act 1986, Sch B1, para 83 for CVL or presentation of a winding-up petition for compulsory liquidation.

326   Insolvency Act 1986, Sch B1, para 84.

327   An administration may end automatically by effluxion of time (Sch B1, para 76); on an application to court by the administrator (Sch B1, para 79); on the filing of a notice by the administrator that the statutory purpose has been achieved (Sch B1, para 80); on an application to court by a creditor (Sch B1, para 81); on a public interest winding up (Sch B1, para 82); by moving into CVL (Sch B1, para 83); by moving into dissolution (Sch B1, para 84); or by compulsory winding up.

328   Insolvency Act 1986, Sch B1, para 3(1)(a).

329   Hildyard J declined to decide the point conclusively in *Re Lehman Bros Europe Ltd (No 9)* [2017] EWHC 2031, [84], but observed that the description 'statutory trust' was 'inapposite in the case of administration'.

330   *Davey v Money* [2018] EWHC 766 (Ch), [2018] Bus LR 1903, [323].

331   Insolvency Act 1986, Sch B1, para 111(1).

(1)   The administrator of a company must perform his functions with the objective of –
    (a) rescuing the company as a going concern, or
    (b) achieving a better result for the company's creditors as a whole than would be likely if the company were wound up (without first being in administration), or
    (c) realising property in order to make a distribution to one or more secure or preferential creditors.

7.129 Paragraph 3(3) states that an administrator must perform his or her functions with the first objective in para 3(1)(a) unless the administrator 'thinks' that it is either 'not reasonably practicable to achieve' it,[332] or that the second objective in para 3(1)(b) 'would achieve a better result for the company's creditors as a whole'.[333] Paragraph 3(4) provides that the third objective in para 3(1)(c) may only be pursued where the administrator 'thinks that it is not reasonably practicable to achieve either' the first or second objectives,[334] subject to the further proviso that the administrator 'does not unnecessarily harm the interests of the creditors of the company as a whole' in doing so.[335] In this way, para 3 requires an administrator to pursue one of the objectives in para 3(1) in a conditional descending hierarchy of priority, based on what the administrator 'thinks' is 'reasonably practicable'.

7.130 It is expressly provided by para 3 of Sch B1 that the interests of the creditors as a whole are relevant at every stage; the words 'the company's creditors as a whole' or the substantively identical 'creditors of the company as a whole' appear in each of the four subparas of para 3 of Sch B1. Those interests may only be suborned to those of the secured creditor(s) in limited circumstances: the prohibition on an administrator who is pursuing the third objective in para 3(1)(c) from doing anything that will 'unnecessarily harm' the creditors as a whole means that those interests are never entirely out of the picture, even in cases where distributions only to the secured creditor(s) are anticipated.

7.131 The hierarchy of objectives and the additional protections for unsecured creditors mean that an administrator's duties differ in a significant way from a receivership or a pre-Enterprise Act 2002 administrative receivership. Snowden J drew this distinction in *Davey v Money*[336] as follows:

> A receiver or administrative receiver owes his primary duties to his appointor and is generally free to determine when and how to realise assets to repay the secured debt without consideration for the interests of the unsecured creditors or the company itself. In contrast, in deciding how to run the administration, an administrator is required to have regard to the interests of all of the company's creditors, and he can only limit his ambition to asking to realise assets to repay the secured creditor if he thinks that it is not reasonably practicable to achieve anything else. Even then, he must not unnecessarily harm the interests of the creditors as a whole.[337]

7.132 This relentless focus on the interests of creditors, together with the hierarchy of statutory objectives in para 3(1) of Sch B1, is the key distinguishing feature of administration as a process.

---

332 Ibid., Sch B1, para 3(3)(a).
333 Ibid., Sch B1, para 3(3)(b).
334 Ibid., Sch B1, para 3(4)(a).
335 Ibid., Sch B1, para 3(4)(b).
336 [2018] EWHC 766 (Ch), [2018] Bus LR 1903.
337 Ibid., [254].

7.133   The prominence that is given to the interests of the creditors in Sch B1 occasionally gives rise to the shorthand suggestion that administrators' duties are owed to the creditors, as distinct from owed to the company.[338] In the Court of Appeal's detailed review of this question in *Oldham v Kyriss*,[339] Jonathan Parker LJ held that:

> Given the nature and scope of an administrator's powers and duties, I can for my part see no basis for concluding that an administrator owes a duty of care to creditors in circumstances where a director would not owe such a duty to shareholders. In each case the relevant duties are, absent special circumstances, owed exclusively to the company.[340]

7.134   *Oldham v Kyriss* concerned a pre-Enterprise Act 2002 administration, but it is submitted that the passage above remains an accurate statement of the position and, save in exceptional circumstances, an administrator's duties are owed to the company in administration, not its creditors. The specific application of an administrator's duties in any particular case is determined by the asset and liability position of the company in the administration. This approach maintains consistency with the position of a director of a company outside a formal insolvency process and a liquidator of a company in liquidation, both of whom owe their duties to the company in question, rather than to the members or creditors as the case may be.

7.135   The shorthand reference to an administrator owing their duties to the creditors does no harm where a company is demonstrably insolvent and the shorthand description is intended to refer to the creditors as a class. In such a case its use will amount to a distinction without a difference. But the fact that administration is not necessarily a terminal process, combined with the priority given to the rescue objective, means that it does not fully encompass an administrator's duty and should be avoided in the interests of clarity. While the interests of the creditors are given overarching priority by Sch B1, other interests are also within the scope of the administrator's duty to the company.

7.136   In many cases where a company is in administration, the members will not have any economic interest by reason of the company's insolvency. But that will not be every case: companies that face immediate and unmanageable cash-flow insolvency, but are balance-sheet solvent, may be among the most suitable for the administration procedure.[341] Cases that begin as insolvencies may produce an unexpected surplus.[342] In *Re ASA Resource Group plc (in administration); Dearing v Skelton*,[343] ICC Judge Jones made the following observation about cases in this category:

> Whilst administrations exist in the context of actual or likely insolvency, they can, as here, be concerned with companies unable to pay their debts as they fall due but balance sheet solvent. When they cease, they may leave a solvent company. Therefore, whilst there will be administrations where the only interested party will be the creditors, for others the interests of the company and, therefore indirectly the members will be relevant.[344]

---

338   *SNR Denton UK LLP v Kirwan* [2013] ICR 101, [38]; *Re One Blackfriars Ltd (in liq); Hyde v Nygate* [2021] EWHC 684 (Ch), [231].

339   [2003] EWCA Civ 1506, [2004] BCC 111

340   Ibid., [146].

341   *Re Hat & Mitre plc (in admin)* [2020] EWHC 2649 (Ch), [186]–[187].

342   *Re Lehman Bros (in admin) (No 8)* [2019] 1 WLR 2173, [2].

343   [2020] EWHC 1370 (Ch).

344   Ibid., [22].

Similarly, in *Re Zinc Hotels (Holdings) Ltd (in administration)*,[345] the unexpected emergence **7.137** of the possibility of a surplus of assets over liabilities for the members introduced previously unforeseen conflicts of interest that required management.[346] In *Re Hat & Mitre plc (in administration)*,[347] Trower J held that administrators in balance sheet solvent administrations have a duty to have regard to the interests of the members as a whole when deciding on the appropriate action. Trower J considered this to be 'plain' from the drafting of para 74 of Sch B1, which may give members a remedy where the acts of administrators cause unfair harm to them.[348]

Moreover, from a wider policy perspective, the elevation of rescue as a going concern as the **7.138** highest objective of administration is a measure that has the effect of promoting the member interest. The qualified priority given to the first objective demonstrates this. As noted above, unless the exception in para 3(3)(b) applies,[349] an administrator is under a duty to pursue the first objective in para 3(1)(a) if it is reasonably practicable to do so. Snowden J in *Davey v Money* explained that the first objective is: 'a result in which all creditors are paid in full and the company is restored to financial health for the benefit of its shareholders'.[350]

As such, achievement of the first objective will be of greatest benefit to the member class inter- **7.139** est and, perhaps, wider economic policy goals that the rescue culture seeks to promote.

That said, it is important to note that even where the members' interests are relevant, the **7.140** administrator remains subject to the overarching duty in para 3(2) of Sch B1 to perform their functions in the interests of the company's creditors as a whole: the creditors remain to the fore. In this respect, an administrator's duty where the company in administration is or becomes solvent is significantly different from a director's duty to a solvent company outside administration. A director of a solvent company is under a duty to promote the success of that company for the benefit of its members as a whole and is not required to have regard to the interests of creditors until the company is either insolvent or likely to become insolvent.[351] By contrast, an administrator of a company that turns out to be solvent continues to be required by para 3(2) to exercise their functions in the interests of the creditors as a whole and this will remain the case even when achieving the rescue objective in para 3(1)(a). Most strikingly, the duty in para 3(3)(b) may require the administrator to pursue the second statutory objective in para 3(1)(b) instead of rescue if he or she thinks it would achieve a better result for the company's creditors as a whole, even if rescue is reasonably practicable (and even if the members are pressing for it, as in practice they may well be).

Accordingly, and while an administrator in an appropriate case is under a duty to have regard **7.141** to the interests of the members as discussed above, the administrator's duty to the company is always potentially in conflict with the members' interests, even where the company is solvent,

---

345   [2018] EWHC 1936 (Ch),2018] BCC 968.
346   Ibid., [91].
347   [2020] EWHC 2649 (Ch).
348   Ibid., [204].
349   Namely that the second objective in para 3(1)(b) would achieve a *better* result for the company's creditors as a whole than the first objective.
350   [2018] EWHC 766 (Ch), [2018] Bus LR 1903, [253].
351   Companies Act 2006, s.172(1); *BTI 2014 LLC v Sequana SA* [2019] EWCA Civ 112, [2019] 2 All ER 784, [126]–[127].

unlike that of a director of a solvent company, who need look only to the members' interests in discharging their duty.

4. Officeholders' statutory duties and powers

(a) Codification and case law

7.142 An officeholder's statutory powers and duties are derived principally from the Insolvency Act 1986 and the Insolvency Rules 2016. In the modern era an officeholder's role is codified to a considerable extent, but certain common law rules outside the statutory regime continue to apply and the door is not necessarily closed on further extra-statutory judicial development. The courts may, however, be slower to permit this than was once the case. In *Re Lehman Bros International (Europe) (in administration) (No 4)*,[352] Lord Neuberger PSC articulated the position as follows:

> despite its lengthy and detailed provisions, the 1986 legislation does not constitute a complete insolvency code. Certain long-established judge-made rules, albeit developed at a time when the insolvency legislation was far less detailed, indeed by modern standards sometimes positively exiguous, none the less survive…Provided that a judge-made rule is well-established, consistent with the terms and underlying principles of current legislative provisions, and reasonably necessary to achieve justice, it continues to apply. And, as judge-made rules are ultimately part of the common law, there is no reason in principle why they cannot be developed, or indeed why new rules cannot be formulated. However, particularly in the light of the full and detailed nature of the current insolvency legislation and the need for certainty, any judge should think long and hard before extending or adapting an existing rule, and, even more, before formulating a new rule.[353]

7.143 The ability of the common law to supplement the insolvency regime by incremental development, therefore, may be limited to aspects where the legislation is silent. Subsequent cases have been consistent with this view.[354]

(b) Duty to maintain records

7.144 Both liquidators and administrators, as IPs, are governed by the Insolvency Practitioners (Amendment) Regulations 2015.[355] They provide that in respect of each case in which an IP acts, the IP shall maintain records containing information sufficient to show and explain – (a) the administration of that case by the IP and the IP's staff; and (b) any decisions made by the IP which materially affect that case.

---

352 *Re Lehman Bros International (Europe) (in admin) (No 4)* (known as '*Waterfall I*') [2017] UKSC 38, [2018] AC 465.
353 [2018] AC 465, para 13.
354 In *Re Lehman Bros Europe Ltd (No 9)* [2017] EWHC 2031, Hildyard J suggested at [54] that the Insolvency Act 1986 might be supplemented 'particularly in areas where there is an apparent gap which might be covered or plugged by recourse to other legislation which is not expressly ousted or confined'. Henry Carr J held in *Zinc Hotels (Holdings) Ltd (in admin)* [2018] EWHC 1936, [2018] BCC 968, [51]–[63], that a judge is not entitled to formulate a new rule where the Insolvency Act 1986 already provided a relevant gateway and mandatory conditions for its use had not been complied with.
355 Insolvency Practitioners (Amendment) Regulations 2015 (SI 2015/391) reg 3.

(c) Liquidators' statutory duties
(i) Control by the liquidator

In drawing a distinction between liquidation and administration, David Richards J explained **7.145**
that:

> The sole purpose of a liquidation is to realise the assets of the company and to distribute the proceeds
> to the company's creditors. The liquidator is under a statutory duty to ensure the company's assets
> are got in, realised and the proceeds distributed to the creditors: see the Insolvency Act 1986, section
> 143(1) (compulsory winding-up) and section 107 (voluntary winding-up).[356]

This is the primary duty of a liquidator and it reflects the fact that liquidation is a terminal **7.146**
process. Section 143 of the Insolvency Act 1986 is the centrepiece of this regime in compulsory
liquidation and, in support of this, s 144 imposes a duty on a liquidator to take custody or
control of all property or things in action to which the company is or appears to be entitled.
Liquidators in CVLs have similar obligations to those specified in s 143.

The concept of taking custody or control does not require the liquidator to have done any- **7.147**
thing to take actual possession or other control of the company's assets. It describes the
post-liquidation governance position, where rights have shifted from the directors to the
liquidator, rather than necessarily reflecting any physical state of affairs on the ground. In *Re
MK Airlines Ltd (in liquidation)*,[357] Sir Andrew Morritt C rejected a submission that custody or
control on the part of a liquidator referred to a sub-category of a company's property requiring
something to have been done to achieve custody or control of it. The Chancellor explained the
concept by reference to the comparative rights of the liquidator and the directors respectively,
as follows:

> ...the concept or other fiduciary taking custody or control of an asset is of long-standing and in the
> nature of a term of art...

> The contrast is not between having and not having custody or control but between the custody and
> control of the directors and that of the liquidators or administrators...In all cases the property right
> remains vested in the company but its custody and control passes from the directors to the administra-
> tors or liquidators on appointment and without the need for any further action on their part.[358]

The precise manner in which these duties are carried out is, for the most part, entrusted to the **7.148**
good judgment of the liquidator. The liquidator, like directors, is given a large degree of discretion and power in what he or she does. This, therefore, means that they need to be accountable
for what they do.

The getting in of assets may involve the need for the liquidator to institute legal proceedings **7.149**
against persons or companies that have possession of the company's assets or have funds that
are the company's under contract or other cause of action, or as provided for under statute. We
will discuss this further when considering the power of the liquidator to take legal action.

---

356   *Re MF Global UK Ltd (in special admin)* [2012] EWHC 3068 (Ch), [2013] 1 WLR 903, [32].
357   [2012] EWHC 1018 (Ch), [2012] 3 All ER 781.
358   Ibid., [14]–[15].

7.150   Realisation will involve the liquidator disposing of property of the company by private treaty, auction or some other appropriate way in order that the most benefit will redound on the company, and hence the creditors.

(ii)   Transparency in liquidation

7.151   A number of statutory duties are imposed on liquidators to ensure that those interested in the company's estate are aware of the liquidation. Notice of the commencement of both voluntary and compulsory liquidations must be publicised in the *Gazette* and filed with the registrar of companies. A voluntary liquidator must, within 14 days of appointment, publish in the *Gazette* and deliver to the registrar of companies a notice of appointment in the prescribed form.[359] Where a winding-up order has been made, the court must deliver notice of the fact in the prescribed form[360] and two sealed copies of the order[361] to the OR as soon as reasonably practicable. The OR (who as a consequence of the winding-up order is in office as liquidator) must, as soon as reasonably practicable, then deliver a sealed copy of the order to the company and to the registrar of companies, and cause notice of the order to appear in the *Gazette*.[362]

7.152   A liquidator in compulsory winding up who has been appointed by the Secretary of State must give notice of their appointment to the company's creditors, or the court may give directions for that appointment to be advertised. In either case, the liquidator must explain to the creditors the procedure for establishing a liquidation committee under s 141.[363] From the commencement of both voluntary and compulsory liquidation, every invoice, letter or order form issued by the company or the liquidator, as well as all the company's websites, must contain a statement that it is being wound up.[364]

7.153   Where the directors fail to comply with their duty in a CVL to lay a statement of affairs before the creditors within seven days of the resolution of winding up[365] or to seek a nomination for liquidator from them,[366] then within seven days of the later of the liquidator's appointment by the members or on becoming aware of the default, the liquidator is under a duty to apply to court for directions.[367] This very tight timescale reflects the importance attached to ensuring that an insolvent liquidation is conducted in a timely fashion in the interests of the company's creditors. An onerous control obligation is imposed on the members' choice of voluntary liquidator to ensure that everything is done properly where the winding up is taking place out of court.

7.154   Where a liquidator concludes that a company in MVL is in fact insolvent, within seven days of forming that opinion, they are under a duty to make a statement of affairs in the prescribed

---

359   Insolvency Act 1986, s 109(1).
360   Insolvency Rules 2016, r 7.21.
361   Ibid., r 7.22(1).
362   Ibid., r 7.22.
363   Insolvency Act 1986, s 137.
364   Ibid., s 188.
365   Ibid., s 99.
366   Ibid., s 100(1B).
367   Ibid., s 166(5)–(6).

form[368] and send it to the company's creditors.[369] Such a liquidator is under a duty to seek a nomination of a person to be liquidator from the company's creditors. Whether or not the MVL liquidator continues in office once the company enters CVL is a matter for the creditors; on insolvency, control of the winding up shifts from the members to the creditors to reflect the actual economic interest in the insolvent company.[370]

(iii) Duty to report

In order to enhance transparency and accountability, liquidators, like directors with their annual **7.155** directors' reports, are obliged to provide annual reports. In creditors' voluntary liquidation, the liquidator must produce an annual progress report.[371] This must be sent to both the members and the creditors.[372] The reports must cover the periods of 12 months starting on the date the liquidator is appointed and each subsequent period of 12 months.[373] The liquidator must send a copy of each progress report within two months after the end of the period covered by the report to the registrar of companies; the members; and the creditors.[374]

The liquidator in a compulsory liquidation must also send an annual progress report to the **7.156** registrar of companies; the members; and the creditors.[375] As with voluntary liquidations, the reports must cover the periods of 12 months starting on the date the liquidator is appointed and each subsequent period of 12 months.[376] The liquidator is required to send reports to those mentioned earlier within two months of the end of the period covered by the report.[377] The contents of annual progress reports are set out in r 18.3 of the Insolvency Rules 2016.

If the liquidator does not file, deliver or make any report and fails for 14 days to make good **7.157** the default after service on him or her of notice requiring the making good of the default, the court may,[378] on an application by a creditor or contributory or by the registrar of companies, order the liquidator to make good the default within a specified time,[379] and, also, order that the liquidator pay the costs of and incidental to any application.[380]

In all types of liquidation, once it appears to the liquidator that the winding up is complete, **7.158** a final account must be prepared showing how the liquidation has been conducted and the company's property has been disposed of.[381] The account must include those matters set out in r 18.14. In CVL and compulsory winding up, the creditors must be given a notice explaining

---

368 Ibid., s 95(4).
369 Ibid., s 95(1A).
370 Ibid., s 95(4C).
371 Ibid., s 92A(1) (MVL); s 104A(1) (CVL). The relevant rules are found at Insolvency Rules 2016, rr 18.3, 18.4, 18.6.
372 Ibid., s 104A(1).
373 Insolvency Rules 2016, r 18.7(2).
374 Ibid., r 18.7(6). Also, see s 192.
375 Ibid., r 18.8(5). Also, see s 192.
376 Ibid., r 18.8(2).
377 Ibid., r 18.8(5).
378 Insolvency Act 1986, s 170(1).
379 Ibid., s 170(2).
380 Ibid., s 170(3).
381 Ibid., s 94(1) (MVL); s 106(1) (CVL) and s 146 (compulsory liquidation).

the effect of the provision dealing with the liquidator's release from liability and how they may object to that release.[382] Any objections must be reported to the registrar of companies.[383]

(iv) Duty to investigate

7.159 It has been held that a liquidator conducting an investigation into a contentious issue in arising in a company's affairs should strive to gather and review all readily available evidence on that issue on an impartial basis and re-evaluate evidence as the investigation progresses.[384]

7.160 Part VI of the First Group of Parts to the Act,[385] which comprises ss 233–237 of the Insolvency Act 1986, contains extensive powers in support of the liquidator's duty to investigate, take control of, and get in the company's property. The relevant provisions apply to administrators, administrative receivers, liquidators and provisional liquidators.[386]

7.161 Section 234 provides an officeholder with the power to apply to court for an order to direct any person who has property or books and records of the company to provide such material over to the liquidator.[387] An officeholder may also use s 235 ('Duty to co-operate with office-holder') to require the co-operation of a class of persons, including those who have at any time been directors of the company, employees and, where the company is in compulsory liquidation, those who have acted as officeholders.[388] The section imposes a positive duty on the parties falling within its scope to provide co-operation. Section 235 does not require a court order for the duty to co-operate to engage.

7.162 Where co-operation is not forthcoming under s 235, the officeholder may make an application to court under s 236 ('Inquiry into company's dealings, etc.'). On an application under this section, the court may order co-operation from a director, a person known or suspected to have possession of any property of the company or indebted to it, or any person whom the court thinks capable of giving information concerning the promotion, formation, business, dealings, affairs or property of the company. That co-operation may include provision of information in writing or for a private examination at court.[389]

7.163 An application under s 236 of the Act may be made against a wider class of persons than are identified in s 235. A person within the scope of s 235 is under a duty to answer when examined under s 236.[390] An order under s 236 is more likely to be made against an officer of the company because an officer is already under a fiduciary duty to the company, which includes the duty to provide an account.[391]

---

382 Ibid., s 106(2)(c) (CVL), s 146(3)(b) (compulsory liquidation).

383 Ibid., s 106(3)(b) (CVL), s 146(4)(b) (compulsory liquidation).

384 *Guardian Care Homes (West) Ltd (in liquidation); Hellard v Graiseley Investments Ltd* [2018] EWHC 2664 (Ch), [116].

385 Insolvency Act 1986, ss 233–237.

386 Ibid., s 234(1).

387 Ibid., s 234.

388 Ibid., s 235.

389 Ibid., s 236. For a detailed discussion of this provision and its application, see, A Keay, *McPherson and Keay's The Law of Company Liquidation* (5th ed, Sweet & Maxwell, 2021), 1040–1084.

390 *Bishopsgate Investment Management Ltd (in provisional liq) v Maxwell* [1993] 2 AC 1, 59B–D.

391 *Re Cloverbay Ltd (No. 2)* [1991] Ch 90, 102G-103B. See also *Shierson v Rastogi* [2003] 1 WLR 586, [48]–[49]; *Re Westmead Consultants Ltd* [2002] 1 BCLC 384, 387A–B.

The Company Directors Disqualification Act 1986 provides that where a company is in liq- **7.164** uidation, administration or administrative receivership, the officeholder is required to prepare a conduct report about the conduct of each person who was a director of the company on the insolvency date or at any time during the three years prior to that.[392] The report must be sent to the Secretary of State to assist in deciding whether to exercise the power under s 7(1) or 7(2A) to seek a disqualification order or undertaking.[393]

The OR is under a duty to investigate the cause of the failure of the company.[394]   **7.165**

In a winding up by the court, the OR may apply to the court under s 133 for the public exami- **7.166** nation of any person who has acted as an officer of the company, or liquidator or administrator, or has been concerned with the promotion, formation or management of the company.[395] The OR is under a duty to make such an application if requested to do so by one-half in value of the creditors, or three-quarters in value of the company's contributories.[396] If a public examination is granted, the liquidator of the company has the power to take part in it.[397]

A liquidator in a winding up by the court who is not the OR is also under a duty to provide **7.167** the OR with information and assistance that the OR may reasonably require in carrying out its functions in relation to the winding up. This is a recognition of the duty on the OR to carry out an investigation into the company's failure in a compulsory winding up.

If the liquidator is not the OR, they must furnish such information, produce and permit **7.168** inspection of books, papers and other records, and give such other assistance, as the OR may reasonably require.[398]

(v) Duty to maintain records and accounts

When demanded, a liquidator must produce to the Secretary of State, and permit him or her to **7.169** inspect, any accounts, books and other records maintained either by the liquidator by a prede- cessor in office.[399] The liquidator must permit the Secretary of State to remove and take copies of any of the accounts, books and records kept by the liquidator wherever kept.[400]

Liquidators in both compulsory and creditors' voluntary liquidations must prepare and keep **7.170** separate financial records in respect of each company; and such other financial records as are required to explain the receipts and payments entered in the financial records, including an explanation of the source of any receipts and the destination of any payments.[401] The Regulation provides that in the case of a winding up by the court, the liquidator is to obtain and keep bank

---

392   Company Directors Disqualification Act 1986, s 7A(1).
393   Ibid., s 7A(3).
394   Insolvency Act 1986, s 132.
395   Ibid., s 133(1). For a detailed discussion of this provision and its application, see, A Keay, *McPherson and Keay's The Law of Company Liquidation* (5th ed, Sweet & Maxwell, 2021), 1028–1040.
396   Insolvency Act 1986, s 133(2).
397   Ibid., s 133(4)(b).
398   Ibid., s 143(2).
399   Insolvency Regulations 1994 (SI 1994/2507) reg 15(1).
400   Ibid., reg 15(2).
401   Ibid., reg 10(2).

statements relating to any local bank account in the name of the company.[402] A liquidator must submit financial records to the liquidation committee when required for inspection.[403]

7.171   All records maintained by the liquidator are to be retained by him or her for a period of six years following one of: vacation of office; release as liquidator under s 174 (for the OR), unless they are delivered to another liquidator who succeeds him or her in office.[404] Where the liquidator is succeeded in office by another liquidator, the records are to be delivered to that successor forthwith, unless, in the case of a winding up by the court, the winding up is for practical purposes complete and the successor is the OR, in which case the records are only to be delivered to the OR if the latter so requests.[405]

7.172   If required by the Secretary of State, the liquidator is to send to him or her an account in relation to the liquidator's receipts and payments covering such period as the Secretary of State may direct, and such account, if the Secretary of State requires, is to be certified by the liquidator.[406] If a liquidator vacates office prior to the finalisation of the winding up pursuant to s 146 then the liquidator shall, within 14 days of vacating office, send to the Secretary of State an account of receipts and payments covering such period not covered by a previous account sent to the Secretary of State.[407] If no account has been sent previously by the liquidator then he or she is to send an account for the whole of the period of office.[408]

(vi) Duty to settle a list of contributories

7.173   The court has the duty to settle a list of contributories[409] and this power is delegated to liquidators in compulsory liquidations.[410] Also, under s 165(4)(a) the liquidator in a voluntary liquidation is given the power of the court to settle a list of contributories. This process involves the liquidator ascertaining those members who are liable to contribute to the funds to pay expenses and then, if there are sufficient funds, be available to the creditors.

(vii) Duty to determine creditor claims

7.174   Section 153 of the Insolvency Act 1986 provides that the court is empowered to fix a time or times within which creditors are to prove their claims. The power of the court is delegated to the liquidator pursuant to s 160(1), and the liquidator has the duty of determining what claims creditors have. The liquidator will call for claims, and creditors will seek to claim what is owed to them and they will lodge proofs of debt, which are written claims of debt.

---

402   Ibid, reg 10(3).
403   Ibid, reg 10(4).
404   Ibid., reg 13(1).
405   Ibid., reg 13(2).
406   Ibid., reg 14(1).
407   Ibid., reg 14(2). This regulation has not been amended to make it accord with changes to the Act and the Rules relating to the abolition of final meetings under s 146. The text has been written to take into account the situation as it now applies under the Insolvency Act and Rules.
408   Ibid., reg 14(2).
409   Insolvency Act 1986, s 148(1).
410   Insolvency Rules 2016, r 7.79.

A proof of debt that is submitted must be dated and authenticated and made out by or under **7.175**
the directions of the creditor, and it must state all those matters set out in r 14.4(1). They are:

- the creditor's name and address;
- the total amount of the creditor's claim on the date of liquidation;
- whether or not the amount includes outstanding uncapitalised interest;
- particulars of how and when the debt was incurred by the company;
- particulars of security held, the date when it was given and the value put on it by the creditor;
- details of any reservation of title in respect of goods to which the debt relates;
- details of any document by reference to which the debt can be substantiated; and
- the name, address and authority of the person who authenticated the proof (if not the creditor).

Even though a person may appear to have a good claim according to the company's books and **7.176**
accounts, a liquidator cannot admit a person as a creditor unless the creditor actually does make
a claim.[411]

As far as the creditors are concerned, liquidators have two principal functions in the winding **7.177**
up: they must endeavour to ascertain all the debts and liabilities of the company, and they must
deal with all the proofs submitted to them by admitting or rejecting them or requiring further
evidence in support of them.

Liquidators have the right to allow proofs, which have been lodged with them, to be inspected **7.178**
at all reasonable times on any business day by creditors, except those whose proofs have been
wholly rejected, who have submitted proofs; contributories of the company; and/or any person
acting on behalf of creditors who have submitted proofs, members or contributories.[412] A liquidator is only required to permit inspection if the request is made by a creditor, member, contributory or person acting on their behalf who can show a legitimate interest in inspection.[413]

The liquidator determines whether a proof should be admitted or rejected, and in performing **7.179**
this function the liquidator acts in a quasi-judicial capacity.[414] In discharging the duty to
adjudicate on claims a liquidator may question and investigate, but where evidence has been
submitted, he or she must examine it.[415]

If the liquidator decides to reject a proof in whole or in part, he or she is to prepare a written **7.180**
statement containing the reasons for the decision and this is to be sent as soon as reasonably
practicable to the creditor.[416] The statement should advise the creditor that he or she may
appeal against the decision of the liquidator.

---

411   *Re Compania de Electricidad de la Provincia de Buenos Aires Ltd* [1980] Ch 146; [1978] 3 All ER 668.
412   Insolvency Rules 2016, r 14.6. For a case where inspection was rejected, see *Re MG Rover Group Ltd* [2012] BPIR 590.
413   *Burnden Group Holdings Ltd v Hunt* [2018] EWHC 463 (Ch), [2018] 2 BCLC 122.
414   *Tanning Research Laboratories Inc v O'Brien* (1990) 169 CLR 332, (1990) 8 ACLC 248; *Re Menastar Finance Ltd* [2003]
      BCC 404, [2003] 1 BCLC 338, [44].
415   *Re JPF Clarke (Construction) Ltd* [2020] BPIR 194, [10].
416   Insolvency Rules 2016, r 14.7(2).

7.181   If liquidators fail to carry out their duties in respect of calling for and adjudicating on proofs, creditors may apply to the court either pursuant to s 112 in a voluntary liquidation, which allows one to ask the court to determine any question arising in the liquidation, or pursuant to s 167(3) in a compulsory liquidation, which empowers the court to control liquidators.

7.182   If a decision is made by a liquidator to accept or reject a proof a creditor who is dissatisfied with the liquidator's decision may appeal to the court to reverse or vary that decision.[417] An appeal against a rejection of a proof must be instituted within 21 days of the creditor receiving the notice (under r 14.7(2)) setting out the reasons for rejection of the proof.[418] This obviously will ensure that the liquidator has to be accountable for his or her decision on the proof.

(viii)Duty to distribute the company's assets

7.183   Both compulsory and voluntary liquidators are under a duty to make distributions to proving creditors whenever they have sufficient funds in hand for the purpose.[419] The starting point is that distribution is made pari passu, but that starting point is significantly circumscribed by other factors. First, assets that are subject to fixed charge security or retention of title clauses do not fall into the assets available for distribution. In liquidation, the secured assets are outside the statutory trust for creditors[420] and even where there is no statutory trust secured assets are to be regarded as outside the insolvency.[421] The same goes for assets covered by a retention of title clause as the assets do not pass to the company. Secondly, pari passu distribution yields to the statutory scheme for distribution, which provides for certain classes of claims to be paid in priority to others. While pari passu distribution continues to apply within interest classes (i.e., as between claims standing in the same right), in modern times the statutory scheme is the dominant driver of who receives what in a corporate insolvency.

7.184   In summary terms, the statutory order of priority that an officeholder must follow when making distributions in winding up and administration is as follows:

- fixed charge creditors;[422]
- moratorium debts and priority pre-moratorium debts in relation to a moratorium under Part A1 of the Insolvency Act 1986;[423]
- expenses of the insolvency proceedings;
- preferential creditors;[424]
- floating charge creditors;
- unsecured provable debts;
- statutory interest;

---

417   Ibid., r 14.8(1). See, for an e.g., *Re BCCI (No. 6)* [1994] 1 BCLC 450.
418   Ibid., r 14.8(2).
419   Ibid., r 14.27.
420   *Re Oasis Merchandising Services Ltd* [1998] Ch 170, 181A–B.
421   *Insolvency Law and Practice: Report of the Review Committee*, Cmnd.8558, para 17, p 12.
422   Their interest is not part of the liquidation.
423   Insolvency Act 1986, s 174A(2) (liquidation), Sch B1, para 64A(2) (administration). This is where the proceedings for the winding up were commenced or the entering into of administration occurred before the end of the period of 12 weeks beginning with the day after the end of the moratorium under Part A1 of the Insolvency Act 1986.
424   These creditors effectively only take precedence over floating charges where there is an insufficiency in funds payable to unsecured creditors in order to pay the preferential debts in full.

- non-provable liabilities; and
- shareholders.[425]

A version of the foregoing summary was laid down by Lord Neuberger PSC in *Re Nortel GmbH* **7.185**
(in administration),[426] having been derived, in relation to liquidation, from ss 107, 115, 143,
175, 176ZA and 189 of the Insolvency Act and rr 4.181 and 4.218 of the Insolvency Rules
1986 (since replaced by rr 6.42, 7.108 and 14.12 of the Insolvency Rules 2016); and, in relation
to administration, from paras 65 and 99 of Sch B1 to the Act and rr 2.67 and 2.88 of the 1986
Rules (since replaced by rr 3.51 and 14.23 of the 2016 Rules).[427] One addition has been made to
Lord Neuberger's summary, which is the super-priority afforded to certain debts arising from
a moratorium under Part A1 of the Insolvency Act 1986. This was introduced by s 174A of the
Act and para 64A of Sch B1, which were inserted by s 2(1) of the Corporate Insolvency and
Governance Act 2020, in relation to liquidation and administration respectively.

An administrator does, however, have a power under para 66 of Sch B1 to make a payment   **7.186**
otherwise than in accordance with the statutory scheme, if 'he thinks it likely to assist achievement of the purpose of administration'. Authority on another provision using this subjective
language ('thinks') suggests that the administrator's judgment is likely to be subject to a generous standard of review by the court, with the administrator's judgment, as long as it is bona fide
and rational, likely to carry considerable weight.[428] Nonetheless, authority specifically on para
66 indicates that administrators ought to apply to the court for directions before making such
a payment, to avoid future challenge.[429]

(d) Liquidators' statutory powers

Section 165 (in the case of voluntary liquidation) and s 167 (in the case of compulsory liquida-   **7.187**
tion) provide that a liquidator may exercise any of the powers specified in Parts 1–3 of Sch 4 to
the Insolvency Act 1986. The powers in Part 1 include the power to pay any class of creditors
in full,[430] the power to enter into a compromise with creditors[431] or others in relation to assets
or liabilities,[432] or to bring legal proceedings under the Insolvency Act 1986.[433] The last power
covers the liquidator's right to bring proceedings personally under several provisions in the
Act. These provisions grant the liquidator a personal right to institute proceedings. Since the
coming into force of the Small Business, Enterprise and Employment Act 2015 these powers
may now be exercised by a liquidator in the exercise of their discretionary judgment without
sanction from the court or the creditors. It might be thought that this lessens the degree of

---

425   They will receive nothing in a liquidation involving an insolvent company.
426   [2013] UKSC 52, [2014] AC 209, [39].
427   Insolvency Act 1986, s 386 and Sch 6 (both dealing with preferential debts) might also usefully be added to the list of
       provisions relevant to distribution.
428   See *Davey v Money* [2018] EWHC 766, [255], in the context of Sch B1, para 3.
429   *Re TXU UK Ltd (in administration)* [2002] EWHC 2784 (Ch), [2003] 2 BCLC 341, [18]–[19].
430   Insolvency Act 1986, Sch 4, Part I, para 1.
431   Ibid., Sch 4, Part I, para 2.
432   Ibid., Sch 4, Part I, para 3.
433   Ibid., Sch 4, Part I, para 3A. These being officeholder claims under ss 213 (fraudulent trading), 214 (wrongful trading),
       238 (transaction at undervalue), 239 (preference), 242 (gratuitous alienations (Scotland)), 243 (unfair preferences
       (Scotland)) or 423 (transactions defrauding creditors). Prior to the introducing of the Small Business, Enterprise and
       Employment Act 2015, sanction was required to bring such proceedings.

a liquidator's accountability. Nevertheless, the liquidator will be responsible for the exercise of the powers and could be held liable if he or she did not act carefully or for improper reasons.

7.188 Other powers in Sch 4 include the power to bring or defend legal proceedings in the name and on behalf of the company,[434] the power to carry on the business of the company so far as may be necessary for its beneficial winding up,[435] power to sell any of the company's property by public auction or private contract,[436] claim in other insolvencies,[437] raise money on the security of the company's assets,[438] and appoint agents to do any business that the liquidator is unable to do themselves.[439] The exercise of any of the powers in Sch 4, including those that formerly required sanction, is a commercial decision for the liquidator, with which the court would not generally interfere.[440] Decision-making by officeholders and the way it which it may be subject to challenge is examined in Chapter 8.

7.189 The powers reflect the need for the liquidator to fulfil his or her duties. In particular, they assist the liquidator in his or her work to get in the company's assets, as required by s 143.

7.190 One of the most controversial powers can be the power of the liquidator to initiate legal proceedings, whether on behalf of the company or personally. Exercising this power might well incur a lot of expense which could denude the company's estate if proceedings do not succeed. Unless the creditors agree to fund actions, something which they might be reluctant to do, or there are substantial funds held by the company, the liquidator will need to seek funding from outside parties, usually from specialist litigation funders.[441]

7.191 While the exercise of the powers mentioned above is no longer subject to the need for sanction, Snowden J in *Re Longmeade (in liquidation)*[442] laid down a list of matters which liquidators might consider. Of prime importance is that liquidators should normally give weight to the reasoned views of the majority of creditors, provided that those views were uninfluenced by extraneous considerations and if all those who were interested in the insolvent estate are fully informed and are unanimously of the same view, the liquidators should ordinarily give effect to their wishes.

7.192 These powers are widely drawn and the final paragraph of Sch 4 grants the liquidator the power to do all such other things as may be necessary for winding up the company's affairs and distributing its assets.[443] Although widely drawn, however, it should nonetheless be noted that

---

434 Insolvency Act 1986, Sch 4, Part II, para 4. This is to be contrasted with para 3A which covers proceedings brough in the liquidator's own name.
435 Ibid., Sch 4, Part II, para 5.
436 Ibid., Sch 4, Part III, para 6.
437 Ibid., Sch 4, Part III, para 8.
438 Ibid., Sch 4, Part III, para 10.
439 Ibid., Sch 4, Part III, para 12.
440 *Re Longmeade (in liq)* [2016] EWHC 356 (Ch), [2016] BPIR 666, [2017] 1 BCLC 605, [56]–[66].
441 For a discussion of funding in the context of liquidation, see, A Keay, *McPherson and Keay's The Law of Company Liquidation* (5th ed, Sweet and Maxwell, 2021), 605–611, and for a discussion in a more general sense in insolvency, see P Walton *Insolvency Litigation Funding – in the Best Interests of Creditors?* (April 2020) a research report commissioned by Manolete Partners plc and supported by the ICAEW and IPA.
442 [2016] EWHC 356 (Ch), [2016] BPIR 666, [2017] 1 BCLC 605.
443 Insolvency Act 1986, Sch 4, Part III, para 13.

the focus is limited to winding up and distribution. It should be noted in particular that, as noted above, a liquidator may only continue to trade a company so far as may be necessary for its beneficial winding up,[444] and not with a view to its continuance.[445]

The historical differences between the powers of voluntary and compulsory liquidators (and the underlying processes more generally) are significantly reduced by s 112 which confers an important power on a voluntary liquidator to apply to the court to have determined any question arising in the winding up, or to exercise any power that the court might exercise in a compulsory winding up.[446]   **7.193**

(e) Administrators' statutory powers and duties

As explained above, a number of powers available to liquidators are also available to other officeholders including, of course, administrators. In addition, further specific powers and duties of an administrator are extensively codified. Some of these provisions have much in common with those applicable to liquidators.   **7.194**

A number of provisions impose a duty on a newly appointed administrator to do certain things 'as soon as is reasonably practicable following appointment'. Among these, an administrator must: **7.195**

- send a notice of appointment in the prescribed form to the company;[447]
- publish a notice of appointment in the prescribed manner, which means gazetted and publicised in such other manner as the administrator thinks fit;[448]
- obtain a list of the company's creditors;[449]
- send a notice of appointment to each creditor of whose claim and address the administrator is aware;[450] and
- send a notice in the prescribed form to require one or more 'relevant persons' within the meaning of Sch B1, para 47(3) (most usually one or more directors of the company) to provide a statement of affairs of the company.[451]

Before the end of seven days after the date of the court's order (in the case of appointments by the court) or the date on which the administrator receives notice of their appointment under para 20 or para 32 of Sch B1 (in the case of out-of-court appointments), the administrator must: send a notice of appointment to the registrar of companies;[452] and send a notice of   **7.196**

---

444 Ibid., Sch 4, Part II, para 5.
445 *Re Wreck Recovery and Salvage Company* (1880) 15 ChD 353 (CA).
446 Insolvency Act 1986, s 112.
447 Ibid., Sch B1, para 46(2)(a). Rules 3.24 to 3.26 of the Insolvency Rules 2016 set out the prescribed forms.
448 Ibid., Sch B1, para 46(2)(b). Rule 3.27 of the Insolvency Rules 2016 set out the prescribed requirements.
449 Ibid., Sch B1, para 46(3)(a).
450 Ibid., Sch B1, para 46(3)(b).
451 Ibid., Sch B1, para 47. The time for compliance by the '*relevant person*' nominated is quite short: 11 days beginning with the day on which the person receives notice of the requirement (para 48(1)), although the administrator has the power to revoke or extend the period for compliance (para 48(2)). Detailed provisions in relation to the statement of affairs are found at Insolvency Rules 2016, rr 3.28–3.34.
452 Insolvency Act 1986, Sch B1, para 46(4). The requirements for this notice are set out in Insolvency Rules 2016, r 3.27(4).

appointment to the persons specified in r 3.27(3), including any receiver, petitioning creditor, provisional liquidator and CVA supervisor.[453]

7.197   From the outset of the administration, every business document issued by or on behalf of the company or the administrator, and all the company's websites, must state the name of the administrator and that the affairs, business and property of the company are being managed by the administrator.[454] If the administrator, an officer of the company, or the company itself permits a contravention of that requirement, then they commit an offence.[455]

7.198   The administrator is under a duty on appointment to 'take custody or control of all the property to which' the administrator 'thinks the company is entitled'.[456] As noted above, the concept of 'custody or control' refers to the comparative rights of the directors on the one hand and the officeholder on the other.[457] Use of the word 'thinks' has been held to indicate that the duty is subject to the administrator's subjective assessment, which is not lightly to be second-guessed by the court, and is subject to a generous standard of review of good faith and rationality.[458] In the context of a wrongful interference claim against administrators, the court observed in *Blue Monkey Gaming Ltd v Hudson*[459] that administrators come to a company as strangers and it is the duty of a person claiming ownership to identify their own property, not for the administrators to do so.[460]

(i)   Duty to select objective and put proposals to creditors

7.199   In parallel with these immediate duties, the administrator is also required to prepare a statement of proposals for the administration under para 49 of Sch B1.[461] This too must be done as soon as reasonably practicable after the company enters administration, with a backstop requirement that the proposals must be sent to the registrar of companies, creditors and members before the end of eight weeks after that time.[462]

7.200   A key aspect of the duty to prepare a statement of proposals is the requirement that the administrator must make a statement setting out proposals for achieving the purpose of administration.[463] As explained above, the 'the purpose of administration' means 'an objective specified in paragraph 3'.[464]

7.201   The regime does not go as far as to impose a duty on the administrator to select one objective in particular in the proposals, but the point must nonetheless be addressed in the proposals in a reasoned way. In particular, para 49(2)(b) requires that where the administrator 'thinks' that

---

453   Insolvency Rules 2016, r 3.27(3). The requirements for this notice are set out in Insolvency Rules 2016, r 3.27(4).
454   Insolvency Act 1986, Sch B1, para 45(1).
455   Ibid., Sch B1, para 45(2).
456   Ibid., Sch B1, para 67.
457   *Re MK Airlines Ltd (in liq)* [2012] EWHC 1018 (Ch), [2012] 3 All ER 781, [14]–[15].
458   See *Davey v Money* [2018] EWHC 766, [2018] Bus LR 1903, [255], in the context of Sch B1, para 3.
459   [2014] All ER (D) 222 (Jun).
460   Ibid., [157].
461   Insolvency Act 1986, Sch B1, para 49 and Insolvency Rules 2016, r 3.35.
462   Ibid., Sch B1, paras 49(4)-(5).
463   Ibid., Sch B1, para 49(1).
464   Ibid., Sch B1, para 111.

the objective mentioned in para 3(1)(a) or 3(1)(b) cannot be achieved, they must explain why.[465] The governance purpose of this duty was explained in *Davey v Money*.[466] Snowden J held that it is there for the protection of unsecured creditors, even in cases where that class has no economic interest in the company. The context for this is that where the administrator thinks that neither of the objectives in para 3(1)(a) and (b) can be achieved, there is no need for the creditors' approval of the proposals[467] to be sought unless requested to do so.[468] Snowden J held that this feature underpins the need for an explanation in the proposals:

> The requirements of paragraph 49(2)(b) of Sch B1 to the 1986 Act are designed to fulfil the goal of reporting and transparency – primarily where unsecured creditors are not to be given the opportunity of having a meeting to approve the administrator's proposals because the administrator considers that there will be nothing in the administration for them.[469]

Snowden J rejected a submission, however, that a breach by administrators of the requirement to provide such an explanation thereby invalidated their subsequent conduct of the administration.[470] Nonetheless, it is submitted that the requirement should be seen as an important component of an administrator's statutory duty and is there to provide transparency to the unsecured creditors. **7.202**

In practice, an administrator's proposals are often expressed with a degree of flexibility, rather than to specify a single objective. For example, it is not uncommon for administrators to include a statement to the effect that the administration currently appears to be one where the second objective will be achieved, but that the shareholders are attempting to formulate funding proposals to rescue the company, and the administrators will pursue that higher objective if funding transpires. Alternatively, where the position is less promising, an equivalent conditional statement referring to the second objective and the third objective may be included. The selection of the objective has been described as a 'dynamic and iterative process'[471] to be kept under review during the course of the administration as circumstances change or further information emerges. **7.203**

Snowden J held in *Davey v Money* that an administrator's decision in relation to which objective in para 3(1) to pursue is a commercial one for the administrator.[472] As such, a test of good faith and rationality of the kind applied to other exercises of discretionary judgment by officeholders, as found in cases such as *Re Edennote Ltd*[473] and *Re Longmeade Limited (in liquidation)*,[474] applies to the selection of the objective.[475] The judge considered that this followed from the mixture of subjective and objective language in para 3 and held that the choice of **7.204**

---

465 Ibid., Sch B1, para 49(2)(b).
466 *Davey v Money* [2018] EWHC 766 (Ch), [2018] Bus LR 1903.
467 Insolvency Act 1986, Sch B1, para 52(1)(c).
468 Ibid., Sch B1, para 52(2).
469 *Davey v Money* [2018] EWHC 766 (Ch), [2018] Bus LR 1903, [322].
470 Ibid., [324].
471 *Re One Blackfriars Ltd (in liq); Hyde v Nygate* [2021] EWHC 684 (Ch), [205], [207].
472 [2018] EWHC 766 (Ch), [2018] Bus LR 1903, [255]. See also *Key2Law (Surrey) LLP v Gaynor De'Antiquis* [2011] EWCA Civ 1567, [2012] BCC 375, [33]; *Re One Blackfriars Ltd (in liq); Hyde v Nygate* [2021] EWHC 684 (Ch), [205].
473 [1996] BCC 718.
474 [2016] EWHC 356, [2017] 2 All ER 244.
475 The standard of review for officeholder decision-making is addressed in Chapter 9.

the word 'thinks' rather than, for example, 'reasonably believes' was a clear indication that the legislature intended that a degree of latitude should be given to an administrator in deciding upon the objective to be pursued.[476]

7.205   This deferential standard of review does not, however, extend to the 'methods adopted' to pursue the particular objective selected. In particular, Snowden J considered that the objective language in para 3(4)(b) providing that an administrator may pursue the third objective 'only if…he does not unnecessarily harm the interests of the creditors of the company as a whole' invited 'a more objective standard of review',[477] which indicates a duty of care akin to that applied in professional negligence generally. The distinction between commercial judgments and other types of conduct falling into the 'methods adopted' category is discussed in Chapter 8.

7.206   The administrator's statement of proposals may not include any action which affects the right of a secured creditor to enforce that security or affect the priority of preferential debts.[478] That restriction does not apply to action to which the secured creditor consents, or to the inclusion of proposals for three specified forms of collective restructuring: a CVA, a scheme of arrangement under Part 26 or a restructuring plan under Part 26A of the Companies Act 2006.[479]

7.207   The administrator is required by para 51 of Sch B1 to seek a decision from the company's creditors on the proposals[480] within the period of ten weeks from the company's entry into administration.[481] An administrator commits an offence if this duty is breached without reasonable excuse.[482]

7.208   Where, however, the administrator thinks that the creditors will be paid in full or the company has insufficient property to make a distribution to unsecured creditors other than under the prescribed part, or that neither of the objectives in para 3(1)(a) or (b) can be achieved, then no decision from the creditors need be sought.[483]

7.209   That starting point may be displaced if at least 10 per cent of the creditors by value request that the administrator seeks a decision.[484] As noted above, the possibility that the control function of the creditors may be dispensed with on the exercise of an administrator's judgment underpins the requirement for an explanation in the administrator's proposals under para 49(2)(b). A similar further duty is imposed on an administrator by para 56 to seek a decision from the creditors on a matter if it is requested by at least 10 per cent of the creditors by value, or if the

---

476   [2018] EWHC 766 (Ch), [2018] Bus LR 1903, [255]. See also *Key2Law (Surrey) LLP v Gaynor De'Antiquis* [2011] EWCA Civ 1567, [2012] BCC 375, [33]; *Re One Blackfriars Ltd (in liq)*; *Hyde v Nygate* [2021] EWHC 684 (Ch), [205].
477   Some years prior to the point being addressed in the case law, the mixture of subjective and objective language in Sch B1, para 3 and its possible implications was discussed in detail in John Armour and Rizwan Mokal, 'Reforming the Governance of Corporate Rescue: The Enterprise Act 2002', ESRC Centre for Business Research, University of Cambridge, Working Paper No 289, June 2004, pp 19–26.
478   Insolvency Act 1986, Sch B1, para 73(1).
479   Ibid., Sch B1, para 73(2).
480   Ibid., Sch B1, para 51(1).
481   Ibid., Sch B1, para 51(2).
482   Ibid., Sch B1, para 51(5).
483   Ibid., Sch B1, para 52(1).
484   Ibid., Sch B1, para 52(2).

court directs the administrator to do so.[485] An administrator commits an offence if the duty to seek a decision from the creditors under para 56 is breached without reasonable excuse.[486]

Where the creditors take a decision on whether or not to approve the administrator's proposals, **7.210** those proposals may either be approved without modification or with modifications to which the administrator consents.[487] The requirement that the administrator must consent to any modifications indicates that power continues to reside with the administrator to an extent, although ultimately the creditors can continue to withhold support from the unmodified proposals, resulting in deadlock. Any decision must be reported as soon as reasonably practicable to the court, the registrar of companies, the creditors and every other person to whom a copy of the statement of proposals was delivered.[488] An administrator commits an offence if the duty to report the creditors' decision is breached without reasonable excuse.[489]

Where the administrator proposes a revision to the proposals and 'the administrator thinks **7.211** that the proposed revision is substantial', para 54 of Sch B1 requires the administrator to seek a decision from the creditors. It is clear from the wording of both this paragraph and of para 68 that, where the administrator proposes a revision and does not think it is substantial, he or she need not seek the creditors' approval. Again, the word 'thinks' is important here in indicating that the administrator's judgment on this point is subject to a test of good faith and rationality. This gives an administrator a generous latitude in managing matters day-to-day, in what will frequently be changing conditions on the ground. Where a creditors' decision is sought, it must be reported to the court, the registrar of companies, the creditors and every other person to whom a copy of the original statement of proposals was delivered. An administrator commits an offence if the duty to report the decision is breached without reasonable excuse.[490]

(ii) Administrator's statutory powers

An administrator is given wide discretionary powers by para 59(1) of Sch B1: 'The administra- **7.212** tor of a company may do anything necessary or expedient for the management of the affairs, business and property of the company.'

Paragraph 59(2) adds that a provision of Sch B1 that expressly permits the administrator to do **7.213** a specified thing is without prejudice to the generality of sub-para (1), which appears to amount to something close to a blanket discretion on the part of the administrator. This reflects the unfettered ability of an administrator to trade a company in administration with the principal objective of returning it to financial health as a going concern, which contrasts sharply with the limited ability of a liquidator to trade discussed earlier in this chapter.

Paragraph 60 provides that an administrator has the extensive further powers in Sch 1 to the **7.214** Insolvency Act 1986. Schedule 1 runs to 23 paragraphs and its provisions encompass corporate

---

485   Ibid., Sch B1, para 52(1).
486   Ibid., Sch B1, para 56(2).
487   Ibid., Sch B1, para 53(1).
488   Ibid., Sch B1, para 53(2); Insolvency Rules 2016, r 3.41.
489   Ibid., Sch B1, para 53(3).
490   Ibid., Sch B1, para 54(7). Under para 55 where the administrator reports that the creditors have failed to approve the original proposals or a revision of them, the court may provide for the appointment of the administrator to cease to have effect or to make any other order it thinks appropriate.

powers of the widest kind, including the power to sell,[491] borrow money and grant security;[492] appointing solicitors, accountants[493] or other agents;[494] bring, defend[495] or compromise[496] litigation; pay money;[497] carry on the business of the company;[498] establish subsidiaries;[499] grant or accept the surrender of leases;[500] make calls;[501] claim in other insolvency processes;[502] and present or defend a petition for winding up.[503]

7.215   An administrator may remove or appoint a director of the company under para 61.[504] By para 62, an administrator may call a meeting of members of the company or seek a decision on any matter from the company's creditors. Paragraph 64 provides that the administrator has the power to consent to the exercise by the company or its officers of a general or specific management power. Unless such consent is given, no such management power may be exercised once the company is in administration, other than by the administrator themselves.[505] This power may be utilised in what have become known as 'light touch' administrations, where a company's existing directors may be authorised to continue to trade the business. For example, in *Re Debenhams Retail Ltd (in administration)*,[506] the administrators' proposals included the granting of consent to the existing management to exercise operational powers during the COVID-19 uncertainty in the interests of stabilising the business and pursuing a going concern rescue within the meaning of para 3(1)(a) of Sch B1.[507]

7.216   An administrator has the power under para 70 to dispose of or take action relating to property which is subject to a floating charge as if it were not subject to the charge.[508] The holder of the floating charge takes the same priority in respect of the property acquired (i.e., the proceeds of sale) as that holder had in respect of the property disposed of.[509]

7.217   With the permission of the court, the administrator may dispose of property subject to fixed charge security. The test is that the court must think that the disposal of the property would be likely to promote the purpose of administration in respect of the company.[510] Such an order is subject to the condition that there shall be applied towards discharging the sums secured by the

---

491   Ibid., Sch 1, para 2.
492   Ibid., Sch 1, para 3.
493   Ibid., Sch 1, para 4.
494   Ibid., Sch 1, para 11.
495   Ibid., Sch 1, para 5.
496   Ibid., Sch 1, para 18.
497   Ibid., Sch 1, para 13.
498   Ibid., Sch 1, para 14.
499   Ibid., Sch 1, para 15.
500   Ibid., Sch 1, para 17.
501   Ibid., Sch 1, para 19.
502   Ibid., Sch 1, para 20.
503   Ibid., Sch 1, para 21.
504   Ibid., Sch B1, para 61.
505   Ibid., Sch B1, para 64.
506   [2020] EWHC 921 (Ch), [2020] 3 All ER 319.
507   Ibid., [20]. See also discussion of Insolvency Act 1986, Sch B1, para 64 in *Re One Blackfriars Ltd (in liq); Hyde v Nygate* [2021] EWHC 684 (Ch), [271].
508   Insolvency Act 1986, Sch B1, para 70(1).
509   Ibid., Sch B1, para 70(2).
510   Ibid., Sch B1, para 71.

security both the net proceeds of disposal of the property and any additional money required so as to produce the amount determined by the court as the net amount that would be realised on a sale of the property at market value.[511] There is similar provision in relation to the disposal of goods in the possession of the company under a hire-purchase agreement.[512]

(iii) Duties and powers in the performance of an administrator's 'functions'

Paragraph 68 imposes a duty on the administrator to manage the company's affairs, business **7.218** and property in accordance with any proposals approved under para 53, any revision of those proposals made by the administrator and that the administrator does not consider substantial, and any revision made under para 54.[513] That duty is subject to the requirement that the administrator must comply with any directions given by the court in relation to the administrator's management of the company's affairs, business or property,[514] but the court may only give such directions in the limited circumstances set out in para 68(3). Once proposals have been approved or revised, a degree of latitude is shown by the courts towards an administrator's conduct of the estate where it can be shown to be in accordance with those proposals.

Schedule B1 imposes various duties in relation to the administrator's 'functions'. An adminis **7.219** trator 'must perform his functions':

- pursuing one of the objectives in para 3(1);[515]
- in the interests of the company's creditors as a whole;[516] and
- as quickly and efficiently as possible.[517]

An administrator is also placed under a duty by para 57(3) to provide any creditors' committee **7.220** with information about the exercise of their 'functions'[518] and may apply for directions in connection with them.[519] In exercising their 'functions', an administrator acts as the company's agent.[520] Where there is a joint appointment, para 100 requires that it must specify which 'functions' are to be exercised jointly and which by any or all of the persons appointed.[521] A joint appointee is not necessarily liable for any wrongs committed by the other appointee and will not be where they have no reason to suppose that their joint appointee is acting carelessly or improperly.[522]

Despite the repeated references to 'functions' in Sch B1, and the imposition on administrators **7.221** of duties in relation to these, the term 'functions' is not expressly defined in the Insolvency

---

511   Ibid., Sch B1, para 71(3).
512   Ibid., Sch B1, para 72.
513   Ibid., Sch B1, para 68(1).
514   Ibid., Sch B1, para 68(2).
515   Ibid., Sch B1, para 3(1).
516   Ibid., Sch B1, para 3(2).
517   Ibid., Sch B1, para 4.
518   Ibid., Sch B1, para 57(3).
519   Ibid., Sch B1, para 63.
520   Ibid., Sch B1, para 69.
521   Ibid., Sch B1, para 100(2).
522   *PJSC Uralkali v Rowley* [2020] EWHC 3442 (Ch), [539]–[548].

Act 1986.[523] The words 'Functions of Administrator' appear as a heading to para 59 to para 75 inclusive of Sch B1, although it is submitted that it is likely that the entirety of an administrator's powers and duties under the legislative scheme and the general law will fall under the wider description 'functions'. It may be the case that 'functions' was intended by the draftsman to capture within its remit both duties and powers without the need continually to refer to both.

7.222   An important question is whether the nature of the duty imposed by para 3(1) means that *every* exercise of a 'function' by an administrator must be performed directly for and only for the purpose of administration (i.e., one of the objectives in para 3(1)(a)–(c)),[524] or whether matters ancillary to that purpose may also be undertaken. The case law is currently unsettled on this point.

7.223   On the one hand, in *Re Lehman Bros Europe Ltd (in administration) (No 9)*,[525] Hildyard J rejected the suggestion that an administrator may perform any of his or her functions as long as doing so does not conflict with the statutory purpose of the administration.[526] Instead, the judge held that any action taken by the administrators would necessarily need to further the statutory purpose in order for it to be pursued.[527] However, Vos C declined to follow Hildyard J when a similar question arose in *Re Lehman Brothers International (Europe) (in administration)*.[528] The Chancellor held that there must be 'an element of pragmatism' and that there was no requirement that 'every exercise of every power must be capable of being shown specifically to advance the statutory objective in a definable way'.[529] As long as the statute authorised the function in question and the administrator was faithfully pursuing the statutory objective, no further causative analysis was required. Anything else, considered Vos C, would be unworkable.[530]

7.224   It is respectfully submitted that the approach of Vos C should be preferred in the interests of the practical governance of companies in administration. If administrators were required to consider whether or not each and every step they wished to take was directly referable to the statutory purpose, it would risk imposing unmanageable practical and administrative burdens on administrators. This might be particularly acute in trading administrations, where numerous decisions must be taken each day that have as their immediate focus the needs of an ongoing business. To require an administrator to be able to tie each decision, act or omission in a direct causal way to the overall purpose of the administration would give rise to an additional level of exposure to those discharging what is, on any view, already a very challenging and demanding role.

---

523   *Re Lehman Bros Europe Ltd (in admin) (No 9)* [2017] EWHC 2031 (Ch), [2018] 2 All ER 367, [61]; *Re Lehman Brothers International (Europe) (in admin)* [2020] EWHC 1932 (Ch), [39].
524   Insolvency Act 1986, Sch B1, para 111.
525   [2017] EWHC 2031 (Ch), [2018] 2 All ER 367.
526   Ibid., [60]–[64].
527   Ibid., [94].
528   [2020] EWHC 1932 (Ch), [2020] Bus LR 1875.
529   Ibid., [41].
530   Ibid.

(iv) Power and duty to distribute the company's assets

Paragraph 65 of Sch B1 provides that the same order of priority of distribution set out in s **7.225**
175[531] that applies in liquidation also applies in administration.[532] The administrator may make
a distribution to either secured or preferential creditors but may only distribute to unsecured
creditors[533] by way of the prescribed part under s 176A(2)(a) or if the court gives permission.[534]

As is generally the position in administration, the relevant questions the court will ask in any **7.226**
application for permission to distribute to unsecured creditors will include whether the proposed distribution will be conducive to the purpose of administration and in the interests of the
creditors as a whole.[535]

Where an administrator is not pursuing the first objective in para 3(1) of Sch B1 and the **7.227**
company has assets, the administrator will be required to make a distribution.[536] Subject to
the restrictions on the administrator's ability to make a distribution to unsecured creditors,
the principles governing the distribution of a company's assets are essentially the same in both
liquidation and administration. The starting point is that an officeholder is under a duty to
distribute the company's assets pari passu: on an equal footing.[537]

The above rules for distributions to creditors are subject to a caveat where the company has **7.228**
been subject to a statutory moratorium under Part 1A of the Insolvency Act 1986 which has
terminated and the administration has commenced within 12 weeks of that termination.[538]
In such cases, the administrator is under a duty to make a distribution to the creditors of the
company who are owed debts incurred during the moratorium and any pre-moratorium debts
which are given statutory priority.[539] The distribution to moratorium-related debts takes priority over any distribution to floating charge holders, payments due under contracts entered into
during the administration, payments due to employees whose contracts of employment have
been adopted by the administrator and the administrator's own fees and expenses.[540] In cases
where such moratorium debts exist, they must be paid in full before the administrator may
exercise the power under para 65 to pay any other creditor of the company.

(v) Duties and powers in relation to termination of administration

The appointment of an administrator automatically ceases to have effect after one year.[541] An **7.229**
administrator has the power to extend the appointment out of court by creditor consent once

---

531 And also under Insolvency Act 1986, s 176AZA which applies effectively the same priority in relation to relevant financial institutions.
532 Insolvency Act 1986, Sch B1, para 65(2).
533 Interpreted to mean a creditor who in respect of the debt owed does not hold security over the property of the company
(ibid., s 248).
534 Ibid., Sch B1, para 65(3).
535 *Re MG Rover Belux SA/NV (in administration)* [2007] BCC 446, [7].
536 *Re Nortel GmbH (in admin)* [2013] UKSC 52, [2014] AC 209, [39].
537 The pari passu principle is applied to compulsory liquidation and administration by Insolvency Rules 2016, r 14.12 and
to voluntary liquidation by Insolvency Act 1986, s 107.
538 Insolvency Act 1986, Sch B1, para 64A(1).
539 Ibid., s 174A.
540 Ibid., Sch B1, para 64A(3) cross referring to paras 70 and 99.
541 Ibid., Sch B1, para 76(1).

and for a period of up to one year.[542] Otherwise, the court may order an extension for a speci-fied period.[543] Any extension must be obtained before the administration automatically comes to an end; it cannot be extended retrospectively.[544] Repeat applications may, and in practice frequently are, made to the court for periodic extensions. Where an extension is granted, the administrator must notify the registrar of companies as soon as reasonably practicable[545] and commits an offence if they do not without reasonable excuse.[546]

7.230   An administrator is under a duty to make an application to court for their appointment to cease to have effect under three specified circumstances:

- if the administrator thinks that the purpose of administration cannot be achieved;
- if the administrator thinks that the company should not have entered administration; or
- if the company's creditors have decided that such an application should be made.[547]

7.231   An administrator who has been appointed by the court must also make an application for their appointment to cease to have effect where the administrator thinks that the purpose of the administration has been sufficiently achieved in relation to the company.[548]

7.232   Paragraph 83 of Sch B1 provides for an out-of-court mechanism to enable a company to exit administration into voluntary liquidation. That may be done where the administrator thinks that the total amount that each secured creditor of the company is likely to receive has been paid or set aside for that creditor and that a distribution (other than by way of the prescribed part) will be made to unsecured creditors.[549] In such a case, the administrator may send the registrar of companies a notice, file a copy with the court and send a copy to each creditor.[550] Once the registrar of companies has registered the notice, the appointment of the administrator ceases to have effect and the company shall be wound up as if a resolution for voluntary winding up under s 84 had been passed on the day on which the notice was registered.[551] It appears that the administrator's discretion to exit administration using para 83 is not fettered by the requirement under para 79 to apply to court in certain circumstances.[552]

7.233   Where an administrator has been appointed out of court and thinks that the purpose of the administration has been sufficiently achieved, they may file a notice in the prescribed form with the court and with the registrar of companies,[553] which causes the appointment to cease to have

---

542   Ibid., Sch B1, para 76(2)(b). Under para 78, the administrator will need to obtain the consent of each secured creditor In addition, if unsecured creditors are likely to receive a payment apart from under the prescribed provision of s 176A, a decision of the creditors must also be sought. If the unsecured creditors are not likely to be in the money but preferential creditors are, a decision of the preferential creditors will need to be sought in addition to the consent of the secured creditors.
543   Ibid., Sch B1, para 76(2)(a).
544   Ibid., Sch B1, para 77(1).
545   Ibid., Sch B1, para 77(2).
546   Ibid., Sch B1, para 77(3).
547   Ibid., Sch B1, para 79(2).
548   Ibid., Sch B1, para 79(3).
549   Ibid., Sch B1, para 83(1).
550   Ibid., Sch B1, para 83(3)–(5).
551   Ibid., Sch B1, para 83(6).
552   *Re Ballast plc (in administration)* [2003] EWHC 2356 (Ch), [2005] 1 BCLC 446, [15].
553   Insolvency Act 1986, Sch B1, para 80(2).

effect.[554] Where the administrator files such a notice he or she shall also send a copy to every creditor of the company.[555] An administrator who fails to comply with this notice requirement commits an offence.[556]

Where an administrator thinks that the company has no property that might permit a distri-   **7.234** bution to its creditors, para 84 imposes a duty on them to send a notice to that effect to the registrar of companies,[557] file a copy with the court and send a copy to the creditors.[558] An administrator commits an offence if the duty to file a copy at court or send a copy to creditors is not complied with without reasonable excuse.[559] At the end of three months from the date of registration, the company will automatically be deemed dissolved[560] unless an application is made by the administrator or 'another interested person' for the period to be extended or suspended or the deeming provision to be disapplied.[561] Where an order is made under those provisions, the administrator is under a duty to notify the registrar of companies as soon as reasonably practicable.[562]

Where any order is made under Sch B1 providing for the appointment of an administrator to   **7.235** cease to have effect, the administrator is under a duty to send a copy to the registrar of companies within 14 days and commits an offence if they fail to do so without reasonable excuse.[563] Where an administrator vacates office automatically as a consequence of ceasing to be qualified as an IP in relation to the company,[564] they are under a duty to give notice to the court (in the case of an appointment by administration order) or to the party that appointed them (in the case of an out-of-court appointment).[565] An administrator who fails without reasonable excuse to comply with that notice requirement commits an offence.[566]

(f) Seeking assistance and advice[567]

Officeholders have the power to seek assistance and advice in the course of carrying out their   **7.236** function.

Liquidators and administrators may, from time to time, need to seek guidance in the perfor-   **7.237** mance of their duties. They are entitled to assistance and advice from a range of sources and these are discussed below.

---

554   Ibid., Sch B1, para 80(3).
555   Ibid., Sch B1, para 80(4).
556   Ibid., Sch B1, para 80(6).
557   Ibid., Sch B1, para 84(1). The administrator's appointment ceases when this notice is registered under para 84(4).
558   Ibid., Sch B1, para 84(5).
559   Ibid., Sch B1, para 84(9).
560   Ibid., Sch B1, para 84(6).
561   Ibid., Sch B1, para 84(7).
562   Ibid., Sch B1, para 84(8).
563   Ibid., Sch B1, para 86.
564   Ibid., Sch B1, para 89(1).
565   Ibid., Sch B1, para 89(2).
566   Ibid., Sch B1, para 89(3).
567   Parts of this section of the chapter draw on some material contained in Andrew Keay, *McPherson and Keay on the Law of Company Liquidation*, (5th ed, Sweet & Maxwell, 2021), 586–595.

(i) Liquidation and creditors' committees

7.238 As discussed in detail in Chapter 9 a liquidation committee may be constituted in a liquidation and a creditors' committee may be established in an administration. Liquidators and administrators may go either to their liquidation committee or creditors' committee for assistance and advice. Sometimes creditors have knowledge which may be helpful to officeholders. Officeholders may wish to seek advice from liquidation committees or creditors' committees on their views concerning prospective litigation, and this might well occur in potentially costly litigation or where the liquidation or administration is complex. Also, officeholders may consult their committees concerning possible conflict issues which officeholders might have.[568]

(ii) Special manager

7.239 Special managers are discussed in more detail in Chapter 10, but we will mention them in the context of liquidation here. Courts may appoint[569] a special manager of the business or property of the company that is in liquidation on the filing of both the application of the liquidator and a report setting out the reasons for the application.[570] The report is to include the liquidator's estimate of the value of the assets over which the manager is to be appointed.[571] Liquidators may make an application when they are of the opinion that the nature of the business or property of the company, or the interests of the company's creditors or contributories or members generally, require the appointment of another person to manage the business or property.[572] The Insolvency Service has established a Special Manager Panel for appointments.[573] The Insolvency Service issued guidelines and criteria for those who wish to be placed on the panel and to provide special manager services in relation to complex compulsory liquidations.[574]

7.240 The appointment of a special manager may be renewed from time to time.[575] The remuneration of the manager is fixed by the court from time to time.[576] Just as it is with a liquidator, the acts of a special manager are valid notwithstanding a defect in appointment or qualifications.[577]

7.241 Corporate governance not only covers liquidators, but it also affects any special managers that are appointed. They are officers of the court and under its control. The duties of a special manager are set out in s 177(5). In accordance with the need for accountability and transparency managers must prepare and keep such accounts as prescribed and produce the accounts in accordance with the Rules to the Secretary of State or to such other persons as prescribed.[578]

---

568 *Re VE Interactive Ltd* [2018] EWHC 186, [2019] BPIR 437. This case related to administration but is equally applicable to liquidation.
569 Insolvency Act 1986, s 177.
570 Insolvency Rules 2016, rr 6.37(1) (creditors' voluntary) and 7.93(1) (compulsory). An example of a recent appointment is in relation to the liquidation of British Steel plc (see *Re British Steel Ltd* [2019] EWHC 1304 (Ch), [2019] BCC 974).
571 Ibid., rr 6 37(2), 7.93(2)
572 Insolvency Act 1986, s 177(2).
573 Dear IP Issue No 109, September 2020 announced this intention which has been carried out.
574 Ibid.
575 Insolvency Rules 2016, rr 5.17(4), 6.37(4), 7.93(4).
576 Ibid., rr 5.17(3)(k), 6.37(3)(k), 7.93(3)(j).
577 Ibid., rr 5.17(5), 6.37(5), 7.93(6).
578 Insolvency Act 1986, s 177(5).

The accounts must contain details of receipts and payments,[579] and special managers must produce the accounts to liquidators.

If the liquidator decides that a special manager is no longer necessary or profitable for the company then the liquidator is to apply to the court for directions and the court may order the termination of the appointment.[580] Similarly, in a creditors' voluntary liquidation the liquidator is to apply to the court where the creditors decide that an appointment should come to an end.[581] In a compulsory winding up, the liquidator is to apply to the court where the creditors decide that an appointment should end.[582]   **7.242**

Usually, applications to appoint a special manager are made only where the business or affairs of the company are too large, too remote or too specialised for the liquidator to be able to exercise personal control over their conduct or administration.[583]   **7.243**

(iii) Legal advice

Liquidations and administrations will often require consideration of issues that require examination of elements that are of a technical legal nature. These include the conveyancing of real property, contracts for the sale of assets, initiating and defending legal actions, making applications to court, and conducting examinations of officers and other persons. Most officeholders are accountants, and thus they are entitled to appoint solicitors to assist them in the performance of their duties by undertaking professional legal work and giving advice on matters of law and practice.[584] This does not relieve officeholders of their duties and particularly the fact that they must personally conduct the winding up. The solicitor properly comes on the scene only when his or her client, the officeholder, requires assistance, and to that end instructs him or her. Solicitors are not entitled to do work on their own initiative.[585]   **7.244**

An officeholder does not need to seek approval for the appointment of a solicitor, but should take some care in making a choice and must, in compulsory windings up, give notice to the liquidation committee of his or her decision to appoint a solicitor.[586] Choosing someone to whom the officeholder knows the liquidation committee or the creditors' committee will object, or whose independence may be affected by reason of being the employer of a member of the liquidation committee or creditors' committee,[587] or of being a partner of the officeholder, should be avoided.[588] It is often the practice, and is permitted,[589] that the solicitors who acted on behalf of the petitioner in getting a winding-up order or an administration order are instructed   **7.245**

---

579 Insolvency Rules 2016, rr 5.20(1), 6.40(1), 7.96(1). Details relating to the keeping of accounts are set out in rr 5.20(2), 6.40(2), 7.96(2).
580 Ibid., rr 5.21(1), 6.41(1), 7.97(2).
581 Ibid., r 6.41(2).
582 Ibid., r 7.97(3).
583 See, e.g., *Re U.S. Ltd* (1983) 1 BCC 98, 985 (where a special manager was appointed to sell certain goods of the company).
584 *Re Home and Colonial Insurance Co Ltd* [1930] 1 Ch 102, 125.
585 *Reekie v Dingwall* 1911 SC 808, 809 and 815.
586 Insolvency Act 1986, s 167(2)(b).
587 Compare *Re F. T. Hawkins & Co* [1952] Ch 881.
588 *Re Universal Private Telegraph Co* (1870) 23 LT 884.
589 *Re Baron Investments (Holdings) Ltd* unreported, 16 April 1999 Ch D.

as solicitors for the liquidator or administrator. However, it has been stated[590] that instructing the solicitors for the petitioner could be inappropriate in some cases as a conflict might well arise for the solicitors.[591] The officeholder may change solicitors at any time[592] but a solicitor's retainer is not affected by the removal of the liquidator or administrator.[593]

7.246   It has been held that an application could be made to have the solicitor for the liquidator removed by the court,[594] and, it is submitted, the same could apply in an administration.

7.247   The solicitor is entitled to charge for professional services, though not for administrative work[595] performed in the course of the winding up or administration. The solicitor must, however, rely on the assets of the company for payment, with the liquidator or administrator not being personally liable,[596] unless there is some agreement to that effect.[597] Solicitors are entitled to a lien in respect of moneys and documents of the company which come into their possession prior to liquidation or administration but not in respect of those which were acquired during the course of the winding up or administration.[598]

(iv) Judicial advice

7.248   Officeholders have the right to apply to the court for advice when encountering situations where real doubt exists as to what they should do; they can apply for directions although courts do not agree to exercise the power to give such directions as a matter of course. An example of where a liquidator should seek directions is where there is significant doubt about whether to admit a particular debt or claim to proof in the winding up.[599] An officeholder has a duty to seek directions if there is a difficulty at any stage during the course of the winding up or administration of the company's affairs.[600] As provisions apply to companies in compulsory liquidations, in creditors' voluntary liquidation and administration and to permit ease of exposition, we shall tackle them separately, although there are many similarities with obtaining judicial advice in relation to all three regimes and thus there are overlaps.

7.249   In compulsory winding up the liquidator should apply under s 168(3) or the inherent jurisdiction of the court for directions. While the creditors cannot apply for directions,[601] as they can in a creditor's voluntary liquidation, they may put in train a decision procedure to enable them to obtain a decision from creditors to direct the liquidator to seek directions.

---

590   *Avonwick Holdings Ltd v Shlosberg* [2016] EWCA 1138.
591   The case involved a bankruptcy but what the court had to say applies equally to liquidations.
592   *Re Continental Fire & Casualty Co* [1924] 3 DLR 9.
593   *R. v Lord Mayor of London* [1893] 2 QB 146.
594   See, e.g., *Re Recover Ltd (in liq)* [2003] EWHC 536 (Ch), [2003] 2 BCLC 186, [2003] BCC 976.
595   Compare *Re Pryor* (1888) 59 LT 256.
596   *Re Anglo-Moravian Ry Co* (1876) 1 Ch D 130; *Re Nation Life Insurance Co Ltd* [1978] 1 WLR 45, 47.
597   See *Stevensdrake Ltd (t/a Stevensdrake Solicitors) v Hunt* [2017] EWCA Civ 1173; [2017] BCC 611 for an unusual case where the officeholder was personally liable to pay a solicitor's fees under a conditional fee agreement.
598   *Re Capital Fire Insurance Association* (1883) 24 Ch D 408; *Re Anglo-Maltese Hydraulic Dock Co* (1885) 54 LJ Ch 730; *Re Rapid Road Transit Co* [1909] 1 Ch 96; *Re Meter Cabs Ltd* [1911] 2 Ch 557.
599   Compare *Re Banque des Marchands de Moscou; Wilenkin v Liquidator (No 2)* [1953] 1 WLR 172.
600   *Re Windsor Steam Coal Co* [1929] Ch 151, 159; *Re Timberland Ltd; Commissioner for Corporate Affairs v Harvey* (1979) 4 ACLR 259; *Pace v Antlers Pty Ltd (in liq)* (1998) 16 ACLC 261, 273.
601   Pursuant to s 112 of the Insolvency Act 1986.

The role of s 168(3) is to provide a procedure for a liquidator to obtain some guidance from the **7.250**
court so as to give protection against a claim for breach of duty.[602] The provision is essentially
concerned with action which is prospective at the time of the application. Although a direction
given on such an application does not amount to a judicial determination raising an estoppel,[603]
the advantage of using this procedure is that, having obtained and followed the directions of the
court, the liquidator is then protected against any possible allegations of breach of duty which
might subsequently be made by creditors or contributories of the company.[604] In fact the courts
have said that in cases of real doubt the correct procedure for a liquidator is to seek directions.

Liquidators are effectively obliged to inform the court of difficult issues that confront them and **7.251**
to seek directions.[605] In one Australian case directions were given where the proposed decision
of the liquidator was being criticised by a creditor as being evidence of bad faith.[606] Liquidators
have been given directions where they have been confronted with charges of acting unreasonably, and this is the case even where the matter involves commercial judgment.[607] Liquidators
may get directions in such situations where there is the prospect of attack by creditors or
others.[608]

Courts will decline to give directions where the liquidator seeks to have the court make a com- **7.252**
mercial decision for the liquidator.[609] Giles J said in *Re Spedley Securities Ltd (in liquidation)*:[610]

> It is generally not appropriate in an application for directions to make the liquidator's commercial
> decisions for him where he has full power to act … and the liquidator should not seek directions as
> a kind of insurance that he has made the right commercial decision.[611]

Furthermore, liquidators should not seek directions where there is a dispute between two third **7.253**
parties over company funds. In such a case the appropriate course of action is for the liquidator
to commence substantive proceedings against the two parties and seek a declaratory order.[612]

If a court is of the opinion that an application for directions was inappropriate, it can decline **7.254**
to order that the liquidator's costs of the application be paid from company funds as a cost
of the winding up.[613] On occasions judges have complained that liquidators have applied for
directions in respect of issues which fall within the commercial judgment of liquidators.

---

602   *State Bank of NSW v Turner Corp Ltd* (1994) 14 ACSR 480, 483. Also, see *Rodger v Gourlay* (1984) 73 FLR 264, 265, (1984) 2 ACLC 594, 595.
603   *Re Blackbird Pies (Management) Pty Ltd (No 2)* [1970] QWN 14; *TTC (SA) Pty Ltd (in liq), formerly Tom the Cheap (SA) Pty Ltd* (1983) 1 ACLC 914.
604   *Re Atkinson* [1971] VR 612, 615–616; *TRe Lemon Tree Passage & Districts RSL and Citizens Club Co-Operative Ltd* (1988) 6 ACLC 24, 27; *Coats v Southern Cross Airlines Holdings Ltd* (1998) 145 FLR 386, (1998) 16 ACLC 1393.
605   *Re Windsor Steam Coal Co* [1929] 1 Ch 151, 159.
606   *Re Addstone Pty Ltd (in liq)* (1997) 25 ACSR 357, 363. See this case for an instance where the court felt it should give directions in a situation where the commercial decision of the liquidator was involved (at 371).
607   *Sanderson v Classic Car Insurances Pty Ltd* (1985) 10 ACLR 115, (1986) 4 ACLC 114; *Re Dungowan Manly Pty Ltd (in liq)*[2018] NSWSC 1083, [17].
608   *Re Dungowan Manly Pty Ltd (in liq)*[2018] NSWSC 1083, [17].
609   *Shiraz Nominees (in liq) v Collinson* (1985) 3 ACLC 706; *Re Dungowan Manly Pty Ltd (in liq)* [2018] NSWSC 1083.
610   *Re Spedley Securities Ltd (in liq)* (1992) 10 ACLC 1742.
611   Ibid., 1744–1745. Also, see *Re Ansett Australia Ltd and Korda* (2002) 40 ACSR 433, [66].
612   *Re Everything Australian Pty Ltd* (1993) 11 ACLC 50, 51; *Re AMN Pty Ltd (in liq)* (1997) 15 ACLC 368.
613   See, e.g., *Re AMN Pty Ltd (in liq)* ibid.

7.255   In making an application the liquidator must be totally transparent and has the responsibility of making a full and fair disclosure to the court of the material facts and the court's function is not to resolve factual conflicts.[614]

7.256   While courts have generally said that they are unable to bind other parties, they have made orders declaratory of substantive rights which are intended to be binding on parties to proceedings where the proceedings have commenced as a liquidator's application for directions.[615]

7.257   If liquidators in voluntary windings up need to obtain the advice of the court they are to apply under s 112 of the Insolvency Act for the determination of any question arising in the winding up of the company. In fact, any creditor or contributory can also utilise this provision. Section 112 permits a court to exercise any of the powers which it may exercise in a compulsory winding up. The test to be applied on an application made pursuant to s 112 is, according to *Re Autobrokers Ltd*,[616] that which was stated in *Re Barings plc*[617]: whether it will be conducive to both the proper operation of the process of liquidation and provide justice for all those interested in the liquidation.

7.258   Although there was an indication in *Re County Marine Insurance Co*[618] that the jurisdiction of both ss 112(1) and 168(3) is much the same, the more recent case of *Kean v Lucas*[619] does not appear to support that view. Registrar Briggs (as he then was) observed that s 112 included wider language than s 168 and this latter provision did not include a threshold requirement, while s 112 did.[620] The requirement is that a liquidator, creditor or contributory who makes the application has to demonstrate that the 'determination of the question or the required exercise of power will be just and beneficial'. In an Australian case it has been said that the court may, under the equivalent of s 168(3), direct the liquidator, its officer, to commit a breach of trust or to do something which it is arguable that the liquidator has no power to do, while under the equivalent of s 112(2) the court is only given power to avoid expensive procedures.[621]

7.259   Judicial policy has been to apply s 112 liberally,[622] to the point where it even includes the jurisdiction to grant an injunction preventing a meeting[623] but in *IRC v Blueslate Ltd*,[624] Hart J stated that an application under the section can only be entertained where its purpose is a legitimate purpose of winding up. This comment obviously ties up with the requirement in s

---

614   *Re Magic Aust Pty Ltd (in liq)* (1992) 7 ACSR 742, 746; *Re Dungowan Manly Pty Ltd (in liq)* [2018] NSWSC 1083.
615   *Re Staff Benefits Pty Ltd (in liq)* (1979) 1 NSWLR 207, (1979) 4 ACLR 54; *Re GB Nathan & Co Pty Ltd (in liq)* (1991) 24 NSWLR 674, 680, (1991) 5 ACSR 673, 678.
616   *Re Autobrokers Ltd* [2015] EWHC 2691 (Admin).
617   *Re Barings plc* [2001] 2 BCLC 159.
618   *Re County Marine Insurance Co* (1870) LR 6 Ch App 104, 114–115.
619   *Kean v Lucas* [2017] EWHC 250 (Ch), [2017] BPIR 689, [16].
620   Ibid.
621   *Dean-Willcocks v Soluble Solution Hydroponics Pty Ltd* (1997) 15 ACLC 833, 835.
622   *Re Union Bank of Kingston-upon-Hull* (1880) 13 Ch D 808. While this is the case, the court's role is to decide matters according to the law: *Dean-Willcocks v Soluble Solution Hydroponics Pty Ltd* ibid, 836.
623   *Kean v Lucas* [2017] EWHC 250 (Ch), [2017] BPIR 689; [2017] BCC 311, [16].
624   [2003] EWHC 2022.

112 referred to above by Registrar Briggs. The liberal construction of s 112 has precipitated the bringing of a wide range of matters before the court.[625]

While the actual jurisdiction of the court is extremely wide, its exercise is a matter of discre- **7.260**
tion,[626] as clearly set out in s 112(2), since an application of this kind will not be entertained unless the court is satisfied that the determination of the question posed will meet the require-ment identified by Registrar Briggs above. That required an objective consideration of class interests.[627] The courts could always come to the conclusion that the requested exercise of power could be just and beneficial for the winding up, but in their discretion decline to exercise the power.[628]

It is not easy to ascertain the exact limits that are imposed by the requirement that the court **7.261**
must be satisfied that there will be a just and beneficial determination. There have been few reported cases in which applications have been refused. It seems, however, that s 112(1) is to be regarded as providing a summary procedure which is not intended as a means of trying issues involving complex questions of fact[629] or the assessment of claims for unliquidated damages,[630] which could more properly and more conveniently be made the subject of ordinary proceedings at common law.[631] Hart J in *IRC v Blueslate Ltd*[632] said that an application under s 112 would only be considered where its purpose was a legitimate purpose of winding up. The case provided us with a situation where directions were denied to the applicant. The applicant had asked for an order that a company's liquidators disclose documents in their possession or control. The applicant was contemplating taking action under s 212 (the misfeasance provision) against the company's liquidators and directors. The court said that the application really was an attempt to obtain pre-action disclosure. Hart J refused to make an order as he said that the application did not involve a legitimate purpose of the winding up.

As with applications made under s 168(3), courts will not, with s 112 applications, make a com- **7.262**
mercial decision for the liquidator. The courts have made it plain that directions on matters which fall within the liquidator's discretion should not be sought where the intention is to enable the liquidator to be absolved of responsibility for making a difficult commercial decision.

A court may decline to hear an application under s 112 where a company has sufficient funds **7.263**
and the matter can be best dealt with pursuant to ordinary litigation.[633] Even if the applicant for directions is using the process for a collateral purpose, such as to discover whether the company may have a cause of action against the liquidator, the court may still hear the application.[634]

---

625 For a listing of some of the kinds of applications that have been successful, see Andrew Keay, *McPherson and Keay on the Law of Company Liquidation*, (5th ed, Sweet & Maxwell, 2021), 591–592.
626 *Re Centrifugal Butter Co* [1913] 1 Ch 188.
627 *Kean v Lucas* [2017] EWHC 250 (Ch), [2017] BPIR 689, [16].
628 Ibid.
629 See *Re Centrifugal Butter Co* [1913] 1 Ch 188 as explained in *Re F. & E. Stanton Ltd* [1929] 1 Ch 180.
630 *Crawford v McCulloch*, 1909 SC 1063.
631 Ibid., 1067.
632 [2003] EWHC 2022 (Ch), [15].
633 Ibid.
634 *Re Movitex Ltd* [1992] BCC 101.

7.264 Any application that is made under the section should be made to the court which has jurisdiction to wind up the company.

7.265 Most of the comments that were made in relation to compulsory and voluntary liquidations, such as the fact that courts will not give directions where a matter involves something for the commercial judgment of the officeholder, are pertinent to administrations and will not be repeated. In this section we simply discuss the specific legislative provisions that apply to administrators.

7.266 Paragraph 63 of Sch B1 to the Insolvency Act provides, like s 168(3) does for liquidators in compulsory liquidations, that administrators may apply to the court for directions in connection with their functions. The provision enables an extremely broad range of matters in relation to which an administrator may seek directions, such as to whether pre-administration payments were susceptible as preferences[635] and whether a contract is enforceable.[636] Many of the comments made in relation to liquidations above apply equally to administrators. For instance, just as in liquidations courts will decline to give directions where the administrator is essentially seeking to have the court make a commercial decision for the administrator[637] or make other decisions for which the administrator is responsible.[638] Also, while there is no specific provision permitting creditors in administrations to do so, creditors may, like creditors in voluntary liquidations, apply for directions pursuant to the court's inherent general power to control administrators because they are officers of the court.[639]

7.267 Somewhat connected to para 63 is para 68(2). Paragraph 68(1) states that an administrator is to manage the company's affairs, business and property in accordance with any proposals approved under para 53, any revision of those proposals which is made by him or her and which the administrator does not consider substantial, and any revision of those proposals approved under para 54. Paragraph 53 provides that the company's creditors may approve proposals made by the administrator concerning the company and the administrator is required to report any decision taken by the company's creditors to the court, the registrar of companies, and such other persons as may be prescribed. Paragraph 54 simply deals with the situation where there are modifications to the proposals. If the administrator thinks that the modifications are substantial, then a further creditors' decision has to be sought in relation to the modified proposals. Any decision of the creditors must be reported to the court, the registrar of companies, and such other persons as may be prescribed. Paragraph 68(2) provides that if the court gives directions to the administrator of a company in connection with any aspect of the administrator's management of the company's affairs, business or property, the

---

635 *Re Lewis's of Leicester* [1995] BCC 514.
636 Louis Doyle QC, Andrew Keay and Joseph Curl QC (eds), *Insolvency Legislation: Annotations and Commentary* (9th ed, LexisNexis, 2020), 749.
637 *Re T & D Industries plc* [2000] 1 All ER 333, 344J. Compare the situation in *Heis v Financial Services Compensation* [2018] EWCA Civ 1327, [2018] BCC 921 where the court said that what was involved was for the administrator to do something that was outside his commercial judgment.
638 See *RAB Capital plc v Lehman Brothers International (Europe)* [2008] EWHC 2335 (Ch), [2008] BCC 915, [4].
639 *Re Mirror Group (Holdings) Ltd* [1992] BCC 972, 976 and applying *Re Atlantic Computer Systems* [1990] BCC 859, 881G.

administrator shall comply with the directions. But, according to para 68(3), the court may give directions only if—

(a)   no proposals have been approved under paragraph 53,
(b)   the directions are consistent with any proposals or revision approved under paragraph 53 or 54,
(c)   the court thinks the directions are required in order to reflect a change in circumstances since the approval of proposals or a revision under paragraph 53 or 54, or
(d)   the court thinks the directions are desirable because of a misunderstanding about proposals or a revision approved under paragraph 53 or 54.

While the emphasis in this chapter is on liquidators and administrators as the overseers of collective type insolvency regimes, we should mention that the supervisor of a CVA is entitled under s 7(4)(a) of the Insolvency Act to apply to the courts for directions in relation to any particular matter arising under the voluntary arrangement.   **7.268**

5.   Officeholders' general duties

The following discussion centres on liquidators and administrators. Besides being subject to statutory duties, which we considered earlier in the chapter, these officeholders owe duties that are not set out in statute. These general duties, as they are known, are clearly owed to the company and not to the creditors,[640] but the Privy Council has acknowledged that it is arguable that a duty is also owed to its creditors, as a body, in the distribution of the company's assets,[641] and if officeholders fail to fulfil this duty then the creditors may take action against the office-holders. It is emphasised that this duty owed to creditors is owed to them as a class and not to each of them individually.[642]   **7.269**

The general duties are, as with the general duties of directors of companies, separated into two: the duty of care and fiduciary duties.   **7.270**

Duties are a way of making those on whom they are imposed accountable for what they have done. So, in the context of officeholders, these professionals must ensure that they can explain and justify what they have done as being within their duties. They might be accountable to the liquidation or creditors' committee, the creditors or the contributories. Obviously if they do not account when asked to do so, they may be forced to give an account in a court, if proceedings are initiated for a breach of duty or for a review of their actions.   **7.271**

(a)   Duty of care

Although not expressly stated in the Insolvency Act 1986, liquidators and administrators will owe a duty of care at common law to the company. They are appointed and paid to exercise a particular professional skill, and a high standard of care and diligence is required in the   **7.272**

---

640   *Kyrris v Oldham* [2003] EWCA Civ 1506, [2004] BCC 111. In *MacDonald v Carnbroe Estates Ltd* [2019] UKSC 57, [38] there is a comment that possibly a duty is owed to the creditors, but this is as a class as far as the realising of the assets is concerned.
641   *Hague v Nam Tai Electronics Inc* [2008] UKPC 13, [2008] BCC 295. See, *Pulsford v Devenish* [1903] 2 Ch 625, 632 and 637; *James Smith & Sons (Norwood) Ltd v Goodman* [1936] Ch 216, 231–232; *A & J Fabrications Ltd v Grant Thornton* [1998] 2 BCLC 227, 231.
642   *Hague v Nam Tai Electronics Inc* [2008] UKPC 13, [2008] BCC 295, [2008] BPIR 363; *MacDonald v Carnbroe Estates Ltd* [2019[UKSC 57, [38].

performance of duties.[643] The duty is to exercise reasonable care and skill in the performance of their functions to the standard of the reasonably skilled and careful IP.[644] An officeholder is not to be judged by the standard of the most meticulous and conscientious member of the profession; instead, anyone claiming against an officeholder must establish that an error has been made that a reasonably skilled and careful IP would not have made.[645] it is not every error of judgment that will be accounted negligence on the part of an officeholder.[646] An error of judgment will amount to negligence only if it is such as to show that the officeholder does not possess the necessary qualifications for the position which is occupied,[647] and an officeholder will be guilty of negligence only where there is failure to display that degree of skill and care which, by accepting office, the officeholder has held himself or herself out as possessing.

7.273 Allowing a company in liquidation[648] or administration[649] to continue to trade to the prejudice of creditors may give rise to a breach of the duty of skill and care. For instance, in *Re Centralcrest Engineering Ltd*[650] a liquidator was held liable for misfeasance in circumstances, where, inter alia, she allowed the continuation of trading when it was clear that she should have realised the assets quickly.

7.274 The duty to take reasonable care when selling company property to obtain the best price that the circumstances permit is an aspect of the common law duty of care[651] and perhaps the most frequently litigated. As well as owing the usual direct duty to the company subject to the insolvency process, where a person can show an economic interest in the equity of redemption, then an officeholder will owe a duty to that person to take reasonable care to obtain the best price that the circumstances permit. This duty is derived from the duty owed to a mortgagor by a mortgagee when exercising its power of sale. Power of sale has often been exercised by a receiver and most of the case law in the insolvency context concerns receivers and in that context the application of the duty is well-settled by authority. The precise scope of its application to administrators has only comparatively recently been the subject of detailed scrutiny. A case is still awaited in the context of liquidation, but it is likely that a similar approach is employed.

7.275 The comprehensive review of the relevant principles in the mortgage context was delivered by Lightman J giving the judgment of the Court of Appeal in *Silven Properties Ltd v Royal Bank of Scotland plc*[652] (a case concerning a sale of properties by receivers appointed by a bank). The Court of Appeal rejected the contention that a receiver appointed by a mortgagee owed any

---

643   *Re Windsor Steam Coal Co* [1929] Ch 151, 165; *Re Home and Colonial Insurance Co Ltd* [1930] 1 Ch 102, 125; *Charlie Pace v Antlers Pty Ltd (in liq)* (1998) 16 ACLC 261, 273.
644   *Re One Blackfriars Ltd (in liq); Hyde v Nygate* [2021] EWHC 684 (Ch), [205], [207].
645   *Re Charnley Davies Ltd (No 2)* [1990] BCC 605, 618D–E.
646   *Re George Bond & Co* (1932) 32 SR (NSW) 301, 306.
647   Ibid.
648   *Re Centralcrest Engineering Ltd* [2000] BCC 727.
649   *Parkinson Engineering Services plc (in liq) v Swan* [2009] EWCA Civ 1366, [2010] PNLR 17, [2]–[3]
650   [2000] BCC 727.
651   *Re One Blackfriars Ltd (in liq); Hyde v Nygate* [2021] EWHC 684 (Ch), [211]; *Davey v Money* [2018] EWHC 766 (Ch), [2018] Bus LR 1903, [622]; *Brewer (joint liquidator of ARY Digital UK Ltd) v Iqbal* [2019] EWHC 182 (Ch), [2019] BCC 746, [52]–[56].
652   [2003] EWCA Civ 1409, [2004] 1 WLR 997, [13]–[20]

heightened duty to the mortgagor or those interested in the equity of redemption than a mortgagee. Lightman J said[653] that receivers owed the same equitable duty to the mortgagor and others interested in the equity of redemption as is owed by the mortgagee in the exercise of the power of sale. Both are obliged to take care to obtain the best price reasonably obtainable.[654] In the absence of a provision to the contrary in the mortgage or the terms of the receiver's appointment, the receiver must be active in the protection and preservation of the charged property over which they are appointed. The duty owed by receivers to mortgagors was not owed to them individually but to them as persons interested in the equity of redemption. The duty of care owed by a mortgagee and a receiver of property is owed to all those interested in the equity of redemption.[655]

By way of summary, the duty of care owed by a mortgagee and a receiver is limited to taking reasonable care to obtain the best price in the circumstances at the time of sale. The choice of when to sell is entirely up to the receiver (looking only to the need to repay the secured debt). It is important to note that the duty is not to obtain a proper price, but only to take reasonable care to obtain a proper price. The duty is to take care when taking a particular step, not a duty to achieve a particular outcome from taking that step.   **7.276**

To what extent, and in what way, this duty of care applied to officeholders in collective insolvency processes was until relatively recently confined to judicial observations that were either *obiter* or made in the absence of argument. In *Re Charnley Davies Ltd*,[656] Millett J (as he then was) recorded that it had been common ground before him that an administrator owed a duty to the company over which they were appointed to take reasonable steps to obtain a proper price for its assets.[657] But Millett J went on to draw a distinction between the duty owed by a mortgagee or a receiver where security was enforced by or on behalf of the mortgagee from the nature of the duty that, in his Lordship's view, was owed in a collective insolvency process (i.e., liquidation and administration) as follows: **7.277**

> A mortgagee is bound to have regard to the interests of the mortgagor, but he is entitled to give priority to his own interests, and may insist on an immediate sale whether or not that it calculated to realise the best price … An administrator, by contrast, like a liquidator, has no interest of his own to which he may give priority, and must take reasonable care in choosing the time at which to sell the property.[658]

Patten J cited this passage at first instance in *Silven Properties Ltd v Royal Bank of Scotland plc*[659] and, in the course of Patten J's decision being upheld by the Court of Appeal, Lightman J commented as follows: **7.278**

> In the case of agent appointed to manage his principal's property on his behalf alone, general agency principles will apply. The agent will be obliged to pursue single-mindedly the interests of his principal

---

653   *Silven Properties Ltd v Royal Bank of Scotland plc* [2004] 1 WLR 997, [21]–[29].
654   *Cuckmere Brick Co v Mutual Financial Ltd* [1971] Ch 949; *Downside Nominees Ltd v First City Corp Corpn* [1993] AC 295; *Yorkshire Bank plc v Hall* [1991] 1 WLR 1713, 1728E–F; *Medforth v Blake* [2000] Ch 86, 98H–99A; *Raja v Austin Gray* [2003] 1 EGLR 91, [55].
655   *Alpstream AG v PK Airfinance SARL v Alpstream AG* [2015] EWCA Civ 1318, [115]–[116].
656   [1990] BCC 605.
657   Ibid., 618A.
658   Ibid., 618A–C.
659   [2003] BPIR 171, 219–220.

for which the claimants contend. This is reflected in the passage in the judgment of Millett J in *In re Charnley Davies Ltd* ... cited by Patten J. The administrator as agent for the company owes a duty of care to the company in the choice of the time to sell and (by parity of reasoning) in the decision whether to take the appropriate available advantageous pre-marketing steps which are calculated to achieve the best price.[660]

7.279   Lightman J's comments in *Silven* indicated a difference between the duty of a mortgagee or receiver on the one hand, and an administrator on the other. A degree of uncertainty lingered, not only because of the *obiter* nature of Lightman J's observations, but also because of the possible implications of the introduction of the new administration regime in Sch B1 by the Enterprise Act 2002, which came into force on 15 September 2003: *Silven* was argued prior to that date, but judgment was delivered afterwards, and it was not obvious whether the reforms had been taken into account in Lightman J's brief comparison. It remained arguable that a new-style administrator pursuing the third objective in para 3(1)(c) of Sch B1 (i.e., realising property in order to make a distribution to one or more secured or preferential creditors) was performing a role akin to that of a receiver and, accordingly, the same kind of duty should be owed.

7.280   The position, at least as far as administrators are concerned, was resolved by the decisions of Snowden J in *Davey v Money*[661] and Mr John Kimbell QC (sitting as a deputy High Court judge) in *Re One Blackfriars Ltd (in liquidation); Hyde v Nygate*.[662] Having cited both *Charnley Davies* and *Silven*, Snowden J endorsed in *Davey v Money* the view that a post-Enterprise Act 2002 administrator is required by the hierarchy of objectives in para 3(1) of Sch B1 to 'have regard to the interests of a wider group of stakeholders rather than simply the holder of the qualifying floating charge who appointed them'. This had an important implication for the timing of any sale:

> ... the administrator cannot simply decide to sell the company's assets at a time to suit the interests of the secured creditor, if by doing so he causes harm to the unsecured creditors which is not necessary for the protection of the interests of the secured creditor. The interests of the unsecured creditors in an administration therefore receive enhanced protection in an administration compared with a receivership.[663]

7.281   This was described by Snowden J as the 'inherent potential conflict between the interests of a secured creditor in achieving a sale at a level which sees it paid out, and the interests of the unsecured creditors in holding out or doing more to achieve a sale at a higher level'. In *One Blackfriars Ltd (in liquidation)*, this stakeholder conflict had been acknowledged by the administrators themselves at the material time, rightly drawing a contrast between the administrator's statutory duty in para 3 of Sch B1 and the secured creditor's commercial objectives.[664] The secured creditor in *One Blackfriars Ltd* had favoured a lower offer because it carried a smaller execution risk, whereas the administrators' duty to exercise their functions in the interests of the creditors as a whole required them to explore other options.[665]

---

660   *Silven Properties Ltd v Royal Bank of Scotland plc* [2004] 1 WLR 997, [25].
661   [2018] EWHC 766 (Ch), [2018] Bus LR 1903.
662   [2021] EWHC 684 (Ch).
663   *Davey v Money* [2018] EWHC 766 (Ch), [2018] Bus LR 1903, [392].
664   *Re One Blackfriars Ltd (in liq); Hyde v Nygate* [2021] EWHC 684 (Ch), [104].
665   Ibi.d, [138].

While there appears to be no decision on this point in relation to a liquidator, it is submitted **7.282** that (as Millett J suggested in *Charnley Davies*) the position of a liquidator is the same as an administrator:[666] as an officeholder owing duties to the company subject to the process that requires regard to be had to all the creditors, not just the secured creditor, the sale of company property must be done in a way that is consistent with those duties. Following these cases, the duty remains one to take reasonable care to obtain the best price that the circumstances permit, not an unqualified duty to achieve such a price;[667] nonetheless, in deciding on the timing of any sale, an administrator is required to have regard to the interests of the creditors as a whole, not simply the secured creditor.

The use of selling agents gives rise to a further key difference between the liability of receivers **7.283** and that of other officeholders. A receiver is liable to the mortgagor for loss occasioned by the negligence of an agent employed by the receiver.[668] By contrast, an administrator (and, it is submitted, a liquidator) is not liable if the advice received appears competent, their reliance on the advice was reasonable, and the decision in question is within the officeholder's powers.[669] The logic for this difference is that a receiver is to be treated in the same way as a mortgagee[670] and a mortgagee cannot set up its own agent's negligence as a defence to a claim by an aggrieved mortgagor; the mortgagor would not necessarily have any direct cause of action against the mortgagee's agent, whereas the mortgagee would.[671] By contrast, an administrator (and it is submitted a liquidator) has no interest in the property and since the agent would be engaged on behalf of the company, any cause of action would be an asset of the company, which could sue the negligent agent itself.[672] Accordingly, such an officeholder is entitled to rely on the advice of agents that is apparently competent to take steps within the officeholder's powers without attracting liability.[673]

It is plain that officeholders must exercise reasonable care in both choosing the time when to **7.284** sell company assets and obtaining the best price in the circumstances.[674]

(b) Fiduciary duties

A fiduciary duty is owed where a party has undertaken to act for or on behalf of another in **7.285** circumstances that give rise to a relationship of trust and confidence.[675] Liquidators and administrators both occupy a personal office under the Insolvency Act 1986 and are fiduciaries for the company in liquidation or administration. As discussed earlier in this chapter, a liquidator

---

666 See *Top Brands Ltd v Sharma* [2014] EWHC 2753 (Ch), [2015] 1 BCLC 546, [2015] BPIR 621, [28]; and affirmed on appeal at [2014] EWCA Civ 761.

667 A submission that an administrator owes an unqualified duty to obtain the best price reasonably obtainable at the time of sale was considered and rejected by the deputy judge in *Re One Blackfriars Ltd (in liq); Hyde v Nygate* [2021] EWHC 684 (Ch), [210]–[211].

668 *Raja v Austin Gray* [2003] Lloyd's Rep PN 126, [29]–[32].

669 [2018] EWHC 766 (Ch), [2018] Bus LR 1903, [451]; *Re One Blackfriars Ltd (in liq); Hyde v Nygate* [2021] EWHC 684 (Ch), [223]).

670 *Medforth v Blake* [2000] Ch 86.

671 *Raja v Austin* [2003] Lloyd's Rep PN 126.

672 *Re One Blackfriars Ltd (in liq); Hyde v Nygate* [2021] EWHC 684 (Ch), [221].

673 *Davey v Money* [2018] EWHC 766 (Ch), [2018] Bus LR 1903, [450]–[451]; *Re One Blackfriars Ltd (in liq); Hyde v Nygate* ibid., [221]–[223].

674   *MacDonald v Carnbroe Estates Ltd* [2020] UKPC 57, [38].

675 [1998] Ch 1, 18A–B.

is a trustee of the statutory trust that arises on the commencement of winding up. An administrator is an agent, and accordingly a fiduciary, for the company in administration.[676] Like any fiduciary duty,[677] the content and scope of the fiduciary duties owed by insolvency officeholders will depend upon the nature of the particular obligation giving rise to that duty.

7.286   It is frequently repeated, but should be emphasised, that not every duty owed by a fiduciary (including an insolvency officeholder) is a fiduciary duty.[678] Millett LJ explained in the classic exposition of the distinction between fiduciary and non-fiduciary duties in *Bristol and West Building Society v Mothew*[679] that:

> The expression 'fiduciary duty' is properly confined to those duties which are peculiar to fiduciaries and the breach of which attracts legal consequences differing from those consequent upon the breach of other duties. Unless the expression is so limited it is lacking in practical utility.[680]

7.287   Accordingly, it is not the case that a given breach of duty by an insolvency officeholder is necessarily to be regarded as a breach of fiduciary duty. Many breaches of duty by an officeholder will not be fiduciary in character. The limits of this principle in the officeholder context were tested at length in *Davey v Money*,[681] in which the claimant argued that administrators had committed a number of breaches of fiduciary duty in the course of an administration. The administrators in that case had been appointed by a QFCH over a single-asset company that owned a development site in the Docklands. Following a decision not to pursue a planning application, the asset was sold and a distribution was made only to the QFCH. The company's shareholder and director, who had also personally guaranteed the company's debt to the QFCH, brought proceedings against the former administrators under para 75 of Sch B1, which enables the court to inquire into potential misfeasance by an administrator on the application of a creditor or contributory.

7.288   The applicant alleged that the administrators had acted in breach of duty in the administration throughout, by surrendering their discretion to the QFCH and failing to exercise independent judgment in relation to matters such as the appointment of the selling agent for the property and whether or not to pursue a planning application. As a consequence of these failures, it was submitted that the administrators had failed to obtain a proper price for the asset.[682] As the company was a single-asset vehicle for the development of the asset in question, the sale was at the heart of all aspects of the applicant's allegations, as it was the main opportunity for any loss to have been suffered by the company and those interested in the equity of redemption.

7.289   It was submitted that by reason of the administrators being fiduciaries, they should be subject to the same equitable duties and standards as a trustee when selling property of the company under their control, as set out in the case law concerning express trustees.[683] This meant that

---

676   Insolvency Act 1986, Sch B1, para 69.
677   *Henderson v Merrett* [1995] 2 AC 145, 206B–D; *Re Medstead Associates Ltd* [2019] EWCA Civ 83, [2019] 1 WLR 4481, [45].
678   Paul Finn, *Fiduciary Obligations* (Law Book Co, 1977), p. 2; cited with approval by Millett LJ [1998] Ch 1, 18C.
679   [1998] Ch 1.
680   Ibid., 16C–D.
681   [2018] EWHC 766 (Ch), [2018] Bus LR 1903.
682   Ibid., [251].
683   The principal authority relied on was *Killearn v Killearn* [2011] EWHC 3775 (Ch).

administrators were obliged to sell property 'under every possible advantage' to the beneficiaries in order to ensure the best price was obtained. It was also contended that, as fiduciaries, the administrators bore the burden of justifying the sale, rather than the applicant having to establish a breach of duty in order to make out her claim.[684] As fiduciary agents in respect of the company's property, the applicant contended that each of the breaches of duty alleged on the part of the administrators were breaches of fiduciary duty.[685] Snowden J rejected the breadth of these submissions and, applying *Mothew*,[686] held that not all duties owed by a person who may occupy a fiduciary person are fiduciary duties. In particular, the administrators' duty of care and selling duty were not fiduciary duties.[687]

A breach by an officeholder of their duty to take care when selling company property will not **7.290** of itself constitute a breach of fiduciary duty. It is, however, possible that further facts could give rise to a breach of fiduciary duty in the context of a sale of company assets (e.g., where an officeholder positively prefers the interests of the purchaser over the interests of the company) but a conventional breach of the selling duty by way of an undersale of company property will not be in the nature of the breach of fiduciary duty.

A fiduciary obligation has at its core an obligation of single-minded loyalty by the fiduciary **7.291** towards the principal. In order to establish a breach of fiduciary duty, the claimant must show a breach of this core obligation of loyalty; mere incompetence is not enough.[688] In the case of liquidators and administrators, that means loyalty towards the company over which they have been appointed. Examples of the core duty of loyalty include the requirement for the fiduciary to act in good faith, not to make a profit out of their position, and not to act in a position where their duty and interest conflict.[689] These, of course, are duties pertinent on all fiduciaries and they are clearly imposed on company directors who are also fiduciaries.

(i)   Duty to act independently

Officeholders are required to exercise independent judgment and retain a discretion to act, **7.292** which is an obvious consequence of the fact that the offices of administrator and liquidator are personal offices under the Insolvency Act 1986 and the relevant authority and statutory powers are given to the administrator or liquidator and not anyone else.[690]

This duty demands that officeholders are required to use their own discretion in the manage- **7.293** ment of the affairs and property of the company and the distribution of the assets;[691] they are not to rely on others, other than for advice, and they must not regard themselves beholden to anyone.

---

684   *Davey v Money* [2018] EWHC 766 (Ch), [2018] Bus LR 1903, [381].
685   Ibid., [615].
686   Ibid., [621].
687   Ibid., [622].
688   *Bristol and West Building Society v Mothew* [1998] Ch 1, 18F.
689   Ibid., 18A–C.
690   *Davey v Money* [2018] EWHC 766 (Ch), [2018] Bus LR 1903, [590].
691   See *Re London and Mediterranean Bank; Ex parte Birmingham Banking Co* (1868) 3 Ch App 651; *Re Allebart Pty Ltd* [1971] 1 NSWLR 24; compare *Re International Properties Pty Ltd* (1977) 2 ACLR 477.

7.294   If officeholders surrender their discretion to act to some third party, or act to serve the interests of a third party, rather than the company, they are in breach of their duty to act independently.[692] Such a duty does not preclude officeholders from considering the wishes of those who will be affected by any decisions which they will make. Indeed, it may be prudent to seek the wishes of relevant parties. This is particularly the case when contemplating the instigation of significant litigation or any other action that might be costly and time-consuming. However, while officeholders may ascertain the wishes of others, the final decision on any matter must be theirs and theirs alone.

7.295   This duty is linked to the fact that an officeholder must act impartially and not act or be seen to be acting in the interests of any particular party. In acting impartially the officeholder is maintaining independent judgment and not compromising his or her discretion.

(ii)   Duty to act in good faith and for proper purposes

7.296   Officeholders must exercise their powers in good faith and for a proper purpose, i.e., not capriciously.[693] The requirement to act for proper purposes will extend to a prohibition on acting perversely or irrationally or for extraneous reasons, and includes the requirement for officeholders to take reasonable steps to acquire information on relevant matters and, where appropriate, to follow professional advice.[694]

(iii)   Duty to avoid conflicts of interest

7.297   A critical aspect of any fiduciary's role is that he ensures that he avoids any conflict between his own interests and those of the one for whom he is to act.[695] The rule is applied strictly.[696] A fiduciary is not only to avoid a conflict but also the possibility of a conflict.[697]

7.298   An important consequence of the fiduciary relationship is that officeholders are not permitted, either directly or indirectly, to profit from their office otherwise than to the extent expressly allowed by law or else them might be placing themselves in a conflict situation.[698] Their profit will usually be limited to their reasonable remuneration to which they are entitled as professionals.

7.299   Officeholders are generally not permitted to enter into contracts with the company as this might open up the possibility of conflict.

7.300   If, during the course of an administration or liquidation, the officeholder discovers that he or she has a conflict of interest the appropriate course might be to seek directions from the court. In the most extreme cases it is probably appropriate that the officeholder resigns.

---

692   *Davey v Money* [2018] EWHC 766 (Ch), [2018] Bus LR 1903, [624].
693   Ibid., [622]–[623].
694   G Lightman, G Moss, H Anderson, I Fletcher and R Snowden *Lightman & Moss on the Law of Administrators and Receivers of Companies*, (6th ed., Sweet & Maxwell, 2017), [12–037].
695   If authority is necessary, see *Boardman v Phipps* [1967] 2 AC 46; *Aberdeen Rly Co v Blaikie Bros* [1854] 2 Eq Rep 1281, (1854]) 1 Macq 461, [1843–1860] All ER Rep 249 (HL); *Ultraframe (UK) Ltd v Fielding* [2005] EWHC 1638 (Ch).
696   See, e.g., *Re Gertzenstein Ltd* [1937] Ch 115. In the context of company directors, see *Regal (Hastings) Ltd v Gulliver* [1967] 2 AC 134 (HL).
697   *Boardman v Phipps* [1967] 2 AC 46, 124 (HL).
698   *Re Gertzenstein Ltd* [1937] Ch 115.

(iv) Benefits of claiming a breach of a fiduciary duty

Claimants will frequently seek to argue that the breach of which they complain is a breach **7.301**
of fiduciary duty because the remedies available for a breach of fiduciary duty compared with
a non-fiduciary duty tend to be more flexible and attractive from a claimant's point of view. As
Millett LJ explained in *Mothew*, the equitable remedies available 'are peculiar to the equitable
jurisdiction and are primarily restitutionary or restorative rather than compensatory'.[699] The
practical effect of this is that the restitutionary or restorative measure may permit a claimant
to elect to receive what is known as a 'substitutive performance' measure of loss. Where an
asset has been wrongly disposed of by a fiduciary, the substitutive performance measure may
require the fiduciary to pay the value of the asset to be determined at the date of judgment,
rather than the date of the breach of duty as is the case with the compensatory measure.[700] In
a rising market, the value of the asset at the date of judgment may well be more attractive to
the claimant. Where the substitutive performance measure applies and a defaulting fiduciary
is required to restore the estate, the ordinary rules of causation and remoteness of loss do not
apply. The measure is the objective value of the property lost is determined at the date of trial
and with the benefit of hindsight.[701]

A good practical illustration of these principles working in the insolvency context is provided **7.302**
by *Brewer (joint liquidator of ARY Digital UK Ltd) v Iqbal*.[702] An administrator had sold the
company's principal assets, which were of a highly-specialised kind, to a newly incorporated
company that was associated with the directors of the company in administration. In proceedings brought by the subsequently appointed liquidators, it transpired that, despite the administrator's unfamiliarity with the particular asset class, he had concluded the sale without first
obtaining an independent valuation of the assets and having relied on what the directors had
told him about the value of the assets. The administrator also relied on the directors for advice
about marketing and the timing of the sale. Such advertising of the assets as had been undertaken had excluded the name of the company and its location, which was a deliberate decision
on the administrator's part in order to avoid detrimentally affecting the overall brand associated
with the global corporate group of which the company in administration was a member.[703]

Chief ICC Judge Briggs held that in taking advice from the potential buyers about value, adver- **7.303**
tising and timing, failing to take independent advice, and taking into account the interests of
the wider brand instead of the interests of the creditors of the company itself, the administrator
had not merely been negligent, but had breached his fiduciary duty.[704] As a consequence, the
award of compensation to the liquidators was based on the value of the assets at the date of trial,
not the date of breach, which represented a windfall to the estate.[705]

---

699   [1998] Ch 1, 18A–B.
700   For a recent discussion by the Court of Appeal of the distinction between the two categories of equitable compensation,
        see *Interactive Technology Corporation Ltd v Ferster* [2018] EWCA Civ 1594, [16]–[21].
701   *Libertarian Investments Ltd v Hall* (2013) 17 ITELR 1, [168]; *AIB Group (UK) Ltd plc v Mark Redler & Co Solicitor*
        [2014] UKSC 58, [2015] AC 1503, [135].
702   [2019] EWHC 182 (Ch), [2019] BCC 746.
703   Ibid., [75], [81], [89].
704   Ibid., [90], [94].
705   Ibid., [110].

7.304   Also, in seeking relief for breach of a fiduciary duty a claimant might well have more and different remedies available. For instance, the claimant can seek an account of profits which would not be available for breaches of non-fiduciary duties.

8

THE CONTROL OF INSOLVENCY PRACTITIONERS

A. OFFICEHOLDER DECISION-MAKING

1.   The standard of review

8.001   Officeholders' powers and duties are such that it will frequently be necessary for them to take specific discretionary decisions, often requiring commercial judgment, on behalf of the company that is subject to an insolvency proceeding. Evaluative judgments of this kind may require the weighing-up of various factors, often in fast-moving situations or conditions of imperfect information. A considerable degree of deference is shown by the court towards an officeholder's decision-making where it falls into this category. If it were otherwise, and such decisions fell to be scrutinised after the event and criticised where they were less than perfect, then anyone still willing to act as an officeholder under such conditions would probably be reluctant to take any decision without first seeking directions from the court.[1]

8.002   Where a decision falls into this category, then unless it is perverse or irrational, the court will not interfere with it. In *Leon v York-O-Matic Ltd*,[2] a contributory who was also a creditor sought an injunction to restrain a liquidator from selling certain company assets. Plowman J indicated that two conditions must be satisfied before a court might interfere with a liquidator's judgment: First, was the liquidator's discretion exercised *bona fide*? Secondly, had the liquidator acted in a way in which no reasonable liquidator could have acted?[3] In essence, the test is one of perversity.[4] It recognises that in matters of discretionary judgment, there is often a range of reasonable positions that could properly be adopted by officeholders, and their conduct should not be judged with hindsight. In *Re Buckingham International plc (in liquidation) (No 2)*, Robert Walker LJ held that in such cases 'the court will be very slow to substitute its judgment for the liquidators on what is essentially a businessman's decision…'.[5]

---

1   For discussion about directions, see para 8.007.
2   [1966] 1 WLR 1450.
3   Ibid., 1455C–D.
4   *Re Hans Place Ltd* [1992] BCC 737, 746; *Hamilton v Official Receiver* [1998] BPIR 602, 605; *Davey v Money* [2018] EWHC 766, [2018] Bus LR 1903, [255].
5   [1998] BCC 943, 961.

Precise verbal formulations vary, but the following characterisations of the test appear in the   **8.003**
cases:

...so utterly unreasonable and absurd that no reasonable man would have done it.[6]

...so perverse that no reasonable liquidator could have entered into the agreement.[7]

...The administrators have made a commercial judgment and have explained why they made it. It is not for the court to interfere with such a decision unless it is based on a wrong appreciation of the law...or is conspicuously unfair to a particular creditor or contractor.[8]

...open to challenge [only] if it was made in bad faith or was clearly perverse...[9]

This principle applies equally to liquidators,[10] administrators[11] and (although beyond the scope   **8.004**
of this book) trustees in bankruptcy.[12] In the discussion that follows, references to the 'perversity' or 'deferential' or 'good faith and rationality' standards of review should be treated synonymously as descriptions of the test applicable to discretionary or commercial decision-making.

Many of the cases falling into this category and capable of attracting the deferential standard   **8.005**
of review have concerned the exercise of the officeholder's dispositive power.[13] Other decisions regarded as exercises of discretionary or commercial judgment include a decision whether or not to disclaim a lease,[14] commence litigation,[15] compromise a claim,[16] assign a claim,[17] and how far to push a preferred bidder to increase its offer.[18] Where statutory language is apt to confer a discretionary power, the commercial judgment standard will apply; for instance the selection of which objective in para 3(1) of Sch B1 to the Insolvency Act 1986 to pursue in order to achieve the statutory purpose of administration will also fall into this category,[19] as will the exercise of an administrator's power to compromise a claim in para 60 of Sch B1,[20] and the

---

6   *Re Edennote Ltd* [1996] BCC 718, 722.
7   *Mahomed v Morris* [2001] BCC 233, [17].
8   *Re Zegna III Holdings Inc (in administration); BLV Realty* [2009] EWHC 2994, [2010] BPIR 277, [22];
9   *Davey v Money* [2018] EWHC 766, [2018] Bus LR 1903, [255].
10   *Leon v York-O-Matic Ltd* [1966] 1 WLR 1450, 1454B–1455D; *Re Edennote Ltd* [1996] BCC 718, 722; *Re Longmeade Ltd (in liq)* [2016] EWHC 356, [2017] 2 All ER 244, [54]–[55].
11   *CE King Ltd* [2000] 2 BCLC 297, 303 (Neuberger J); *Davey v Money* [2018] EWHC 766, [2018] Bus LR 1903, [255].
12   *In re a Debtor, ex parte Debtor v Dodwell* [1949] Ch 236, 241.
13   *In re Peters, Ex parte Lloyd* (1882) 47 LT 64, 65; *Leon v York-O-Matic Ltd* [1966] 1 WLR 1450, 1455C–1455G; *Re Edennote Ltd* [1996] BCC 718. Robert Walker LJ made the observation in *Re Buckingham International plc (in liq) (No 2)* [1998] BCC 943, 961 that all the cases considered by Nourse LJ on the point in *Re Edennote Ltd* had concerned decisions as to the disposal of assets.
14   *Re Hans Place Ltd* [1992] BCC 737, 746.
15   *Re Longmeade (in liq)* [2016] EWHC 356, [2017] 2 All ER 244.
16   *Mahomed v Morris (No 2)* [2001] BCC 233, [32].
17   *Hamilton v Official Receiver* [1998] BPIR 602.
18   *Davey v Money* [2018] EWHC 766, [2018] Bus LR 1903, [543]; *Re Capitol Films Ltd (in admin)* [2010] EWHC 3223 (Ch), [2011] 2 BCLC 359, [84].
19   *Davey v Money* [2018] EWHC 766, [2018] Bus LR 1903, [255].
20   *In re MF Global UK Ltd (in special administration) (No 5)* [2014] EWHC 2222 (Ch), [2014] Bus LR 1156, [41]. In *Re Lehman Brothers International Europe (in admin)* [2013] EWHC 1664, [2014] BCC 132, the administrators applied to court for directions in relation to a settlement agreement to which they had already committed the company, not because they required the court's approval to enter into it, but in order to give assurance to the counterparty officeholder under the settlement (being the US bankruptcy trustee appointed for the liquidation of Lehman Brothers Inc) that it would be performed: [9]–[10].

decision whether or not to cause a company to move from administration to creditors' voluntary liquidation ('CVL').[21]

8.006 This standard of review is derived from fiduciary principles and is generally the same as that applied to exercises of commercial judgment by company directors. In *Re Windsor Steam Coal Company (1901) Ltd,* Lord Hanworth categorised directors and liquidators together in this respect: 'Now it is quite true that the Court ought to be very tender with persons who are placed in the difficult positions of directors or liquidators, and should not judge their conduct in the light of subsequent events.'[22]

8.007 The converse of this is that officeholders are expected to use their discretionary powers without first seeking the guidance of the court and are discouraged from applying too readily for directions when it comes to this category of decision-making. It has been said that the court is not to be used as a 'rubber stamp'.[23] The court's attitude is perhaps best encapsulated in the following observation of Neuberger J in *In re T & D Industries plc*:[24]

> an administrator may be called upon to make important and urgent decisions. He has a responsible and potentially demanding role. Commercial and administrative decisions are for him, and the court is not there to act as a sort of bomb shelter for him.[25]

8.008 This is not to suggest that an officeholder may never justifiably apply for directions. Rather, an officeholder will be expected to show that the application is necessary to resolve a difficult question, or concerns a 'particularly momentous'[26] decision for which the officeholder needs the blessing of the court. Where there is a genuine need for the court's direction, officeholders will not be criticised for seeking it. For instance, in *In re MF Global UK Ltd (in special administration) (No 5)*, it was necessary for the administrators to apply for directions because they were involved on both sides of a compromise of claims[27] and in *Re Longmeade Ltd (in liquidation)*, it was appropriate for the liquidators to have 'some reassurance' from the court given the highly unusual circumstances.[28]

8.009 In taking discretionary or commercial decisions, an officeholder may take into account the views of creditors or contributories. This is, however, subject to some qualifications. These were explored in detail by Snowden J in *Re Longmeade Ltd (in liquidation)*,[29] which concerned whether or not a liquidator should commence litigation in the face of opposition from the

---

21 *In re Kilnoore Ltd (in liq); Unidare plc v Cohen* [2005] EWHC 1410 (Ch), [2006] Ch 489, [71]; *Re Ballast plc* [2004] EWHC 2356 (Ch), [2005] 1 All ER 630, [15].

22 [1929] 1 Ch 151, 159.

23 *Re Nortel Networks UK Ltd* [2014] EWHC 2614 (Ch), [38].

24 [2000] 1 WLR 646. The case concerned a pre-EA 2002 administration, but has been applied both to a post-EA 2002 administration (see *In Re Transbus International Ltd* [2004] EWHC 932 (Ch), [2004] 1 WLR 2654, [9]; and a liquidation (see *Re Comet Group Ltd (in liq); Kahn v ICAEW* [2018] EWHC 1378, [9]).

25 [2000] 1 WLR 646, 657F–G.

26 *The Public Trustee v Cooper* [2001] WTLR 901, 923.

27 [2014] EWHC 2222 (Ch), [2014] Bus LR 1156, [41].

28 [2016] EWHC 356, [2017] 2 All ER 244, [71].

29 Ibid.

large majority of creditors.[30] Some general principles towards discretionary officeholder decision-making may be extracted from that case.

First, in order for a party to have the necessary kind of interest in the decision in issue for its **8.010** views to be relevant, that party must show that they have a financial interest in the estate. It is important to note that a contributory will only be able to satisfy this requirement if there is the possibility of a surplus for them,[31] which for obvious reasons will tend to be rare where the company is subject to an insolvency process. This important principle is discussed further later in this chapter.

Secondly, although the officeholder may consult creditors before taking a decision, there is no **8.011** obligation to do so.[32] Snowden J concluded in *Re Longmeade Ltd* that there is no requirement for a liquidator to hold a meeting of creditors[33] or consult with creditors or contributories with an interest in the estate.[34] In a similar vein, the same judge subsequently held in *Davey v Money* that there was no absolute requirement on an administrator to consult with the directors and shareholders over whether the rescue of the company as a going concern was feasible before taking the decision not to pursue that objective,[35] even though, by definition, the shareholders will have a financial interest if the company resumes profitable trading as a going concern. It follows from these cases that even a party with a financial interest in the estate will face an uphill struggle in impugning a discretionary or commercial decision by an officeholder on the basis of an allegation that they were not consulted in advance.

Thirdly, although the reasoned views of creditors will ordinarily carry great weight, the majority **8.012** position is not decisive. In particular, where creditors are 'influenced by extraneous considerations…' or 'not promoting a view based upon their capacity as such…', then those views should be discounted or not given effect.[36] This reflects the class-based nature of insolvency proceedings: a party wishing to have their views taken into account must not only have the necessary economic interest in the estate, but must also be acting in that capacity and in the interests of the class of which they are a member. Snowden J indicated that an exception to this third qualification applies where all persons having an interest in the insolvent company are fully informed and of the same view; in those circumstances the officeholder will ordinarily be obliged to give effect to that view.[37] This unanimity exception is derived by analogy from the well-established principle concerning the rights of beneficiaries under a trust in *Saunders v Vautier*,[38] or the ability of corporate members in a solvent company to take informal decisions where they act unanimously in *In re Duomatic Ltd*.[39]

---

30   Ibid.
31   *Re Longmeade Ltd (in liq)* [2016] EWHC 356, [2017] 2 All ER 244, [53].
32   Ibid., [66].
33   Ibid., [50].
34   Ibid., [66].
35   *Davey v Money* [2018] EWHC 766, [2018] Bus LR 1903, [287].
36   *Re Longmeade Ltd (in liq)* [2016] EWHC 356, [2017] 2 All ER 244, [51]–[52].
37   Ibid., [53].
38   (1841) 4 Beav 115.
39   [1969] 2 Ch 365. But decision-making under these principles really must be unanimous: on its unusual facts, over 99.73 per cent of the creditors in *Re Longmeade Ltd (in liq)* were opposed to bringing the claim, but the matter remained one for the liquidator's commercial judgment unless full unanimity was established.

2.   Advice and investigation

8.013   There is an important qualification to the latitude that will be shown towards an officeholder's decision-making: the reasonable officeholder is taken to be one who is properly advised.[40] Where an officeholder fails to take advice before making a decision on a point where such advice was properly required, then the officeholder will not meet the threshold standard of being a 'reasonable' one, which is a necessary condition for the court's deference to engage. In *Re Comet Group Ltd (in liquidation)*,[41] Sir Nicholas Warren rejected the suggestion that the court was being asked to substitute its own judgment for the commercial judgment of the liquidators. Instead, the judge held that there was 'real and justified concern' that the officeholders' decisions in question 'do not reflect a properly informed exercise of commercial judgment.' This was because:

> The complaint is not that, on the basis of all the material available, the Liquidators have made decisions outside the range of reasonable decisions, but that they have (i) made their decisions without proper consideration of the material which is available and (ii) made their decisions without proper investigation of matters which should have been investigated.[42]

8.014   This illustrates some similarities between aspects of an officeholder's position and that of a company director, in that the substitution of an objective for a subjective standard of review of directors' conduct may likewise be made where a director has unreasonably failed to take into account a very material interest before taking a decision.[43]

8.015   Conversely, an officeholder who has properly based their discretionary or commercial decision-making on advice will not be criticised where that decision turns out to have been wrong. For instance, in *In re Kilnoore Ltd (in liquidation)*,[44] the administrator had exercised a discretion under para 83 of Sch B1[45] and, while Lewison J considered the administrator's decision to be objectively wrong, it had nonetheless been formed on reasonable grounds by reason of the administrator having taken appropriate legal advice.[46]

8.016   The fact that judges show deference to officeholders might, rightly, be seen as circumscribing accountability in that while officeholders will be required to disclose the facts of any particular situation to a judge and explain and justify what has been done, the questioning and judgment aspects of accountability, described in Chapter 2, will be somewhat limited. To an observer this might seem that officeholders may not be held to account sufficiently. However, it may be said, and following on from what has been said earlier in this chapter, if the questioning and judgment was overly evaluative officeholders might simply not take up nominations or limit the decisions they make. The latter could be damaging to the administration of an insolvent

---

40   *Re Edennote Ltd* [1996] BCC 718, [723]–[724], citing in support *Re Hans Place Ltd (in liq)* [1993] BCLC 768, 778.

41   [2018] EWHC 1378 (Ch).

42   *Re Comet Group Ltd (in liq)* [2018] EWHC 1378 (Ch), [173], see also [117] and [153]. See also *Top Brands Ltd v Sharma* [2014] EWHC 2753 (Ch), [2016] BCC 1, [33], [183], upheld by the Court of Appeal [2015] EWCA Civ 1140 [2017] 1 All ER 854.

43   *Re HLC Environmental Projects Ltd (in liq)* [2013] EWHC 2876 (Ch), [2014] BCC 337, [92(c)].

44   [2005] EWHC 1410 (Ch), [2006] Ch 489.

45   This provision is one of a number in Sch B1 based on what the administrator '*thinks*', which indicates that it is subject to a test of good faith and rationality: *Davey v Money* [2018] EWHC 766, [2018] Bus LR 1903, [255].

46   [2005] EWHC 1410 (Ch), [2006] Ch 489, [71]–[72].

company. Also, as we explain in the next section deference must be distinguished from ignoring negligence.

3. Distinction between deferential standard and negligence standard

It is important to distinguish the deference extended to specific discretionary or commercial **8.017** decisions from conduct that falls to be assessed by reference to duty of care (i.e., negligence) standard of review.[47] The deferential standard of review discussed above applies to decisions taken by officeholders that are within their powers. Negligent conduct is, by definition, outside those powers. Snowden J distinguished in *Davey v Money* in practical terms between these categories. In that case, the administrators' decision to pursue the third objective in para 3(1) of Sch B1 attracted the deferential good faith and rationality standard of review.[48] This was to be distinguished from the 'methods adopted' by them to pursue that chosen course, to which a less deferential and objective standard of 'an ordinary skilled practitioner' would apply.[49] In order for the claimant to establish a breach of duty on the part of an administrator in the course of selling company property, it was necessary to show that the administrator made an error that a reasonably skilled and careful insolvency practitioner (IP) would not have made.[50] That objective negligence standard was applied in *Davey v Money* to a series of decisions taken in the sale of the company's principal asset, including the decisions not to pursue an existing planning application,[51] not to instruct an investment agent,[52] not to run a 'beauty parade' of possible selling agents,[53] not to advertise,[54] to accept their agent's advice on the contents of a targeted marketing list,[55] and not to invite conditional offers.[56] A similar distinction was drawn in *Re One Blackfriars Ltd (in liquidation)* and a negligence standard was applied to decisions to appoint a particular expert,[57] to not pursue a varied planning consent,[58] to seek an unconditional sale without an overage provision,[59] and in relation to marketing and sale strategy.[60]

At an analytical level, the distinction is clear: the deferential standard of review applies to **8.018** decisions taken by officeholders that are within their powers; a duty of care standard applies to determine whether conduct amounts to a breach of duty. It is submitted, however, that the distinction may not always be easy to draw in practice, at least in advance of a judicial determination. As noted above, many of the decisions on the discretionary or commercial judgment standard concern officeholder decisions over whether or not to exercise the officeholder's dispositive power in relation to company property. It is submitted that the line between the

---

47   *Davey v Money* [2018] EWHC 766, [2018] Bus LR 1903, [383]–[384].
48   Ibid., [371]–[393].
49   Ibid., [256].
50   Ibid., [383]–[384].
51   Ibid., [413].
52   Ibid., [428].
53   Ibid., [434].
54   Ibid., [464].
55   Ibid., [477].
56   Ibid., [513].
57   [2021] EWHC 684 (Ch), [302].
58   Ibid., [370].
59   Ibid., [393].
60   Ibid., [412].

decision whether or not to sell (which will attract the subjective deferential standard of review) and the methods adopted in effecting the sale (which will be assessed by reference to the objective standard of the ordinary skilled practitioner) may not always be clear-cut, particularly in fast-moving administrations. Claimants will naturally try to present cases as falling into the 'methods adopted' category in order for the negligence standard to apply, whereas officeholders will endeavour to pull the case back over the discretionary judgment line requiring them only to show that their decision was not perverse. The distinction between breach of duty and the review of other forms of officeholder conduct is discussed further below.

4.   Distinction between discretionary decisions and matters of law

8.019   The deferential good faith and rationality standard of review will not apply to a decision that is based on a question of law. The distinction emerged in the Court of Appeal decision *Re Buckingham International plc (in liquidation) (No 2)*.[61] In that case, two unsecured judgment creditors of a company attempted to garnish debts owed to the company in Florida. On learning of the steps being taken, the receivers of the company presented a winding-up petition in England and caused provisional liquidators to be appointed. The provisional liquidators filed a petition in Florida seeking to restrain the creditors from perfecting their writs of garnishment. An application was made by the creditors to the English court seeking an order to permit the garnishment proceedings to proceed. At first instance, the court dismissed the creditors' application, having treated the liquidators' decision as subject to a test of perversity.[62] The Court of Appeal reversed that decision and held that the intervention in Florida had not been an exercise of discretion subject to the deferential standard of review. Robert Walker LJ accepted a submission that cases in the category of *Leon v York-O-Matic* and *Re Edennote Ltd* were distinct from the position in *Re Buckingham International* on the basis that:

> …The liquidators' application to the American insolvency court was … of a different character. It was concerned with competing creditors: in particular, with the efforts of one pair of judgment creditors to put themselves into the position of secured creditors before the position was frozen by the onset of the winding up…This is eminently a matter for the Companies Court, or for liquidators acting under the control of the Companies Court. It is not a matter for the liquidators to decide at their own discretion in the way in which they might take decisions as to the disposal of their company's assets.[63]

8.020   This approach was applied to administration in *Re Capitol Films Ltd (in administration)*.[64] In that case, the joint administrators sought to resist an adverse costs order following their unsuccessful pursuit of an application under para 71 of Sch B1 to dispose of property subject to security as if it were not subject to security. The administrators argued that their decision to bring the application had been a commercial judgment taken to realise the assets of the company in administration and, as such, the court should not make an order against them simply because they failed, provided that they had behaved rationally.[65] The court rejected the administrators' arguments, on the basis that an application under para 71 raised additional and different issues, requiring:

---

61   *Re Buckingham International plc (in liquidation) (No 2); Mitchell v Buckingham* [1998] BCC 943.
62   [1998] BCC 943, 953.
63   Ibid., 961.
64   [2010] EWHC 3223 (Ch).
65   Ibid., [83].

...the court to determine whether it is appropriate to prevent the holder of a fixed charge from enforcing his security rights and to permit the administrator to undertake a sale which promotes the purposes of the administration more generally. Such an application requires the court to balance the competing rights and interests of the holders of fixed charges with the rights and interests of the other creditors...On that type of issue, the court does not simply apply the Edennote approach and defer to the administrators' business judgment provided that it is rational: the court will decide for itself how to resolve the competing interests of creditors...[66]

The readiness of the court to review issues of this kind plainly creates an incentive for applicants to try to bring their grievance within this category. Such an attempt failed in *Mahomed v Morris (No 2)*,[67] where the Court of Appeal considered the liquidators' act to have been concerned with the compromise of a dispute, which had called for a commercial decision to be taken and 'did not involve purely legal issues'.[68] **8.021**

The distinction was invoked in *Stevanovich v Wide & McDonald (as joint liquidators of Barrington Capital Group Ltd (in liquidation))*.[69] A former director of a company in insolvent liquidation in the British Virgin Islands made an application[70] seeking to have set aside the liquidators' decision to admit a proof of debt lodged by a US trustee in bankruptcy based on a judgment obtained in Minnesota in default of an appearance by the company. The applicant former director argued that the company had not submitted to jurisdiction in Minnesota and, as such, the judgment was unenforceable in the BVI.[71] The applicant successfully argued that the question was one involving purely legal issues. Wallbank J shrewdly observed that if the perversity test applied, the applicant former director would have had a much higher hurdle to overcome in seeking to have the liquidators' decision set aside, demonstrating the importance of the side of the line on which a challenge to an officeholder's decision falls.[72] The judge held that the provability of a debt was a question of law and the factual inquiry was a component of that greater legal issue of provability. Ultimately, either the debt was provable or it was not: that decision involved no compromise nor any exercise of discretion on the part of the liquidators.[73] **8.022**

It is submitted that identifying the precise line of demarcation between exercises of discretion and questions of law may throw up difficult cases at the margins, with the claimants and defendants seeking to argue in different directions in order to raise or lower the hurdle as the case may be. **8.023**

---

66 Ibid., [84]–[86]. On the facts of the case, the deputy judge did not, in any event, believe that the administrators' conduct in pursuing the application had been either rational or reasonable.
67 [2001] BCC 233.
68 Ibid., 242.
69 A decision of Wallbank J in the BVI Commercial Court, BVIHCM 2013/0043, 5 December 2018.
70 Under s 273 of the British Virgin Islands Insolvency Act, 2003, which is in equivalent terms to s 168(5).
71 Following the decision of the Supreme Court of the UK in *Rubin v Eurofinance SA* [2012] UKSC 46.
72 BVIHCM 2013/0043, 5 December 2018, [50].
73 Ibid., [52].

B. REVIEW OF OFFICEHOLDER CONDUCT

1. The tangible economic interest principle

8.024   There are a number of statutory gateways in the Insolvency Act 1986[74] for an officeholder's conduct to be reviewed by the court. Generally speaking, and subject to certain limited exceptions, a party seeking to be heard will need to show that they have a tangible economic interest in the assets available for distribution in the insolvency and a legitimate interest in the relief being sought in order to establish standing.

8.025   It is an inevitable feature of most insolvencies that a range of interests will be affected as a consequence. Frequently one or more parties will express discontent with the officeholder's conduct of the estate. Often the primary source of such a party's grievance will be the insolvency and the inevitable losses suffered as a consequence of that, rather than anything the officeholder is or is not doing. As the personal manifestation of the insolvency process, however, the officeholder will tend to be the focus of discontent. If all such parties were allowed to apply to challenge the governance of companies subject to collective insolvency proceedings, then it would be difficult for officeholders to get on with their jobs. The following observation made by Harman J in *Debtor v Dodwell*[75] (a bankruptcy case but equally relevant to corporate insolvency) continues to apply: 'Administration in bankruptcy would be impossible if the trustee must answer at every step to the bankrupt for the exercise of his powers and discretions in the management and realisation of property.'[76]

8.026   If challenges to officeholder conduct were freely permitted, the value of assets otherwise available for distribution would be wasted in investigating or dealing with challenges from parties remote from any realistic economic interest in that value. For this reason, a principle resembling a preliminary filter has developed, which runs through a number of governance aspects of companies that are subject to formal insolvency processes. The general rule is that a party will seldom be heard by the court in relation to an insolvent company unless they can show a tangible economic interest in the assets available for distribution. This provides an important control function in the corporate governance of insolvent companies. Accountability and transparency in the context of involvement in court proceedings in relation to insolvent companies means, as a general rule, accountability and transparency to those with an economic interest in a future distribution. The relevant interests are the collective interests of the class or classes entitled to a distribution.

8.027   Subject to limited exceptions, this principle tends to be followed irrespective of whether the wording of any particular statutory gateway appears wide enough to include anyone, or whether it prescribes the class of persons that may apply under it. The only principled exceptions arise either where the statutory provision expressly provides otherwise[77] or, it appears, where the

---

74   All references to sections are to the Insolvency Act 1986 unless it is indicated otherwise.
75   [1949] Ch 236. Harman J's words have been cited in company cases, e.g., *Leon v York-O-Matic Ltd* [1966] 1 WLR 1450, 1455 per Plowman J; and *Re Hans Place Ltd*, [1992] BCC 737, 745 per Edward Evans-Lombe QC (sitting as a deputy High Court judge).
76   [1949] Ch 236, 241.
77   In particular s 212(6).

party seeking to apply is able to show that jurisdiction to commence the proceedings in which they seek to be heard was lacking altogether.[78]

The earliest manifestations of the principle concerned the initiation of company winding up by **8.028** shareholders. In *In re Rica Gold Washing Company*,[79] a fully paid-up shareholder in an insolvent company petitioned for a winding-up order so that an alleged fraud by the company's promoters could be pursued. The petitioner was held not to have standing because, as a shareholder in an insolvent company, he was unable to show a tangible interest in the assets then available for distribution.[80] The petitioner could not establish the necessary interest by asserting that a surplus might be produced by means of recoveries from future litigation to be brought within the liquidation itself; only once recoveries were made might a shareholder properly present a petition to enable the surplus to be divided up in liquidation.[81] There is no exception merely because it is contended that the company's affairs required investigation[82] and the principle continues to be robustly applied today.[83]

This principle also applies as the starting point to establish standing to be heard on a winding-up **8.029** petition presented by someone else.[84] An established practice has developed in the Companies Court (now the companies list in the Business and Property Courts) that a contributory is not permitted to appear on a petition unless a contingent surplus can be demonstrated, to be departed from only in exceptional circumstances.[85] It also applies to standing to apply to rescind a winding-up order under r 12.59 of the Insolvency (England and Wales) Rules 2016.[86] This has been reflected in the relevant practice direction for many years, which provides that applications to rescind will only be entertained if made by (a) a creditor; (b) a contributory; or (c) by the company jointly with a creditor or with a contributory.[87]

The tangible economic interest principle was applied in the context of a petition for the **8.030** appointment of an administrator in *Re Chelmsford City Football Club (1980) Ltd*.[88] Shareholders opposed to the making of an administration order sought to be heard on the footing that they had a sufficient interest by reason that, although the company was currently insolvent, the pro-

---

78   See *PricewaterhouseCoopers v Saad Investments Co Ltd* [2014] 1 WLR 4482 and *Carter v Bailey (as foreign representatives of Sturgeon Central Asia Balanced Fund Ltd (in liq)* [2020] EWHC 123 (Ch), [2020] 1 BCLC 600.

79   (1879) 11 Ch D 36.

80   Ibid., 43.

81   Ibid.

82   *Re Othery Construction Ltd* [1966] 1 WLR 69, 74–75. A similar argument was also unsuccessful in *Re Chesterfield Catering Co Ltd* [1977] 1 Ch 373, 387.

83   *Gamlestaden Fastigheter AB v Baltic Partners Ltd* [2007] UKPC 26, [2007] Bus LR 1521, [31]–[32].

84   (1870) 5 Ch App 600.

85   *The Charit-Email Technology Partnership LLP v Vermillion International Investments Ltd* [2009] EWHC 388, [2009] BPIR 762. The case concerned a limited liability partnership rather than a company, but this makes no difference to the point in issue.

86   SI 2016/1024. All references to rules or to the Insolvency Rules 2016 are to the Insolvency (England and Wales) Rules 2016 unless it is indicated otherwise. Insolvency Rules 2016, r 12.59, formerly Insolvency Rules 1986, r 7.47. See also *Re Mid East Trading Ltd; Lehman Bros Inc v Phillips* [1997] 3 All ER 481,486f–j; the matter went to the Court of Appeal on other points, but the rescission point was not appealed: see [1998] BCC 726, 744.

87   *Practice Direction: Insolvency Proceedings* [2020] BCC 698, para 9.10.3. The wording (with very minor differences) first appears at *Practice Note (Winding Up Order: Rescission) (No 2)* [1971] 1 WLR 757.

88   [1991] BCC 133.

spective administrator had opined that it could be rescued as a going concern, which by definition would mean that the members held the necessary interest. The court refused the opposing
shareholders leave to appear on the basis that no sufficient interest had yet been established.[89]

8.031   A widely-followed modern exposition of the principle was given by Lord Millett in *Deloitte &*
Touche AG v Johnson in an appeal to the Privy Council from the Cayman Islands.[90] A former
auditor of the company in liquidation, against whom the liquidators had caused the company to
commence proceedings for negligence, applied to remove the liquidators on grounds of conflict
of interest. The application was made under the Cayman Islands equivalent to s 108 of the
Insolvency Act 1986,[91] which enables the court to remove a liquidator on 'cause shown'.[92] As
with its English equivalent,[93] the provision does not contain any express limitation or prescrip-
tion in relation to the class of persons entitled to apply under it. Lord Millett nonetheless held
that the former auditors had no standing to be heard on any conflict of interest:

> '...the court has consistently regarded the creditors (in the case of an insolvent liquidation) and the
> contributories (in the case of a solvent liquidation) as the proper persons to make the application, being
> the only persons interested in the liquidation'.[94]

8.032   As outsiders to the liquidation, the auditors could have no interest in the assets available for
distribution irrespective of the company's solvency position and, accordingly, had no standing.
Lord Millett went on to scrutinise the nature of their motive for making the application and
held that, on the particular facts of the case, not only did the auditors lack a legitimate interest,
their interest as counterparties to the negligence claims was one that was positively adverse to
the interests of the liquidation:

> The plaintiff is not merely a stranger to the liquidation; its interests are adverse to the liquidation and
> the interests of the creditors. In their Lordships' opinion, it has no legitimate interest in the identity of
> the liquidators, and is not a proper person to invoke the statutory jurisdiction of the court to remove
> the incumbent office-holders...[95]

8.033   Lord Millett's comparatively short speech in *Deloitte & Touche AG v Johnson* has been widely
applied and embodies the modern approach to the tangible economic interest principle for
those seeking to be heard in insolvency proceedings. It gives rise to a two-stage approach. At
the first stage, the party must show that they have the necessary economic interest in the estate.
In an insolvent company, this will typically and most readily be satisfied where the applicant is
a creditor. A contributory will only have the necessary interest where the company is or might
be solvent. Parties who are altogether strangers to the estate (such as the auditors in the *Deloitte*
case) will not be able to satisfy this requirement whether the company is solvent or insolvent.
Establishing this formal capacity at the first stage will not necessarily, however, be sufficient to
be heard. At the second stage, the court must be satisfied that the applicant has a 'legitimate

---

89   Ibid., 135. See also *Re Kaupthing Capital Partners II Master LP Inc (in admin)* [2010] EWHC 836, [2011] BCC 338,
       [82].
90   [1999] 1 WLR 1605.
91   Section 106(1) of the Companies Law (1995 rev.).
92   Ibid.: 'Any official liquidator may resign or be removed by the court on due cause shown; ...'; compared with s 108(2) of
       the Insolvency Act 1986: 'The court may, on cause shown, remove a liquidator and appoint another.'
93   Insolvency Act 1986, s 108(2).
94   [1999] 1 WLR 1605, 1610D–E.
95   Ibid., 1611H.

interest' in the relief being sought, which will require the court to scrutinise the real capacity in which the application is made.[96] The second stage will require a careful evaluative judgment to be made by the court. In *Brake v Lowes*, the Court of Appeal applied the Privy Council's reasoning in *Deloitte & Touche AG v Johnson* and held that, at the second stage, there is neither an absolute requirement that an applicant's real capacity must be positively adverse to the estate in order for standing to be denied, nor that the applicant has a direct financial interest in the relief sought in order for standing to be established.[97] As such, the second stage admits of a subtle and nuanced inquiry by the court into the real capacity of the applicant as a matter of substance. The cases show that it is possible for a party to satisfy the first stage by showing that they have an economic interest in the estate by virtue of being a creditor, but to be denied standing at the second stage as a consequence of acting other than in the interests of the creditors as a class.[98]

2.   Gateways to review a liquidator's conduct

Section 167(3) provides that in a compulsory liquidation: **8.034**

> The exercise by the liquidator in a winding up by the court of the powers conferred by this section is subject to the control of the court, and any creditor or contributory may apply to the court with respect to any exercise or proposed exercised of those powers.

In practice, the use of s 167(3) tends to overlap with s 168(5). Section 168(5) provides that: **8.035**

> If any person is aggrieved by an act or decision of the liquidator, that person may apply to the court; and the court may confirm, reverse or modify the act or decisions complained of, and make such order in the case as it thinks just.

The provisions now found at ss 167(3) and 168(5) were described by Plowman J in *Leon v*   **8.036**
York-O-Matic Ltd[99] as being 'somewhat similar' to each other. Robert Walker LJ remarked in *Re Buckingham International plc (No 2)* that the 'basic issue' in that case was 'the same under either provision'.[100] Where applications are made to challenge the liquidator's conduct, it is common to see both provisions relied on in the alternative.

Both provisions require an applicant to show the necessary interest in the insolvent estate,   **8.037**
despite s 167(3) apparently permitting 'any creditor or contributory' to apply and s 168(5) containing no words of limitation beyond the condition that the applicant be 'aggrieved'.[101] It is frequently the case in liquidation that there will be no shortage of persons who appear to satisfy the latter requirement, but the scope of a 'person aggrieved' has consistently been limited by the courts to avoid wasteful applications.[102]

---

96   *Nero*, [59], [73].
97   *Brake v Lowes* [2020] EWCA (Civ) 1491, [2021] PNLR 269, [83]–[84].
98   Ibid., [100]-[104]; *Walker Morris v Khalastchi* [2001] 1 BCLC 1, 9a–b.
99   [1966] 1 WLR 1450. The case concerned ss 245(3) and 246(5) of the Companies Act 1948, which were the almost identically worded predecessors to the Insolvency Act 1986, ss 167(3) and 168(5).
100 [1998] BCC 943, 959.
101 This formulation first appeared in company legislation in the Companies Act 1890 and was derived from similar words in s 20 of the Bankruptcy Act 1869.
102 *Ex parte Sidebotham* (1880) 14 Ch D 458, 465. This case was decided under s 20 of the Bankruptcy Act 1869, from which s 168(5) of the Act was derived.

8.038   The Court of Appeal considered standing to apply under s 168(5) of the Insolvency Act 1986 in *Re Edennote Ltd*.[103] The court considered that it was 'neither necessary nor desirable' to classify the extent of persons 'aggrieved', but made clear that an 'outsider to the liquidation' would not have locus standi to apply.[104] Such an 'outsider' would include a party whose only interest was that they had not been given the opportunity to make an offer to the liquidator for an asset of the company. In a subsequent judgment in the same liquidation, Lightman J spelt out that prejudice to a party as a prospective purchaser of the company's assets was irrelevant to the liquidator's decision-making.[105] The Court of Appeal applied *Re Edennote Ltd* in *Mahomed v Morris (No 2)*[106] and held that '[i]t could not have been the intention of Parliament that any outsider to the liquidation, dissatisfied with some act or decision of the liquidator, could attack that decision'.[107] In that case, the applicant was a surety asserting purported security rights by way of subrogation. The Court of Appeal held that a party asserting such rights was not a creditor in the liquidation but was instead seeking to enforce rights outside the liquidation.[108] As such, the applicant did not have a tangible economic interest in the insolvent estate.

Even where an applicant has such an interest in the estate, they may still be denied standing to apply under s 168(5) if the court is satisfied that the application is made in a different capacity. Lord Millett's approach in *Deloitte & Touche AG v Johnson* discussed above was applied to an application under s 168(5) by the Court of Appeal in *Brake v Lowes*. In that case, standing was denied to a number of applicants, despite their being unsecured creditors, because they were seeking to advance interests other than those of the unsecured creditors as a class.[109]

8.039   Peter Gibson LJ recorded in *Mahomed v Morris (No 2)* that the only case cited to the court in which a person other than a creditor or contributory had been permitted to apply under s 168(5) as a 'person…aggrieved' was *Re Hans Place Ltd*.[110] In that case, a landlord had challenged a liquidator's decision to disclaim a lease as onerous property. This was described as an 'exception' in *Mahomed v Morris (No 2)*[111] on the footing that the landlord in *Re Hans Place Ltd* had been someone 'directly affected by the exercise of the power'.[112] It is respectfully submitted that *Re Hans Place Ltd* should not be regarded as a true exception, in that the landlord's grievance concerned an interest in the capacity of creditor in relation to the rent that would have fallen due had the disclaimer not taken place. The landlord was denied that status only by the same exercise of the liquidator's discretion that he sought to challenge. As such, he was a creditor but for the same act of the liquidator of which complaint was made. Accordingly, even this instance can, and it is submitted should, be understood in conventional terms.[113]

---

103   [1996] BCC 718.
104   [1996] BCC 718, 721.
105   *Re Edennote Ltd (No 2)* [1997] 2 BCLC 89, 94i–95a.
106   [2001] BCC 233.
107   Ibid., [26].
108   Ibid., [27].
109   *Brake v Lowes* [2020] EWCA (Civ) 1491, [2021] PNLR 269, [100]–[104]. See also *Walker Morris v Khalastchi* [2001] 1 BCLC 1, 9a-b, where standing was similarly denied to a creditor where they were acting adversely to the interests of the estate.
110   [1992] BCC 737.
111   [2001] BCC 233, [24].
112   Ibid., [26].
113   See the discussion of the point by the Court of Appeal of the Eastern Caribbean Supreme Court in *Re Fairfield Sentry Ltd (in liq); ABN Amro Fund Services (Isle of Man) 24 Nominees Ltd v Krys* [2017] ECSCJ No 255 [21] of equivalent words in s 273 of the Virgin Islands Insolvency Act 2003.

Sections 167(3) and 168(5) are expressed to apply only in compulsory liquidation. The signifi- **8.040**
cance of the distinction between compulsory and voluntary liquidation is reduced by s 112. This
provides for 'any creditor or contributory' to apply 'to determine any question arising in the
winding up' or for the court to exercise 'all or any of the powers which the court might exercise
if the company were being wound up by the court'. Section 112 may be used in a voluntary
liquidation as a gateway to invite the court to exercise its powers under either s 167(3)[114] or s
168(5)[115] as if it were a compulsory liquidation. This provision has the effect of greatly reducing
the practical differences between compulsory and voluntary liquidation for the purposes of
seeking to challenge the act or decision of the liquidator, although these differences have not
been eliminated for all purposes.[116]

3.   Gateways to review an administrator's conduct

(a) Directions

Paragraph 63 of Sch B1 to the Insolvency Act 1986 provides for an administrator to apply to **8.041**
court for directions in connection with their own functions. There is no express provision for
a person other than the administrator themselves to apply. It was held in cases decided under
the pre-Enterprise Act 2002 regime that the court may nonetheless give directions to control
an administrator's acts or decisions by reason of their being an officer of the court[117] and the
position must be the same under Sch B1. In order to invoke that jurisdiction against an officer
of the court, it is necessary to satisfy the usual tangible economic interest test.[118]

There is further limited scope for directions to be sought and given under para 68 of Sch B1. **8.042**
Paragraph 68(2) provides that an administrator must comply with any directions given by the
court in connection with any aspect of his management of the company's affairs, business or
property. But para 68(3) goes on to provide that such directions may only be given where no
proposals have been approved under para 53, or the directions are consistent with any proposals
or revision approved under paras 53 or 54, or the court thinks that the directions are required in
order to reflect a change in circumstances since such approval, or required because of a misunderstanding about proposals or a revision approved under paras 53 or 54. In short, the existence
of approved proposals significantly limits what directions can be given.

Paragraph 68 does not specify who may apply under it. In *Four Private Investment Funds v* **8.043**
Lomas,[119] Blackburne J accepted that any person with a genuine and legitimate interest in the
directions sought may apply, which need not necessarily be confined to a creditor or member.[120]

---

114   *Cooper v PRG Powerhouse Ltd (in liq)* [2008] EWHC 498 (Ch), [2008] BCC 588, [9].
115   *Re Hans Place Ltd* [1992 BCC 737, 741; Walker Morris v Khalastchi [2001] 1 BCLC 1, 3f-g.
116   See *Donaldson v O'Sullivan* [2008] EWCA Civ 879, [2009] 1 WLR 924, [38]–[41]; *Kean v Lucas* [2017] EWHC 250
        (Ch), [2017] BPIR 702, [22]; Singularis Holdings Ltd v PricewaterhouseCoopers [2014] UKPC 36, [2014] 2 BCLC
        597, [25], [113].
117   *Re Mirror Group (Holdings) Ltd* [1992] BCC 972, 976G–H; *Re Atlantic Computer Systems Plc* [1992] Ch 505, 543G;
        Insolvency Act 1986, Sch B1, para 5.
118   *Brake v Lowes* [2020] EWCA Civ 1491, [2021] PNLR 10, [63]; applied to administration in *PJSC Uralkali v Rowley*
        [2020] EWHC 3442 (Ch), [386].
119   [2008] EWHC 2869 (Ch), [2009] 1 BCLC 161.
120   Ibid., [41].

(b) Unfair harm

8.044 In practice, where a party other than the administrator has grounds to challenge the act or decision of the administrator or otherwise to ask the court to direct the administrator to conduct the administration in a different way, the applicant will usually make their application under para 74 of Sch B1. This empowers the court to grant relief on the application of a creditor or member where the administrator is acting or has acted so as 'unfairly to harm', or proposes to act in a way that would 'unfairly harm', the interests of the applicant, whether alone or in common with some or all other members or creditors.[121] Relief may also be granted on the application of a creditor or member where the administrator is not performing their functions as quickly or as efficiently as reasonably practicable.[122]

8.045 An application may only be made while the company is '*in administration*', but where an application is properly made and the company subsequently goes into liquidation, the application may continue to be pursued, although the fact of the liquidation will shape the relief that may be available.[123] Paragraph 74(3)(e) allows the court to make any order it thinks appropriate on such an application and para 74(4) sets out a series of possible orders that may be made, including an order to regulate the exercise of the administrator's functions, to do or not do a specified thing, for a decision to be sought from the company's creditors, or for the administrator's appointment to cease to have effect.

8.046 It should be emphasised at the outset that para 74 is distinct from the directions gateways referred to above and the misfeasance provisions discussed below. Paragraph 74 concerns the review of an administrator's conduct, but on the particular basis of 'unfair harm'. This is not the same as misconduct[124] or negligence,[125] both of which fall under the misfeasance provisions dealt with below. Significantly, para 74(5)(a) specifically provides that 'unfair harm' within the meaning of that paragraph may arise whether or not the administrator is acting within their powers under Sch B1.

8.047 Paragraph 74 of Sch B1 is principally concerned with regulating the administration and is not a mechanism for the payment of compensation to individual creditors or members. While Norris J acknowledged in *Re Coniston (Kent) LLP (in liquidation)* that the strict wording of para 74 admitted the possibility of the payment of compensation by an administrator to a creditor who had been unfairly harmed, this was an argument that could only arise in an 'exceptional case', where the 'unfairness cannot be undone by regulating the conduct of the administration differently'.[126] Norris J declined to decide the point definitely and there does not appear to be any reported case where compensation has been ordered be paid by administrators under para 74, either to the insolvent estate or to individual creditors or members. Instead, para 74 is

---

121 Insolvency Act 1986, Sch B1, para 74(1). See *Lehman Bros Australia Ltd (in liq) v MacNamara* [2020] EWCA Civ 321, [2021] Ch 1, [70].
122 Ibid., Sch B1, para 74(2). The wording of this provision indicates that it is directed at a breach of the statutory duty in Sch B1, para 4.
123 *Re Coniston (Kent) LLP (in liq)* [2013] BCC 1, [2015] BCC 1, [68].
124 *Re Coniston Hotel (Kent) LLP (in liq)* [2015] EWCA Civ 1001, [30].
125 *Re Hat & Mitre plc (in admin)* [2020] EWHC 2649 (Ch), [180].
126 [2013] BCC 1, [2015] BCC 1, [35].

primarily a means for 'regulating the conduct of the administration itself'[127] and its 'management'.[128] This is consistent with the class-based nature of administration.[129]

Where orders under para 74 have been made, these have directed an administrator in relation to a particular aspect of their conduct. Orders made under para 74 have included a refusal to admit a proof in a sum higher than the mistaken sum embodied in a claims determination deed[130] and a refusal to assign a cause of action.[131] Paragraph 74 has been held to be wide enough to include an order to remove administrators and replace them with others.[132] Reported cases where relief has been granted, however, are markedly less common than those where it has been refused.[133] The hurdle for an applicant is a high one.   **8.048**

It is not enough simply to come within the category of creditor or member in order to be able to apply. In order to obtain relief, the applicant must have suffered 'unfair harm' in that capacity.[134] Paragraph 74 is 'directed to the protection of his [a creditor or member's] interests as such'.[135] This necessarily means that the applicant must have the usual tangible economic interest in the assets available for distribution, for otherwise they will not be able to show any 'harm' in their capacity of creditor or member. Moreover, the applicant must also be applying in the same capacity in which they raise their complaint. For instance, in *Re Zegna III Holdings Inc (in administration)*, the applicant was a creditor, but its interests as a creditor were unaffected; its real complaint was that its interests as a contractor had been treated less favourably after the date of administration than those of other contractors.[136] Similarly, in *Fraser Turner Ltd v PricewaterhouseCoopers LLP*,[137] an applicant's complaint was not made in its capacity as creditor; its grievance was that the administrators had not assisted it in its private capacity to obtain a new post-administration right to an ongoing royalty from the purchaser of the company's assets.[138]   **8.049**

---

127   Ibid., [35].
128   Ibid., [69].
129   *Re Zegna III Holdings Inc (in admin)* [2009] EWHC 2994 (Ch), [2010] BPIR 277, [20].
130   *Lehman Bros Australia Ltd v MacNamara* [2020] EWCA Civ 321, [2021] Ch 1, [2], [103]–[104].
131   *Hockin v Marsden (joint administrators of London & Westcountry Estates Ltd)* [2014] EWHC 763 (Ch), [2017] BCC 433, [49]–[53].
132   *Clydesdale Financial Services Ltd v Smailes* [2009] EWHC 1745 (Ch), [2009] BCC 810, [15]; see also *SISU Capital Fund Ltd v Tucker* [2005] EWHC 2170 (Ch), [2006] BCC 463, [88]; *Re Zegna III Holdings Inc (in admin)* [2009] EWHC 2994 (Ch), [2010] BPIR 277, [13].
133   Relief under Sch B1, para 74 was refused in *In re Kilnoore Ltd (in liq)* [2005] EWHC 1410 (Ch), [2006] Ch 489; *SISU Capital Fund Ltd v Tucker* [2005] EWHC 2170 (Ch), [2006] BCC 463; *Four Private Investment Funds v Lomas* [2008] EWHC 2869 (Ch), [2009] 1 BCLC 161; *Re Zegna III Holdings Inc (in admin)* [2009] EWHC 2994 (Ch); [2010] BPIR 277; *Re Coniston (Kent) LLP (in liq)* [2013] BCC 1, [2015] BCC 1; *In re Meem SL Ltd (in admin)* [2017] EWHC 2688 (Ch), [2018] BCC 652, [33]–[34]; *LF2 Ltd v Supperstone* [2018] EWHC 1776 (Ch) *Re Zinc Hotels (Holdings) Ltd* [2018] EWHC 1936 (Ch), [2018] BCC 968; *Re ASA Resource Group plc (in admin)* [2020] EWHC 1370 (Ch), [2020] BCC 730; *Re Hat & Mitre plc (in admin)* [2020] EWHC 2649 (Ch) [180].
134   *Hockin v Marsden (joint administrators of London & Westcountry Estates Ltd)* [2014] EWHC 763 (Ch), [2017] BCC 433, [14].
135   *Re Coniston (Kent) LLP (in liq)* [2013] BCC 1, [2015] BCC 1, [35] (undisturbed on appeal).
136   *Re Zegna III Holdings Inc (in admin); BLV Realty* [2009] EWHC 2994, [2010] BPIR 277, [24].
137   [2019] EWCA Civ 1290, [2019] PNLR 33.
138   Ibid., [77].

8.050 A person who wishes merely to purchase a claim belonging to a company in administration as an investment is not within the scope of para 74.[139] Nor is a disappointed bidder in a bidding process.[140] Where an applicant under para 74 was a member but also the putative defendant to proceedings that might be brought by the company, their interests as such were regarded as collateral to, and in direct conflict with, the interests of the members as a whole.[141]

8.051 It is insufficient simply to show 'harm'; the harm must also be 'unfair'.[142] This may or may not involve discriminatory treatment of a particular creditor[143] and differential or unequal treatment of a creditor or member will not necessarily be unfair.[144] Norris J emphasised in *Re Zegna III Holdings Inc (in administration)* that administration is a class remedy and that it might be in the interests of the creditors as a whole to terminate a particular contract with a creditor if there were sound commercial reasons relating to the interests of the creditors as a whole for doing so.[145] The concept of 'unfair harm' may also extend to something that harms the creditors as a whole,[146] for otherwise 'an idiotic decision by an administrator which affected all creditors equally' would be incapable of challenge.[147] It is submitted that, in practice, most cases under para 74 will be likely to concern less favourable treatment of a particular creditor or member; this was described as 'the paradigm case' in *Re Meem SL Ltd (in administration)*.[148]

8.052 As to the meaning of 'unfair harm' for the purposes of para 74 of Sch B1 and its relationship with an administrator's decision-making, the first instance authorities have not entirely spoken with one voice. Some judges have applied what appears to be the same deferential standard of good faith and rationality as applies to the review of decision-making by officeholders, while others (including the most recent appellate authority on the point[149]) have applied a distinctive approach derived from the specific wording of para 74. The cases on this aspect are summarised in the following paragraphs.

8.053 In *Re Zegna III Holdings Inc (in administration)*, Norris J observed that the court would not interfere under para 74 with differential treatment of creditors where it was based on a commercial judgment supported by an explanation, unless it was based on a wrong appreciation of the law.[150] In *Re Meem SL Ltd (in administration)*, it was held that for differential treatment to be unfair, an applicant needed to show that the decision could not be justified by reference to the interests of the creditors as a whole or to achieving the objective of administration. Where

---

139 *Hockin v Marsden (joint administrators of London & Westcountry Estates Ltd)* [2014] EWHC 763 (Ch), [2017] BCC 433, [14].

140 *PJSC Uralkali v Rowley* [2020] EWHC 3442 (Ch), [386].

141 *Re Hat & Mitre plc (in admin)* [2020] EWHC 2649 (Ch), [205].

142 *Four Private Investment Funds v Lomas* [2008] EWHC 2869 (Ch), [2009] 1 BCLC 161, [37]; *Hockin v Marsden (joint administrators of London & Westcountry Estates Ltd)* [2014] EWHC 763 (Ch), [2017] BCC 433, [19].

143 *Lehman Bros Australia Ltd v MacNamara* [2020] EWCA Civ 321, [2021] Ch 1, [83].

144 *Re Zegna III Holdings Inc (in admin); BLV Realty* [2009] EWHC 2994, [2010] BPIR 277, [24].

145 Ibid., [20].

146 *Hockin v Marsden (joint administrators of London & Westcountry Estates Ltd)* [2014] EWHC 763 (Ch), [2017] BCC 433, [19]-[20]; *Re Meem SL Ltd (in admin)* [2017] EWHC 2688 (Ch), [2018] BCC 652, [33]–[34].

147 *Hockin v Marsden (joint administrators of London & Westcountry Estates Ltd)* [2014] EWHC 763 (Ch), [2017] BCC 433, [17].

148 *Re Meem SL Ltd (in admin)* [2017] EWHC 2688 (Ch), [2018] BCC 652, [44].

149 *Lehman Bros Australia Ltd v MacNamara* [2020] EWCA Civ 321, [2021] Ch 1.

150 *Re Zegna III Holdings Inc (in admin); BLV Realty* [2009] EWHC 2994, [2010] BPIR 277, [22].

there was no differential treatment, the court would only interfere with the decision where it did not withstand logical analysis, which the deputy judge in *Re Meem SL Ltd (in administration)* considered 'probably means the same thing as perversity'.[151] Conversely, in *Hockin v Marsden*, the deputy judge specifically rejected a submission that the perversity test in *Edennote* applied and held that: 'Unlike ss 167, 168 and 303,[152] it lays down its own test for interference, a test of unfair harm. That is evidently not the same thing as a test of perversity…In my view, the statutory test applies without further gloss.'[153]

The subsequent comments of Vos C in the Court of Appeal *Fraser Turner Ltd v PricewaterhouseCoopers LLP* in refusing relief under para 74 appeared consistent with the perversity standard of review: **8.054**

> …there could be no unfairness sufficient to engage paragraph 74 without a suggestion that the administrators were acting otherwise than in accordance with their obligations under Schedule B1 of the Insolvency Act 1986 or an order of the court…the Administrators were, as it seems to me, acting in good faith to carry out their functions in the interests of the creditors as a whole. Accordingly, the judge was right here too to hold that any harm that might have been caused…could not have been caused 'unfairly' within the meaning of paragraph 74.[154]

Most recently, however, a different emphasis was applied by the Court of Appeal in *Lehman Bros Australia Ltd (in liquidation) v MacNamara*.[155] It is submitted that previous authorities should now be read in light of this decision, which bears two significant features. First, David Richards LJ held that even where an administrator was carrying out statutory functions in the interests of creditors as a whole, unfair harm may still be inflicted on a particular creditor.[156] Secondly, his Lordship highlighted that para 74(5) specifically provides that a claim may be made under para 74(1) whether or not the conduct in question is within the administrator's powers under Sch B1[157] and distinguished Vos C's approach in *Fraser Turner Ltd v PricewaterhouseCoopers LLP* as follows: **8.055**

> Where, as noted by the Chancellor, an administrator is acting in accordance with his *obligations* under schedule B1, there can be no question that he is causing *unfair* harm. Where, however, the administrator is exercising his discretion, but does so in a manner which unfairly harms a creditor, I see no reason in the terms of paragraph 74 or in its evident purpose why the court should not in an appropriate case grant relief.[158]

It is submitted that the distinction between 'obligations' and 'discretions' may not always be easy to draw and may introduce a degree of uncertainty in identifying the correct test in a given case. For instance, when an administrator discharges their duty to make a statement of proposals under para 49,[159] they are placed under an *obligation* to exercise a *discretion* concerning their   **8.056**

---

151   *In re Meem SL Ltd (in admin)* [2017] EWHC 2688 (Ch), [2018] BCC 652, [44].
152   Insolvency Act 1986, ss 167 and 168 are discussed in 8.034 above. Insolvency Act 1986, s 303(1) applies in bankruptcy and is similar to s 168(5) but refers to a person being 'dissatisfied' rather than 'aggrieved' by the officeholder's conduct.
153   *Hockin v Marsden (joint administrators of London & Westcountry Estates Ltd)* [2014] EWHC 763 (Ch), [2017] BCC 433, [16].
154   [2019] EWCA Civ 1290, [2019] PNLR 33, [76].
155   [2020] EWCA Civ 321, [2021] Ch 1, [70].
156   Ibid., [84].
157   Ibid., [81].
158   Ibid., [82]. Emphasis in original.
159   Insolvency Act 1986, Sch B1, para 49(1).

decision-making in relation to the statutory objective in para 3(1). Paragraph 49(2) provides that:

> A statement under sub-paragraph (1) *must*, in particular…where applicable, explain why the administrator *thinks* that the objective mentioned in paragraph 3(1)(a) or (b) cannot be achieved.[160] (emphasis added)

8.057   The dividing line between the obligatory ('must') and discretionary ('thinks') elements of that single process may not be clear-cut in practice. Moreover, there may be a degree of tension between the conclusion that discretionary aspects of an administrator's office are subject to an 'objective standard of fairness' for the purposes of para 74[161] and the well-established position that the good faith and rationality standard of review generally applies to such discretionary decisions.[162]

8.058   It is likely, however, that cases where the court is prepared to impugn an administrator's conduct on the application of the objective standard of fairness in circumstances where that conduct would be secure under the subjective standard of good faith and rationality will tend to be rare in practice. Moreover, para 74(6)(c) provides that an order may not be made under para 74 if it would impede or prevent the implementation of proposals approved under paras 53 or 54 of Sch B1 more than 28 days before the day on which the application for relief under para 74 was made. Accordingly, dissentient creditors and members have only a short window to challenge the administrator's proposals where these have been approved; after that, the administrator will be free to act in accordance with those approved proposals without challenge on grounds of 'unfairness'.

4.   Misfeasance

8.059   Provisions exist in both liquidation[163] and administration[164] to permit certain categories of applicant to pursue in their own name causes of action belonging to the company and seek redress on behalf of the company for wrongs done to it. These provisions have a long history, having been derived from s 165 of the Companies Act 1862.

(a) Applicants and respondents

8.060   Section 212 applies where a company is being wound up. An application may be made under s 212 by the official receiver, or the liquidator, or 'any creditor or contributory'. Such an application may be made against an officer or former officer, or a person who has acted as a liquidator or administrative receiver of the company, or a person who is or has been concerned or has taken part in the promotion, formation or management of the company. It applies where it appears that the respondent has misapplied or retained or become accountable for any money or other property of the company, or been guilty of any misfeasance or breach of any fiduciary or other duty in relation to the company.

---

160   Ibid., Sch B1, para 49(2).
161   *Lehman Bros Australia Ltd v MacNamara* [2020] EWCA Civ 321, [2021] Ch 1, [84].
162   *Re Kilnoore Ltd (in liq); Unidare plc v Cohen*, [71]; *Davey v Money* [2018] EWHC 766, [2018] Bus LR 1903, [255]; *Zinc Hotels (Holdings) Ltd (in admin)* [2018] EWHC 1936, [2018] BCC 968.
163   Insolvency Act 1986, s 212.
164   Ibid., Sch B1, para 75.

Administrators were formerly among the category of persons that may be respondents to an **8.061** application brought under s 212, but on the introduction of Sch B1 to the Insolvency Act 1986,[165] references to administrators were removed from s 212 and replaced with a new provision in para 75 of Sch B1. The class of possible applicants under para 75 is the same as under s 212, save that it includes an administrator of the company.[166] Possible respondents under para 75 are limited to persons who are or have been administrators or purported administrators of the company.[167]

Although the present discussion concerns applications made against officeholders, it should be **8.062** noted that, in practice, s 212 is frequently used by liquidators to pursue delinquent directors for wrongdoing that took place prior to liquidation. By contrast, directors are not within the class of possible respondents under para 75 of Sch B1, which means that an administrator may not similarly pursue directors during an administration. Lloyd LJ suggested in *Irwin v Lynch*[168] that the reason for this may be that an administrator is not normally in office for long so that, unless the company emerges from administration as a viable undertaking, there will be a liquidator in place who can bring a claim under s 212. While an administrator may cause the company itself to commence a misfeasance claim in its own name against defaulting directors,[169] it is more usual for a company to enter liquidation if such claims are available to be brought.

Historically, the tangible economic interest principle applied to statutory misfeasance claims **8.063** brought under what is now s 212. The principle was applied with full rigour in *Cavendish Bentinck v Thomas Fenn*,[170] in which the House of Lords dismissed the appeal of a fully paid-up shareholder and with it his summons commenced under s 165 of the Companies Act 1862.[171] Lord Macnaghten held that 'As a contributory it is utterly impossible, upon the facts as stated by himself, that he could ever derive any benefit from this litigation.'[172] The position has now been modified by the terms of s 212. Section 212(5) expressly provides that, while a contributory requires the leave of the court to make an application, a contributory's power to make an application 'is exercisable notwithstanding that he will not benefit from any order that the court may make on the application', thereby expressly disapplying the tangible economic interest principle in the case of a contributory under s 212. No similar qualified disapplication appears in the analogue provision for administration in para 75 of Sch B1, which appears to continue to apply with full force to that provision.

For instance, in *Re Coniston Hotel (Kent) LLP (in liquidation)*,[173] Morgan J had to consider an **8.064** application to dismiss summarily an application brought by two members of a company formerly in administration under, inter alia, para 75 of Sch B1. In acceding to the application and

---

165   From 15 September 2003 on the introduction of the Enterprise Act 2002.
166   Insolvency Act 1986, Sch B1, para 75(2)(b).
167   Ibid., Sch B1, para 75(1).
168   [2010] EWCA Civ 1153, [2011] 1 WLR 1364, [4].
169   [2010] EWCA Civ 1153, [2011] 1 WLR 1364, [10].
170   (1887) 7 App Cass 652.
171   The summons in that case was against the company's director, rather than its liquidator, but the point of principle (i.e., standing to apply) is unaffected.
172   (1887) 7 App Cass 652, 672. Lord Herschell (at 664–665) and Lord Watson (at 666–667) also expressed similar views on the point.
173   [2014] EWHC 1100 (Ch).

dismissing the claim, the court accepted a submission that applicants under para 75, whether creditors or members, must show that they have sufficient interest in the relief sought.[174] Somewhat ironically, Morgan J cited in support of this view *Cavendish Bentinck v Thomas Fenn*, which concerned liquidation but had by that point been disapplied (subject to obtaining leave of the court) by s 212(5) in relation to applications by contributories in liquidation. The Court of Appeal upheld the decision and drew attention to the fact that whatever happened with the members' claim, the value in the company would inevitably break in the secured creditor's interest, with nothing for unsecured creditors or members.[175] This critical difference in approach between standing to apply under s 212 and para 75 indicates the overarching force of the tangible economic interest principle and shows that when it is not to apply the legislature says so.

(b) Types of conduct giving rise to claims against officeholders

8.065   The officeholder duties whose breach may give rise to a claim under these provisions were discussed in Chapter 7. Breaches of those duties are often discussed under the umbrella term 'misfeasance', although this is a word without a clear-cut definition.[176] The current versions of s 212 and para 75 are widely drafted and have been held to include negligence,[177] which had been outside the scope of their predecessors.[178]

8.066   It is important to distinguish the type of conduct that is subject to review under the misfeasance provisions from other kinds of applications to review officeholder conduct. The types of conduct falling within s 212 and para 75 are all by definition wrongful, although cases may vary significantly in gravity. As such, these applications are necessarily concerned with conduct falling outside an officeholder's powers, not a review of the exercise of those powers.[179] As Norris J put it in *Re Coniston Hotel (Kent) LLP (in liquidation)*, 'Paragraph 74 is about management and para 75 is about misconduct.'[180] Both provisions provide in some way for administrators to be accountable.

8.067   It is, however, not unusual to find applications in relation to officeholder conduct to be made under both types of provision, presumably on the basis that if the conduct is not outside the officeholder's powers and accordingly misfeasant, it is nonetheless appropriate for the court to review it. This is particularly the case in administration, where the same facts will frequently be put on the basis both of para 74 (unfair harm) and para 75 (misfeasance).[181]

8.068   Misfeasance claims brought against officeholders may include allegations of inadvertent negligence or, less commonly, breach of fiduciary duty and, still less commonly, may extend to

---

174   Ibid., [52].
175   [2015] EWCA Civ 1001, [65].
176   *Re B Johnson & Co (Builders) Ltd* [1955] Ch 634, 648. Lord Evershed MR's observations about the scope of 'misfeasance' concerned Companies Act 1948, s 333, which was a predecessor to Insolvency Act 1986, s 212.
177   *Re D'Jan of London Ltd* [1993] BCC 646.
178   *Re Kingston Cotton Co (No 2)* [1896] 2 Ch 279, 283.
179   *Lehman Bros Australia Ltd v MacNamara* [2020] EWCA Civ 321, [2021] Ch 1, [81].
180   [2013] EWHC 93 (Ch), [2015] BCC 1, [69].
181   See, e.g.: *Zinc Hotels (Holdings) Ltd (in admin)* [2018] EWHC 1936, [2018] BCC 968, [2]; *Fraser Turner Ltd v PricewaterhouseCoopers LLP* [2019] EWCA Civ 1290, [2019] PNLR 33; *Taylor Pearson (Construction) Ltd (in admin)* [2020] EWHC 2933 (Ch), [3].

serious wrongdoing. Examples from the reported cases include a claim by a creditor under s 212 in *Re Centralcrest Engineering Ltd*[182] alleging that a liquidator had carelessly allowed a company to trade in liquidation without sanction in circumstances where she should have realised its assets quickly after her appointment. The court in that case required the liquidator to pay compensation for the full trading loss during the relevant period. A similar claim was brought under s 212 in *Parkinson Engineering Services plc (in liquidation) v Swan* by a liquidator against the former administrators of a company alleging that they had negligently traded a company in administration and should pay compensation for the trading losses.[183]

Findings of negligence and breach of fiduciary duty were made in *Top Brands Ltd v Sharma* **8.069** on an application under s 212 by creditors against a former liquidator, arising from the former liquidator's failure adequately to investigate the company's affairs before making payment away of company money.[184] Proceedings were brought under para 75 by a contributory in *Re Rhino Enterprises Properties Ltd* against former administrators, alleging that a lack of independence from the qualifying floating charge-holder ('QFCH') that appointed them led them to breach their duty to the company in failing to investigate and pursue claims against that QFCH.[185] In *Re AMF International Ltd*,[186] a former liquidator who had treated the liquidation as solvent and paid away the company's money to a contributory before dealing with its liabilities was ordered to pay compensation on an application under s 212 made by a subsequently appointed liquidator jointly with a creditor.[187] A common subject-matter of misfeasance applications in recent years has been in relation to alleged undersales of company assets by administrators, commenced either by subsequently appointed liquidators (as in *Brewer (joint liquidator of ARY Digital UK Ltd) v Iqbal*[188] and *Re One Blackfriars Ltd (in liquidation); Hyde v Nygate*[189]), or by contributories (as in *Davey v Money*[190] and *Zinc Hotels (Holdings) Ltd (in administration)*[191]).

Where a claim is made out, both s 212 and para 75 grant the court jurisdiction to order the **8.070** respondent to repay, restore or account for money or property or pay compensation to the company, together with interest.[192] The reference to 'repay, restore or account' indicates that an order under these provisions may include proprietary relief, as would be the case where the company itself pursued a breach of fiduciary duty.

---

182   [2000] BCC 727. Sanction to trade a company in liquidation was at that time required under Insolvency Act 1986, s 167.

183   [2009] EWCA Civ 1366, [2010] PNLR 17, [2]–[3]. The proceedings concerned the pre-EA 2002 version of Insolvency Act 1986, s 212, which included administrators among the class of respondent. Today such an application would be made under Sch B1, para 75.

184   *Top Brands Ltd v Sharma* [2014] EWHC 2753 (Ch), [2016] BCC 1, [172]–[175], upheld by the Court of Appeal [2015] EWCA Civ 1140, [2017] 1 All ER 854.

185   [2020] EWHC 2370 (Ch), [2021] BCC 18, [15]. These proceedings against the former administrators were subsequently summarily struck out: [2021] EWHC 2533 (Ch).

186   [1996] BCC 335.

187   [1996] BCC 335, 337A–B, 340A–B.

188   [2019] EWHC 182 (Ch), [2019] BCC 746.

189   [2021] EWHC 684 (Ch).

190   [2018] EWHC 766 (Ch), [2018] Bus LR 1903.

191   [2018] EWHC 1936, [2018] BCC 968.

192   Insolvency Act 1986, s 212(3); Sch B1, para 75(4).

(c) Nature of the causes of action

8.071   Neither s 212 nor para 75 confer any substantive new rights on the applicant. They are simply a procedural gateway to enable a member of the named class of applicant to pursue in their own name claims vested in the company for the benefit of that company. In *Re Eurocruit Europe Ltd*,[193] Blackburne J held that:

> In each case…the claimant is in substance the company; the relief which is granted under s 212(3) is for the repayment, restoration or accounting (to the company) of the money or property of the company or for a contribution to be made 'to the company's assets by way of compensation' for the wrong in question. This is so whether the claim is brought by the company or by the liquidator or, for that matter, by a creditor or contributory…there is only a single cause of action, that of the company. All that s 212 does is give to the liquidator, if he wishes, the right to bring the claim in his own name.[194]

8.072   Relief may be granted on an application under s 212 or para 75 only in favour of the company, not the particular applicant. As mentioned above, Norris J left open the possibility in *Re Coniston (Kent) LLP (in liquidation)* that it was arguable that in an exceptional case compensation might be ordered to be paid under para 74 directly by an administrator to a creditor.[195] By contrast, there is no such possibility under s 212 or para 75: all relief is directed to restoring the insolvent estate for the benefit of all those interested in it.[196] Norris J explained in the same case:

> The court cannot order the wrongdoing administrator[197] to pay equitable compensation for breach of fiduciary duty or damages for breach of some other duty to an individual creditor or to a contributory. If there is a deficiency in the insolvency then the payment goes for the benefit of the creditors as a class: and if the company proves solvent in administration then the benefit goes to the contributories as a class.[198]

8.073   The significant consequence of this is that, despite the standing vested in creditors and contributories to apply for relief under s 212 and para 75, it does not imply any additional duty on the part of officeholders to such categories of applicant. Save in exceptional circumstances, an officeholder in a collective insolvency process does not owe any direct duty to individual creditors or members of the company. A question that arises from this position is how the officeholder is to be made accountable to those with the relevant interest in the company's assets available for distribution to them, without the imposition of any direct duty. The answer is that the process is an indirect one, with the rights of those interested in the company's assets generally continuing to be mediated through the company, as they were prior to the commencement of the process. In a case brought under s 212 against a misfeasant liquidator, His Honour Judge Barker QC (sitting as a High Court judge) explained that: 'Creditors, who have an indirect or

---

193   [2007] EWHC 1433 (Ch), [2007] BCC 916.
194   *Re Eurocruit Europe Ltd (in liq)* [2007] EWHC 1433 (Ch), [2007] BCC 916, [24]. Applied by the Court of Appeal in *Parkinson Engineering Services plc (in liq) v Swan* [2009] EWCA Civ 1366, [2010] 1 BCLC 163, [12]. See also *In re Oasis Merchandising Services Ltd* [1998] Ch 170, 181F–G; *Re Continental Assurance Company of London plc* [2001] BPIR 733, [393]; *Cohen v Selby* [2002] BCC 82, [20]; *Wightman v Bennett* [2005] BPIR 473 [12]; *Re Mama Milla Ltd* [2016] BCC 1, [38].
195   [2013] EWHC 93 (Ch), [2015] BCC 1, [35].
196   Ibid., [69].
197   The position will be identical where the respondent is a wrongdoing liquidator.
198   [2013] EWHC 93 (Ch), [2015] BCC 1, [40].

derived interest in the proper exercise by a liquidator of his/her duties, are authorised to hold a liquidator to account for the benefit of the company.'[199]

Any 'benefit' accruing to the company following such a holding to account will ultimately devolve on those interested in the company, to the extent that there is sufficient for distribution to the interest class of which they are a member.   **8.074**

(d) Permission to bring misfeasance proceedings

Misfeasance proceedings may be brought using the procedural gateways in s 212 and para 75 even after the officeholder has received their statutory release from liability.[200] In order to bring such proceedings after release, however, the permission of the court is required.[201] There are two principal criteria for the grant of permission: first, whether a reasonably meritorious cause of action has been shown, and, secondly, whether giving permission is reasonably likely to result in benefit to the estate. The test is the same whether sought under s 212[202] or para 75.[203] Other factors of relevance are delay and whether or not a reasonable litigant would be justified in bringing the litigation.[204] In cases where permission is granted, a claim may be pursued using the gateway in s 212 in circumstances where an officeholder would have had a complete defence had an identical cause of action been pursued in the name of the company.[205]   **8.075**

The need for permission has been held to perform two distinct functions, depending upon the identity of the applicant under s 212 or para 75. In cases where the applicant is a party other than another officeholder (i.e., a creditor or contributory), it provides a filter to prevent discharged officeholders from being pursued by vexatious claims. This principle is derived from the bankruptcy case *Brown v Beat*,[206] but has been held to apply to misfeasance claims against discharged officeholders.[207] Where the applicant is a subsequently appointed officeholder, the filter has been held to be required because the former officeholder no longer has the assets of the estate in his or her possession with which to indemnify himself or herself in respect of unmeritorious claims.[208]   **8.076**

(e) Exculpation from liability

An officeholder is entitled to invoke s 1157 of the Companies Act 2006 where 'proceedings for negligence, default, breach of duty or breach of trust' are brought against them in their capacity   **8.077**

---

199   *Top Brands Ltd v Sharma* [2014] EWHC 2753 (Ch), [2016] BCC 1, [37], upheld by the Court of Appeal [2015] EWCA Civ 1140 [2017] 1 All ER 854.

200   Insolvency Act 1986, s 173 (voluntary liquidation), s 174 (compulsory liquidation) or Sch B1, para 98 (administration).

201   Ibid., s 212(4) (in the case of claims against former liquidators) and Sch B1, para 75(6) (in the case of claims against former administrators).

202   *Parkinson Engineering Services plc (in liq) v Swan* [2009] EWCA Civ 1366, [2010] 1 BCLC 163, [34].

203   *Katz v Oldham* [2016] BPIR 83; *Re Rhino Enterprises Properties Ltd* [2020] EWHC 2370 (Ch), [2021] BCC 18; *Re One Blackfriars Limited (in liq)* [2021] EWHC 684 (Ch).

204   *Re One Blackfriars Limited (in liq)* [2021] EWHC 684 (Ch), [26].

205   *Parkinson Engineering Services plc (in liq) v Swan* [2009] EWCA Civ 1366, [2010] 1 BCLC 163, [41]; *Irwin v Lynch* [2010] EWCA Civ 1153, [2011] 1 WLR 1364.

206   [2002] BPIR 421.

207   *Katz v Oldham* [2016] BPIR 83, [6].

208   *Re Hellas Telecommunications (Luxembourg) II SCA* [2011] EWHC 3176 (Ch) [96]; *Re One Blackfriars Limited (in liq)* [2021] EWHC 684 (Ch), [22]–[23].

as an officer of the company. Section 1157 permits the court to excuse an officer of a company from liability, either wholly or in part, even where it appears to the court that they may be liable. The section is more commonly relevant to proceedings against company directors but insolvency officeholders have also been held to be within its scope.[209] Two conditions must be satisfied for liability to be excused: first, the officeholder must have acted honestly, and, secondly, they must have acted reasonably. Even where both conditions are satisfied, the court retains a discretion whether or not to grant exculpation having regard to all the circumstances of the case. As the cases concerning directors show, the requirement of honesty is usually satisfied, but the further necessary condition of reasonableness often prevents the section from engaging. It tends to be difficult to show that any breach of duty was done 'reasonably'. For instance, in *Top Brands Ltd v Sharma*,[210] the respondent liquidator sought exculpation in proceedings brought under s 212 on the ground that she had taken legal advice. However, no proper advice was taken, because the instructions the liquidator had given to her solicitor were flawed. The solicitor's 'advice was geared to his instructions and [the liquidator's] instructions were woefully incorrect and inadequate'.[211] Accordingly, the liquidator could not show that she acted reasonably for the purposes of s 1157.

(f)   Personal claims by creditors, shareholders or others

8.078   The reference to 'personal claims' in the subheading above is intended to denote claims brought against insolvency officeholders on the claimant's own behalf, i.e., not claims brought on behalf of the company for the benefit of the company's insolvent estate as a whole of the kind discussed above. Such claims are sometimes attempted by creditors, shareholders or others who wish to challenge, for their own benefit, the officeholder's conduct of the insolvency. To succeed, they must establish direct liability on the part of the officeholder to the particular claimant, which is seldom possible because the duties of officeholders in collective corporate insolvency proceedings are as a general rule owed to the company, not its individual stakeholders.

8.079   Direct liability on the part of an officeholder leading to relief for an individual creditor arises only in exceptional circumstances. *Pulsford v Devenish*[212] was a rare case where a negligent former liquidator was fixed with direct liability to a creditor. A claim was brought by a creditor against the liquidator after the company had been dissolved. It appears to have been a clear case of negligence, where the liquidator simply failed to pay the claimant creditor, despite having paid others of the same class. Farwell J identified that during the currency of a liquidation, i.e., prior to the company's dissolution, such a creditor could have brought an action against the liquidator under the predecessors to s 212,[213] which would have provided for recoveries to have been made for the benefit of the estate as a whole. As the company had been dissolved, that avenue of redress was now closed. Farwell J declined to leave the creditor without a remedy

---

209   *Re Home Treat Ltd* [1991] BCC 165, 169E–170E. This case was decided under the similarly worded s 727 of the Companies Act 1985.

210   [2014] EWHC 2753 (Ch), [2016] BCC 1.

211   Ibid., [30]–[34], [183] undisturbed on appeal.

212   [1903] 2 Ch 625, 627. This was a voluntary liquidation where a new company had covenanted to pay all debts and liabilities of the liquidating company.

213   Ibid., 632–633. Farwell J made reference to s 138 of the Companies Act 1862 and s 10 of the Companies Act 1890, the latter being the direct predecessor to s 212 of the Insolvency Act 1986, derived from s 165 of the Companies Act 1862.

and held that where the statutory remedy had ceased to exist because the company had been dissolved, the liquidator's duty was directly actionable by the creditors.[214]

Subsequent authorities indicate that the grant of a direct remedy to an aggrieved creditor as in *Pulsford v Devenish* is to be closely confined in two ways. First, it is restricted as a matter of principle to cases where the company in question has been dissolved.[215] Secondly, the case has been interpreted in recent times as further confined by the personal nature of the loss suffered by the creditor, which arose from the liquidator's failure to pay a distribution to that creditor in particular, rather than in relation to the liquidator's conduct of the estate as a whole. In *Re HIH Casualty and General Insurance Company Ltd,*[216] David Richards J (as he then was) explained that *Pulsford v Devenish* had been a case where the aggrieved creditor's claim was a personal one arising from the creditor's right to the proper administration and distribution of assets in accordance with the statutory scheme,[217] which was to be contrasted with claims 'as regards management, disposal of assets and so on', which were 'class claims',[218] and in relation to which neither an administrator nor a liquidator owed a duty of care to individual creditors.[219]   **8.080**

The approach in *Re HIH Casualty and General Insurance Company Ltd* was developed in *Fraser Turner Ltd v PricewaterhouseCoopers LLP.*[220] At first instance, the deputy judge held that the mere fact that the company had been dissolved, and that therefore no statutory misfeasance action could be advanced under para 75 of Sch B1, did not of itself lead to the conclusion that the claimant creditor's claims could be brought.[221] A distinction was required between, first, a breach of duty owed to the company such as a failure to obtain a proper price for the assets, and, secondly, a breach of duty concerned with the distribution of the assets to creditors. Whether the company had been dissolved or not, the first kind of claim would remain a company claim and therefore not actionable by individual creditors. If the company had been dissolved, the claim would have been bona vacantia, rather than transformed into one available to a creditor. To bring a claim in the first category, a dissolved company would first have to be restored to liquidation.[222] Only the latter type of claim, concerned with personal loss to a creditor, fell 'within the special class of breach actually considered in *Pulsford v Devenish*'.[223]   **8.081**

The detailed review of this area by the Court of Appeal in *Oldham v Kyrris* concerned a claim of the kind described as a 'class claim'[224] in *Re HIH Casualty and General Insurance Company*   **8.082**

---

214   Ibid., 633.
215   *Oldham v Kyrris*, [2004] BCC 111, [154]–[163].
216   [2005] EWHC 2125. There was no discussion of the *Pulsford v Devenish* category of case when the first instance decision in *Re HIH Casualty and General Insurance Ltd* was upheld in the Court of Appeal [2006] EWCA Civ 732, [2007] 1 All ER 177 or reversed (on an unrelated point) in the House of Lords [2008] UKHL 21, [2008] 1 WLR 852.
217   Ibid., [115]–[116].
218   Ibid., [118]–[119].
219   Ibid., [115]–[121]. See also *Lomax Leisure Ltd (in liq) v Miller* [2007] EWHC 2508, [2008] BCC 686, [34].
220   [2018] EWHC 1743 upheld by the Court of Appeal, [2019] EWCA Civ 1290, [2019] PNLR 33.
221   Ibid., [69].
222   That course was not available at the time of *Pulsford v Devenish*, a point discussed in *James Smith & Sons (Norwood) Ltd v Goodman* [1936] Ch 216, 236. This was a rare case where *Pulsford v Devenish* was applied. Like *Pulsford v Devenish* itself, it concerned a company that had been dissolved. It was a factually extreme case, where a voluntary liquidation had been part of a 'deliberate attempt by a solvent company to get rid of onerous leases without making provision for the landlords.
223   [2018] EWHC 1743, [66], [69].
224   [2005] EWHC 2125, [118]–[119].

Ltd and a 'cause of action that would be part of the insolvent estate'[225] in *Fraser Turner Ltd v PricewaterhouseCoopers LLP*. It was alleged in *Oldham v Kyrris* that the administrators of a limited partnership[226] had owed an unsecured creditor a duty of care in negligence and what was described as a 'fiduciary duty to ensure that [the creditor's] interests were protected'.[227] It was expressly contended that these duties were owed in addition to the availability of the statutory misfeasance gateway in s 212.[228] Moreover, the applicants sought damages for their own benefit and not by way of a contribution to the assets of the liquidation.[229]

8.083   At first instance, the court held that unless there was a direct contract between the administrator and an individual creditor,[230] or some negligence giving rise to special damage on the part of a creditor that differentiated them from other creditors,[231] there was no general right for individual creditors to sue administrators for their own benefit outside the statutory gateway providing for collective relief. The judge struck out that part of the claim.[232] In upholding that decision, the Court of Appeal agreed that, absent some special relationship, an administrator appointed under the Insolvency Act 1986 does not owe a general common law duty of care or a fiduciary duty to unsecured creditors.[233] It is submitted that Jonathan Parker LJ's use of the word 'exclusively' in the following passage should be noted:

> Given the nature and scope of an administrator's powers and duties, I can for my part see no basis for concluding that an administrator owes a duty of care to creditors in circumstances where a director would not owe such a duty to shareholders. In each case the relevant duties are, absent special circumstances, owed exclusively to the company.[234]

8.084   The Court of Appeal held that it would apply the same approach to determining the existence of any direct duty on the part of an administrator towards individual creditors as it would to the existence of such a duty by company directors towards shareholders.[235] There is nothing in the office itself that gives rise to such a duty. The mere fact that the officeholder is aware of the creditor's circumstances is insufficient to create the necessary special relationship,[236] as

---

225   [2018] EWHC 1743, [66], [69].
226   The case concerned the administration and subsequent liquidation of a partnership, not a company, but this makes no relevant difference to the point of principle discussed here.
227   [2004] BCC 111, [6].
228   At the time, the statutory gateway for bringing a misfeasance claim against an administrator or former administrator was found in s 212 of the Insolvency Act 1986. Since the coming into force of the Enterprise Act 2002 on 15 September 2003 the relevant gateway has been found at Sch B1, para 75 and is no longer included in s 212.
229   [2004] BCC 111, [78].
230   Such as in *A & J Fabrications (Batley) Ltd v Grant Thornton* [1999] BCC 807: see *Oldham v Kyrris* [2004] BCC 111, [82]–[83].
231   Such as in *Pulsford v Devenish* [1903] 2 Ch 625 and *James Smith & Sons (Norwood) Ltd v Goodman* [1936] Ch 216: see *Oldham v Kyrris* [2004] BCC 111, [82]–[83].
232   Ibid., [87].
233   Ibid., [141]–[143].
234   Ibid., [146].
235   Ibid., [143]–[146]. For examples of that approach in the company director context, see *Williams v Natural Life Health Foods Ltd* [1998] 1 WLR 830; *Peskin v Anderson* [2001] BCC 874; and *Sharp v Blank* [2015] EWHC 3220, [2017] BCC 187.
236   *Charalambous v B&C Associates* [2009] EWHC 2601 (Ch), [2013] BCC 491, [22].

is the mere fact that the party will suffer loss.[237] Something more, showing an assumption of responsibility, is required.[238]

Oldham v Kyrris was an administration case. It was applied by the Privy Council in the context **8.085** of liquidation[239] in *Hague v Nam Tai Electronics*.[240] In the latter case a creditor issued proceedings against the company's liquidator in its own name and not under the applicable statutory gateway providing for collective relief in the liquidation.[241] The Privy Council held that the proceedings as constituted were misconceived and disclosed no cause of action vested in the creditor, because the liquidator did not owe any duty to each creditor individually.[242] Instead, the appropriate remedy would have been the commencement of proceedings under the equivalent of s 212.[243]

Lord Scott accepted the liquidator's submission that the breaches of duty alleged in the cred- **8.086** itor's statement of claim were not breaches of duties owed to individual creditors, but rather a duty owed to the company in liquidation. His Lordship went on, however, to observe that, 'It is well arguable that the duties owed by a liquidator in an insolvent liquidation are owed also to the creditors as a class.'[244] It is submitted that in the case of a demonstrably and categorically insolvent company of the kind before the Privy Council in *Hague v Nam Tai Electronics*, this is a distinction without a difference, in that for all practical purposes the interests of such a company are to be equated, as a matter of substance, with the interests of the creditors.[245] In such a case there is no other class with any interest in the assets available for distribution. To that extent, it is submitted that the concept of owing an additional duty to the only class with an economic interest in a company's assets adds no practical content to a duty owed to the company.

There are good reasons underlying the default position that officeholders owe no direct duty **8.087** to individual creditors, shareholders or other parties. Where a company is insolvent, there is an inherent conflict between the interests of any individual creditor and the creditors as a class: any individual creditor's interest is in realising the maximum value possible on their claim, whereas the class interest is in the total assets being swelled to ensure the highest possible pari passu distribution for the creditors as a whole. This inherent conflict was explained by the Court of Appeal in *Fraser Turner Ltd v PricewaterhouseCoopers LLP*.[246] In that case, a lessee of

---

237 Ibid., [19].
238 *Fraser Turner Ltd v PricewaterhouseCoopers LLP* [2019] EWCA Civ 1290, [2019] PNLR 33, [71]; *PJSC Uralkali v Rowley* [2020] EWHC 3442 (Ch), [324], [355]–[360].
239 This was an insolvent liquidation under the BVI Companies Act. It is clear that the position would be identical under the Insolvency Act 1986 in similar circumstances.
240 [2008] UKPC 13, [2008] BCC 295.
241 BVI Companies Act, s 191, which was to the same effect as Insolvency Act 1986, s 212.
242 [2008] UKPC 13, [2008] BCC 295, [13].
243 Ibid., [15].
244 Ibid., [13]. The point was expressed in similarly cautious terms in the Supreme Court in the Scottish appeal *MacDonald v Cranbroe Estates Ltd* [2019] UKSC 57, [2020] BCC 294. Having cited *Hague v Nam Tai Electronics Inc* and *Oldham v Kyrris* [2004] BCC 111, Lord Reed JSC stated at [38] 'A liquidator is under a fiduciary duty to the company, and possibly its creditors as a class, to exercise the professional care and skill of an insolvency practitioner in realising the assets of an insolvent company…'.
245 *BTI 2014 LLC v Sequana SA* [2019] EWCA Civ 112, [2019] 2 All ER 784, [220]–[222].
246 [2019] EWCA Civ 1290, [2019] PNLR 33.

a mine in Africa and its parent company became insolvent. The claimant company had acted as a consultant to the insolvent companies and had been receiving a royalty from the mine under a royalty deed. The same IPs were appointed both as receivers of the lessee company and as administrators of the parent, following which they sold the business of the lessee to a buyer who was unaware of, and not bound by, any obligation to pay a royalty to the claimant. Having proved as a creditor for the future royalties that would not now be paid by reason of the insolvency, the claimant contended that it had been led to believe that the administrators would do everything necessary to draw the royalty deed to the attention of any purchaser and ensure that the purchaser would agree to take on responsibility for the ongoing royalty.[247] The claimant accepted that in order to succeed on the breach of duty claims, it had to show, first, a special relationship between it and the administrators, and, secondly, the existence of special circumstances. It said that the first requirement was satisfied by assurances given by the administrators in relation to the royalty deed, and the second by the special damage said to have been caused to the claimant in particular, as distinct from the creditors as a whole, arising from its loss of rights under the royalty deed.[248]

8.088 Summary judgment was sought by the administrators, on the basis that they owed no direct duty to the claimant and were simply not at liberty to do anything to improve the lot of one unsecured creditor. At first instance, the deputy judge pointed out that to have acted in the way that the claimant submitted the administrators should have acted would reasonably have been expected to be positively against the interests of the remaining creditors. The following passage illustrates the incompatibility between the existence of a direct duty on the part of an officeholder towards individual members of a class and the class interest as a whole:

> …it would have been highly surprising if any such assumption of responsibility or special relationship did arise given that the interests of the Claimant in this context were potentially adverse to those of the remaining creditors and would potentially have caused significant difficulties for the administration. The wish of the Claimant, that any purchaser of the assets…should take on responsibility for the Royalty, was likely to result in a reduction in the consideration realised on sale and thereby to cause prejudice to other creditors.[249]

8.089 As for the discussions with the administrators that the claimant argued gave rise to a reasonable belief on its part that the administrators would try to secure a royalty from any purchaser, Vos C held on appeal:

> All that happened here was what happens in hundreds of administrations every year. A creditor bought its particular problem to the attention of the administrator, who listened politely and said he would look into it. No promises were made, nor are any alleged. All that is alleged is that [the claimant's director] believed that the Administrators would do as he had asked. If he did so believe … he was, I am afraid to say, commercially naïve. It was the duty of the Administrators … to achieve the best realisation of its assets for the benefit of all the creditors. It would not have been open to them to prefer the interests of one creditor over the others….[250]

---

247 Ibid., [12].
248 Ibid., [39].
249 [2018] EWHC 1743, [64]; referred to with obvious approval by the Court of Appeal at [2019] EWCA Civ 1290, [2019] PNLR 33, [41].
250 [2019] EWCA Civ 1290, [2019] PNLR 33, [72].

Parties who are not even creditors or shareholders are still more remote from any direct duty on **8.090** the part of an officeholder. An unsuccessful bidder for an insolvent company's assets brought a claim against the company's former administrators in *PJSC Uralkali v Rowley*,[251] based on an allegation that the former administrators had acted in breach of a direct duty of care owed to the bidder. The court applied *Fraser Turner Ltd v PricewaterhouseCoopers LLP* and held that, as agents of the company, administrators did not owe any duty of care to particular creditors simply by virtue of their office or as a consequence of knowing that those creditors might be adversely affected by their actions. Miles J observed that the 'position must be a fortiori where the putative claimant is not even a creditor of the company'.[252]

No special circumstances giving rise to a duty of care to the individual bidder were found **8.091** in *PJSC Uralkali v Rowley*. A bidding process was 'an entirely routine function'[253] for an administrator to run, during which the administrator might make 'countless statements to an array of different parties'.[254] In communicating matters to other bidders and the company's stakeholders, the administrator knew that all such parties were interested in the outcome of the process and each stood in varying ways to be adversely affected by his decisions. Accordingly, if an individual duty to the clamant existed, then such a duty would also be owed to 'a broad and uncontrolled class of potential claimants'.[255] In dismissing the claim, Miles J demonstrated the unworkability of such duties. As in *Fraser Turner Ltd v PricewaterhouseCoopers LLP*, the duties would be owed to parties with individual interests that conflicted with the collective interests of the administration and the court should be very slow to impose a duty that might cut across or subvert the statutory purpose of administration.[256] Miles J concluded:

> The task of administrators is demanding and exacting enough without requiring them to have to look over their shoulders for personal claims by bidders. I consider that the imposition of a personal duty of care on the administrators on facts such as the present would be inimical to the single-minded duty placed on administrators to act in the interests of the company's creditors. One can never say never, and there may be exceptional cases where administrators will be found to have taken on a personal responsibility to third parties. But there is nothing in the present situation to justify a personal duty of care.[257]

C. REMOVAL AND REPLACEMENT OF THE OFFICEHOLDER

1. Introduction

The identity of the officeholder is a frequent source of dispute between stakeholders with **8.092** competing interests in insolvent companies. Such disputes often raise arguments over conflicts of interest or allegations of a lack of independence on the part of the officeholder and are the source for a number of the authorities on these issues. Once again, the collective interests of

---

251 [2020] EWHC 3442 (Ch).
252 Ibid., [355].
253 Ibid., [356].
254 Ibid., [361].
255 Ibid., [378].
256 Ibid., [379].
257 Ibid., [387].

the estate as a whole, not the individual interests of stakeholders, are to the fore in the court's approach.

2.   Out-of-court removal or replacement

(a) Out-of-court removal or replacement of liquidators

8.093   A liquidator may be removed from office by a decision of the members in the case of a members' voluntary liquidation ('MVL'),[258] or the company's creditors made by a qualifying decision procedure in the case of CVL and compulsory liquidation.[259] In the case of CVL, where the liquidator was appointed by the court under s 108, then a decision procedure may be instigated only if the liquidator thinks fit, the court so directs, or it is requested by one-half or more in value of the company's creditors.[260] Otherwise, the threshold for instigating a decision procedure in CVL is the usual one of 25 per cent in value of the company's creditors, excluding those who are connected with the company.[261] The position for instigating a qualifying decision procedure is less clear in the case of compulsory liquidation and, on the face of the rules,[262] it appears that in many cases an application to court for a direction that such a procedure be instigated will be required.[263]

(b) Out-of-court removal or replacement of administrators

8.094   Detailed machinery dealing with the replacement or substitution of an administrator is contained in paras 87–99 of Sch B1. In the case of replacement, if the appointment was made by the court, then the court will make an appointment.[264] Where the appointment was made out of court, then the same party that made the initial appointment may make the replacement.[265] In the case of appointment by a QFCH under para 14, the QFCH alone makes the decision.[266] If the appointment was made by the company or the directors under para 22, the consent of any QFCH is required for such replacement.[267]

8.095   In the case of substitution, where the administrator has been appointed by a QFCH under para 14, the holder of a prior QFC may apply to the court for substitution.[268] Where the appointment has been made by the company or directors under para 22 and there is no QFCH, then the creditors may substitute a different administrator by a qualifying decision procedure.[269]

---

258   Insolvency Act 1986, s 171(2)(a), (3).
259   Ibid., s 171(2)(b), (3A) (CVL), 172(2), (3).
260   Ibid., s 171(3A).
261   Insolvency Rules 2016, r 15.18(4).
262   Section 172(3) provides for a qualifying decision procedure to be instigated by not less than one-quarter in value of the creditors only in limited circumstances and there is no equivalent to r 15.18(4) in the Insolvency Rules 2016 for compulsory liquidation.
263   Provision for an application to court to be made for a qualifying decision procedure to be instigated is included in the case of both CVL (r 6.27(1)) and compulsory liquidation (r 7.65(1)) in the Insolvency Rules 2016.
264   Insolvency Act 1986, Sch B1, para 91.
265   Ibid., Sch B1, paras 92–94.
266   Ibid., Sch B1, para 92.
267   Ibid., Sch B1, paras 93(2), 94(2).
268   Ibid., Sch B1, para 96.
269   Ibid., Sch B1, para 97.

Accordingly, governance rights in filling a vacancy or making a substitution in administration **8.096** follow the same hierarchy as applies throughout administration: first, any QFCH (and if there is more than one QFCH, then taking precedence in chronological order of the creation of the QFCs); secondly, the general body of creditors (subject to the consent of any QFCH); and, thirdly, the company or its directors.[270] Responsibility to decide on the replacement falls on the party responsible for the appointment in the first place, subject to the court deciding to make a contrary order.[271]

(c) Restraint of out-of-court removal

The court may grant an order restraining a creditors' meeting from being convened if removal **8.097** would be against the interests of the estate as a whole, even where an officeholder is under a mandatory statutory duty to requisition one.[272] In *Re Barings plc (No 6)*,[273] a company in compulsory liquidation was in the process of bringing a £1 billion claim against its former auditors for negligence. About a month before the trial of that action was listed to commence, a creditor served on the liquidators a requisition notice under s 168(2) requiring them to convene a meeting of creditors for the purpose of replacing them. The liquidators applied to court for an order directing them not to comply with the requisition. Sir Andrew Morritt VC noted that it was common ground between the parties that, although s 168(2) imposed a duty on the liquidator, the court had jurisdiction to override that duty, citing the bankruptcy cases *Re Mansel, ex parte Sayer*[274] and *Re Burn, ex parte Dawson*.[275] The court held that in deciding such an application, the appropriate questions for the court were whether the meeting 'will be conducive to both the proper operation of the process of liquidation and to justice as between all those interested in the liquidation'.[276] Granting the application to restrain the meeting, the court held that neither limb of this twofold test justifying a meeting was satisfied: there was an obvious conflict of interest between the different classes of creditor and there were justified concerns that the creditor that had requisitioned for the liquidator's replacement was acting only in its own interests and not those of the creditors as a whole.[277] As such, both the proper operation of the process of liquidation and justice as between all those interested in the assets required a direction that no meeting be held.[278]

The existence of the court's jurisdiction to direct that the liquidators need not requisition **8.098** a meeting for their own removal was conclusively determined by Patten J in *Carman v The Cronos Group SA*.[279] Patten J observed that s 168(2) imposed a duty on a liquidator to summon meetings requisitioned by creditors, but imposed no specific sanction if the liquidator declined to do so. The judge held that the duty fell to be regulated by the rest of s 168, which gave

---

270 Ibid., Sch B1, paras 91–94.
271 Ibid., Sch B1, paras 93(2)(b), 94(2)(b), 95.
272 This jurisdiction is likely to extend to the requisitioning of a qualifying decision procedure.
273 [2001] 2 BCLC 159.
274 (1887) 19 QBD 679.
275 [1932] 1 Ch 247.
276 [2001] 2 BCLC 159, [47].
277 Ibid., [52].
278 Ibid., [53].
279 [2006] EWHC 1390 (Ch). The question of jurisdiction had been common ground in *Re Barings plc (No 6)*.

a liquidator the right to apply for directions and such directions could include a direction that the meeting should not be held, under s 168(3).[280]

8.099 *Re Barings plc (No 6)* was applied in the context of CVL in *Fielding v Seery*.[281] A creditor against whom the company in liquidation had significant claims applied for the liquidator's removal and the court appointment of another liquidator 'independent of both sides'.[282] The court refused to order the liquidator's removal and further directed the liquidator not to hold a creditors' meeting for that purpose. The court held that although the majority vote of the creditors should normally prevail, creditors holding the majority vote did not have an absolute right to choose the liquidator.[283] A liquidator should not be the choice of a person against whom the company had hostile or conflicting claims[284] or whose conduct in relation to the affairs of the company was under investigation through the liquidator.[285] By contrast, it was not an objection to a liquidator that he was the choice of a person concerned to pursue the claims of the company through the liquidator.[286]

8.100 Such applications are not always successful. The court refused to restrain a creditors' meeting to remove voluntary liquidators in *Autobrokers Ltd v Dymond*.[287] The liquidators applied under s 112 for an order directing them not to call a meeting that had been validly requisitioned to consider a resolution for their removal. Removal of the liquidators was sought by certain creditors concerned over the level of fees charged and other aspects of the conduct of the liquidation. The liquidators contended that a creditor seeking to challenge fees should make that challenge under the relevant machinery in the rules, where such a challenge fell to be funded by the applicant creditor, rather than by seeking the appointment of a new liquidator, whose investigation into the fees issue would be at the expense of the estate as a whole. The court rejected that argument on the ground that whether to use the funds in the estate or funds to be externally provided was a decision that the creditors themselves were competent to take, acting in their own interests as they saw them, acting by a majority.[288]

8.101 It appears that the critical distinction between the position in *Fielding v Seery* (where a meeting was restrained) and *Autobrokers Ltd v Dymond* (where majoritarian decision-making prevailed) was the absence from the latter case of any evidence of motive on the part of the majority creditors that was adverse to the class interest of the creditors or the insolvent estate as a whole.[289] The considerations in *Autobrokers Ltd v Dymond* may have been different, it is submitted, had there been a significant minority creditor interest before the court objecting on reasoned grounds, and by reference to the interests of the estate as a whole, to the replacement of the liquidators. As discussed further below, authority indicates that officeholders themselves are

---

280 Ibid., [23]–[25].
281 [2004] BCC 315.
282 Ibid., [1], [29].
283 Ibid., [33].
284 Ibid., [33] citing *Re City & County Investment Co* (1877) 25 WR 342 and *Deloitte & Touche AG v Johnson* [1999] 1 WLR 1605.
285 Ibid., [33] citing *Re Charterland Goldfields* (1909) 26 TLR 132.
286 Ibid.
287 [2015] EWHC 2691 (Admin), [2017] BCC 291.
288 Ibid.
289 This point was acknowledged by Judge Cooke at [2015] EWHC 2691 (Admin), [2017] BCC 291, [17].

generally expected to take a neutral line where an argument relates to whether or not they remain in office and it may have been significant that the judgment contains no reference to any expressions of support for the liquidators' position from creditors.[290]

3.   Resignation of liquidators and administrators

Appointment as an officeholder is not something to be entered into lightly. A liquidator or an administrator may only resign their appointment under the following limited circumstances: **8.102**

*   on grounds of ill health;
*   because of the intention to cease to practise as an IP;
*   because the further discharge of their duties is prevented or made impractical by a conflict of interest or a change of personal circumstances.[291]

In addition to the circumstances set out above, an administrator may, with the permission   **8.103** of the court, resign on other grounds.[292] In the case of liquidation, an additional ground for resignation may arise where two or more liquidators are acting jointly and it is the opinion of both or all of them that it is no longer expedient that there should continue to be that number of liquidators.[293]

A person who ceases to be qualified to act as an IP vacates office as liquidator automatically at   **8.104** once on ceasing to be qualified, but retains a residual capacity to apply under s 108 for another IP to be appointed in their place.[294] An administrator also vacates office automatically on ceasing to be qualified as an IP without any need for an application[295] and is required to give written notice to the party that appointed them.[296]

In the case of liquidation, before resigning, the liquidator must give notice to the members (in   **8.105** the case of MVL)[297] or the creditors (in the case of CVL and compulsory liquidation).[298] In the case of CVL and compulsory liquidation, the notice must invite the creditors by a decision procedure, or by deemed consent procedure, to consider whether a replacement liquidator

---

290   The court also declined to exercise the jurisdiction to restrain the holding of a validly requisitioned meeting to remove CVL liquidators in *Kean v Lucas (as liquidator of J&R Builders (Norwich) Ltd* [2017] EWHC 250 (Ch), [2017] BCC 311. The court held that there was no requirement on a creditor to provide any reason for wishing to requisition a removal meeting and creditors were entitled to such a meeting in most circumstances, save where an abuse could be demonstrated to the court's satisfaction, [27]–[28].
291   Insolvency Rules 2016, rr 3.62(1) (administration); 5.6(1) (MVL); 6.25(1) (CVL); 7.61(1) (compulsory liquidation). Resignation by administrators on grounds of conflict of interest under r 3.62(1)(c)(i) was addressed in *Re Ve Vegas Interactive Ltd (in admin)* [2018] EWHC 186 (Ch), [2019] BPIR 438. On the particular facts of that case, which are discussed further below, removal was ordered instead of permitting the administrators to resign [16] (Registrar Jones).
292   Ibid., r 3.62(2).
293   Ibid., rr 5.6(1)(d) (MVL); 6.25(1)(d) (CVL); and 7.61(1)(d) (compulsory).
294   *Re A J Adams (Builders) Ltd*, [1991] BCC 62, [65]–[66] (Warren J).
295   Insolvency Act 1986, Sch B1, para 89(1); *Re Stella Metals Ltd* [1997] BCC 626.
296   Ibid., Sch B1, para 89(2).
297   Insolvency Rules 2016, r 5.6.
298   Ibid., rr 6.25, 7.61.

should be appointed[299] and may suggest the name of a replacement liquidator.[300] The decision date must be not more than five business days before the date on which the liquidator intends to give notice of resignation to the registrar of companies (in the case of CVL)[301] or to the court (in the case of compulsory liquidation).[302]

8.106   In the case of administration, at least five business days' notice of an intention to resign or apply to the court for permission to resign must be delivered by an administrator to, among others, the company's creditors.[303] Where the appointment was made by a QFCH under para 14 of Sch B1, or by the company or the directors under para 22 of Sch B1, then the appointor must receive notice of any intention to resign.[304] Resignation is then effected by delivering notice under para 87 of Sch B1 to the person who made the appointment. A copy of that notice must be delivered to the registrar of companies and other prescribed persons.[305] The ability to appoint a replacement administrator is set out in paras 90–95 of Sch B1 and follows a similar structure (including the hierarchy of governance rights) to that which applies to an initial appointment.[306]

8.107   As a matter of professional conduct, an IP is required to 'end' an appointment if threats to compliance with the fundamental principles of ethics for IPs[307] in the Code of Ethics cannot be reduced to an acceptable level.[308] The Code of Ethics is discussed further later in this chapter.

4.   Removal and replacement by the court

(a) Standing to apply to remove

8.108   The tangible economic interest principle discussed earlier in this chapter applies where an order for the removal or replacement of an officeholder is sought from the court. In *Re Corbenstoke Ltd (No 2)*, the court held that a shareholder did not have standing to apply to remove a liquidator on the ground that 'the court should not be troubled … by persons not having any real interest'.[309] Even where the necessary interest is present, the court will still scrutinise the applicant's motives and the real capacity in which removal is sought. This point is discussed further below.

(b) Officeholder neutrality on questions of appointment

8.109   The authorities indicate that, as a general rule, officeholders are expected to remain neutral before the court on the merits of any dispute over whether or not that IP should be appointed, or remain appointed, as the officeholder of any particular company. On an application to

---

299   Ibid., rr 6.25(2), 7.61(2). This requirement does not apply where one or more jointly appointed liquidators remains in office.
300   Ibid., rr 6.25(4) (CVL), 7.61(4) (compulsory).
301   Ibid., r 6.25(6); Insolvency Act 1986, s 171(5).
302   Ibid., r 7.63(6); Insolvency Act 1986, s 172(6).
303   Ibid., r 3.62.
304   Ibid., r 3.62(4).
305   Ibid., r 3.63.
306   See 7.033.
307   Code of Ethics, 2100.
308   Ibid., R 2116.1.
309   (1989) 5 BCC 767, 768. This case was applied by Lord Millett in *Deloitte & Touche AG v Johnson* [1999] 1 WLR 1605 discussed earlier in this chapter.

remove liquidators under s 108 in *Re Core VCT plc (in liquidation)*,[310] the Court of Appeal indicated that the role of the incumbent liquidators should be confined to providing information to the court,[311] save where the grounds of an application reflected on the liquidators' competence or integrity or suggested that their conduct required investigation. This approach appears to apply to any proceedings concerned with the identity of the officeholder. For instance, in *Re Roselmar Properties Ltd*[312] and *In re Lubin, Rosen and Associates Ltd*,[313] incumbent voluntary liquidators were criticised for opposing petitions for compulsory winding up. Similarly, in *Re Ariadne Capital*[314] the same approach was taken to an administrator who took a partisan position before the court over whether or not he should be appointed liquidator. In such cases, the incumbent officeholder's personal interest in remaining in office is potentially in conflict with the interests of the estate as a whole or, put another way, their position renders them unable to assess the issue of whether or not they remain in office disinterestedly.

(c)   Initial appointment compared with applications for removal

It appears that the court's approach to disputes over the choice of officeholder at the commencement of an insolvency process, compared with applications to remove or replace an officeholder who has been in place for some time, are in principle the same. For instance, in *Med-Gourmet Restaurant Ltd v Ostuni Investment Ltd*,[315] Lewison J (as he then was) applied without qualification principles derived from *Fielding v Seery*,[316] which was a case concerning the removal of a liquidator who had been in office for some time, to a contested initial appointment of administrators.   **8.110**

While the approach is the same in principle, however, it should be emphasised that, once an officeholder has been in place for some time, persuading a court to remove and replace that officeholder will tend to give rise to different or wider considerations compared with a contested initial appointment. Certain features that weigh in the scales in deciding whether an incumbent officeholder should be removed are less likely to exist on initial appointment. This may present a higher hurdle for the party seeking removal.   **8.111**

For instance, once an officeholder has been in office for a period and incurred costs, it will be more difficult to justify another officeholder starting from scratch and potentially duplicating some or all of those costs. The possible impact on the officeholder's professional standing if the court orders removal may also become a relevant factor where removal is sought,[317] which will obviously not arise on a dispute about initial appointment where there is no incumbent officeholder capable of being affected in that way. Accordingly, a party whose merits are such that their preferred candidate might well have succeeded in achieving appointment by the court at the outset in a straightforward bilateral competition with another candidate will not necessarily   **8.112**

---

310   [2020] EWCA Civ 1207, [2021] BCC 46.
311   Ibid., [40].
312   (1986) 2 BCC 99, 157.
313   [1975] 1 WLR 122.
314   [2018] Lexis Citation 545, [7]–[9].
315   [2010] EWHC 2832 (Ch), [2013] BCC 47, [18].
316   [2004] BCC 315.
317   *Re Edennote* [1996] 2 BCLC 389, 398f.

succeed with the same grounds in a later application for removal and replacement against an established incumbent.

(d) Statutory gateways for removal in liquidation

8.113   There are multiple statutory gateways for removal by the court in liquidation. Section 108(2) applies to voluntary winding up and provides that 'The court may, on cause shown, remove a liquidator and appoint another.' Mr Justice Etherton observed in *Re Buildlead Ltd (No 2)*[318] that these words 'have appeared in substantially the same form in company legislation for over 140 years'.[319] Section 108 does not apply directly to compulsory liquidation but r 7.65(2) as well as past case law indicates that the same criteria as that stated in s 108 apply and thus there is no distinction in approach between the two different types of liquidation.

8.114   In addition to this, ss 171(2) and 172(2) grant the court an apparently unfettered power to remove a liquidator from office in voluntary and compulsory winding up respectively.

(e) Statutory gateways for removal in administration

8.115   The primary statutory gateway for court removal of an administrator is para 88 of Sch B1, which provides simply that: 'The court may by order remove an administrator from office.'

8.116   An administrator may also be removed by the court under para 74(3) of Sch B1. As discussed earlier in this chapter, para 74 enables a creditor or member of a company in administration to apply to court claiming that unfair harm has been or will be caused to their interests by the administrator. On such an application, para 74(3) permits the court to make any order it thinks appropriate. Paragraph 74(4) sets out examples of orders that may be made, including that the appointment of an administrator shall cease to have effect.[320] There is no express reference in para 74 to the appointment of a replacement administrator, but the court held in *Clydesdale Financial Services Ltd v Smailes*[321] that the court's powers under para 74(3) of Sch B1 extend to the ability to remove an administrator and appoint a replacement, although the breadth of para 88 means that it is likely to be unnecessary to rely on para 74 for such a step.[322]

(f) The court's approach to removal and replacement

8.117   The requirement in s 108 that there be 'cause shown' for the removal of a liquidator has been applied by case law to the other statutory gateways for officeholder removal. Despite the absence of any words of limitation in either s 171(2) or s 172(2), Nourse LJ held in *Re Edennote Ltd*[323] that the difference in language between s 108(2) and s 172(2) was 'immaterial' and that 'it is not easy to think of any circumstances in which the court would remove a liquidator without

---

318   [2004] EWHC 2443 (Ch), [2006] 1 BCLC 9.

319   Ibid., [155].

320   Insolvency Act 1986, Sch B1, para 74(4)(d).

321   [2009] EWHC 1745 (Ch), [15].

322   Ibid. Warren J referred to the possible use of para 74 as a means of causing the appointment of an administrator to cease to have effect in *SISU Capital Fund Ltd v Tucker* [2005] EWHC 2170 (Ch), [2006] BCC 463, [88]. It was common ground before Norris J in *Re Zegna III Holdings Inc (in admin)* [2009] EWHC 2994 (Ch), [2010] BPIR 277, [13] that para 74(3) enabled the court to remove an administrator and appoint another.

323   [1996] 2 BCLC 389, 397h–i.

cause being shown'.[324] In *SISU Capital Ltd v Tucker*,[325] Warren J found Nourse LJ's approach in *Re Edennote Ltd* to be applicable both to the test for removal of a voluntary liquidator under s 171(1) and to the removal of administrators under para 74 and para 88 of Sch B1.[326] In short, it appears that the 'cause shown' test is common both to liquidation (corporate and voluntary) and administration and applies regardless of which statutory gateway is employed.

The courts have repeatedly made clear that the circumstances that will justify removal for 'cause shown' cannot be prescribed and should not be fettered. At all times, the overriding consideration is the proper interests of the insolvency process. This point has been repeatedly made in the case law since Victorian times. The following summary provided by Bowen LJ in *In re Adam Eyton Ltd*[327] remains authoritative: **8.118**

> ...the due cause is to be measured by reference to the real, substantial, honest interests of the liquidation, and to the purpose for which the liquidator is appointed. Of course, fair play to the liquidator himself is not to be left out of sight, but the measure of due cause is the substantial and real interest of the liquidation.[328]

Bowen LJ's encapsulation of 'due cause shewn' as being 'by reference to the real, substantial, honest interests of the liquidation, and the purpose for which the liquidator is appointed' continues to be described as 'the touchstone for appraisal' of the test.[329] **8.119**

Neuberger J gave the following summary of the court's approach in *AMP Enterprises Ltd v Hoffman*: **8.120**

> As a matter of ordinary principle and statutory interpretation, that seems to me to suggest as follows: (a) the court has a discretion whether or not to remove and replace the liquidator, (b) it will do so on good grounds, (c) it is up to the person seeking the order to establish those grounds, (d) whether good grounds are established will depend on the particular case, (e) in general it is inappropriate to lay down what facts will and what facts will not constitute sufficient grounds.[330]

An evaluative judgment ('a difficult balancing exercise'[331]) will be undertaken by the court. As such, it is impossible to be definitive in any discussion of removal and replacement. Allegations of misconduct are neither a necessary nor sufficient condition for removal. The following principles may, however, be identified. **8.121**

(i) Matters requiring investigation will usually lead to removal

Allegations of misconduct or negligence on the part of the officeholder that have sufficient foundation to require further investigation will usually lead to their removal from office.[332] The **8.122**

---

324 For a consideration of the law on removal for 'cause shown' see Andrew Keay, *McPherson and Keay's The Law of Company Liquidation* (5th ed, Sweet & Maxwell, 2021), 529–536.
325 [2005] EWHC 2170 (Ch), [2006] BCC 463.
326 Ibid., [87]–[88].
327 (1887) 36 ChD 299. This was an application to remove a liquidator in a compulsory liquidation 'on due cause shown' under a previous statutory formulation of the test in s 93 of the Companies Act 1862.
328 Ibid., 306.
329 *Re Buildlead Ltd (No 2)* [2004] EWHC 2443 (Ch), [2006] 1 BCLC 9, [168].
330 [2002] EWHC 1899 (Ch), [2003] 1 BCLC 319, [21].
331 Ibid., [23].
332 *Re John Moore Gold Mining Company* (1879) 12 ChD 325, 328–329.

basis for this is that all officeholders are required to be independent of any particular interest and an incumbent officeholder cannot investigate themselves in a disinterested way.

8.123   When addressing the requirements for showing cause for removal on grounds of misconduct, Jacob J explained in *Shepheard v Lamey* that: 'You do not have to prove everything in sight; you do not have to prove, for example, misfeasance as such; you do not have to show more than that there may well be a case of misfeasance or, indeed, incompetence.'[333] This observation should not, however, be read in isolation from the further judicial observations under the next heading.

(ii)   Unsubstantiated allegations of misconduct will not be sufficient

8.124   Officeholders will not be removed merely on the basis of allegations of misconduct. For example, in *Re Zinc Hotels (Holdings) Ltd*,[334] a series of allegations were advanced against a range of parties, including the administrators.[335] Henry Carr J considered the evidence and decided that there was not 'even arguably' a breach of duty on the part of the administrators.[336] Similarly, in *Memon v Cork*,[337] removal of liquidators was refused despite the articulation of serious allegations against them of misconduct, including the suggestion that they had fabricated documents.[338] ICC Judge Barber observed that here 'The Court should be slow to permit such tactics to trigger a removal.'[339]

8.125   As with all cases of removal, the court will undertake an assessment of the merits on the basis of the evidence before it. It is likely that the applicable test will be akin to the familiar 'triable issue' test for resisting a winding-up petition or summary judgment. In *Clydesdale Financial Services Ltd v Smailes*,[340] the court ordered the removal of administrators where the evidence raised 'a serious issue for investigation' and 'a seriously arguable issue'.[341] That case concerned a pre-pack administration, where the self-investigation difficulty is particularly to the fore by reason of the structural conflicts of interest inherent in that process. The issues arising from pre-packs are addressed separately below.

8.126   When a removal application is made on the basis of misconduct, officeholders are accountable for how they have administered the company's affairs but as we discussed above, any allegations will need to be supported by evidence of substance.

(iii)   Removal may be justified even without any misconduct or personal unfitness

8.127   There is no requirement that there be an allegation of actual positive wrongdoing for removal to be justified. In *Re Keypak Homecare Ltd*,[342] Millett J rejected a submission that the case law indicated that 'very special circumstances' must exist before the power to remove a liquidator

---

333   [2001] BPIR 939, 940.
334   [2018] EWHC 1936 (Ch), [2018] BCC 968.
335   Ibid., [21], [92], [121], [129].
336   Ibid., [134]–[146].
337   [2018] EWHC 594.
338   Ibid., [28].
339   Ibid., [146].
340   [2009] EWHC 1745 (Ch), [2009] BCC 810.
341   Ibid., [26].
342   (1987) 3 BCC 558.

should be exercised where no personal misconduct or unfitness could be shown. Millett J held that:

> On the contrary, the words of the statute are very wide and it would be dangerous and wrong for a court to seek to limit or define the kind of cause which is required. Circumstances vary widely, and it may be appropriate to remove a liquidator even though nothing can be said against him, either personally or in his conduct of the particular liquidation.[343]

Having undertaken a survey of the case law up to that point, Etherton J applied this approach in *Re Buildlead Ltd (No 2)*[344] and held that: **8.128**

> ... it is quite clear from the entire line of authority stretching back to 1867 that, in appropriate circumstances, there may be good cause to remove a liquidator, notwithstanding the failure of the applicant to prove misfeasance as such, and even though no reasonable criticism can be made of his conduct.[345]

(iv) Removal is not taken lightly: there must be good grounds for it

Notwithstanding the position under the previous subheading, the court will not lightly remove a properly appointed officeholder. In *Re Edennote Ltd*,[346] the Court of Appeal agreed that an officeholder should not remain in office if the creditors no longer have confidence in his ability to realise the assets of the company to their best advantage and to pursue claims with due diligence. The court emphasised, however, that such a loss of confidence must be reasonable and that the court will have regard to the impact of an order for the removal on that IP's professional standing and reputation.[347] **8.129**

An officeholder should not be removed simply because they have 'fallen short of ideal'.[348] In *AMP Enterprises Ltd v Hoffman*, Neuberger J made the realistic observation that, once a liquidation has been conducted for some time, there can almost always be criticism, in the sense that things can be identified that could have been done better, or done earlier. Neuberger J considered that: **8.130**

> It is all too easy for an insolvency practitioner, who has not been involved in a particular liquidation, to say, with the benefit of the wisdom of hindsight, how he could have done better. It would mean that any liquidator who was appointed, in circumstances where there was support for another possible liquidator, would spend much of his time looking over his shoulder, and there would be a risk of the court being flooded with applications of this sort.[349]

Neuberger J's observations in this respect are consistent with the court's general reluctance to second-guess decision making by officeholders and tendency to leave them to get on with it, without the need to seek the protection of directions from the court before acting.[350] **8.131**

---

343   Ibid., 564.
344   [2004] EWHC 2443 (Ch), [2006] 1 BCLC 9.
345   Ibid., [167].
346   [1996] 2 BCLC 389.
347   Ibid., 398f (Nourse LJ). See also *Hobbs v Gibson* [2010] EWHC 3676 (Ch), [47].
348   *AMP Enterprises Ltd v Hoffman* [2002] EWHC 1899 (Ch), [2002] BCC 996, 1001H.
349   Ibid., 1001H–1002B.
350   See *Re T & D Industries plc* [2000] 1 WLR 646, 657F–G.

(v) Officeholder's complacency or failure to act quickly may justify removal

8.132 Where there is reason to think that a particular officeholder has not acted with appropriate speed or diligence, this may justify their removal. *Re Keypak Homecare Ltd*[351] was an early case under the Insolvency Act 1986 in which the facts indicated that an unattractive phoenix arrangement had been effected, about which the liquidator appeared unconcerned. In what appears to have been a robust policy decision designed to signal a profound change with the unregulated pre-1986 insolvency culture,[352] Millett J ordered the liquidator's removal on the basis that the creditors were perfectly reasonable in their view that the liquidator had 'adopted a relaxed and complacent attitude' and appeared 'not likely to pursue the directors with anything like sufficient vigour'.[353]

(vi) Creditors' views are not decisive

8.133 In deciding whether or not to order removal, the court will consider, but may not be persuaded by, the wishes of the majority of creditors.[354] Simply counting the value on either side will not be conclusive. Regard will be had to the creditors' motives in adopting whatever stance they have taken and whether or not it is consistent with the class interest of the creditors as a whole. Less weight, or no weight at all, may be attributed to creditors who are motivated by extraneous considerations. In *Re Zegna III Holdings Inc (in administration)*, a creditor's standing to apply for, among other things, the removal of administrators was discounted in circumstances where the real capacity in which it applied was as a contractor seeking to be restored as development manager of a project being undertaken by the company in administration, rather than in its capacity as creditor.[355]

5. Conflicts of interest and removal

8.134 The existence of a potential conflict of interest will not of itself require the removal of the officeholder. Conflicts of interest are so widespread in insolvent situations that the approach of the courts has necessarily been pragmatic. Where there is a potential or actual conflict of interest, it neither precludes an initial appointment nor requires the removal of a serving officeholder. Instead, the relevant inquiry is into whether or not the conflict can be managed appropriately. The court's approach in this respect reflects IPs' professional regulatory obligations, which are considered separately later in this chapter.

8.135 Conflicts of interest as they affect fiduciaries, including officeholders, are heavily fact contingent and almost infinitely various, but at the level of general principle there are two kinds. First, there is the conflict of duty and duty. A common example of this kind of conflict in the insolvency context may arise in the insolvencies of corporate groups, where an officeholder holds appointments over two or more companies with claims arising between them, perhaps in both directions. Here the officeholder may find himself both advancing and adjudicating claims in the simultaneous capacities of creditor and debtor.

---

351 (1987) 3 BCC 558.
352 Peter Millett QC (as he then was) had been a member of the Review Committee that produced the Cork Report leading to the Insolvency Act 1986.
353 (1987) 3 BCC 558, 564.
354 *Cash Generator Ltd v Fortune* [2018] EWHC 674 (Ch), [2018] 4 All ER 325, [29].
355 [2009] EWHC 2994 (Ch), [2010] BPIR 277, [24].

Secondly, there is the conflict of duty and interest. In its simplest form, this kind of conflict will **8.136**
arise where a fiduciary has a personal interest in an estate (such as being a counterparty to some
transaction with it or a debtor or creditor of it in their personal capacity) that is in conflict with
their duty to act independently of all such interests. Plainly an IP cannot be appointed over an
estate where they hold such an interest.[356]

In the insolvency context, examples of the duty and interest conflict are more likely to arise **8.137**
where allegations of substance are made about the officeholders' conduct of the estate. As noted
above, where the conduct requires investigation, then it will be impossible for the officeholder
to investigate themselves with the necessary disinterest and objectivity.

More complex is the situation where it is considered that the officeholder or proposed office- **8.138**
holder is too close to a particular stakeholder, usually the one that introduced them to the
appointment. This may give rise to a conflict of duty and duty, with the nominated IP moving
from a situation where pre-appointment advice has been provided to the directors or the secured
creditors (as the case may be) to acting as officeholder of the company. But situations of this
kind may also be presented as a conflict of duty and interest, in that it may be suggested that the
IP's relationship with the stakeholder will incentivise the IP, once appointed as officeholder, to
advance the interests of that stakeholder in particular, rather than the interests of the insolvent
estate as a whole, perhaps with a view to obtaining further work for themselves or their firm.

(a)   Group insolvencies

There will frequently be potential or actual conflicts of interest between associated insolvent **8.139**
companies, particularly where there have been mutual dealings between them giving rise to
inter-company proofs of debt. If it were necessary to eliminate all actual or potential conflicts
from appointments across associated companies, group insolvencies could become unwieldy,
duplicative and expensive. The firm policy of the courts in such situations has for many years[357]
been that the same individuals, or at least members of the same firms, are not precluded from
taking multiple appointments in group insolvencies. Usually, the benefits of such appointments
will outweigh the disadvantages and, generally speaking, the policy is that conflicts should be
managed as and when they emerge. The following passage from the judgment of Hoffmann J
in *Re Arrows Ltd*,[358] where IPs from the same firm had been appointed provisional liquidators
over a company as well as receivers of 80 associated companies, reflects the orthodox position
on the authorities:

> ...it is very difficult to see how the necessary process of investigation could have been efficiently con-
> ducted if there were separate firms representing all, or worse still some of the receivership companies,
> and another firm representing the provisional liquidators. It is by no means uncommon in the case of
> the insolvency of a substantial group of companies for cross-claims and conflicts of interest to arise
> between companies within the same group. That does not usually deflect the court from appointing

---

356   For an extreme example, see *Re Corbenstoke Ltd (No 2)* (1989) 5 BCC 767, 772, where the same individual was simultaneously liquidator and director of the company in liquidation, as well as creditor (in his capacity as trustee in bankruptcy
of the principal shareholder) and a debtor of the company.
357   For early examples see *Re Western Life Assurance Society ex parte Willett* (1870) LR 5 Ch App 396, 399; *Re British Nation
Life Assurance Association* (1872) LR 14 Eq 492, 498–499.
358   [1992] BCC 121.

a single firm of insolvency practitioners in the first instance to deal with the whole insolvency of the group, leaving the question of potential conflict of interests to be dealt with if and when it arises.[359]

8.140 In *SISU Capital Fund Ltd v Tucker*,[360] Warren J summarised the case law up to that point and concluded that even an actually existing conflict would not necessarily preclude a group appointment. Warren J held that if the correct approach as set out in *Re Arrows Ltd* was to allow the same officeholders to act where there was a potential conflict, but to ensure that the conflict was managed if and when it became an actual conflict, then there was no reason why an actually existing conflict should necessarily preclude appointment, if it was capable of being effectively managed.[361] His Lordship set out the following summary of the appropriate principles of conflict management:

    (a)   Licensed insolvency practitioners are professional men who are well accustomed to dealing with conflicts.

    (b)   In general it is in the interests of creditors, at least in the first instance, to appoint a single officeholder and any conflicts are usually best left to be managed if and when that becomes necessary.

    (c)   If and when it becomes clear that any conflict is sufficiently material to require to be managed, one of a variety of different approaches may be appropriate depending on all the circumstances.

    (d)   Such different approaches may include, for example, obtaining legal advice, the appointment of an additional partner from the same firm or the appointment of an independent partner from a different firm.[362]

8.141 An argument that the pragmatic 'management' approach should be limited solely to 'large scale multi-national groups of companies' was rejected in *Re TPS Investments (UK) Ltd (in administration)*.[363] The court went further than simply rejecting the distinction and held that the justification for a 'pragmatic moderating approach' to the management of conflicts might be said to apply 'equally if not more strongly' in smaller group situations, where the level of assets meant that costs considerations were further to the fore.[364] Practical means of managing conflicts when they emerged might include measures such as the provision of separate legal advice (either on a joint or separate instruction),[365] the appointment of an additional administrator, or separate representation in an application to court to determine the point in issue.[366]

8.142 In *Beattie v Smailes*,[367] the possibility of a conflict of duty had to be balanced against the real disadvantage that would be suffered if the liquidators were removed. The same IPs were liquidators of two members of the same group where there had been mutual dealings and the companies' affairs, including their respective responsibility for tax liabilities, were in a confused state.[368] Having acknowledged the potential for conflict between the two companies'

---

359   Ibid., 123G–H (Hoffmann J). Some years later, Lord Hoffmann (as he had by then become) reached an almost identical conclusion in delivering the advice of the Privy Council on an appeal from the Cayman Islands in *Parmalat Capital Finance Ltd v Food Holdings Ltd (in liq)* [2008] UKPC 23, [2009] 1 BCLC 274, [13].

360   [2005] EWHC 2170 (Ch), [2006] BCC 463.

361   *SISU Capital Fund Ltd v Tucker* [2005] EWHC 2170 (Ch), [2006] BCC 463, [108].

362   Ibid., [103] (Warren J).

363   [2018] EWHC 360 (Ch), [2019] 1 BCLC 61.

364   Ibid., [35]. A similar view is expressed at [97].

365   Obtaining legal advice from separate solicitors had been approved by the court as a way of managing a conflict in a group insolvency by the mid-Victorian era, see *Re Western Assurance Society ex parte Willett* (1870) LR 5 Ch App 396, 399.

366   [2018] EWHC 360 (Ch), [2019] 1 BCLC 61, [96].

367   [2011] EWHC 1563 (Ch), [2012] BCC 205.

368   Ibid., [10], [13].

positions,[369] Norris J considered that there had been 'good sense' in appointing the same liquidators to enable 'pooling of the resources to investigate both sides of the relevant transactions'.[370] Moreover, the liquidators were pursuing litigation against the companies' directors for fraudulent trading and their removal would require conditional fee agreements and after the event insurance to be renegotiated with no certainty of outcome.[371] Taking these factors into account, Norris J held that balancing the theoretical conflict of interest between the companies' respective claims (which could be dealt with, if necessary, by seeking directions from the court to approve any compromise) against prejudicing the conduct of the fraudulent trading claim, the balance came down in favour of leaving things as they were.[372]

The most common form of practical conflict management in group situations is the appoint-   **8.143**
ment of an additional officeholder. Such an appointment may be a general one, or the additional officeholder's role may be limited to a specific aspect of the insolvency that is affected by the conflict. In *Re York Gas Ltd (in liquidation)*,[373] Newey J (as he then was) allowed an appeal against the dismissal of an application by liquidators to appoint an additional conflict liquidator to deal with a claim between two group companies. Newey J agreed with the liquidators that, as a matter of principle, a conflict of interest faced by officeholders could be managed by a division of responsibilities and that the authorities showed that the appointment of an additional IP from the same firm as the existing officeholders could potentially be an acceptable way to manage a conflict of interest.[374]

(b) Relationship between officeholder and stakeholder

A different kind of potential for conflict may arise where the officeholder or their firm has some   **8.144**
kind of pre-appointment relationship with a party interested in the insolvency. On the basis of the current system by which officeholders are appointed, the mere fact that an IP is nominated by a party with an interest in the estate cannot be an objection to their holding office, for almost all insolvency appointments are made following the nomination of a particular IP by someone with such an interest. This may arise where the officeholder has advised the company, acting by its directors, prior to the commencement of CVL. Alternatively, it is common for an IP to be at least introduced to a struggling company by one of its major creditors.[375]

A prior relationship may also exist where an IP has been instructed to undertake pre-appointment   **8.145**
work, often by the secured creditor, and subsequently taken an appointment. This is particularly common in the case of administrations, by reason of the prominent role of the QFCH in that process. Relationships between IPs and secured creditors is an area that continues to attract controversy, and some litigation,[376] in light of the repeat-player nature of many secured creditors and the dominant position of the QFCH in the insolvency regime. Where the line

---

369   Ibid., [17].
370   Ibid., [19].
371   Ibid., [27].
372   Ibid., [28].
373   [2010] EWHC 2275 (Ch), [2011] BCC 447.
374   Ibid., [11].
375   *PJSC Uralkali v Rowley* [2020] EWHC 3442 (Ch), [441].
376   For example *Davey v Money* [2018] EWHC 766, [2018] Bus LR 1903, [259]; *Re Zinc Hotels (Holdings) Ltd (in admin)* [2018] EWHC 1936, [2018] BCC 968, [3]; *Re Rhino Enterprises Properties Ltd* [2020] EWHC 2370 (Ch), [2021] BCC 18, [15].

should be drawn in such relationships is a policy decision and some would draw it in a different place.[377] This aspect has informed the debate over proposals for regulatory reform in recent years and is discussed further below.

8.146   The point has been made a number of times in the cases that, in most insolvencies of any size or complexity, the proposed officeholders will have been engaged prior to the commencement of the insolvency proceedings by one or more creditors, or the directors, or a regulator.[378] In *Re Zinc Hotels (Holdings) Ltd (in administration)*, Henry Carr J pointed out that specific provision is now included in the Insolvency Rules 2016 for disclosure in an administrator's statutory statement of proposals of costs incurred by the administrators prior to their appointment and recovery of those costs from the estate.[379] Self-evidently, the inclusion of such costs in the regime puts beyond argument any suggestion that there is anything necessarily wrong with pre-appointment engagement by IPs who later take an appointment as administrator.

8.147   Indeed, it has been held that undertaking such pre-administration work may render a creditor's nominee particularly suitable: in *Re Maxwell Communications Corporation plc*,[380] the bank creditors' nominee had already undertaken 7,000 hours of pre-administration work on their instructions by the time the administration application was made.[381] Hoffmann J decided that the prior knowledge that the banks' nominees' firm had obtained in doing that pre-appointment work would enable the administration to be carried out more cheaply, effectively and quickly than had the nominee of the directors been appointed.[382] In a similar vein, Norris J found in *Re Zegna III Holdings Inc (in administration)*[383] that such a prior relationship was not only no impediment to the administrators continuing in office, but in fact underlined that there was a 'unity of purpose' between interests in the administration.[384]

8.148   Similarly, the fact that a solicitor who previously advised the creditor has been retained by the officeholder does not give rise of itself to an unmanageable conflict.[385] Again, authority is to the effect that it may be positively beneficial in terms of avoiding duplication of work. For instance, in *Shlosberg v Avonwick Holdings Ltd*,[386] Arnold J (as he then was) held that:

---

377   See, for example, Tomlinson, L. 'The Tomlinson Report' (2013) (www.tomlinsonreport.com/docs/tomlinsonreport .pdf). Shortly before this book went to press, the All Party Parliamentary Group on Fair Business Banking (APPG) published a report titled *Resolving Insolvency: Restoring confidence in the system* (September 2021). The APPG's report proposed far-reaching regulatory and statutory reform, including a 'ban' on all conflicts of interest in IP appointments, a move to a single regulator supported by an ombudsman, and 'placing the Code of Ethics on a statutory footing'.

378   [2018] EWHC 1936 (Ch), [2018] BCC 968, [77]; *SISU Capital Fund Ltd v Tucker* [2005] EWHC 2170 (Ch), [2006] BCC 463, [114].

379   [2018] EWHC 1936 (Ch), [2018] BCC 968, [78]. The relevant rules are found at Insolvency Rules 2016, rr 3.35(10(a), 3.36 and 3.52.

380   [1992] BCLC 465.

381   *Re Maxwell Communications Corporation plc* [1992] BCLC 465, 467b.

382   Ibid., 469b–d.

383   [2009] EWHC 2994 (Ch), [2010] BPIR 277.

384   *Re Zegna III Holdings Inc (in admin)* [2009] EWHC 2994 (Ch), [2010] BPIR 277, [26]; *Re Zinc Hotels (Holdings) Ltd* [2018] EWHC 1936 (Ch), [2018] BCC 968, [86]–[92].

385   *Re Zegna III Holdings Inc (in admin)* [2009] EWHC 2994 (Ch), [2010] BPIR 277, [26].

386   [2016] EWHC 1001 (Ch), [2017] Ch 210. This was a personal insolvency case but it is clear that Arnold J was talking about corporate insolvency as well.

… there is nothing inherently objectionable about the solicitor acting for both a trustee in bankruptcy or liquidator and a major creditor of the bankrupt or insolvent company. On the contrary, it has been recognised that this may well be convenient because of the creditor's familiarity with the debtor's affairs and because of absence of any real likelihood of a conflict of interest between the trustee and liquidator and the creditor.[387]

Whether or not it is appropriate to instruct a solicitor or other agent who has previously advised a particular creditor depends on whether there is a realistic prospect of conflict between that creditor and the class interest of the creditors as a whole[388] or, put another way, whether the proposed solicitor or agent is able to discharge their fiduciary duties to the company.[389] *Re Zinc Hotels (Holdings) Ltd*[390] provides a useful practical illustration of the dynamic nature of an insolvent company's conflict profile and the officeholders' response to it. At the commencement of the administration, the administrators had taken the view, on advice, that the value of the estate would break in the secured creditors' interest.[391] As such, the possibility of any conflict between the interests of the secured creditors and the administrators' duties was remote.[392] Accordingly, there was no reason why the administrators should not instruct the solicitors that had acted for the lenders pre-administration. In relation to aspects of the administration where there might be a conflict, such as legal actions that the shareholders had identified as potentially available against the lenders, the administrators instructed a separate firm of solicitors to advise. Later in the administration, it appeared that there would, after all, be a surplus of assets available for the shareholders.[393] This changed the conflict profile of the estate and meant that there was now a realistic possibility of conflict between the interests of the lenders in having their secured debt repaid and the duties of the administrators, which now involved taking into account the interests of unsecured creditors and shareholders. Once the possibility of a surplus had emerged, the administrators decided to replace both the original solicitors and the additional firm advising on the lender claims with a single, new, unconflicted firm.[394] Such pragmatic responses to a changing situation were regarded as entirely appropriate by the court.[395] This need to keep the position under review was emphasised in *Re Comet Group Ltd (in liquidation)*:[396] even if the conflicts an officeholder is under are not sufficient to require them to refuse an appointment at the outset, conflicts should nonetheless be addressed with procedures put in place to deal with situations as they arise or where they might be perceived as having an influence on their conduct of particular aspects of the case.[397] **8.149**

In cases of this kind, where stakeholder interests in the same estate conflict, the court may not be as ready to order a joint appointment as the appropriate way of managing conflicts as in the group insolvency situation discussed earlier. For instance, in *Oracle (Northwest) Ltd v Pinnacle* **8.150**

---

387 Ibid., [46].
388 *Re One Blackfriars Ltd (in liq)* [2021] EWHC 684 (Ch), [298].
389 *Davey v Money* [2018] EWHC 766, [2018] Bus LR 1903, [340].
390 [2018] EWHC 1936 (Ch), [2018] BCC 968, [88].
391 Ibid., [17].
392 Ibid., [89].
393 Ibid., [36].
394 Ibid., [91].
395 Ibid., [90].
396 [2018] EWHC 1378 (Ch).
397 Ibid., [31].

(UK) Ltd,[398] competing applications for the appointment of an administrator were made, respectively, by a company's directors and an unsecured creditor. Each applicant nominated a different IP to be the administrator, although the directors ultimately took the position that they would accept a joint appointment of both nominated IPs. The court rejected that proposal on the ground that it might create more problems than it solved, considering the lack of any agreed strategy or any proposal for the sharing of tasks between the officeholders, the risk of disagreement and the need for expensive applications to court for directions. As the administration was for the ultimate benefit of creditors, the court held that the choice of the unsecured creditors should prevail in preference to that of the directors.[399]

8.151   Similarly, in *Re Zinc Hotels (Holdings) Ltd*,[400] Henry Carr J held that even if the court had enjoyed jurisdiction to grant the shareholders' request and appoint an additional 'conflict administrator', it would not have done so. The application had been made on the express basis that the new joint administrator's role would be to 'represent the interests of the shareholders' and was opposed by the existing administrators and the appointing QFCH. The court concluded that a joint appointment in such circumstances 'would be likely to cause stalemate in progressing the administration and might well prevent the realisation of the assets of the companies in administration'.[401] A further factor that concerned the judge was that a joint appointment in those circumstances would require 'repeated supervision by the court',[402] which would be inconsistent with the court's general desire to keep applications to court by officeholders to a minimum.[403]

(c) Pre-pack administration

8.152   It appears that the court is more likely to order removal on grounds of conflict in cases involving 'pre-pack' administrations than in other kinds of insolvency proceedings. A pre-pack, in its typical form, will see an IP engaged prior to administration to advise on a sale of the company's business and undertaking to a connected party. Generally, the sale will be negotiated in principle prior to the IP's appointment as administrator and will complete immediately or shortly after that appointment. In most cases the unsecured creditors will not know about the sale until it has completed. Although they have many advantages as a restructuring tool and can be a useful means of preserving going concern value, pre-packs have always attracted controversy and have recently been made the subject with a greater degree of regulation, which is discussed elsewhere in this book.[404]

8.153   Conflicts of interest are inherent in the pre-pack structure. A company's director in a pre-pack negotiation may be faced with perhaps the most fundamental of fiduciary conflicts, in that they are on both sides of the pre-pack deal: simultaneously as a director of the selling company and also as a potential purchaser. By the time the negotiation takes place, the interests of the

---

398   [2008] EWHC 1920 (Ch), [2009] BCC 159. This was an initial appointment case, not a removal case, but it usefully illustrates the conflict point.
399   Ibid., [20].
400   [2018] EWHC 1936 (Ch), [2018] BCC 968.
401   Ibid., [69].
402   Ibid., [142].
403   *Re Transbus International Ltd* [2004] EWHC 932 (Ch), [2004] 1 WLR 2654, [9].
404   See para 8.203.

company are usually, as a matter of substance, those of the creditors rather than the shareholders by reason of the company's insolvency, and the potential for conflict between those interests is inherent in the structure. The IP is engaged prior to their appointment as administrator in order to prepare for that conflicted sale to take place on their authority as administrator.[405]

David Richards J observed in *Clydesdale Financial Services Ltd v Smailes*[406] that: **8.154**

> As is notorious there has been widespread public concern in relation to pre-pack administrations in terms of whether they achieve the best outcome for creditors. This is not to say that in any particular case or even in the generality of cases they do not achieve the best outcome but the hallmarks of a lack of widespread marketing of the business, often combined with the involvement of the directors of the insolvent company in the purchaser, create conditions in which the result may be called into question.[407]

Where an undersale is alleged following a pre-pack sale and an investigation is required, an **8.155** incumbent administrator is unable to investigate, because the investigation concerns the probity of a commercial deal in which they themselves were intimately involved. This is a conflict of interest that cannot be managed in the way other conflicts might be. In *Clydesdale Financial Services Ltd v Smailes*,[408] David Richards J ordered the removal of administrators on the ground that the evidence raised 'a serious issue for investigation'.[409] His Lordship emphasised that this conclusion did not mean that any investigation would finally disclose that there was anything untoward in the sale; it simply meant that the administrator and his firm were so closely involved in the negotiations that he could not be expected to conduct an independent investigation.[410]

In *Re Ve Interactive Ltd (in administration)*,[411] ICC Judge Jones was critical of pre-pack **8.156** administrators who had not recognised and taken steps to address their inability to investigate whether or not the best price for the company's business was achieved. Judge Jones held that:

> In my judgment the [administrators] ought to have concluded, effectively from the date of their appointment or soon thereafter, that they as members of [their firm] were conflicted and could not carry out those investigations. [The administrators' firm] were inextricably bound up in the process by reason of their contractual retainer and, therefore, so were the Respondents. This is not technical legal analysis. It is obvious.

That does not necessarily mean they should have resigned from their appointments. It may be there were alternative solutions. For example, the appointment of an additional administrator or replacement by only two new administrators who would be specifically and only responsible for the investigations.[412]

---

405   *Re Kayley Vending Ltd* [2009] EWHC 904 (Ch), [2009] BCC 578, [2].
406   [2009] EWHC 1745 (Ch), [2009] BCC 810, [15].
407   Ibid., [6].
408   Ibid., [15].
409   Ibid., [26].
410   Ibid., [30].
411   [2018] EWHC 186 (Ch), [2019] BPIR 438.
412   Ibid., [25]–[26].

8.157   The judgment in *Re Ve Interactive Ltd (in administration)* caused a degree of disquiet in the insolvency profession, for although the judge observed that it was 'not a case where removal will or should encourage unjustified applications or cause officeholders to have to look over their shoulders',[413] it is submitted that the features that led to the problematic conflict in that case were ones that will tend to be present in every or almost every pre-pack administration by reason of its structure. That being so, it is unclear what would constitute an 'unjustified' application on the logic of the judgment. It remains to be seen whether or not the new regulatory regime for pre-packs will deal satisfactorily with the issue.[414]

8.158   It appears that a distinction should be drawn between the uniquely challenging self-investigation conflict present in a pre-pack administration and the position in other insolvency processes. This distinction was addressed by Norris J in *Re Zegna III Holdings Inc (in administration)*.[415] The nature of the alleged conflict in that case was pre-appointment advice to the QFCH and the retention by the administrators of the same solicitor as had previously advised that creditor. Norris J considered the conflict to be unproblematic and went on to distinguish the situation in *Re Zegna III* from the self-investigation issue in the pre-pack case *Clydesdale Financial Services Ltd v Smailes*. Norris J held that:

> The circumstances of the decision making are, it seems to me, miles away from those considered in *Clydesdale Finance v Smailes*…to justify removal of an administrator and thereby facilitate examination of a 'pre-pack' sale on questionable terms which he himself had negotiated immediately before appointment.[416]

8.159   Similarly, in *Re Zinc Hotels (Holdings) Ltd*,[417] the shareholders sought removal of administrators appointed by the QFCH under para 14 of Sch B1 on the grounds that, first, the administrators had provided pre-appointment advice to the QFCH and, secondly, that the administrators' solicitors had previously acted for the QFCH. The shareholders referred both to *Clydesdale Financial Services Ltd v Smailes* and to the extract from the then-recent decision in *Re Ve Interactive Ltd (in administration)* set out above. In deciding that the shareholders had not shown a serious issue to be tried in *Re Zinc Hotels (Holdings) Ltd*, Henry Carr J firmly distinguished the case before the court from the position in the pre-pack cases, holding that the conflict in those cases had arisen because the administrators could not investigate their own conduct, which did not arise in *Re Zinc Hotels (Holdings) Ltd*.[418]

D. REGULATION OF IPS

1.   Qualification and authorisation of IPs

8.160   Prior to the introduction of the Insolvency Act 1986, there was no requirement for IPs to be professionally qualified. At that time, the only regulation of those taking appointment was the

---

413   Ibid., [36].
414   See para 8.203.
415   [2009] EWHC 2994 (Ch), [2010] BPIR 277.
416   Ibid., [26].
417   [2018] EWHC 1936 (Ch), [2018] BCC 968.
418   Ibid., [67]–[68], [84].

requirement that the Department of Trade should certify the suitability of the person appointed at the meeting of creditors.[419] But, as noted by the Insolvency Law Review Committee chaired by Sir Kenneth Cork in its report entitled '*Insolvency Law and Practice*' (the Cork Report), the practice of the Department of Trade was to certify anyone who had given the necessary security provided that they had not on some previous occasion been removed from a trusteeship or liquidation.[420] That was plainly a low hurdle. The Cork Report noted that the lack of any minimum professional qualification had been the subject of much criticism, with a number of proposals advanced, many of which had been put forward by IPs themselves.[421] It concluded that such qualification and control was essential, both to ensure a high standard of competence and to maintain integrity, in order to command public confidence.[422]

Part 13 of the Insolvency Act 1986 adopted many of the recommendations made by the Cork Report and in certain respects went further. Its key requirement was that IPs should be members of Recognised Professional Bodies (RPBs), which were to be responsible for their licensing and regulation. The Insolvency Act 1986 gave power to the Secretary of State to declare by order that a body was an RPB, with further provisions for the authorisation of IPs by the RPBs, and of the RPBs themselves by the Secretary of State.[423]   **8.161**

For a body to be eligible to be declared an RPB by the Secretary of State, it must be one that regulates the practice of a profession and must maintain and enforce rules for securing that its insolvency specialist members are fit and proper persons to act as IPs, and that they meet acceptable requirements as to education and practical training and experience.[424] In practice, the functions of the Secretary of State under the Act are discharged by the Insolvency Service, which acts as '*oversight regulator*'.[425] The Insolvency Service is an 'executive agency'[426] of the Department for Business, Energy and Industrial Strategy and does not have a legal personality separate from the Department.[427]   **8.162**

To become qualified to act as an IP, a person must be a member of one of the RPBs and permitted to act as an IP under the rules of that RPB.[428] Seven bodies were declared to be RPBs by the Insolvency Practitioners (Recognised Professional Bodies) Order 1986,[429] which came into   **8.163**

---

419   *Insolvency Law and Practice: Report of the Review Committee*, Cmnd.8558, 1982 ('Cork Report'), para 739.
420   Cork Report, para 740.
421   Ibid., para 735.
422   Ibid., para 756.
423   Insolvency Act 1986, ss 391–398.
424   As enacted, these requirements were found in Insolvency Act 1986, s 391(2); the provision in restated form is now at s 391(4).
425   See *Insolvency practitioner regulation – regulatory objectives and oversight powers: Legislative changes introduces on 1 October 2015*, Insolvency Service, December 2015, p 3 and https://www.gov.uk/government/publications/insolvency-service -as-oversight-regulator-of-the-insolvency-profession/insolvency-service-as-oversight-regulator-of-the-insolvency -profession-in-detail, (17 February 2017).
426   It is considered in Chapter 11.
427   *Sebry v Companies House* [2015] EWHC 115 (QB), [2016] 1 WLR 2499, [6] (Edis J). This case concerned Companies House, another 'executive agency' of the Department of Business, Innovation and Skills (the predecessor to the Department of Business, Energy and Industrial Strategy), but its status appears to be identical to that of the Insolvency Service.
428   Insolvency Act 1986, s 390A(2).
429   SI 1986/1764.

force on 10 November 1986.[430] These were the Chartered Association of Certified Accountants (ACCA),[431] the Insolvency Practitioners Association (IPA), the Institute of Chartered Accountants in England and Wales (ICAEW), the Institute of Chartered Accountants in Ireland (CAI), the Institute of Chartered Accountants of Scotland (ICAS), the Law Society,[432] and the Law Society of Scotland.[433] Until 30 September 2016, the Secretary of State also had a power to grant direct authorisation to act as an IP, with that function being discharged on its behalf by the Insolvency Practitioner Section of the Insolvency Service.[434]

8.164 The Insolvency Practitioner Regulations 1990[435] came into effect on 1 April 1990. These required applicants for authorisation to act as an IP to have passed the examinations set by the Joint Insolvency Examination Board (JIEB).[436] The regulations also set out detailed requirements for an IP to provide security[437] and to keep records and make them available for inspection.[438] These regulations were repealed and replaced by the Insolvency Practitioner Regulations 2005, with effect from 1 April 2005.[439] The existing key requirements for authorisation as an IP (i.e., to pass the JIEB examination,[440] provide security,[441] and maintain records for inspection[442]) were all maintained.

8.165 Acting as an IP without qualification is an offence, unless the person acting is the official receiver.[443] A person acts as an IP in relation to a company when they act as its liquidator, provisional liquidator, administrator, administrative receiver or monitor of a moratorium under Part A1 of the Insolvency Act 1986, or as the nominee or supervisor of an approved CVA.[444] It should be noted that the provision does not include receivers other than administrative receivers. At first glance this may appear anomalous, but it is explicable on the footing that receivership is a security enforcement process rather than a collective insolvency process.[445]

---

430 See para 8.239 for the current position in relation to RPBs.
431 Since 1996 known as the Association of Chartered Certified Accountants (ACCA), but still referred to by its former name in the Order. In 2019 ACCA sought to have its standing as a recognised body revoked and this was acceded to. As from 31 December 2019 ACCA ceased all regulatory activities as a recognised professional body in relation to insolvency practitioners. See, Insolvency Practitioners (Recognised Professional Bodies) (Revocation of Recognition) Order 2021.
432 The Law Society of England and Wales was such a body until it sought to have its standing revoked in 2015. See, Insolvency Practitioners (Recognised Professional Bodies) (Revocation of Recognition) Order 2016.
433 SI 1986/1764, Sch 1, para 1. The Law Society of Scotland also was a recognised body until 2015 when it sought revocation of this standing. See, Insolvency Practitioners (Recognised Professional Bodies) (Revocation of Recognition) Order 2016.
434 The power was conferred by Insolvency Act 1986, ss 392 and 393. Those sections were revoked by the Deregulation Act 2015, Sch 6, para 21 with effect from 1 October 2015 with transitional provisions under Sch 6, para 23 coming to an end on 30 September 2016.
435 SI 1990/439.
436 Ibid., Part II. Provision was made to dispense with the requirement to pass the JIEB for those already authorised to act as IPs who held a certain amount of appointment-taking experience.
437 Ibid., Part III.
438 Ibid., Part IV.
439 SI 2005/524.
440 Ibid., Part 2.
441 Ibid., Part 3 and Sch 2.
442 Ibid., Part 4.
443 Insolvency Act 1986, s 389.
444 Ibid., s 388(1).
445 *Re MF Global UK Ltd (in special admin)* [2012] EWHC 3068 (Ch), [2013] 1 WLR 903, [66].

As mentioned above, the examinations for authorisation as an IP are set and administered by **8.166** the JIEB. Candidates are eligible to sit the exams if they satisfy the requirement that they are the member of an RPB under s 391 of the Insolvency Act 1986. There are two papers, one on corporate insolvency and one on personal insolvency, each lasting three-and-a-half hours. The exams are noted for their challenging nature, requiring candidates to have an understanding of insolvency practice, including its taxation, accountancy and legal dimensions. A further qualification, the Certificate of Proficiency in Insolvency (CPI), is set by the IPA. The CPI is intended to provide a practical professional grounding in insolvency practice, perhaps as an intermediate stage before attempting the JIEB exams, but does not formally count towards qualification as an IP.

2.   Joint Insolvency Committee

Since 1999, co-ordination between the RPBs has been maintained by the Joint Insolvency **8.167** Committee (JIC). The JIC was formed in 1999 with the objective of providing a forum to promote common standards and a consistency of approach across the RPBs. It is currently composed of representatives from each of the four current RPBs,[446] five lay members (most of whom represent creditors),[447] and representatives from the Insolvency Service and the Insolvency Service Northern Ireland. Representatives from the Association of Business Recovery Professionals (the trade body for the insolvency and restructuring profession, known as R3) and the Law Society of Scotland attend as observers. Other observers may attend by arrangement. The JIC is responsible for issuing the Insolvency Code of Ethics (Code of Ethics), the Statements of Insolvency Practice (SIPs), and Insolvency Guidance Papers (IGP). Each of these regulatory sources is approved by each of the RPBs.

3.   The Code of Ethics

The Code of Ethics is the primary source of mandatory profession regulatory guidance for **8.168** IPs. Its current version was introduced on 1 May 2020 and has been approved in substantially similar form by each of the RPBs. IPs are required to observe and comply with the Code of Ethics,[448] and apply it at all times in relation to the conduct of insolvency appointments or circumstances that might lead to an insolvency appointment.[449] The Code of Ethics is based on principles, which require the exercise of professional judgment, rather than prescriptive rules. At its core are the five 'Fundamental Principles',[450] which are supported by the 'Conceptual Framework'.[451] IPs are required to comply with each of the Fundamental Principles, which are briefly summarised below.[452]

---

446   These being (May 2021) the IPA, the ICAEW, the CAI and ICAS.
447   Currently (May 2021) the Association of British Insurers, the British Property Federation, Her Majesty's Revenue and Customs and the Chartered Institute of Credit Management.
448   Code of Ethics, R2000.5.
449   Ibid., R2000.7.
450   Ibid., R2100.1 A1.
451   Ibid., R2110.1.
452   Ibid., R2100.2.

(a) The Fundamental Principles
(i) Integrity

8.169   This principle requires an IP to be straightforward and honest in all professional and business relationships.[453] The Code of Ethics states that an IP must not knowingly be associated with reports, returns, communications, or other information that are false or misleading, contain statements or information provided recklessly, or omit or obscure required information where such omission or obscurity would be misleading.[454]

(ii) Objectivity

8.170   The requirement of objectivity engages, as a matter of regulation, some of the themes already addressed in this chapter that are prevalent in insolvency practice. Objectivity is described by the Code of Ethics as 'the state of mind which has regard to all considerations relevant to the task in hand but no other'.[455] This principle requires an IP not to compromise professional or business judgment because of bias, conflict of interest or undue influence of others.[456] The threats to compliance with the Fundamental Principles that are identified in the Conceptual Framework[457] are largely focused on matters going to objectivity and a further section of the Code of Ethics is specifically devoted to conflicts of interest.[458]

(iii) Professional competence and due care

8.171   This principle requires the IP to attain and maintain professional knowledge and skill, based on current technical and professional standards and relevant legislation, and to act diligently and in accordance with applicable technical and professional standards.[459] An IP is also required to take reasonable steps to ensure that those working under their authority have appropriate training and supervision.[460] Further regulatory guidance on the delegation or sharing of work-loads, either within firms or between them, with staff or other IPs, is addressed in the IGP on 'Control of Cases'.[461]

(iv) Confidentiality

8.172   An IP is required by this principle to report on their acts and dealings as fully as possible given the circumstances of the case,[462] thus providing accountability and transparency. This must be done while simultaneously respecting the confidentiality of information acquired as a result of professional and business relationships.[463] Of particular note is the requirement not to use confidential information acquired as a result of professional and business relationships for the personal advantage of the IP or the advantage of a third party.[464] Various exceptions to the

---

453   Ibid., R2101.1.
454   Ibid., R2101.2.
455   Ibid., 2102.1 A1.
456   Ibid., R2102.1.
457   Ibid., 2110.1 to 2116.2.
458   Ibid., 2310.1 to 2316.1.
459   Ibid., R2103.1.
460   Ibid., R2103.2.
461   Insolvency Guidance Paper: Control of Cases (July 2005).
462   Code of Ethics, R2104.2.
463   Ibid., R2104.3.
464   Ibid., R2104.3(e).

general confidentiality requirement are identified, such as producing statutory reports for the creditors, submitting reports on the conduct of the directors, or producing documents in the course of legal proceedings.[465]

(v) Professional behaviour

This principle requires an IP to comply with relevant law and regulations and avoid any **8.173** conduct that the IP knows or should know might discredit the profession. They may not knowingly engage in any business, occupation or activity that impairs or might impair the integrity, objectivity or good reputation of the insolvency profession.

(b) The Conceptual Framework

The Code of Ethics realistically recognises that the 'circumstances in which insolvency prac-   **8.174** titioners operate might create threats to compliance with the fundamental principles'.[466] The Conceptual Framework is intended to identify such threats, evaluate the threats identified, and address them by eliminating them or reducing them to an acceptable level.[467] A key point to note at the outset is that the presence of these 'threats' does not of itself preclude appointment, but rather acts as a red flag for further consideration, which may require specific steps to manage the risk or, if the risk cannot be managed, to decline the appointment.

Five types of threat to the Fundamental Principles are identified in the Conceptual Framework. **8.175** Some of the examples given in the Code of Ethics for each of the threats are summarised below.

(i)   Self-interest threat

Examples of the self-interest threat include an individual within the IP's firm having an interest **8.176** in a creditor or potential creditor with a claim that requires subjective adjudication, or having an interest in a party to a transaction. It may also include situations where an IP has concerns about the possibility of damaging a business relationship.[468]

(ii) Self-review threat

An example provided in the Code of Ethics is where an IP has previously carried out profes- **8.177** sional work of any description, including sequential insolvency appointments, for an entity.[469]

(iii) Advocacy threat

This may arise where an IP has advised a creditor of an insolvent entity or for the entity itself **8.178** prior to its insolvency.[470]

---

465   Ibid., 2104.3 A1.
466   Ibid., 2110.1.
467   Ibid., 2110.2.
468   Ibid., 2114.1 A5(a).
469   Ibid., 2114.1 A5(b).
470   Ibid., 2114.1 A5(c).

(iv) Familiarity threat

8.179 A familiarity threat may arise where an IP or an individual within their firm or an immediate family member has a close professional or personal relationship with the insolvent entity or a purchaser of the insolvent entity's assets.[471]

(v) Intimidation threat

8.180 An IP may be affected by an intimidation threat where an individual within their firm is threatened with dismissal or replacement, litigation, complaint or adverse publicity, or violence or other reprisal.[472]

(c) The threats to compliance in practice

8.181 It will be noted that several of the threats will tend to arise in the ordinary course of routine insolvency practice. Further, and as the Code of Ethics expressly notes, a circumstance might create more than one threat, and a threat might affect compliance with more than one fundamental principle.[473] Take, for instance, a case where an IP has advised a secured creditor prior to accepting an appointment by that creditor as administrator. Based on the examples summarised above, such an appointment could feasibly give rise to each of (a) a self-interest threat (the perception that the IP was concerned to preserve their business relationship with the appointing creditor); (b) a self-review threat (if the administrator was subsequently appointed liquidator); (c) an advocacy threat (by reason of having advised the creditor pre-appointment); and (d) a familiarity threat (if the secured creditor was a potential purchaser of the insolvent company's assets).

8.182 Where the IP identifies a threat to compliance with the Fundamental Principles, they must evaluate whether such a threat is at an acceptable level.[474] An IP is required to use professional judgment in assessing a threat and in doing so is to use the 'reasonable and informed third party test', i.e., whether the same conclusions would be reached by such a third party. The reasonable and informed third party is one that weighs all the relevant facts and circumstances that the IP knows or could reasonably be expected to know at the time the conclusions are reached. They need not be an IP but would possess the relevant knowledge and experience to understand and evaluate the appropriateness of the IP's conclusions in an impartial manner.[475] For a threat to at an acceptable level, it must be level where an IP, using the reasonable and informed third-party test, would likely conclude that the IP complies with the Fundamental Principles.[476] Where the threat cannot be eliminated or reduced to an acceptable level, the IP should decline or end the appointment in question.[477]

(d) Conflicts of interest under the Code of Ethics

8.183 A further section in the Code of Ethics is devoted to conflicts of interest, which are specifically identified as a threat to the principle of objectivity and might also create threats to compliance

---

471   Ibid., 2114.1 A5(d).
472   Ibid., 2114.1 A5(e).
473   Ibid., 2114.1 A6.
474   Ibid., R2115.1.
475   Ibid., 2113.1 A1.
476   Ibid., 2115.1 A1.
477   Ibid., R2116.1; R2311.2.

with the other Fundamental Principles.[478] The key requirement is that an IP 'shall not allow a conflict of interest to compromise professional or business judgment'.[479] Central to this is the concept of a 'Significant Professional Relationship' or a 'Significant Personal Relationship', which is a relationship where no action can be taken to eliminate a threat or reduce it to an acceptable level. Where such a relationship exists, the IP shall not accept the appointment.[480] Risks of conflict will be increased where IPs or their firm have carried out previous assignments for the entity, its group, its chargeholders or stakeholders.[481]

The Code of Ethics requires a thorough assessment to be carried out by an IP contemplating **8.184** appointment to ensure there is no prior relationship that would make it inappropriate to accept it. The IP is required to have policies and procedures to identity relationships[482] and must take reasonable steps to identify circumstances and relationships that may create conflicts of interest.[483] This must be kept under review throughout the appointment,[484] including changes in circumstance.[485]

Prior to accepting an appointment, an IP should consider making disclosure to the court or the **8.185** creditors of the existence of any threat, together with any safeguard identified and applied.[486] It should be noted that this only requires the IP to *consider* making such disclosure; there is no absolute requirement to do so. The Code of Ethics spells out that it is a matter of professional judgment for the IP to determine whether the nature and significance of a conflict of interest are such that specific disclosure and explicit consent is necessary when addressing the threat created by the conflict of interest.[487] In reaching their view the IP must always consider the perception of others in deciding whether to accept an appointment.[488] The IP must document their courses of action, judgments made and decisions taken[489] sufficiently to enable a reasonable and informed third party to reach a view on the appropriateness of their action.[490]

As noted above, there are relatively few hard-and-fast rules in the Code of Ethics, but the **8.186** appropriateness of a number of specific kinds of appointment is considered. An IP 'may normally' accept appointment as an administrator or liquidator where an individual within their firm has previously acted as supervisor of a CVA;[491] or appointment as a liquidator where an individual within their firm has acted as administrator.[492] In both cases they must consider whether there are any circumstances that give rise to an unacceptable threat to compliance with

---

478   Ibid., 2310.2.
479   Ibid., R2311.1.
480   Ibid., 2312.7.
481   Ibid., 2311.2.A2.
482   Ibid., 2312.3.
483   Ibid., 2312.4.
484   Ibid., 2312.4.A1.
485   Ibid., 2313.1.
486   Ibid., 2210.5 A3.
487   Ibid., R2315.4.
488   Ibid., R2312.8.
489   Ibid., 2312.9.
490   Ibid., 2319.10.
491   Ibid., 2520.2.
492   Ibid., 2520.3.

the fundamental principles. In these categories of case, the risk of conflict is plainly reduced given the collective nature of the respective processes.

8.187   More problematic are cases where an IP proposes to take any appointment where an individual within their firm has previously acted as administrative or other receiver. In these cases, 'it is unlikely' that the threat can be reduced to an acceptable level and the IP should not take the appointment.[493] The scope for conflict here is clear: the previous appointment will have involved acting solely for the appointing secured creditor and not for those interested in the company as a whole.

8.188   The Code of Ethics considers that a Significant Personal Relationship precluding appointment 'will normally arise' where the IP's firm or an individual within the firm has carried out audit related work involving the entity within the previous three years. Where the audit work was more than three years before the proposed date of the appointment, the IP must nonetheless evaluate the threat. This prohibition does not apply to an MVL appointment.[494] The basis for this exception is that where the company is solvent, there is no potential conflict between audit work undertaken for the ultimate benefit of the members and appointment by the members to undertake a solvent liquidation.

8.189   A further circumstance requiring particular attention is where an IP proposes to take an appointment where their firm or an individual within the firm was previously instructed by or at the instigation of a creditor or a party with a financial interest in the company to investigate, monitor or advise in relation to its affairs. Whether or not a Significant Personal Relationship arises depends on close scrutiny of the nature of the previous involvement.[495]

(e) Code of Ethics and the substantive law

8.190   The substantive law is referred to relatively briefly in the Code of Ethics and goes no further than to make clear that IPs are required to comply with it. An IP is expressly required by the Code of Ethics to comply with statute or secondary legislation,[496] any relevant judicial authority relating to their conduct and any directions given by the court,[497] act in a manner appropriate to their position as an officer of the court where applicable, and in accordance with any quasi-judicial, fiduciary or other duties that they may be under.[498]

8.191   While departure from the Code of Ethics by an IP may give rise to regulatory action by that IP's RPB, such a departure by an officeholder will not, of itself, necessarily give rise to a breach of duty that is susceptible to review by the court. The courts have approached allegations based on regulatory departures with a degree of ambivalence, as discussed in more detail below.

---

493   Ibid., 2520.1.
494   Ibid.
495   Ibid., 2510.2.
496   Ibid., R2200.4.
497   Ibid., R2200.6.
498   Ibid., R2200.7.

(f) Summary

The thrust of the Code of Ethics can be seen as fostering accountability and transparency in **8.192** many different ways. Many of the virtues included in the Code contribute to better accountability and transparency. For instance, integrity and professionalism should demand that the IPs disclose their position and account for what they have done. The Code is designed to ensure that IPs provide disclosure where it is appropriate and to advise how they have carried out their functions.

4. Statements of Insolvency Practice

The Statements of Insolvency Practice ('SIPs') are issued to IPs under procedures agreed **8.193** between the RPBs acting through the JIC[499] and are periodically updated[500] and occasionally withdrawn. SIP 1 (*An introduction to statements of insolvency practice*) states that the SIPs set principles and key compliance standards with which IPs are required to comply and, accordingly, compliance with the SIPs is mandatory. IPs are warned by SIP 1 that: 'Failure to observe the principles and/or maintain the standards set out in a SIP is a matter that may be considered by a practitioner's regulatory authority for the purposes of disciplinary or regulatory action....'[501]

SIPs are not, however, statements of law and do not set out obligations imposed by the **8.194** insolvency legislation itself.[502] SIP 1 states that the SIPs exist to promote and maintain high standards and to harmonise the approach of IPs. It adds that the SIPs 'apply in parallel to the prevailing statutory framework'.[503] This parallel relationship between the regulatory and wider statutory regimes is addressed further below.

A number of SIPs are focused on matters of accountability and transparency and as such are **8.195** of relevance to the issues discussed in this book. Indeed, several of the more recent SIPs state at or near their start that the 'particular nature of an [IP's] position renders transparency and fairness in all dealings of primary importance',[504] or words to similar effect. The summary below touches briefly on those SIPs that are of particular relevance to the issues discussed in this book.

(a) SIP 3.2: Company Voluntary Arrangements[505]

SIP 3.2, *Company Voluntary Arrangements*,[506] sets out compliance standards for IPs when advis- **8.196** ing at different stages in the CVA process. It identifies that an IP is likely to act in a number of different capacities (the provision of initial advice to the directors, assisting in the preparation of the proposal, acting as nominee, and acting as supervisor) and requires IPs to differentiate clearly between these stages.[507] An IP must act with objectivity[508] and be satisfied that the

---

499 SIP 1, para 9 (1 October 2015).
500 Most recently, SIPs 3.2, 7 and 9 were updated on 1 April 2021 and SIPs 13 and 16 were updated on 30 April 2021.
501 SIP 1, para 6.
502 Ibid., para 8.
503 Ibid., para 1.
504 SIP 3.2, para 1; SIP 7, para 2; SIP 9, para 1; SIP 16, para 2.
505 SIP 3.2 (1 April 2021).
506 Ibid.
507 Ibid., para 3.
508 Ibid.

proposal 'is achievable and that a fair balance is struck between the interests of the company and its creditors'.[509] This last statement is interesting from a corporate governance perspective. Where a company is insolvent, the interests of that company ought to be equated as a matter of substance with the interests of its creditors. As such, there ought to be no need to balance the interests of the company with those of its creditors, because they should amount to the same thing. It appears likely that, in context, the reference to 'company' is probably being used in SIP 3.2 as shorthand for the members' interests represented by the directors proposing the CVA, but this ambiguous usage highlights the difficult task for any IP in balancing exactly what interests are in issue when an insolvent company, acting by its directors, proposes a CVA.

8.197 SIP 3.2 recognises that the maintenance of objectivity in voluntary arrangements is particularly challenging, given the IP's personal involvement in the preparation of the proposal and the need for any IP acting as adviser and nominee to put aside their commercial self-interest in becoming supervisor when deliberating on proofs for voting purposes. The kinds of challenges to objectivity that are present in voluntary arrangements generally are evident from some of the case law on IVAs.[510]

(b) SIP 6: Deemed Consent and Decision Procedures in Insolvency Proceedings[511]

8.198 SIP 6, *Deemed Consent and Decision Procedures in Insolvency Proceedings*, identifies that stakeholder involvement in decision-making is essential to the maintenance of trust and confidence in insolvency proceedings.[512] It sets out principles and compliance standards for IPs requiring that they take reasonable steps to ensure that those entitled to participate in deemed consent and decision procedures are treated fairly and are able to participate on an informed basis.[513] Information presented must be 'transparent, consistent and useful'.[514] SIP 6 also requires IPs to put in place 'sufficient and proportionate safeguards' against participation by those not entitled to do so.[515] The IP is required to exercise 'reasonable professional judgment' in these respects.[516] Much of SIP 6 is concerned specifically with IPs who assist in obtaining deemed consent or the convening of a decision procedure in CVL. In such cases, a threat to an IP's objectivity and a conflict of interest is potentially present in the IP's role advising the directors prior to becoming liquidator. SIP 6 seeks to manage that threat by requiring IPs to disclose the extent of their or their firm's prior involvement, any threats identified, and the safeguards applied to mitigate those threats.[517] A detailed list of key information likely to be of interest to prospective participants in addition to that required by statute is set out in SIP 6.[518]

---

509   Ibid., para 7.
510   *Royal Bank of Scotland plc v Munikwa* [2020] EWHC 786 (Ch).
511   SIP 6 (1 January 2018).
512   Ibid., para 1.
513   Ibid., para 4.
514   Ibid., para 7.
515   Ibid., para 8.
516   Ibid., para 9.
517   Ibid., para 11.
518   Ibid., para 12.

(c) SIP 7: Presentation of Financial Information in Insolvency Proceedings[519] and SIP 9: Payments to Insolvency Officeholders and their Associates from an Estate[520]

SIP 7, *Presentation of Financial Information in Insolvency Proceedings*, and SIP 9 *Payments to Insolvency Officeholders and their Associates from an Estate*, may be appropriately taken together. Both are concerned with ensuring accountability and transparency to creditors and others with a statutory right to information about an officeholder's receipts and payments.[521] A particular focus of these SIPs is the need for accountability and transparency in relation to payments from insolvent estates to parties associated with the officeholder. This has been a particular focus of concern in recent times. Until April 2021, SIP 9[522] distinguished between expenses and disbursements. 'Expenses' were payments properly made directly from the insolvent estate that were not the officeholder's remuneration or a distribution to creditors. Such expenses could include legal or agent's fees. 'Disbursements' were expenses initially met by the officeholder and subsequently reimbursed to the officeholder from the estate. Such disbursements were split into two types: 'category 1 disbursements', which were 'payments to an independent third party where there is a specific payment referable to the appointment in question';[523] and 'category 2 disbursements', which were 'expenses that are directly referable to the appointment in question but not a payment to an independent third party'.[524] Category 1 disbursements could be reimbursed from the estate without approval, while category 2 disbursements required approval in the same manner as an officeholder's remuneration. **8.199**

Varden Nuttall Ltd (in administration) v Nuttall[525] concerned an IP who had operated a dishonest scheme to increase fees in IVAs, by treating category 2 disbursements as if they were category 1 disbursements. Following that case, SIP 9 was redrafted and, from April 2021, no longer includes the distinction between expenses and disbursements. There are now only expenses, which are separated into two types: 'category 1 expenses' are payments to persons who are not an 'associate' of the officeholder; and 'category 2 expenses' are payments to 'associates' or that have an element of shared costs. The former may be paid without prior approval, while the latter requires approval.[526] Accordingly, whether or not prior approval is required for a payment is simplified, with the determining factor now being solely the identity of the person being paid, with the initial source of the payment (i.e., whether officeholder or estate) and the question of reimbursement no longer relevant to whether or not approval is needed. **8.200**

As updated in April 2021, both SIP 7 and SIP 9 require officeholders to take a more expansive view of the concept of 'associate' than that set out in the legislation. An officeholder is required to 'consider the substance or likely perception of any association between' the IP, their firm or an individual within their firm, and the recipient of any payment. The test to be applied is that of the 'reasonable and informed third party', which is widely employed in the Code of Ethics. Where that third party might consider there to be an 'association', payments should be treated **8.201**

---

519   SIP 7 (1 April 2021).
520   SIP 9 (1 April 2021).
521   SIP 7, para 4; SIP 9, para 2.
522   SIP 9, *Payments to Insolvency Officeholders and their Associates* (1 December 2015), see in particular paras 23 and 26–27.
523   SIP 9 (1 December 2015), para 22.
524   Ibid., para 23.
525   [2018] EWHC 3868 (Ch), [2019] BPIR 738, [73]–[75].
526   SIP 9 (1 April 2021), para 30.

as being to an associate, notwithstanding that the association might not strictly fall within the definition of associate in the Insolvency Act 1986.[527] In this way, SIP 7 and SIP 9 have been brought into line with the Code of Ethics and toughened up in a way addressed at the type of abuse seen in *Varden Nuttall Ltd (in administration) v Nuttall*.

8.202   In addition to this, SIP 7 sets out principles and compliance standards in relation to an office-holder's reporting obligations. It sets out in some detail how types of payments should be categorised and presented.[528] Requests for further information must be viewed on their individual merits by the officeholder and treated in a fair and reasonable way.[529] SIP 9 sets out principles and compliance standards in relation to payments to an officeholder or their associates. An officeholder is required to inform creditors and other interested parties of their rights under the legislation (which will include the right to challenge remuneration) in the first communication and in each subsequent report.[530] When reporting to creditors and other interested parties: 'Any disclosure by an office-holder of payments should be of assistance to those who have a financial interest in the level of payments from an estate in understanding what was done, why it was done, and how much it costs.'[531]

(d)   SIP 13: Disposal of Assets to Connected Parties in an Insolvency Process[532] and SIP 16: Pre-packaged Sales in Administrations[533]

8.203   SIP 13, *Disposal of Assets to Connected Parties in an Insolvency Process*, and SIP 16, *Pre-packaged Sales in Administrations*, may usefully be taken together. Both SIPs concern disposals to connected parties. New versions of these SIPs were introduced on 30 April 2021, primarily to ensure that the regulatory regime was fully aligned with the Administration (Restrictions on Disposal etc. to Connected Persons) Regulations 2021,[534] concerning pre-pack arrangements, that came into force on the same day. The regulations require an administrator to obtain either the approval of the company's creditors or a 'qualifying report' from an 'evaluator' before entering into a pre-pack disposal of a company's assets. Pre-pack administrations are dealt with elsewhere in this book.

8.204   SIP 13 applies to all connected party disposals in any insolvency process both corporate and personal,[535] whereas SIP 16 specifically concerns pre-pack administrations only. SIP 16 is concerned with all pre-pack administrations, whether they are to connected parties or not (although most are), while SIP 13 deals only with connected party sales. Each of the scenarios covered by SIP 13 and SIP 16 share the same sources of heightened concern from the point of view of accountability and transparency, which are the potential for an absence of proper scrutiny of the transaction and the risk that the IP will become affected by a serious conflict of interest. There is considerable overlap between the contents of SIP 13 and SIP 16 in these respects.

---

527   SIP 7, para 3; SIP 9, para 2.
528   Ibid., paras 7 onwards.
529   Ibid., para 17.
530   SIP 9 (1 April 2021), para 15.
531   Ibid., para 34.
532   SIP 13 (30 April 2021).
533   SIP 16 (30 April 2021).
534   SI 2021/427.
535   It does not apply to MVL disposals, these being solvent, not insolvent, processes under the Insolvency Act 1986.

Both SIP 13 and SIP 16 emphasise at the outset that transparency is of primary importance.[536] **8.205**
SIP 13 notes that the disposal of assets to a connected party may give rise to concerns that the
disposal has been at less than market value or on more favourable terms than may have been
available to a third party.[537] SIP 16 states that the IP should assume, and plan for, greater interest in and scrutiny of pre-pack sales where the purchaser is connected.[538]

The source of the heightened sensitivity towards an IP's role in connected party sales and **8.206**
pre-pack administrations is the different, and potentially conflicting, roles that the IP may
play. SIP 13 and SIP 16 both identify the same essential principles, namely that an IP should
be clear about their role in the pre-appointment period and ensure that their role is explained
to the directors and the creditors.[539] When advising an insolvent company, the IP must make
it clear that their role is not to advise any parties connected with the purchaser, such as the
directors, who must seek their own advice.[540] This will often be an acutely delicate task for the
IP, given that the insolvent company in such a case will be acting by its directors, who in most
cases will also be connected to the potential purchaser. Directors will often find it difficult to
distinguish in the necessary way between the capacities in which they act, and shareholders may
find it difficult to accept that the company's insolvent position has reduced or eliminated their
immediate economic interest in its assets.

SIP 13 and SIP 16 provide that an IP should exercise professional judgment in advising a client **8.207**
whether a formal valuation of assets is necessary. Where something other than an independent
valuation is relied on, this should be disclosed and an explanation must be provided.[541] An
officeholder must provide creditors and other interested parties with sufficient information
such that the reasonable and informed third party would conclude that the transaction was
appropriate and the officeholder acted with due regard for creditors' interests.[542] An officeholder
should keep a detailed record of both their decision-making and all alternatives considered.[543]

SIP 13 requires that a proportionate and sufficiently detailed justification of why a sale to **8.208**
a connected party was undertaken, together with alternatives considered, should be made in the
next report to creditors after the sale has taken place.[544] SIP 16 contains additional marketing
and disclosure requirements for pre-pack sales. Marketing is regarded as an important element
in ensuring that the best available price is obtained in the interests of the creditors as a whole,
and will be a key factor in providing reassurance to creditors.[545] A detailed narrative explanation
and justification for the decision to undertake a pre-pack sale must be provided to the creditors
to demonstrate that the administrator has acted with due regard for their interests.[546] This
is referred to as the 'SIP 16 statement' and should be provided with the first notification to

---

536   SIP 13, para 2; SIP 16, para 2.
537   SIP 13, para 1.
538   SIP 16, para 3.
539   SIP 13, para 6; SIP 16, para 7.
540   SIP 13, para 6; SIP 16, para 9.
541   SIP 13, para 8; SIP 16, para 15.
542   SIP 13, para 7; SIP 16, para 8.
543   SIP 13, para 10; SIP 16, para 13.
544   SIP 13, para 11.
545   SIP 16, para 16.
546   Ibid., para 19.

creditors and in any event within seven days of the transaction.[547] A bullet-point summary of 'Marketing Essentials' and a detailed list of matters to be addressed in the SIP 16 statement are contained in an appendix to SIP 16. These matters include explanations of the alternatives that were considered, any decision not to consult with major or representative creditors, any decision not to trade the business and offer it for sale as a going concern, and details of any attempts to arrange working capital.

5.   Insolvency Guidance Papers (IGP)

8.209   There are currently six IGPs in place, which have been developed and approved by the JIC and adopted by each of the RPBs. Unlike the Code of Ethics and the SIPs, which set out mandatory practice that IPs are required to comply with as a matter of professional conduct, the IPGs contain guidance only. IPs may develop their own different approaches to the issues covered by the IPGs.

8.210   Three IPGs are within the scope of this book. Firstly, 'Control of Cases' deals with the need for IPs to maintain and demonstrate appropriate control where work is delegated to staff or joint appointments are taken. This may be particularly important where joint appointments are proposed as a way of managing conflicts.[548] Secondly, 'Succession Planning' explains the importance of IPs having in place a system to ensure continuity in the event of death, incapacity or retirement, with the overriding principle being the need to ensure that the interests of creditors and other stakeholders should not be prejudiced.[549] Thirdly, 'Dealing with Complaints' sets out good practice for IPs when dealing with complaints professionally and expeditiously. It contains the interesting observation that actions or outcomes that may seem obvious to an IP may be seen as wrong or unfair by complainants.[550] This aspect is returned to below.

6.   Dear IP

8.211   A further source of guidance for IPs is the 'Dear IP' letters issued by the Insolvency Service from time to time. These contain technical updates or other practical information. The precise status of guidance given by way of Dear IP may sometimes be ambiguous; it has been described by R3 as a means of introducing 'quasi-legislation' at a time when formal legislation has been delayed.[551]

7.   Complaints to RPBs

8.212   Each RPB has governance structures in place to separate its membership function from its regulatory function. On the regulatory side, each has disciplinary arrangements in place that are

---

547   Ibid., para 20.
548   *Insolvency Guidance Paper: Control of Cases* (July 2005).
549   *Insolvency Guidance Paper: Succession Planning* (July 2005).
550   *Insolvency Guidance Paper: Dealing with Complaints* (October 2009).
551   R3, *Regulation of Insolvency Practitioners – Review of the Current Regulatory Landscape – R3 response* (October 2019), p 18, para 91.

governed by sets of rules and bye-laws.[552] Anyone may make a complaint to an IP's RPB, which the RPB will then investigate under its internal arrangements.

Since June 2013, the Insolvency Service has operated an online function known as the **8.213** 'Complaints Gateway'. This is a single point of entry for those wishing to complain about IPs, regardless of which RPB regulates them. The Insolvency Service only refers on to the relevant RPB those cases that require consideration by that RPB and otherwise rejects them. In recent years, approximately 50 per cent of complaints to the 'Complaints Gateway' have been referred on to an RPB.[553]

One of a number of important differences between the right to complain about an IP to their **8.214** RPB and standing to ask the court to review an officeholder's conduct is that, in order to complain to an RPB, there is no requirement to show a tangible interest in the estate. As discussed earlier in this chapter, a threshold condition has developed in the case law to the effect that an applicant seeking to be heard by the court in an insolvency proceeding must show an economic interest in the estate in order to ground standing. This has the effect of filtering out certain applications from disgruntled shareholders or unsecured creditors whose unhappiness may well have its basis in the fact that the company is insolvent, rather than the officeholder's conduct. The principle has no application to complaints to IPs' regulators. As the Insolvency Service has made clear, RPBs are expected to assess and undertake 'thorough investigation of complaints from all sources, including debtors, creditors, regulators and other insolvency practitioners'.[554] While this does not necessarily indicate that the RPBs are more likely to tolerate unjustified or vexatious grievances than the court, it nonetheless illustrates the point that the function of professional regulation is distinctly different from the function of the court.

The detail of the disciplinary arrangements of RPBs varies between each of them. Typically, **8.215** however, a complaint will fall to be considered by an investigating officer and, if appropriate, will be escalated to a higher level of assessment where it will be determined whether a prima facie case is disclosed by the complaint. If it does, then the IP may be offered the option of entering into an agreed order, where the complaint is admitted by them and a particular outcome (typically a reprimand with or without a fine) applied. Where the IP does not admit the complaint, it may proceed to a contested hearing before a tribunal, at which the IP may be legally represented, with a right of appeal to an appellate tribunal. Tribunal hearings are usually held in public. A range of sanctions may be imposed, ranging from exclusion from membership, withdrawal of authorisation to act as an IP for a period, a reprimand or severe reprimand, or a fine. The outcomes of complaints that are found to be proved (whether by agreement or following an adversarial hearing) are published on the RPBs' websites. Since 1 November 2014, all published disciplinary sanctions of the RPBs have also been published on the Insolvency Service's website in an agreed format. If the IP remains unhappy after their hearing before the

---

552 Insolvency Service, *Review of the monitoring and regulation of insolvency practitioners* (September 2018), p 8.

553 The numbers of complaints and the proportion referred on to RPBs have been remarkably stable in recent years. Numbers of complaints (with the percentage referred to the relevant RPB) are 2016: 849 (57 per cent); 2017: 757 (48 per cent); 2018: 830 (46 per cent); 2019: 856 (50 per cent). See Insolvency Service, *Call for Evidence – Regulation of insolvency practitioners: Review of current regulatory landscape* (July 2019), p 13; and Insolvency Service, *Annual Review of Insolvency Practitioner Regulation 2019* (26 August 2020), para 3.

554 Insolvency Service, *Insolvency Practitioner Regulation – regulatory objectives and oversight powers: Legislative changes introduces on 1 October 2015* (December 2015), p 7.

appellate tribunal, then they may apply for a judicial review of the decision. A good summary of the procedure employed by ACCA, from an initial complaint being made to its disposal by an appellate tribunal, is set out in *R (Mond) v Association of Chartered Certified Accountants*.[555]

8.216 When it comes to judicial reviews of the decisions of RPBs, the reported cases indicate that tribunal decisions tend to be treated deferentially by the courts and are usually left alone. This is consistent with the court's approach to disciplinary decisions of professional regulators more generally. The courts recognise that professional regulation has a fundamentally distinct purpose compared with court proceedings. In *Bolton v Law Society*, Sir Thomas Bingham MR held that, although there is sometimes a punitive or deterrent element, the orders of disciplinary tribunals are primarily directed at, first, ensuring that the offender does not have the opportunity to repeat the offence, and, secondly, maintenance of the reputation of the profession in question and protection of the public.[556] In the insolvency context, an illustration of this approach is evident in *R (Eliades) v Institute of Chartered Accountants in England and Wales*,[557] where an application for leave to seek judicial review was dismissed. The IP complained that his RPB's licensing committee had withdrawn his authorisation to practise in advance of a hearing taking place and that this had been unfair and oppressive. Newman J held that, in the circumstances of the case, the RPB would have been in danger of being criticised for acting in dereliction of its duty to the public if it had failed to take action.[558] The deferential approach of the courts on applications for judicial review is similarly apparent from *R (Hollis) v ACCA*,[559] where the application was dismissed and the decision of the RPB upheld.

8. Regulatory reform in recent years

8.217 There has been significant debate, and a degree of controversy, over the regulation of IPs over the last decade. It is submitted that, at times, criticism of existing regulatory provision or proposals for its reform have been in substance criticisms of the underlying insolvency regime that are really beyond the scope of professional regulation. At the time of writing, a review by the Insolvency Service of insolvency practitioner regulation is underway.[560] This section summarises the key debates over regulation in recent years that have led to this review.

(a) OFT Report and the Kempson Report

8.218 In June 2010, the Office of Fair Trading published 'The market for corporate insolvency practitioners: a market study' (OFT Report),[561] which was followed in July 2013 by 'Review of Insolvency Practitioner Fees: Report to the Insolvency Service' by Professor Elaine Kempson (Kempson Report).[562] The focus of both the OFT Report and the Kempson Report was the level of IPs' fees (i.e., their remuneration) and expenses.

---

555 [2005] EWHC 1414 (Admin), [2006] BPIR 94.
556 [1994] 1 WLR 513, 518F–519A. That case concerned a solicitor, but it applies with equal force to other professions, included chartered accountants: *R (Coke-Wallis) v ICAEW* [2011] UKSC 1, [2011] 2 AC 146, [60].
557 [2001] BPIR 363.
558 Ibid., [22], [31]–[33].
559 [2014] BPIR 1317.
560 Insolvency Service, *Call for Evidence – Regulation of insolvency practitioners: Review of current regulatory landscape* (July 2019).
561 Office of Fair Trading, *'The market for corporate insolvency practitioners: A market study'*, OFT1245 (June 2010).
562 Kempson, E., *'Review of Insolvency Practitioner Fees: Report to the Insolvency Service'* (July 2013).

The OFT Report reached the conclusion that there were identifiable market failures in **8.219** corporate insolvency appointments, particularly administration, and proposed reforms to the regulatory regime with a view to remedying the position. The OFT Report's overarching view was that the dependence of IPs on secured creditors for appointments made them particularly responsive to the secured creditors' wishes. It found that in the 63 per cent of cases where the secured creditor was not paid in full, the market 'appears to work reasonably well',[563] owing to the secured creditors' continuing economic interest in the level of fees charged by the office-holder, i.e., the direct effect that such fees would have on the level of distribution they would receive.[564] In the remaining 37 per cent of cases where the secured creditor was paid in full, however, there was evidence that 'like-for-like fees paid to the IP' were approximately 9 per cent higher than where the secured creditor retained an interest in them. The OFT Report suggested that a lack of understanding of insolvency processes, as well as a comparatively modest economic interest in the outcome, meant that unsecured creditors were not engaged with the process in a remotely comparable way to secured creditors.[565]

Three years later, the Kempson Report suggested a similar explanation for non-attendance by **8.220** unsecured creditors at creditors' meetings, including opportunity cost (such as lost earnings and out-of-pocket expenses) and a belief that they would not have any influence even if they did attend, particularly when the sum of money they were owed by the insolvent company represented only a small proportion of its overall debtors.[566] The OFT Report had found that a creditors' committee was formed in only 3 per cent of administrations,[567] commenting that 'there appears to be little regulatory focus on encouraging' such committees.[568] The Kempson Report identified similar issues[569] and found that, through their panels of approved IPs, the major banks were able to negotiate discounts (varying from 10 to 40 per cent) or run tendering processes at the outset, requiring an estimate of likely fees and a cap. The implicit sanction underpinning all such negotiations was to remove a firm from the panel.[570]

The OFT Report proposed reform to the regulatory system to address the market failure it had **8.221** identified. In doing so, it made clear that it was concerned with the market for corporate IPs and not with what it described as 'the insolvency process itself', save 'insofar as it affects the market for corporate IPs'.[571] In taking this approach, the OFT proceeded on two implied assumptions. The first implied assumption was that the operation of the market for corporate IPs could be analysed as a phenomenon in its right, rather than as a product of the legal and normative content of the insolvency process itself. The effect of this assumption was that any criticisms of existing outcomes, or proposals for rectifying perceived failures that the OFT Report wished to make, had to be grounded in causes or solutions external to the legislative regime. In taking this approach, the OFT Report arguably impoverished its ability to analyse the market, for it was unable to consider the possibility that the market it wished to examine was entirely a product of

---

563   OFT Report, paras 1.6, 1.12.
564   Ibid., para 1.12; para 4.29.
565   Ibid., paras 4.87–4.88.
566   Ibid., para 4.2.1, p 19; Kempson Report; para 4.2.3, p 22.
567   OFT Report, para 4.50.
568   Ibid., para 6.13.
569   Kempson Report, para 4.
570   Ibid., para 4.1.1.
571   OFT Report, para 2.7.

the complex interplay of priorities and interests produced by the underlying insolvency regime. The OFT report did not consider this aspect and instead concluded, without argument, that:

> ... in over a third of administrations and CVLs the market for IPs in corporate insolvencies fails. The current regulatory system for IPs does not appear to correct this failure, which indicates that there are problems with the regulatory system itself.[572]

8.222   This conclusion embodied the second implied assumption, i.e., that it is a function of professional regulation to exercise downward pressure on officeholder fees, of a kind capable of replicating the effect of the competitive market in insolvencies where there are repeat-player QFCHs.

8.223   Had it considered the underlying regime, it is possible that the OFT Report may have concluded that the market failure it identified was a result of the elevated position of secured debt, and in particular the dominant status of the QFCH, in that regime. That may have led it to consider the possibility that the outcomes it deprecated were neither the result of inadequate regulation nor susceptible to effective or efficient modification by means of regulatory reform. No consideration was given to the possibility that regulation was the wrong target.

8.224   The OFT Report noted that there were, at that time, no defined regulatory objectives for the RPBs. Drawing guidance from the *Clementi Review* on legal services,[573] it proposed the following regulatory objectives:

> *Promoting growth by maximising long-term returns to the body of creditors:* the primary responsibility of an IP is maximising the returns to the insolvent company from which the whole body of creditors benefit, and this should be the primary responsibility of their regulatory bodies. This usually means sustainably reforming businesses where possible, and efficiently disbanding them where necessary. In the process it should promote confidence and trust in lending, and in the fairness of the insolvency process.

> *Correct market failure by protecting the interests of vulnerable creditors:* Regulation should seek to correct the power imbalances in the market that can lead to market failure. In the market for corporate insolvency, at present this would involve ensuring that unsecured creditors' interests are sufficiently protected.

> *Ensuring an independent and competitive IP industry:* Ensure healthy competition between IPs delivers efficiency and innovation. Ensure IPs act in the wider public interest.[574]

8.225   The Kempson Report recommended a more extensive code of practice and identified considerable variation in the level of compliance monitoring then undertaken by the RPBs. A case could be made, Professor Kempson considered, for a reduction in the number of RPBs, perhaps by setting a minimum threshold for the number of IPs they regulated. Ultimately, Professor Kempson concluded, there was a case for a single regulator of IPs. As long as there continued to be a number of self-regulating bodies, the Insolvency Service needed to play an active role in ensuring that they operate to common standard of compliance monitoring and enforcement.[575]

---

572   Ibid., para 5.2.
573   Clementi, D., *'Review of the Regulatory Framework for Legal Services in England and Wales: Final Report'* (December 2004).
574   OFT Report, para 6.6.
575   Kempson Report, para 6.1.6.

(b) The 2015 reforms

Significant changes to the regime were made by Sch 6 of the Deregulation Act 2015 (DA 2015)   **8.226**
and Part 10 of the Small Business, Enterprise and Employment Act 2015 (SBEEA 2015).
Both sets of amendments were effective from 1 October 2015. The DA 2015 introduced new
ss 390A and 390B to the Insolvency Act 1986,[576] which provided for IPs to be authorised by
an RPB to act only in relation to companies or only in relation to individuals. Previously, IPs
could be authorised only in relation to both types of appointment. A considerable number of
the existing provisions in Part 13 of the Insolvency Act 1986 were repealed.[577]

The SBEEA 2015 introduced a further new version of s 391 and new ss 391A–391T to the   **8.227**
Insolvency Act 1986.[578] These provisions provided for a revised regulatory regime dealing
with the application process for a body to become recognised by the Secretary of State as an
RPB[579] and the introduction for the first time of defined 'regulatory functions' and (as had been
proposed in the OFT Report) 'regulatory objectives' for RPBs.[580] They also included powers
vested in the Secretary of State (which in practice means the Insolvency Service in its capacity
as oversight regulator) to:

- discipline RPBs;[581]
- revoke an RPB's authorisation;[582]
- discipline IPs directly;[583]
- obtain information from RPBs, IPs, or persons connected to IPs;[584] and
- apply to court to secure compliance with requirements under Part 13.[585]

Finally, the SBEEA 2015 conferred a power on the Secretary of State to make regulations to   **8.228**
designate a single body to act as the regulator of IPs, which may be either a body corporate
established by the regulations themselves, or a body already in existence.[586] A 'sunset clause'
provided that the power to designate a single regulator would expire at the end of seven years
from its coming into force.[587] The power will expire in October 2022.

This raft of powers and measures was discussed in the explanatory notes to the SBEEA 2015,   **8.229**
which observed that, as things stood, the Secretary of State had only one sanction against an
RPB that was not regulating effectively, which was to revoke its recognition. That ultimate
sanction, the explanatory notes said, would be disproportionate in all but the most serious
circumstances and had never been used. The stated purpose of the amendments made by the
SBEE 2015 was to amend Part 13 of the Insolvency Act 1986 to introduce a range of sanctions

---

576   DA 2015, s 17(3).
577   Insolvency Act 1986, ss 389(1A), 389(A) and 392 to 398, were repealed by DA 2015, Sch 6.
578   SBEEA 2015, ss 137–143.
579   Insolvency Act 1986, ss 391 and 391A.
580   Ibid., ss 391B and 391C.
581   Ibid., ss 391D–391K.
582   Ibid., ss 391L–391N. This was not strictly a new power, as the Secretary of State had previously had the power under s
       393 to 'withdraw' authorisation, but the power was heavily recast.
583   Ibid., ss 391O–391R.
584   Ibid., s 391S.
585   Ibid., s 391T.
586   SBEEA 2015, s 144.
587   Ibid., s 146.

against an RPB that was not adequately fulfilling its role as a regulator or, where it was in the public interest to do so, to apply to court for a direct sanctions order against an IP.[588]

8.230   Perhaps the most interesting aspect of the amended regime is the definition of 'regulatory functions' in s 391B and the introduction of specified 'regulatory objectives' by s 391C of the Insolvency Act 1986.[589] Section 391B provides that in discharging its regulatory functions (essentially authorising and regulating IPs[590]), an RPB must, so far as reasonably practicable, act in a way that is compatible with and in which the RPB considers most appropriate for the purpose of meeting those 'regulatory objectives'.

8.231   Section 391C(3) sets out the 'regulatory objectives' as follows:

> 'Regulatory objectives' means the objectives of –
>
> (a)   having a system of regulating persons acting as insolvency practitioners that –
>   (i)   secures fair treatment for persons affected by their acts and omissions,
>   (ii) reflects the regulatory principles, and
>   (iii) ensures consistent outcomes,
> (b)   encouraging an independent and competitive insolvency-practitioner profession whose members –
>   (i)   provide high quality services at a cost to the recipient which is fair and reasonable,
>   (ii) act transparently and with integrity, and
>   (iii) consider the interests of all creditors in any particular case,
> (c)   promoting the maximisation of the value of returns to creditors and promptness in making those returns, and
> (d)   protecting and promoting the public interest.

8.232   No further guidance was provided in the explanatory notes to the SBEE 2015 to assist in the interpretation of the 'regulatory objectives'. This lack of definition raises again the tension between the outcomes driven by the values and priorities in the statutory insolvency regime and the role of regulation in moderating or altering those outcomes. It is not clear, for example, whether the objective at s 391C(3)(a)(i) of having a system that secures fair treatment for persons affected by IPs' acts and omissions intends to refer to securing substantively fair outcomes for those affected by insolvency, or whether it refers to fair treatment in the conduct of the regulatory process itself. If the former, then it is difficult to see how the provision can be interpreted (whether by IPs or anyone else) without having regard to values that are found outside the regulatory objectives themselves: does 'fair treatment' mean fairness by reference to the statutory regime, or does it refer to a more general concept of fairness? It is submitted that where there is a deficiency of assets against liabilities, and losses must be suffered somewhere, what is fair or unfair will often depend upon an affected party's point of view. Measured against anything other than the values and priorities embodied in the legislation, it may not be straight-forward for IPs to interpret this objective in a principled way.

8.233   This tension has been noted by the JIC. The IGP *Dealing with Complaints* notes that:

> It is a feature of the work of insolvency practitioners that complaints may arise because of an incomplete understanding of the insolvency legislation under which insolvency officeholders are required

---

588   Ibid., Explanatory Notes, paras 72–73.
589   Ibid., s 138.
590   Insolvency Act 1986, s 391C(2).

to act. In many cases, actions or outcomes that are obvious to insolvency practitioners may be seen as wrong or unfair by complainants, as the duties of the officeholder may be misunderstood.[591]

Guidance published by the Insolvency Service shortly after the regulatory objectives were enacted also anticipated this difficulty. The Insolvency Service said: **8.234**

> It is for the RPB to exercise their expertise and judgment in deciding on what fair treatment means in an insolvency context. It is recognised that the person impacted by an insolvency practitioner's decision may not always feel fairly treated if they disagree with the way legislation is framed for example, but the RPB should be able to explain how they have dealt fairly with all parties in the circumstances that have arisen.[592]

These passages indicate that the regulatory objective of 'fair treatment' is interpreted by the JIC and the Insolvency Service as procedural rather than substantive, and neither regards it as opening up a wider conception of fairness outside or inconsistent with the underlying legislative regime. This relationship between outcomes produced by the insolvency regime, perceptions of what is fair, and the role of regulation in this, is returned to below. **8.235**

Other provisions introduced by the SBEE 2015 at ss 391D–391N have given the Secretary of State various powers to regulate the conduct of an underperforming RPB. Prior to the introduction of these measures, the Secretary of State (acting by the Insolvency Service as oversight regulator) had no power other than withdrawal of recognition to discipline RPBs. These powers may be invoked where the Secretary of State is satisfied that an act or omission, or series of acts or omissions, of the RPB in discharging one or more of its regulatory functions has had or is likely to have an adverse impact on the achievement of one or more of the regulatory objectives. The powers include the ability to give a direction,[593] impose a financial penalty,[594] or give a reprimand[595] to an RPB. The Secretary of State continues to be able to revoke the recognition of an RPB.[596] **8.236**

Further provision is made for the Secretary of State to impose direct sanctions against individual IPs. This gives the Secretary of State the power to act as a super-regulator, should the circumstances require it. Where it appears in the public interest to do so, the Secretary of State may apply to the court for a direct sanctions order against an IP.[597] Such an order may withdraw or suspend the IP's authorisation, or require them to make a contribution to one or more creditors, not to exceed the amount of remuneration the IP has received from the case.[598] The grounds for such an order include that the IP has failed to act in accordance with the rules of the RPB or any standards, or code of ethics, for the insolvency profession adopted from time to time by the RPB.[599] This is a particularly interesting development, as such an application **8.237**

---

591 *Insolvency Guidance Paper: Dealing with Complaints* (October 2009).
592 Insolvency Service, *'Insolvency practitioner regulation – regulatory objectives and oversight powers: Legislative chances introduced on 1 October 2015'*, December 2015, p 6. The Insolvency Service restated the point in updated but similar language in *'Call for evidence: Regulation of insolvency practitioners: Review of current regulatory landscape'* (July 2019), para 5.1.1.
593 Insolvency Act 1986, ss 391D, 391E.
594 Ibid., ss 391F, 391G
595 Ibid., ss 391J, 391K.
596 Ibid., ss 391L, 391M.
597 Ibid., s 391P.
598 Ibid., s 391O.
599 Ibid., s 391Q.

by the Secretary of State would see the court deliberating on a cause of action against an IP founded directly on a failure to comply with some aspect of professional regulation, rather than a breach of duty under the substantive law. To date, it appears that none of the direct powers to sanction either individual RPBs[600] or individual IPs have been exercised by the Insolvency Service, so there has been no opportunity to see how this regime would work in practice. The court's current attitude to attempts by litigants to draw on regulatory material in proceedings against officeholders is discussed further below.

(c) Call for Evidence 2019

8.238 As noted above, the Secretary of State's power to move to a single regulator is to expire in October 2022. The Insolvency Service is currently considering whether or not that power will be exercised and published a call for evidence in July 2019, which closed on 4 October 2019 (Call for Evidence 2019).[601] The stated objective of the Call for Evidence 2019 is to gather evidence to gauge the impact of the introduction of the 'regulatory objectives' and how the current regime is working, to help inform the decision on whether or not the government should consult on a move to a single regulator, or consider other improvements to the regulatory framework.[602]

8.239 The power bestowed on the Secretary of State in the SBEE 2015 to designate a single regulator has been overtaken to an extent by events, as the number of regulators has declined significantly in recent years. Both the Law Society and the Law Society of Scotland made a request to the Secretary of State in 2015[603] that their status as RPBs be revoked. At the point at which the Law Society requested that its status be revoked, it authorised only 129 solicitor IPs, of whom only around 22 took appointments.[604] Both requests were granted and the Law Society of Scotland's status as an RPB was revoked with effect from 18 January 2016,[605] with the Law Society's status similarly revoked with effect from 15 April 2016.[606] From 1 January 2017, ACCA transferred its monitoring and regulatory functions to the IPA.[607] On 2 February 2019, ACCA asked the Secretary of State to consider its request under s 391N that it should cease to be an RPB. The Secretary of State granted that request and revoked ACCA's status as an RPB with effect from 1 March 2021.[608] ICAEW now assists ICAS with its IP monitoring work,[609] which means that the number of regulators has declined from eight in 2015 to either three or four, depending whether or not ICAS is counted separately. The vast majority of IPs are now regulated either by the IPA or the ICAEW.

---

600   IPA, *Insolvency Service Review of Current Regulatory Landscape: Insolvency Practitioners Association Position Paper* (3 October 2019), p 18, para 41; ICAEW Representation 107/19 (4 October 2019), p 3, para 8; p 34.

601   Insolvency Service, *Call for evidence: Regulation of insolvency practitioners: Review of current regulatory landscape*, Insolvency Service (July 2019).

602   Ibid., p 3.

603   Insolvency Act 1986, s. 391N.

604   Solicitors Regulation Authority, *Regulation of insolvency practice: consultation response* (17 March 2015), para 2.

605   Insolvency Practitioners (Recognised Professional Bodies) (Revocation of Recognition) Order 2015/2067, art 2.

606   Insolvency Practitioners (Recognised Professional Bodies) (Revocation of Recognition) Order 2016/403, art 2.

607   Insolvency Service, *Review of the monitoring and regulation of insolvency practitioners* (September 2018), p 3.

608   Insolvency Practitioners (Recognised Professional Bodies) Order 2021/110.

609   ICAEW Representation 107/19 (4 October 2019), p 3, para 6.

In their responses to the Call for Evidence 2019, the two biggest RPBs (the IPA and the ICAEW) both indicated their opposition to a move to a single regulator.[610] By contrast, the ACCA (having recently ceased to be an RPB) not only supported the move to a single new regulator established by regulations, but considered the single regulator model to be the only one that would address the perception of conflict of interest and inconsistency of regulation of IPs.[611]   **8.240**

In a 2019 survey, R3 found that the profession was split: 39 per cent of respondents favoured some sort of single regulator, while 57 per cent were in favour of retaining a multi-regulator structure.[612] R3 submitted that a switch to a single regulator would not automatically solve current concerns and observed that many practitioners felt that the Insolvency Service was pushing the RPBs towards a tick-box or compliance-driven approach to regulation. It added: **8.241**

> A not uncommon complaint from members at R3 listening events has been that, as a result, an insolvency practitioner can be 100% compliant with regulation, but is still able to bring the profession into disrepute – and to get away with it.[613]

At the time of writing, it is not known what conclusions will be drawn from the evidence gathered by the Call for Evidence 2019. For the reasons explored above, there remain unanswered questions concerning the correct interpretation of the regulatory objectives and their relationship with the underlying legislative regime. In terms of further regulatory reform, it is submitted that there may be an expectation gap between the aspirations that some have for professional regulation and the reality. As a matter of substance, certain issues that are presented as matters concerned with the regulation of IPs, particularly in relation to the control that secured creditors have over the appointment of officeholders[614] or their fees,[615] are really criticisms of the role of secured debt, and especially the dominant position of the QFCH, in the statutory insolvency regime. That is a legitimate subject for debate (and has been one for a long time[616]) but it is better to approach it for what it is, namely a fundamental issue going to the heart of the corporate governance of insolvent companies, rather than something marginal that can be regulated away.[617]   **8.242**

---

610   IPA, *Insolvency Service Review of Current Regulatory Landscape: Insolvency Practitioners Association Position Paper* (3 October 2019), p 4, para (i); ICAEW Representation 107/19 (4 October 2019), p 10, paras 42–43.

611   ACCA, *Regulation of insolvency practitioners: Review of the current regulatory landscape* Ref: TECH-CDR-1836 (4 October 2019), pp 6–7.

612   R3, *Regulation of Insolvency Practitioners – Review of the Current Regulatory Landscape – R3 response* (October 2019), p 19, para 94. Broken down fully between the detailed options, a more diffuse picture was presented: (a) 28 per cent: a 'single regulatory process' (where existing regulators share a single monitoring, complaints and disciplinary process); (b) 25 per cent: a 'single, independent regulator'; (c) 17 per cent: the existing framework to stay the same; (d) 14 per cent: one of the existing regulators becoming a 'single regulator'; (e) 13 per cent maintaining the existing framework but with fewer regulators: p 18, para 93.

613   Ibid., p 6, paras 27–28.

614   Tomlinson, L. *'The Tomlinson Report'* (2013) (www.tomlinsonreport.com/docs/tomlinsonreport.pdf).

615   OFT Report, para 5.2.

616   See remarks of Lord Macnaghten in *Salomon v A Salomon & Co Ltd* [1897] AC 22, 53 and Lord Walker's discussion of the point in *Re Spectrum Plus Ltd (in liq)* [2005] 2 AC 680, [132].

617   Shortly before this book went to press, the All Party Parliamentary Group on Fair Business Banking (APPG) published a report titled *Resolving Insolvency: Restoring confidence in the system* (September 2021). The report proposed a number of regulatory and statutory reforms, including a 'ban' on all conflicts of interest in IP appointments, a move to a single regulator supported by an ombudsman, and 'placing the Code of Ethics on a statutory footing'. These reforms were

9.   Relationship between regulatory control and control by the court

8.243   As noted above, the functions of professional regulators and the courts are distinct, although there appear to be increasing references to regulatory material in litigation. This section looks first at the reluctance of the courts to encroach on the territory of professional regulation, before considering the way that regulatory material may nonetheless have a role to play in litigation over officeholder duties.

8.244   The difference in function between the regulators and the courts is significant. For instance, a departure from best practice that has caused no loss (such as, for instance, a failure to maintain records or file reports on time) might be susceptible to regulatory censure, but an absence of loss will be a complete answer to a misfeasance claim irrespective of the surrounding conduct.[618] The regulator is using its powers to ensure high standards of conduct by IPs, whereas the court is primarily concerned with rectifying the particular economic wrongs before it. Moreover, and as noted above, regulators are not concerned only with those with an economic interest in the estate, but also with those who may otherwise have been affected by an insolvency. That will include considering complaints by out-of-the-money parties, particularly debtors, who would not have standing before the court by reason of their lack of interest in the assets available for distribution.

8.245   This difference in function is observed by the courts. A breach of a regulatory obligation will not, of itself, give rise to an actionable breach of duty with which the court will engage. In *SISU Capital Fund Ltd v Tucker*, Warren J dealt with applications to revoke or suspend approval of two related company voluntary arrangements, which were alleged to be unfairly prejudicial within the meaning of s 6 of the Act. The respondent officeholders were said to have been subject to conflicts of interest that made their positions impossible.[619] In support of this, the applicants sought to rely on what is referred to in the judgment as 'the applicable [ICAEW] Guidance'.[620] Warren J did not consider that the regulatory guidance 'really adds anything to the applicants' case save for the forensic point that, not only have the respondents acted when suffering from alleged irreconcilable conflicts but those conflicts are ones specifically to be avoided in accordance with professional rules'.[621] In Warren J's view, the relevant statutory provision was 'the beginning and the end of the case' and any suggestion that the fact that an officeholder may be in breach of their professional rules was enough, by itself, to establish unfair prejudice for the purposes of the statute was rejected.[622]

8.246   In reaching this conclusion, Warren J adopted a distinction between 'the interests of the insolvency administration' on the one hand, and 'professional guidance/standards' on the other. The relevant ultimate question for the court was whether there was unfair prejudice; a breach of regulatory guidance of itself did not amount to that. In support of this view, Warren J cited an

---

described as 'simple changes' in the foreword to the report, but it is submitted that they are, in fact, far-reaching and profound. The debate is certain to continue for some time to come.

618   *Re Derek Randall Enterprises Ltd* [1990] BCC 749, 760H; *Lomax Leisure v Miller* [2007] EWHC 2508, [2008] 1 BCLC 262, [37]; *Re E D Games Ltd* [2009] EWHC 223, [16]; *Re One Blackfriars Ltd (in liq)* [2021] EWHC 684 (Ch), [255].
619   *SISU Capital Fund Ltd v Tucker* [2005] EWHC 2170 (Ch), [2006] BCC 463, [91].
620   Ibid., [93].
621   Ibid., [132].
622   Ibid., [91].

earlier observation of Millett J in *Re Polly Peck International plc*,[623] where a similar distinction had been drawn between 'the interests of the administration' (with which the court was concerned) and 'the integrity and objectivity' of IPs (with which the regulator was concerned).[624]

Similar arguments were raised in reliance on the Code of Ethics in *Re Zinc Hotels (Holdings)* **8.247** *Ltd*. Citing Warren J in *SISU Capital Fund Ltd v Tucker* and Millett J *Re Polly Peck*, Henry Carr J summarised the position in the following stark terms: 'There is a distinction between professional guidance given to practitioners and the interests of the relevant insolvency proceedings, and the court is primarily concerned with the latter rather than the former.'[625]

Consistently with this approach, David Richards J did not entertain a suggestion that a failure **8.248** by administrators to comply with SIP 16 was a ground for their removal in *Clydesdale Financial Services Ltd v Smailes*.[626]

Re Comet Group Ltd (in liquidation)[627] was a comparatively high-profile example of the different **8.249** functions of the regulators and the courts. In this unusual case, some voluntary liquidators applied under s 112 for directions. The liquidators had formerly been administrators and their firm had advised the secured creditor prior to the commencement of the administration. The ICAEW had investigated a number of complaints against the liquidators concerning, amongst other things, alleged threats to their objectivity arising from their prior professional relationship with the secured creditor and their alleged failure to investigate the enforceability of the secured creditor's charge and the directors' conduct. A draft report by the ICAEW had found a prima facie case to be referred to a disciplinary tribunal.[628] The liquidators applied to the court, naming the ICAEW as respondent, and at the hearing sought directions that they be permitted to form their own view of the merits of the enforceability of the charge and the possible claims against the directors.[629] They contended that they had obtained advice that the security was valid and wished to continue the liquidation on the basis of that advice. The court recorded that the liquidators perceived that the ICAEW was interfering in the liquidation when it had no right to do so and that the liquidators were concerned that they faced regulatory consequences and possible disciplinary proceedings if they failed to comply with what they saw as directions from the ICAEW.[630]

The judge declined to grant any relief, principally on the basis that the liquidators did not need **8.250** a direction from the court in order to form their own views or to make their own decisions: they were entitled to do that without launching an application. Sir Nicholas Warren (sitting as a High Court judge) cited Neuberger J's 'bomb shelter' dictum from *In re T & D Industries*

---

623   *Re Polly Peck International plc*, unreported, 2 February 1992.
624   *SISU Capital Fund Ltd v Tucker* [2005] EWHC 2170 (Ch), [2006] BCC 463, [130].
625   *Re Zinc Hotels (Holdings) Ltd* [2018] EWHC 1936 (Ch), [2018] BCC 968, [81]. The judge nonetheless went on to consider the administrators' conduct by reference to the Code of Ethics and did not accept that there had been any breach of it.
626   [2009] EWH 1745 (Ch), [2009] BCC 810, [32], [34]. The officeholder in that case was removed on other grounds [39].
627   [2018] EWHC 1378 (Ch).
628   Ibid., [23]–[24].
629   Ibid., [8].
630   Ibid., [3]–[4].

plc[631] discussed earlier in this chapter and observed that the purpose of the application could only be to protect the liquidators in some way from disciplinary actions that the ICAEW may take.[632] If the directions the liquidators sought were granted, the judge considered, then the risk of disciplinary proceedings would be hugely reduced, if not altogether eliminated, because it would be difficult to criticise the liquidators if directions were made and the liquidators were then to act in accordance with them.[633] Accordingly, the court refused to grant the directions the liquidators requested.

8.251 It is submitted that the decision in *Re Comet Group Ltd (in liquidation)* can be interpreted as an example of the court not wishing to involve itself in, or encroach upon, an RPB's ability to regulate its own members, or to allow officeholders to outflank a regulatory investigation by means of directions from the court. The decision in *Re Comet Group Ltd (in liquidation)* underlines the different functions that professional discipline and the legislative insolvency regime perform and the reluctance of the court either to adopt or usurp the role of the RPBs in matters of regulation. In this respect, it is consistent with the established approach taken by the court when judicially reviewing decisions of regulatory tribunals discussed above.

8.252 Regulatory material has, however, informed the court's approach in other contexts. In *Re Kayley Vending Ltd*,[634] HHJ David Cooke (sitting as a High Court judge) said that in most cases where an application for an administration order is made in a pre-pack case, provision of the information in SIP 16 would fall within the requirement in what is now r 3.6(3)(g)[635] to inform the court of 'any other matters which, in the applicant's opinion, will assist the court in deciding whether to make such an order' and so should be included. Judge Cooke considered that this was an aspect of the need in pre-pack cases for the court to 'be alert to see, so far as it can, that the procedure is at least not being obviously abused to the disadvantage of creditors'.[636]

8.253 In *Re Moss Groundworks Ltd*,[637] Snowden J declined to grant an application for an administration order where the evidence in support of it was 'wholly inadequate' to explain how the 'marketing essentials' contained in the appendix to SIP 16 had been complied with.[638] Unless a better explanation were provided for the apparent inconsistency between the company's book value and the consideration proposed under the pre-pack sale, the court was unable to be satisfied that the type of abuse referred to in *Re Kayley Vending Ltd* was not present.[639] The case was adjourned specifically for the company and the proposed administrators to reconsider, amongst other things, their compliance with SIP 16.[640] When the matter came back before HHJ Eyre QC (sitting as a High Court judge), accompanied by much improved evidence and a SIP 16 compliant report, an administration order was made and the judge observed that:

---

631   [2000] 1 WLR 646. See para 8.007 above.
632   [2018] EWHC 1378 (Ch), [15]–[16].
633   Ibid., [17]–[18].
634   [2009] EWHC 904 (Ch), [2009] BCC 578.
635   The rule in force at the time was Insolvency Rules 1986, r 2.4(2)(e).
636   [2009] EWHC 904 (Ch), [2009] BCC 578, [24].
637   [2019] EWHC 2825 (Ch).
638   Ibid, [27].
639   Ibid, [28].
640   Ibid, [29].

Evidence of compliance with those steps is likely to be sufficient in very many, perhaps in most, cases to assuage the court's concerns. Conversely, a party who has failed to take those steps will need to explain all the more clearly why it can be said that the risk of abuse is not significant.[641]

The approach that has developed here is interesting, because while compliance with SIP 16 is not a part of the statutory procedure for an administration application, the courts have nonetheless developed a practice of regarding the information in SIP 16 as a benchmark by which the adequacy of the evidence filed in support of an administration application can be measured. In this way, the regulatory regime has informed the statutory test and, by means of case law, become a part of it for all practical purposes. **8.254**

A tendency has also begun to emerge in recent cases to regard non-compliance with regulatory guidance as evidence of breaches of actionable duties. It should be emphasised that the following cases are not authority for the proposition that breaches of regulatory guidance are actionable by the court in and of themselves, but rather that departures from good practice may be indicative of breaches of duty. In *Brewer v Iqbal*,[642] an administrator had entered into a related-party sale, but had thought SIP 16 did not apply and admitted that he had not considered SIP 13. Chief ICC Judge Briggs considered that these features meant that the administrator 'had not acted in accordance with best practice'[643] and held that they were 'strong indicators of a failure to act with due care and skill'.[644] The judge accepted expert evidence that a competent officeholder would have complied with the 'Acting with sufficient expertise'[645] section of the Code of Ethics and obtained appropriate knowledge and understanding of the entity and acquired an appropriate understanding of the complexities of the business.[646] The administrator's failure to do so led to a failure properly to market the assets, which constituted a failure to act with reasonable care and skill. **8.255**

The breach of duty in *Brewer v Iqbal* was not in the administrator's failure follow regulations: in the case of the SIPs, the departure from best practice was evidence of negligence; in the case of the Code of Ethics, the failure to follow the guidance had caused the administrator to fail to market the assets adequately. This approach was adopted in *Re One Blackfriars Ltd (in liquidation)*,[647] where the deputy judge held that a breach of the Code of Ethics 'may well be an indicator or even a strong indicator of a failure to act with due care and skill' and that it was open to the applicant liquidators to rely on the Code of Ethics to assist the court on whether the respondent administrators had acted in breach of their duties, despite the lack of a pleaded case based on the Code of Ethics. The deputy judge further held that: 'Behaviour constituting a breach, for example, of Fundamental Principle (a) (Integrity) or (b) (Objectivity) as described in the Code of Ethics may well be strong or very strong evidence of a breach of duty of care or a fiduciary duty.'[648] **8.256**

---

641   [2019] EWHC 3079 (Ch), [8].
642   [2019] EWHC 182 (Ch), [2019] BCC 746.
643   Ibid., [66].
644   Ibid., [80].
645   Code of Ethics, 2300.1.
646   Ibid., 2300.3 A4.
647   [2021] EWHC 684 (Ch).
648   Ibid., [251]–[252].

8.257 It is submitted that these cases show that regulatory guidance is being used to set something like an objective standard for competent officeholder conduct, against which the duty of care will be measured. As noted earlier in this chapter, the negligence standard is an objective one, namely that of an ordinary skilled practitioner.[649] Significant departures from that standard will amount to negligence and in that sense regulatory guidance may provide a benchmark.

---

649   *Davey v Money* [2018] EWHC 766, [2018] Bus LR 1903, [256].

9

CREDITORS' AND LIQUIDATION COMMITTEES

A. INTRODUCTION

When a company enters administration or administrative receivership a creditors' committee **9.001** may be convened. In liquidation a similar kind of committee, known as a liquidation committee, may be established which is made up solely of creditors, although in one particular situation contributories may also be members of the committee. These committees can be seen as analogous to a board in a solvent company. Just as a board is to oversee the directors' management of the company, so these committees, where appointed, are to oversee the work of the relevant officeholder. Obviously a meeting of all contributories or a meeting of all creditors would be too large and cumbersome to be able to assist in and supervise the insolvency regime, and this is most obvious where the company's affairs are complex. Thus, as with a board in the company situation, in insolvency a group of people are deputed to represent the interests of what could be a large body of people.

The chapter aims primarily to explain the appointment, constitution, role, position, functions, **9.002** and operation of the aforementioned committees, although it will deal with a few other issues that are relevant. Much of the law is procedural and contained in the Insolvency Act ('the Act') or the Insolvency Rules 2016 ('the Rules'). One chapter of the Rules, Chapter 17, is set aside for committees. We do not mention every aspect that the Rules consider as that would be tedious and would not fulfil the aim of the book.[1] There is relatively little case law that addresses the committees and that does leave, in places, a lacuna in the law. The law tends to treat creditors' committees and liquidation committees in the same manner, under the latest iteration of the insolvency rules, and, for most purposes, we do so likewise in the chapter. However, in some places we have discussed the different committees separately as the law treats them differently.

---

1   For the Rules and commentary thereon, see L Doyle QC, A Keay and J. Curl QC (eds), *Insolvency Legislation: Annotations and Commentary,* (10th ed, Lexis, 2021).

B. APPOINTMENT AND CONSTITUTION

9.003 The creditors of the company have the right to appoint a creditors' committee in an administrative receivership where the receiver has prepared a report under s 48 of the Act. Such a report includes such things as reporting on the events leading up to the appointment of the receiver, the disposal of property, the payment of amounts to the receiver's appointors (the relevant debenture-holders) and what is available to pay to other creditors.[2]

9.004 The creditors of a company that enters administration, through whatever gateway (by way of court order or out of court), also have the option of forming a creditors' committee.[3]

9.005 For committees in both administrative receivership and administration there must be at least three members appointed and not more than five members.[4]

9.006 The right to have a similar committee applies to the creditors in a liquidation.[5] They can establish what is called a liquidation committee, although it may only be appointed where there is a compulsory[6] or creditors' voluntary winding up.[7] Like creditors' committees in administrative receivership and administration, for creditors' voluntary windings up[8] and a compulsory winding up[9] a liquidation committee must have at least three members, but no more than five.

9.007 While creditors will populate the committees discussed, in a creditors' voluntary liquidation if there is a liquidation committee, the company may, either at the meeting at which the resolution for voluntary winding up is passed or at any subsequent time in general meeting, appoint such number of persons as they think fit to act as members of the committee, not exceeding five.[10] However, the creditors may, if they think fit, decide that all or any of the persons appointed by the company ought not to be members of the liquidation committee. If the creditors make that decision those persons are not then, unless the court otherwise directs, qualified to act as members of the committee; and on any application to the court under s 101(3) the court may, if it thinks fit, appoint other persons to act as such members of the committee in place of those persons.

9.008 In compulsory liquidations where companies are ordered to be wound up because of insolvency the contributories will not be entitled to be members of a liquidation committee except in limited circumstances.[11] If the creditors do not decide that a committee should be established or decide that a committee should not be established, the contributories may decide to appoint

---

2   Insolvency Act 1986, s 48(1).
3   Ibid., para 57(1) of Sch B1.
4   Insolvency Rules 2016, r 17.3(1).
5   In liquidations where the company was not insolvent contributories may also be members of a committee. See ibid., r 17.3(3)(b).
6   Insolvency Act 1986, s 141.
7   Ibid., s 101.
8   Insolvency Rules 2016, r 17.3(2); Insolvency Act 1986, s 101(1).
9   Ibid., r 17.3(3).
10 Insolvency Act 1986, s 101(2).
11 Where the grounds on which the company was wound up do not include inability to pay its debts and where the contributories so decide, the committee may have up to three contributory members elected by the contributories: r 17.3(3)(b).

one of their members to apply to the court for an order requiring the liquidator to seek a further decision from the creditors on whether a liquidation committee should be established.[12] The court may, if it thinks that there are special circumstances to justify it, make such an order and the creditors' decision sought by the liquidator in compliance with the order is deemed to have been a decision under s 141 of the Act.[13] If the creditors, when making a decision that the court requires them to make, decide not to establish a committee the contributories may do so.[14] The committee must then consist of at least three, and not more than five, contributories elected by the contributories and r 17.5 (the rule on establishment of committees), applies. It is submitted that it will be very unusual to see the contributories getting involved in the manner just outlined.

9.009 There is no provision for contributories to be members of creditors' committees in either administrative receivership or administration.

9.010 It has been held in Australia that if it is clear that creditors will not receive full payment from the winding up, then providing that all other matters are equal all members of the committee should represent creditors.[15] In any event, it is unlikely that there will be any interest amongst contributories to have any input into most insolvent liquidations. The exception might be where contributories believe that the company should be able to make large claims against third parties that will see the company become solvent again when recoveries have been received. In such a case, obviously, contributories might receive a pay-out.

9.011 The court has no express power to interfere with the composition of a validly appointed committee, but, in exercising its general powers in relation to winding up, it has been said that the court should consider influencing the composition of the committee so that no creditor or class of creditors with a substantial interest is excluded from the representation which it seeks.[16]

9.012 If there are more than five creditors seeking to be members of a creditors' committee or liquidation committee, the appropriate way to proceed is for the officeholder (if chair/convenor) to choose the five creditors who attracted the greatest number of votes by value on a single ballot.[17]

9.013 As far as membership of the committees is concerned, any creditor is eligible to be a member of a creditors' or liquidation committee if that creditor has proved for a debt which is not fully secured and that proof has not been wholly disallowed for voting purposes or wholly rejected for the purpose of distribution or dividend.[18] No person may be a member of a liquidation committee as both a creditor and a contributory.[19] A body corporate may be a member of a creditors' committee, but it may only act by a properly authorised representative.[20]

---

12   Insolvency Rules 2016, r 17.6(1)(2).
13   Ibid., r 17.6(2).
14   Ibid., r 17.6(3).
15   *Re James; In re Cowra Processors Pty Ltd* (1995) 15 ACLC 1582.
16   *Radford & Bright Ltd, Re* [1901] 1 Ch 272 at 277, *Re James; In re Cowra Processors Pty Ltd* (1995) 13 ACLC 1582.
17   *Re Polly Peck International plc* [1991] BCC 503, 508.
18   Insolvency Rules 2016, r 17.4(1)(2).
19   Ibid., r 17.4(3).
20   Ibid., r 17.4(4). A representative is duly authorised under the provisions of r 17.17.

9.014 A liquidation committee is established if both the company's creditors and contributories take the decision to establish a committee.[21] If only the creditors or only the contributories decide in favour, a liquidation committee is to be established unless the court orders otherwise.[22] Where the official receiver is the liquidator, in a compulsory liquidation, then, although a committee may be established, it is neither able nor can it be required to carry out its functions, those being vested in the Secretary of State.[23]

9.015 If a liquidator is not advised of the establishment of a liquidation committee, it is for the liquidator to determine whether or not to request the creditors and contributories to decide to establish a committee, but the liquidator is obliged if requested to do so by one-tenth in value of the company's creditors.[24] In complex liquidations, in particular, in which there is likely to be controversy or substantial litigation the liquidator may well decide to instigate a decision procedure to seek a decision from the creditors as to whether a committee should be established. The establishment of a committee would enable the liquidator to be in a position where he or she can obtain advice and support.

9.016 It should be noted that if a company commenced winding up as a creditors' voluntary liquidation, but it is found that the company is in fact solvent and the creditors are paid in full, company members could not be appointed to the liquidation committee if it were necessary to secure a decision of the liquidation committee because, on payment of their debts, the creditors who were members of the committee had their membership terminated under r 17.11 and so no committee existed to which the company members could be appointed.[25]

9.017 Once a decision has been made to establish a creditors' or liquidation committee, the convener of the decision procedure or deemed consent process (or chair where the decision procedure involves a meeting), if not the officeholder, must inform the officeholder of the decision and, if members have been elected, provide the names and addresses of those elected to be members of the committee.[26] Should a decision be made to establish a committee but not as to its membership, the officeholder must seek a decision from the creditors, and, where applicable, the contributories, as to nature of the membership.[27]

9.018 The committee is not established and cannot act until the minimum number of persons required by r 17.3 have agreed to act as members of the committee and the relevant officeholder has delivered a notice to that effect to the registrar of companies.[28] The notice must contain the following: a statement that the committee has been duly constituted; identification details for any company that is a member of the committee; and the name and address of each member. The notice must be authenticated and dated by the officeholder,[29] and must be delivered to the registrar of companies as soon as reasonably practicable after the minimum membership of

---

21   Insolvency Act 1986, s 141(2).
22   Ibid., s 141(3).
23   Ibid., s 141(4).
24   Ibid., s 141(3B).
25   *Re Future Route Ltd* [2017] EWHC 3677 (Ch) at [15]–[22].
26   Insolvency Rules 2016, r 17.5(1).
27   Ibid., r 17.5(4).
28   Ibid., r 17.4(5)(9).
29   Ibid., r 17.5(7).

three have agreed to act as members and have been elected.[30] The fact that a notice has been delivered by a liquidator to the registrar does not necessarily mean that the committee has been constituted properly and can stand. In *Re W & A Glaser Ltd*[31] the court held, under previous rules, that a committee was not constituted properly, notwithstanding the certificate (equivalent to the notice) of the liquidator (in this case), on the basis that the creditor members of the committee were in fact not creditors. Any irregularity in the establishment of a committee does not, however, invalidate the acts of a committee.[32]

9.019 As far as all of the regimes that have committees and which we discuss in this chapter, a creditor is eligible to be a member if: the person has proved for a debt; the debt is not fully secured; and neither the proof has been wholly disallowed for voting purposes nor has it been wholly rejected for the purpose of distribution or dividend.[33]

9.020 Where an administration is followed by a creditors' voluntary winding up, the creditors' committee continues in existence as if appointed as a liquidation committee.[34]

9.021 There are special rules in relation to the case where an administration precedes a winding up by the court. But they only apply where:[35]

- the winding-up order has been made by the court upon an application under para 79 of Sch B1 to the Act;
- the court makes an order under s 140(1) appointing as liquidator the person who was previously the administrator;
- a creditors' committee was established before the winding up commenced.

9.022 Where a creditors' committee in administration existed before the company entered into compulsory liquidation, it continues in existence after the date of the order as if appointed as a liquidation committee under s 141.[36] However, subject to r 17.8(3)(a), the committee cannot act until the minimum number of persons required by r 17.3 have agreed to act as members of the liquidation committee (including members of the former creditors' committee and any others who may be appointed under r.17.8) and the liquidator has delivered a notice of continuance of the committee to the registrar of companies.[37] The notice must be delivered as soon as reasonably practicable after the minimum number of persons required have agreed to act as members or, if applicable, been appointed[38] and it must contain those matters stated in r 17.29(5). The notice must be authenticated and dated by the liquidator.[39]

---

30 Ibid., r 17.5(8).
31 [1994] BCC 199.
32 Insolvency Rules 2016, r 17.27(1). See *Testro Bros Consolidated Ltd, Re* [1965] VR 18, 23.
33 Ibid., r 17.4(2).
34 Insolvency Act 1986, para 83(8)(f) of Sch B1.
35 Insolvency Rules 2016, r 17.29(1).
36 Ibid., r 17.29(2).
37 Ibid., r 17.29(3).
38 Ibid., r 17.29(4).
39 Ibid., r 17.29(6).

C. ROLE, POSITION AND FUNCTIONS OF COMMITTEES

9.023   Committees discussed in this chapter play a number of roles. The Rules specifically state that the committees are given a general role in assisting the officeholder in discharging the officeholder's functions and acting in relation to the officeholder in such manner as may from time to time be agreed.[40] Therefore the committee, rather than acting simply as an administrative or supervisory body, is established to provide assistance to the officeholder by way of consultation and consensus.[41] In a liquidation the committee can be regarded by the liquidator as providing a useful forum of accredited representatives of the creditors and contributories to which the liquidator can turn for advice and guidance on questions of policy. There is authority for the view that the committee has an oversight role on behalf of the creditors,[42] and in this respect it is a body to which the liquidator is accountable.

9.024   It appears that the administrative receiver is in control of the creditors' committee in administrative receivership in that its functions have to be agreed with him or her, and this position may be compared with that of a liquidation committee which appears to be more powerful.[43]

9.025   The administrator in an administration is to place an appropriate degree of importance on what the committee states, with or without a vote, but the administrator has the sole responsibility for discharging powers and duties in an administration. A court will only authorise an administrator to act in a way that is contrary to the resolution of the committee in very exceptional circumstances.[44] It is submitted that this would also be the case in relation to committees in other regimes.

9.026   While not expressed in the law, it is clear, as mentioned above, that another one of the foremost roles that committees have is to act as bodies that can call the officeholder to account for what he or she has done. This can be done in the following ways. First, administrative receivers and administrators can be required by committees to attend a meeting and explain how they are discharging their functions.[45] This can occur where a committee in an administration resolves under para 57(3)(a) of Sch B1 to require the attendance of an administrator, or a committee in an administrative receivership resolves under s 49(2) to require the attendance of the administrative receiver.[46] A meeting with the officeholder is to be held on a business day fixed by the committee, but the time and place is determined by the officeholder.[47] The committee members are to be given written notice of five business days unless there is a waiver. In the case of such a requisitioned meeting the members of the committee elect a chair from one of their own number.[48] The notice delivered to the officeholder must be accompanied by a copy of the resolution and authenticated by a member of the committee.[49] A member's representative

---

40   Ibid., r 17.2.
41   E Bailey and H Groves, *Corporate Insolvency Law and Practice* (5th ed, Lexis, 2017), [10.104].
42   *Southern Cross Airlines Holdings Ltd v Arthur Anderson & Co* (1998) 16 ACLC 485.
43   E Bailey and H Groves, *Corporate Insolvency Law and Practice* (5th ed, Lexis, 2017), [11.73].
44   *Re C E King Ltd* [2000] 2 BCLC 297, 306.
45   Insolvency Act 1986, s 49(2) (administrative receiver); para 57(3) of Sch B1 (administrator).
46   Insolvency Rules 2016, r 17.22(1).
47   Ibid., r 17.22(4).
48   Ibid., r 17.22(5).
49   Ibid., r 17.22(2).

may authenticate the notice for a committee member.[50] Where the officeholder attends, the committee may elect one of their number to be chair of the meeting in place of the officeholder or an appointed person.[51]

While the views of a committee should be considered by an officeholder as representing the views of the creditors and, where appropriate, the contributories, it is not for the committee to decide how a regime should be conducted. That is a matter for the officeholder.[52] Thus, while the officeholder is accountable for the (non-) exercise of his or her powers and functions, they are exercised at his or her discretion.   **9.027**

Secondly, to provide information. In administrations and administrative receiverships a committee may require the officeholder to furnish it with such information concerning the running of the administration or administrative receivership as it may reasonably require, so it will be a matter for the committee when they require information and what information is required. A liquidator is required to deliver a report to every member of the liquidation committee containing the information required by r 17.23(3) not less than once in every period of six months (unless the committee agrees otherwise) and when directed to do so by the committee.[53] The report must set out both the position generally in relation to the progress of the liquidation and also any matters arising in connection with the liquidation which the liquidator considers should be drawn to the committee's attention.[54] The liquidator must, as soon as reasonably practicable after being directed by the committee, deliver any report directed to be provided and comply with a request by the committee for information.[55] Yet there remains a degree of autonomy and discretion in the liquidator as a liquidator is not obliged to comply with a direction for a report where it appears to the liquidator that: **9.028**

(a)   the direction is frivolous or unreasonable;
(b)   the cost of complying would be excessive, having regard to the relative importance of the information; or
(c)   there are insufficient assets to enable the officeholder to comply.[56]

If a liquidator were to not comply for any of the above reasons, his or her decision could be the subject of review by a court on an application by a creditor or contributory.[57]   **9.029**

In the situation where the committee was established more than 28 days after the appointment of the liquidator, the liquidator is required to provide a summary report to the members of the committee of what actions he or she has taken since being appointed, and must answer such questions as they may put to him or her relating to his or her conduct of the proceedings so far.[58] This is a classic instance of accounting where there is disclosure, explanation and questioning of   **9.030**

---

50   Ibid., r 17.22(3).
51   Ibid., r 17.22(5).
52   *Re Brilliant Independent Media Specialists Ltd* [2015] BCC 113, [2014] BPIR 1395.
53   Insolvency Rules 2016, r 17.23(1)(2).
54   Ibid., r 17.22(3).
55   Ibid., r 17.23(4).
56   Ibid., r 17.23(5).
57   Insolvency Act 1986, s 168(5) (compulsory liquidations) and via s 112 for voluntary liquidations.
58   Insolvency Rules 2016, r 17.23(6).

the accountor, as discussed in Chapter 2. A person who becomes a member of the committee at any time after its first establishment is not entitled to require a report under this rule by the officeholder of any matters previously arising, other than a summary report.[59] The committee, or any member of it, is entitled to have access to the liquidator's record of the proceedings, and to seek an explanation of any matter provided it is within the committee's responsibility.[60]

9.031 While committees are given quite broad rights to information and to require the officeholder to account, there is authority for the proposition that committees are not entitled to inspect, or ask the officeholder questions concerning documents passing between the officeholder and the Department of Business Energy and Industrial Strategy relating to the possible disqualification of directors of the company.[61]

9.032 An aspect of the consulting role of committees is for an officeholder to consult the committee concerning possible conflict issues which the officeholder might have.[62] This role will require the officeholder to be transparent concerning the state of the company and the progress with the insolvency regime.

9.033 Committee views may be influential in the courts ascertaining the views of the creditors as a whole on any particular matter.[63]

9.034 Where there is a change in membership of the committee the officeholder has the obligation to deliver or file a notice[64] which includes: the date of the original notice in respect of the constitution of the committee and the date of the last notice of membership given under this rule (if any); a statement that this notice of membership replaces the previous notice; identification details for any company that is a member of the committee; the full name and address of any member that is not a company; a statement whether any member has become a member since the issue of the previous notice; the identification details for a company or otherwise the full name of any member named in the previous notice who is no longer a member and the date the membership ended.[65] The officeholder has to authenticate and date the notice.[66] The officeholder must, as soon as reasonably practicable, deliver the notice to the registrar of companies.[67]

9.035 During the time of the regime's existence, there may, from time to time, become a vacancy among the creditor members, through resignation, automatic termination or removal. The vacancy need not be filled where the liquidator and a majority of the creditor members agree provided that the total number of members does not fall below three.[68] The officeholder may appoint any creditor to fill the vacancy provided that the creditor is so qualified, the majority of

---

59   Ibid., r 17.23(7).
60   Ibid., r 17.23(8).
61   *Re W&A Glaser Ltd* [1994] BCC 199, 205. This case related to a liquidation.
62   *Re VE Interactive Ltd* [2018] EWHC 186, [2019] BPIR 437. This case related to administration.
63   *Re WSBL Realisations 1992 Ltd* [1995] BCC 1118, 1120; *Re C E King Ltd* [2000] 2 BCLC 297, 306. Both cases dealt with administrations.
64   Insolvency Rules 2016, r 17.7(1).
65   Ibid., r 17.7(2).
66   Ibid., r 17.7(3).
67   Ibid., r 17.7(4).
68   Ibid., r 17.8(2).

the other creditor members (provided that there are two) agree, and the creditor consents.[69] As an alternative the officeholder make seek the views of the creditors' meeting and it may resolve that a creditor, be appointed (with his or her consent) to fill the vacancy.[70] In the circumstances where the vacancy is filled by an appointment made by a decision of creditors which was not convened by the officeholder, the convener or chair is to report to the officeholder the appointment which has been made.[71]

Where there is a vacancy among the contributory members, similar rules apply. The vacancy **9.036** need not be filled if the officeholder and a majority of the remaining contributory members (provided that there are two) agree provided that in a situation where the committee is one of the contributory members only, and in the case of a committee of contributories only, the total number of members does not fall below three.[72] The officeholder may appoint any contributory to fill the vacancy provided that the contributory is so qualified, the majority of the other contributory members agree and the contributory consents.[73] As with the situation where there is a committee with only creditor members, an alternative process is provided for, namely the meeting of contributories may resolve that a contributory be appointed (with his or her consent) to fill the vacancy.[74] In the circumstances where the vacancy is filled by an appointment made by a decision of contributories which was not convened by the liquidator, the convener or chair shall report to the officeholder the appointment which has been made.[75]

Members of the committee are fiduciaries,[76] and they occupy a fiduciary position in relation to **9.037** the creditors (and, in some cases, to the contributories)[77] which prevents them from deriving a profit from their office or from allowing their private interests to conflict with their duty as committee members. We shall return to this shortly.

In an administration the committee may apply to the court for the replacement of an adminis- **9.038** trator where a vacancy has occurred as a result of any of the matters referred to in para 90 of Sch B1 transpiring, and the administrator was appointed by way of administration order.[78]

The liquidation committee is not able, or required, to carry out its functions at any time **9.039** when the official receiver is liquidator.[79] Where there is for the time being no liquidation committee, and the liquidator is a person other than the official receiver, the functions of such a committee are vested in the Secretary of State except to the extent that the rules otherwise provide.[80]Therefore, where a provision in the legislation empowers a liquidator to act with the consent of the liquidation committee, and there is no committee, the liquidator must obtain the

---

69   Ibid., r 17.8(3).
70   Ibid., r 17.8(4).
71   Ibid., r 17.8(5).
72   Ibid., r 17.9(2).
73   Ibid., r 17.9(3).
74   Ibid., r 17.9(4).
75   Ibid., r 17.9(5).
76   *Re F. T. Hawkins & Co* [1952] Ch 881.
77   *Re Geiger* [1915] 1 KB 439, 447; *Re Bulmer* [1937] Ch 499, 502; *Re Standard Insurance Co Ltd (in liq)* [1970] 1 NSWR 392; *Re Security Directors Pty Ltd (in liq)* (1997) 24 ACSR 558.
78   Insolvency Act 1986, para 91(1)(a) of Sch B1.
79   Ibid., s 141(4).
80   Ibid., s 141(5).

consent of the Secretary of State. The Rules provide that where the functions of the committee are vested in the Secretary of State, the official receiver may exercise them.[81]

9.040 Finally, in relation to the subject of this part of the chapter we have noted how the officeholder is accountable to the committee, but there is no provision for committees' accountability. Unlike a board of directors which is accountable to the general meeting of members, creditors in committees, who represent the creditors in general, are subject to no reporting requirement to the creditors or anyone else for that matter. Thus, there are no clear mechanisms for holding committees accountable for what they have done. Committee members are not required to inform the creditors what they have done and to explain the reason(s) for their actions. The only mechanism that might be seen as accounting is where there is a need for a court application and the court might seek to know what a committee's views are and the reasons why they are held. But this is not accountability in the strict sense of the term. This lack of accountability might be regarded as an omission given the government's concern for sound corporate governance in insolvency.

D. THE OPERATION OF COMMITTEES

9.041 The officeholder may call a meeting, at his or her discretion.[82] The first meeting of the committee must be held within six weeks after it is first established[83] and five business days' notice of each meeting must be given.[84] However, where the officeholder has determined that a meeting should be conducted remotely under r 17.20, the notice period is seven business days.

9.042 After the calling of the first meeting, the officeholder must call subsequent meetings if so requested by a member of the committee or the member's representative. The meeting is then to be held within 21 days of the request being received by the officeholder, and for a specified date, if the committee has previously resolved that a meeting be held on that date.[85]

9.043 The chair at a meeting of a committee must be the officeholder or an appointed person.[86]

9.044 As far as the quorum is concerned, a meeting of a committee is duly constituted if due notice of it has been delivered to all the members, and at least two of the members are in attendance or represented.[87]

9.045 Committee members may be represented by others in the disposal of committee business.[88] Thus, persons who represent creditor or contributory members may attend meetings of the committee if duly authorised by the member for that purpose.[89] Such persons must hold letters

---

81   Insolvency Rules 2016, r 17.28(2).
82   Ibid., r 17.14(1).
83   Ibid., r 17.14(2).
84   Ibid., r 17.4(4).
85   Ibid., r 17.14(3).
86   Ibid., r 17.15.
87   Ibid., r 17.16.
88   Ibid., r 17.17(1).
89   Ibid.

of authority signed by the committee member authorising them to act.[90] A proxy or an instrument conferring authority (in respect of a person authorised to represent a corporation) is to be treated as a letter of authority to act generally (unless the proxy or instrument conferring authority contains a statement to the contrary).[91] The chair at a meeting has the power to exclude a person from the meeting where the latter attends on the basis of being a representative of a member and where a letter of authority cannot be produced at, or by the time of, the meeting, or the chair opines that the authority is deficient.[92] Certain persons are disqualified from representing a committee member, namely: another member of the committee; a person who is at the same time representing another committee member; a body corporate; an undischarged bankrupt; a person whose estate has been sequestrated and who has not been discharged; a person to whom a moratorium period under a debt relief order applies; a disqualified director; or a person who is subject to a bankruptcy restrictions order (including an interim order), a bankruptcy restrictions undertaking, a debt relief restrictions order (including an interim order) or a debt relief restrictions undertaking.[93]

Where the officeholder considers it appropriate, a meeting of the committee may be conducted **9.046** and held remotely, namely in such a way that persons who are not present together at the same place may attend.[94] A person attends such a meeting who is able to exercise that person's right to speak and vote at the meeting.[95] Someone is able to speak at a meeting when he or she is in a position to communicate during the meeting to all those attending the meeting any information or opinions which he or she has in relation to the business of the meeting.[96] A person is able to vote at a meeting when he or she is able to vote, during the meeting, on resolutions or determinations put to the vote at the meeting, and that person's vote can be taken into account in determining whether or not such resolutions or determinations are passed at the same time as the votes of all the other persons attending the meeting.[97]

When a meeting is to be held the officeholder must make whatever arrangements he or she **9.047** considers appropriate to enable those attending the meeting to speak or vote and to verify the identity of those attending the meeting and to ensure the security of any electronic means used to enable attendance.[98] This demand may be satisfied by specifying the arrangements the officeholder proposes in order to enable persons to exercise their rights to speak or vote where in the reasonable opinion of the IP a meeting will be attended by persons who will not be present together at the same place and it is unnecessary or inexpedient to specify a place for the meeting.[99] In the course of doing this the IP must have regard to the legitimate interests of the committee members or their representatives attending the meeting in the efficient despatch of the business of the meeting.[100] The liquidator must specify a place for the meeting if at least

---

90   Ibid., r 17.17(2).
91   Ibid., r 17.17(3).
92   Ibid., r 17.17(4).
93   Ibid., r 17.17(5).
94   Ibid., r 17.20(1).
95   Ibid., r 17.20(2).
96   Ibid., r 17.20(3).
97   Ibid., r 17.20(4).
98   Ibid., r 17.20(5).
99   Ibid., r 17.20(6).
100 Ibid., r 17.20(7).

one member of the committee requests the officeholder to do so in accordance with r 17.21.[101] These requirements all work towards good corporate governance in the sense that the committee members get the opportunity to engage with the officeholder and each other concerning issues relating to the affairs of the company. This is likely to engender greater transparency and accountability.

9.048 Rule 17.21(2) provides that any request by a committee member to the officeholder to specify a place for a meeting must be made within three business days of the date on which the officeholder delivered the notice of the meeting in question. Where the officeholder considers that the request has been properly made in accordance with this rule, the officeholder must: deliver notice to all those previously given notice of the meeting (that it is to be held at a specified place, and as to whether the date and time are to remain the same or not); fix a venue for the meeting, the date of which must be not later than seven business days after the original date for the meeting; give three business days' notice of the venue to all those previously given notice of the meeting.

9.049 At meetings each member or his or her representative has one vote.[102] A resolution is passed when a majority of the members attending or represented have voted in favour of it.[103] Every resolution passed must be recorded in writing and authenticated by the chair, either separately or as part of the minutes of the meeting, and the record must be kept with the records of the proceedings.[104] To facilitate committee business the officeholder may send out by post a proposed resolution and the members can indicate on the proposal whether they agree or disagree.[105] Any creditor member of the committee may, within seven business days from the date of the officeholder sending out the proposed resolution, require the officeholder to call a meeting of the committee to consider the issues raised by the resolution.[106] If there is no request for a meeting, once the officeholder receives an indication from a majority of the members (excluding those not permitted to vote by way of r 17.25(4)[107]) the resolution is deemed to have been passed by the committee.[108] A copy of every resolution passed and a note that the committee's agreement was secured, are to be kept as part of the records of the regime.[109]

9.050 Actions of committees are valid notwithstanding any defect in the appointment, election or qualifications of any member of the committee or any committee member's representative or in the formalities of its establishment.[110]

9.051 The liquidation committee has a number of powers that it can carry out in compulsory winding up, *such as* being able: to be entitled to receive notice that the liquidator is going to dispose of

---

101 Ibid., r 17.20(8).
102 Ibid., r 17.18(1).
103 Ibid., r 17.18(2).
104 Ibid., r 17.18(3).
105 Ibid., r 17.19(1), (2).
106 Ibid., r 17.19(3).
107 This paragraph excludes those members from voting in relation to a resolution that involves approving a benefit that would redound to those members, because they would benefit from the approval.
108 Insolvency Rules 2016, r 17.19(4).
109 Ibid., r 17.19(5).
110 Ibid., r 17.27(1).

property to a person connected with the company;[111] to be entitled to receive notice that the liquidator is going to employ a solicitor to assist in the carrying out of his or her functions;[112] to direct the liquidator to deliver information to it;[113] to determine the basis for the remuneration of the liquidator.[114]

The liquidation and creditors' committees have the power to approve remuneration that **9.052** exceeds the fee estimate where the committee has fixed the basis for the remuneration,[115] and to determine a dispute as to remuneration where there are joint officeholders who are unable to agree between themselves how the remuneration that is payable should be apportioned.[116]

E. DEALINGS, EXPENSES AND REMUNERATION OF COMMITTEE MEMBERS

As mentioned earlier, committee members are fiduciaries and this limits their dealings with **9.053** the company. The starting point with members of the committee is that they should not derive a profit from their office.[117] The conflicts rules that apply in relation to a fiduciary will apply to members of the committee, that is, the committee members must not be in a position where their personal interests conflict with their duty as committee members. The fact that a person is a member of the committee does not prevent that person from dealing with the company. Dealings by members are dealt with separately as far as liquidation on the one hand, and administration and administrative receivership on the other hand, are concerned.

First, liquidation. In *Re F. T. Hawkins & Co,*[118] a firm of solicitors appointed to assist the **9.054** liquidator were refused profit costs on the ground that their managing clerk was a member of the committee of inspection [a former title for the liquidation committee] which approved the appointment of the firm as solicitors to the liquidator. The decision turned principally upon the construction of the Companies (Winding-up) Rules 1949. Rule 163 provided, inter alia, that no profit from a transaction arising out of a liquidation could be received by a member of a committee 'except under and with the sanction of the court'. Such a rule has been interpreted to mean that sanction must be secured before the transaction leading to the profit occurs.[119] Now the matter is regulated by r 17.25 for the members of liquidation committees.[120] This provides that a person who has been, during the last 12 months, any of the following: a com-

---

111   Insolvency Act 1986, s 167(2)(a).
112   Ibid., s 167(2)(b).
113   Insolvency Rules 2016, r 17.23.
114   Ibid., r 18.20(2).
115   Ibid., r 18.30(2)(a).
116   Ibid., r 18.17(a).
117   *Re F T Hawkins & Co Ltd* [1952] Ch 881, [1952] 2 All ER 467.
118   [1952] Ch 881.
119   *Re Gallard* [1896] 1 QB 68, 72–73; *Re F. T. Hawkins & Co* [1952] Ch 881, 884.
120   Insolvency Rules 2016, r 17.26 deals with administration and administrative receivership.

mittee member, a representative of a committee member, or a person who is an associate of a committee member or a committee member's representative, is not permitted to:[121]

- receive as an expense of the liquidation out of the company's assets any payment for services given or goods supplied in connection with the winding up;
- obtain any profit from the winding up;
- acquire any assets of the company that form part of the insolvent estate.

9.055 This prohibition does not occur when: the prior approval of the committee is obtained, and where it is satisfied (after full disclosure of the circumstances) that the person will be giving full value in relation to the transaction, the prior approval of the court is secured, or, where the person enters the transaction as a matter of urgency, or by way of a contract already in force before the company went into liquidation, and he or she obtains the leave of the court for the transaction, having applied for it without delay.[122] In the latter instance no member or representative of a member of the committee who is to participate directly or indirectly in the transaction may vote.[123] The New South Wales Supreme Court in *Re DH International Pty Ltd (No 2)*[124] gave approval to the liquidators assigning to a member of the liquidation committee claims which the company had against former directors and officers of the company on the basis that there was unanimous support from the creditors and the liquidators, there was no possibility of the company being able to pursue the claims as the liquidators had no funds and no one else had offered to purchase the claims or fund the litigation.

9.056 The court is empowered by r 17.25(5), on the application of an interested person, to set aside a transaction that contravenes r 17.25 and it may make any other order that it sees as just, including requiring a person to whom the rule applies to account for any profits obtained from the transaction and to compensate the estate for any resultant loss.[125] The court will not make an order to set aside where a person who is an associate of a member or of a representative of a member is involved and the court is satisfied that he or she entered into the transaction without having any reason to suppose that in doing so there would be a contravention of r 17.25.[126] The costs of the application are not payable as an expense of the insolvency proceedings unless the court orders otherwise.[127]

9.057 Secondly, as far as administration and administrative receivership are concerned, r 17.26 is relevant and provides, to some degree, a different approach compared with a liquidation committee. A member of a creditors' committee may deal with the company (for instance buying assets from the company) while the regime is operating so long as the transaction is in good faith and for value.[128] Just as under r 17.25, on the application of an interested person to set aside a transaction that contravenes r 17.26 the court may make any other order that it sees as

---

121 Ibid., r 17.25(1), (2).
122 Ibid., r 17.25(3).
123 Ibid., r 17.25(4).
124 [2017] NSWSC 871.
125 Insolvency Rules 2016, r 17.25(5).
126 Ibid., r 17.25(6).
127 Ibid., r 17.25(7).
128 Ibid., r 17.26(1), (2).

just, including requiring a person to whom the rule applies to account for any profits obtained from the transaction and to compensate the estate for any resultant loss.[129]

There is a specific defence for associates of members of committees; no order is to be made against an associate of a member or of a member's representative where the court is satisfied that the associate or representative entered into the relevant transaction without having any reason to suppose that in doing so he or she would contravene the conflict rule.[130] The costs of the application are not payable as an expense of the insolvency proceedings unless the court orders otherwise.[131]   **9.058**

An officeholder is required to defray out of the company's assets any reasonable travelling expenses directly incurred by members of committees or their representatives in relation to attendance at meetings of the committee or on the committee's business.[132] Payment is to be made in accordance with the priority structure set out in r 3.51(2) (administration), r 6.42(4) (creditors' voluntary liquidation) or r 7.108(4) (compulsory liquidation).[133]   **9.059**

There is no statutory provision for remuneration of the committee. The only law that we have relates to liquidation committees. That law provides that before a committee member receives anything by way of remuneration, prior sanction of the committee or the prior approval of the court must be obtained,[134] and this accords with the law relating to members benefitting from transactions.[135] Approval of the court will not ordinarily be forthcoming unless the committee has rendered special services in the course of the regime. An example of a case where remuneration was approved was in the Australian liquidation case of *Re Security Directors Pty Ltd (in liquidation)*.[136] In that case the liquidator applied to the court to enable him to pay A\$5,000 to each of the six members of the committee as the liquidator wished to make the payments as recognition of the 'remarkable services performed by the members during a period of six years'.[137] In deciding whether it was appropriate to grant leave, the Victorian Supreme Court said that while the court's discretion cannot be fettered, courts should consider previous decisions on the matter and regard the comments in the cases as guidelines.[138] The court opined that generally the work of a committee member is to be regarded as honorary, so, remuneration would only be received in exceptional circumstances.[139] The court said that financial considerations are an element to be taken into account in making a decision, in that the court must consider what effect an award of remuneration would have on the creditors' dividends.[140]   **9.060**

---

129 Ibid., r 17.26(3).
130 Ibid., r 17.25(6).
131 Ibid., r 17.25(7).
132 Ibid., r 17.24(1). This excludes a meeting held within six weeks of a previous meeting unless the meeting was summoned by the officeholder: r 17.24(2).
133 The expenses fall under r 3.51(2)(g) (administration) r 6.42(4)(f) (creditors' voluntary liquidation) or r 7.018(4)(m) (compulsory liquidation).
134 *Dowling v Lord Advocate* 1963 SLT 146.
135 Insolvency Rules 2016, r 17.25(3).
136 (1997) 24 ACSR 558.
137 Ibid., 560.
138 Ibid., 569.
139 Ibid.
140 Ibid., 570.

9.061 Other matters to be taken into account are whether the services provided could normally be provided without payment and whether the creditors benefit more from receiving the services from the member of the committee rather than from a stranger.[141] Because of the substantial work performed by the members of the committee[142] the court in *Re Security Directors Pty Ltd (in liquidation)*[143] said that the amount sought to be paid was modest as it could not 'represent the proper value of all the work performed, the time contributed and the inconvenience borne'.[144] The sum to be paid to the members was classified as a gift.[145]

F. END OF APPOINTMENT

9.062 A committee member may resign by notice in writing, which must be delivered to the officeholder.[146] There is no power in the court to remove a member of the committee,[147] but membership is automatically terminated, for instance, if a member becomes bankrupt,[148] or if the member is absent from three consecutive committee meetings,[149] or the member ceases to be,[150] or is found never to have been a creditor.[151] The court in *Re Rubber & Produce Investment Trust*[152] took the view that the decision to remove had to be taken by the committee itself without any further guidance by the court as to what the creditors had to take into consideration when assessing whether another member of the committee should be removed. What a court can do is to direct the liquidator to convene a meeting of the creditors and contributories to achieve the removal purpose.[153]

9.063 A creditor may be removed from office by a decision of the creditors through a decision procedure and a contributory member of the committee may be removed by a decision of contributories through a decision procedure.[154] At least 14 days' notice must be given of a decision procedure.[155]

---

141   Ibid.
142   Ibid., 576.
143   (1997) 24 ACSR 558.
144   Ibid., 575.
145   Ibid.
146   Insolvency Rules 2016, r 17.10.
147   *Re Rubber & Produce Investment Trust* [1915] 1 Ch 382.
148   Insolvency Rules 2016, r 17.11(a). The member is replaced by his or her trustee in bankruptcy.
149   Ibid., r 17.11(c). This does not apply where at the third of the meetings it is resolved that this paragraph is not to apply in the relevant case.
150   Hence, if a creditor is paid off he or she is unable to continue to act as a member of the committee as the person is no longer a creditor.
151   Insolvency Rules 2016, r 17.11(e).
152   [1915] 1 Ch 382.
153   *Re Radford & Bright Ltd* [1901] 1 Ch D 272.
154   Insolvency Rules 2016, r 17.12(1).
155   Ibid., r 17.12(2).

In a liquidation where the creditors have been paid in full together with interest in accordance **9.064** with s 189 of the Act, the liquidator must deliver to the registrar of companies a notice to that effect[156] and on the delivery of the notice the liquidation committee ceases to exist.[157]

G. CONCLUSION

The Act and the Rules lay down requirements that mean an officeholder must account to **9.065** creditors' and liquidation committees. This includes the fact that committees can require both meetings to be held and the provision of information. From an accountability perspective it is perhaps unfortunate that creditors' committees are not mandatory. They will only operate where creditors are willing to engage with the insolvency regime and anecdotal evidence suggests that many creditors will not engage as they feel that they are 'throwing good money after bad' in dedicating time to such engagement. However, it might be argued that changes to the Rules in recent years have provided the foundation for more engagement in that meetings may be held remotely. Nevertheless, there are many regimes where there is no committee and, effectively, no one to whom IPs need to account, short of a court hearing.

This is likely to be the case in all but the largest insolvencies or where there is clear suspicion of **9.066** improper conduct on the part of the directors.

---

156 Ibid., r 17.13(1).
157 Ibid., r 17.13(2).

10

SPECIAL MANAGERS

A. INTRODUCTION

10.001   When a company has entered liquidation or provisional liquidation, in addition to the appointment of the liquidator the court may be asked to make an additional appointment to the role of special manager.[1]

10.002   In the era since the Insolvency Act 1986 came into force, appointments of special managers have become less likely for the reason that only licensed insolvency practitioners or the official receiver may be appointed as liquidators. The qualification and experience of such officeholders are usually sufficient to deal with any managerial issues which might arise in a liquidation.

10.003   Appointments of special managers have been made in recent years in cases where there is a clear public interest in the continued operation of the business of the company. Examples of this include the compulsory liquidations of Carillion plc,[2] British Steel Ltd[3] and Thomas Cook Group plc.[4]

B. ORIGINS OF POWER TO APPOINT

10.004   The power to appoint a special manager has its origins in nineteenth-century bankruptcy law. During the 1800s there was almost a continuous running battle between advocates of the bankruptcy process being under the control of the creditors (sometimes referred to as 'voluntaryism') and those who believed that bankruptcy required a public official to oversee it

---

1   Insolvency Act 1986, s 177.
2   *Re Carillion plc* (unreported 15 January 2018).
3   *Re British Steel Ltd* [2019] EWHC 1304 (Ch), [2019] BCC 974.
4   *Re Thomas Cook Group plc* [2019] EWHC 2626 (Ch).

('officialism').[5] The role of the official assignee (a predecessor of today's official receiver) was introduced in 1831 and abolished in 1869 only to return in the form of the official receiver in the Bankruptcy Act 1883. The system of appointing officials to deal with bankruptcy estates was initially popular and effective but fell into disrepute due to the personal advantage acquired by the officials. Prior to 1861, in addition to the appointment of an official assignee, there were also officials called 'messengers' who got in and realised the bankrupt estate.

The Bankruptcy Act 1861 had sought a form of compromise between the powers of officials   **10.005**
on the one hand and the powers of creditors to control the bankruptcy on the other. Although an official assignee was still initially appointed in a bankruptcy, s 122 of the 1861 Act provided the creditors with a power to choose their own creditors' assignee (the equivalent of today's private sector trustee in bankruptcy) to replace the official assignee. At the same time as making this decision, the creditors were also provided with a power to appoint, in addition to their creditors' assignee, a manager to collect in and wind up the bankrupt's estate. The possibility for nepotism and lack of accountability between the parties was predicted in Parliamentary debates at the time and the need to appoint any manager in addition to the creditors' assignee was questioned.[6]

The role of official assignee disappeared under the Bankruptcy Act 1869 when the creditors   **10.006**
took full control over the bankruptcy process. Following further concerns about fraudulent practices[7] officialism made a permanent comeback under the Bankruptcy Act 1883. The 1883 bankruptcy procedure remained largely in place until the Insolvency Act 1986 completely over-hauled the bankruptcy system, but the power to appoint a special manager remains.[8]

An outline of the 1883 procedure will help in understanding where special managers came   **10.007**
in. When a bankruptcy petition was successful, it led to a two-stage process. The court would make an order, a receiving order, which had one of two possible results. It might lead to a com-position of debts or a scheme of arrangement if such was feasible or it might lead to an adju-dication of bankruptcy. If an adjudication order was made, a meeting of creditors was called to decide whom to appoint as trustee in bankruptcy. The receiving order, in and of itself, did not make the debtor bankrupt. As soon as a receiving order was made, its effect was to constitute the official receiver the receiver of the debtor's property.[9] It generally also stayed proceedings by unsecured creditors.

---

5   HC Deb 19 March 1883 vol 277 cc 816 et seq Joseph Chamberlain explained that the decision in 1869 to return the
     control of bankruptcies to creditors alone without any public official in place 'led to absolute chaos and gave general
     dissatisfaction'.
6   HL Deb 16 April 1861 vol 162 cc 623 et seq Lord Chelmsford:
         could not for the life of him understand why there should be any such paid agent appointed, for if the creditors'
         assignee were not competent why should he be appointed, and if he were competent why was he to be supplanted by
         the appointment of a paid agent?
7   See the discussion below in Chapter 11 as to the history of the Insolvency Service.
8   See now Insolvency Act 1986, s 370 for the power of the court to appoint a special manager in bankruptcy.
9   Bankruptcy Act 1883, s 66.

10.008 If required to do so by the creditors, the official receiver had the power to appoint a special manager of the debtor's business to act, but only until a trustee in bankruptcy was appointed.[10] The special manager had such powers (including any of the powers of a receiver) as were entrusted to him by the official receiver. The special manager had to give security for the appointment and had a duty to account.[11] The special manager's remuneration was decided on by the creditors.[12] If no special manager was appointed, the official receiver acted as manager.[13]

10.009 The general utility of a power to appoint a manager when a company had entered liquidation appears to have been recognised around this period. As official receivers were not necessarily people with the skills or resources to run a business, the ability to appoint a special manager to operate the business of a company,[14] at least for a short time as part of the liquidation, was introduced into corporate insolvency not long after the 1883 Act.

10.010 Section 5 of the Companies (Winding-Up) Act 1890 adopted the special manager power found in the Bankruptcy Act 1883. There were some differences. An amendment made on the suggestion of Sir Horace Davey[15] in Parliament required the official receiver, who was liquidator of a company (whether provisionally or otherwise) to apply to the court for the appointment of a special manager. It was no longer just a decision for the official receiver at the behest of the creditors. It was now the court's decision on the application of the official receiver.

10.011 The official receiver had to be satisfied that the nature of the company's estate or business (or the interests of creditors or contributories) required a special manager.[16]

10.012 There was no temporal limit on the appointment. It was not in essence a temporary appointment pending the appointment of a liquidator as it was in bankruptcy. The appointment could last for such time as the court directed.[17]

10.013 The court had a wide discretion to entrust the special manager with whatever powers it directed, with the express example of the powers of a receiver and manager.[18]

---

10   Ibid., s 12. There was also a power to appoint a special manager where the official receiver was appointed interim receiver under s 10 before the petition was heard (see, e.g., *Re A, B & Co (No 2)* [1900] 2 QB 429).

11   Ibid., s 12(2).

12   Ibid., s 12(3).

13   Ibid., s 70.

14   In the context of bankruptcy see HC Deb 19 March 1883 vol 277 cc 860–861 where Joseph Chamberlain explained that where for example, the official receiver was appointed over 'a large mill employing some hundreds of hands, or of a bank with 80 or 90 employees' was just the sort of case where a special manager might be appointed.

15   HC Deb 4th July 1890 vol 346 c842. As Lord Davey he would later chair the Report of the departmental committee appointed by the Board of Trade to inquire what amendments are necessary in the acts relating to joint stock companies incorporated with limited liability under the Companies Acts, 1862 to 1890 (1895 c 7779).

16   Companies (Winding-Up) Act 1890, s 5(1).

17   Ibid., s 5(1).

18   Ibid., s 5(1). This was significant as by 1890 the court had become accustomed to appointing receivers and managers in debenture holder actions in the context of companies subject to a floating charge. On the distinction between receivers on the one hand and receivers and managers on the other, see *Re Manchester & Milford Ry Co* (1880) 14 Ch D 645 at 653 per Jessel MR.

To similar effect to the 1883 bankruptcy provisions, the special manager was required to   **10.014**
provide security and to account in such manner as the Board of Trade directed.[19]

The special manager's remuneration was to be fixed by the court not the creditors.[20]   **10.015**

The power to appoint a special manager in identical terms continued through the Companies   **10.016**
Act 1908,[21] the Companies Act 1929,[22] Companies Act 1948[23] and Companies Act 1985.[24] It
is now found in s 177 of the Insolvency Act 1986 with one significant amendment which is
considered below.

C. POWER TO APPOINT

Under s 177 of the Insolvency Act 1986 ('the Act') where a company has gone into liquidation   **10.017**
(or a provisional liquidator has been appointed) the court may, on the application of the liquidator or provisional liquidator, appoint any person to be the special manager of the business
or property of the company.[25] It is no longer only open to the official receiver to apply for such
an appointment. Any liquidator, whether the liquidation is compulsory or voluntary, solvent or
insolvent, or a provisional liquidator may apply to the court.

Since a liquidator has available the alternative of appointing an agent with the required skill-set   **10.018**
under Sch 4 para 12 of the Act, one might expect the power to appoint a special manager to
be exercised only in rare circumstances. Although such appointments are indeed unusual, they
have become relatively common in recent times where the businesses operated by certain large
insolvent companies have had a significant public interest element.

In the cases of *Re Carillion plc*,[26] *Re British Steel Ltd*[27] and *Re Thomas Cook Group plc*[28] a compul-   **10.019**
sory liquidation was ordered with the official receiver appointed as liquidator.

In these three cases, there were overwhelming reasons why administration or a liquidation   **10.020**
with a private sector liquidator were not feasible. There was little if any money in any of the
companies. Secured creditors were unwilling to fund any administration. Each company
carried on business with potentially catastrophic consequences to the public if their businesses
were not continued at least for a period. The respective compulsory liquidations allowed for

---

19   Ibid., s 5(2). The security required to act as a special manager was the same as for a liquidator under r 67 of the
Companies Winding-Up Rules 1890.
20   Ibid., s 5(3).
21   Companies Act 1908, s 161.
22   Companies Act 1929, s 209.
23   Companies Act 1948, s 263. The official receiver had to provide an opinion on how much remuneration should be paid
to the special manager and once the court had decided upon the remuneration it had to be stated in the order appointing
unless the court directed otherwise r 50(1) and (2) Companies (Winding-Up) Rules 1949 (SI 1949/330).
24   Companies Act 1985, s 556.
25   Insolvency Act 1986, s 177(1).
26   Unreported 15 January 2018.
27   [2019] EWHC 1304 (Ch), [2019] BCC 974. See A Keay and P Walton 'British Steel: is it a wind up?' (2019) 4
Corporate Rescue and Insolvency 125.
28   [2019] EWHC 2626 (Ch).

an orderly winding up and, amongst other things, completion of major public sector building projects (Carillion), averting an environmental disaster and fulfilling current and future order books (British Steel) and the repatriation of millions of British holiday makers abroad (Thomas Cook).

10.021   Each compulsory liquidation required the appointment of a public sector official due to the public interests at large. The official receiver needed the help of major insolvency practitioner firms acting as special managers to complete these tasks. If the government had not agreed to indemnify for the costs of these liquidations it is unlikely they would have been successful as there would not have been funding available to pay for the specialist private sector special managers. No private sector insolvency practitioner was willing to take on the possible role as administrator mainly due to the uncertainty around funding available for fee payment. The role of special manager with a government indemnity covering their fees and expenses was feasible. These are the sort of cases where special managers have a role.

10.022   The grounds for the application for a special manager remain essentially unchanged from 1890. The application must be made to court and may be made in any case where it appears to the liquidator or provisional liquidator that the nature of the business or property of the company, or the interests of the company's creditors or contributories or members generally, require the appointment of another person to manage the company's business or property.[29] Under the Insolvency (England and Wales) Rules 2016[30] an application for such an appointment must be supported by a report setting out the reasons for it. In *Re British Steel Ltd*,[31] for example, the official receiver's report included reasons relating to the size and complexity of the business, ongoing press comment on the state of the company, and the many work-streams that needed to be attended to simultaneously. It also gave reasons for the appointment of the particular persons proposed as special managers.

10.023   The appointment in such cases is likely to be made at the same time that the court makes the winding-up order.[32]

D. POWERS AND DUTIES

10.024   The special manager has whatever powers are given by the court making the appointment. There is no longer a specific reference in the section to the powers of a receiver and manager but clearly they remain the likely blueprint for any court-entrusted powers. Although the powers entrusted to the special manager must be included in the order making the appointment, somewhat surprisingly, there is a lack of transparency about which powers have been granted as in

---

29   Insolvency Act 1986, s 177(2).

30   SI 2016/1024 ('Insolvency Rules 2016') r 7.93. The references in the following footnotes are to the provisions in the Insolvency Rules 2016 which apply to special managers appointed in a compulsory liquidation but equivalent provisions exist for members' voluntary liquidations (Chapter 3 of Part 5) and creditors' voluntary liquidations (Chapter 5 of Part 6).

31   [2019] EWHC 1304 (Ch), [2019] BCC 974.

32   As was the case in all of *Re Carillion plc* (unreported 15 January 2018), *Re British Steel Ltd* [2019] EWHC 1304 (Ch), [2019] BCC 974 and *Re Thomas Cook Group plc* [2019] EWHC 2626 (Ch).

practice this part of the judgment is not made public.[33] The detail of the powers is something between the court, the liquidator and the special manager.

The court may direct that any provision of the Act that has effect in relation to the liquidator or provisional liquidator of a company shall have the like effect in relation to the special manager for the purposes of the carrying out any of the functions of the provisional liquidator or liquidator.[34]   **10.025**

Once appointed, a special manager derives authority directly from the court and will not be an agent of the liquidator or provisional liquidator. If the liquidator is of the view that the employment of the special manager is no longer necessary or profitable for the company, the liquidator must apply to the court for directions and the court may terminate the appointment.[35] The liquidator must make the same application if the creditors pass a decision requesting the appointment be terminated.[36]   **10.026**

The court decides upon the remuneration of the special manager.[37]   **10.027**

Although a special manager does not need to be licensed as an 'insolvency practitioner'[38] in reality they will be insolvency practitioners. The security requirements for a special manager are likely to be satisfied by the general bond requirements of an insolvency practitioner. A person appointed as special manager may give security either specifically for a particular winding up, or generally for any winding up in relation to which that person may be appointed as special manager. The amount of the security must be not less than the value of the business or property in relation to which the special manager is appointed, as estimated in the liquidator's report which accompanied the application for appointment.[39]   **10.028**

Interestingly, the security requirements for a special manager may be seen as potentially inadequate.[40] In the case of *Re British Steel Ltd* the company had an annual turnover £1.2 billion with debts in the region of £880 million. It was anticipated that unsecured creditors would be unlikely to receive any dividend in the liquidation beyond the prescribed part payment under s 176A of the Act which at the time was set at a maximum of £600,000. The official receiver took   **10.029**

---

33   Insolvency Rules 2016, r 7.93(3)(g).
34   Insolvency Act 1986, s 177(4).
35   Insolvency Rules 2016, r 7.97(2).
36   Ibid., r 7.97(3).
37   Ibid., r 7.93(5). The appointment implies the payment of reasonable remuneration (*Re US Ltd*) (1983) 127 SJ 748. The Right Honourable Frank Field MP, chair of the House of Commons Work and Pensions Committee, is reported in *The Times* (7 February 2019) as commenting on the payment in fees of £44.2m to special managers by the government in the Carillion compulsory winding up in the following terms: 'In this way they are ably assisted by a merry little bank of advisors and auditors, conflicted at every turn and with every incentive to milk the cash cow dry.'
38   Insolvency Act 1986, ss 230 and 388(1). Under Insolvency Rules 2016, r 7.93(6) the acts of a special manager are valid notwithstanding any defect in the special manager's appointment or qualifications.
39   Ibid., s 177(5) and Insolvency Rules 2016, r 5.18. When the special manager has provided the security to the liquidator, the liquidator must file with the court a certificate as to the adequacy of the security. The cost of providing the security must be paid in the first instance by the special manager, but the special manager is entitled to be reimbursed as an expense of the winding up.
40   The Government's First Review of the Insolvency (England and Wales) Rules 2016: Call for evidence (March 2021) specifically identifies possible changes to the requirements around special manager bonding.

the view, with which the court agreed, that the value of the business or property in relation to which the proposed special managers were to be appointed was that which would ultimately be available to the unsecured creditors. Despite this limited valuation, it appears the court recognised that the company's total assets were valued at over £5 million. The court appears to have used by analogy the requirement under the Insolvency Practitioners Regulations[41] that where the value of the insolvent's assets is more than £5 million the specific penalty sum shall be £5 million. The security provided by the special managers was therefore limited to a bond in the sum of £5 million per special manager.

10.030 Special managers must prepare and keep accounts recording receipts and payments for each three-month period which must be submitted to the liquidator for approval but are not made available publicly. Once approved the special manager's receipts and payments are added to those of the liquidator so there is an element of transparency about the financial dealings of the special manager.[42]

E. CONCLUSION

10.031 It is interesting to consider the historical development of special managers. They were introduced in bankruptcy largely to do the day-to-day getting in and realisation of property. They were intended as only a temporary appointment pending the appointment of a permanent officeholder. Their role has changed in modern times. They have played a major role in some recent large liquidations.

10.032 Although special managers do not need to be licensed insolvency practitioners, the Insolvency Service has a panel of firms, all of whom are insolvency practitioners, who are able and willing to act as special managers at short notice in the event of a large compulsory winding up whose management is beyond the expertise of capacity of the official receiver's office.

10.033 Although the Insolvency Service, through its official receivers will therefore select potential special managers in such cases, they must still be appointed by the court. They will be officers of the court and under the court's control. Although this provides the public with some confidence that their actions are firmly under the control of the court, the powers given to them and details of their remuneration are not necessarily made available publicly which calls into question the transparency which one would expect in relation to their appointment, powers and recompense.

10.034 Although special managers are not often encountered in practice they do fill a necessary role where the official receiver has to act as liquidator of last resort. Where there are no funds to pay the fees of a private sector administrator or liquidator, the official receiver will be appointed as liquidator. It is unlikely that the official receiver will have available resources to conduct an

---

41   SI 2005/524, Sch 2 para 7.

42   Insolvency Rules 2016, r 7.96. The requirements for the official receiver to report financial information to creditors are far more 'light touch' than for a private sector liquidator. The reporting requirements of Part 18 of the Insolvency Rules 2016 do not apply to the official receiver when acting as an officeholder.

effective winding up of any major undertaking and so the appointment of special managers by the court is an important power.

The cost of special managers is likely to fall on the public purse in such cases and not on secured **10.035** creditors or receivables financiers who are permitted to protect their respective positions and not have their security used to fund any orderly winding up.

11

ROLE OF THE INSOLVENCY SERVICE

A. INTRODUCTION

11.001   The Insolvency Service is an executive agency within the Department of Business, Energy and Industrial Strategy ('BEIS'). It is responsible for leading on the government's insolvency law policy and the regulation of the insolvency profession. It has a number of operational, investigatory and enforcement functions which date back to the nineteenth century. It has long been accepted that some form of officialism, or official intervention and oversight, is needed in cases involving insolvency. Where there is wrongdoing, culpable behaviour must be investigated and wrongdoers pursued whether the result is a director's disqualification or a criminal sanction. Official receivers are employed by the Insolvency Service and are appointed in bankruptcies and compulsory liquidations.

B. ORIGINS OF OFFICIALISM

11.002   The history of insolvency regulation is a tale of disparate, and at times desperate, attempts to try to arrive at an appropriate balance between the rights of creditors on the one hand and the public interest on the other. Prior to the late nineteenth century most legislative action was in the area of personal insolvency as companies registered under the Companies Acts were comparatively rare up to that point.

11.003   Parliament had passed numerous Bankruptcy Acts over the centuries since the first Bankruptcy Act in 1542.[1] Although it is not easy to discern a clear pattern from the provisions of this long succession of statutes, it is clear that they were designed, to a greater or lesser extent, to combat fraudulent conduct by bankrupts (and others) but also to give control of a bankrupt's estate to creditors or their representatives. When creditors, and their representatives, were given too much control, there was the capacity for fraud. When the courts, and those appointed by the courts, were given too much say in the way bankrupts and their property were dealt with,

---

1   34 & 35 Hen 8, c 4.

different vested interests took unfair advantage of the creditors. The power over a bankrupt's assets and the power to investigate and take action in relation to culpable behaviour periodically passed to and from the courts and the creditors.

The breakthrough in these struggles to find an acceptable compromise in regulating bankruptcy **11.004** came with the Bankruptcy Act 1883. In Parliamentary debates, the then President of the Board of Trade, Joseph Chamberlain, famously explained the rationale of the 1883 regime,[2] a system which effectively survives today in terms of its main characteristics in both personal and corporate insolvency.

Prior to 1831, creditors had full control of the administration of bankrupt estates. This form **11.005** of voluntaryism was deeply unpopular. Due to a number of frauds perpetrated by creditors and their representatives, the Bankruptcy Act 1831[3] introduced a system which took effective control of bankruptcies away from creditors and handed it to court-appointed official assignees. This was the first time that a system of official administration had been used in bankruptcy. Such official assignees controlled bankruptcies and investigated allegations of fraud and corruption.

Although initially a popular system, this system of officialism slowly fell into disrepute due **11.006** mainly to the enormous profits made personally by the official assignees and others who were part of the bankruptcy apparatus. It was impractical for the courts to exercise proper supervision over the appointment and conduct of the official assignees. Assignees were appointed based on their connections not their abilities. Assignees were accused of 'jobbery' and there were instances of embezzlement of funds by official assignees.

The Bankruptcy Act 1861 very much limited the function and duties of official assignees. **11.007** The Bankruptcy Act 1869 went further and abolished them. Bankruptcy returned control to the creditors, a system of voluntaryism, 'which again led to absolute chaos and gave general dissatisfaction'.[4]

The Bankruptcy Act 1883 saw a permanent return to a form of officialism which was deemed **11.008** necessary in order to bring an element of control and transparency to the process of bankruptcy. Chamberlain explained in Parliament that this time things would be different.[5] The new system of official receivers would be under the control of a responsible government department, the Board of Trade, not the courts. The guiding principle of the system was to incorporate the best aspects of the previous systems. Official interference was limited to a level of supervision which was needed to protect minority creditors to ensure honest dealing in relation to the bankruptcy estate. Despite the necessary appointment of the official receiver in all bankruptcies, the 1883 system still enabled creditors to take complete and effective control over the estate with the appointment of their own trustee in bankruptcy who would replace the official receiver when the creditors wished to appoint their own person.

---

2   HC Deb 19 March 1883 vol 277 cc 816 et seq.
3   Known also as Lord Brougham's Act due to the steadfast work of its main architect.
4   HC Deb 19 March 1883 vol 277 c 825.
5   Ibid., cc 825–826.

11.009   The 1883 Act introduced three guiding public policy principles to ensure fairness and transparency:

- There is a need for a public inquiry into the reasons for a bankruptcy;
- There was a need for the appointment of a public official (the official receiver) to conduct this inquiry;
- Official receivers would be attached to all courts with bankruptcy jurisdiction but were fully responsible to the Board of Trade which was, in turn, responsible to public opinion and Parliament.

11.010   As it became progressively easier and more common to incorporate trading companies with limited liability under the Companies Acts in the latter part of the nineteenth century, there appeared a need to introduce similar official controls over company liquidations as there were over personal bankruptcies. The Companies (Winding-Up) Act 1890 in effect incorporated into compulsory winding up the same oversight and control of the official receiver as had been seen to work in bankruptcies. Again the principal reason given for extending the remit of the official receiver to company liquidations was the need to exercise financial control in each case and to enable investigations and action where improper conduct was uncovered.[6]

11.011   As the commercial needs of the country changed so the role of the Board of Trade expanded. The Companies Act 1928 first introduced the possibility of company directors found guilty of fraudulent trading to be disqualified.[7] The role of the official receiver and other Board of Trade officials has expanded in this regard incrementally, and directors' disqualification is now a major function of public officials.[8]

11.012   Various administrative tasks and investigatory powers and duties have also been added over the years to arrive at the current system. The major changes made by the Insolvency Act 1986 saw, for example, the need to regulate a new profession, that of the licensed insolvency practitioner.[9] Although greatly expanded since it began, the current system of officialism is recognisably based upon the 1883 system and retains its very strong public sector ethos.

C. FUNCTIONS OF THE INSOLVENCY SERVICE

11.013   The nineteenth-century Board of Trade has changed its name several times over the years. Its current incarnation is BEIS. Since 1990 the Insolvency Service has been an executive agency[10] within the successors to the Board of Trade. Wherever statute requires action by or reporting

---

6   HC Deb 04 July 1890 vol 346 cc 842 et seq (comments by the then President of the Board of Trade, Sir Michael Hicks Beach).

7   Companies Act 1928, ss 75 and 76. These provisions followed recommendations of the Greene Committee (the *Company Law Amendment Committee* Cmd 2657 (1925–6)). Section 84 of the 1928 Act introduced disqualification from acting as a director of a company for undischarged bankrupts.

8   See above Chapter 4.

9   See above Chapter 8 above.

10   Executive agencies were introduced into government following a government Efficiency Unit report to the Prime Minister entitled *Improving Management in Government: the next steps* (1988) which may be found at: https://www.civilservant.org.uk/library/1988_improving_management_in_government_the%20next_steps.pdf.

to the Secretary of State for BEIS in the context of insolvency matters, it is invariably the Insolvency Service which will have that function delegated to it. The Secretary of State retains the power to appoint official receivers who act under the general instructions of the Secretary of State but are also officers of the court.[11]

The Insolvency Service's functions include the following: **11.014**

- to administer bankruptcies and debt relief orders (where debtors themselves will be applying administratively for the order);[12]
- to investigate the affairs of companies in liquidation, making reports of any director misconduct;[13]
- to investigate trading companies and take action to wind them up and to consider taking action to disqualify the directors where there is evidence of misconduct;[14]
- to act as trustee in bankruptcy or liquidator where no private sector insolvency practitioner is in place;[15]
- to act as the regulator of private sector insolvency practitioners;[16]
- to operate a single gateway complaints procedure dealing with complaints relating to all things insolvency, including the Insolvency Service itself, an official receiver, an insolvency practitioner,[17] a bankrupt or directors or their companies suspected of fraud or misconduct.
- to issue redundancy payments from the National Insurance Fund;[18]
- to act to disqualify unfit directors in all corporate failures;[19]
- to deal with bankruptcy restrictions orders and undertakings and debt relief restrictions orders and undertakings;[20]
- to act, in the best interests of the public, as an impartial source of information for the public on insolvency and redundancy matters;

---

11   Insolvency Act 1986, ss 399 and 400.
12   Adjudicators (who cannot be official receivers) are appointed by the Secretary of State and decide upon applications for bankruptcy made by debtors (Insolvency Act 1986, Part IX, Chapter A1). Official receivers are empowered to make debt relief orders on the application of debtors under Insolvency Act 1986, Part 7A.
13   Insolvency Act 1986, s 132, the official receiver owes a duty to report misconduct to the court which is a separate duty to that to report unfit conduct for the purposes of the Company Directors Disqualification Act 1986, s 7A.
14   See the powers, e.g., in Companies Act 1985, s 447 and Company Directors Disqualification Act 1986, s 8.
15   These respective roles are carried out by official receivers.
16   An Insolvency Service consultation in 2014 called *Strengthening the Regulatory Regime and Fee Structure for Insolvency Practitioners* led to a substantially new regulatory framework being introduced partly by the Deregulation Act 2015 and partly by the Small Business, Enterprise and Employment Act 2015. Subsequently, there has been a significant reduction in the number of bodies able to authorise and regulate IPs. The Secretary of State ceased to be a competent authority for the purposes of authorisation and regulation with regulatory action now falling to the remaining professional bodies who license IPs. Where such action is deemed necessary but has not been taken, the Secretary of State retains various significant powers which may be exercised on the advice of the Insolvency Service against the professional bodies (see, e.g., Insolvency Act 1986, s 391T which deals with compliance orders).
17   Complaints about IPs pass through the single Complaints Gateway (see https://www.gov.uk/complain-about-insolvency -practitioner) which operates as a conduit for complaints to be passed onto the appropriate licensing professional body. The operation of the Complaints Gateway is governed by a memorandum between the Secretary of State and the recognised professional bodies.
18   The Insolvency Service operates the Redundancy Payments Service on behalf of the Secretary of State which permits employees of insolvent employers to claim certain statutory payments from the National Insurance Fund.
19   This power if primarily exercised under Company Directors Disqualification Act 1986, s 6.
20   See Insolvency Act 1986, s 281A giving effect to Sch 4A and s 251V giving effect to Sch 4ZB. The Insolvency Service also keeps online Individual Insolvency Register which is available online.

- to provide statistics on corporate and personal insolvencies;
- to advise BEIS ministers and other government departments and agencies on insolvency and redundancy related issues; and
- to investigate and prosecute breaches of company and insolvency legislation and other criminal offences on behalf of BEIS.[21]

D. CONCLUSION

11.015   Although only becoming an executive agency in 1990, the Insolvency Service was effectively established in 1883 for bankruptcy and extended its remit to insolvent companies in 1890. Its functions have expanded further over the decades but it has retained its public service emphasis. Although on occasion it may have been suspected of trying to make money from insolvency,[22] it has remained true to its initial purposes of ensuring that insolvent estates are dealt with honestly and transparently, more generally protecting the public from culpable behaviour and to uphold a sense of commercial morality. It has a strong commitment to those purposes and contributes to confidence in the market. Its annual report is presented to Parliament for scrutiny as well as being made public.[23]

---

21   See Insolvency Act 1986, Sch 10 for the long list of criminal offences which may be committed under the Act.
22   See the discussion in P Walton 'It's Officialism – the uncertain past, present and future of the Insolvency Practitioner Profession in the United Kingdom' [2017] *Gore-Browne on Companies Special Release* 97.
23   The annual report is presented to the House of Commons pursuant to Government Resources and Accounts Act 2000, s 7.

INDEX